Advanced PowerBuilder® 6 Techniques

Ramesh Chandak

Purshottam Chandak

Derrik Deyhimi

David Mosley

WILEY COMPUTER PUBLISHING

John Wiley & Sons, Inc.
New York • Chichester • Weinheim • Brisbane • Singapore • Toronto

The co-authors of this book, Ramesh and Purshottam, would like to dedicate this book to Rajita.

Publisher: Robert Ipsen
Editor: Robert M. Elliott
Managing Editor: Marnie Wielage
Electronic Products, Associate Editor: Mike Sosa
Text Design & Composition: Publishers' Design and Production Services

Designations used by companies to distinguish their products are often claimed as trademarks. In all instances where John Wiley & Sons, Inc., is aware of a claim, the product names appear in initial capital or ALL CAPITAL LETTERS. Readers, however, should contact the appropriate companies for more complete information regarding trademarks and registration.

This book is printed on acid-free paper. ∞

This publication is designed to provide accurate and authoritative information in regard to the subject matter covered. It is sold with the understanding that the publisher is not engaged in professional services. If professional advice or other expert assistance is required, the services of a competent professional person should be sought.

Library of Congress Cataloging-in-Publication Data:

ISBN: 0-471-29792-5

Printed in the United States of America.

10 9 8 7 6 5 4 3 2 1

CONTENTS

Acknowledgments   xv
About the Authors   xv
Foreword   xvii

PART I   OVERVIEW

Chapter 1   Introduction   3

What's New with PowerBuilder 6?   4
About This Book   5

Chapter 2   Application Architectures   7

Tiered Architecture   8
    Two-Tiered Architecture   *9*
    Three-Tiered Architecture   *10*
    Services Architecture   *12*
    Email   *13*
PowerBuilder Object Orientation   17
    Inheritance   *18*
The Component World   25
    COM   *25*
    DCOM   *26*
    CORBA   *27*
    PowerBuilder's Object Generation Infrastructure   *27*
PowerBuilder Class Libraries   28
    Foundation Class   *30*
    Extension Class   *31*
Sharing PowerBuilder Objects   32

PART II   **DEVELOPMENT CONCEPTS**

Chapter 3   **DataWindows**   **35**

DataWindow Objects   36
    Data Sources   *36*
    Presentation Styles   *41*
    Groups   *57*
    Filters   *58*
    Sorting   *60*
    Sliding Columns   *61*
    Data Validation   *61*
    Display Formats and Edit Marks   *73*
    Computed Columns and Fields   *79*
    Update Properties   *85*
    New Objects for the DataWindow   *89*
    Child DataWindows   *91*
DataWindow Controls   96
    DataWindow Buffers   *96*
    Drag-and-Drop   *98*
    Transaction Processing   *100*
    Dynamic DataWindows   *111*
    Query Mode and Prompt for Criteria   *121*
    DataWindow Save As   *126*
Design Considerations   127
    Embedded SQL   *127*
    Direct Data Access   *128*
    Handling Large Result Sets   *135*
    Shared Result Sets   *138*
    Retrieve As Needed   *140*
    DataWindows as Buffers and DataStore Objects   *143*
    Code Tables   *146*
    Using a DDDW versus Filling a DDLB   *152*
    Using Bitmaps with DataWindows   *152*
    Using a Computed Field   *157*
    OLE Columns   *160*
    Creating a DataWindow Architecture   *168*

Chapter 4   **Multiple Document Interface (MDI) and Windows**   **171**

MDI Applications   172
    Types of MDI Applications   *172*
    MDI Components   *173*
    Creating and Manipulating an MDI   *176*
    Menus and Toolbars   *178*
    MicroHelp   *186*
Windows   187
    Types of Windows   *187*

Window Events	*192*
PowerBuilder Functions	*195*
Calling Events and Functions	*196*
PowerBuilder Variables	*197*
Window Datatypes	*199*
Window Controls	*200*
Window Attributes	*217*
Window Paradigms	*219*

Chapter 5   Menus   **227**

Types of Menus	227
Menu Bar	*227*
Popup Menus	*228*
Inheritance	229
Menu Events, Scripts, and Functions	234
Menu Events	*235*
Menu Functions	*236*
Menus within MDI Applications	237
Toolbars	239
Drop-Down Toolbars	241
Integrating with an .INI File	242
Accelerator and Shortcut Keys	248
Menuitem Properties	248
Design Considerations	250
Suggested Reading	*250*

Chapter 6   Structures, Functions, and User Objects   **251**

Structures	251
Creating and Declaring Structures	*251*
Types of Structures	*252*
Functions	253
Types of Functions	*253*
Declaring External Functions	*255*
Parameter Passing	*257*
Object-Oriented Programming and Functions	*263*
User Objects	271
Types of User Objects	*271*
Interfacing between Windows and User Objects	*304*
Dynamic User Objects	*307*
Object-Oriented Programming and User Objects	*313*

Chapter 7   Graphs and Reporting   **321**

Graphs	321
Parts of a Graph	*321*
Using Graphs	*325*

Reports 339
Report Painter/InfoMaker 339
Presentation Styles 340
Printing Reports 345
Saving Reports 348

Chapter 8 Printing and File I/O 350

Printing 351
How Microsoft Windows Printing Works 351
Printing Functions 352
Print Area 352
Printing Single DataWindows 354
Printing Multiple DataWindows 358
Printing PowerBuilder Objects 363
Printing Graphs 364
Print All Capabilities 364
Changing Microsoft Windows Print Settings 364
Creating Print Dialog Boxes 365
File and I/O 373
File I/O Functions 373
Reading Files that Exceed 32,766 Bytes 374
Writing a File Copy Function 375
ImportFile Function 376
Simulating the ImportFile Function 377
Environment Variables 378
Directory I/O 380
Initialization (.INI) Files 385
Registry Functions 392

Chapter 9 Debugging 393

Debug Painter 393
Breakpoints 394
Watch List 396
Variables 396
Source 399
Source Browser 401
Source History 402
Call Stack 402
Objects in Memory 402
Just In Time Debugging 402
Using the Debugbreak( ) Function 404
Runtime Debug 404
Trace Debug 407
Custom Debug Methods 415
Writing Variables to a File 415
Messages 417

Third-Party Debug Tools 418
Spy or Win View *418*
HeapWalker *418*
Unload Utilities *418*
Code View *420*
Windows Profiler *420*

Chapter 10 Creating Windows Help Files 421

Microsoft Windows 95 Help 422
Topic Files *422*
Help Topic Components *422*
Graphics *424*
Project File *424*
Contents File *424*
Context-Sensitive Help in PowerBuilder 424
Creating Help with Third-Party Products 427

PART III ADVANCED DEVELOPMENT CONCEPTS

Chapter 11 Email Interfaces 431

Messaging Standards 431
MAPI and VIM *431*
X.400 *432*
PowerBuilder's DDE Interface 432
PowerBuilder's MAPI Interface 435
PowerBuilder Library for Lotus Notes 443
Email APIS 446

Chapter 12 Open Repository CASE API (ORCA) 447

Case Tools and Methodology 447
Powersoft's Vision and the Code Initiative 448
Open Repository CASE API (ORCA) 449
ORCA Architecture *449*
ORCA Features *449*
ORCA Functions *451*
PowerBuilder ORCA Header File *452*

Chapter 13 External Interfaces 454

The Windows API 454
Making Windows API Calls *454*
Windows Messages *455*
DDE (Dynamic Data Exchange) 462
PowerBuilder DDE Functions/Attributes *462*
DDE to Microsoft Word and Microsoft Excel *462*

OLE (Object Linking and Embedding) 467
Microsoft OLE 2 Features 468
PowerBuilder OLE 2 Control Properties 469
PowerBuilder OLE 2 Functions 469
PowerBuilder OLE 2 Container Application Support 471
PowerBuilder OLE 2 Sample Code 475
Inbound OLE Automation 477
Creating OLE Automation Server 480
OLE Custom Controls (OCX) 484
Windows DLLs 489
Why Write Your Own DLLs? 490
DLLs and Applications 490
How to Write a DLL 491
Cross-Platform Issues 498

Chapter 14 Network Considerations **499**

The OSI Model 499
Application Layer 500
Presentation Layer 500
Session Layer 500
Transport Layer 500
Network Layer 501
Datalink Layer 501
Supporting Multiple Protocols 501
Interfacing with a Network Operating System (NOS) 503
Networking with Distributed PowerBuilder 504
Middleware 504
RPCs and Message-Passing 505
DCE and CORBA 508
DRDA 509
Database Gateways 509
Transaction Processing Monitors 510

PART IV   DATABASE CONNECTIVITY

Chapter 15 Open Database Connectivity (ODBC) **515**

Advantages of ODBC 516
Disadvantages of ODBC 516
ODBC SQL Processing 517
ODBC Conformance Levels 518
API Conformance Levels 518
SQL Conformance Levels 521
PowerBuilder's Support for ODBC 522
.INI File Settings 522

ODBC Driver Manager Initialization File (odbc.ini) — *522*
ODBC Installation Initialization File (odbcinst.ini) — *522*
PowerBuilder ODBC Configuration File (pbodb60.ini) — *523*
Registry Settings — 523
Connecting to ODBC from PowerBuilder — 525
Database Profile Painter and DBParm Settings — *526*
Setting Up ODBC on the Client — 530

Chapter 16   SQL Anywhere and Other Databases   532

SQL Anywhere — 532
Database Architecture and Features — *533*
The PowerBuilder System Tables — *542*
Datatypes — *543*
ORACLE — 544
Database Architecture and Features — *544*
Connecting to Oracle from PowerBuilder — *557*
The PowerBuilder System Tables — *561*
Datatypes — *562*
SQL Server — 562
Database Architecture — *563*
Connecting to SQL Server from PowerBuilder — *565*
The PowerBuilder System Tables — *573*
Datatypes — *573*
Informix — 574
Database Architecture and Features — *575*
Connecting to Informix from PowerBuilder — *578*
The PowerBuilder System Tables — *579*
Datatypes — *580*

PART V   ADMINISTRATION

Chapter 17   Project Standards and Naming Conventions   585

Programming Standards — 585
Hard-Coded References — *586*
Code Modularization — *588*
Encapsulation — *590*
Comments — *590*
Function Visibility — *591*
Naming Conventions — 591
Objects — *591*
Variables — *592*
Datatypes — *592*
Controls — *593*
Database Objects — *594*
Window Type Standards — 594

SDI   *594*
MDI   *596*
GUI Standards   596
Error Handling   597
Database Error Handling   *598*
The Error and External/Exception Events   *599*
System Error Handling   *601*
Error Handling When Calling Dynamic Link Libraries   *603*

**Chapter 18   Creating an Executable and Testing PowerBuilder
Applications**   **606**

What Happens when Building the .EXE   606
Machine Code versus P-Code   *607*
Using .PBDs or .DLLs   *607*
The Library Search Path   *608*
Resource Files   *608*
Optimizing .PBLs   *610*
The PowerBuilder Project Painter   610
Building the Executable   *611*
Executable and Resource Filenames   *611*
The PowerBuilder Virtual Machine   *613*
Component Generators   *613*
PowerBuilder Synchronization Tool   *614*
Testing PowerBuilder Applications   614
Testing Relative to the Systems Development Life Cycle (SDLC)   *615*
Application Test Stages   *616*
Testing Tools   *623*
Sample Testing Forms   631

Chapter 19   PowerBuilder Software Migration   **640**

Software Development Life Cycle   640
File Types and Locations   *642*
Directory Structure   *644*
An Example of a Typical Software Management Environment   646
Version Control within PowerBuilder   *647*
Using ObjectCycle   *650*
Migration Forms   658

Chapter 20   Performance Considerations   **661**

Client Configuration   662
Network Architecture   663
Database Design   665
PowerBuilder Application Design Issues   665
Partitioning Application Components   *666*

When to Use Database Triggers 666
When to Use Stored Procedures 666
When to Perform Validation 667
PowerScript Functions versus External Functions 668
One EXE versus Several EXEs 668
Building PBLs into Both EXE and the PBDs or DLLs 668
Distribution of Application Components 670
Preloading Objects 671
Choosing PowerBuilder Controls 671
PowerBuilder Application Development 675
Scope of Variables and Functions 675
Managing the PowerBuilder Libraries 675
PowerScript Coding Considerations 676
New Features in PowerBuilder 6 683

Chapter 21 The Data Pipeline 685

Creating a Data Pipeline Object 685
Table 689
Options 689
Commit 689
Key 690
Max Errors 690
Extended Attributes 690
Column Definition 690
Executing A Data Pipeline 691
Using Pipelines within the Development Environment 691
Using Pipelines within an Application 692
Data Pipeline Object Attributes, Events, and Functions 700

PART VI DISTRIBUTED APPLICATION AND INTERNET DEVELOPMENT

Chapter 22 Distributed Application Development 705

Overview of Distributed PowerBuilder 705
DPB Classes and Concepts 706
DPB Classes 707
Some Uses of DPB 712
Distributed PowerBuilder Drivers and Configuration 712
Communication Driver Platform Requirements and Usage 712
Transaction Server Support 713
Sybase Transaction Server (Jaguar CTS) 714
Microsoft Transaction Server 714
When Should You Use a Transaction Server? 715
Open Technology Support 715

Chapter 23   Advanced Distributed Application Development   **717**

Development Methodology 718
Creating Shared Objects 718
Running the Application *719*
Designing the Application *720*
Server Push 728
Running the Application *728*
Designing the Application *730*
Asynchronous Processing 737
Running the Application *737*
Designing the Application *738*
DataWindow Synchronization 749
Running the Application *750*
Designing the Application *751*

Chapter 24   PowerBuilder Foundation Class (PFC) Library   **761**

What is PFC? 761
PFC Services Architecture 761
PFC Libraries *762*
PFC Extension Layers *762*
Application Services *763*
DataWindow Service *768*
Window Services *769*
PFC Objects *773*
PFC Object Hierarchy 778
PFC Process Flows 779
Third-Party PFC-Based Products 780
Third-Party Class Libraries 780

Chapter 25   Using Internet Tools   **781**

DataWindow Plug-In 781
Window Plug-In 783
Window ActiveX Control 786
Customizable Web Jumps 789
Secure Mode 789
Restricted PowerBuilder Functions *790*
Running the Window ActiveX Control in Secure Mode *791*
Running the Window Plug-In in Secure Mode *791*
Running the DataWindow Plug-In in Secure Mode *792*
Synchronizer 792
Building the Synchronization Data File *792*
Running Synchronizer as a Stand-Alone Application *796*
Using the Sync ActiveX Control *796*
HTML Table Generation 797

Web.pb 799
web.pb Wizard *800*
web.pb Class Library *802*

Chapter 26 **Learning HOW to Build PowerBuilder Applications** **803**

Introduction 803
Installing HOW *804*
Editions and Components *804*
Using HOW to Build PowerBuilder Applications 805
Create a Project and Library *806*
Create a Domain with Class Objects *808*
Create Attributes for the Class Objects *810*
Establish an Association between the Class Objects *810*
Generate a Data Model Based on the Domain *812*
Synchronize the Data Model and Bring the Physical Data Model
Information into HOW *814*
Create the Windows and Controls *815*
Create the Tasks that Use the Windows, Controls, Queries, and the
Given Navigations between the Windows *816*
Specify the Navigation between the Windows to Establish the
Program's Flow *817*
Add Parameters and Links *819*
Generate the PowerBuilder Application *819*
Run the Application *821*
Examine the Objects that HOW Generates *821*
Generate Documentation for the Project by Using HOW *822*

Appendix **What's on the CD-ROM?** **823**

Source Code from the Book 823
English Wizard 823
Demo Utilities Toolkit 824
PowerDrops *824*
PowerGraph *824*
PowerUndo *824*
PB Developer Tools & Services 825
Interspace 825
PowerDoc 825

Index **827**

Acknowledgments

Publishing a book is the result of the combined effort of a number of different people. The coauthors of this book, Ramesh Chandak and Purshottam Chandak, would like to thank Robert Elliott for giving us the opportunity to be part of this book. We would like to thank Martha Kaufman and Brian Calandra for their support and patience in answering our questions while we were writing this book. We would also like to thank Chiman Jagani for his helpful tips and insights into PowerBuilder 6. Last, but not least, we would like to thank our two best Jijajis in this world, Shriniwas Soni and Satyanarayan Bihani, for their unconditional love, care, and support throughout our careers.

About the Authors

RAMESH CHANDAK

Ramesh Chandak graduated with a Fellowship in Advanced Engineering Study from MIT (Cambridge, MA) and has a total of 8 years of work experience in the IT industry. Ramesh has worked extensively with Internet, Microsoft, Sybase, Powersoft, and Java technologies. In addition, Ramesh has authored 10 books, tech edited 14 books, and published over 25 technical articles for several leading publishers on client/server, databases, multimedia, and Internet technologies.

PURSHOTTAM CHANDAK

Purshottam Chandak, a Windows application developer, has 5 years experience in designing and developing client/server and Web applications. Purshottam has worked extensively with Microsoft, Powersoft, Oracle, and Internet technologies, and has developed corporate applications and products for the niche markets. In addition, Purshottam coauthored a book on Microsoft tools and technologies, a book on Oracle 8, and published an article on distributed PowerBuilder application development.

DERRIK DEYHIMI

Derrik Deyhimi, a cofounder of EnterpriseWorks, has served as Director, Chief Executive Officer, and President since the company's inception. He was Executive Vice President and Chief Technology Officer, as well as a Director on the board for Business Solutions, Inc. Derrik also served in a variety of technical leadership positions at BSG Consulting, Compaq Computer Corporation, and Texaco specializing in the design of client/server and distributed application architectures and is a recognized technology leader and actively lectures at universities and industry conferences.

DAVID MOSLEY

David Mosley is the Vice President of Product Development and Services for Dealer Solutions, a software development company that develops enterprise systems for automobile dealerships. David has over 11 years of experience in the design and implementation of departmental and enterprise-wide client/server systems using distributed technologies. David's specialty is in the area of relational databases and client/server technical architectures. David has been working with PowerBuilder since version 1.0.

Foreword

As I write this Foreword, PowerBuilder is no longer just a development tool to hundreds of thousands of professional enterprise developers and independent software vendors, but an industry that has taken on a life of its own. This book in itself is an outstanding representation of that industry.

It has been an absolutely amazing journey since my involvement with the first alpha release of PowerBuilder began in early 1990. At that time, very few developers really understood the impact PowerBuilder would have on their lives and the types of enterprise applications they would be delivering to their customers as the year 2000 approached. Many products have come and gone since 1990, failing to keep up with the advances in hardware and software technologies and never seeing a second release. PowerBuilder, however, has broken all the rules. Now in its sixth release, with more coming, you are about to experience what many hundreds of thousands of developers have been experiencing—a product that keeps going and going and going, a product that leverages advances in object-oriented technologies, relational databases, Internet, distributed computing, user-interface design, and more.

By picking up this book, you have already begun a wonderful journey into the world of advanced technologies that are core to PowerBuilder. In particular, I think you will enjoy the coverage of all the new features found in PowerBuilder 6. The authors have done a wonderful job tackling some of the more complex topics that had not been covered in print in the past. In fact, when I first picked up the manuscript of this book, I immediately flipped to the chapter on

"Advanced Distributed Application Development" where I found myself poring over the great code examples and picking up some tips myself. Yes, even the Vice President of Technology learns a few new tricks now and again. I expect you will enjoy the coverage of Internet technologies in this book, I know I did.

Developers using PowerBuilder today are very focused on building first-class distributed component architectures for their next generation applications. This book will give you all the great tips, tricks, and advice for helping you build these best-in-breed enterprise applications. In addition, many developers are interested in preserving their existing investments in both knowledge and code in PowerBuilder, but also want to take advantage of emerging technologies like the Internet. This book will provide you with all the basic knowledge necessary to leverage these new technologies using PowerBuilder. I think you will also find the code examples very valuable—there is nothing like having a chunk of code to help you understand some of the more complex topics in building enterprise applications.

Openness has always been a key mantra during the creation of the various releases of PowerBuilder. In fact, when PowerBuilder was first being developed, technologies like COM+ and JavaBeans didn't exist. In fact, the TLA (three letter abbreviation) DDE didn't exist at the time PowerBuilder 1.0 was first released. Over the course of time, as these new technologies rolled out of the various research and development labs of many different software companies, PowerBuilder was one of the first enterprise-development tools to take advantage of these new technologies in a very elegant manner. In fact, PowerBuilder was one of the first tools to support technologies such as ODBC, Windows 3.1, and OCX technologies.

Keeping PowerBuilder moving forward as new technologies emerge has always been a high priority for the PowerBuilder team. This book does a great job introducing the developer to several of these new advanced technologies with special focus on the latest release of PowerBuilder, Version 6.0.

PowerBuilder 6 represents one of the most feature-rich enterprise development tools on the market today. In fact, it has so many powerful features that having this book by the side of your personal computer will be quite helpful. But, wait, it may not be a PC—not to worry—with PowerBuilder 6, we complete our mission of providing mainstream cross-platform support for Solaris, HP, and IBM. So if you are sitting beside a UNIX workstation, that is perfectly fine with us (and PowerBuilder 6).

In my capacity as Vice President of Technology and Sybase Fellow at Sybase, Inc., I have one of the best jobs at the company (just don't tell anyone). I get to travel all over this beautiful planet and spend time with lots of people who "geek out" every day on PowerBuilder. In addition, I spend a great deal of time researching and investigating new technologies that will impact our development tools into the future. I am also lucky to have the keys to the doors that allow passage into the R&D labs of PowerBuilder in Concord, MA. It is absolutely fantastic to see what is being developed every day in this lab, by some of the best and brightest software engineers in the industry. This advanced work will be the foundation for the evolution of PowerBuilder that will no doubt continue to leave a positive impact on the industry and on many professional software developers who have invested time and energy learning about PowerBuilder and its capabilities. From rich multi-tier distributed applications to enterprise Web applications, PowerBuilder is responsible for helping developers make the transition from the old to the very latest in application development tool technology.

I'm confident that you will enjoy this book and that the Power-Builder industry will continue supporting the latest and greatest new technologies well into the next millennium. Speaking on behalf of the entire PowerBuilder team, we absolutely appreciate your support of our product and wish you well in learning the concepts found in this great book.

BOB ZUREK
Vice President of Technology and
Sybase Fellow, Sybase, Inc.

PART I

Overview

CHAPTER 1

Introduction

Since corporations have begun migrating their applications from traditional mainframe-based systems to a LAN-based client/server environment, the need for powerful yet easy-to-use application development tools has grown rapidly. PowerBuilder has, in a relatively short time, become one of the leading client/server development tools in the market today. PowerBuilder's object-based development environment, its ability to handle large-scale, multideveloper projects, and its open systems approach sets it apart from other products. Version 6, which in this text we will refer to as *PowerBuilder 6,* strengthens PowerBuilder's position as an industry-leading development tool by adding improved support for distributed application development, including Internet and intranet applications, asynchronous processing, server push, shared objects, Object Linking and Embedding (OLE) automation, compiled code, PowerBuilder Foundation Classes, transaction server, open technology standards, ObjectCycle library management, and improved performance over version 5, along with several other enhancements.

Client/server technology has been advancing at an increasing rate and will continue to do so in the years to come. This rate of advancement has moved us away from the single-vendor solution of the past into a more open environment. Within the client/server arena are a number of technologies and vendors, each providing a solution for the different parts of a system. When developing mission-critical applications or products within this environment, you must insist on an open and scalable architecture. It is important that applications and development tools be interoperable with other vendors' products and open enough to take advantage of emerging technologies. Powersoft has positioned PowerBuilder as an open development environment that is capable of tightly integrating with third-party software products such as project management tools, transaction processing monitors, version control software, Computer-

Aided Software Engineering (CASE) tools, object libraries, and others. This enables your organization to put together a "best-of-breed" client/server and Internet software solution.

WHAT'S NEW WITH POWERBUILDER 6?

Internet and intranet application development by using the integrated Internet tools.   The Internet tools include web.pb DLLs, class libraries, and wizards you can use to create a powerful and interactive data-driven application for the Internet.

Improved support for distributed application development.   Includes asynchronous processing, server push, shared objects, named server utility, and DataWindow synchronization. Easy synchronization of a DataWindow control on the client with a data store on the server lets you exploit the DataWindow architecture to its fullest to develop n-tier applications.

New object generation infrastructure.   Lets you create components by using PowerBuilder, C++, and more. In addition, you can deploy the components on Sybase's Jaguar Component Transaction Server (CTS) and Microsoft Transaction Server. Future updates of PowerBuilder are expected to include component builders for JavaBeans, Common Object Request Broker Architecture (CORBA), and Component Object Model (COM).

New Window ActiveX control.   Acts as a wrapper that can run PowerBuilder windows within a browser.

Enhanced PowerBuilder Foundation Class Library.   Includes new services such as DataWindow resize, calendar, calculator, application preference, most recently used window, linked list, timer, broadcaster, metaclass services, and more.

New DataWindow enhancements.   Includes support for button objects and group box objects on the DataWindow. Centered checkboxes and complete scrolling within print preview mode are yet another set of enhancements to the DataWindow. In addition, the DataWindow control includes a new RowFocusChanging event.

Developer productivity enhancements.   Includes a new debugger, adding extensive just-in-time debugging capabilities and an innovative user interface to the debugging painter. In addition, a trace engine and an application profiler capture are extremely useful development tools for tuning your application's performance.

Modeling tool.   PowerBuilder now comes bundled with HOW, Riverton's component-based application modeling tool.

PowerBuilder 6 supports heterogeneous platforms.   PowerBuilder now supports HP/UX and IBM AIX platforms, along with Sun Solaris, Windows 95, Windows NT, and Macintosh OS platforms.

New UNICODE-enabled version.   Lets you develop multilingual business applications at an international level.

Arabic and Hebrew language support.   The Enterprise Edition includes support for Arabic and Hebrew languages when run on Windows 95's Arabic or Hebrew versions. PowerBuilder 6 includes new functions and an EditMask character to handle the Arabic and Hebrew characters and numbers.

ActiveX controls.   PowerBuilder 6 includes a component gallery of ActiveX controls. The gallery includes ActiveX controls for message handling, database and network access, multimedia functions, telecommunications, and so on.

Component generators.   PowerBuilder 6 supports component generators. By using the component generators, you can create C++ classes, ActiveX controls, Java components, and so on from custom class user objects.

ABOUT THIS BOOK

This book provides PowerBuilder developers, designers, and administrators a resource to use when dealing with the full range of issues encountered when building client/server, Internet, and intranet applications. It is not meant to replace the PowerBuilder documentation but rather to serve as an extension of it. In some cases, this extension relates not only to PowerBuilder itself but to include the other areas of a client/server system such as email and other external interfaces, network considerations, performance considerations, and so on.

This book is written for the novice who wants to improve his or her skills as well as for the advanced user. The authors assume that the reader has, at a minimum, a basic knowledge of PowerBuilder. You can achieve this level by taking an introductory PowerBuilder class or by doing some PowerBuilder design and development. Although not required, the reader also benefits by having a working knowledge of Windows programming and SQL. While this book provides numerous examples of working source code for some intermediate to advanced PowerBuilder topics, the authors hope that the reader learns as much about *why* to do certain things as *how* to do them.

Part I of the book includes Chapters 1 and 2. Chapter 1 provides an overview of the book. Chapter 2, "Application Architecture," addresses the topic of application architecture and discusses the various options and design concepts that you should consider when building a client/server and Internet system. This chapter also includes a discussion of object orientation and how you can implement object-oriented programming within PowerBuilder.

Part II of the book discusses the different development concepts focusing specifically on the PowerBuilder development environment. This section includes Chapter 3, "DataWindows," Chapter 4, "Multiple Document Interface (MDI) and Windows," Chapter 5, "Menus," Chapter 6, "Structures, Functions, and User Objects," Chapter 7, "Graphs and Reporting," Chapter 8, "Printing and File I/O," Chapter 9, "Debugging," and Chapter 10, "Creating Windows Help Files." This section is intended mainly for application developers and designers and includes several code examples and valuable tips and techniques.

Part III of the book covers advanced development concepts and focuses on the interfaces between PowerBuilder and external tools and resources. This section includes Chapter 11, "Email Interfaces," Chapter 12, "Open Repository CASE API (ORCA)," Chapter 13, "External Interfaces," and Chapter 14, "Network Considerations." This section, which also includes several code examples and techniques, includes a discussion on how to write 16- and 32-bit dynamic linked libraries. With Powersoft strategically positioning its development tools as open systems, the need to understand these interfaces is critical. This section is intended for both application developers and designers.

Part IV addresses database connectivity. This section includes Chapter 15, "Open Database Connectivity (ODBC)" and Chapter 16, "SQL Anywhere and Other Databases." Some of the issues related to connecting from a PowerBuilder application to a database, including a brief description of the architecture of some of the more popular relational database management systems (RDBMSs), are discussed. This section is intended for developers, designers, and administrators.

Part V covers administration. It includes Chapter 17, "Project Standards and Naming Conventions," Chapter 18, "Creating an Executable and Testing PowerBuilder Applications," Chapter 19, "PowerBuilder Software Migration," Chapter 20, "Performance Considerations," and Chapter 21, "The Data Pipeline."

Part VI covers distributed application and Internet development. This part includes Chapter 22, "Distributed Application Development," Chapter 23, "Advanced Distributed Application Development," Chapter 24, "PowerBuilder Foundation Classes (PFC) Library," Chapter 25, "Using Internet Tools," and Chapter 26, "Learning HOW to Build PowerBuilder Applications." Chapter 22 covers the concepts of distributed application development by using PowerBuilder. Chapter 23 covers advanced distributed application development concepts, including asynchronous processing, server push, creating and using shared objects, and DataWindow synchronization. Chapter 24 covers enhancements to the PFC. Chapter 25 covers designing and developing web applications by using the integrated Internet tools. Chapter 26 covers a third-party product, Riverton Software's HOW, that Powersoft bundles with PowerBuilder 6's Enterprise Edition.

We hope you enjoy using PowerBuilder as much as we do. It's a powerful tool that has far-reaching capabilities within the world of emerging technologies.

CHAPTER 2

Application Architectures

This chapter will focus on the different ways an application architect can develop an application. The chapter will discuss some of the high-level concepts, while other concepts relevant to building applications with PowerBuilder are discussed throughout the book.

Developing applications is like building a house, and an application's architect is like a house's architect. An architect who is hired to build a house delivers the blueprint of the house to be constructed after several hours of work. This is very similar to what an application architect does. The blueprint that the application architect delivers is called the *system architecture*. The building blueprint can be for a one-, two-, or three-story building. Similarly, the system architecture can be for a one-, two-, or three-tier system. A building architect, when designing the blueprint, can take advantage of several industry standards and accepted methods related to different aspects of the building or house about to be constructed. The application architect can—and should—take advantage of several standards when designing an architecture for an application. Some of these system standards include MAPI, CORBA, X.500, COM, DCOM, DCE, VIM, X.400, and ODBC. These standards can complement or compete with each other, but each in its own way can assist the application architect in designing the system architecture. The most important thing that architects must base the entire architecture or blueprint on is the client's requirements. Based on the customer's requirements, the architect can determine the architecture's framework or direction. A client's requirements for building a house can include the geographic location. For example, if the architect will construct the house on the West Coast of the United States, the house's structure must comply with the region's earthquake standards. Another requirement is the house's location. Will the architect build the house on a hill, near the ocean, or on flat ground? Similarly, when developing an application there are requirements that can affect a system's architecture. Performance, maintenance, data distribution, and scalability are a few of the customer requirements that can affect a system's architecture.

When implemented correctly, an application architecture can bring several benefits to the application developer, the customer, and the user. These benefits include reduced development time, reuse of major application components across other applications, scalability of applications, ease of maintenance, and better application performance. However, developing an application architecture for the first time requires much more initial planning and investment than simply developing the first application. But without this investment, the customer or user will have duplicate work, produce high-maintenance applications that do not comply with the common standards set by an architecture, duplicate testing and documentation, and the developer will have a very difficult time satisfying the customer's ever-changing business needs. In short, if an organization or customer is planning to develop only one application, the investment in an application architecture may not be justified. But, as each additional application is developed, the organization or customer and the developers will quickly enjoy the rewards of their investment in an application architecture.

Before reading on, there are a few terms that are important to remember:

Object/component library.   An object library is a set of independent objects or components you can use together or individually to develop an application. Typically, more development is necessary to create a foundation for developing an application.

Object framework.   In PowerBuilder, an object framework is a group of components or templates that have already been developed as either windows or user objects that you can use to develop an application. This approach provides much of the development that is necessary for building an application. In earlier versions of PowerBuilder, several developers or class library software companies provided pre-developed business models such as master-detail, form, and list, so developers could simply inherit the window or user object. The business model was mostly functional. In PowerBuilder 6, the emphasis is on user objects, both visual and nonvisual, and a new, more services-based approach has gained popularity. This approach recommends that the developers write most of their code within nonvisual objects. Then instead of having a deep hierarchy of objects, different services or nonvisual objects are instantiated based on the attributes or services the developer desires.

Foundation classes.   This approach is basically an underlying structure from which you can develop both frameworks and object libraries.

This chapter will cover the following application architecture issues:

- Tiered architecture
- Services architecture
- PowerBuilder object orientation
- PowerBuilder class libraries

TIERED ARCHITECTURE

When developing a PowerBuilder client/server application based on the application or enterprise requirements, having different types of architectures would make sense. This section discusses two types of tiered architectures. When you can divide an application's logical section into categories or tiers, it is called a *tiered architecture*. This section discusses two-tiered and three-tiered architectures.

Two-Tiered Architecture

A two-tiered architecture is the traditional client/server environment that divides the application into the graphical user interface (GUI) (the client) and the data (the server). You can develop the GUI by using a product like PowerBuilder, and you can set up the data by using a relational database management system (RDBMS), as shown in Figure 2.1.

The GUI is often referred to as the *presentation layer*. Within the two-tiered environment, all the application's pieces are either on tier one (the client) or tier two (the server). For example, if the application has a number of business rules that it needs to process, then the business rules either reside on the client or the server. If the business rules are on the client, then you write the code as part of the DataWindow, as a window level function, or as user objects (see Figure 2.2).

The other alternative is to write the business rules on the server tied to the RDBMS, as shown in Figure 2.3. In this case, you can write the business rules in the form of stored procedures, functions, triggers, or any other RDBMS vendor-specific method.

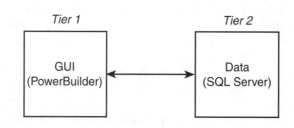

Figure 2.1   **A two-tiered architecture.**

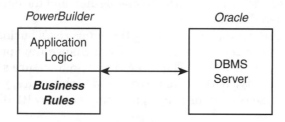

Figure 2.2   **Business rules residing on a two-tiered architecture's client side.**

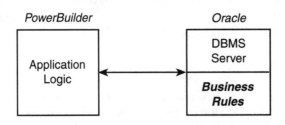

Figure 2.3   **Business rules residing on a two-tiered architecture's server side (RDBMS server).**

For the most part, within a two-tiered environment, you write all the application's components either on the client (tier one) or the server (tier two) pieces of the application. This method has some advantages and disadvantages.

One advantage of a two-tiered approach is that there are only two pieces to deal with, and in most cases there are only two vendors, the GUI tool vendor (e.g., Powersoft) and the RDBMS vendor (e.g., Microsoft, Sybase, Oracle). Developers need not learn multiple products, and the development time is faster.

A disadvantage is that you must write all the rules either on the client tool or on the RDBMS. The problem is, if you write the business rules on the RDBMS, when you change the RDBMS from SQL Server to Oracle, you must rewrite all the rules for Oracle. This may not be a serious issue if there are only a few business rules, but in most cases you have made a large investment in the development of the business rules.

The same holds true for the client tool. If you write all the business rules with a third-party 4GL development tool other than PowerBuilder, if you decide to switch to PowerBuilder you will have to rewrite the code.

Also, you cannot share the business rules with other non-PowerBuilder-based applications. Reuse across multiple applications is limited to PowerBuilder applications.

Another disadvantage of a two-tiered application or architecture is limited scalability. Only a few of the several advantages and disadvantages are mentioned here.

Three-Tiered Architecture

A three-tiered architecture divides an application into three logical categories, or tiers. The three tiers are the presentation or GUI, the business rules, and the data server tiers. Figure 2.4 shows a three-tiered architecture.

With a three-tiered architecture, by separating the enterprise's business rules, you will not lose your investment in the business rules if you change the applications, application development tools, or RDBMSs. The three-tiered architecture also solves the problems of reuse and scalability. Within the three-tiered architecture, you design the business rules as a separate, so you can use any application(s) or any RDBMS, as shown in Figure 2.5.

You can design the business rules as components, such as nonvisual PowerBuilder user objects, ActiveX controls, Java applets, JavaBeans, C++ objects, and so on. You

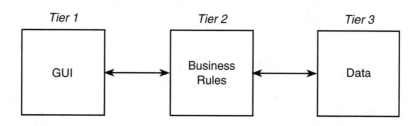

Figure 2.4   **A three-tiered architecture.**

can host these components on Sybase's Jaguar Component Transaction Server (CTS). Jaguar CTS integrates very well with Sybase tools, including PowerBuilder, and acts as the middle tier within a three-tier client/server architecture. In addition, the Jaguar CTS includes both a transaction processing (TP) monitor and an object request broker (ORB) that you can use to develop high-performance, multitier WebOLTP (on-line transaction processing) applications. The Jaguar CTS supports a number of back-end databases, including Sybase Adaptive Server, Sybase SQL Anywhere, Microsoft SQL Server, and Oracle 7.x. The Jaguar CTS connects and communicates with these databases through a number of connection protocols, including ODBC, JDBC, Sybase Open Client, and CTLib. For more information on TP monitors, see Chapter 14, "Network Considerations." For more information on the Jaguar CTS, see Chapter 22, "Distributed Application Development." You can also visit the site at www.sybase .com/products/jaguar/index.html. For Jaguar CTS code samples, visit the site at www.powersoft.com/products/jaguar/protected/sampcode.html. To download an eval-

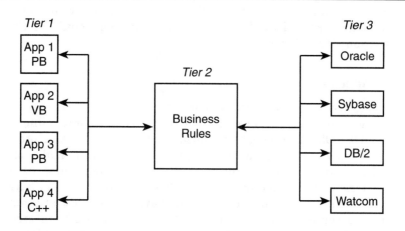

Figure 2.5   **A three-tiered architecture with the business rules as a separate tier (shared by any tier 1 client and tier 3 RDBMS).**

uation copy of the Jaguar CTS, visit the site at www.powersoft.com/products/jaguar/protected/betasrc.html.

It does not always make sense to jump into a three-tiered architecture, because there are some disadvantages. The first is the setup cost. It will take more investment in time and resources to put a three-tiered architecture in place. Second, a three-tiered architecture's administration can be more complex than that of a two-tiered system. Third, the technologies you use are newer and the skill set within the industry is often not available, and when it is, it is more expensive. Fourth, you will usually need an additional vendor, so another mechanism that could break is introduced into the architecture. But for enterprise-wide applications, a three-tiered architecture is most often recommended to deliver a truly successful system.

Both architectures have advantages and disadvantages. You should not make a decision until you have carefully examined the goals of the users, application, department, and the enterprise. Once you have gathered the overall requirements, extending beyond just one application, you can choose a more calculated architecture. Several developers fall into the trap of quickly building an application without considering the entire department or even the enterprise's objectives; then, issues such as scalability and reuse arise. The classic example of this is a prototype or small departmental application that gets turned into an enterprise application. After the small departmental application gains popularity and the demand for it extends beyond the department and spans the enterprise, scalability issues arise. Again, you can avoid this situation by gaining an understanding of the enterprise's goals before quickly building an application to satisfy a user or department's short-term needs.

In PowerBuilder 5, Powersoft introduced distributed PowerBuilder. In PowerBuilder 6, Powersoft has enhanced distributed PowerBuilder. Distributed PowerBuilder is a mechanism for distributing business logic that you write in the form of nonvisual objects. To execute these objects, you can deploy them on a server. This approach permits the development of a three-tiered application without introducing an additional vendor. For more information on distributed application development using PowerBuilder, see Chapter 22, "Distributed Application Development," and Chapter 23, "Advanced Distributed Application Development."

Services Architecture

A services architecture is a very critical piece of a system. In most cases, the applications perform services such as printing, email, fax, data access, error handling, Dynamic Data Exchange (DDE), Object Linking and Embedding (OLE), and several others. You should decouple these services from a particular application so that several applications or, potentially, the entire corporation can reuse them. When designing these services, you should also decide if you would like to build all or some of these services by using a distributed architecture. You can achieve this by having a server that contains the different distributed services. This can be much more involved than creating reusable modules in the form of Dynamic Link Libraries (DLLs), but it should be a consideration based on the architecture's requirements.

This section discusses some of the several services that you could include as part of a services architecture. Figure 2.6 shows how some services are separate from the application, via a generic services interface. You can access the service modules shown in the figure, such as email, input/output (I/O), pager, and error services, via a common interface.

Separating the services from the application permits more reuse throughout the organization. In addition to reuse, there are several other advantages, such as ease of maintenance. Assume you have developed the following architecture and you have integrated some services, such as email, with 20 different applications across the company. The huge advantage gained here—with regard to maintenance—is that if you switch the email service from cc:Mail to MS Mail, for example, you need to make the changes only within the email service module, and the 20 or more applications that interface with the email service remain untouched. Traditionally you would have to recompile each of the 20 applications to incorporate changes within all of the modules. You can achieve this advantage not only by building the services separate from the application but by enabling some object-oriented concepts and hiding the complexities of the individual services by incorporating stub layers throughout the architecture. You can incorporate additional object-oriented components, such as broker agents, authentication, and object repositories into a services-based architecture. What follows is a discussion of a simple approach to building service modules.

Email

Integration with an email service has been very popular within the client/server environment. This integration has included sending someone mail from within an applica-

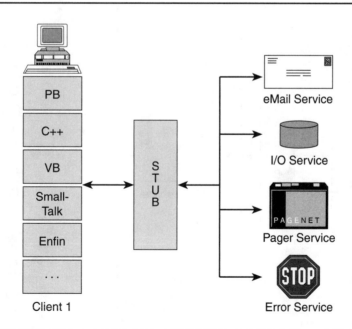

Figure 2.6   Services separate from the application via a generic services interface.

tion by invoking the email software to providing full integration by being able to send and receive reports from within an application. There are several different methods for implementing an email service. The sections that follow discuss a simple and practical solution. Figure 2.7 shows the separation of the email service from the application.

An Email Service Architecture Figure 2.8 shows the email service's three logical layers. The first layer is the application and a generic service stub (Stub 1). The second layer contains a generic email stub (Stub 2) and the different messaging APIs. The third layer is the actual email service, such as Lotus Notes, Lotus cc:Mail, Microsoft Exchange, or any other email package.

You use Stub 1 to provide a common interface to the different services, email being one of those services. From the PowerBuilder application, a generic **DoService( )** function is called. It specifies the particular service (e.g., email), the specific subservice (Send-Mail) within the service, and a structure as the DoService( ) function's third parameter. The structure will pass the data that needs to be sent. You can use this common interface for any service. The DoService( ) function can map the service and subservice requests to the appropriate service agent and send across the appropriate data.

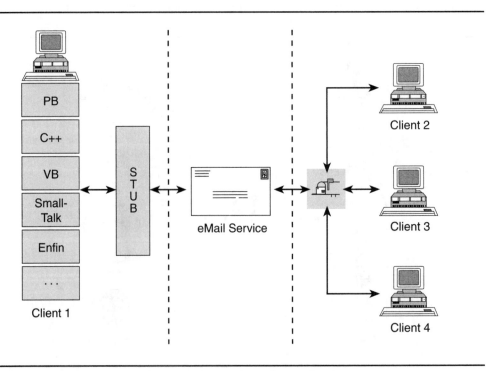

Figure 2.7   **Separation of the email service from the application.**

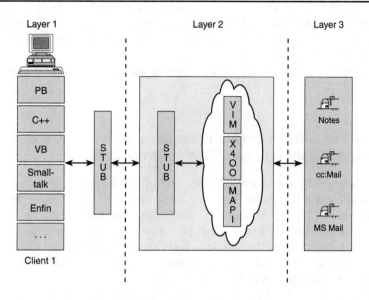

Figure 2.8   The email service's three layers.

T IP The first and second layers can exist on the same PC or on a network in the form of a DLL. Within a distributed service environment, the second layer will exist on a separate server not known to the first layer. Within a distributed approach, you can implement remote procedure calls (RPC) or messaging architectures. The architect can design the Stub 1 layer to interface with a broker to determine the requested service's location. At runtime, this location can be a distributed server that you can invoke via an RPC call or the location can be a DLL on the network that you can invoke via a normal function call.

The next step is within the second layer. Once the service and subfunction have been invoked, the Stub 2 functionality will determine which mail service is active, and it will map the subfunction to the appropriate messaging Application Programming Interface (API). For example, if you use Microsoft Mail, the Stub 2 functionality is smart enough to interface with the Microsoft Messaging Application Programming Interface (MAPI). This method is useful because the applications and the general services stub do not care about the details of the vendor API or even which API will be used. This approach provides a very maintainable interface not only from within the applications that interface with the service but from within the service itself.

Within the email service of the vendor you are using, you can swap APIs with no changes to the applications, no changes to the services architecture, and minimal changes within the email service itself. You can build the functionality within the email service to determine which vendor API to use. If that functionality is built in, switching between the different vendor APIs will also result in no changes to the email service.

The final step is for the vendor API to interface with the third layer, which is the vendor mail engine, and to send the mail.

The next section briefly defines some other services you can develop by using the same architecture.

Other Services

You can implement several different services by using a generic services architecture. This section discusses some of the services with an explanation of each.

Data Access The data access object can contain any and all data access mechanisms for any and all PowerBuilder applications. You can locate all the data access methods within a data access library that all the applications share. The individual applications do not interact with the data directly but, rather, call generic functions within the data access layer that, in turn, interface with the data sources. One advantage of doing this is that when you change the data source or attributes, you affect only the data access layer. You will not need to modify any of the applications.

The preceding description is for a PowerBuilder-based data access layer. There are different ways to implement a data access solution that is not PowerBuilder-based and supports distribution. There are messaging or RPC-based mechanisms that provide for a more open data access service. In fact, because Powersoft is committed to working with vendors to provide extensions to PowerBuilder, several vendors have introduced new interfaces. Although one of PowerBuilder's strengths is its data access capabilities, you must keep in mind ways to reuse an architecture to its full potential.

Print.   This service includes print functionality for all the applications.

OLE.   This service includes OLE functionality for all the applications.

DDE.   This service includes DDE functionality for all the applications.

Clipboard.   This service includes clipboard functionality for all the applications.

Security.   This service includes security for the applications. You develop all the methods and attribute structures for application security and put them within the nonvisual architecture object. You can develop security at either the macro-application level or down to the micro-level of objects. You can develop a security mechanism within PowerBuilder as a nonvisual PowerBuilder object that you can use across PowerBuilder applications. This security user object can interface with an external security service that is used across other applications. For distributed applications, the security service should be able to interface with the Kerberos Authentication Security Service.

For more information on the Kerberos Authentication Security Service, visit the following sites:

www.transarc.com/afs/transarc.com/public/www/Public/Partners/ocsg.html

www.oit.duke.edu/~rob/kerberos/kerbdetails.html

www.cifs.com/2ndcifsconf/Microsoft-Leach3/sld017.htm

www.roxen.com/rfc/rfc1510.html

www.ini.cmu.edu/NETBILL/pubs/pkda.html

consult.stanford.edu/tmp/afsinfo/AFS_Kerberos.html

For a list of frequently asked questions (FAQs) on the Kerberos Authentication Security Service, visit the following site:

www.lanl.gov/divisions/cic/ComputingAtLANL/services/kerberos/

For a list of white papers on the Kerberos Authentication Security Service, visit the following sites:

www.tgv.com/customer_support/white_papers/kerb1000.html

www.suite.com/whitepapers/wp5.html

Modem This service includes modem communication functionality for all the applications. Applications need not be concerned with the functionality specific to the different modems. Instead, they call generic functions that provide an interface to a modem.

Drag-and-Drop This service includes drag-and-drop functionality for all the applications.

Fax This service includes fax functionality for all the applications.

DOS/File I/O This service includes file I/O functionality for all the applications. If an application needs access to an environment variable, the application developer makes a simple call to a generic environment variable function.

Multimedia This service includes sound and image functionality for all the applications. Within the Windows environment, the multimedia API is mmsystem.dll.

EDI This service includes electronic data interchange (EDI) functionality for all the applications.

POWERBUILDER OBJECT ORIENTATION

The design stage is often the most important stage in building applications. This section discusses some important design concepts of object-oriented systems. Other design concepts relevant to building applications within PowerBuilder are discussed throughout the book.

Object orientation has become a relatively popular approach to application design and development. It is based on breaking an application down into a set of objects, each object having a defined set of attributes and behaviors.

Within an object-oriented system, you design each object to accomplish a specific application task. Objects communicate with each other by passing messages. Objects react to the messages passed to them by doing something.

When implemented correctly, object-oriented design and development can bring several benefits to both the application developer and the end user. These benefits include reduced development time and better application performance. However, using object orientation requires much more initial planning and investment than does a traditional approach. Without this investment, developing within an object-oriented environment can be difficult and result in a slower, less efficient application.

This section presents four major topics:

- Inheritance
- Encapsulation
- Polymorphism
- Binding

Inheritance

Inheritance is a mechanism that lets an object obtain its attributes and behaviors from another object. This allows development of a basic set of objects, known as *base classes* or *superclasses*, that contain a set of attributes reusable by the "descendant" objects (i.e., those that inherit attributes and/or behaviors from other objects).

Inheritance is established in the form of an object hierarchy. This hierarchy is generally in the form of an inverted tree, with the more generic functionality defined within the objects at the top of the hierarchy and more specific functionality defined within the objects at the bottom of the hierarchy (see Figure 2.9).

True inheritance lets descendant objects both extend and override their ancestors' properties. Because the code is passed to the descendant objects instead of being merely copied, a descendant class can change some of the attributes or behavior of its ancestor while maintaining the core set of functionality built into the ancestor. A well-designed object hierarchy makes use of the *virtual classes* of objects. A virtual class is an object class that is not intended to be used directly but to serve as an object from which you can inherit other objects. For example, within the inheritance structure just described, the top and middle layers of the objects could serve as virtual classes. You will then inherit all the objects from one of these classes, and the descendants will extend or override the functionality built into these classes.

Advantages of Inheritance

Code Reusability Because you need not rewrite the code inherited from another object class within the descendant class, inheritance provides a method of code reusability. This also reduces the amount of code you need within the descendant classes.

Code Sharing Code sharing is one of the major benefits of object-oriented development. Building a common set of functionality into a class library provides all the developers of a given application the ability to inherit from these classes, extending or overriding the code of the ancestors as needed. Code sharing increases when you inherit multiple classes from a single base class. For example, an architecture could define a ReportWin class and a QueryWin class, each inherited from StdWindow (see Figure 2.10).

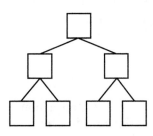

Figure 2.9   **The inheritance tree structure.**

In this situation, inheritance provides the StdWindow's code to ReportWin and QueryWin.

Code Reliability Using inheritance makes code more reliable because you define the code contained within ancestor objects in a single place, and you need not duplicate the code within different objects. Eliminating duplicate code reduces the chances for errors and provides an easier way to track and correct bugs. When you correct an error within an ancestor object, the error is corrected throughout the entire application.

For example, suppose for every window within an application, the application displays a message box asking the user to save any changes to the window. With inheritance, this code can be part of a virtual class, eliminating the need to have the code within every window of the application. You can trace any errors within this functionality encountered during development or testing to a single location and correct it there for all the windows of the application.

Interface Consistency Providing a consistent interface throughout an application can be difficult for large applications that are being developed by several people. Inheritance ensures interface consistency by guaranteeing that all objects inherited from a base class provide a common interface. You should establish interface standards within your corporation and build them into the virtual classes.

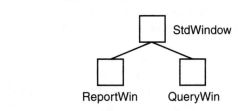

Figure 2.10   **The sample inheritance tree.**

Code Maintenance One of the biggest advantages of inheritance is the increased code maintainability. Sharing code throughout an application obviously reduces the maintenance effort. Eliminating duplicate code also makes error tracing much simpler, thus reducing the time required to find and correct bugs.

Disadvantages of Inheritance

Execution Speed Some people mistakenly believe that inheritance alone hampers performance. This is simply not true. While a poorly designed object hierarchy can hurt performance, a well-designed object hierarchy can actually improve both performance and memory efficiency.

Program Size The use of object libraries obviously adds to the application's size, although this is becoming less of an issue as the price of memory decreases. Most people are willing to put up with this disadvantage to gain the several benefits of inheritance.

Program Complexity Applications that use inheritance may be more complex than traditional, structured applications because code can be in different locations throughout an object hierarchy. The ability to extend and override ancestor events and functions adds complexity to an application's flow. The ease of maintenance resulting from the use of inheritance, however, often outweighs the disadvantage of increased complexity.

Inheritance in PowerBuilder In its ability to inherit windows, menus, and user objects, PowerBuilder provides full inheritance capabilities. Other tools offer the capability to copy or reuse code but do not let the code be passed on to the descendant objects. By using such tools, you lose the benefit of ease of maintenance. As stated earlier, when you create a PowerBuilder descendant object, you can extend or override the events and functions associated with the ancestor object, but all the benefits of inheritance survive.

PowerBuilder lets the developer create an unlimited number of descendants for an object, each of which can, in turn, be an ancestor. Extending an ancestor event or function results in the execution of the ancestor code plus the execution of any code you define for the event within the descendant object. Overriding an ancestor event or function results in the execution of only the code you define within the descendant object. Taken together, the true inheritance provided within PowerBuilder provides maximum code reusability and ease of code maintainability.

Design Considerations When designed correctly, an object hierarchy can provide several benefits, including improved performance. It is important you define only the appropriate levels of inheritance and that you inherit as much code as possible from the set of virtual classes.

You should define interface standards such as screen layout, colors, fonts, and menus within virtual classes, along with the basic functionality necessary at each level. Examples of common functionality you can include within ancestor scripts include standard error trapping routines, exit functionality, window initialization, and database connectivity.

An example of a type of function you should include within a virtual class inheritance structure is the use of a common exit from a window. You should define such basic functionality only once and inherit it for the lower windows. This is a basic example of the type of code you could use (later chapters show further working examples of inheritance):

```
/* if the user made changes, allow to save */
If hasChanged( ) Then
    If not askSave("Exit") Then
            Return False
    End If
End If
```

This is a generic close function you should define within the base ancestor class. All normal shutdown will be funneled through this function. This function calls another function, **hasChanged( )**, to determine if the user has made changes. If the user has made a change, you can call the function **askSave( )** to save the changes before exiting. Because you defined the function within the base ancestor class, you can implement the function for the entire application.

You should define object hierarchies for all possible objects, and not only for windows. The higher-level objects should perform a broad range of generic functionality with the descendant objects performing the specific tasks. To provide a method of inheriting the DataWindow controls (or other window controls), the developer can define a user object virtual class that has a DataWindow control within it. You can also encapsulate events and functions that pertain to the DataWindow control within this user object (see the next section). You can then include the user object within one of the virtual window classes or within an application window. This lets you define and test more complex items at the ancestor level so that all the descendants can use them and you do not have to reinvent them every time you require them. The example in Figure 2.11 illustrates the use of user objects at different levels within the inheritance structure.

Encapsulation

Encapsulation is the concept of packaging a set of attributes and behaviors into an object. This allows the definition of data, functions, and variables at the object level, meaning that you group all the functionality of an object into a single integrated package.

A major benefit of encapsulation is the ability to hide information and shield complexity from the object's users. You achieve information hiding because you only need to know how to interface with a particular object, and not the specific details of how that object accomplishes its tasks.

For example, you can develop the code to enable or disable menu options based on a user's security privileges to a particular object as a window function of a virtual window class. A descendant window only needs to know how to call this function and what the function returns. The descendant window does not need to know how the function determines whether the menu option should be enabled or disabled.

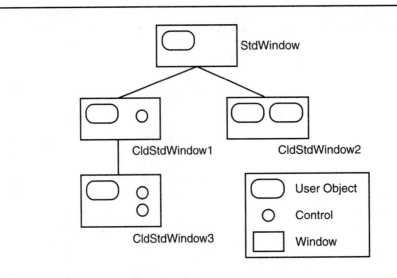

Figure 2.11   **The virtual class window with user object.**

Encapsulation in PowerBuilder PowerBuilder supports the encapsulation of variables, events, and functions at the object level for windows, menus, and user objects. Through the use of instance variables, standard and user-defined events, and object-level functions, you can encapsulate all the data and behaviors of an object into a single package.

Design Considerations You should implement all interaction with an object's attributes through the interface functions, rather than reference the attribute directly. For example, to check an instance variable's value, you should call a function that returns the variable's value rather than reference the variable directly. This method of encapsulation achieves information hiding and thus simplifies application maintenance.

  As mentioned earlier, you can encapsulate a DataWindow control's functionality (or any other window control) within a user object. For example, suppose you want to develop a master-detail maintenance conversation. Within the conversation, you need a master DataWindow control and a detail DataWindow control. These two types of Data-Window controls have some common functionality, but they also contain functionality specific to each DataWindow control. You can encapsulate the functionality for each type of DataWindow control within a separate virtual user object class, and you can then use them as ancestors to any master-detail maintenance conversations within the application(s).

  Within the DataWindow user object, you should include all the different types of functionality that you will need. Types of DataWindow functionality might include functions to enable or disable the fields within the DataWindow, validate text entries, and trap errors. An example of the functionality you should include within an encapsulated DataWindow is the DataWindow's initialization by using the PowerBuilder function **SetTransObject( )**:

```
/*
Initialize the DataWindow. Fill in our parent reference so we can
call functions and trigger events, and set the transaction.
*/
i_dwParent = aParent
If useTransObj Then
    SetTransObject(this,aTransaction)
Else
    SetTrans(this,aTransaction)
End If
Return True
```

Polymorphism

Polymorphism is a function's ability to behave differently, depending on the context within which you call the function. This allows the definition of functions at a high level, with the function's details handled by each individual object at the lower levels. To create a drawing application by using traditional programming techniques, for example, you need to define the functions to draw each type of object (rectangle, circle, line, etc.). The main function then needs to know the type of object to draw so it can call the appropriate function.

With polymorphism, you can define a class for each object type; each class contains a draw function. You will define the draw function at a higher level of detail, making it more functional. Because the main program does not need to know the type of object to be drawn, it simply tells the object to "draw." The object receiving the request will handle the details. This approach also allows the addition of new objects to the draw function with no impact on the main program because the interface to draw the new objects will be the same as the existing interface. You could add a triangle object with its own function, for example, and with no other changes, the application can draw triangles.

Overloading Polymorphism provides the ability to overload both functions and operators. A function is overloaded if two or more function bodies contain the same name. In the preceding example, the draw function is an overloaded function.

You may define overloaded functions with different argument lists and different argument types. PowerBuilder uses the argument list and argument types to determine which version of an overloaded function to execute. For example, assume an application needs to display messages containing both integer and string data. You could define a function named **displayMessage** to accept a single string argument. You can then overload this function to accept a single integer argument. Within the application, a call to displayMessage with either a string or integer argument will execute the correct function.

Overloading is not restricted to functions; you can also overload operators. Overloaded operators work in a manner similar to overloaded functions. For example, you can define the + operator to behave differently depending on the operands with which you use the operator. With two string operands, you can define the + operator to concatenate the two strings, while with two integer operands it will perform an addition operation.

TIP Unfortunately, PowerBuilder does not permit user-defined operator over-loading.

Overriding Much of the power of object orientation lies within the ability to override an ancestor object's attributes or behaviors within the descendant objects. Without the ability to override the ancestor objects' functionality, you will lose much of the flexibility and power of object orientation.

Polymorphism in PowerBuilder PowerBuilder supports polymorphism in the form of over-loaded functions and the capability to override ancestor functions and events. Polymorphism lets you define generic types of functionality within virtual class windows. This, in turn, provides the flexibility of having different routines at specific object levels to handle generic functionality such as printing, enabling, and disabling windows.

A good example of polymorphism is the following razor object. If a male uses the razor object, it will be used primarily for grooming facial hair. The same razor object, when used by a female, however, will be used to groom leg hair. Even though the ancestor object tells both people to perform the function **shave**, the function actually does different things.

Design Considerations When building different applications, it is a good idea to create windows that have generic references that can use the aspects of polymorphism. These references let the objects be reused again and again by other coding with generic references. An example of this is a function you can include within the DataWindow user object to disable a DataWindow. The ancestor object calls a function to disable the DataWindow. If there are two different descendant objects, each might logically carry out the same type of functionality, but the code might be different.

One of the descendant objects might handle disabling of the DataWindow with this code:

```
This. Modify (colname+".color=~""+DISABLED_COLOR+&
   "~""+colname"+.pointer=~"Arrow!~""+&
   colname+".TabSequence=0")
Return True
```

while the other object might handle the disabling of the DataWindow in the following manner:

```
This.Enabled = False
Return FALSE
```

Thus the two descendant objects achieve disabling of a DataWindow in different ways.

Binding

Binding is the association of an object attribute and its meaning. This can be broken down into:

- The binding of an identifier with its type
- The binding of a message to an object's method

One issue within object-oriented programming concerns the time at which binding occurs. Binding can occur at compile, linkage, or execution time. Binding at compile or linkage time is known as *static binding*; binding at execution time is known as *dynamic binding*.

With static binding, the meaning and types of all the attributes must be known at compile time. Programming languages that require binding at compile time are said to be "strongly typed." PowerBuilder 6 allows dynamic binding. The default within Power-Builder is static. Dynamic binding is at the control of the developer.

On the other hand, dynamic binding binds all the attributes at execution time. This provides greater flexibility because, for example, you can use a single identifier differently throughout an application.

Design Considerations There is one basic trade-off between static and dynamic binding: performance versus flexibility. Static binding results in better performance than dynamic binding because dynamic binding requires the extra step of matching an identifier with its type or a message with its method at runtime.

Error detection is also much simpler when using static binding because any errors are found at compile time, which makes it easier to know the error's location. With dynamic binding, errors often go undetected and are much more difficult to locate when they occur at runtime.

THE COMPONENT WORLD

Microsoft's object specification includes the Component Object Model (COM) and the Distributed Component Object Model (DCOM). Microsoft's ActiveX technology is based on COM and DCOM. In this section, you learn more about COM, DCOM, ActiveX controls, and the advantages of using COM. In addition, you learn about a sample ActiveX control—the label control—that Internet Explorer 4's setup utility will install on your system when you install Internet Explorer 4. You learn about the label control's interface including the control's properties, methods, and events. By understanding the control's interface, you will understand how you can use the control within your application and what you can do with the control. The control's interface defines the control's behavior.

COM

Microsoft and Digital Equipment Corporation first proposed the Component Object Model (COM). The model is based on the theory of creating, using, and reusing objects to build applications irrespective of the objects' language or origin. In other words, you may use Visual Basic to create a COM-compliant object and then use Visual C++ to create another COM-compliant object, but the two objects can interact and communicate with each other because they are both COM compliant. As a result, you can use both the objects as part of your application's building blocks.

Microsoft's COM specification includes the following:

- A set of standard application programming interfaces (API)
- A set of standard protocols
- A set of network interfaces

OLE, ActiveX controls, and Java ActiveX objects are examples of COM-compliant objects. You can create COM-compliant objects by using a variety of tools. You can use Visual Basic and Power++ to create ActiveX controls. You can use Visual C++ to create both OLE and ActiveX controls. In addition, you can create Java ActiveX objects by using Visual J++. As a result of the COM standard, you can use an ActiveX control created by using Power++ within your PowerBuilder application. This saves time and effort because you can reuse the ActiveX control you create by using Power++ within an application you create by using a different tool such as PowerBuilder, Visual Basic, Visual C++, and so on. For example, you can use the spell checker object you create by using Power++ within your PowerBuilder application. This saves you the trouble of writing a spell checker user object within PowerBuilder. Easy creation, simple integration, and maximum object reuse are COM's underlying principles.

TIP   Java applets are not COM-compliant objects, whereas Java ActiveX objects are COM compliant. Today, Visual J++ is the only Java integrated development environment (IDE) on the market supporting the integration of ActiveX controls and Java applets within your Java applications.

To understand a COM-compliant object so you can use it easily within your application, you must understand the object's interface. The COM object's interface is the object's outside layer, which is important to the outside world. The outside world includes applications that would like to use the COM-compliant object. The calling application sends a message to the object, and the object, in turn, responds with the results. The calling application is not interested in how the object derives the results. The calling application is also not interested in the programming language or platform you used to create the COM-compliant object. The calling application is interested only in the results from the object. A COM-compliant object's interface includes the following important components:

Properties. The object's properties define the object's appearance.

Methods. The object's methods define the object's behavior.

Events. The object's events define the events to which the object responds.

PowerBuilder 6 includes full support for COM. As a result, you can integrate ActiveX controls within your PowerBuilder 6 applications. In addition, you can use the integrated C++ Class Builder within PowerBuilder 6's Enterprise Edition to create C++ class objects and Windows DLLs.

DCOM

While COM constitutes the communication backbone of the objects residing on the same client machine, Distributed Component Object Model (DCOM) forms the communication backbone of the objects across networks on different machines. Objects conforming to the DCOM protocol can communicate and interact with each other across distributed, heterogeneous networks. An object residing on one machine within a network can communicate with another object residing on another machine within a different network by using the DCOM protocol.

CORBA

The Common Object Request Broker Architecture (CORBA) sets the standard for distributed object computing. The CORBA architecture allows you to define an abstract object model. Once you lay out the object model, the next step is to define the various components of this model. Having done this, you then go on to lay out the interface for each of these components. (However, components developed on one platform would need to be recompiled for other target platforms.) CORBA also defines a standard for inter-ORB communication that allows two compliant ORB implementations to invoke methods on objects on different machines.

PowerBuilder's Object Generation Infrastructure

PowerBuilder 6's object-oriented development environment remains unchanged from PowerBuilder 5. You can create a new PowerBuilder object such as window, DataWindow, user object, and so on, or inherit from existing PowerBuilder objects. You can define events to which the objects will respond. In addition, you can add new methods to the objects. You can provide varying degrees of data encapsulation by defining an object's method as public, private, or protected. You can define the following three types of methods:

Public. Any object can call the object's public method.

Private. Only that object's other methods can call the private method.

Protected. No other object or object's method can call the method.

You cannot use the native PowerBuilder objects within other development environments because PowerBuilder 6 objects are not COM compliant. Powersoft is expected to provide support for creating COM-compliant objects, including ActiveX controls, OLE controls, and so on, in PowerBuilder's future versions. Examples of the native PowerBuilder objects include PowerBuilder windows, DataWindows, and user objects. Also, PowerBuilder 6 does not support multiple inheritance; rather, PowerBuilder 6 supports only single inheritance. Although you cannot create COM-compliant objects by using PowerBuilder 6, you can integrate and use COM-compliant objects including ActiveX and OLE controls within your PowerBuilder 6 applications.

In addition, PowerBuilder 6 supports creating proxy objects for your distributed applications. A *proxy object* is a copy of the actual user object that resides on both the client and the server, thus facilitating communication between them. To learn more about how you can create a proxy object within PowerBuilder 6, see Chapter 23, "Advanced Distributed Application Development."

POWERBUILDER CLASS LIBRARIES

So far, this chapter has discussed several different concepts, from tiered architectures to inheritance. Several of these concepts are an application architecture's foundation. One additional component of an application architecture that the chapter has not discussed in detail is the presentation layer or the PowerBuilder GUI architecture. With PowerBuilder, you can develop an architecture to complement the development of PowerBuilder applications at the presentation layer. PowerBuilder is an object-oriented application development environment. As such, it provides the developer with several tools and facilities to enable the rapid development of client/server applications. However, in an ever-changing business environment, PowerBuilder needs to be extended so that you can use reusable class libraries in order to react in a timely manner to your customers' requests. The PowerBuilder class libraries should be the PowerBuilder version of the presentation or GUI layer within the tiered architectures explained earlier. You can either purchase or develop these class libraries. An example of a class library you can purchase is the PowerBuilder Library for Lotus Notes. A number of consulting firms and vendors also provide class libraries. You should study these class libraries closely and match them to your specific business needs. Your other option is to develop a custom set of class libraries. Suggestions on developing different modules of the class libraries are given next.

An overall application architecture can extend PowerBuilder to create an environment suited to building corporate application systems. Such an architecture consists of a PowerBuilder application, class hierarchies of reusable system objects, common functions, and object construction tools that support both the development and execution environments.

The overall PowerBuilder class library in Figure 2.12 shows the basic structure of a suitable application architecture within the PowerBuilder environment. This figure shows the dependence of the applications on the architecture. If an application architecture did not exist, you will need to develop all the code and logic for each application, reducing productivity and increasing application delivery time. After you have made the initial investment within an application architecture, all applications can take advantage of much of the functionality built into the architecture. Each application can take advantage of the architecture's visual, business, and service objects. You can share all the components of the architecture between different applications.

When developing PowerBuilder class libraries, the architect must have an understanding of the overall application development vision for the corporation. The architect must have established frequent communication with each application's project manager, lead designers, and analysts to understand the common modules within each application. These common modules can be visual, business, or service objects or modules. Through a series of ongoing meetings, the architect determines the level of commonality between the applications.

Developers can also determine the unique pieces of an application that they should build into the corporate application architecture for future flexibility, reusability, and modularity. There is often functionality that is unique to an application but common to all the different pieces of the application. Each application can also have its own individual architecture that the developer builds by using the objects within the application architecture. You should develop an individual application's architecture to minimize or eliminate duplicate design and development.

All conversations within medium- and large-scale application systems have similar features and functionality. In addition, the architecture's specification requires that conversations follow a certain protocol (e.g., a tab folder protocol) to take advantage of these similarities. This situation presents a two-fold problem. First, the requirement of architecture-support code and common functions within every conversation creates a very repetitive recoding task for each conversation. Second, it is extremely important within large-scale applications that you handle common functionality, errors, and other standard operations consistently from both a code maintenance and user interface standpoint. A good application architecture addresses both of these issues by defining common code within class hierarchies from which all the system components inherit. This structure produces a system of reusable component objects that takes full advantage of such object-oriented programming concepts as inheritance, encapsulation, and polymorphism. In addition, the architecture's object construction facility should create reusable open boxes, search boxes, and lookup dialog boxes as well as almost-functional standard maintenance conversation—all within a tab folder (or any other) interface.

Figure 2.13 shows examples of visual objects, business objects, and service or nonvisual objects. Visual objects and service objects are, in most cases, technology or interface based. You define business objects specifically to address the corporation's business requirements. By using object-oriented analysis and design, you break down the business requirements into business objects with attributes and methods that you can build into the application architecture.

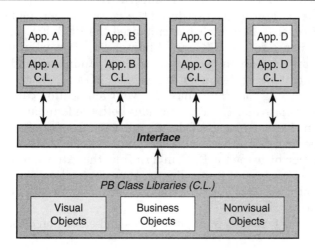

Figure 2.12   The corporate application structure in support of multiple PowerBuilder applications.

An architecture's visual objects are technology-based objects that are visible to the user. These objects can include windows, menus, toolbars, tabs, DataWindows, and other objects. You can break down these high-level objects into more detailed specific objects by taking advantage of inheritance.

Unlike visual objects, the user cannot see the service or nonvisual objects. These are the objects that add service-level functionality to an application. Some examples of service objects are data access objects, OLE objects, print objects, and several more. You give an application or a window access to a print object so it can print windows or a specific window. You can develop a print object once and add the object to the application architecture, allowing each application that needs some level of print functionality to simply add the print object to the application's window(s). Details about visual, business, and service or nonvisual objects follow.

A corporate PowerBuilder class library should also provide tools that facilitate the building of screens and interfaces. In Visual C++, Wizards, a standard object constructor empowers the developer with an easy interface to the architecture. Wizards automatically construct screens and code by simply requiring the developer to input some specific information about the screen being developed. Such automatic construction of application code becomes more imperative as the underlying architecture increases in complexity and functionality. In addition to a standard object constructor, the application architecture should include a security maintenance application for building the security module and a workstation painter for creating icon-based, workstation-style menu screens. There should also be a configuration utility that permits developers or administrators to create DLLs, INI files, EXEs, and PBDs and provides the ability to modify global parameters, such as color and font, on demand throughout the application objects.

Within any environment in which you build multiple PowerBuilder applications, the investment in a PowerBuilder class library is imperative.

With PowerBuilder 5, Powersoft introduced the PowerBuilder Foundation Classes (PFC). With PowerBuilder 6, Powersoft has enhanced the PFC. For more information on the new enhancements to the PFC, see Chapter 24, "PowerBuilder Foundation Classes (PFC)." PFC provides an ancestry of objects you can inherit and use to simplify and reduce your application's development time. The PFC's cornerstone is its service-based architecture. By using the PFC's ancestry, your application can readily use the services the PFC objects provide. The PFC includes both the foundation and extension classes. The extension classes are a set of classes inherited from the foundation classes. You must not change or modify the foundation and extension classes. To build your PowerBuilder application by using the PFC, inherit from the extension set of classes, not from the foundation set of classes. Depending on your application's requirements, you may want to build another level of ancestor objects specific to your application inherited from the extension set of classes.

The PFC includes the following foundation class and extension class objects:

Foundation Class

pfcapsrv.pbl. The pfcaprsrv.pbl includes foundation objects for application services.

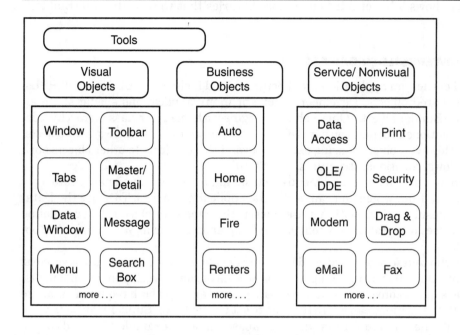

Figure 2.13   **Example of a PowerBuilder class library breakdown.**

pfcdwsrv.pbl.   The pfcdwsrv.pbl includes foundation objects for DataWindow services.

pfcmain.pbl.   The main foundation class .pbl.

pfcutil.pbl.   The pfcutil.pbl includes foundation objects for utility services.

pfcwnsrv.pbl.   The pfcwnsrv.pbl includes foundation objects for window services.

Extension Class

pfeabsrv.pbl.   The pfeabsrv.pbl includes extension objects for application services.

pfedwsrv.pbl.   The pfedwsrv.pbl includes extension objects for DataWindow services.

pfemain.pbl.   The main extension class .pbl.

pfeutil.pbl.   The pfeutil.pbl includes extension objects for utility services.

pfewnsrv.pbl.   The pfewnsrv.pbl includes extension objects for window services.

TIP You will find the PFC PBLs within the \adk\pfc directory of your Power-Builder 6 installation.

Table 2.1 shows a list of third-party class libraries that work with PowerBuilder's PFC.

SHARING POWERBUILDER OBJECTS

As described earlier, an application architecture should include a .PBL (or set of .PBLs) to store the shared objects. Developers of one or many applications should share all types of PowerBuilder objects. Object sharing begins with an object class hierarchy's definition. As mentioned earlier, you can define a class hierarchy for windows, user objects, and menus. However, object sharing extends beyond these objects to other objects such as DataWindows, functions, structures, and SQL.

For windows, user objects, and menus, you should build the functionality into a set of virtual classes from which you can derive the application objects. To share the Data-Windows, encapsulate them within a user object. By using user objects, you can define the virtual classes of DataWindow controls and implement them as you would other object hierarchies.

Through the course of application design and development, it usually becomes clear that different functions within an application will have some overlapping components. For example, a query conversation and a reporting conversation both require a database connection. Both functions can share the code to set up the PowerBuilder transaction object and handle the communication with a database. Another example of shared code is a function to generate sequential numbers. This generic type of code can provide functionality common to several application functions.

To share SQL, store the common queries within files. You can then use these files as a data source for any other application's DataWindow.

One of the most valuable benefits of object-oriented development is this ability to share objects. A correctly built PowerBuilder application uses the power of inheritance to minimize coding and maximize efficiency. Sharing objects then increases code reliability and interface consistency, and eases the task of code maintenance by reducing or eliminating the need for duplicate code.

Table 2.1   Third-Party Class Libraries

Library	URL
CornerStone	www.findyn.com
APOL	www.janiff.com/docs/softw.htm
PowerTOOL	www.powercerv.com/Tools/PowerTOOL/index.htm
PFCtool	www.powercerv.com/Tools/PFCtool/index.htm
PowerClass	www.serverlogic.com/tools.htm

PART II

Development Concepts

CHAPTER 3

DataWindows

The DataWindow object provides a simple way to retrieve, display, and update data from a specified data source. Although the data source is usually a database, it can be other things such as a text file or data structure. The DataWindow object lets you define not only the data source but a data set's presentation style, edit masks, and validation criteria.

The DataWindow control, on the other hand, is a window control that lets you incorporate DataWindow objects within a PowerBuilder window or user object. The DataWindow control has a set of events encapsulated within it that provide a great deal of flexibility, including the ability to dynamically bind to the different DataWindow objects at runtime.

This chapter discusses the following topics related to DataWindow objects, DataWindow controls, and related design considerations:

- DataWindow objects
  - Data sources
  - Presentation styles
  - Groups
  - Filters
  - Sorting
  - Sliding columns
  - Data validation
  - Display formats and edit masks
  - Computed columns and fields
  - Update properties
  - New objects in DataWindow
  - Child DataWindows
- DataWindow controls

- DataWindow buffers
- Drag-and-drop
- Transaction processing
- Dynamic DataWindows
- Query mode and prompt for criteria
- DataWindow Save As
- Design considerations
  - Embedded SQL
  - Direct data access
  - Handling large result sets
  - Shared result sets
  - Retrieve As Needed
  - DataWindows as buffers and DataStore objects
  - Code tables
  - Using a DDDW versus filling a DDLB
  - Using bitmaps within DataWindows
  - OLE columns
  - Stop light reports
  - Creating a DataWindow architecture

DataWindow objects and controls work together to provide a much simpler and more efficient database interface than writing the data access code from scratch. Because a great deal of functionality is encapsulated within both the DataWindow object and DataWindow control, you need not write a large amount of database access code.

DATAWINDOW OBJECTS

Data Sources

The DataWindow data source options are Quick Select, SQL Select, Query, External, and Stored Procedure. This section provides a brief overview of each option.

Quick Select

The Quick Select option provides a fast method for choosing the tables and columns that provide a DataWindow object's data source. The Quick Select window lets you select from the available tables within the current database. When you select the initial table, the Tables box lists all the tables with a primary or foreign key relationship with the initial table. For example, when you select the PowerSoft sample database's employee table from the Quick Select dialog box, PowerBuilder displays the screen shown in Figure 3.1.

TIP PowerBuilder displays the table comments when you select the table from the Tables box. To view a column's comments, press the right button of your mouse down while positioning the cursor on the column name.

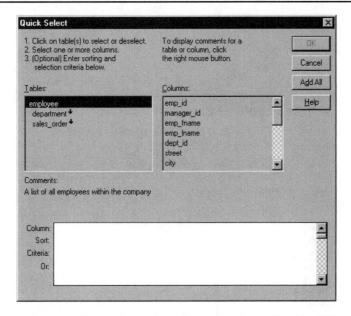

Figure 3.1   **Selecting employee data by using the Quick Select dialog box.**

Notice that PowerBuilder displays the employee table's columns within the Columns box and shows all the tables within the database that have a key relationship with the employee table indented under the employee table within the Tables box. If you then select one of the indented tables, PowerBuilder adds the list of columns from that table to the Columns box. For example, if you select the department table from the dialog box shown in Figure 3.1, the dialog box changes to that shown in Figure 3.2.

Once you select the query's tables and columns, you can specify the selection and sorting criteria within the Quick Select window by entering the criteria in the grid at the bottom of the window. For example, selecting employee records for all the department numbers over 200 sorted in descending order by the employee's last name is done on a Quick Select window that looks like Figure 3.3. This query's SQL syntax is:

```
SELECT "department"."dept_id", "employee"."emp_lname",
   "employee"."emp_fname"
FROM "employee", "department"
WHERE ( "employee"."dept_id" = "department"."dept_id" ) and
   ((("department"."dept_id" > 200)))
ORDER BY "employee"."emp_lname" DESC
```

Notice that PowerBuilder automatically adds the join between the employee and

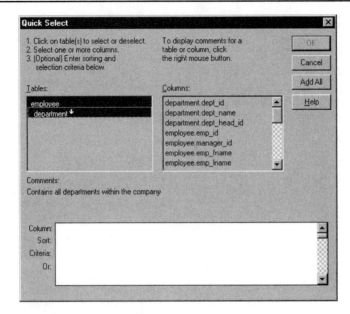

Figure 3.2 **Selecting department and employee data by using the Quick Select dialog box.**

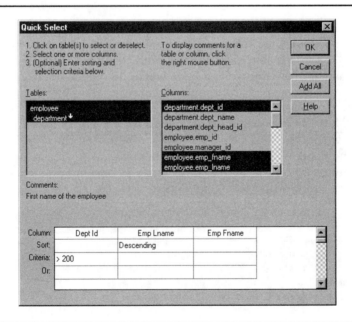

Figure 3.3 **Adding selection criteria to the Quick Select dialog box.**

department tables. PowerBuilder adds the join to the Where clause based on the defined key relationship between the two tables.

The Quick Select data source is good to use for relatively simple queries. It does not let you specify retrieval arguments or a table join (other than the join that a key relationship specifies), but you can add these later with the Select painter, at which point the query generated with a Quick Select data source is no different than a query generated with a SQL Select data source.

TIP When selecting from more than one table by using Quick Select, PowerBuilder adds only one set of join criteria to the Where clause of the resulting Select statement for each pair of tables. If more than one primary or foreign key relationship exists between two tables, verify that the correct join criteria is specified by looking at the Select statement's syntax within the Select painter.

SQL Select

The SQL Select data source is a DataWindow object's most common data source. Like the Quick Select, the SQL Select involves selecting tables and columns to construct the query. The SQL Select lets you define all aspects of a query, however, rather than just the selection columns, sort order, and limited selection criteria. Use the SQL Select data source generally for more complex queries, including those containing joins, Group By clauses, and Having clauses.

To define each element of the query, the Select painter uses a tab interface combined with drag-and-drop. For example, to sort a list of employees by last name, click the **Sort** tab and drag the emp_lname column from the list of columns on the left to the box on the right as shown in Figure 3.4.

Query

You can also use the PowerBuilder query objects as a DataWindow object's data source. To use this type of data source, simply choose the query object from the appropriate .PBL. This is a good approach to use when there is a query that you use often within an application and can save it as a file.

External

External data sources represent the data that the application does not retrieve from an application database. When creating a DataWindow with an external data source, you must define a result set. This result set is a listing of columns and their datatypes. One reason for using the DataWindow objects with external data sources is to enable the validation and editing capabilities built into the DataWindow object. You can also use the external data sources when the data is stored with the DataWindow object instead of retrieved from a database. For example, to store a list of states within a DataWindow, define an external data source with a code and description element and store the state information within the DataWindow as shown in Figure 3.5.

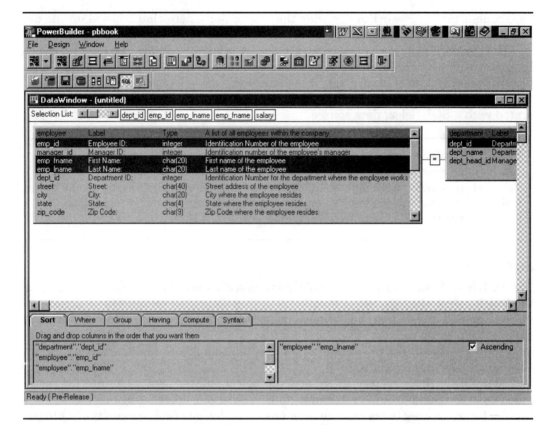

Figure 3.4 Sorting a list of employees by last name by using the Select painter.

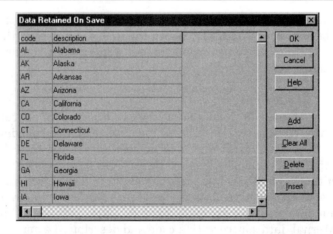

Figure 3.5 Storing a list of states within a DataWindow by using an external data source.

TIP It is highly recommended to use an external DataWindow instead of placing direct controls like single-line edit boxes, multiline edit boxes, and drop-down list boxes. By using an external DataWindow, you can better format and more easily validate the data.

Stored Procedures

If an application RDBMS supports stored procedures, you can use them as a DataWindow object's data source. To use a stored procedure as a data source, the stored procedure must have the ability to return the result sets to PowerBuilder. Most RDBMSs that support stored procedures have this capability, but using an Oracle stored procedure as a data source works a little differently. Refer to Chapter 16, "SQL Anywhere and Other Databases," for a description of how to use Oracle7 stored procedures as a DataWindow data source.

You have the choice of letting the stored procedure define the result set or building the result set manually. By default, PowerBuilder automatically builds the result set based on the stored procedure's output values. To override this feature and build the result set manually, check the Manual Result Set checkbox when choosing the stored procedure, as shown in Figure 3.6.

Presentation Styles

This section provides a brief description of the different DataWindow object presentation styles that PowerBuilder supports. For a more detailed description of each presentation style, refer to the PowerBuilder documentation.

Composite

A composite DataWindow consists of multiple DataWindows or reports within a single DataWindow. This feature, referred to as *nested* or *composite* reports, lets existing DataWindows or reports be added to any band of a DataWindow of any presentation style. You can include multiple reports within a single DataWindow, and composite reports print on the same page as the DataWindow when you print the DataWindow.

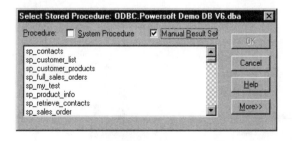

Figure 3.6   **Building a Stored Procedure's result set manually.**

A composite report may or may not be related to the DataWindow to which you add the report. Use the composite reports not related to the DataWindow to place multiple reports on the same page. For example, it may be desirable to have three DataWindows that display a single data set by using different presentation styles on a single page. Composite reports provide a simple way to do this. To create a set of nonrelated reports, select Composite as the new DataWindow's presentation style. This then displays a dialog box of all the available DataWindows. From this list, select all of the DataWindows that you want to include within the base DataWindow.

If a composite report is related to the DataWindow, the data within the composite report is in some way dependent on the data within the DataWindow. To specify the relationship between the composite report and the DataWindow, use the DataWindow painter's Specify Retrieval Criteria dialog box. For example, suppose we want to list the department ID and name within one DataWindow and include a DataWindow listing all the employees of the department as a composite report within the department DataWindow. To do this, first create the department DataWindow as shown in Figure 3.7.

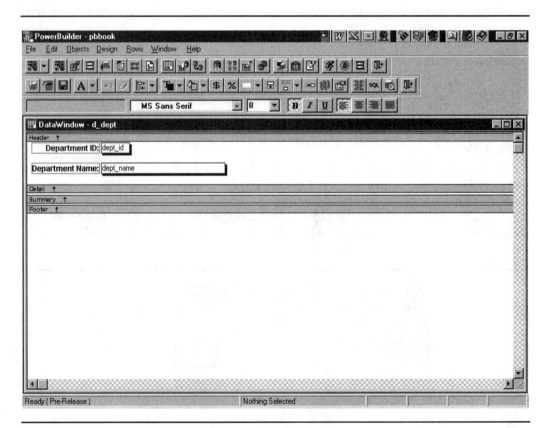

Figure 3.7   Creating the Department DataWindow.

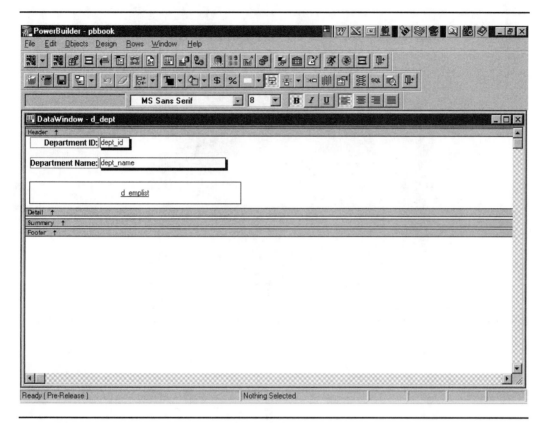

Figure 3.8   Adding the employee list DataWindow.

Next, click the report icon from the DataWindow PainterBar. PowerBuilder, in turn, displays a dialog box that lists all the available DataWindows. From this list, choose the employee list DataWindow (d_emplist) and place the DataWindow below the department name, as shown in Figure 3.8.

To define the relationship between the nested report and the DataWindow, select the **Criteria** tab of the report's Properties sheet (display the Properties sheet by clicking the right button of your mouse while positioned on the report), as shown in Figure 3.9.

The **Criteria** tab displays each column of the nested DataWindow and allows the entry of selection criteria for the nested report. Values within this dialog box may either be constants or names of columns from the base DataWindow. For this example, retrieve all the employees whose department ID is the same as the base DataWindow's department ID, as shown in Figure 3.10.

If the nested report contains retrieval arguments, specify them by using the Retrieval Arguments dialog box. To display this dialog box, select the **Arguments** tab of the report's Properties sheet, as shown in Figure 3.11.

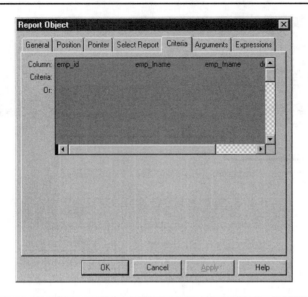

Figure 3.9 Defining the relationship between the nested report and the DataWindow.

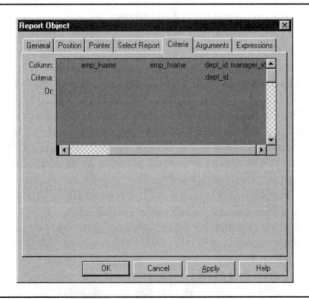

Figure 3.10 Specifying criteria for the nested report.

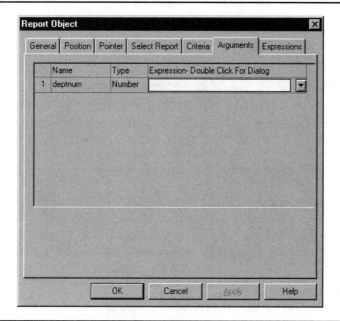

Figure 3.11   Specifying the retrieval arguments for the nested DataWindow.

The **Arguments** tab displays each retrieval argument defined for the nested DataWindow and lets you select the columns from the base DataWindow or an expression's definition. For this example, select the dept_id column. PowerBuilder uses the base DataWindow's dept_id value when retrieving data into the nested DataWindow, as shown in Figure 3.12.

Next, PowerBuilder retrieves all the employees for the current department, as shown in Figure 3.13.

Composite reports simplify the development of DataWindows with a master/detail relationship. Instead of using two (or more) separate DataWindow controls for the master and detail DataWindows—each of which must have code written to set the DataWindow's transaction object, retrieve, update, and so on—composite reports let you use a single DataWindow control and are more efficient because they require only one transaction.

TIP Although a good data source, composite reports support no more than 23 nested reports. Also, all composite reports display with the print preview on at runtime.

Crosstab

The Crosstab presentation style presents data within a matrix format, as shown in Figure 3.14.

Figure 3.15 shows the Crosstab Definition dialog box for the preceding example.

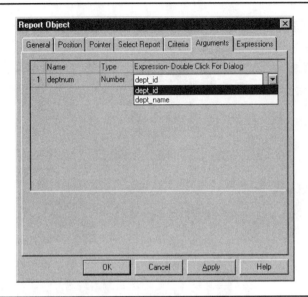

Figure 3.12   Selecting the base DataWindow's dept_id value.

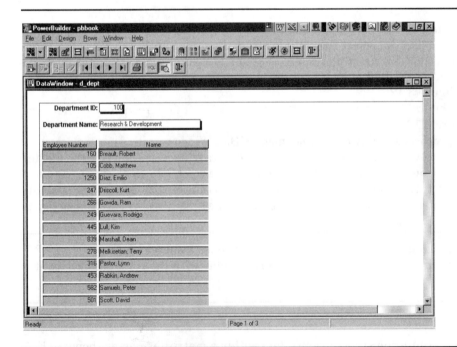

Figure 3.13   Retrieval of all the employees for the current department.

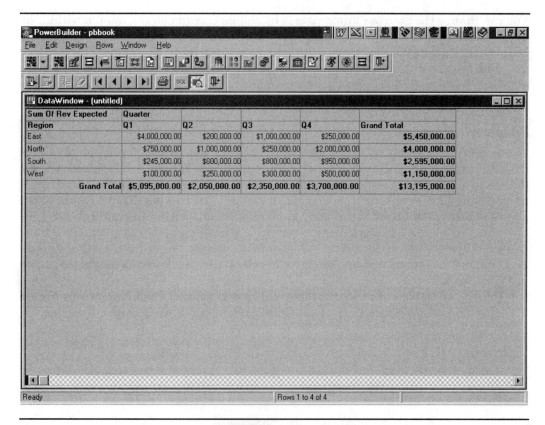

Figure 3.14   A sample Crosstab DataWindow.

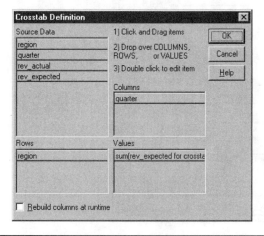

Figure 3.15   The Crosstab Definition dialog box.

You can change the Source column names by double-clicking on the column within the Crosstab Definition dialog box's Source Data list. To do this at runtime, modify the DataWindow's DataWindow.Crosstab.Sourcenames attribute. You can do this by using the **Modify( )** function or by referencing the DataWindow object directly using the dot notation. To display the Crosstab Definition dialog box at runtime, call the DataWindow function **datawindow.CrosstabDialog( )**.

Freeform

The freeform presentation style, generally used for data entry forms, places fields down the page, with labels next to each data column. PowerBuilder lets you modify the default field placement of the freeform DataWindows. You can do this by specifying a wrap height. The wrap height, measured in inches, specifies the default height of the DataWindow's detail band. This lets you place the fields within the multiple columns of the detail band. For example, to specify a wrap height of one inch, select the freeform presentation style and click the Options... button on the new DataWindow dialog box. In the Options dialog box, enter (or select) the desired wrap height, as shown in Figure 3.16.

The default DataWindow then creates multiple columns of fields if necessary. Figure 3.17 shows an example default freeform DataWindow with a wrap height of one inch.

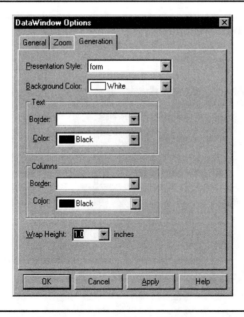

Figure 3.16   Specifying a wrap height within the Options dialog box.

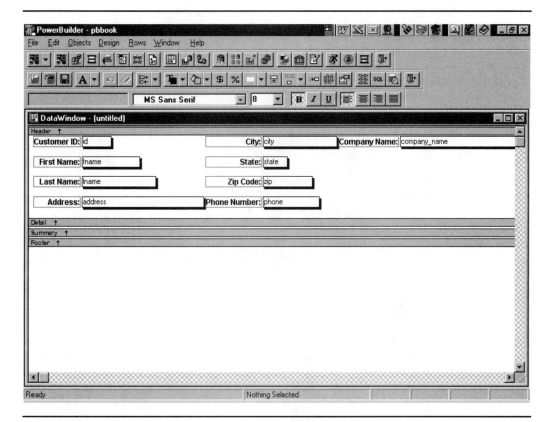

Figure 3.17   A sample freeform DataWindow with a wrap height of one inch.

TIP While this previous example shows only one row, you can display additional rows by scrolling down the page. If you want to show only one row, size the DataWindow control to show only a single row and configure to not allow scrolling.

Graph

The graph presentation style lets you choose from a wide range of graph types to present the DataWindow data. Chapter 7, "Graphs and Reporting," further discusses graphs.

Grid

The grid presentation style presents the data within a row-column format. Rows and columns are separated by grid lines, and you can resize the columns.

Click the right button of your mouse on the grid DataWindow object and select **Prop-**

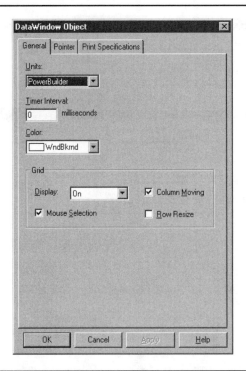

Figure 3.18 Use the DataWindow Object Properties Sheet to set the DataWindow Object's properties.

erties. PowerBuilder, in turn, displays the DataWindow Object Properties Sheet (see Figure 3.18), which you can use to set the various grid properties for the DataWindow.

TIP You can change the column placement as well as the size of the column during the preview mode.

Group

The group presentation style lets you define the groups when PowerBuilder creates the DataWindow. The next section discusses groups in more detail.

Label

The label presentation style is a customized report style you can use to print mailing labels. You can define the label's size, printing sequence, and other attributes by using the label specification dialog box, as shown in Figure 3.19.

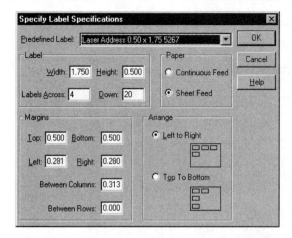

Figure 3.19   The Label Specification dialog box.

N-Up

The N-Up presentation style lets you display the rows side by side within the Data-Window. You can define the number of rows to display within the DataWindow's detail band.

This presentation style is enhanced within PowerBuilder 6. Powersoft has improved the way in which PowerBuilder displays the row selection within an N-Up DataWindow object. When the user selects a specific row, only that row is highlighted. Formerly, PowerBuilder highlighted that row and all the other rows occurring on the same detail line as the selected row.

OLE 2

With an OLE 2 presentation style, you can pass the data that the application retrieves into a DataWindow to an OLE 2 server application by simply double-clicking to activate the OLE 2 server application. To create a DataWindow with an OLE 2 presentation style, select the OLE 2 presentation style with the desired data source. You can use any data source in combination with the OLE 2 presentation style. After building the Select statement for the DataWindow, PowerBuilder displays the Insert Object dialog box, as shown in Figure 3.20.

This dialog box lets you choose the type of object to include within the DataWindow. You have the option of creating the OLE object as a new object, creating the object from an existing file, or inserting a custom control. To create a new object, select the type of object to create from the list of available object types on the **Create New** tab of the Insert Object dialog box. For example, suppose we want to graphically display the number of employees within each department by using Microsoft Graph. To do this, select the dept_id and emp_id columns from the employee table and complete the Insert Object dialog box.

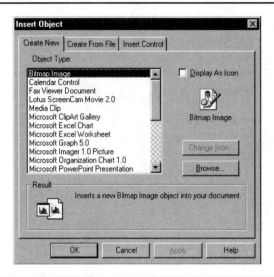

Figure 3.20   The Insert Object dialog box.

Notice in Figure 3.21 that the **Display as Icon** option is selected. This means that that object is represented by an icon, rather than by the object's contents. After the Insert Object dialog box is completed, the DataWindow painter looks like Figure 3.22.

Next, we need to specify which data you want to pass from the DataWindow to the Microsoft Graph OLE server. Within our example, we need to group the data by de-

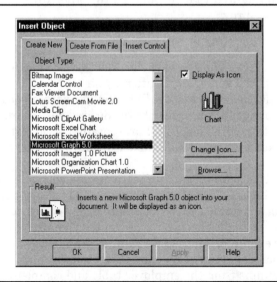

Figure 3.21   Creating a new Microsoft Graph OLE Object.

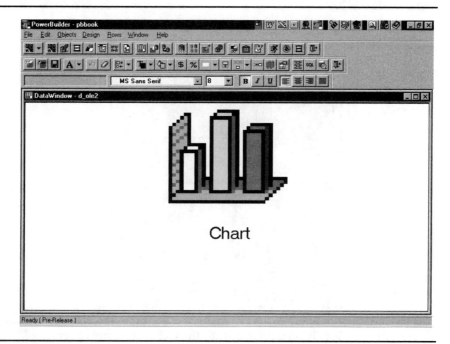

Figure 3.22   The DataWindow painter with a Microsoft Graph OLE object.

partment ID and pass the department ID along with the number of employees within each department to Microsoft Graph. To do this, complete the **Data** tab of the object's properties sheet as shown in Figure 3.23.

Also, to pass the name of the chart to Microsoft Graph, complete the **Options** tab of the properties sheet as shown in Figure 3.24. The **Options** tab also lets you set other object options. The **Contents** option specifies whether the object is embedded or linked, or if either method is allowed if the object is inserted programmatically. **Display Type** specifies whether the object's contents are displayed or an icon represents the object. The **Activation** option specifies how the object is activated, either by double-clicking or programmatically. The **Link Update** option specifies whether the link to the object is updated automatically or manually. Updating the link automatically means the link is updated when the object is opened and whenever the object changes within the server application.

When data is retrieved into the DataWindow, double-clicking on the icon opens Microsoft Graph and passes the data specified within the **Data** tab from the DataWindow to Microsoft Graph, the OLE 2 server application. After some cosmetic changes to the graph object itself, Figure 3.25 shows the resulting graph.

To insert a file's contents as an object, select the **Create From File** tab on the Insert Object dialog box and enter the file's name. Creating the OLE object from a file lets that file be activated at runtime by using the application that created it. For example,

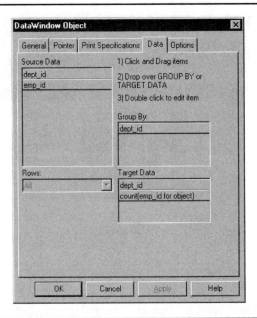

Figure 3.23 Specifying data to pass to the OLE Server application.

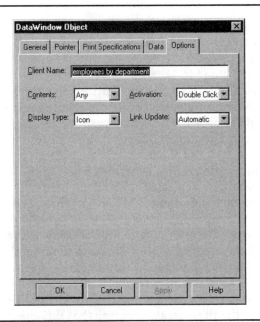

Figure 3.24 Completing the Options tab.

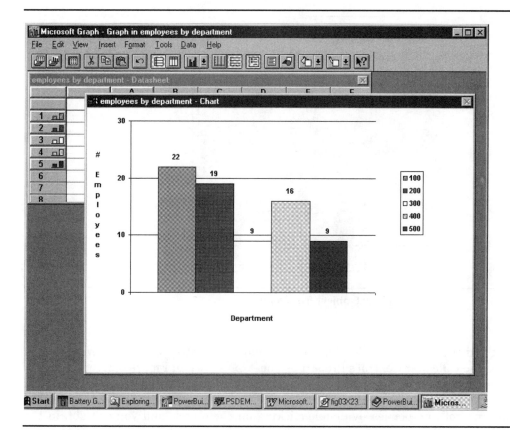

Figure 3.25   The resulting Microsoft Graph object.

to insert the Microsoft Word document mailmerg.doc as an object within a DataWindow, complete the Insert Object dialog box as shown in Figure 3.26.

When creating an object from a file, you have the option to Link the object to the selected file. This means that any changes to the selected file are reflected within the object. If you do not select the Link option, PowerBuilder inserts the file's contents into the DataWindow as an object, meaning that any changes to the selected file are not reflected within the object.

You also have the option of displaying the object as an icon, rather than the object's contents. In this example, the object is linked to mailmerg.doc, and PowerBuilder displays the object as an icon.

The third option is to insert a custom control. To do this, click the **Insert Control** tab on the Insert Object dialog box. A list of registered custom controls available for use within a PowerBuilder application (either within a DataWindow object or a Window control) are displayed. For example, to insert the Calendar Control, select the control from

Figure 3.26 Creating an OLE object from a file.

the list and click OK. PowerBuilder, in turn, adds the control to the DataWindow and displays the Calendar Control's Properties sheet, as shown in Figure 3.27.

The properties for a custom control are divided into control-specific properties (shown in Figure 3.27) and PowerBuilder OLE object properties. You can obtain the custom control's properties by double-clicking on the object, and you can obtain the PowerBuilder OLE object properties by selecting the **Properties...** option of the control's popup menu (display by clicking the right button of your mouse while positioned on the object).

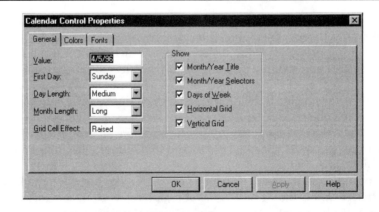

Figure 3.27 The Calendar Control's Properties sheet.

RichText

The RichText presentation style is a sophisticated style that lets you load RTF (Rich Text Format) files and provides enhanced editing capabilities within a DataWindow. For more information on the RichText presentation style, see Chapter 7, "Graphs and Reporting."

Tabular

The tabular presentation style presents data in the format of columns across the page with a header above each column. The tabular format is very similar to the Grid format; both are used to display several rows of data at once. However, in the case of grid presentation style, the user can size the columns and rows at runtime. The tabular presentation style does not allow this.

Groups

PowerBuilder lets related rows be grouped together for the purposes of formatting or performing group-related functions such as group sums, averages, and the like. Using a PowerBuilder group is different from adding a Group By clause to a Select statement because the grouping is done on the client rather than the server.

    You can create groups either by specifying a group presentation style when creating a new DataWindow or by selecting the **Create Group...** option from the DataWindow painter's **Rows** menu. PowerBuilder assigns a sequential number (beginning with 1) as the group name. To show an average salary for all the employees by manager within a department, first create a group break on the dept_id and manager_id columns within the employee table, as shown in Figure 3.28. Next, create a computed field with

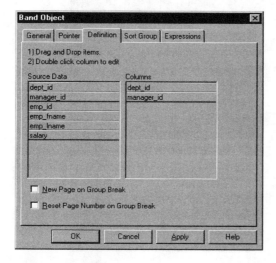

Figure 3.28   **Specifying the Group Columns.**

the expression shown in Figure 3.29. PowerBuilder displays the employee data as shown in Figure 3.30.

PowerBuilder performs the group calculations only after retrieving all the data from the database. If rows are inserted, deleted, or modified during a user session, it may be necessary to repeat the group calculation on the new set of rows. Rather than retrieving the data again, you can perform the calculation by calling the PowerBuilder **GroupCalc( )** function.

TIP It is important to make sure you sort the data before using the data within a group. You can do the sorting either on the server, by adding an Order By clause to the Select statement, or on the client, by specifying the sort criteria when creating the DataWindow or by using the **Sort( )** function.

Filters

Filters provide a way to limit the part of a result set a user interacts with. A filter is different from a Where clause within the DataWindow's Select statement in that it is used on the client instead of the server. With a filter, the server returns all the data from a Select, and then PowerBuilder filters the data. A filter is a Boolean expression you define by using the PowerBuilder functions. You can define the filter shown in Figure 3.31 for the preceding example to limit the data displayed within the DataWindow to those rows within which dept_id = 100.

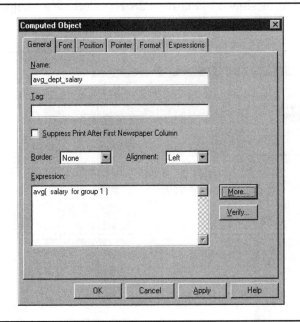

Figure 3.29   **Creating a computed field.**

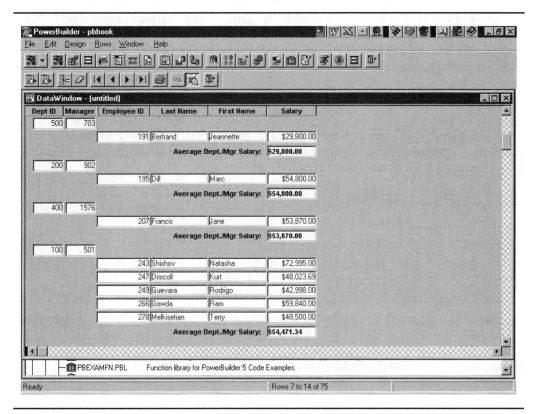

Figure 3.30   PowerBuilder displaying the employee data.

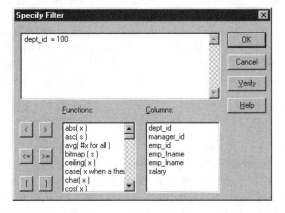

Figure 3.31   Specifying a filter.

You can modify the filters dynamically by using the **SetFilter( )** and **Filter( )** functions. SetFilter( ) lets you define a new filter for a DataWindow, while Filter( ) actually applies the filter to the DataWindow. For example, to change the filter in the last example from dept_id = 100 to dept_id = 200, PowerBuilder executes the following script:

```
dw_emp.SetFilter("dept_id = 200")
dw_emp.Filter( )
```

To determine how many rows have been filtered out, use the **FilteredCount( )** function. For example, the following script uses FilteredCount( ) to tell how many employees work within departments other than 200:

```
dw_emp.Retrieve( )
dw_emp.SetFilter("dept_id = 200")
dw_emp.Filter( )
If dw_emp.FilteredCount( ) > 0 Then
    // Processing for non dept. 200 employees
End If
```

Using filters provides some flexibility with regard to which data is displayed within a DataWindow. Filters can also improve performance by limiting the number of required database retrievals. They do, however, add some overhead on the client. In addition, instead of retrieving a large result set and using filters, it is generally better to use a Where clause to restrict the amount of data the server returns.

Sorting

Like filters, you can do sorting on the client as well as the server. You can accomplish sorting on the server by using an Order By clause within a SQL Select statement. When sorting on the client, the server returns all the data from a Select to the client and then PowerBuilder sorts the data. This provides a method of off-loading the sorting process from the server to the client.

You can change a DataWindow sort order dynamically by using the **SetSort( )** and Sort( ) functions. SetSort( ) defines a DataWindow's sort order, while Sort( ) actually performs the sort operation on the data. For example, the following script changes a DataWindow's sort order to sort on the manager_id field. The script then sorts the data:

```
dw_emp.SetSort("manager_id")
dw_emp.Sort( )
```

Whether to sort on the client or the server depends on the result set's size, the resources available on the server and client, and how often the sorting criteria are to be changed. If server resources are available, you can do the sorting more quickly on the server, but if you must sort the data multiple times within an application, sorting on the client usually results in better overall performance than executing the query multiple times on the server.

Sliding Columns

Sliding columns provide a way to remove the excess space between the columns within a DataWindow. Three options are available for sliding columns:

Left. Slides the selected column to the left, removing the excess space between the selected column and the column to its left. One popular use of sliding the columns to the left is the removal of space between the first and last name. Without this capability, presenting the first and last name with a single space between the two usually requires creating a computed field or including the concatenation within the DataWindow's Select statement. This feature makes it easier to present the data in this fashion.

Up-All Above. Slides all the columns positioned above the selected column up, removing the excess vertical space between the columns. You can use this for such things as mailing labels.

Up-Directly Above. Slides only the columns positioned directly above the selected column up, removing the excess vertical space between the columns.

TIP To use the sliding columns, set the column's AutoSize Height attribute to True. This is because blank columns still have a height that you must be able to change in order to slide the column.

For example, suppose we want to retrieve a list of employees and display the first and last name with a single space between them. By default, the data is presented as shown in Figure 3.32.

To slide the last name column to the left, select the last name column, click the right button of your mouse on the column and set the Slide attribute to On. PowerBuilder, in turn, displays the list with a single space between the first and last name, as shown in Figure 3.33.

Data Validation

One benefit of using DataWindows is the built-in validation capabilities. To better understand how validation works, it is necessary to look at how PowerBuilder actually represents a DataWindow to the user. A DataWindow consists of two logical pieces—a presentation layer (consisting of a floating "edit control") and the underlying DataWindow buffer. The user enters the data into the edit control. The application must then validate this data before passing the data to the DataWindow buffer, as shown in Figure 3.34.

In this example, the salary retrieved from the database for the first employee is $41,023.69. After retrieval, this value is within both the edit control and the DataWindow buffer. When the user changes this value to $50,000.00, the change is recognized only within the edit control. The DataWindow buffer does not receive the new value until the data is validated.

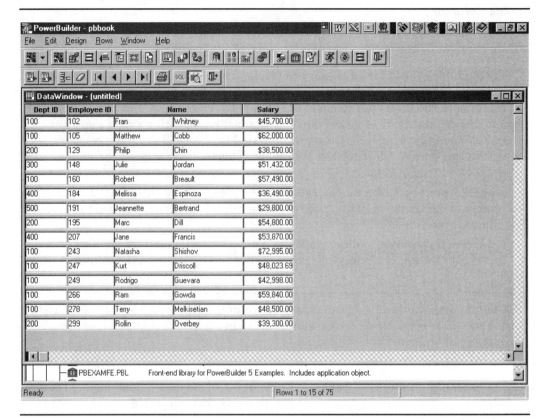

Figure 3.32 The default listing of employee first and last name.

TIP You can make changes to the DataWindow buffer directly by using the **SetItem( )** function or by using dot notation. This bypasses all the validations other than the datatype validation.

Any of the following can trigger validation:

- The user attempts to leave the column.
- The user presses the Enter key.
- The **AcceptText( )** function is executed.

These events cause PowerBuilder to begin its three-step validation process:

1. Datatype validation
2. Validation Rules validation
3. ItemChanged Event validation

The following sections discuss these steps.

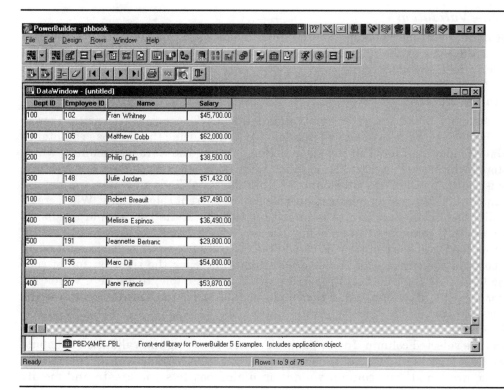

Figure 3.33   Result of sliding the last name column.

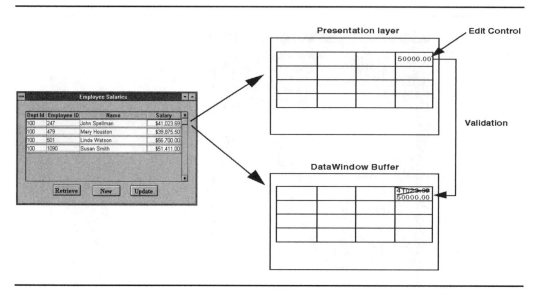

Figure 3.34   Validation of the data that the user enters into the edit control.

Datatype Validation

In the datatype validation step, PowerBuilder makes sure that the datatype the user enters is the same as the column's datatype. For example, if a user enters "ABC" into a numeric field, an error occurs.

Validation Rules

PowerBuilder lets you create custom validation rules. These rules consist of Power-Script Boolean expressions that you can define either by using the Database painter or the DataWindow painter. The rules you define by using the Database painter, which are stored within the PowerBuilder system tables as extended attributes, are available for reuse with any DataWindow column. Within the DataWindow painter, you can use a default validation rule or create a new rule for the current column only. When creating validation rules, therefore, it is important to know if the rule should be shared among multiple columns within any application.

From the Database painter, you can define the rules in two ways. The first method is to position the cursor over the desired column and click the right button of your mouse to display the column's Properties sheet. For example, to create a validation rule for the dept_id column within the employee table, click the **Validation** tab on the dept_id's Properties sheet, as shown in Figure 3.35.

PowerBuilder, in turn, displays a list of all the rules defined for the same data-type as the selected column. In our example, when selecting the validation attribute for the dept_id column, all the rules for the integer type columns within the current database are listed. The column validation dialog box lets you create and modify rules, along with the setting of an initial value for the column.

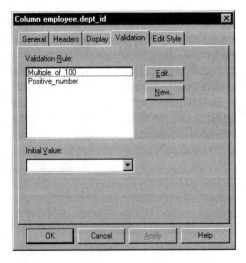

Figure 3.35 Creating a validation rule for the dept_id column.

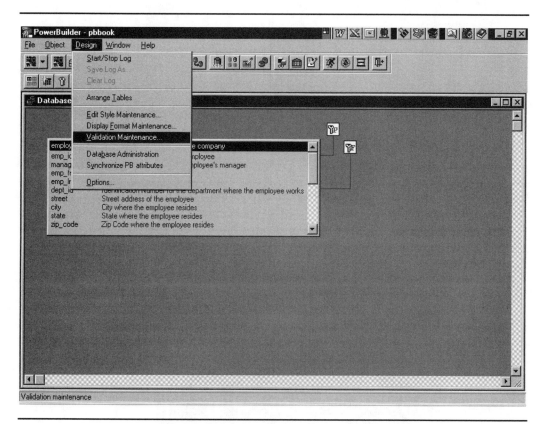

Figure 3.36   Selecting the Validation Maintenance... option.

The second method is to select the **Validation Maintenance...** option from the Database painter's **Design** menu, as shown in Figure 3.36.

PowerBuilder, in turn, lists all the defined rules for the current database, as shown in Figure 3.37.

When you define a rule for a column by using the Database painter, the rule is used whenever the column is included as part of a DataWindow. When you place the column onto a DataWindow, any changes made to the rule subsequently are not reflected within the column on the DataWindow.

To define a rule from the DataWindow painter, select the **Validation** tab from the Properties sheet of the desired column (obtained by selecting the column and clicking the right button of your mouse). PowerBuilder, in turn, displays the column validation definition dialog box, on which the validation rule and default validation error message are defined, as shown in Figure 3.38. For information on the set of PowerBuilder functions available for use within rule expressions, see the PowerBuilder Function Reference.

You should realize that any rules that you define from the DataWindow painter are not stored within the system tables, so other columns cannot use them.

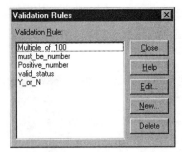

Figure 3.37 A listing of all the defined validation rules.

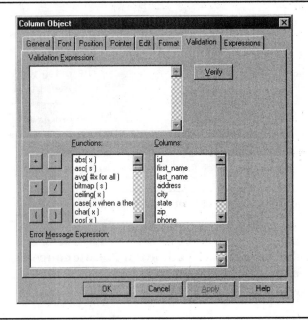

Figure 3.38 Defining a validation rule from the DataWindow painter.

Changing Rules Dynamically

You can change rules at runtime by using the **GetValidate( )** and **SetValidate( )** functions. GetValidate( ) retrieves a DataWindow column's current rule into a string variable. SetValidate( ) redefines a column's rule. Generally you use these functions to temporarily change a rule during execution and later reset the rule to its original value. You can accomplish this same functionality by using the dot notation to reference the validation and validationMsg attributes directly. For example, the following code changes the ID column's validation rule within DataWindow dw_custlist to "Number(GetText( )) > 100" (meaning that the value that the user enters within the ID column must be greater than 100):

```
dw_custlist.Object.id.validation = "Number(GetText( )) > 100"
```

You can use the same method to change the ID column's validation message within the DataWindow dw_custlist to "ID must be numeric":

```
dw_custlist.Object.id.validationMsg = "ID must be numeric"
```

TIP For performance reasons, you should try to minimize the number of times you change a rule.

ItemChanged Event

The ItemChanged event is triggered whenever data in a column is changed and the column loses focus. Within columns with a DropDownListBox edit style, the ItemChanged event is triggered when a user selects an item within the list but before the column loses focus. In either case, usually you use the ItemChanged event to validate any business rules pertaining to the column. This is the validation process's final step.

It is important that the code within the ItemChanged event does not cause another ItemChanged event to be triggered, resulting in an endless loop. To keep this from occurring, you should not put the **AcceptText( )**, **SetColumn( )**, and **SetRow( )** function calls into the ItemChanged script. In addition, because the **Update( )** function does an AcceptText( ) by default, you should call the Update( ) function only with the first parameter set to False to keep AcceptText( ) from being executed.

The ItemChanged event has a set of return codes associated with it that let you specify the action that is taken when the event occurs. For the ItemChanged event, the valid return codes are:

0 to accept the data value (default)

1 to reject the data value and do not allow the focus to change

2 to reject the data value but allow the focus to change

Process Flow

Figure 3.39 shows the validation process flow diagram. It is important to note that the validation process occurs only if data is changed. To determine whether data is changed, compare the value within the edit control to the item within the DataWindow buffer. Because PowerBuilder does not make this comparison until the column loses focus, the situations in which a user makes a change and reenters the original value before leaving the column are not considered changes.

As each level of validation is passed, PowerBuilder performs the test at the next level (if available). If any of the steps fail, PowerBuilder triggers the ItemError event. If there is no error-handling code within the ItemError event, PowerBuilder handles

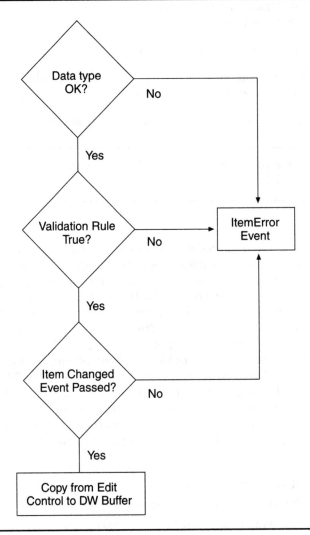

Figure 3.39   The validation process flow.

the error by displaying a message box similar to the one in Figure 3.40. At this point, the cursor returns to the field in question and the user must reenter the value.

TIP To restore the original value from the DataWindow buffer into the edit control, press the Escape key.

Figure 3.40 PowerBuilder's standard DataWindow error message box.

ItemError Event

You can use the ItemError event to code customized error handling such as writing to an error log when an error occurs or changing the message displayed to the user. You can place the following code within a DataWindow control's ItemError event to change the error message displayed to the user:

```
string sColName

// Get the current column name by using the dwo event argument
sColName = dwo.name

// Call the function to display the custom error message
DisplayMsg("Validation Error", "'" + data + "' is not valid for
column '" + & sColName + "'")

// Return 1 to not display system message
Return 1
```

This code uses the event argument dwo to determine the name of the column for which the ItemError event was executed. The dwo argument is of type DWObject, which is used specifically as a reference to a DataWindow column. Also, the ItemError event uses its data argument to display the value that the user enters and return codes to determine how the error is handled. The valid return code values for the ItemError event are:

0 to reject the data value and show a system error screen (default)

1 to reject the data value but do not show a system error screen

2 to accept the data value

3 to reject the data value but allow the focus to change

TIP Include a call to AcceptText( ) within the DataWindow control's LoseFocus event to make sure the data at the current position within the DataWindow is validated.

Protecting Columns

The Protect column attribute provides a way to prevent users from entering a column without the need to set the tab order to 0. The Protect attribute can be a constant or an expression, and you can set the attribute by using the **Expressions** tab of the column's Properties sheet, as shown in Figure 3.41.

If the expression defined for a column's Protect attribute evaluates to True, the column is protected and the user cannot enter the column. If the expression evaluates to False, the column is not protected, and the user can enter the column. The Protect attribute provides a simple way of conditionally protecting a column by using such things as row or column status and the value of other columns to determine if a column should be protected. For example, if a column should be protected for the existing rows and unprotected for new rows, you could define the protect expression as shown in Figure 3.42.

The Protect attribute provides a way to protect a column without requiring additional code to set the column's tab order.

RowFocusChanging Event

PowerBuilder 6 provides a new RowFocusChanging event for the DataWindow control. This event occurs just before the RowFocusChanged event. The RowFocusChanging event is fired when the current row is about to change within the DataWindow. This event provides two arguments, namely, currentrow (the row number for the current row) and newrow (the row number to which the DataWindow control changes focus).

Figure 3.41   A DataWindow column's Expressions tab.

Figure 3.42   **Defining the Protect attribute expression.**

This event returns 0 to continue processing and 1 to stop the user from changing the current row.

This event is a winner for PowerBuilder developers as you can do a lot of validations before you let the user change the row. Remember, in the master detail relationships in which you wanted to do some validations before letting the user change the master row, this event provides you the opportunity to code them easily.

Code Tables

Code tables provide a method of validation by ensuring that the data the user enters is within a predefined table of codes. The section on design considerations later in this chapter discusses the code tables in further detail.

Finding Required Columns

To find all the required DataWindow columns that contain Null, use the **Find-Required( )** DataWindow function. This function's syntax is:

```
datawindowname.FindRequired ( dwbuffer, row, colnbr, colname, updateonly )
```

where:

> **datawindowname.**   The name of the DataWindow control in which to find the required columns that have Null values.

dwbuffer. A dwBuffer enumerated datatype indicating the DataWindow buffer to search for the required columns (Primary!, Filtered!).

row. The row at which to begin searching (1 to search all the rows). Find-Required( ) increments the row number automatically after it validates the row within all the columns. When it finds a row with a required column with a Null value, its row number is stored within row. After FindRequired( ) validates the last column within the last row, it sets row to 0.

colnbr. The number of the column at which to begin searching (1 to search all the columns). After validating the last column, FindRequired( ) sets colnbr to 1 and increments the row. When FindRequired( ) finds a required column without a Null value, the function stores the column number in colnbr.

colname. String variable in which to store the name of the required column containing a Null value (colnbr's name).

updateonly. Indicates whether to validate all the rows and columns or only the rows that are inserted or modified. (True validates only those that changed. Setting updateonly to True enhances performance within large DataWindows. False validates all the rows and columns.)

Starting at row colnbr within datawindowname, FindRequired( ) finds the row and column location of a required column that contains a Null value and stores the row number within row, the column number within colnbr, and the column name within colname. If updateonly is True, FindRequired( ) checks only the rows that are inserted or modified.

To prevent sending an Insert or Update statement that is known to cause an error, you should call FindRequired( ) before updating a DataWindow. The following code illustrates the use of FindRequired( ):

```
long    ll_row
int     li_colnum
string  ls_colname

ll_row = 1
li_colnum = 1

// Loop to find all the instances
Do While ll_row <> 0
    // Exit if an error occurs
    If dw_master.FindRequired (Primary!, ll_row, li_colnum, ls_colname, &
                        True) < 0 Then
        Exit
    End If

    // If ll_row is not 0, a required row, column was found without a
    // value.
    // Display a message indicating the row and column in error
```

```
        If ll_row <> 0 Then
            MessageBox("Required Value Missing","Enter a value in " + &
                       ls_colname +"Row " + string (ll_row) )
            // Go to the row and column in error
            dw_master.SetColumn(li_colnum)
            dw_master.ScrollToRow(ll_row)
            Exit
        End If


        // This row and column was ok, continue
    Loop
```

Display Formats and Edit Masks

Display formats control how PowerBuilder displays the data to the user; an edit mask defines the way the user must enter the data. While these two things have a great deal in common, they can be different for a given column. For example, a phone number may have an edit mask of ########## and a display format of (###) ###-####.

PowerBuilder lets you create custom display formats and edit masks by using either the Database painter or the DataWindow painter. PowerBuilder stores the formats and edit masks you define by using the Database painter within the PowerBuilder system tables as extended attributes and are available for reuse with any DataWindow column. Within the DataWindow painter, you can use a default format or edit mask or you can create a new edit mask for the current column only. When creating a display format or edit mask, therefore, it is important to know if multiple columns within any application will share the format or mask.

From the Database painter, you can define the display formats in two ways. The first method is to position the cursor over the desired column and click the right button of your mouse to display the column's Properties sheet. For example, to create a display format for the dept_id column within the employee table, click the **Display** tab on the dept_id's Properties sheet, as shown in Figure 3.43.

PowerBuilder displays a list of all the display formats defined for the same datatype as the selected column. In our example, when selecting the display format for the dept_id column, PowerBuilder lists all the display formats for the integer type columns within the current database. The display dialog box lets you create and modify the display formats, along with the column's justification, display height, and display width.

For the edit masks, select the **Edit Style** tab from the column's Properties sheet, as shown in Figure 3.44. This dialog box lists all the edit styles defined for the current database.

To modify an existing edit mask, select the edit style and press the **Edit...** button. To create a new edit mask for a dept_id column that only allows three numbers, click the **New...** button on the Edit Style dialog box and complete the dialog box as shown in Figure 3.45.

The second method you can use to define the display formats and edit masks from the Database painter is by selecting the **Edit Style Maintenance...** and **Display Format Maintenance...** options from the Design menu, respectively, as shown in Figure 3.46.

Figure 3.43   The Display tab for the dept_id column.

When you define a display format or edit mask for a column by using the Database painter, the format or mask is used whenever you include the column as part of a DataWindow. When you place the column onto a DataWindow, the changes you make to the format or edit mask subsequently are not reflected within the column on the DataWindow.

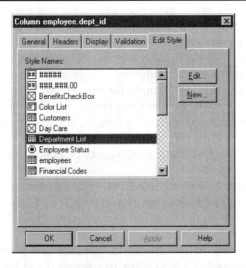

Figure 3.44   The Edit Style tab for the dept_id column.

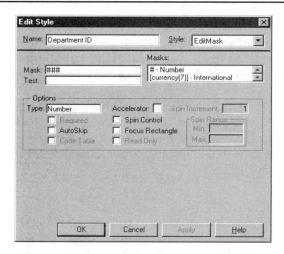

Figure 3.45   Defining a new Edit Mask.

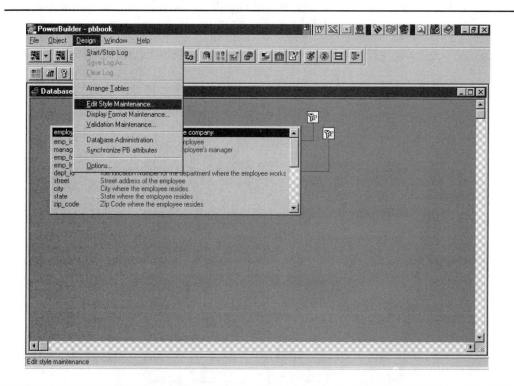

Figure 3.46   Defining the edit styles and display formats from the Database painter's
                    <u>D</u>esign menu.

To define a display format from the DataWindow painter, select the **Format** tab from the Properties sheet of the desired column (obtained by selecting the column and holding down the right button of your mouse). PowerBuilder, in turn, displays all the formats defined for the column's datatype. In our example, with the dept_id column, the display format dialog box displays all the defined formats for an integer datatype, as shown in Figure 3.47.

To define an edit mask from the DataWindow painter, select the **Edit** tab from the Properties sheet and select **Edit Mask** from the Style drop-down listbox. PowerBuilder, in turn, displays all the edit masks defined for the column's datatype. In our example, with the dept_id column, the Edit dialog box displays all the defined edit masks for an integer datatype, as shown in Figure 3.48.

Changing Display Formats

You can change the display formats dynamically at runtime by using the **GetFormat( )** and **SetFormat( )** functions. GetFormat( ) retrieves a DataWindow column's current display format into a string variable. SetFormat( ) redefines a column's display format. Generally, you use these functions to temporarily change a display format during execution and later reset the format to its original value. To illustrate the changing of display formats, suppose the format of a string DataWindow column changes depending on the value retrieved from the database. For example, if the value is a phone number, the display format is (@@@) @@@–@@@@, but if the value is a social security number, the format is @@@-@@-@@@@. To do this, you need to add the following code within the

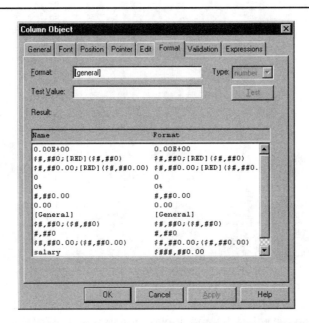

Figure 3.47   The Format tab for the dept_id column.

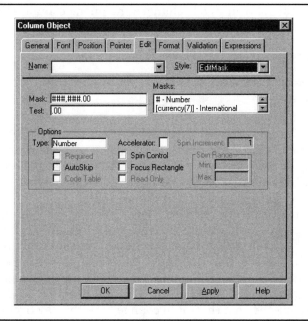

Figure 3.48   **Listing all the edit masks for the integer columns.**

Retrieve command button's clicked event (assume the instance variable is_NumType is previously set):

```
int     li_RetCode
string ls_OldFormat

ls_OldFormat = dw_master.GetFormat("num_col")

Choose Case is_NumType
    Case "PHONE"
        dw_master.SetFormat("num_col","(@@@) @@@-@@@@")
    Case "SOCIAL_SEC"
        dw_master.SetFormat("num_col","@@@-@@-@@@@")
End Choose
li_RetCode = dw_master.Retrieve ( )

If (li_RetCode = -1) Then
  MessageBox("Select Error", SQLCA.SQLERRTEXT)
End If
```

Like the validation attribute described earlier, you can also change the display format programmatically by using the dot notation to reference the format attribute directly. For example, the following code changes the phone column's display format within the DataWindow dw_master to "(@@@) @@@-@@@@":

```
dw_master.Object.phone.format = "(@@@) @@@-@@@@"
```

Using the dot notation provides a simpler, more direct way to modify all the DataWindow attributes.

Spin Controls

A spin control is a type of edit mask that lets the users increment and decrement a value by clicking an up or down arrow on the control. To define a spin control, you need to check the Spin Control checkbox in the Edit Mask definition window. On checking this option, the data is displayed as shown in Figure 3.49.

You can define spin controls for numbers, dates, and strings. For numbers, a spin control uses the values you enter within the Spin Range group box and increments/decrements the value by the number within the Spin Increment column.

The same is true for dates, except that the values you enter within the Spin Range group box must be valid dates. When changing the date values with a spin control, you must change the day, month, and year individually. For example, to change 01/28/93 to 02/01/93 requires using the spin control to change both the day (from 28 to 01) and the month (from 01 to 02). You cannot make the change by selecting the entire date and clicking the up arrow four times.

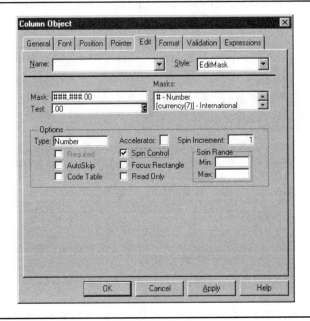

Figure 3.49   Defining a spin control.

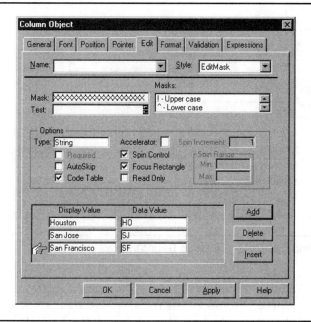

Figure 3.50 Defining a spin control for a list of cities.

For strings, what is within the code table display determines the range of values. For example, to use a spin control to choose between a set of cities, define the edit mask as shown in Figure 3.50. The user can then scroll through the list of cities by using the spin control.

Computed Columns and Fields

You can greatly enhance the DataWindows through the use of computed columns and fields. Computed columns are additional columns that you can add to a DataWindow as part of the SQL Select statement used to retrieve the DataWindow's data. Computed columns can consist of columns, RDBMS functions (not PowerScript functions), operators, and retrieval arguments. Because they are within the Select statement, computed columns are calculated only when the DataWindow's **Retrieve( )** function is executed. The two important things to remember about computed columns are that they are an extension of the RDBMS language (not PowerScript), and, because they are part of the Select statement, you can use them only within a DataWindow's detail band.

For example, the following SQL statement creates a computed column with each product's total price, calculated as the product's unit price multiplied by the number of products ordered:

```
SELECT prod_num, prod_price, prod_qty, product_price * qty FROM Products;
```

Computed fields, on the other hand, are fields that PowerBuilder creates dynami-

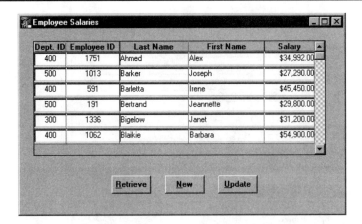

Figure 3.51 The employee salary tracking DataWindow.

cally *after* the DataWindow's Retrieve( ) function is executed. You can change computed fields, which you can use within all the DataWindow bands (header, group headers, detail, group trailers, summary, and footer), based on the DataWindow object's contents. Unlike computed columns, computed fields are not restricted to the RDBMS functions. They can contain both built-in and user-defined PowerScript functions, columns, operators, retrieval arguments, and references to other computed fields.

Computed fields are commonly used to provide summary information (both overall and by group), concatenated data ("Average salary for Dept." + dept_id + ":"), and system information (date, userid, etc.). For example, assume the DataWindow shown in Figure 3.51 is used to track employee salary information and suppose you want to enhance this DataWindow to do the following:

- Show each employee's average monthly salary
- Group the list by department and show the average monthly salary for the employees within the department
- Add a page number to the bottom of each page

To show the average monthly salary for each employee, create the computed field as shown in Figure 3.52.

Place the new computed field at the end of the DataWindow's detail band, as shown in Figure 3.53.

Next, group the list by department by selecting the **Create Group...** option from the **Rows** menu, as shown in Figure 3.54.

There are two ways to create the calculated field to compute the average monthly salary within each department. The first way is by clicking the icon to create a computed field and placing the field onto the DataWindow. Doing this displays the Computed Field Definition window. When completed, this window looks like the one in Figure 3.55.

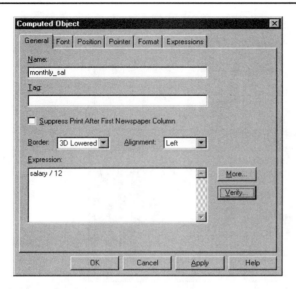

Figure 3.52   Creating a computed field for average salary.

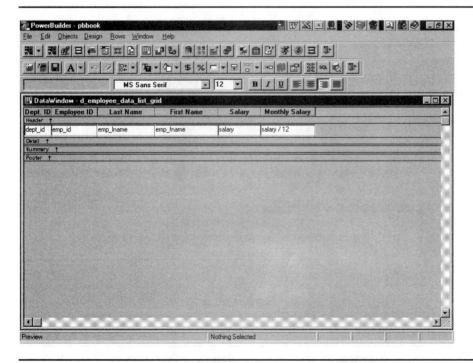

Figure 3.53   Placing the computed field on the DataWindow.

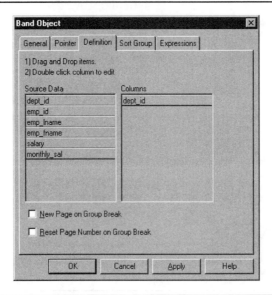

Figure 3.54   Grouping the list by department.

Figure 3.55   Creating a computed field for the average monthly salary within each department.

The second way of creating the computed field is by using the DataWindow painter's **Objects** menu. This menu provides a quick way to create the more commonly used computed fields, including column averages, column counts, page numbers, column summations, and the current date.

For this example, select the monthly salary computed field and choose the **Average** option from the **Objects** menu, as shown in Figure 3.56. PowerBuilder automatically creates the computed field, using the selected computed field's expression (monthly_sal) within its definition.

Both methods result in the same definition for the new computed field. After adding the new group and creating the computed field, the DataWindow looks like the one in Figure 3.57.

As mentioned earlier, you can add the page number by using the **Objects** menu and clicking somewhere within the footer band to place the computed field onto the DataWindow. With a few other cosmetic modifications, the new DataWindow at runtime looks like the one in Figure 3.58.

In deciding whether to use computed columns or computed fields, consider the following:

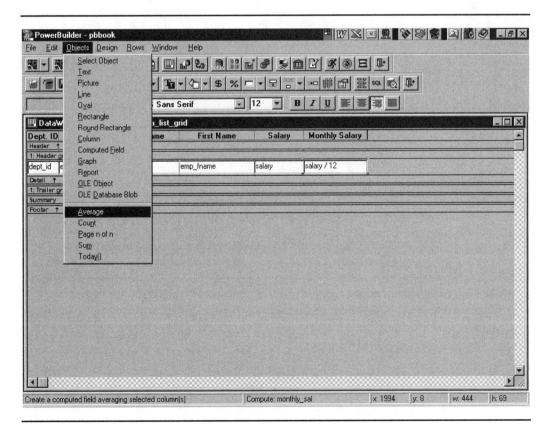

Figure 3.56   Creating a computed field by using the Objects menu's Average option.

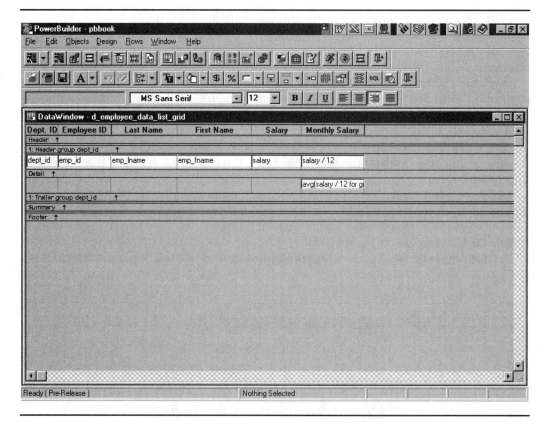

Figure 3.57 The DataWindow with the new group and computed field.

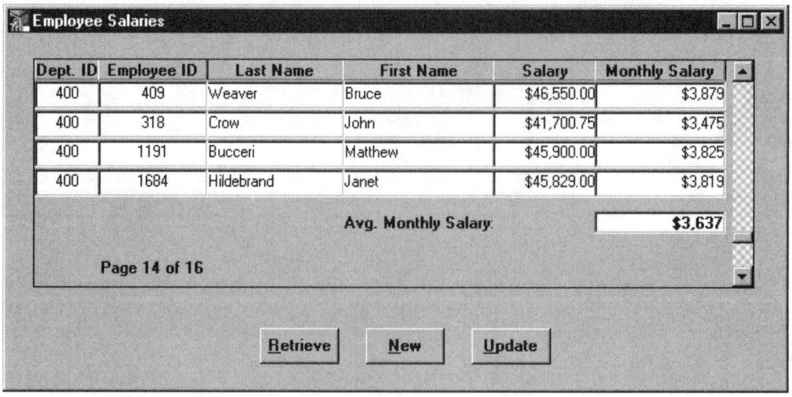

Figure 3.58 The completed DataWindow at runtime.

- If it is best to perform the calculations on the database server, use a computed column.
- If the value is to appear on any DataWindow band other than the detail band, you must use a computed field.
- If the value cannot be computed by using only the syntax of the RDBMS language, you must use a computed field.

PowerBuilder provides an excellent list of functions that you can use within computed fields. These functions make the computed fields one of the strongest features of the DataWindow. It is a good idea to browse through each one of them. Here are three cases that you may find very useful:

Use case statements.   You can use the case statement instead of the nested if statements. This makes your code within the computed column very readable.

The [-1] feature.   You can refer to the column's value within the previous row with the [-1] syntax.

Use cumulative sum.   The cumulative sum function provides a great way to display the running totals.

Update Properties

You can specify the SQL statement that PowerBuilder sends to the database by selecting the **Update Properties...** option from the **Rows** menu within the DataWindow painter, as shown in Figure 3.59.

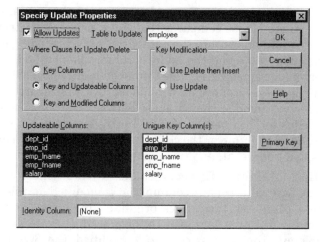

Figure 3.59   The Update Properties dialog box.

This window is very important because its contents determine how PowerBuilder builds the default SQL statement it uses when executing the DataWindow **Update( )** function. This window lets you specify the:

- Table to update
- Where clause for the updates and deletes
- Key modification
- Updatable columns
- Key columns

The following sections discuss each of these options.

Table to Update

PowerBuilder lets you update only one table through a DataWindow. You select this table from the drop-down listbox at the top of the window. You must code any other updates that need to be performed when the Update( ) function is executed, either by using the **Modify( )** function, by using the dot notation to modify the DataWindow directly, or through embedded SQL.

Where Clause for Updates and Deletes

PowerBuilder provides three ways of structuring an Update or Delete statement's Where clause:

Key columns. This option builds a Where clause consisting of only the selected table's key values. The Where clause compares the value originally retrieved for the key value(s) against the key column(s) within the database. For example, if the key column for a table of customers is custnum, the Where clause that PowerBuilder generates is like the one shown in Figure 3.60.

Key and updatable columns. This option builds a Where clause consisting of the key values and original values of any column identified as updatable for the selected table. The Where clause compares the values originally retrieved for these columns against the columns within the database. In the preceding example, if address and city are updatable and the address column is modified, the SQL statement that PowerBuilder generates is like that shown in Figure 3.61.

Using this method, an error occurs if you modify any of the updatable columns and another user saves them to the database between the time the user retrieves the row and performs the Update( ) function. In this example, if a second user updated either the address column or the city column of this row between the time the first user selects and updates it, an error occurs.

Key and modified columns. This option builds a Where clause consisting of the key values and original values of any column that is modified for the selected table. The Where clause compares the values originally retrieved for these columns against the columns within the database. In the preceding example, if address and city are updatable and the address column is modified, the SQL statement that PowerBuilder generates is like that shown in Figure 3.62.

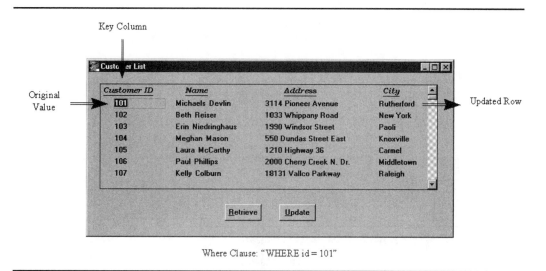

Figure 3.60   Using key columns to build the Where clause.

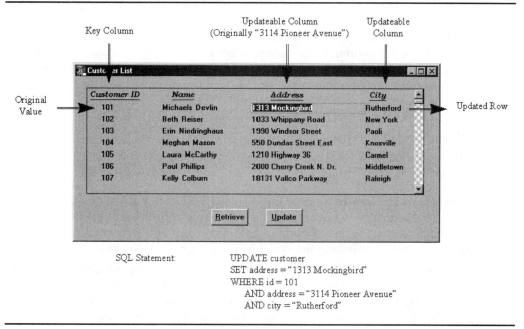

Figure 3.61   Using key and updatable columns to build the Where clause.

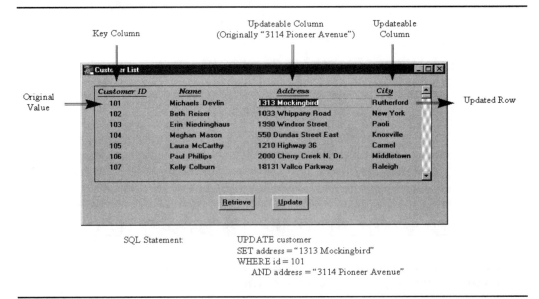

Figure 3.62 Using key and modified columns to build the Where clause.

The only difference between this Update statement and the last one is that it does not contain the portion of the Where clause that checks the city. This is because only the address column is modified.

Using this method, an error occurs if you modify the modified column and another user saves the column to the database between the time the user retrieves the row and performs the Update( ) function. In this example, if a second user updated the address column of this row between the time the first user selects and updates it, an error occurs.

Key Modification

PowerBuilder generates one of the two SQL statements whenever you modify a key column (specified within the Unique Key Column(s) box). These two statements are:

Issuing a Delete then Insert. This is the default method. This method deletes the row with the modified key and inserts a new row with the new key value. Using this method ensures that any Delete or Insert triggers are performed and provides a reliable method of handling the multiple rows with modified keys.

Issuing an Update. This method updates the row with the modified key by replacing the value within the key column with the new key value. This method ensures that any Update triggers are fired, but does not fire any Delete or Insert triggers. With this method, there may also be problems updating multiple rows within which the key value has changed.

The decision of which of the two methods to use should be based on the extent to which the application uses triggers and referential integrity constraints. In general, however, key columns should not be modifiable.

Updatable Columns

This option lets you specify the updatable columns. As mentioned before, because you use this in building the SQL Update statement, choosing this option can have performance implications. You should include only the columns that the user can modify within this list. If you disable a column or the column has a tab order of 0, and thus the user cannot modify the column, you should not include the column in this list.

Key Columns

This option lets you specify which columns are included as part of the key for the selected table used within the DataWindow Update( ) function. Columns specified as key columns are included within the Where clause for all the Update statements PowerBuilder generates. Consequently, they can also have performance implications. You should include only the true key columns for the selected table within this list. For automatic selection of the key columns, click the **Primary Key** command button on the window.

New Objects for the DataWindow

Button Object

PowerBuilder 6 provides a button object for the DataWindow object. This button object can be of a command or picture button. You can attach any one of the 21 predefined actions for the button (see Figure 3.63). Table 3.1 defines the predefined actions that you can attach to the button object within a DataWindow.

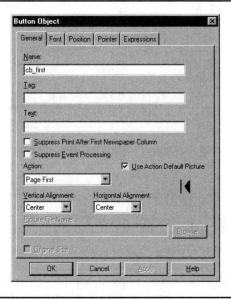

Figure 3.63   Defining the button object's properties.

Table 3.1 The Predefined Actions for the Button Object within a DataWindow Object

Action	Description
AppendRow	Insert a new row at the end.
Cancel	Cancel a retrieval that is started.
DeleteRow	If the button is placed within the detail band, delete the row associated with button, else delete the current row.
Filter	Display the filter dialog and apply the filter as specified.
InsertRow	If the button is placed within the detail band, insert the row by using row number, else insert the row by using the current row.
PageFirst	Scroll to the first page.
PageLast	Scroll to the last page.
PageNext	Scroll to the next page.
PagePrior	Scroll to the prior page.
Preview	Toggle between preview and print preview.
PreviewWithRulers	Toggle Rulers on and off.
Print	Print the DataWindow.
QueryClear	Remove the WHERE clause from a query.
QueryMode	Toggle query mode between on and off.
QuerySort	Specify sort criteria for the query.
Retrieve	Retrieve rows from the database.
Retrieve (Yield)	Retrieve rows from the database with the yield option. This lets the Cancel action take effect during a long retrieve.
SaveRowsAs	Display the Save As dialog box and save rows within the format specified.
Sort	Display the Sort dialog box and sort as specified.
Update	Save changes to the database. If the update is successful, issues a COMMIT. If the update fails, issues a ROLLBACK.
UserDefined	Lets you program the action within the ButtonClicked and ButtonClicking events.

When the user clicks the button at runtime, the new ButtonClicking event on the DataWindow control is fired. PowerBuilder executes the code within the ButtonClicking event (if any).

If the ButtonClicking event returns 0, PowerBuilder then executes the predefined action assigned to the button. Upon executing this action or if the ButtonClicking event returns 1, the ButtonClicked event on the DataWindow control is fired.

Group Box Object

Examine Figure 3.64 carefully. All the button objects are placed together within a group box. The group box is a new PowerBuilder 6 object now available within the DataWindow object.

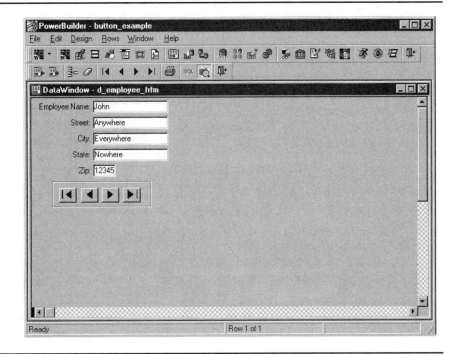

Figure 3.64   A sample DataWindow object with the button objects.

Child DataWindows

A child DataWindow is defined as a DropDownDataWindow (DDDW) within a Data-Window object. You can think of this as a DataWindow within a DataWindow.

For example, assume the DataWindow d_cities retrieves a list of cities from the database. You can use this DataWindow as a child DataWindow to any other DataWindow that needs a list of cities. In the customer list example, you can define the city column as a DDDW with the definition as shown in Figure 3.65.

TIP You can specifiy the number of lines within the drop-down DataWindows in the properties sheet. If more rows are retrieved than specified, you need to provide a vertical scroll bar to the drop-down DataWindow.

The data within the child DataWindow d_cities is retrieved, once and only once, when the application calls either the Retrieve( ) or **InsertRow( )** function for the parent DataWindow d_custlist. The user can then select from the list of cities retrieved by using d_cities, as shown in Figure 3.66.

When you define the child DataWindow to accept retrieval arguments, you must call the Retrieve( ) function for the child DataWindow (with the retrieval arguments)

Figure 3.65   Defining a DropDownDataWindow.

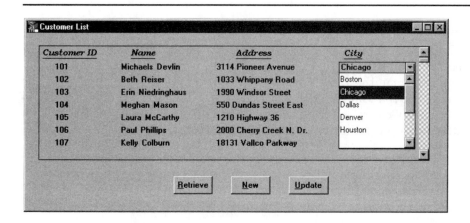

Figure 3.66   The DropDownDataWindow for cities at runtime.

before the Retrieve( ) function for the parent DataWindow. This is necessary to keep the Specify Retrieval Arguments dialog box from displaying to prompt the user to enter the retrieval arguments.

The child DataWindow must also be retrieved after executing a Modify( ) against the DDDW. This is because PowerBuilder automatically performs a Retrieve( ) after performing a Modify( ) against a DDDW. The next section describes retrieving the child DataWindow.

TIP If you have a retrieval parameter for the child DataWindow, make sure that you retrieve the child DataWindow before you retrieve or insert records within the main DataWindow. Alternatively, when you create the data object for the child DataWindow, add a row to the DataWindow. To add a row to the DataWindow object at design time, select **Data** from the **Rows** menu. Power-Builder, in turn, displays the Data Retained on Save dialog box. Add a blank row, click OK, and save the DataWindow object. Now, even if you have a retrieval parameter for the child DataWindow, PowerBuilder does not prompt you with the retrieval argument dialog box as a blank row always exists within the DataWindow.

Calling the Retrieve( ) function for the child DataWindow requires the use of the GetChild( ) function to obtain a handle to the child DataWindow. After obtaining the handle, you can use the handle within all of the DataWindow-related functions.

To illustrate, assume that in the preceding example a clerk can only enter customer records for the customers within his/her home state. Retrieve this value into the instance variable i _sMyState, and then, pass this value to the Retrieve( ) function for the DDDW d_cities. For this example, assume the state code is TX and this value already exists within i_sMyState. To pass this value to the DDDW d_cities's Retrieve( ) function, you could place the following code within the main DataWindow's constructor event:

```
// Declare the child DataWindow variable dw_child
DataWindowChild   dw_child
int               iRtn

// Get the handle of the child DataWindow into dw_child
iRtn = dw_master.GetChild("city",dw_child)

// Check for errors
If iRtn = -1 Then
    MessageBox ("Error", "Error obtaining the child DataWindow handle")
Else
    // Set the transaction object for dw_child and retrieve
    dw_child.SetTransObject(SQLCA)
    dw_child.Retrieve(i_sMyState)
End If
```

Within this example, since the value passed to the Retrieve( ) function of the DDDW d_cities is static (it is always TX), it is more efficient to put the code within the main DataWindow's constructor event, where it is executed only once. Putting this code into an event such as the **Retrieve** command button's clicked event results in the same code being executed needlessly if the command button is clicked more than once.

If the argument passed to the Retrieve( ) function is dynamic, however, place the code where it is executed before the main DataWindow's Retrieve( ) or InsertRow( ) functions. For example, within a master/detail conversation, to display only the valid cities within a detail DataWindow's DDDW for a state listed within the master DataWindow, call the DDDW's Retrieve( ) function before the detail DataWindow's Retrieve( ) function:

```
// Declare the child DataWindow variable dw_child
DataWindowChild   dw_child
int               iRtn

// Get the child DataWindow's handle into dw_child
iRtn = dw_master.GetChild("city",dw_child)

//Check for errors
If iRtn = -1 Then
     MessageBox ("Error", "Error obtaining child DataWindow handle")
Else
     // Set the transaction object for dw_child and retrieve
     // for the child. Pass the state as retrieval argument.
     dw_child.SetTransObject(SQLCA)
     dw_child.Retrieve(dw_master.object.state[1])
End If
```

Exclusive DDDWs

There may be instances when you may want to create a DataWindow containing only DDDWs. In such cases, there would be no data source for the main DataWindow and therefore no Retrieve is required. Although it may not seem necessary to have another DataWindow, a main DataWindow is always required to use a DDDW. You can handle this situation by specifying an external data source for the main DataWindow and performing an InsertRow( ) on this DataWindow instead of a Retrieve( ). Because the main DataWindow does not retrieve the data, you must call InsertRow( ) to display the single row that any child DataWindows use. For example, to view a list of customers for a particular city, create another DataWindow that contains only the DDDW d_cities. The user then uses this DataWindow to choose a city, as shown in Figure 3.67.

When the user selects a city, data is retrieved into the customer list, as shown in Figure 3.68.

To perform the Retrieve of the child DataWindow, place the following code into the top DataWindow's constructor event (this assumes the use of i_sMyState to select only the cities from the clerk's state):

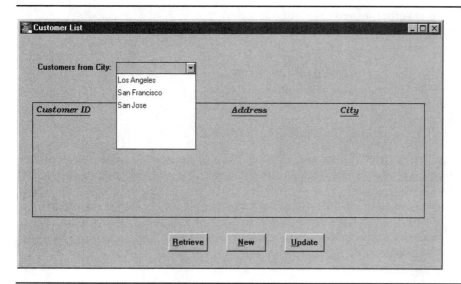

Figure 3.67   **An exclusive DropDownDataWindow.**

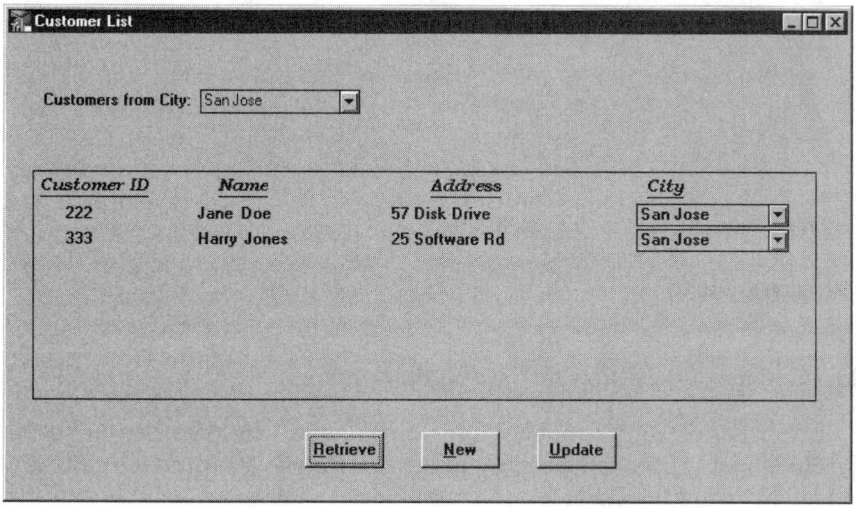

Figure 3.68   **Retrieving the data into customer list based on city.**

```
// Declare the child DataWindow variable dw_child
DataWindowChild   dw_child
int               iRtn


// Get the child DataWindow's handle into dw_child
iRtn = dw_city_select.GetChild("city",dw_child)
// Check for errors
If iRtn = -1 Then
    MessageBox("Error","Error obtaining child DataWindow handle")
Else
    // Set the transaction object for dw_child and retrieve
    dw_child.SetTransObject(SQLCA)
    dw_child.Retrieve(i_sMyState)
End If


// Perform insertrow( ) to display a row within dw
dw_city_select.InsertRow (0)
```

To retrieve the data into the customer list DataWindow, place the following code into the Retrieve command button's clicked event:

```
int    iRtn


// Retrieve the data for the customer list
// Get the data from the DDDW in dw_city_select
iRtn = dw_custlist.retrieve(dw_city_select.object.city[1])
If (iRtn = -1) Then
  MessageBox("Select Error", SQLCA.sqlerrtext)
End If
```

DATAWINDOW CONTROLS

DataWindow Buffers

PowerBuilder provides four different DataWindow buffers:

Primary!   The primary DataWindow buffer contains all the data visible to the user. This includes any rows retrieved by using the Retrieve( ) function plus any new rows added by using the InsertRow( ) function.

Filter!   The filtered buffer contains any rows filtered from the primary buffer by using the Filter( ) function.

Delete!   The delete buffer contains any rows deleted by using the **DeleteRow( )** function that are not yet deleted from the database.

Original!   The original buffer contains data used to generate the Where clause that is used within the DataWindow Update( ) function.

PowerBuilder uses these filters to create the SQL statements used in executing the DataWindow Update( ) function. The data deleted when executing the Update( ) function is the data within the Delete! buffer. If a DataWindow does not allow updates, the Delete! and Original! buffers are not maintained.

You can retrieve data from any of the buffers by using the dot notation. For example:

```
integer  li_filterval
li_filterval = dw_master.object.city.filter[1]
```

This code retrieves the integer value located within the city column of the Filter! buffer's first row.

PowerBuilder provides the following DataWindow control functions to manipulate data within the different DataWindow buffers:

RowsCopy( ).   Lets you copy the rows from one DataWindow buffer to another. You can use this function to copy the rows between the different buffers of the same DataWindow control or between the buffers of the different DataWindow controls. You can also do this by using dot notation. The **RowsCopy( )** function's syntax is

```
datawindow.RowsCopy ( startrow, endrow, copybuffer, targetdw,
beforerow, targetbuffer )
```

where:

> **datawindow** is the source DataWindow control's name.
>
> **startrow** is the number of the first row to copy (Long).
>
> **endrow** is the number of the last row to copy (Long).
>
> **copybuffer** is the buffer from which to copy the rows (Primary!, Delete!, Filter!).
>
> **targetdw** is the name of the DataWindow control where the rows are to be copied. This can be different than the source DataWindow control.
>
> **beforerow** is the number of the row before which to insert the copied rows (Long). To insert after the last existing row, use any value that is greater than the number of existing rows.
>
> **targetbuffer** is the buffer to which the rows are copied (Primary!, Delete!, Filter!).
>
> **RowsCopy( )** is the function that copies the rows within the datawindow's copybuffer beginning with startrow and ending with endrow and inserts them within targetdw before beforerow within the targetbuffer.

For example, to copy all the rows from the dw_1's Delete! buffer to the dw_2's Primary! buffer, call RowsCopy( ):

```
dw_1.RowsCopy(1, dw_1.DeletedCount( ), Delete!, dw_2, 1, Primary!)
```

The RowsCopy( ) function gives you the ability to move data quickly between the different DataWindows and their respective buffers.

RowsMove( ).   Lets you move the rows from one DataWindow buffer to another. This function is basically the same as RowsCopy( ); the only exception is that the rows are removed from the source buffer once they are copied to the target buffer. **RowsMove( )** provides a simple way of "undeleting" the rows deleted from the Primary! buffer. To do this, call RowsMove( ) as shown:

```
dw_1.RowsMove(1, dw_1.DeletedCount( ), Delete!, dw_1, 1, Primary!)
```

RowsDiscard( ).   Lets you permanently remove the rows from a DataWindow buffer. The **RowsDiscard( )** function's syntax is:

```
datawindow.RowsDiscard(startrow, endrow, buffer)
```

where:

datawindow is the DataWindow control's name.

startrow is the number of the first row to discard (Long).

endrow is the number of the last row to discard (Long).

buffer is the buffer from which to discard the rows (Primary!, Delete!, Filter!).

RowsDiscard( ) permanently deletes the rows within a DataWindow, beginning with the startrow and ending with the endrow within the buffer DataWindow buffer. For example, to permanently delete all the rows within dw_1's Delete! buffer, call Rows-Discard( ) as shown:

```
dw_1.RowsDiscard(1, dw_1.DeletedCount( ), Delete!)
```

Drag-and-Drop

Drag-and-drop is a type of graphical interface that can make an application intuitive and friendly to the user. Adding products to an order within an order entry system, for example, can be as simple as dragging a product from a list of products into an order (located somewhere else in the window). PowerBuilder provides drag-and-drop capabilities for all controls other than drawing objects. These controls have two attributes:

DragAuto.   A Boolean value used to automatically place a control into drag mode when the user clicks on the control.

DragIcon.   The icon to display when the user drags the control.

In addition to these two attributes, each control has four events and two functions pertaining to drag-and-drop. The events are:

DragDrop.   When the user drops a dragged control on a target control.

DragEnter.   When a dragged control enters a target control.

DragWithin.   When a dragged control is within a target control.

DragLeave.   When a dragged control leaves a target control.

The drag-and-drop functions are:

Drag( ).   Starts or ends the dragging of a control based on the value of the argument passed to it. Valid arguments are:

Begin!.   Begin dragging the control.

Cancel!.   Stop dragging the control and do not trigger a DragDrop event.

End!.   Stop dragging the control and trigger a DragDrop event if positioned over a target control.

DraggedObject( ).   Returns a reference to the control being dragged. You can access this value by using the **TypeOf( )** function.

To illustrate a simple use of drag-and-drop, assume a list of customers as shown in Figure 3.69.

To enable printing of a customer record by using drag-and-drop, add a picture control to the window. This picture control is the target object. Records from the customer DataWindow are printed by dragging a row from the DataWindow and dropping the row on the picture control.

Next, place the following code within the DataWindow control's clicked event:

```
/*******************************************************************
** If we have not clicked within a column or label, start dragging his
** dw object. Because the DataWindow is editable, we do not want to
** drag if a column is clicked.
*******************************************************************/
If dwo.name = "datawindow" And row > 0 Then
    drag(begin!)
End If
```

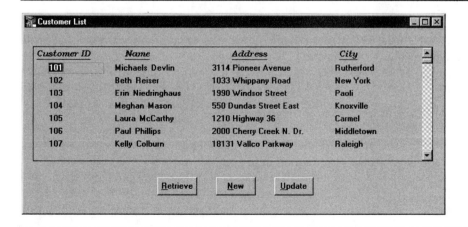

Figure 3.69   A sample customer list.

TIP The value "datawindow" listed for dwo.name in the preceding code example, ple is the value contained within dwo.name when a click occurs somewhere within the DataWindow control where no object exists (column or label in this case). In this example, dragging begins only if the user clicks within an open space within the DataWindow control. You could do additional checking to begin dragging if a click occurs on the labels.

After selecting the drag icon for the DataWindow (the Question! icon in this example), create the picture control and add the following code to the dragdrop event:

```
// determine which control type was dropped by using the
// event argument "source" (type DragObject)
Choose Case TypeOf(source)
    Case DataWindow! // If DW, print the current row & invert the
                     // picture
        dw_custlist.PrintRow() // Object function to print row data
        invert = False
    Case Else
       // Error handling
End Choose
```

Finally, to invert the picture object when the dragged control is within the picture control, add the following line to the picture control's dragenter event:

```
invert = True
```

To restore the picture control to its original state after the dragged control leaves the picture control, add the following line to the picture control's dragleave event:

```
invert = False
```

When the user clicks within the DataWindow (but not on a column or label), the drag icon appears as shown in Figure 3.70.

When the dragged icon enters the picture control, the control is disabled, as shown in Figure 3.71.

When the icon is dropped, the current row within the DataWindow is printed.

Transaction Processing

Transaction processing is a key element within most PowerBuilder applications. Any application that accesses a database must have the ability to create and manage a transaction. This includes creating a connection, sending commands to the database, and error handling. This section discusses the following topics related to transaction processing:

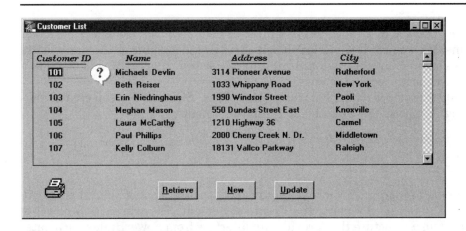

Figure 3.70   Displaying the drag icon.

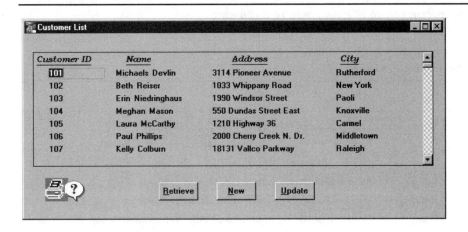

Figure 3.71   Disabling the picture control when the dragged object enters.

- Transaction objects
- Associating transaction objects with a DataWindow control
- The Retrieve( ) and Update( ) functions
- Error handling (embedded SQL)
- Error handling (DataWindows)
- The logical unit of work

Transaction Objects

PowerBuilder manages its connection to a database through the use of a transaction object. A transaction object is a special, nonvisual object that contains the parameters necessary for establishing and maintaining a database connection. Table 3.2 shows a list of the transaction object's elements.

PowerBuilder provides the global transaction object, SQLCA. You can create additional transaction objects by using the following statements:

```
// Create transaction object mytran
transaction mytran
mytran = CREATE transaction
```

These statements first create a variable (mytran) of type transaction, and then create the transaction's instance by using the Create statement. The transaction object is nothing more than a structure that provides an interface from PowerBuilder to a database.

Before connecting to a database, you must fill the transaction object's elements lappropriately. The elements required for the transaction object may vary among the different databases. The following example shows the code for creating a transaction object and connecting to an SQL Anywhere database:

Table 3.2   The Transaction Object's Elements

Attribute	Data Type	Description
DBMS	String	The database vendor's name (e.g., Sybase, Oracle, ODBC).
Database	String	Name of the specific database to which you are connecting.
UserID	String	User ID of the user connecting to the database.
DBPass	String	Password of the user connecting to the database.
LogID	String	Logon ID used to connect to the database server.
LogPass	String	Password of the logon used to connect to the database server.
ServerName	String	Name of the server where the database is located.
DBParm	String	RDBMS-specific.
AutoCommit	Boolean	Used for automatically committing after each database activity (must be TRUE to create the temporary tables).
Lock	String	Lock isolation level (RDBMS-specific).
SQLCode	Long	A database operation's success code: 0 — Success; 100 — No result set returned; -1— Error.
SQLNRows	Long	Number of rows affected by a database operation (RDBMS-specific).
SQLDBCode	Long	RDBMS vendor's specific error code.
SQLErrText	String	RDBMS vendor's specific error message.
SQLReturnData	String	RDBMS-specific.

```
// Open the script for myapp. Sets up the transaction object mytran, reads
// the parameters from myapp.ini, and connects to the database
transaction mytran
mytran                  = CREATE transaction
mytran.DBMS             = ProfileString("myapp.ini","mytran","dbms","")
mytran.database         = ProfileString("myapp.ini","mytran","database","")
mytran.userid           = ProfileString("myapp.ini","mytran","userid","")
mytran.dbpass           = ProfileString("myapp.ini","mytran","dbpass","")
mytran.logid            = ProfileString("myapp.ini","mytran","logid","")
mytran.logpass          = ProfileString("myapp.ini","mytran","logpass","")
mytran.servername       = ProfileString("myapp.ini","mytran","servername","")
mytran.dbparm           = ProfileString("myapp.ini","mytran","dbparm","")
Connect;
If (mytran.sqldbcode) <> 0 Or (mytran.sqlcode) <> 0 Then
  MessageBox ("Sorry! Cannot Connect to Database", mytran.sqlerrtext)
End If

Open(w_main)
```

This example obtains the values for the transaction object from the file myapp.ini. This method of storing the connection parameters provides some flexibility over hard-coding the values into the script. This flexibility comes from the fact that you can make any changes in the parameters within the .INI file and do not require changes to the application code. The myapp.ini's mytran section then looks something like:

```
[mytran]
dbms=ODBC
database=MYDB
userid=DBA
dbpass=SQL
logid=
logpass=
servername=
DbParm=DataSource='MYDB',Connectstring='DSN=MYDBL;UID=DBA ;PWD=SQL'
```

Chapter 16, "SQL Anywhere and Other Databases," discusses the details of creating a transaction object for each of the major RDBMSs that PowerBuilder supports.

Associating Transaction Objects with a DataWindow Control

After creating a transaction object, you can associate the object with a DataWindow control, by using either the **SetTrans( )** or **SetTransObject( )** function. SetTrans( ) and SetTransObject( ) differ in the way they manage the database connection. SetTrans( ) connects and disconnects to the database for each database transaction; SetTransObject( ) leaves it up to you to code the Connect, Disconnect, Commit, and Rollback statements.

While using SetTransObject( ) may seem like more work for you, the function provides more control over transaction management and generally yields better performance than using SetTrans( ). Figure 3.72 shows the difference between SetTrans( ) and SetTransObject( ), for the retrieval and update of the two DataWindows within a master/detail conversation. The example assumes that SetTrans( ) or SetTransObject( ) is called for both the DataWindows within the window's open event.

As Figure 3.72 shows, using SetTrans( ) doubles the number of connections to the database. Because the Connect operation is generally an expensive one in terms of performance, you should minimize its use. Therefore, you should use SetTrans( ) only for applications where database access is minimal.

The Retrieve( ) and Update( ) Functions

The Retrieve( ) and Update( ) functions are built-in PowerBuilder functions of the DataWindow control that generate and send the SQL code to the database for process-

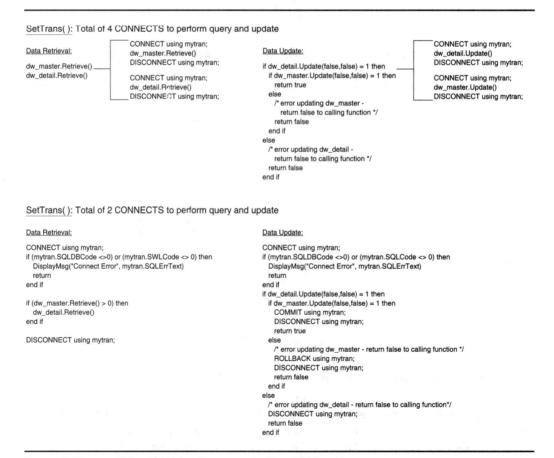

Figure 3.72   Using SetTrans( ) versus SetTransObject( ).

ing. The statement that is generated is dependent upon each row's status within the DataWindow. Rows and columns within a DataWindow can have a status of:

```
New!
NewModified!
NotModified!
DataModified!
```

While rows can have any of these statuses, columns can only have a status of Not-Modified! and DataModified!.

Immediately after issuing a Retrieve( ), each row and column has a status of Not-Modified!. When a column is changed, the status of both the row and column is changed from NotModified! to DataModified!.

When you insert a row into the DataWindow by using the InsertRow( ) function, the row has a status of New! and each column within the row has a status of NotModified!. The column status changes from NotModified! to DataModified! after you change the column's value. When the status of any column within a new row changes to Data-Modified!, the row's status changes from New! to NewModified!. See Figure 3.73 for examples of these functions.

When the Update( ) function is called, PowerBuilder executes the Update or Insert SQL statements based on each row's status within the Primary! or Filter! buffer, and generates the Delete statements for each row within the Delete! buffer. Each row with a DataModified! status causes the execution of an Update statement; each row with a NewModified! status causes the execution of an Insert statement.

The columns included within an Update statement depend on whether the column

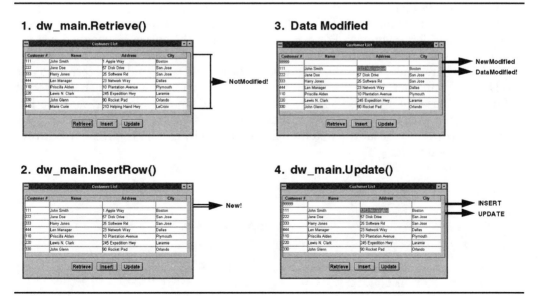

Figure 3.73   RowStatus when using Retrieve( ), InsertRow( ), and Update( ).

is on the list of updatable columns (see the previous section on specifying update properties) and whether it has a status of DataModified!. All the columns displayed within the DataWindow are included within an Insert statement, with blank or empty columns represented as NULL.

You can use the **GetItemStatus( )** and **SetItemStatus( )** functions to modify row and column status programmatically. In addition to these functions, PowerBuilder provides two additional functions for determining the row status: **IsRowModified( )** and **IsRowNew( )**. **IsRowModified( )** returns True if the row is changed. IsRowNew( ) returns True if the row is new. You can use these functions to check a row or column's status to, for example, force a particular SQL statement to be executed (in place of the one that PowerBuilder automatically generates).

Update Flags

PowerBuilder uses the update flags to determine if a DataWindow row or column is modified. For each row within a DataWindow buffer, the update flag is set for each row inserted, updated, or deleted. When the DataWindow Update( ) function is executed, PowerBuilder uses each row's status within the DataWindow with its update flag set to generate the appropriate SQL statement. By default, PowerBuilder resets the update flags of each modified row within the DataWindow if the Update( ) function executes successfully.

There may be situations in which you should not reset a DataWindow's update flags immediately after executing the Update( ) function. For example, to update the two DataWindows within a master/detail situation, PowerBuilder updates the master DataWindow first, followed by the detail DataWindow. Assume that if an error occurs within either DataWindow, PowerBuilder rolls back the transaction and makes no changes to the database.

In this case, if the master DataWindow's update flags are reset and an error occurs in updating the detail window, PowerBuilder rolls back the entire transaction, yet the master DataWindow's update flags are reset, indicating that no changes to the master DataWindow are made. When the data within the detail DataWindow is corrected and the Update( ) function is called again, the master DataWindow does not update the database because the update flags are reset. To avoid this problem, execute the Update( ) function with the Resetflags attribute set to False. Once the two Updates( ) are executed successfully, reset the update flags manually by calling the **ResetUpdate( )** function. For example:

```
Int  iRtn

// Update the master DataWindow without resetting the update flags
iRtn = dw_master.Update(True, False)

// If the master update is successful, update the detail
// DataWindow without resetting its update flags
```

```
If iRtn = 1 Then
    iRtn = dw_detail.Update(True, False)

    // If the detail update is successful, commit the transaction
    // and reset the update flags for both the DataWindows
    If iRtn = 1 Then
        COMMIT using SQLCA;
        dw_master.ResetUpdate( )
        dw_detail.ResetUpdate( )
    Else
        // Detail update failed, so rollback the transaction
        ROLLBACK using SQLCA;
    End If
Else
    // Master update failed, so rollback the transaction
    ROLLBACK using SQLCA;
End If
```

TIP This first parameter passed to the Update( ) function determines whether to perform an AcceptText( ) function before executing Update( ). The default is True, but to specify the resetflag value, you must also include the accepttext value within the call to Update( ). AcceptText( ) applies the current edit field's contents to the current item within the DataWindow after the value passes validation.

Error Handling (Embedded SQL)

The transaction object's SQLCode, SQLDBCode, and SQLErrText elements provide a method of error handling when accessing a database by means other than a DataWindow. (When dealing with a DataWindow, the DataWindow functions' return codes are used instead of these values.) You should check these values when accessing a database by using embedded or dynamic SQL and also when using the CONNECT, DISCONNECT, COMMIT, and ROLLBACK statements.

You can use SQLCode to determine only if a given transaction object's most recent database operation was successful. There are only three possible values for SQLCode:

0 indicates that the operation was successful.

100 indicates that the operation was successful, but no data was returned.

-1 indicates that the operation failed.

You should check SQLCode after every database interaction. The following example shows how SQLCode is checked after an embedded Select statement (by using the transaction object mytran):

```
// Function to select the employee information
SELECT emp_id, emp_fname, emp_lname FROM employee USING mytran;
If mytran.SQLCode <> 0 Then
  MessageBox ("Select Error",mytran.SQLErrText)
  Return False
End If
Return True
```

SQLDBCode provides vendor-specific information regarding a particular error. The information provided from SQLDBCode is more detailed than that provided from SQL-Code. Because SQLCode sometimes returns 0 even if no connection to the database is made, you should also check SQLDBCode when connecting to a database. This was shown within the previous SetTrans( ) example as follows:

```
Connect Using mytran;
If (mytran.SQLDBCode <>0) Or (mytran.SQLCode <> 0) Then
  MessageBox ("Connect Error", mytran.SQLErrText)
End If
...
...
```

SQLErrText contains the vendor-specific text of the error code contained within SQLDBCode. You should use this value to display the error in a more meaningful form.

Error Handling (DataWindows)

Error handling for DataWindows is done differently from the way it is done for embedded SQL. Both the Retrieve( ) and Update( ) functions return values that you should check for errors. The Retrieve( ) function returns the following:

> = 1 indicates success.

0 indicates that no data was returned (no error).

-1 indicates an error.

The following code calls the DataWindow dw_main's Retrieve( ) function and displays a message if an error occurs:

```
int iRtn
iRtn = dw_main.Retrieve( )
If (iRtn = -1) Then
    MessageBox("Select Error", "Error Selecting Data")
End If
```

PowerBuilder also provides the ability to pass more than the necessary number of DataWindow arguments to the Retrieve( ) function. This gives you the flexibility to use a generic Retrieve( ) function that works for any DataWindow having as many or fewer defined arguments than the Retrieve( ) function provides. Of course, the data types of the arguments still must match.

TIP You should not use SQLCode, SQLDBCode, and SQLErrText when handling the DataWindow errors. You should use them only when handling the embedded SQL errors.

The Update( ) function returns one of the two values: 1 if successful or -1 if unsuccessful. When performing an Update( ), you should also do a check similar to the one for the Retrieve( ) function.

The DBError event provides another method of error handling for the DataWindow retrieves and updates. PowerBuilder triggers this event, which is part of the Data-Window control, each time an error occurs when retrieving or updating a DataWindow. You can use this event to trap error codes and messages and for customized error processing.

In previous versions of PowerBuilder, the best way to retrieve the error code and error message was to use the **DBErrorCode( )** and **DBErrorMessage( )** functions, respectively. However, these functions are now obsolete because this data is contained as arguments to the DBError event. Table 3.3 shows a list of arguments to the DBError event.

For example, you could place the following code into a DataWindow's DBError event to display a different message when a user attempts to update a table that he or she does not have access to:

```
/**************************************************************
** Trap any database errors
** If the user does not have update rights, display an informative
** message. NO_RIGHTS is set to the vendor-specific value for
** insufficient privilege at login time.
**************************************************************/

If sqldbcode = NO_RIGHTS Then
  MessageBox ("Insufficient Rights", &
   "You do not have rights to this table. Please check with the DBA.")
Else
    // Other errors
    MessageBox ("Update Error", string(sqldbcode)+"~n"+sqlerrtext)
End If

// Return 1 to avoid displaying the default message
Return 1
```

You can also use the DBError event to determine the row within a multirow DataWindow that caused an error to occur. You can do this by using the row argument.

Table 3.3   A List of Arguments to the DBError Event

Attribute	Data Type	Description
sqldbcode	Long	The RDBMS-specific error code. If there is no error code from the RDBMS, sqldbcode contains one of the following values: -1 Cannot connect to the database because of the missing values within the transaction object. -2 Cannot connect to the database. -3 The key specified within an Update or Retrieve no longer matches an existing row. (This can happen when another user changes the row after you retrieved it.) -4 Writing a blob to the database failed.
sqlerrtext	String	The RDBMS-specific error message.
sqlsyntax	String	The SQL statement's full text sent to the RDBMS when the error occurs.
buffer	DWBuffer	The buffer containing the row involved within the database activity that caused the error.
row	Long	The number of the row involved within the database activity that caused the error, that is, the row being updated, selected, inserted, or deleted.

For example, the following code uses the row argument to display the DataWindow's row that caused the error:

```
// Display the error's location and the error message
MessageBox ("Database Error in Row "+ String(row), sqlerrtext)

// Return 1 to prevent the DataWindow object from displaying its
// error message
Return 1
```

The DBError event provides a method to override PowerBuilder's default DataWindow error processing.

TIP When debugging the DataWindow errors, use the SQLPreview DataWindow event to trap the SQL statements sent to a database from the Retrieve( ), Update( ), and **ReselectRow( )** functions. This event occurs after the function is called but before sending the statement to the database for processing.

PowerBuilder provides two events to the DataWindow control to assist in error handling. The Error event and the ExternalException event, help you trap the runtime errors that may not occur within all instances but only when certain runtime conditions exist. Chapter 17, "Project Standards and Naming Conventions," discusses these two events in detail.

The Logical Unit of Work

A logical unit of work (LUW) is a set of database transactions grouped together as a single transaction. All the database transactions that are part of a LUW are accepted or rejected as a whole. Defining what goes into a LUW is extremely important, and you should define them carefully at design time. If you do not group transactions into a LUW correctly, data integrity problems may result.

Within PowerBuilder, a LUW begins with the Connect or last Commit statement and ends with either a Disconnect, Commit, or Rollback statement. Issuing a Disconnect (which commits before disconnecting) or Commit causes all the transactions sent to the database since the Connect or last Commit was executed to either be committed to the database or rejected. Any single transaction that is not accepted causes *all* the transactions within the LUW to not be accepted.

Issuing a Rollback causes the LUW to end without attempting to commit anything to the database. Both Commit and Rollback cause the closing of any open cursors or procedures and cause the release of any locks held against the database from the transactions within the LUW.

Using **SetTransObject( )** rather than **SetTrans( )** to bind a DataWindow control to a transaction object makes you responsible for managing a LUW. Each LUW should be as short as possible to minimize the resource use and locking problems. Issuing a Commit ends the current LUW and starts a new one. It is recommended that you do Commits as often as possible, even after data retrieval, to release the locks and free the system resources.

Dynamic DataWindows

You can create and modify the DataWindow objects, and all the controls within a DataWindow object, dynamically. Doing this provides a great deal of flexibility within situations where it is impractical to develop a static set of objects to satisfy a wide range of requirements. Providing true ad hoc query capability, for example, lends itself to the use of dynamic DataWindows.

Dynamic DataWindows let the user modify all the attributes of a DataWindow, including columns, colors, fonts, and the result set. Users can then save the DataWindow object within a library for later use.

Creating a DataWindow Dynamically

To create a DataWindow dynamically, you must do two things:

1. Build the DataWindow object's syntax
2. Bind the DataWindow object to a DataWindow control

You can build the DataWindow object's syntax in one of three ways:

By using the SyntaxFromSQL( ) function.   The syntax is:

```
transobj.SyntaxFromSQL(sqlselect, presentation, err)
```

where transobj is the transaction object associated with the function, sqlselect is the SQL Select statement used as the DataWindow's data source, presentation is a string containing the DataWindow's presentation style, and err is a string containing any error information.

The SyntaxFromSQL( ) function returns a string containing the syntax necessary for creating the new DataWindow object. This is the most common way of creating a new DataWindow object.

Exporting an Existing DataWindow Object. You can export an existing DataWindow object's syntax by using the **LibraryExport( )** function. This function returns the DataWindow object's syntax into a string that you can modify to reflect the new DataWindow object's syntax.

Manually. You can create the DataWindow syntax within a string variable. Although this option is not used frequently, it is the only option available for some of the advanced DataWindow attributes, such as group breaks.

When the DataWindow's syntax is known, you can bind the syntax to a DataWindow control by using the **Create( )** function. Its syntax is

```
dw_controlname.Create(Syntax [, errorMsg])
```

where dw_controlname is the name of the DataWindow control that is to be bound to the new DataWindow object, Syntax is a string containing the new DataWindow's source code, and errorMsg (optional) is a string containing any error messages encountered when creating the DataWindow.

The following PowerScript uses SyntaxFromSQL( ) to create a new DataWindow's syntax and Create( ) to actually create the new DataWindow object:

```
string      sSQLSelect, sPresentation, sErrmsg
sSQLSelect      = "SELECT name, address, city FROM customer ORDER BY name"
sPresentation   = "style(type=grid)"
dw_master.Create(SQLCA.SyntaxFromSQL(sSQLSelect, sPresentation, sErrmsg))
dw_master.SetTransObject(SQLCA)
```

Notice that you must execute SetTransObject( ) after the Create( ) command to link a transaction object to the new DataWindow.

Modifying a DataWindow Dynamically

You can modify the DataWindows dynamically with the following two functions:

Describe( ) returns the DataWindow attribute information.

Modify( ) sets the DataWindow attributes.

PowerBuilder also provides the capability to reference the DataWindow attributes directly by using the dot notation. This capability simplifies the access and modification of DataWindow attributes, and significantly reduces the need for both the

Describe( ) and Modify( ) functions. The following examples show both the Describe( ) and Modify( ) methods as well as the direct object reference method.

Describe( ) Describe( ) accepts a property or a list of properties (including the DataWindow expressions) and returns a string value containing the value(s) of the attribute(s). For example, to retrieve the list of columns for the DataWindow shown in Figure 3.74, use Describe( ) as follows:

```
dw_custlist.Describe("DataWindow.objects")
```

The following obtains the same information by using the dot notation:

```
dw_custlist.Object.datawindow.objects
```

In both cases, PowerBuilder returns the following tab-separated string containing all the objects within the DataWindow:

```
id_t    fname_t    address_t    city_t    id    fname    lname    address    city
```

The first four items in the list represent the text column headers' names. The last five items represent the columns' names.

In situations where a name does not exist, PowerBuilder assigns a name beginning with *obj_* to the object. For example, if the Customer ID column header in the last example had no name, PowerBuilder returns the following:

```
obj_16401867    fname_t    address_t    city_t id    fname    lname    address    city
```

If an error occurs, Describe( ) returns an exclamation point (!). If more than one attribute is contained within the function call and an error occurs, PowerBuilder dis-

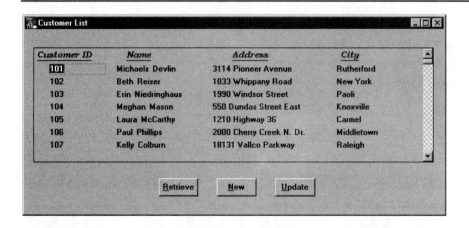

Figure 3.74   **A sample customer list DataWindow.**

plays the values up to the point at which the error occurs. If an attribute does not contain a value, Describe( ) returns a question mark (?).

Continuing with the example, you can obtain the ID column's color and (X,Y) position by using either of the following:

```
dw_custlist.Describe("id.color id.x id.y")
```

or

```
dw_custlist.Object.id.color
dw_custlist.Object.id.x
dw_custlist.Object.id.y
```

Using Describe( ) in the last example returns the color and the X and Y positions separated by a tab character:

```
0    284    4
```

Another good use of obtaining a DataWindow attribute at runtime is when something needs to occur based on the column type. For example, if an error occurs within a DataWindow, you can determine the datatype of the column in error through a call to Describe( ) within the DataWindow's ItemError event:

```
String  sModString, sColType
sModString = string(dwo.Name) + ".coltype"
sColType = This.Describe(sModString)
Choose Case sColType

 Case "number", "long"
    // Numeric error-handling code
    Return 1

 Case "char"
    // Char error-handling code
    Return 1

 Case "date"
    // Date error-handling code
    Return 1

 Case "time"
    // Time error-handling code
    Return 1

 Case "datetime"
    // DateTime error-handling code
    Return 1
End Choose
```

To implement the preceding example by using dot notation, simply replace the first three lines of the code with the following:

```
string sColType
sColType = dwo.coltype
```

As you can see, using dot notation is a simpler and much more straightforward way to obtain the DataWindow attributes. For a list of valid attributes that you can retrieve with Describe( ) or through the dot notation, refer to PowerBuilder documentation.

Modify( ) You can use Modify( ) to do three things with the DataWindows:

Create DataWindow objects.   To dynamically add an object to a DataWindow, call Modify( ) with the CREATE objdef parameter. For example, to add the bitmap named banner.bmp to a DataWindow's header band, call Modify( ) as shown:

```
dw_custlist.Modify("create bitmap(band=header.1 "&
        +"x='1000' y='4' height='138' width='121' "&
        +"filename='C:\RESOURCE\BANNER.BMP' name=banner "))
```

For the syntax required to create each object type, refer to the PowerBuilder User Guide and online documentation.

Destroy DataWindow objects.   To dynamically remove an object from a Data-Window, call Modify( ) with the DESTROY objname parameter. When removing a column, the word *column* must come before objname. For example, to destroy the banner column just created:

```
dw_custlist.Modify("destroy banner")
```

To destroy the city column:

```
dw_custlist.Modify("destroy column city")
```

Assign values to the DataWindow attributes.   This is where you use Modify( ) the most. You can modify the attributes of the DataWindow and any columns or ob-jects within the DataWindow by using Modify( ). As mentioned before, you can use the dot notation instead of Modify( ) to modify the DataWindow attributes directly. The following examples show both the Modify( ) and dot notation methods of mod-ifying the DataWindow attributes.

To illustrate the use of Modify( ), refer to Figure 3.75. In this example, let's assume that only employees from one department at a time are displayed. The user can select a department by using the drop-down listbox, as shown in the figure.

Assume that the salary column should only be displayed if the user is within the "ADMIN" group (a global variable set at login time). For "ADMIN" users, the salary col-umn's color for employees making more than $50,000 should be red with a black back-ground, while the color for all other employees is green with a blue background. Finally, assume the salary column is not defined as updatable within the DataWindow, but it must be updatable for the "ADMIN" users.

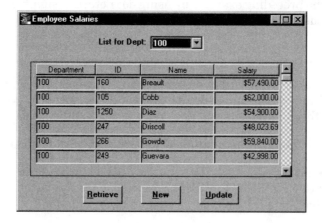

Figure 3.75   **A list of employees for a chosen department.**

The window's open event checks the user type and either destroys the salary object and text (by using Modify( )) or makes the salary column updatable by using the dot notation:

```
/***********************************************************************
** Employee window's open event. Checks global variable for the user
** type. If "ADMIN" user, makes the salary column updatable, else
** destroys the column and the header. Also, if the user is an
** "ADMIN" user, the salary column's color and background are
** changed. Also, get the DataWindow's SELECT statement
** and store the statement within an instance variable for later use.
***********************************************************************/
If g_sUserType <> "ADMIN" Then
   dw_emp.Modify("destroy column salary ~t destroy salary_t")
Else
   dw_emp.Object.salary.Update = "Yes"
   dw_emp.Object.salary.Color = ' 0~t if(salary>50000,255,65280)'
   dw_emp.Object.salary.background.Color = ' 0~t &
                   if(salary>50000,0,16711680)'
End If

// Get the DataWindow's SELECT statement
i_sSQLStmt = dw_emp.Object.DataWindow.Table.Select
```

Notice that the value defined for the salary column's color and background color attributes is the same type of expression that would have previously been included as part of the modstring within the Modify( ) function. Also notice that instead of one call to Modify( ) to set all the three attributes, three separate lines are required when using dot notation.

The cb_Retrieve's clicked event calls the function **my_sql( )**, passing it the department ID from the drop-down listbox:

```
// Call the function to update the SQL statement and retrieve the
// DataWindow
my_sql(ddlb_dept.Text)
```

The function my_sql( ) takes the department ID parameter and uses the dot notation to change the original SQL statement's Where clause. To add the Where clause within this example, it is assumed that the original SQL statement does not contain any clauses (e.g., Where, Order By, Group By) after the From clause. This is because the Where clause is appended to the end of the original statement and is not necessarily placed in the correct position within the Select statement. In a production application, you could parse the string containing the Select statement to find the appropriate place to put the Where clause. The code for my_sql( ) is:

```
/***********************************************************************
** This function changes a DataWindow's SQL statement's Where clause
** based on the passed department id and then retrieves the data
***********************************************************************/
string      sNewWhere, sModTxt
long        lRtn

sNewWhere = " WHERE dept_id = " + as_deptid
sModTxt = i_sSQLStmt + sNewWhere
dw_emp.Object.DataWindow.Table.Select = sModTxt
lRtn =   dw_emp.Retrieve( )
If lRtn = -1 Then
     // Handle error
     Return False
End If
Return True
```

For the "ADMIN" users, the salary column is made updatable, and the values within the salary column have different colors depending on the employee's salary, as shown in Figure 3.76.

For non-"ADMIN" users, the salary column is removed, and the window looks like the one shown in Figure 3.77.

Although there are better ways to achieve this functionality, the method used here is intended to show how you can use the Modify( ) function and dot notation to modify the various aspects of a DataWindow. It is also important to note that PowerBuilder provides the capability to conditionally set the column attributes from the DataWindow painter. To do this, select the **Expressions** tab of the columns Properties sheet, as shown in Figure 3.78.

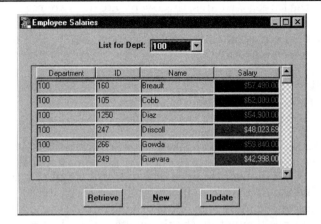

Figure 3.76 Updatable, color-coded salary column for the "Admin" users.

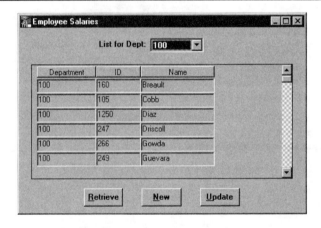

Figure 3.77 The employee window with the salary column removed.

PowerBuilder displays a list of various column properties and their corresponding expressions. Like other expressions, these expressions can contain constants or complex expressions. For example, to set the salary column's color to red for all the employees within department 100, add the expression to the salary column's color attribute as shown in Figure 3.79.

This allows the conditional setting of the column attributes without requiring a runtime modification to the column's attributes by using the Modify( ) function or the dot notation.

You can also modify the DataWindows dynamically to update more than one table when an Update( ) is executed. By default, PowerBuilder lets only one table be updated

Figure 3.78   The salary column's Expressions tab.

Figure 3.79   Setting the salary column's color.

when executing the Update( ) function. To update more than one table, you must change the DataWindow's update properties. The following example shows how to update the department and employee tables by using a single DataWindow (dw_dept). The first example uses the Modify( ) function to change the update properties:

```
int iRtn

// Update the department DataWindow without resetting the
// update flags in case an error occurs on the second update
iRtn = dw_dept.Update(TRUE,FALSE)

// If the update is successful, modify the DataWindow object's update
// properties to update the employee table.
If iRtn = 1 Then
        //Turn off update for the department columns and set the table to employee
        dw_dept.Modify("department_dept_name.Update = No " + &
                        "department_dept_id.Update = No " + &
                            "department_dept_id.Key = No " + &
                            "DataWindow.Table.UpdateTable = ~"employee~"")

        //Turn on the update for the desired employee columns
        dw_dept.Modify("employee_emp_id.Update = Yes "   + &
                        "employee_emp_fname.Update = Yes " + &
                        "employee_emp_lname.Update = Yes " + &
                        "employee_emp_id.Key = Yes")

        // Update the employee table, resetting the update flags
        iRtn = dw_dept.Update( )
        If iRtn = 1 Then
            Commit Using SQLCA;
        Else
            MessageBox("Error","Update of employee table failed. "+ &
                        +"Rolling back changes department and employee.")
        Rollback Using SQLCA;
        End If
Else
        MessageBox("Error","Update of department table failed. " + &
                            +"Rolling back changes to department.")
        Rollback Using SQLCA;
        // Reset the update properties to the department table

End If
```

To do the same thing by using dot notation, change the preceding code to the following:

```
int iRtn

// Update the department DataWindow without resetting the
// update flags in case an error occurs on the second update
iRtn = dw_dept.Update(TRUE,FALSE)

// If the update is successful, modify the DataWindow object's update
// characteristics to update the employee table
If iRtn = 1 Then
    //Turn off update for the department columns and set the table to employee
    dw_dept.Object.dept_name.Update = "No"
    dw_dept.Object.dept_id.Update = "No"
    dw_dept.Object.dept_id.Key = "No"
    dw_dept.Object.DataWindow.Table.UpdateTable = "employee"

    //Turn on update for the desired employee columns
    dw_dept.Object.emp_id.Update = "Yes"
    dw_dept.Object.emp_fname.Update = "Yes"
    dw_dept.Object.emp_lname.Update = "Yes"
    dw_dept.Object.emp_id.Key = "Yes"

    // Update the employee table, resetting the update flags
    iRtn = dw_dept.Update( )
    If iRtn = 1 Then
          Commit Using SQLCA;
    Else
          MessageBox("Error","Update of employee table failed. "+ &
                     +"Rolling back changes department and employee.")
          Rollback Using SQLCA;
    End If
Else
    MessageBox("Error","Update of department table failed. " + &
                       +"Rolling back changes to department.")
    Rollback Using SQLCA;
    // Reset the update properties to the department table
End If
```

Query Mode and Prompt for Criteria

In addition to the methods that have already been discussed, PowerBuilder provides two other ways to dynamically modify a Select statement's Where clause:

- Query Mode
- Prompt for criteria

You can use either method to add Query By Example (QBE) functionality to an application.

Query Mode

You can put a DataWindow into query mode by modifying the DataWindow's Query-mode attribute. The syntax to do this by using dot notation is:

```
dwname.Object.DataWindow.querymode = "Yes"
```

When within query mode, the DataWindow lets the user input the selection and sort criteria. PowerBuilder then appends this information to the DataWindow's Select statement.

When a DataWindow is within query mode, the DataWindow is cleared (any existing data within the DataWindow is hidden) and the user is free to enter the selection and sort criteria. For example, to select all the customers from San Francisco, the query DataWindow looks like the one shown in Figure 3.80.

Notice that the equal sign does not have to be put in front of the value. Notice also that no quotation marks are required around the string datatypes. When all criteria is entered, the Retrieve( ) function executes with a modified Select statement. Assuming no Where clause exists for the DataWindow, the new Where clause is:

```
WHERE (city = 'San Francisco')
```

PowerBuilder adds the AND operators when the selection criteria is put on more than one column for the same row; PowerBuilder adds the OR operators when criteria is entered within more than one row for the same column. Consider the following extension to the last example, as shown in Figure 3.81. This Select's Where clause is:

```
WHERE (id > 300) AND (fname like 'Jo%') AND (city = 'San Francisco')
OR (city = 'Chicago')
```

Notice that it is not possible to add AND or OR operators between the values within

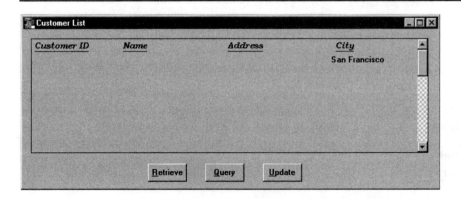

Figure 3.80   Enabling the DataWindow's query mode.

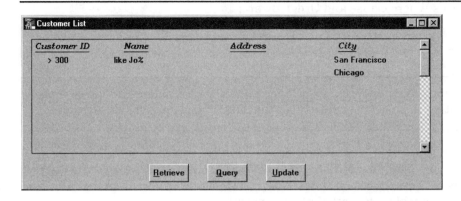

Figure 3.81   Using the AND and OR operators within query mode.

the same column. To do this requires modifying the Where clause by using either the Modify( ) function or the dot notation.

You can add the sort criteria by using the Querysort DataWindow attribute. Set this attribute by using using the dot notation as shown:

```
dwname.Object.DataWindow.querysort = "Yes"
```

This lets you use the query DataWindow's first line for entering the sort criteria. When adding the sort criteria, selection criteria are entered beginning on the second line. In the preceding example, to sort by customer number in ascending order, complete the query DataWindow as shown in Figure 3.82.

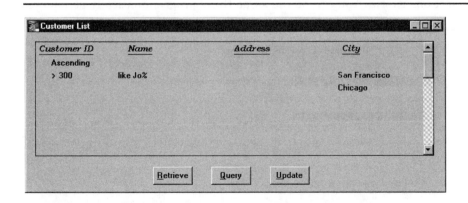

Figure 3.82   The DataWindow within querysort mode.

This Select's Where clause and Order By are:

```
WHERE (id > 300) AND (fname like 'Jo%') AND (city = 'San Francisco')
OR (city = 'Chicago') ORDER BY 1 ASC
```

TIP Setting datawindow.querysort=yes puts a DataWindow into query mode, eliminating the need to explicitly set the datawindow.querymode attribute.

Data entered as either sort criteria or selection criteria does not take effect until the user leaves the field. In addition, you must perform Retrieve( ) to execute the new Select statement. You can obtain the new SQL statement's syntax from the DataWindow's datawindow.table.select attribute, as shown:

```
dwname.Object.datawindow.table.select
```

You can store this value within a local variable or display the value within a MessageBox for debugging purposes (or you can use the DataWindow's SQLPreview event to see the SQL that is sent to the database).

Before executing Retrieve( ), you should reset the DataWindow to its normal state by setting the Querymode attribute to false:

```
dwname.Object.DataWindow.querymode = "No"
```

Prompt for Criteria

Prompt for Criteria provides an interface similar to that used when defining a Quick Select data source. Prompt for Criteria is set on a column-by-column basis either programmatically (by using Modify( ) or dot notation) or through the DataWindow painter by using the **Prompt for Criteria...** option of the **Rows** menu, as shown in Figure 3.83.

The window shown in Figure 3.83 designates the ID and city columns to be prompted for the selection criteria. You can do the same thing programmatically as follows:

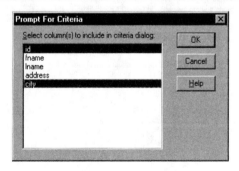

Figure 3.83 The Prompt for Criteria definition dialog box.

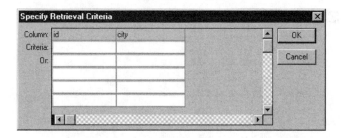

Figure 3.84   The Specify Retrieval Criteria dialog box.

```
dw_custlist.Modify("id.criteria.dialog=yes city.criteria.dialog=yes ")
```

or

```
dw_custlist.Object.id.criteria.dialog   = "yes"
dw_custlist.Object.city.criteria.dialog = "yes"
```

Doing this results in displaying the window in Figure 3.84 when the Retrieve( ) function is called.

The Specify Retrieval Criteria dialog box can be completed just like the Quick Select criteria window. You can use the same operators that you used when completing a query DataWindow (>, <, =, >=, <=, like, in) to complete this window. One difference when using the Prompt for Criteria is that you can specify no sorting criteria. If sorting criteria is required, you must use the Query Mode instead of the Prompt for Criteria.

TIP You should not use the Query Mode and Prompt for Criteria together. Doing so can have mixed results. Generally, if the sort criteria needs to be entered, use the Query Mode. If the number of columns for which the user may enter the selection criteria must be limited, use Prompt for Criteria.

Override Edit and Equality Required

When using either the Query Mode or Prompt for Criteria, you can modify the two other characteristics. These two characteristics are Override Edit and Equality Required.

Override Edit Override Edit lets you override a column's edit characteristics only while within the query mode (or being prompted for criteria). Override Edit changes the column's edit style to the 'edit' style only while selection criteria are entered.

When the selection criteria are entered and the data is retrieved, the column reverts to its defined edit style. Generally you can use this for the columns that have an edit style of something other than the 'edit' style, such as a checkbox, radiobutton, or drop-down listbox. You can set this attribute by selecting the **General** tab of the col-

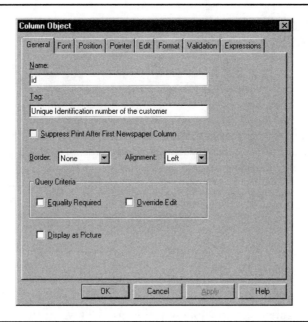

Figure 3.85 Setting the Override Edit and Equality Required column attributes.

umn's Properties sheet (obtained by pressing the right button of your mouse within the column), as shown in Figure 3.85.

You can also do this programmatically as shown:

```
dw_custlist.Modify("id.criteria.override_edit=yes")
```

or

```
dw_custlist.Object.id.criteria.override_edit = "yes"
```

Equality Required Equality Required means that the user can only use the = operator when entering the selection criteria. You can also set this attribute in the **General** tab of the column's Properties sheet, shown in Figure 3.85.

You can also do this programmatically:

```
dw_custlist.Modify("id.criteria.required=yes")
```

or

```
dw_custlist.Object.id.crtiteria.required = "yes"
```

DataWindow Save As

The SaveAs function for the DataWindow control lets you save the data within a DataWindow to other file formats. The function's syntax is:

```
dwcontrol.SaveAs ( { filename, saveastype, colheading } )
```

where:

filename is the name of the file in which you want to save the data.

saveastype is the file format in which you want to save the data. The file formats are described in Table 3.4.

colheading is a boolean value that indicates whether to include the column headings.

All the three agruments are optional. If none of the parameters are provided, PowerBuilder prompts the user with a dialog box for the options. Table 3.4 lists the various file formats.

DESIGN CONSIDERATIONS

Embedded SQL

You often face the question of when to use a DataWindow rather than embedded SQL. As a general rule, you should access the data you display to the user by using a DataWindow whenever possible. In addition to better performance, the functionality built into the DataWindow will save you development time and effort. However, most large development projects cannot rely on the DataWindow alone for data access. You may require embedded SQL for performing such functions as data integrity validations, data definition language (DDL) statements, or any manipulation of nondisplayed data.

Table 3.4   The File Formats for Saving a DataWindow's Data

Format Type	Description
Clipboard!	Save to the clipboard.
CSV!	Comma-separated values.
dBASE2!	dBASE-II format.
dBASE3!	dBASE-III format.
DIF!	Data Interchange format.
Excel!	Microsoft Excel format.
Excel5!	Microsoft Excel 5 format.
HTMLTable!	Text with HTML formatting that approximates the DataWindow layout.
PSReport!	Powersoft Report (PSR) format.
SQLInsert!	SQL syntax.
SYLK!	Microsoft Multiplan format.
Text!	Tab-separated columns with a return at the end of each row.
WKS!	Lotus 1-2-3 format.
WK1!	Lotus 1-2-3 format.
WMF!	Windows Metafile format.

Direct Data Access

In situations that require processing of the data in a row-by-row fashion, the options are to either use a cursor (discussed next) or to use a DataWindow and go through the DataWindow row by row. Previously, going through a DataWindow row by row was usually slower than using a cursor because of all the GetItemXXXX( ) function calls required to get the data from the DataWindow. However, now you can directly access the DataWindow data. The performance difference is significantly reduced to the point that getting the data from a DataWindow requires nothing more than going through an array and is usually as fast or even faster than using a cursor.

You can access and manipulate a DataWindow's data by using the DataWindow's data attribute. This attribute is a two-dimensional array, each element being a data value at a given row and column within the DataWindow. You can reference the data array by using the following syntax:

```
dwcontrol.Object.Data.dwbuffer[row, column]
```

where dwcontrol is the DataWindow control name, dwbuffer is the desired DataWindow buffer (Original, Primary, Delete, and Filter), row is the DataWindow row number, and column is the DataWindow column number. The default for dwbuffer is the Primary buffer. For example, the following line of code obtains the data within the first row, second column of dw_custlist's Primary buffer:

```
dw_custlist.Object.data[1,2]
```

To set this same value to the string "myvalue," use the following code instead of calling the SetItem( ) function:

```
dw_custlist.Object.data[1,2] = "myval"
```

You can also set the value by using a column name within the dot notation.

Static SQL

Embedded SQL exists in either a static or dynamic mode. You can use static SQL for any data manipulation language (DML) statements within which the SQL's structure does not change. While the application may execute the SQL statement multiple times with different values within the program variables used within the Where clause, the statement's structure itself may not change. For example, the following statement is considered to be static SQL:

```
SELECT emp.dept_id, emp_id, emp_fname, emp_lname
FROM emp, dept
WHERE emp.dept_id = dept.dept_id
AND dept_id = :dept_no
USING mytrans;
```

Although the value within the program variable :dept_no may change, this statement is static because the columns the statement selects and the Where clause's structure are constant.

Static SQL also includes cursors, which provide a row-by-row processing capability to what is normally a set-oriented processing model. Within PowerScript, any embedded SQL Select statement that returns more than one row must use a cursor. You can implement cursors by first declaring the cursor, then opening the cursor and fetching one row at a time until the cursor is closed. For example, to go through the customer records one by one, create a cursor and fetch each row until all rows are processed:

```
integer   iCustNum, iLocID
string    sCustName, sAddress, sCity
long      ll_row

ll_row = dw_master.GetRow ()
iLocID = dw_master.Object.loc_id[ll_row]

// Declare a cursor to select the customer data
Declare cust Cursor For
SELECT "customer"."custnum",
"customer"."name",
"customer"."address",
"customer"."city"
FROM "customer"
WHERE location_id = :iLocID
Using SQLCA;

//Open the cursor
Open cust;

// Fetch until all rows are processed
Do While SQLCA.SQLCode = 0
    Fetch cust
    Into :iCustNum,
         :sCustName,
         :sAddress,
         :sCity ;

    //
    // Perform the data manipulation (setItems, etc.)
    //
Loop

// Close cursor
Close cust;
```

TIP For databases that support updatable cursors, you can update the row that the cursor currently holds by using the UPDATE... WHERE CURRENT OF... statement.

Stored procedures are another type of static SQL. Like a cursor, you can use a stored procedure to go through a result set in a row-by-row fashion. For example, the following script executes the preceding example by using the stored procedure process_cust_list, which accepts department ID as an argument:

```
integer    iCustNum, iLocID
string     sCustName, sAddress, sCity
long       ll_row

ll_row = dw_master.GetRow ()
iLocID = dw_master.Object.loc_id[ll_row]

// Declare a procedure to select the customer data
Declare cust_proc Procedure For
process_cust_list @location_id = :iLocID
Using SQLCA;

// Execute the procedure
Execute cust_proc;

// Fetch until all rows are processed
Do While SQLCA.SQLCode = 0
    Fetch cust
    Into :iCustNum,
         :sCustName,
         :sAddress,
         :sCity ;

    //
    // Perform the data manipulation (setItems, etc.)
    //
Loop

Close cust_proc;
```

PowerBuilder's support of stored procedures is RDBMS specific. Chapter 16, "SQL Anywhere and Other Databases," further discusses this topic.

Dynamic SQL

Dynamic SQL differs from static SQL in that it lets a SQL statement's structure change dynamically. Use dynamic SQL when you cannot determine a SQL statement's format until runtime, such as with ad hoc queries. There are four dynamic SQL statement formats (Formats 1–4).

Format 1 Use Format 1 when no input parameters are passed to the SQL statement and the statement does not return a result set. Execute Format 1 SQL statements by using the **Execute Immediate** command. For example, the following script drops a table selected within dw_master:

```
string    sTabName, sSQLStmt
long      ll_row

ll_row   = dw_master.GetRow( )
sTabName = dw_master.object.table_name[ll_row]
sSQLStmt = "DROP TABLE " + sTabName
Execute Immediate :sSQLStmt Using SQLCA;
```

Format 2 Use Format 2 when the input parameters passed to the SQL statement are known and the statement does not return a result set. To accomplish this, Power-Builder uses a dynamic staging area (SQLSA, by default) to store the information about a SQL statement before executing the statement.

The dynamic staging area is used in Formats 2, 3, and 4 to provide a connection between a SQL statement and a transaction object. Place the information about the SQL statement within the dynamic staging area by using the Prepare statement.

The following example shows how you can update the data by using a table and set of columns that the user selects at runtime:

```
string    sSQLStmt, sUpdCol, sUpdVal, sID
int       iID

sID       = sle_id.Text
sUpdCol   = ddlb_cols.Text
sSQLStmt  = "UPDATE employee " + &
     "SET " + sUpdCol + " = ? " + &
     "WHERE emp_id = " + sID
Prepare SQLSA From :sSQLStmt Using SQLCA;

sUpdVal = sle_updval.Text
Execute SQLSA Using :sUpdVal;
```

Notice that the question mark designates an argument that is not known until runtime. For SQL statements that have multiple dynamic parameters, make sure the sequence of the question marks within the statement matches the sequence of arguments within the Execute statement.

Format 3 Use Format 3 when the input parameters and the SQL statement's result set columns are known and the statement returns a result set. Like Format 2, Format 3 uses a dynamic staging area to store the information about the SQL statement before executing the statement.

Format 3 differs from Formats 1 and 2 in that the SQL statement returns a result set. To handle the result set, PowerBuilder uses either a dynamic cursor or dynamic stored procedure. The following example uses a dynamic cursor to process a list of employees based on the job title, experience, and salary that the user enters:

```
string   sSQLStmt, sTitle, sFname, sLname
int      iMonths, iID
long     lSalary

sSQLStmt = "SELECT emp_id, emp_fname, emp_lname FROM employee " + &
           "WHERE title = ? AND exp >= ? AND salary <= ? "

Declare placement_info Dynamic Cursor For SQLSA;
Prepare SQLSA From :sSQLStmt Using SQLCA;

sTitle  = ddlb_title.Text
iMonths = integer(sle_exp.Text)
lSalary = long(sle_salary.Text)

Open Dynamic placement_info Using :sTitle, :iMonths, :lSalary;
Do While SQLCA.SQLCode = 0
     Fetch placement_info INTO :iID, :sFname, :sLname;
   // Process row
Loop

Close placement_info;
```

Format 4 Use Format 4 when the input parameters and the SQL statement's result set columns are not known until runtime and the statement returns a result set. Like Format 3, Format 4 uses a dynamic staging area and either a dynamic cursor or dynamic procedure to process the result set.

Because the input parameters and result set columns are not known until runtime, PowerBuilder uses a dynamic description area (SQLDA, by default) to store the information about these variables. After placing information about the SQL statement into the dynamic staging area (SQLSA) by using the Prepare statement, use a Describe statement to place the information from SQLSA into SQLDA. Then, use SQLDA when opening a dynamic cursor or executing a dynamic stored procedure. Also, use SQLDA with each Fetch statement to return data. The following SQLDA elements are available:

numinputs is the number of input parameters. You can set this attribute. This attribute is set when the Describe statement is executed.

inparmtype is an array of input parameter types. You can set these parameters. These parameters are set when the Describe statement is executed.

numoutputs is the number of output parameters. You can set these parameters. These parameters are set either after the Describe statement or after the first Fetch statement.

outparmtype is an array of output parameter types. You can set these parameters. These parameters are set either after the Describe statement or after the first Fetch statement.

PowerBuilder uses the **SetDynamicParm( )** function to set the SQLDA elements pertaining to the input parameters. You should call the SetDynamicParm( ) function before an Open or Execute statement to assign values to input parameters.

After the SQL statement is executed, you can retrieve the data by using the following functions:

- **GetDynamicDate( )**
- **GetDynamicDateTime( )**
- **GetDynamicNumber( )**
- **GetDynamicString( )**
- **GetDynamicTime( )**

The following example shows how you can use Format 4 Dynamic SQL to provide ad hoc query capability. This example queries the employee information based on the department and columns that the user selects. For example, if the user chooses to display the employee ID, first name, and last name of the employees within department 100, the screen looks like the one in Figure 3.86.

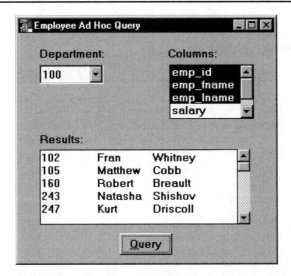

Figure 3.86   An ad hoc query by using Dynamic SQL Format 4.

The script within the query button's clicked event is shown:

```
/****************************************************************
** The following example shows how you can use Dynamic SQL Format 4
** to display the employee information for a department
** that the user selects. The user also specifies the columns
** to be retrieved from the employee table.
****************************************************************/
string    sSQLStmt, sResults, sColList
int       i, iTotCols, iColCount

// Get the list of columns from the listbox
iTotCols = lb_cols.TotalItems( )
For i = 1 To iTotCols
    If lb_cols.state(i) = 1 Then
        iColCount = iColCount + 1
        If iColCount > 1 Then
          sColList = sColList + ", "
        End If
        sColList = sColList + lb_cols.Text(i)
    End If
Next

sSQLStmt = "SELECT " + sColList + " FROM employee " + &
           " WHERE dept_id = " + ddlb_dept.Text

Declare emp_cur Dynamic Cursor For SQLSA;
Prepare SQLSA From :sSQLStmt Using SQLCA;

// Check for Error
If sqlca.sqlcode <> 0 Then
  MessageBox("Prepare Error", SQLCA.sqlerrtext)
  Return
End If

Describe SQLSA Into SQLDA;

// Check for Error
If sqlca.sqlcode <> 0 Then
  MessageBox("Prepare Error", SQLCA.sqlerrtext)
  Return
End If

// Fill the one element of the input descriptor array
// with the value within the department DDLB
SetDynamicParm (SQLDA, 1, ddlb_dept.Text)

Open Dynamic emp_cur Using Descriptor SQLDA ;
```

```
// The output descriptor array contains returned
// values from the result set
Do While SQLCA.SQLCode = 0
    Fetch emp_cur Using Descriptor SQLDA ;
    For i = 1 to SQLDA.numoutputs
        Choose Case SQLDA.OutParmType[i]
        Case TypeString!
            sResults = sResults + GetDynamicString(SQLDA, i) + ' '
        Case TypeDate!
            sResults = sResults + &
                string(GetDynamicDate(SQLDA, i)) + ' '
        Case TypeDateTime!
            sResults = sResults + &
                string(GetDynamicDateTime(SQLDA, i)) + ' '
        Case TypeTime!
            sResults = sResults + &
                string(GetDynamicTime(SQLDA, i)) + ' '
        Case TypeInteger!
            sResults = sResults + &
                string(GetDynamicNumber(SQLDA, i)) + ' '
        Case TypeLong!
            sResults = sResults + &
                string(GetDynamicNumber(SQLDA, i)) + ' '
        End Choose

        sResults = sResults + "~t"
    Next
    sResults = sResults + "~r~n"
Loop
Close emp_cur ;

mle_1.Text = sResults
```

TIP Because PowerBuilder does not support DDL statements within static SQL, you must execute them through dynamic SQL Formats 1 or 2.

Handling Large Result Sets

There may be times when you want to limit the amount of data retrieved from a database into a DataWindow to improve the perceived performance or to keep a user from executing a long-running query and tying up the system resources. To control the large result sets, it is best to either notify the user of a potentially time-consuming query or to impose a limit on the number of rows the application retrieves. There are several ways to accomplish this within PowerBuilder.

Retrieve To Disk

Retrieve To Disk is another method for handing the large result sets. This method is slower to access due to the disk I/O.

Retrieve As Needed

Retrieve As Needed lets a result set be returned to the client in small groups instead of one large data set. This reduces the amount of data initially returned to the client and lets the client cancel the query without returning the entire result set. This section discusses Retrieve As Needed in greater detail later.

Cursors

You can use cursors to limit the data returned to the client by letting only a certain number of rows be fetched from the server. Using a cursor gives you the ability to control when data is sent to the client. For example, the following cursor fetches the rows in groups of 100. When each 100th row is retrieved, the user is prompted to continue. If the user chooses not to continue, the cursor is closed. Otherwise, another 100 rows are fetched:

```
Integer  iCustNum, iMore, iCurRow = 0
string   sCustName, sAddress, sCity

// Declare a cursor to select the customer data
Declare cust Cursor For
SELECT "customer"."custnum",
       "customer"."name",
       "customer"."address",
       "customer"."city"
  FROM "customer" ;


OPEN cust;

// Fetch until done or until the user wants to quit
Do While SQLCA.SQLCode = 0
    Fetch cust Into :iCustNum,
                    :sCustName,
                    :sAddress,
                    :sCity ;
//
// Perform the data manipulation (setItems, etc.)
//

// Increment the row count and check for 100th row
// If multiple of 100th row found, prompt the user to continue
iCurRow ++
If iCurRow = 100 Then
    iCurRow = 0
```

```
    // OKorCancel is a window function that calls MessageBox with
    // the OKCancel! button parameter
        iMore = OKorCancel("Data Retrieval", &
                    "100 rows retrieved. Continue?")
        If iMore <> 1 Then
                // exit the loop and close the cursor
                Exit
            End If
    End If
Loop

Close cust;
```

When using cursors, be careful not to let them remain open for a long period of time. Because opening a cursor locks the data being retrieved, holding a cursor can restrict access of the data to other users. Cursors also consume resources on both the client and server.

The COUNT(*) function

You can execute the **Count(*)** function before a query to determine exactly how many rows are returned. This approach is usually not desirable because of the inefficiency of doing two queries—one to obtain the number of rows and one to perform the retrieve.

The RetrieveRow event

The RetrieveRow event is a DataWindow control event that is triggered each time a row is retrieved from the server to the client. You can use this event to control the number of rows returned to the client by using a row counter similar to the cursor example discussed earlier. In this case, create an instance variable to keep a count of the number of rows retrieved. Then, increment this variable within the RetrieveRow event each time a row is returned to the client. To use the same example as before, the variable i_iCurRow is declared as an instance variable and is incremented within the RetrieveRow event:

```
Integer    iMore
i_iCurRow ++

If i_iCurRow = 100 Then
    i_iCurRow = 0
    // OKorCancel is a window function that calls the MessageBox with the
    // OKCancel! button parameter
    iMore = OKorCancel("Data Retrieval","100 rows retrieved. Continue?")
    If iMore <> 1 Then
        // stop the retrieval
        Return 1
    End If
End If
```

Using the RetrieveRow event can significantly slow the performance because PowerBuilder executes the code within the event every time a row is retrieved. Consequently, you should use the event sparingly.

Shared Result Sets

PowerBuilder lets you share result sets between two or more DataWindow controls within a window. Taking advantage of this capability can reduce the number of queries against the database and thus improve the application performance. To share the data between two DataWindow controls, use the **ShareData( )** function:

```
dwPrimary.ShareData( dwSecondary )
```

where dwPrimary is the primary DataWindow control's name. This DataWindow is the owner of the data and shares its data with one or more secondary DataWindow controls. dwSecondary is the name of the DataWindow control that dwPrimary shares its data with. To share the data with more than one secondary DataWindow control, you must call ShareData( ) once for each secondary DataWindow control.

For example, to share the dw_p1's result set with dw_s1, execute the following script within the window's open event:

```
dw_p1.SetTransObject(SQLCA)
dw_p1.Retrieve( )
dw_p1.ShareData(dw_s1)
```

ShareData( ) allows the sharing of only data between two DataWindow controls. This includes the data within all the three data buffers (Primary!, Filter!, and Delete!) and the sort order. Because the DataWindows do not share the formatting information, shared DataWindows can display the same data with a different appearance.

The Select statement of any DataWindows sharing the data may be different, but the result set description must be the same. Note that although a primary and secondary DataWindow's result set description must be the same, each DataWindow may display different columns. This provides additional flexibility within the appearance of DataWindows sharing a result set. If the result set description is not the same, an error occurs and the secondary DataWindow displays no data. You can also use DataWindows that use a script data source, as long as the columns defined match those of any DataWindow it is sharing data with. For example, the result sets are shared among DataWindows with the following Select statements:

```
SELECT emp_id from employee
SELECT emp_id from employee where dept_id = 300
SELECT emp_id from employee_address
```

However, none of the three DataWindows with the following Select statements could share result sets because of a different result set description:

```
SELECT emp_id from employee
SELECT emp_id, first_name from employee
SELECT emp_id, ss_number from employee
```

Shared DataWindows are treated as independent DataWindow objects. This lets each DataWindow have its own set of attributes that you can retrieve or modify independently. However, because the DataWindow's data is shared, any functions that change the data within a primary or secondary DataWindow result in changes within both the DataWindows (and any other secondary DataWindows). In addition, the following functions are applied to the primary DataWindow control when called for a secondary DataWindow control:

- **Delete( )**
- **Filter( )**
- **ImportClipboard( )**
- **ImportFile( )**
- **ImportString( )**
- **Insert( )**
- **Retrieve( )**
- **Reset( )**
- **SetFilter( )**
- **SetSort( )**
- **Sort( )**
- **Update( )**

To disable the data sharing between two DataWindows, call the **ShareDataOff( )** function:

```
datawindowname.ShareDataOff( )
```

where datawindowname is either the primary or secondary DataWindow control's name. If datawindowname is the secondary DataWindow's name, sharing is disabled only between it and the primary DataWindow. If datawindowname is the primary DataWindow's name, sharing is disabled between the primary DataWindow and all the secondary DataWindows sharing its data. In either case, when you disable sharing, PowerBuilder clears all the secondary DataWindows and no data appears within any of them.

Sharing the data can provide performance gains within situations where you use common data throughout an application. For example, you can share a DataWindow containing employee information that is to appear throughout a set of application functions, such as the employee's name, among multiple secondary DataWindows, as shown in Figure 3.87.

Instead of retrieving the employee name information once for each time it is used, the data from the top DataWindow used in the Employee Address window is shared with the top DataWindow in the Employee Dates window.

While PowerBuilder's implementation of shared DataWindows can reduce the number of database retrievals required and thus improve performance, the implementation does have some limitations. Because all the shared DataWindows use the same data buffer, a secondary DataWindow cannot filter the primary DataWindow's data without changing the data within both the DataWindows. Therefore, it is not possible

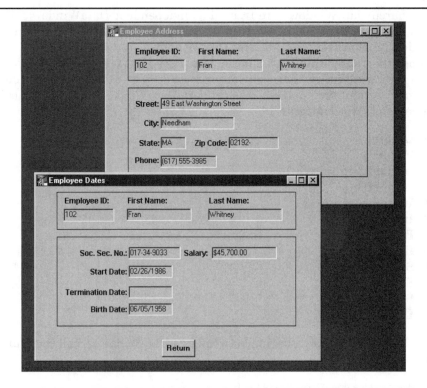

Figure 3.87 Two DataWindows sharing data.

to retrieve a large set of data and apply different filters for the different shared DataWindows.

However, with the RowsCopy( ) function, it is much easier to move the data between the DataWindows, letting data from one DataWindow be copied to another without querying the database more than once. While this is not the same as sharing a DataWindow, RowsCopy( ) does provide a method of taking a single result set and using the result set within more than one DataWindow. You can also use the dot notation to copy the rows.

TIP You can share data between two DataStores as well as between a DataStore and a DataWindow control.

Retrieve As Needed

Retrieve As Needed provides the capability to bring a result set from the server to the client only as the rows are needed for display within a DataWindow. For example, if you size a DataWindow control to show only three rows at a time, Retrieve As Needed initially only brings back enough data from the server to show the first three rows. As the user pages down through the data, PowerBuilder continues to return the data from the server to display within the DataWindow. The user can continue to page down until all the data within the result set is returned to the client. Figures 3.88 and 3.89 illustrate how Retrieve As Needed differs from the traditional data retrieval.

You can implement Retrieve As Needed by selecting the **Rows As Needed** option from the **Retrieve** option of the DataWindow painter's **Rows** menu. PowerBuilder implements retrieve as needed by opening a cursor and maintaining the cursor as rows are retrieved from the server. When data is needed on the client, PowerBuilder simply fetches enough rows from the server (in two-page increments) to update the DataWindow's display.

You override Retrieve As Needed if you perform any sorting, filtering, or aggregate functions (e.g., sum, average) against the DataWindow. This is because PowerBuilder must bring back the entire result set in order to perform any of these functions. You can make sure you do not override Retrieve As Needed by adding an Order By clause to the Select statement to handle the sorting, adding a Where clause instead of using a filter, and placing any computed columns within the Select statement instead of within the DataWindow as computed fields.

Using Retrieve As Needed does not impact the execution of the retrievestart, retrieverow, and retrieveend events. Retrievestart is triggered when the application begins the retrieval and triggers retrieverow for every row the application retrieves. Retrieveend is triggered only when the application retrieves the last row or executes the **dbCancel( )** function.

The Retrieve( ) and Rowcount( ) functions behave differently, however, when using Retrieve As Needed. Retrieve( ) returns only the number of rows initially brought back

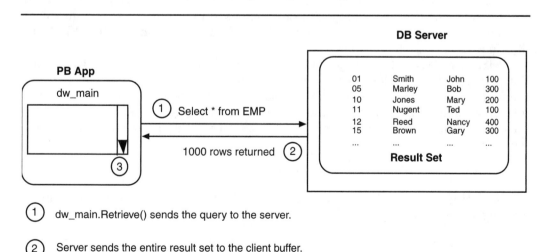

① dw_main.Retrieve() sends the query to the server.

② Server sends the entire result set to the client buffer.

Figure 3.88   **Data retrieval without Retrieve As Needed.**

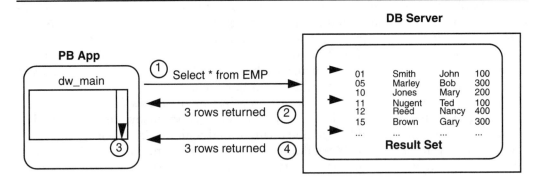

① dw_main.Retrieve() opens a cursor and fetches the first three rows from the server.

② The server only sends the first three rows to the client buffer.

③ The user pages down in dw_main causing the client to fetch the next three rows from the server.

④ The server sends the next three rows to the client. The new rows are added to the client buffer.

Figure 3.89   **Data retrieval with Retrieve As Needed.**

to the client. Rowcount( ) returns the total number of rows that are returned to the client. Using the preceding example, these functions work as illustrated in Figure 3.90. To obtain the total number of rows that satisfy the query, you can use the COUNT(*) SQL function.

Retrieve As Needed also impacts the printing of DataWindows. When you print a DataWindow, PowerBuilder prints only the rows that are returned to the client. To print all the rows of a DataWindow, you must disable Retrieve As Needed. You can do this programmatically by using the dot notation. Setting the Retrieve.AsNeeded DataWindow attribute to "No" causes the result set's remaining rows to be returned to the client:

```
dw_main.Object.DataWindow.Retrieve.AsNeeded = "No"
```

To reset Retrieve As Needed to True after all the rows are returned to the client for printing, do the following:

```
dw_main.Object.DataWindow.Retrieve.AsNeeded = "Yes"
```

The Retrieve As Needed's performance benefits depend on the result set's size and the nature of user interaction with the data. If the user pages through a large per-

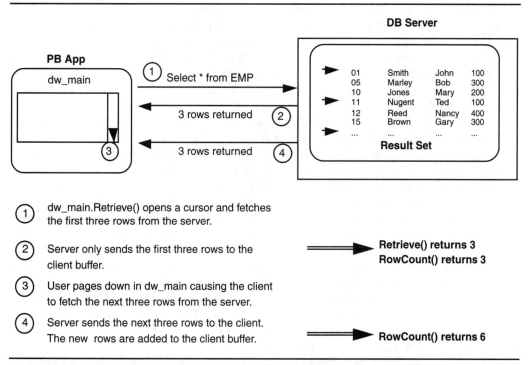

Figure 3.90   Retrieve( ) and RowCount( ) with Retrieve As Needed.

centage of the result set, Retrieve As Needed decreases the perceived performance because the data retrieval is done each time the user scrolls. In this situation, you should
probably not use Retrieve As Needed. However, if a large result set is retrieved and the
user usually does not page through the result set, Retrieve As Needed can provide a big
perceived performance gain.

DataWindows as Buffers and DataStore Objects

In addition to using a DataWindow to present the data to the user, you can also use a
DataWindow as a data buffer. You can take advantage of the great deal of functionality encapsulated within a DataWindow to accomplish such things as storing the application-specific security information, maintaining the user configuration information, or
storing the data read from a file, among others.

One common use of a DataWindow as a buffer is to put the data into a format for
printing. For example, assume we have a data entry DataWindow loading data into an
application database. For the sake of this example, assume that to expedite the data
entry process, this DataWindow includes a very plain, straightforward presentation
style. Also assume there is a need to print the reports to verify the data that the user
enters and that this report's presentation style differs from the data entry form.

A possible solution for this problem is to create a second DataWindow for printing, create a hidden DataWindow control on the data entry window with the "print" DataWindow as its DataWindow object, and copy the desired data to the "print" DataWindow before printing. In this case, the "print" DataWindow is serving only as a data buffer—you do not display the "print" DataWindow to the user. You could also use the RowsCopy( ) and RowsMove( ) DataWindow functions to simplify the transfer of data between the two DataWindows.

PowerBuilder also provides the DataStore object with the capability of retrieving the data into a buffer. A DataStore object is essentially a nonvisual DataWindow control. It is very similar to a DataWindow control, with the exception of some of the DataWindow control's visual attributes. Although the DataStore object is nonvisual, you can still print the data contained within the object.

To use a DataStore, first create the DataStore object within the User Object painter. The DataStore object is a standard nonvisual user object, and you can choose the object from the list of standard class types, as shown in Figure 3.91.

As an example, assume we want to use a DataStore object to store the security information for the application objects. For simplicity's sake, assume the possible rights for a given object are only Update and Read. An object with Update rights allows full select, insert, update, and delete privilege to the user, while Read rights disables the object. After creating the DataStore object, select the DataStore's DataWindow object name (in this case d_security) by opening the object's Properties sheet and entering the DataWindow object's name, as shown in Figure 3.92.

Next, save the DataStore object (u_security_store in this example) and create a global variable gu_secStore of the new DataStore type:

```
u_security_store    gu_secStore
```

Use gu_secStore to store the security information. Creating this as a global variable ensures that security information is available throughout the application's duration. Depending on your particular security requirements, it may be best to create this object as something other than a global variable, but for this example use a global

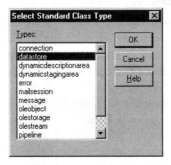

Figure 3.91   Selecting the DataStore object type.

Figure 3.92   Selecting the DataStore DataWindow object.

variable. Next, add the following code somewhere within the application startup process (sometimes before opening an object that needs security checking, most likely immediately after the login process):

```
gu_secStore = Create u_security_store
gu_secStore.SetTransObject(SQLCA)
gu_secStore.Retrieve()
```

This code creates the global DataStore variable, sets the transaction object of the DataStore's DataWindow object, and retrieves the security information into the Data-Store object. Security data is now retrieved and available until you destroy the Data-Store object.

Next, add code to the object's constructor event to check security and disable the object if necessary. The following code uses the **Find( )** function to locate a row within the DataStore object that matches the desired object name ("custobj" in this example). If you find a row, obtain the rights for the object, and if the rights are Read, disable the object. Otherwise, make no changes to the object:

```
Long      lObjRow
string    sRights
lObjRow = gu_secstore.Find("objectname = 'custobj'", 1, &
                           gu_secstore.RowCount())
If lObjRow > 0 Then
     sRights = gu_secstore.Object.Data[lObjRow,2]
     If sRights = "Read" Then
          Enabled = false
     Else
          Enabled = true
     End If
End If
```

Finally, add the following code within the application object's close event to destroy the security DataStore object:

```
destroy gu_sectore
```

Code Tables

Code tables provide a method of reducing the amount of data stored in a database by storing the value's encoded representation. When used within DataWindows, code tables consist of a data value, which is the value retrieved from and stored within a database, and a display value, which is the value the code table shows to the user. You can implement a list of states as a code table, for example, with the state abbreviation being the data value and the state name being the display value:

Data Value	Display Value
CA	California
FL	Florida
TX	Texas
WA	Washington
...	...

Define the code tables through a column's edit style. You can define code tables for the following edit styles:

- Checkbox
- DropDownDataWindow
- DropDownListBox
- Edit Style
- Edit Mask with Spin Control
- Radiobuttons

The following sections discuss each of these edit styles.

Checkbox Code Tables

Although not widely used, code tables can have a checkbox edit style. The value stored is dependent on the checkbox's state, so you can store only three possible values (on, off, or other) for any one column. For example, you can implement a column containing the employee status as a checkbox by defining the On value to mean "active" and the Off value to mean "inactive." The codes AC and IN designate Active and Inactive respectively, as shown in Figure 3.93.

Because a user can choose only between the checkbox's two states, no validation is required.

DropDownDataWindow Code Tables

You can use the DropDownDataWindow (DDDW) edit style to define a child DataWindow as the code table for the column. Generally you use this style for the code tables shared throughout an application. For example, the DataWindow d_dddw_states is defined with the following Select statement as its data source:

```
SELECT state_id, state_name FROM states
```

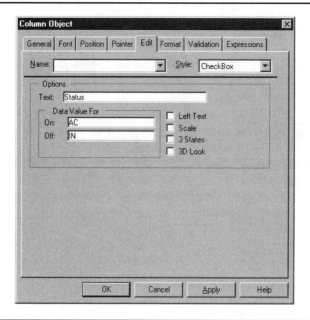

Figure 3.93   The Checkbox edit style.

This DataWindow only displays the state_name column. You can now use d_dddw_ states as a DDDW within any other DataWindow that contains a state column, as shown in Figure 3.94.

If the data you display by using a DDDW is fairly static, storing the data with the DataWindow can improve performance by eliminating the need to retrieve the data from the database. In this example, because the data within d_dddw_states most likely never changes, you should store the data with the DataWindow object. To do this, select the **Data...** option from the **Rows** menu within the DataWindow painter and complete it as shown in Figure 3.95. Should this data change, you need to modify the DataWindow object and redistribute the application.

DropDownListBox Code Tables

You can use a DropDownListBox (DDLB) edit style to define the code table data and display values. For a list of states, complete the DDLB style window as shown in Figure 3.96.

You could either hard-code the values within a DDLB, as shown in Figure 3.96, or fill them from a database programmatically. With DDDWs, filling a DDLB from the database is not necessary.

Edit Style Code Tables

You can define code tables for the edit-style columns by checking the **Use code table** checkbox within the Edit Style window. Checking this column lets you enter the data and display values for the code table, as shown in Figure 3.97.

Figure 3.94   The DropDownDataWindow edit style.

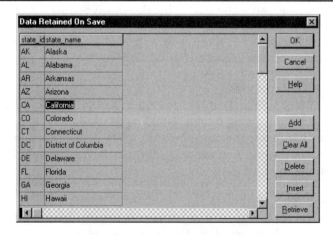

Figure 3.95   Storing the state data with the DataWindow object.

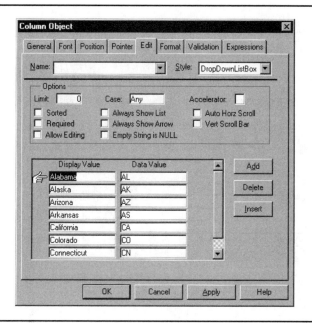

Figure 3.96 The DropDownListBox edit style.

You can validate the edit style columns either by using the code table or through the code you write within the DataWindow control's ItemError event. To use the code table for validation, check the **Validate Using Code Table** checkbox on the edit style window, and do not place any code within the ItemError event. If an error occurs, PowerBuilder displays a message box with a generic message.

To customize the error processing, place code within the ItemError event. For example, to customize the error message if the user enters an invalid employee status code into an edit style column, add the following code to the DataWindow control's ItemError event:

```
// Display the custom error message
MessageBox ("Validation Error", &
          "'" + data + "' is not valid for column '" + dwo.Name + "'")

// Return 1 to not display the system message
Return 1
```

Edit Mask with Spin Control

You can use code tables with spin controls to let the user scroll through the list of code table values. For the list of states example, define the edit mask as shown in Figure 3.98.

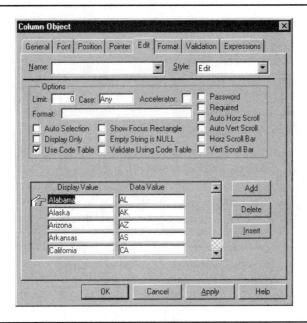

Figure 3.97 The edit style definition dialog box.

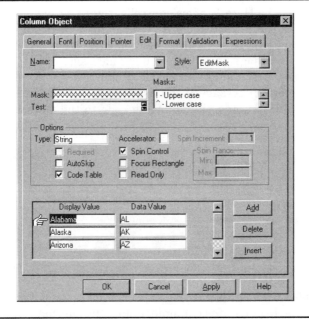

Figure 3.98 Using an EditMask with a Spin Control with a code table.

Radiobuttons

You can use code tables with radiobutton edit styles by defining a fixed number of possible values for a given column. For example, if an employee's status can either be active, terminated, or on leave, you can use radiobuttons with a code table as shown in Figure 3.99.

Radiobuttons are treated much the same way as edit styles. The only difference is that the user must choose one of the possible options (there is no editing capability). Radiobuttons are good for small, static code tables.

Dynamically Changing Code Tables

There may be times when you need to change the values for a code table, such as when a code table's value is dependent on another column's value within the DataWindow. To do this, change the column's values attribute to the new code table.

For example, the following code sets the codes table for the DropDownListBox column "city" to the cities for the state displayed within the state column:

```
string is_StateVal
is_StateVal = dw_1.Object.state[1]

Choose Case is_StateVal
        Case "TX"
                dw_1.Object.city.values = "Houston~tHO/Dallas~tDA"

        Case "CA"
```

continues

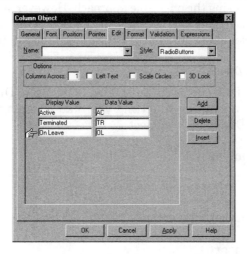

Figure 3.99   **Using a Radiobutton edit style.**

```
            dw_1.Modify("city.values = 'Los Angeles~tLA/San
            dw_1.Object.city.values = "Los Angeles~tLA/San Francisco~tSF"
            ...
            ...
End Choose
```

While all of these code tables (other than the DropDownDataWindow) maintain the code table data within the client application, it is usually desirable to store the code table information within an application database. In this case, you must retrieve the code table data from the database and write any changes to a code table back to the database.

There are two design approaches when storing the code tables within a database. One approach is to store each individual code table as a separate database table. For example, if an application requires code tables to maintain a list of states, a list of company division names, and a list of employee titles, three tables are created, each with the following columns:

```
code              char(10)      Not Null
description       char(40)      Not Null
```

Another approach is to store all code tables within a single database table. In this case, the table must have a column designating the code's type:

```
code_type         char(10)      Not Null
code_char         char(10)      Not Null
description       char(40)      Not Null
```

Deciding which method to use depends on the number of code tables and the frequency with which the code tables are queried and updated. For a larger number of code tables, you can simplify maintenance by using the one-table approach. However, depending upon such things as the nature of transactions against the code tables and the RDBMS, it may be desirable to distribute the code table data among separate database tables.

Using a DDDW versus Filling a DDLB

Use DDDWs instead of filling DDLBs by using embedded SQL. Using DDDWs usually results in better performance, in addition to letting you take advantage of the functionality already built into the DataWindow object.

Using Bitmaps within DataWindows

You can use bitmaps in different ways to enhance a DataWindow's look. You can do this by:

- Setting the Display As Picture attribute
- Using a computed field
- Using **SetRowFocusIndicator( )**

The following sections discuss these methods.

Display As Picture

You can use the Display As Picture attribute to display a bitmap file named within a database column. You usually use this method when the bitmap filename is stored within the database. For example, suppose you define the table part_image, which contains a set of part names and their corresponding bitmap filenames, as:

```
part_name       char(10)        Not Null
bmp_file        char(15)        Not Null
```

Without setting Display As Picture, retrieving this data simply retrieves the part name and the bitmap file's name, as shown in Figure 3.100.

To direct PowerBuilder to display the column as a bitmap, select the **Display As Picture** option from the bmp_file's Properties sheet's **General** tab, as shown in Figure 3.101.

PowerBuilder, in turn, displays the bitmap file itself, rather than just the file's name, as shown in Figure 3.102.

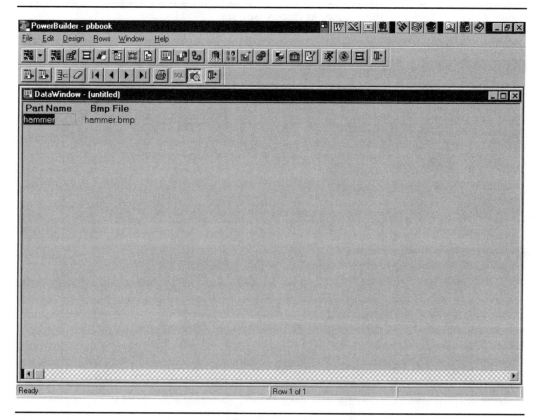

Figure 3.100   Retrieval of part name and bitmap filename only.

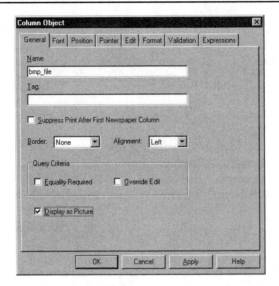

Figure 3.101 Selecting the Display As Picture option.

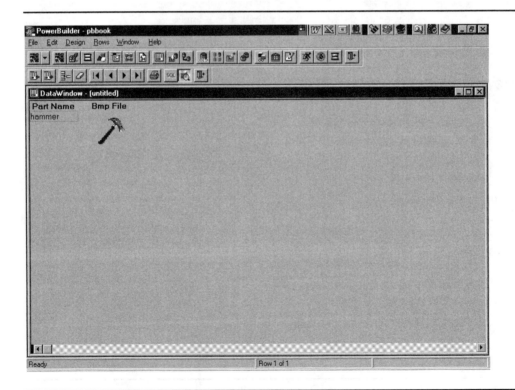

Figure 3.102 Displaying the file as a picture.

As mentioned earlier, you usually use this method of displaying bitmaps within DataWindows when the bitmap's name is stored within the database. Depending on an application's nature, this may or may not be desirable. When dealing with a large volume of image data, this method of image display may be preferable to storing the images within the database. While storing the image data within a database has advantages, it can also significantly slow performance.

Another thing to remember regarding this method of image display is that it does not let you edit the image. You can change the file name, but you cannot modify the image itself. To allow image editing from within a PowerBuilder application, create an OLE column with the bitmap as the data source. OLE columns are discussed later.

A second example using Display As Picture is to use a bitmap to indicate that a row is selected. For example, if the user can select multiple rows within a DataWindow, you can define a column with the Display As Picture attribute set to use a bitmap to indicate that the row is selected. To do this, first modify the DataWindow's Select statement to add a computed column. You can do this by simply adding an empty string to the Select:

```
SELECT ' ', "sales_order"."id",  "sales_order"."cust_id",
    "sales_order"."order_date",  "sales_order_items"."ship_date",
    "sales_order_items"."quantity",  "product"."unit_price"
  FROM "customer",  "sales_order",  "sales_order_items",  "product"
  WHERE ( "customer"."id" = "sales_order"."cust_id" ) and
    ( "sales_order"."id" = "sales_order_items"."id" ) and
    ( "sales_order_items"."prod_id" = "product"."id" )
```

Next, add this column to the DataWindow. Place the column at the leftmost part of the body and select the Display As Picture attribute, as shown in Figure 3.103.

From the Window painter, add the following code to the DataWindow control's clicked event:

```
/**********************************************************************
** If we click within the selection column, then select/deselect this
** row. Indicate the row selection by setting the selection column
** to the name of the bitmap file returned from the selectionBMP( )
** function.
**********************************************************************/
string sSelCol, sTemp

// Only do this if we clicked within our "selection column."
// The selectionColNo( ) function returns the selection column
sSelCol = dwo.Name
If sSelCol = "sel_col" Then
    // First - force to process any changes - only continue if no
    // errors
    If AcceptText() < 0 Then
```

```
                // Error - don't do the rest of this event
                Return 0
          End If
          If row > 0 Then
                // Set this to the current row and get the bitmap file's name
                SetRow(row)
                sTemp = GetItemString (row,"sel_col")

                // If the column is empty, set it to the bitmap file
                // name else, set it to empty string
                If (sTemp = "") or IsNull(sTemp) Then
                      SetItem(row,"sel_col",selectionBMP( ))
                Else
                      SetItem(row,"sel_col","")
                End If
          End If
    End If

    Return 0
```

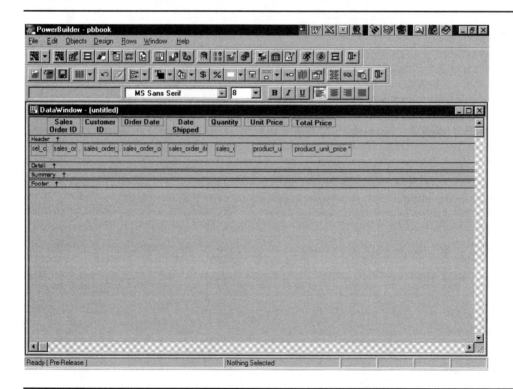

Figure 3.103   Placing a selection column within a DataWindow.

Notice that the script calls the user-defined function **selectionBMP( )**. This function returns a string containing the bitmap file's name used to indicate the row selection ("checkmark.bmp" in this example).

TIP If the same selection column or bitmap is used by multiple DataWindows within an application, it is better to create selectionBMP( ) as a window function of an ancestor window.

When executed, clicking on the selection column toggles between the asterisk and an empty string to indicate whether a row is selected. So, if the first, second, and third rows are selected, the window looks like that shown in Figure 3.104. You should add code to perform some process against each of the selected rows.

Using a Computed Field

Another method for displaying the bitmaps within DataWindows is to use a computed field. The computed field expression uses the **Bitmap( )** function, which takes a single argument that is either a DataWindow column or a string naming the bitmap file to be displayed. Use this function within the computed field's expression to dynamically determine the bitmap to be displayed for each row within the DataWindow.

Using the preceding example, assume we want to display a smiley face if the total order price is greater than $200. To do this, add a computed field to the DataWindow with the expression shown in Figure 3.105.

This example uses the Bitmap( ) function to display smiley.bmp if the total price is greater than $200. Figure 3.106 shows the results.

This method of displaying the bitmaps within a DataWindow provides more flexibility than the preceding method because you can define the computed field so that the bitmap is determined dynamically based on the values of the other columns within the DataWindow.

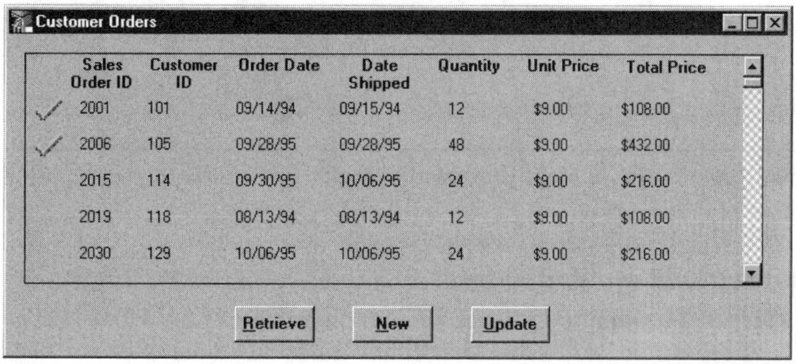

Figure 3.104   Using a bitmap to indicate the selected rows.

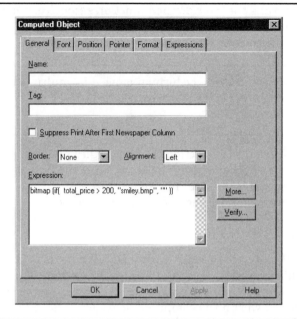

Figure 3.105 Using the Bitmap( ) function within a computed field definition.

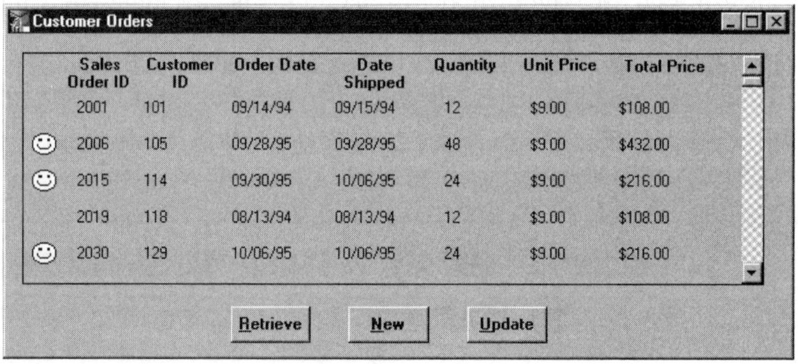

Figure 3.106 The Bitmap( ) function's results.

Using SetRowFocusIndicator( )

You can use bitmaps to indicate the current row within a DataWindow by using the SetRowFocusIndicator( ) function. This function takes either a picture control or a value of the RowFocusInd enumerated datatype. To use a picture control as the row focus indicator, place the picture control on the object containing the DataWindow. You can either hide the picture control or place the control under the DataWindow control to keep the control from displaying on the window. For example, to set the row focus indicator to checkmark.bmp, create a picture control with checkmark.bmp as its picture and call SetRowFocusIndicator before retrieving the DataWindow:

```
int  iRtn

dw_cust_order.SetRowFocusIndicator(p_1)
iRtn = dw_cust_order.Retrieve( )
If iRtn = -1 Then
  MessageBox("Select Error", SQLCA.sqlerrtext)
End If
```

As a result, the DataWindow uses the picture object as the row focus indicator, as Figure 3.107 shows.

The enumerated datatype RowFocusInd contains a set of values that you can use as parameters for SetRowFocusIndicator. This datatype is defined as:

Off!   No indicator.

FocusRect!   Puts a rectangle around the current row.

Hand!   Uses the hand bitmap to indicate the current row.

The SetRowFocusIndicator( ) also takes an X and Y value as parameters to indicate where within the DataWindow control PowerBuilder displays the indicator. Use these arguments only when using a picture control or the Hand! value as the indicator. The defaults for the X and Y position are 0. This displays the indicator at the leftmost side of the DataWindow body. To replace the asterisk previously used with the hand bitmap, change the parameter passed to SetRowFocusIndicator:

	Sales Order ID	Customer ID	Order Date	Date Shipped	Quantity	Unit Price	Total Price
	2001	101	09/14/94	09/15/94	12	$9.00	$108.00
✓	2006	105	09/28/95	09/28/95	48	$9.00	$432.00
	2015	114	09/30/95	10/06/95	24	$9.00	$216.00
	2019	118	08/13/94	08/13/94	12	$9.00	$108.00
	2030	129	10/06/95	10/06/95	24	$9.00	$216.00

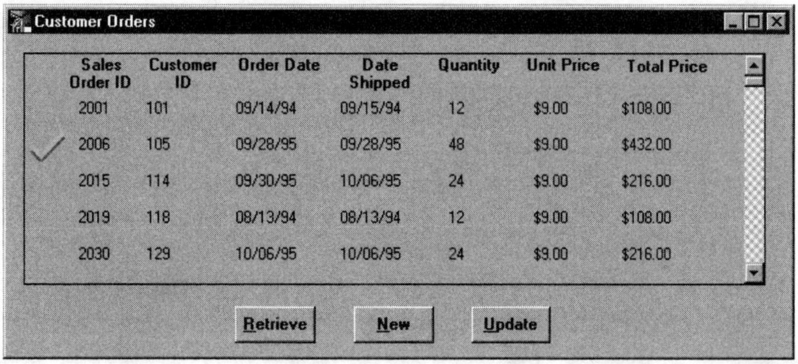

Figure 3.107   Using a picture object as a row focus indicator.

```
int  iRtn

dw_cust_order.SetRowFocusIndicator(Hand!)
iRtn = dw_cust_order.Retrieve( )
If iRtn = -1 Then
  MessageBox("Select Error", SQLCA.sqlerrtext)
End If
```

This code displays the DataWindow as shown in Figure 3.108.

OLE Columns

Microsoft's object linking and embedding (OLE) provides a method of communicating between Windows applications. This method lets you integrate information from a variety of sources into a single document. PowerBuilder supports OLE in the form of a window control as well as in the form of an OLE column within a DataWindow. This section discusses a DataWindow's OLE column only. For a discussion of creating an OLE 2 window control, refer to Chapter 13, "External Interfaces."

You can use OLE DataWindow columns to store the binary large objects (blobs) such as bitmaps, Excel spreadsheets, and Microsoft Word documents within a database.

Table 3.5 defines some of the common terms used with OLE applications.

PowerBuilder uses blobs to store the binary information that OLE requires. Because the blobs are within a database table, PowerBuilder requires at least two columns within a table containing a blob—one for the blob itself and one for a unique identifier of the blob (e.g., a filename or an object number). Usually, you define this column as the table's key.

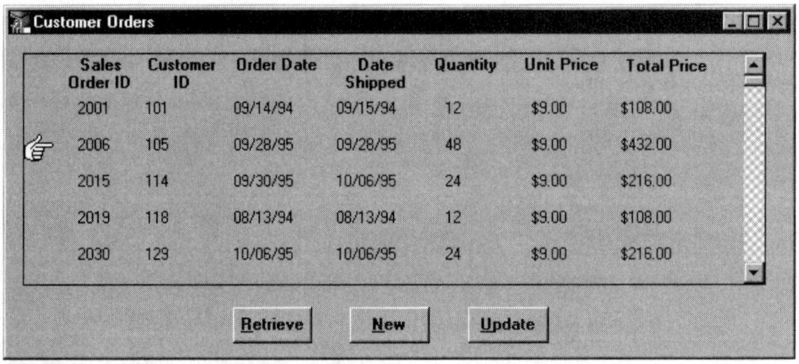

Figure 3.108   Using the Hand! bitmap as a row focus indicator.

Table 3.5 Common OLE Terms

Term	Description
Client Application	The application within which you link or embed an OLE object. If an Excel graph is embedded within a Word document, Word is the client application.
Server Application	The application from which you link or embed an OLE object. If an Excel graph is embedded within a Word document, Excel is the server application.
OLE Client Library	The client application uses this library, olecli.dll, to interact with the OLE protocol. The library contains functions that client applications use.
OLE Server Library	The server application uses this library, olesvr.dll, to interact with the OLE protocol. The library contains functions that server applications use.
Registration Database	You find this database within the shell.dll library. The database contains information that clients and servers need to determine the servers and objects that are available.
Native Data	This is the data that the client stores only for embedded objects. The server document is the embedded object. When a client needs an embedded object manipulated, the client passes this data to the server. Because this data is "native" to the server, PowerBuilder produces a document from the data that can be manipulated just like any of the server's documents. When the user is finished with the server, the server passes the updated native data back to the client for storage.
Presentation Format	This is data that the client stores for both embedded and linked objects. The client application passes this data to the client library so that the object is displayed within the client's document. This data is needed so the client can represent the server's document within its own document. Because the client does not understand the server's native data and therefore cannot display the data, the server must provide a format that the client can use to display the object. This data is the presentation format.
Owner Link	This is the data that a client stores for embedded objects to determine the application that is the server. The server originally passes the data.
Object Link	This is the data a client stores for the linked objects to determine the server and the original file to which the link is made. The server originally passes the data.

For example, create a DataWindow for maintaining a set of employee status and expense reports. This DataWindow contains the employee ID, a week-ending date, and two blob columns—one for the status report (a Word document) and one for the expense report (an Excel spreadsheet). Figure 3.109 shows the SQL Anywhere table definition.

To create a DataWindow with a blob column, first paint a Select statement including the identifier column within the select list, but not the blob. Because PowerBuilder does not directly support the blob datatype, you cannot include the blob column within the select list. Within this example, the emp_id and week_ending columns are selected.

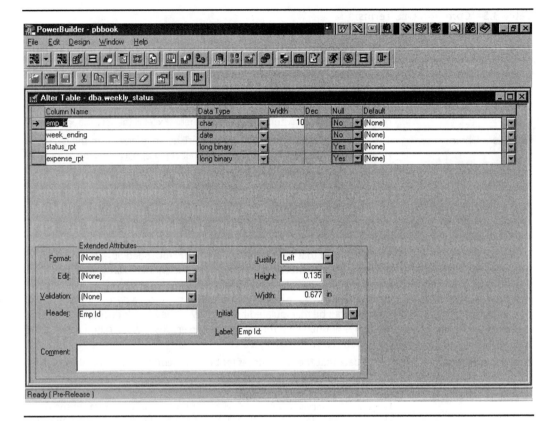

Figure 3.109   Defining a SQL Anywhere table for tracking the employee status and expense reports.

After creating the Select statement, place the blob on the DataWindow by selecting **OLE Database Blob** from the **Objects** menu. After choosing where to place the blob column, display the blob column's Properties sheet's **Definition** tab. Complete this dialog box to create the blob status report as shown in Figure 3.110.

To yield a string that the server application uses as the document's title, concatenate the Client Class, Client Name, and Client Name Expression fields together. The Client Name Expression lets the title be dynamically associated with the runtime values within the client application. For example, the window in Figure 3.110 displays the unique identifiers emp_id and week_ending from the current row within the DataWindow within the phrase *Status report for...* in the titlebar of the server application's window.

Use the Table and Large Binary/Text Columns comboboxes to tell PowerBuilder which column the OLE blob is referring to. Within the window shown in Figure 3.110, weekly_status.status_rpt stores the status report blob. Use the Key clause for retriev-

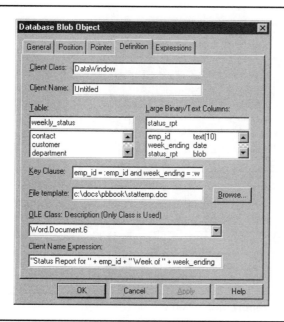

Figure 3.110   Definition of the blob status report.

ing and updating the blobs from the database. The Key clause defines the Where clause needed to identify a specific blob. This example uses the emp_id and week_ending columns within the Where clause to uniquely identify the blob columns.

PowerBuilder uses the File Template field when creating a new blob. If you do an InsertRow( ) within the DataWindow, PowerBuilder creates a new row with an empty blob. By double-clicking on this blob or calling **OLEActivate( )**, PowerBuilder starts the server application that the OLE Class field defines. If there is a filename within the File Template field, the server application displays this file as the default data for the new object. Within our example, PowerBuilder opens the file C:\docs\pbbook \stattemp.doc when creating a new status report.

The OLE Class field is not required if a File Template is entered that contains an extension registered within the OLE registration database. PowerBuilder searches the OLE registration database for the class associated with this extension and starts that class's application.

To define the blob column for the expense reports, repeat the previous steps and complete the blob definition window as shown in Figure 3.111.

After the blob columns are identified, the DataWindow looks something like that in Figure 3.112.

When you execute the expense report example, PowerBuilder displays the existing rows with the two blob columns, as shown in Figure 3.113.

Figure 3.111 The expense report blob's definition.

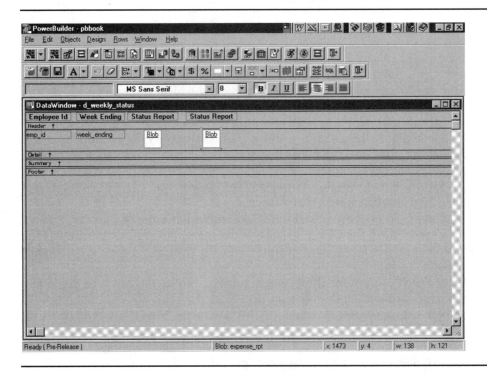

Figure 3.112 The DataWindow after creating the blob column.

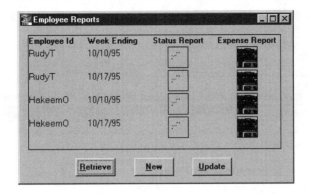

Figure 3.113   The DataWindow at runtime with the blob columns.

Double-clicking on the Microsoft Word icon within the status report column invokes Microsoft Word and opens the document contained within the blob column, as shown in Figure 3.114.

Double-clicking on the Excel spreadsheet icon within the expense report column invokes Excel and opens the document contained within the blob column, as Figure 3.115 shows.

When a new row is inserted, the blob columns are initially blank. Double-clicking on either of the blob columns displays the OLE server application and opens the file that the file template specifies defined within the blob definition window.

TIP To show the users where to click to activate an OLE column, place an object or bitmap behind the blob column.

It is important to note that a blob column does not require a database to start a server and view a specific file. Although this information is never actually embedded within the DataWindow because there is no place to store the information, you can use the blob to let the users look at a specific file from a server application.

For example, to let a user view the Excel file expense.xls from a PowerBuilder application, you can create a DataWindow by using an external data source and a blob column. In this instance, the only meaningful field within the blob definition window is the File Template. You can leave the OLE Class blank and set the Client Class, Client Name, and Client Name Expression to whatever values are appropriate. The Table, Large Binary/Text Columns, and the Key clause can contain anything because the value is not used, but it must contain some value. The File Template field should contain a fully qualified reference to expense.xls.

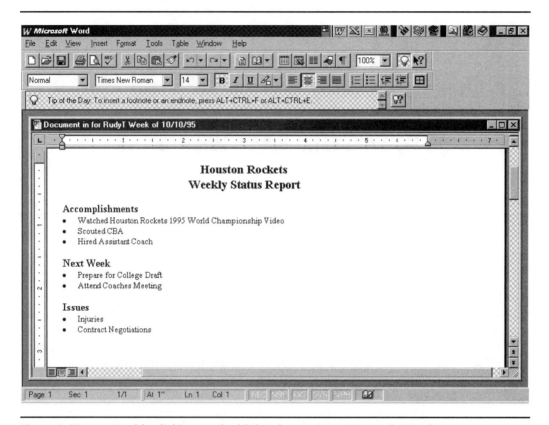

Figure 3.114 Double-clicking on the blob column opens Microsoft Word.

To view the spreadsheet, call InsertRow( ) to create a new row within the DataWindow and double-click on the blob column (or calls OLEActivate( )). PowerBuilder then starts the OLE server application and opens expense.xls because you defined the file as the template file for that OLE column within the DataWindow. It is important to note that this is not the actual expense.xls file. The sheet Excel displays is the OLE object belonging to PowerBuilder, and any changes you make to the sheet are not reflected within expense.xls. Exiting the server returns the presentation data from the server to the DataWindow.

Limitations

According to Microsoft's OLE specifications, the difference between linking and embedding is usually a function of whether the user uses a **Paste** or a **Paste Link** command. Because a DataWindow's functionality does not lend itself to either of these commands, there is no reason to use a Paste or Paste Link command to perform OLE. There is, however, an important distinction between what the client application does to enable linking as opposed to embedding.

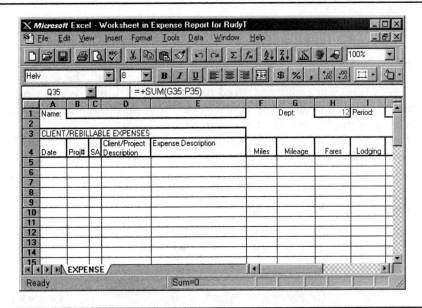

Figure 3.115   Double-clicking on the blob column opens Microsoft Excel.

Embedding is performed if the native data is the first format on the clipboard that the client application can use; otherwise, the format is copied to the client as in a standard cut and paste. If the native data is the first useful format, the client application stores the native, owner link, and useful presentation data. This lets a client represent the server data by calling the client library to draw the object (by using the **OLE-Draw( )** function), but it also lets the client pass the native data back to the appropriate server to be edited (or used in some other manner). The important point to note is that once the data is copied from the server to the client, the client stores the information. There is no way to "link" back to an original source document that the server owns. This is PowerBuilder's current functionality. The database blob stores the native data along with the owner link and presentation data. The OLEActivate( ) function or double-clicking on the blob displays the server application with the native data stored within the database.

In the case of a link, the client application looks for the object link format on the clipboard and uses a presentation format (or a package icon) to display the object within its application. The advantage of a link is that any changes to a file are reflected within the client's application document. In terms of a PowerBuilder application, the object link and presentation format are stored within the database. When the DataWindow retrieves this information, you could use the OLEActivate( ) function or a similar function to update the presentation data to reflect the original document's current state.

Stop Light Reports

You can combine computed columns and bitmaps within a DataWindow to produce what are called *stop light reports*. These reports, generally used within executive information system (EIS) applications, use a background of a specific color to represent a given column's certain status. For example, to represent the urgency of past due account balances, you could use a red background within a balance column for values greater than 1500, yellow for values over 1000, and green for all other values. The DataWindow might look like the one in Figure 3.116.

To do this, create a computed field with the expression shown in Figure 3.117.

Then, place this column behind the balance column within the DataWindow. Next, make the balance column's background transparent to allow the bitmap to show.

Creating a DataWindow Architecture

Through user objects, you can develop a DataWindow architecture in the same manner as windows and menus. Creating a user object hierarchy lets user-defined events, func-

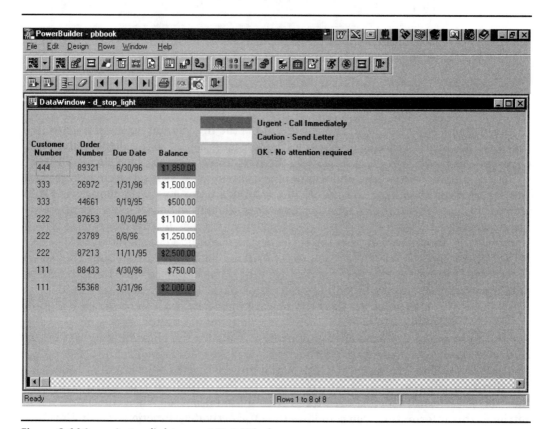

Figure 3.116   A stop light report DataWindow.

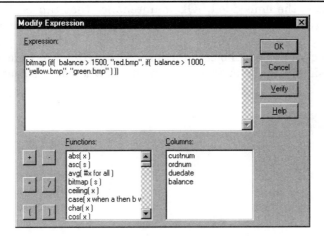

Figure 3.117   Computed field definition for stop light report.

tions, and variables be encapsulated into what is essentially a customized DataWindow. You can build functions such as error handling, set the transaction object, and enable or disable the columns within a DataWindow into an ancestor DataWindow class that is inherited by all the application DataWindows.

Because of the specific maintenance needs of the list DataWindows (e.g., inserting and deleting rows), it may be a good idea to create a List DataWindow class. You can inherit this class from the base class and extend or override the functionality as needed. You could then inherit all the application list DataWindows from this class, while all the others are inherited from the base class directly.

Before designing a DataWindow architecture, you must address the issue of data access in general. A concern among application designers and developers is what to do if the data source(s) for an application change. For example, if an application's data source changes from DB2 to Sybase, how does it affect the application code?

While ODBC attempts to solve this problem, it does not let you take advantage of the various SQL extensions of the different DBMSs. These extensions, while not all accepted as standards, provide you much more flexibility than the standard ANSI SQL. Using these extensions, however, means that a change within RDBMS results in some modification of the application code.

A good data access design can greatly simplify these changes. Abstracting the data access pieces of an application, or set of applications, into an overall data access layer can reduce the development time you need to make the changes required when you change data sources.

You can accomplish data access within a PowerBuilder application by using either a DataWindow or embedded SQL. The DataWindow SQL's maintenance is fairly straightforward. It is the embedded SQL maintenance that can be a problem. You should abstract all the embedded SQL into a set of functions that can be put into a data access .PBL. Within an architecture like the one described earlier, these functions can either be global functions or user object functions. Abstracting this code into a data access layer greatly simplifies the maintenance required when a data source changes.

CHAPTER 4

Multiple Document Interface (MDI) and Windows

The multiple document interface (MDI) is a Windows interface style used to create applications that consist of related subapplications or sheets that contain similar information. An MDI application lets the user interact with several different windows within an application at the same time.

Speaking of Windows, this chapter also discusses the *Window object*, a critical object within the PowerBuilder development environment. You will use the Window object in almost every PowerBuilder application. There are several different types of windows within PowerBuilder. Once you choose the window type, the next important decision is selecting and placing the controls on the window.

This chapter covers:

- MDI applications
  - Types of MDI applications
  - MDI components
  - Creating and manipulating an MDI
  - MicroHelp
- Windows
  - Types of windows
  - Window events
  - PowerBuilder functions
  - Calling events and functions
  - PowerBuilder variables
  - Window datatypes
  - Window controls
  - Window attributes
  - Window paradigms

MDI APPLICATIONS

PowerBuilder lets the developer create several different types of windows. Each window type has a specific purpose, which may differ in functionality depending on the type of application interface you use. The two basic types of application interfaces that PowerBuilder defines are the *single document interface* (SDI) and the *multiple document interface* (MDI). SDI allows the use of one set of screens; MDI allows the manipulation of multiple windows simultaneously.

When used for the right type of application and developed properly, an MDI application with the right type of window selection can provide a very friendly and flexible user interface.

Types of MDI Applications

One of the main differences between an MDI application and a single document interface is that the MDI frame is considered to be the parent window for all of the different windows within the application. Even if a sheet window is a Main window type, it is subordinate to the MDI frame. In addition, each of the other types of windows can be subordinate to the Main window sheet, if needed. Another difference is that PowerBuilder activates the MDI frame and an MDI sheet at the same time.

Some examples of MDI applications are Microsoft Word, Microsoft Excel, and even PowerBuilder. These applications use toolbars, sheets, and MicroHelp to guide their users. When the developer is considering creating an MDI application, there are two basic categories to consider:

- Single task
- Multiple task

Single Task

A single task MDI application consists of a frame window that allows several similar sheets or window instances to perform the same type of task within the application. An example of this type of MDI application is Microsoft Word. This application can display several instances of the main type document for simultaneous use (see Figure 4.1). Another use for this type of MDI would be a contact management application that displays several different types of contacts by business name.

Multiple Task

A multiple task MDI application consists of a frame window that lets you open several different instances of the windows to perform different tasks. The multiple task MDI typically consists of subapplications that may consist of nested windows. An example of this type of MDI application is the PowerBuilder development environment. A user can work within the Library painter and the DataWindow painter within the PowerBuilder application frame at the same time. Because both the painters are considered to be different sheets, or subapplications, the user can switch from the Library painter to the DataWindow painter within the same instance of the PowerBuilder development environment, as shown in Figure 4.2.

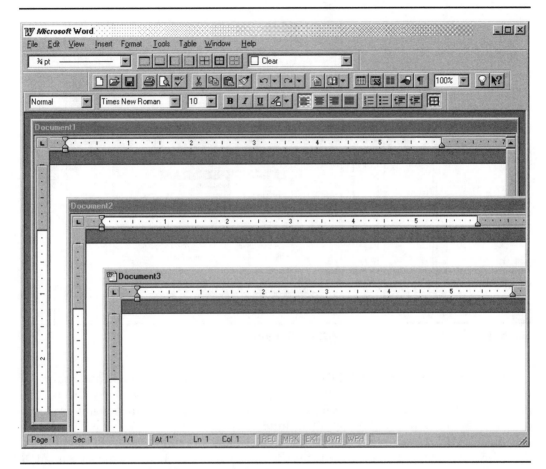

Figure 4.1   The single task MDI application.

You should scrutinize your application to see if its system requirements actually fit the MDI definition. The MDI paradigm is quite popular among developers. While it is intended for displaying multiple instances of the documents or subapplications within a single frame, developers often use it because of MicroHelp and toolbars. Before creating an MDI application, however, make sure it is the appropriate interface for the task.

MDI Components

Frame

The MDI frame is the application shell, and it contains the client area MDI_1, menu, MicroHelp, and all of the related sheets within it. Because you accomplish the majority of the work within the sheets, you should design the MDI frame to have a minimal number of controls.

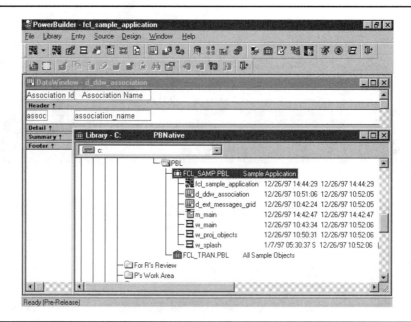

Figure 4.2   **The multiple task MDI application.**

When you create a PowerBuilder MDI frame, PowerBuilder, in turn, automatically creates a client area. This area is the workspace for all of the application's sheets. The client area is the space between the frame's sides, below the standard menu area and above the MicroHelp area. PowerBuilder automatically sizes this area when you create a standard MDI. If you add any controls to the frame, you must resize the client area. Also, PowerBuilder automatically names the client area MDI_1. When you save an MDI frame, PowerBuilder creates the object MDI_1. You can see this object when you browse the list of PowerBuilder objects, but you cannot select MDI_1. In addition, MDI_1 does not have any events associated with it, but it does have alterable attributes and functions. (For further explanation, see the PowerBuilder Objects and Controls manual.)

PowerBuilder generates the MDI frame that contains a border and menu bar with MicroHelp. Each sheet uses the main menu bar when it is activated. To create a standard MDI frame, create a normal window. Next, to make the window into an MDI frame, select **MDI** or **MDI with MicroHelp** in the **Window Type** option under the **Design Properties** menu. The MDI frame should include any functionality that is central to the application and the sheets within the frame.

Sheets

The most important part of the MDI application is the sheet because this is where the user performs the majority of the work. When the MDI is invoked, the application frame acts as the main window and each of the corresponding sheets is subservient to the frame window. Even though the sheets are main windows, they interact with the

MDI frame like child windows within non-MDI applications. Each sheet may also have child windows, but tracking and manipulating nested sheets (i.e., sheets within sheets) is complex, and you should approach such a design cautiously.

An example of child windows that are subordinate to a main window sheet is the Database painter within the PowerBuilder development environment. Each of the separate table windows for a particular database are children to the Database painter sheet window.

Managing Sheets

PowerBuilder provides two functions to assist you in managing MDI sheets: **Get-FirstSheet( )** and **GetNextSheet( )**. These two functions provide a method of programmatically going through the list of open sheets within an MDI application, thus eliminating the need of arrays to maintain the MDI sheets. Basically, PowerBuilder maintains the array for you. The following example uses GetFirstSheet( ) and Get-NextSheet( ) to get the title of all the open sheets in Figure 4.3 and write them to a file.

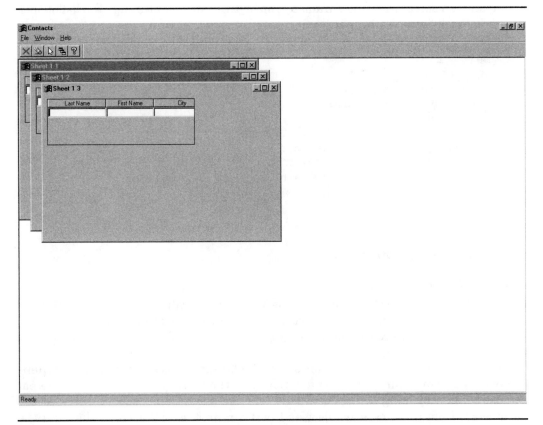

Figure 4.3   Using GetFirstSheet( ) and GetNextSheet( ).

```
// Save the title of all the open sheets to a file
window      currentsheet
string      sText
int         iSheetNum
currentsheet = This.GetFirstSheet( )

Do While IsValid(currentsheet)
    // There is an active sheet, so get its title
    sText = currentsheet.title
    iSheetNum += 1
    SetProfileString("myapp.ini","MyApp","Sheet"+&
        string(iSheetNum),sText)
    currentsheet = This.GetNextSheet(currentsheet)
Loop
Return True
```

The next example, from the PowerBuilder sample application, uses GetFirst-Sheet( ) and GetNextSheet( ) to determine if a particular sheet is already open. This menu function accepts a string parameter, open_title, and goes through the list of open sheets to check for a matching title:

```
window      win

// get the first sheet
win = ParentWindow.GetFirstSheet( )

Do While Isvalid(win) // if we got a valid sheet
        // if the titles match then return true
        If win.Title = open_title Then Return True
        win = ParentWindow.GetNextSheet(win) // get the next sheet
Loop
Return False
```

Creating and Manipulating an MDI

OpenSheet with Parameters

Because PowerBuilder is built on top of the Windows operating system, PowerBuilder can use several of its underlying structures. One of these is the Microsoft Messaging structure. If an event occurs that is not a PowerBuilder-defined event, PowerBuilder uses the Microsoft Message object.

MDI applications can take advantage of the Message object by calling the **Open-SheetWithParm( )** function. This function uses the Message object to store the parameters when opening the sheets. This lets the sheet being opened retrieve the parameters from the Message object and perform processing based on their values.

This is handy in situations such as passing database key values among the MDI sheets.

OpenSheetWithParms( ) is used as follows:

```
OpenSheetWithParm (sheet_refvar, parameter{, window_type}, mdiframe &{,
position {, arrangeopen} } )
```

The Message object lets you pass different types of variables into a sheet for processing. A window function can store a set of variables within the Message object, letting a sheet be opened with the value, or the sheet can store a value within the Message object that another sheet can use. These are some Message attributes you can use to retrieve the arguments passed when opening an MDI sheet:

```
message.DoubleParm        Numeric
message.PowerObjectParm   PowerObject
message.StringParm        String
```

Minimize Sheets within MDI_1

When executing an MDI application, several different sheets can appear within the client area MDI_1. Several users will want to minimize the different sheets that are being used within the application area. This example shows how to minimize a sheet by double-clicking on the sheet's control menu.

First, create a global Boolean variable g_bCloseFrame. Use this variable to determine whether to close or minimize the sheet. Next, within the MDI frame's open event, set g_bCloseFrame to False, meaning that the sheet will be minimized:

```
// Minimize the sheet windows when double-clicking the Control menu
g_bCloseFrame = False

Within the MDI frame's closequery event, reset the variable to True.
// Close the sheet windows
g_bCloseFrame= True
```

Within the MDI sheet w_sheet1 or w_base_sheet's **closequery** event, add the following code:

```
// Check g_bCloseFrame to determine whether to close or minimize the sheets
If Not g_bCloseFrame Then
    This.WindowState = Minimized!
    message.Returnvalue = 1
Else
    message.Returnvalue = 0
End If
```

This lets the user minimize MDI sheets via the **Control** menu.

Finding Active Sheets

When maintaining the different sheets within the MDI frame, you may want to determine which sheet is active. You can use the PowerBuilder function **GetActiveSheet( )** to return the active sheet within an MDI application. Within the following example, the MDI frame window function **Save1( )** uses GetActiveSheet( ) to get the active window's title and write the title to a file:

```
// Save the active sheet's title to a file
window activesheet
string sText
activesheet = w_mdi_frame.GetActiveSheet( )

If IsValid(activesheet) Then
// There is an active sheet, so get its title
        sText = activesheet.Title
End If
SetProfileString("myapp.ini","MyApp","ActiveSheet",sText)
Return True
```

Preventing an MDI Sheet from Maximizing

You may want to prevent a user from maximizing a sheet within an MDI application. You can do this by removing the sheet's maximize attribute. To do this, uncheck **MaximizeBox**, a window attribute. This will keep the user from maximizing the window by dimming the system menu's **Maximize** menu item.

Menus and Toolbars

Another aspect of creating an MDI application is the use of menus and toolbars. Although these items can provide an easy way to navigate through a system, navigating can be cumbersome if you do not design them correctly.

Because MDI applications open multiple instances of the windows, the menus associated with each sheet can sometimes point to the wrong menu instance. When you create multiple instances of a window, PowerBuilder automatically creates a global variable for the menu and an instance of the menu for each window instance. Because the global variable points to the last menu instance that was created, the pointer can sometimes point to the wrong menu. If the code for the menu uses hard-coded references, the menu choices end up referencing the last menu instance that was created instead of the proper menu instance.

For example, within a menu of color choices, you can use the pronoun *This* and the noun *Parent* instead of hard-coding the menu reference to check the selected color and uncheck the other color MenuItems. The script for the MenuItem m_red's clicked event is:

```
This.Check()
Parent.m_blue.Uncheck()
Parent.m_green.Uncheck()
```

Placing the pronoun/noun reference within the script ensures that the code references the menu's current instance.

The second method is to create an instance variable, set the MenuID to the current menu, and point it to the appropriate window instance. This involves the following steps:

1. Create an instance variable called i_active_mnu of type m_stdmnu (your menu name).
2. Within the window w_sheet1's open event, set i_active_mnu = this.menuid. This now becomes a pointer to the menu instance associated with this instance of the window.
3. Create a global variable called g_active_sheet of type w_sheet1.
4. Set g_active_sheet = this within the w_sheet1's activate event. This now properly identifies the window w_sheet1's current instance.

So now the code within the menu will be:

```
g_active_sheet.i_active_mnu.m_color.m_red.Enable()
g_active_sheet.i_active_mnu.m_color.m_blue.Disable()
g_active_sheet.i_active_mnu.m_color.m_green.Disable()
```

Obviously, the use of pronoun references is easier to develop and maintain.

Menus

The MDI application's frame window is the controlling window. It lets the menus associated with the sheet windows pass through the frame window. Because the frame window is the application's central window, the frame window must always have a menu and toolbar associated with it.

Another item to consider when developing menus is the association of menus with the sheets. If a currently active sheet window does not have a menu associated with it, the sheet uses the frame's menu and toolbar. If the designed MDI only has one menu within the main frame area, all of the sheets or subapplication's menus pass through the frame's menu.

A function that you can integrate into an MDI application is the showing of the last n files that the user has saved or opened. PowerBuilder does not automatically handle this functionality, but you can add it programmatically. You will notice this functionality within several third-party products such as Microsoft Word and Microsoft Excel. Unfortunately, PowerBuilder does not let the developer dynamically add and subtract menu items like the lower-level languages do, but you can overcome this by using the functions that read and write information to an initialization file, such as win.ini.

The example in Figure 4.4 opens two sheets within the MDI frame: sheet1–Person and sheet2–Phone. When the user saves each of the sheets, PowerBuilder writes them to the win.ini file and inserts them into the MDI frame menu under the first set of menu items. To do this, create the menus m_stdmnu for the MDI frame and m_stdmdi for the sheets. Within the menu m_stdmnu, create a MenuItem **F**ile with sub-MenuItems **Open**, **Save**, and **E**x**it**, and place two additional items at the end of the MenuItem list. Call these two additional items File1 and File2. Create the same options for m_stdmdi as m_stdmnu under **F**ile but include the MDI functionality of Tile, Cascade, and Layer.

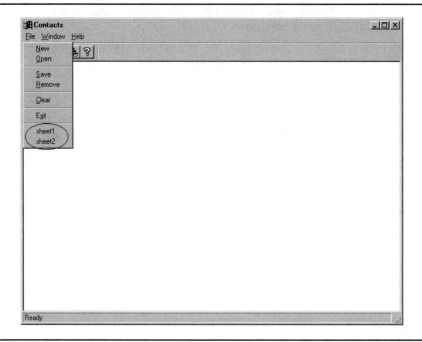

Figure 4.4   Saving previously opened sheets within the MDI frame.

Set the File1 and File2 items's Visible property to False as they will change to visible at runtime to show the two saved file names.

Add the script Close(parentwindow) to the **Exit** MenuItem, to allow closure of each MDI sheet.

Create the MDI frame window as an MDI frame with MicroHelp, and call the window w_mdi_frame. In addition, associate the menu m_stdmnu with the frame. Create each of the sheets, w_sheet1 and w_sheet2, as main windows that have m_stdmdi menu associated with them. The windows w_sheet1 and w_sheet2 retrieve the information from the database about the Person and Phone.

To make this example work, you can facilitate opening of the two sheets by inserting the following into the m_stdmnu's **Open** MenuItem. For this example, hard code the values "w_sheet1" and "w_sheet2" into the sWinName[ ] array:

```
// Open for the 2 sheets
string sWinName[] = {"w_sheet1", "w_sheet2"}
Window WinArray[]
integer i

For i = 1 to 2
    OpenSheet (WinArray [i], sWinName[i],w_mdi_frame,2)
Next
```

Because the sheets are now open, the currently active sheet's menu m_stdmdi controls the MDI frame window. Within m_stdmdi, create the following four menu functions of the Boolean type. The first function, called **LastSheet( )**, reads the value ItemCount from the win.ini file to see how many files are saved for showing within the menu. Based on the number of items that are saved, it will call the functions **save1( )–save3( )**.

```
//Function LastSheet()
//Code for inserting the last 2 files saved
string      sLastFile,sLastFile2
int         iCounter

iCounter=ProfileInt("win.ini", "LastSheet", "ItemCount", 0)
If iCounter = 0 Then
     save1()
ElseIf iCounter = 1 Then
     save2()
ElseIf iCounter = 2 Then
     save3()
Else
        // can add more functions for more sheets
End If
Return True
```

The second function, save1( ), gets the active sheet's title name and saves it to the win.ini file for LastSheet1's value. You will use this function later to add to the MDI frame menu, m_stdmnu.

```
// Function Save1()
// Declare the active sheet (a window datatype)
Window      activesheet
string      sText
activesheet = w_mdi_frame.GetActiveSheet()

If IsValid(activesheet) Then
// There is an active sheet, so get its title
        sText = activesheet.Title
End If

SetProfileString("win.INI","LastSheet","ItemCount","1")
SetProfileString("win.INI","LastSheet","LastSheet1",sText)
Return True
```

The third function, **save2( )**, gets the next active sheet's title name and saves it to the win.ini file for the LastSheet1's value after moving LastSheet1's value to Last-Sheet2's value.

The last menu function, **save3( )**, gets the last active sheet's title name, swaps LastSheet1's value with LastSheet2's value, and inserts the new value into LastSheet1.

```
// Code for saving the last sheet to the INI file
string     sLastFile1
window     activesheet
string     sText

activesheet = w_mdi_frame.GetActiveSheet( )

If IsValid(activesheet) Then
// There is an active sheet, so get its title
       sText = activesheet.Title
End If

sLastFile1 = ProfileString("win.ini", "LastSheet", "LastSheet1", "")
SetProfileString("win.INI","LastSheet","LastSheet2",sLastFile1)
SetProfileString("win.INI","LastSheet","LastSheet1",sText)
Return True
```

After you have created all of the functions, the **Save** option calls the LastSheet( ) function.

Now that you have created the menu functions, you can create a function called **LastFile( )** of type Boolean within the window w_mdi_frame. This function references the MDI frame menu m_stdmnu and pulls the saved LastSheet values from the win.ini. Depending on the sheets, the function will also **Show( )** the additional menu item and change the text to that of the sheet value.

```
// Function LastFile()
// Code for inserting the last 2 files saved
int       iCounter
string sLastFile,sLastFile2

iCounter = ProfileInt("win.ini", "LastSheet", "ItemCount", 0)
If iCounter = 1 Then
    sLastFile = ProfileString("win.ini", "LastSheet", "LastSheet1", "")
    m_stdmnu.m_file.m_file1.Show()
    m_stdmnu.m_file.m_file1.Text=sLastFile
ElseIf iCounter = 2 Then
    sLastFile = ProfileString("win.ini", "LastSheet", "LastSheet1", "")
    sLastFile2 =ProfileString("win.ini", "LastSheet", "LastSheet2", "")
    m_stdmnu.m_file.m_file1.Show()
    m_stdmnu.m_file.m_file2.Show()
    m_stdmnu.m_file.m_file1.Text=sLastFile
    m_stdmnu.m_file.m_file2.Text=sLastFile2
```

continues

```
Else
    // want the default menu to not show file1 & file2
    m_stdmnu.m_file.m_file1.Hide()
    m_stdmnu.m_file.m_file2.Hide()
End If


Return True
```

When you have coded the function LastFile( ), you should create a user-defined event called **refreshmenu.** When you have created the event, you should place the function call to LastFile( ). This custom user event lets you trigger the LastFile( )'s functionality after all of the sheets are closed. In addition, you should call LastFile ( ) from the window w_mdi_frame's open event to let any previously saved files be found when the window is opened. To refresh the list of files when the user clicks the **File** menu item, add the following code to the m_stdmnu.m_file's clicked event:

```
// Code in m_stdmnu File's Clicked event
// Code for saving the last sheet to the INI file
w_mdi_frame      i_parent
i_parent = ParentWindow
i_parent.Event Dynamic Refreshmenu()
```

When you have coded all of the other functions, you can run the application to open each sheet and then save it. When you have closed all of the sheets and view the frame menu, the application lists the last two files saved within the menu. When a sheet is still active, the application displays the sheet menu, so the saved files are not visible. If you require this functionality within the sheet menu, you can use the same code to create it.

In addition, you might add a Clear MenuItem to let the user clear the last two sheets. The Clear MenuItem's code will be:

```
// Code for saving the last sheet to the INI file
w_mdi_frame i_parent
i_parent = ParentWindow
SetProfileString("win.INI","LastSheet","ItemCount","0")
SetProfileString("win.INI","LastSheet","LastSheet1","")
SetProfileString("win.INI","LastSheet","LastSheet2","")
i_parent.Event Post Refreshmenu()
```

Upon the Clear function's execution, the win.ini file looks like this:

```
[Lastsheet]
ItemCount=0
LastSheet1=
LastSheet2=
```

Toolbars

Menu toolbars only work on the MDI frame and MDI sheet windows. If a non-MDI window opens a menu with a toolbar item associated with the menu, the toolbar does not appear. You can create a toolbar easily within the menu painter or you can create the menu as a user object and place it within the object hierarchy.

PowerBuilder lets you create a toolbar within the Menu painter and attach the menu to an MDI frame or sheet like a menu. The toolbar can let the application run other applications outside of PowerBuilder, create or print reports, and perform other user-defined functions.

The toolbar's most common function is to let the toolbar buttons visually mimic the current menu's functionality. Because the toolbar buttons are related directly to the menu items, if you disable the menu item, PowerBuilder also disables the toolbar button, but the toolbar's visible attribute will not change in appearance. In addition, hiding a menu item does not cause a toolbar button to disappear.

Toolbars also have the capability to provide PowerTips, or Timed MicroHelp. You may use the menu painter to create the messages that appear as the user moves the mouse pointer over a toolbar item.

Chapter 5, "Menus," provides a more in-depth discussion of the menus and toolbars.

Creating a Clock on the Frame

A convenient feature for an MDI application is to display the system time in the lower right MicroHelp area on the MDI frame. Unfortunately, PowerBuilder does not include this feature within the MDI frame's creation, but you can add it by creating a popup window that resizes itself within the MDI frame. The result looks like that shown in Figure 4.5.

The first step in doing this is to open the popup window, w_clock, and make the clock visible:

```
// Open and show the clock on the MDI frame. Position the clock within the
// resize event
open(w_clock)
w_clock.show()
```

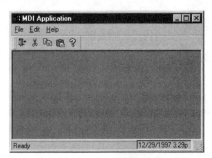

Figure 4.5 Adding a clock to the MDI frame.

The second step is to place the following code within the MDI frame window w_mdi_frame's **resize** event to adjust the popup window's sizing and positioning according to the frame and workspace. If you want to place the clock elsewhere on the MDI frame, you can change the move function coordinates accordingly.

```
// Position the clock in the lower right corner of the MDI frame
integer wx, ww, wy, wh
wx = This.WorkSpaceX()
wy = This.WorkSpaceY()
wh = newheight
ww = newwidth

If IsValid (w_clock) Then
  w_clock.Move(wx+ww - w_clock.width - 80, wy+wh - w_clock.height)
End If

This.Setfocus()
```

The next step is to create a custom user event for the MDI frame w_mdi_frame window called **Move**, and map the event to the PowerBuilder event ID pbm_move. The move event will trigger the resize event to repaint the clock when the user moves the MDI frame within the Windows desktop.

Finally, create a popup window w_clock with a single line edit (SLE) named sle_time. After you create the SLE, you will want to adjust the SLE and the window's size to fit just the date and time and to look good within the application's corner.

To get the clock to adjust the time within the frame, place the code within the popup window's open event. To update the clock, set the timer for 10 seconds. After 10 seconds, the timer event triggers to update the frame with the changed time:

```
sle_time.Weight=300
Timer(10)
This.Event Timer()
```

Within the w_clock's timer event, call a window function called **wf_settime( )** that gathers the system time and formats the time correctly. The function wf_settime( ) is of type Boolean and contains the following code:

```
// Get the date and time for clock
Time          tCurrentTime
date          dCurrentDate
string        sRealTime, sClock, sAmPm

tCurrentTime=Now()
dCurrentDate=Today()
sle_time.Hide()
sle_time.Text=Space(Len(sle_time.Text))
```

continues

```
// format 24-hour clock
If Int(Hour(tCurrentTime)) > 12 Then
        sRealTime = string(int(hour(tCurrentTime)) - 12)
        sAmPm = "p"
Else
        sRealTime = string(hour(tCurrentTime))
        sAmPm = "a"
End If
sClock = sRealTime + ":" + string(minute(tCurrentTime)) + sAmPm
sle_time.Text= String(Month(dCurrentDate))+ "/" + &
        String(day(dCurrentDate)) + "/" + &
        String(year(dCurrentDate)) + " " +sClock
sle_time.Show()
Return True
```

MicroHelp

By using MicroHelp, you can enhance an MDI application by offering additional help text for a menu frame's key items. PowerBuilder creates this facility at the MDI frame's bottom left corner. This area can display a meaningful description about the menu or toolbar items that might be cryptic or hard to define in one word. PowerBuilder lets you include MicroHelp within the Menu painter. To include MicroHelp, enter the Menu painter and then enter the appropriate text within the MDI MicroHelp section.

MicroHelp with Objects

You can also use MicroHelp with controls or objects by using the Tag attribute in conjunction with the **SetMicroHelp( )** function. The Tag attribute lets you tag values to the columns, fields, graphic objects, and user objects. The use of MicroHelp can also be valuable to provide an explanation of the error messages or invalid entries to the user. You can use MicroHelp with the objects in two ways:

- A getfocus event
- A mouse move with a custom event

Getfocus Event For example, to display MicroHelp for a CommandButton cb_close within the MDI sheet window w_sheet1, you need to:

- Assign the desired string as the cb_close's tag value
- Include this statement within the script for cb_close's getfocus event:

```
Parent.SetMicroHelp(This.Tag)
```

Mouse Move To have MicroHelp text change when a user moves the mouse pointer over the window controls, you need to add code within the window controls to change the MicroHelp text. You will:

1. Assign the desired string as the cb_close's tag value.
2. Create a custom user event for the button cb_close called mousemove and map the event to pbm_mousemove.

3. Include this statement within the script for cb_close's mousemove event:

```
Parent.SetMicroHelp(This.Tag)
```

4. To set the MicroHelp back to a value when the mouse leaves the button, place a similar script within the window sheet1's mousemove event:

```
SetMicroHelp("Ready")
```

In conclusion, creating an MDI application can meet several application requirements, but it will create more problems than it solves if you do not design the MDI application properly. You should design an MDI application for an application that requires multiple instances of the nonmodal windows. These windows can be simple windows or subapplications that the user will manipulate simultaneously. You can use the PowerBuilder functions GetActiveSheet( ), GetFirstSheet( ), and GetNextSheet( ) to maintain the sheets within the application. Because of the MDI applications' complexity, if an application needs only the toolbars and MicroHelp, you might consider another interface. If needed and properly created, however, an MDI application can provide a friendly and flexible user interface.

WINDOWS

The next section discusses a critical object within the PowerBuilder development environment—the Window object.

Types of Windows

PowerBuilder provides the developer with several different types of windows. Each window type has a specific purpose, which may differ in functionality depending on the type of application interface you use. The two basic types of application interfaces that PowerBuilder defines are the single document interface (SDI) and the multiple document interface (MDI). SDI allows the use of one set of screens; MDI lets you manipulate multiple windows simultaneously. The application interfaces have already been discussed.

The types of windows within PowerBuilder are:

- Main
- Popup
- Child
- Response
- MDI frame
- MDI frame with MicroHelp

You can select the window type from the **General** tab of the window's Properties sheet (obtain by clicking the right button of your mouse while positioned on the window), as shown in Figure 4.6.

Main Window

The main window type is an independent window that you can use as the SDI application's anchor. A main window can have a title bar, a menu, and a control menu, and you can

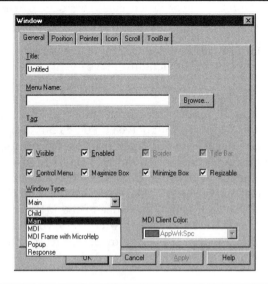

Figure 4.6   Choosing the window type.

maximize or minimize the window. Any other type of window that you open from a main window is subservient to the main window. Consequently, if you minimize a main window, PowerBuilder also minimizes the other windows associated with the main window except in the case of a response window, which this chapter will discuss in more detail later.

For example, you can use a main window with the association and committee information with a child window containing a list of the associations (see Figure 4.7). If you close the main window, the application also closes the subservient window, Child–Sales.

Figure 4.7 also shows that the main window controls the child window's viewing area. When you use child windows in conjunction with the main windows, you can move them only within the main window's area. That is, you cannot move them outside the main window's area. In addition, when you minimize a child window, the child window appears iconized inside the main window.

Popup Window

A popup window acts the same as a child window except its boundaries can extend beyond its parent window's boundaries. Because popup windows can display outside the parent window area, you sometimes use them to display noneditable information or display them as a selection window. A popup window is subservient to its parent window, and thus minimizes if you minimize the parent window. If you minimize only the popup window, however, PowerBuilder shows it iconized at the bottom of the Windows desktop, and not within the parent window (as a child window is).

In Figure 4.8, you use a popup window to make a search list window called w_search for the available customers. The window does not let the user make edits

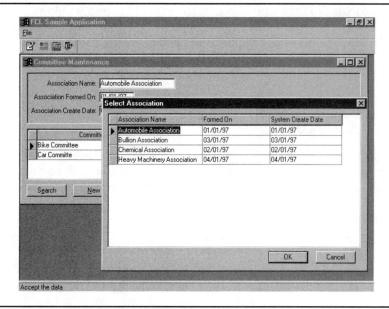

Figure 4.7   Main window and a child window.

within w_search, but it does let the user select a name to be used to populate the parent window or to create a new user.

The example in Figure 4.8 illustrates that you use popup windows as supporting windows because you cannot edit any of the fields. Because popups are supporting windows, it is generally a good idea not to have any complex processing or functionality within them. You should update the tables, for the most part, within either child or main windows. This helps maintain a logical unit of work, and simplifies functionality.

Select Association		
Association Name	Formed On	System Create Date
Automobile Association	01/01/97	01/01/97
Bullion Association	03/01/97	03/01/97
Chemical Association	02/01/97	02/01/97
Heavy Machinery Association	04/01/97	04/01/97

OK   Cancel

Figure 4.8   A popup window.

It is important to note that if you open multiple popup windows from a main window, as shown within the following example, each popup window becomes the parent of the next popup window the application opens.

Within the main window w_mainwindow's open event:

```
Open(w_popupwindow1)
Open(w_popupwindow2)
Open(w_popupwindow3)
Open(w_popupwindow4)
```

For example, w_mainwindow is the w_popupwindow1's parent. When opening the window w_popupwindow2, w_popupwindow1 has focus and therefore becomes the w_popupwindow2's parent. The same concept is true for the rest of the windows.

Child Window

You can open a child window from a main or popup window. A child window does not have a menu.

As an example, take a main window, w_main, which you open with a popup window, w_pop. The window w_pop, in turn, opens the child window w_child. Because the popup window opened the child window, the child window is subservient to the popup window and must stay within the popup window's area. However, because the window w_pop is subservient to the main window, both the popup and child windows are subservient to the main window (see Figure 4.9).

This fairly simple example also shows nested window types within an application. As an application becomes large, it is recommended that you keep nested windows of the different types to a minimum.

Response Window

A response window gives the user information and requires immediate response. Response windows are application modal, and thus do not allow access to another window within the application until the user responds to this window. The user can, however, access the other Windows applications before responding to this window.

Displaying MessageBox-like Response Windows If you want to display a messagebox-like window when a control is modified and the focus changes, you can use a response window rather than a messagebox. A response window allows more flexibility and functionality than a messagebox. The first step will be to create a response window with whatever message and command buttons you require. If a different logic is required depending on which command button the user pressed, you need a way for the window to know which command button the user pushed. One method of communicating between the response window and the main window is by using the **CloseWithReturn( )** function to pass the information back to the main window. Within the main window, you can create a user-defined event. Within this event, you will open the response window and then check what the user did on the response window. If the focus is to remain on the control that has just been modified, add the following lines to the script within the user-defined event, somewhere after the open(responsewindow):

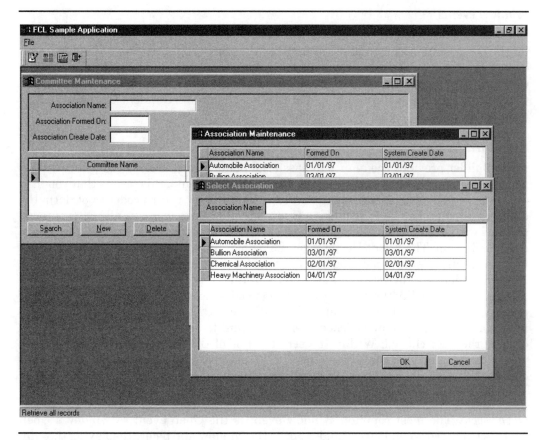

Figure 4.9   A main window with a popup window and a child window.

```
control_n.SetFocus(Parent)      // where control_n is the name of the control on
                                // which to set focus
```

This keeps the focus on the control that the user just modified, rather than letting the focus change to the control that was either tabbed to or mouse-clicked to. Finally, within the control's modified event on the first window, post the user-defined event by adding the following line to the script:

```
This.PostEvent("whatever name you defined the user-defined event with")
```

MDI Frame and MDI Frame with MicroHelp Window

As the name implies, the MDI Frame is used with the MDI application interface. The MDI frame is the MDI application's anchor window, and any window type you open becomes subservient to the MDI frame. MDI applications were discussed ealier in this chapter.

Window Events

The window object and its related controls have several associated events. These events let the user create script to perform functionality based on a user's actions. The window object has 29 different events predefined within PowerBuilder. You can find the complete list of window events and descriptions within the PowerBuilder Objects and Controls manual and online help. In addition to using PowerBuilder's standard control events, you can create custom user events.

Standard Events

PowerBuilder provides the ability to pass arguments to the events, and return values from the events. For the set of standard PowerBuilder events, this means that you may access a predefined set of arguments and specify different return codes to perform the different actions. The **Declare, User Events...** MenuItem displays all the events associated with a window. Pressing the **Args...** button for a specific event will display the event definition. The Event Declaration dialog box, shown in Figure 4.10, looks much like the function definition dialog box. It lets you define a return type and argument(s). For the predefined PowerBuilder events, the return type and argument list are fixed, and you cannot modify them. However, if you need to access an argument for a specific event, you may simply use it like any other variable within the script. For example, suppose that within a window's clicked event, you want to determine which X and Y coordinates the user clicked. Within the script editor of the window's clicked event, the variables xpos and ypos contain the coordinates of the area on the window that the user clicked. Table 4.1 shows the list of standard window events.

Let's discuss some of the more frequently used Window events.

Open Event The most common Window event is the Open event. A window's Open event is triggered when PowerBuilder opens the window and before displaying the window to the user. A common problem in creating windows is coding a large open script

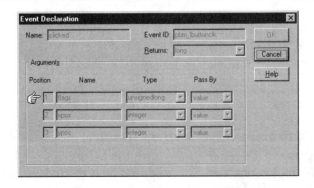

Figure 4.10   The Event Declaration dialog box for a window object's clicked event.

Table 4.1   Standard Window Events

Window Event	Description
Activate	Occurs just before the window becomes active. When the activate event occurs, the first control within the tab order gets focus. If there are no visible objects within the window, the window gets focus.
Clicked	Occurs when a user clicks within the window's unoccupied area.
Close	Occurs just before PowerBuilder removes the window from display to the user.
CloseQuery	Occurs when PowerBuilder removes the window from display.
Deactivate	Occurs when the window becomes inactive.
DoubleClicked	Occurs when the user double-clicks within the window's unoccupied area.
DragDrop	Occurs when a dragged control is dropped on the window.
DragEnter	Occurs when a dragged control enters the window.
DragLeave	Occurs when a dragged control leaves the window.
DragWithin	Occurs when a dragged control is within the window.
Hide	Occurs before PowerBuilder removes a window from the view.
HotLinkAlarm	Occurs after a DDE server application has sent new (changed) data, and the client DDE application has received the data.
Key	Occurs when the user presses a key and the insertion point is not within a line edit.
MouseDown	Occurs when the user presses the mouse button within the window's unoccupied area.
MouseMove	Occurs whenever the user moves the mouse within the window.
MouseUp	Occurs when the user releases the mouse button within the window's unoccupied area.
Open	Occurs before PowerBuilder creates or displays a window.
Other	Occurs when an event other than any of the standard PowerBuilder events occur.
RbuttonDown	Occurs when the user presses the right button of the mouse within the window's unoccupied area.
RemoteExec	Occurs when the client application sends a remote command to the DDE server.
RemoteHotlinkStart	Occurs when a DDE client wants to start a hotlink.
RemoteHotlinkStop	Occurs when a DDE client wants to stop a hotlink.
RemoteRequest	Occurs when a DDE client requests data from the DDE server.
RemoteSend	Occurs when a DDE client application sends the data.
Resize	Occurs when a user or script opens or resizes a window.
Show	Occurs when a script executes the **Show( )** or **Open( )** function. This event occurs before PowerBuilder displays the window.
SystemKey	Occurs when the insertion point is not a line edit, and the user presses the **Alt** key or Alt plus another key.
Timer	Occurs after a specified number of seconds elapses. The number is based on what is passed to the timer function.
ToolbarMoved	An event triggered by moving the frame or sheet toolbar.

for a window that includes database connection, variable declarations, and array declarations. Keep the script for the window's open event to a minimum. Too much processing within the Open event can be very inefficient. Every time PowerBuilder opens the window, PowerBuilder executes all the code within the Open event. This gives the user a perception of a slow application. To avoid this perception, consider displaying the window within the Open event by using the **Show( )** function prior to performing the processing. Another solution is to post a user-defined event so the necessary processing takes place after the window appears.

Activate Event Another important event associated with the window is the Activate event. By placing a large amount of code within the Activate event, you actually misuse the event. The Activate event occurs before the window becomes active, and the first control within the tab order receives focus. This event should contain script that deals with the tab orders or other code that deals with the object focus. The event should not contain a large amount of code pertaining to the window or database connections. A large amount of processing within this event can also affect the window's perceived performance.

CloseQuery Event The CloseQuery event occurs when the user closes a window. Power-Builder must check the active windows to determine if the user can close the window. If the event returns 1 or PowerBuilder determines the Message.ReturnValue's value to be 1, PowerBuilder cannot close the window. You can use this event to perform some processing or variable-checking before the window closes.

Another way to use the CloseQuery event is to create two windows, where the first window, w_cmbo, opens a second window, w_grid, for example. The first window does not retrieve information until the user presses a command button within the second window. Figure 4.11 shows the main window w_cmbo, and the popup window w_grid. The w_grid window's button "Retrieve in w_cmbo" executes the retrieve statement for the main window by using the w_grid's CloseQuery event.

To implement this, first create a user event called getdata in window w_cmbo. Place the code to retrieve the information into the window w_cmbo within the getdata event's script. The code is:

```
// Script to retrieve information into w_cmbo from DB
dw_master.SetTransObject(sqlca)
dw_detail.SetTransObject(sqlca)
dw_master.Retrieve ()
dw_detail.Retrieve ()
```

Next, place the following code within the "Retrieve in w_cmbo" button's clicked event within the window w_grid:

```
Close(Parent)
```

This causes the w_grid's CloseQuery to execute. This event executes the w_cmbo's getdata event by using the **PostEvent( )** function:

```
w_cmbo.PostEvent("getdata")
```

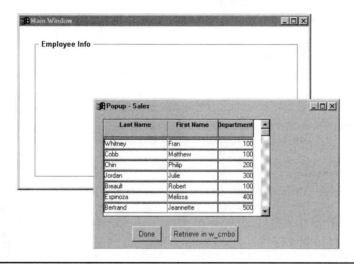

Figure 4.11   Using the CloseQuery event.

Custom User Events

You can also create custom user events for a window or control. Prior to PowerBuilder 5, you had to map the user events to an associated event ID, such as pbm_custom01 or another Windows event ID. Since PowerBuilder 5, this is no longer the case. If a Windows event does not trigger the event, you may defined the custom event without an associated event ID. In this case, the only time the event executes is when the developer triggers it. These changes make events and functions very similar in the fact that they both have arguments and return types, and you can call (trigger or post) them explicitly.

You can use custom user events to call functions, trigger other events on the window, or on the controls within the window, or perform other processing. You can create a custom event by choosing the **Declare, User Events...** MenuItem. To specify a return type and retrieval arguments, click **Args...** in the Event Definition dialog box. PowerBuilder, in turn, displays the Event Declaration dialog box, where you can define a return type and any arguments passed to the event.

PowerBuilder Functions

PowerBuilder lets you create user-defined functions on a window. You may create functions by choosing the **Declare, Window Functions...** MenuItem. You define a function by its arguments and return values. You can post functions as well as overload functions. The following section discusses these two features.

Posting Functions

Direct posting of functions has made it easy to add a function call to the window's queue. The posting of functions works the same way as the posting of events, meaning that PowerBuilder may execute a function immediately (the default) or PowerBuilder may post the function to an object's queue and execute after handling the other messages within the object's queue.

To post a function, include the keyword POST before the function name. For example, to post the function **getdata( )**, call getdata( ) as shown here:

```
POST getdata()
```

To direct PowerBuilder to execute the function immediately instead of posting the function, simply call getdata( ) without putting POST before the function name. This will perform the default behavior, which is to trigger the function rather than post it.

Function Overloading

You can create user-defined functions to take advantage of function overloading. Function overloading lets you create several functions with the same name, but define them differently by the number and/or types of parameters associated with the function. This lets multiple functions share a common name, but the functions use different arguments and may perform different processing. As an example, create two functions, **DisplayText (a_sle)** that accepts a singlelineedit control and **DisplayText (a_st)** that accepts a statictext control. Both functions have the same name, and you may code each one to display the control's text attribute within a messagebox, but the two functions have different arguments. For a detailed discussion of the PowerBuilder functions, refer to Chapter 6, "Structures, Functions, and User Objects."

Calling Events and Functions

With every new release, PowerBuilder has brought events and functions closer together in terms of the parameter passing and return types, and the time of execution (triggering or posting) has also slightly changed the way in which you call an event or function. You can use the following syntax to call object events and functions:

```
{objectname.}{type}{calltype}{when} functionname ({argumentlist})
```

where:

objectname.   The name of the object where you have defined the event/function (or the object's descendant).

type.   Specifies whether the call is to a function (FUNCTION, the default) or an event (EVENT).

calltype.   Specifies whether PowerBuilder will attempt to find the event/function at compile time (STATIC, the default) or at runtime (DYNAMIC). This gives you the ability to include calls to an object event/function that may not exist until runtime without getting a compile error.

when.   Specifies whether the event/function should occur immediately (TRIGGER, the default) or be put at the end of the object's queue and PowerBuilder executes the event/function when PowerBuilder has handled all the other messages within the object's queue (POST).

functionname.   The event or function's name.

argumentlist.   The list of values to pass to the event/function.

To execute an ancestor's version of an event or function explicitly, use the following syntax:

```
ancestorobject :: {type}{when} functionname ({argumentlist})
```

You may also trigger or post global and system functions. The syntax for calling the global and system functions is:

```
{when} functionname ({argumentlist})
```

PowerBuilder also allows calls to more than one event/function to be cascaded into one line of code. You can do this by using the dot notation in combination with an event or function that returns an object that becomes the object for the next function call. For example, if the function **getdw( )** returns a DataWindow control, you could use the following line to retrieve the data into the DataWindow that getdw( ) returns:

```
GetDW().Retrieve()
```

TIP While the ability to cascade function calls provides a great deal of power and flexibility, it does remove the ability to perform error checking on each individual function call.

PowerBuilder Variables

Variable declaration is an important aspect of application design. When considering the use of variables, you must think about memory conservation. To maximize memory efficiency, you must consider several things. First is the type of data the variable represents. Second is whether a variable needs to store positive and negative numbers. A final consideration is the range of values that a variable needs to store.

You can define PowerBuilder variables as local, instance, shared, or global in scope. All the previously mentioned considerations are important when looking at an application as a whole. The proper use of variables can lead to efficient systems, especially within the Windows environment, where different applications share the limited system resources.

The first consideration when declaring a variable is the type of data the variable will represent. Examples include a name/description, quantity, identification number, date, loop/row counter, and error codes. For numeric datatypes, you have a great deal of control regarding the size and range of values for a variable. Because of this, the second consideration is whether a variable needs to store both positive and negative numbers. If it is known that a variable only needs to store positive numbers, you can save memory by declaring the variable as unsigned, rather than signed. This is a very important concept that developers often overlook. Following is the range of signed numbers for variables:

16-bit variable (Integer)-see Figure 4.12
Values range from -32,768 (-2^{15}) to +32,767 ((2^{15}) - 1)

16-bit variable (Unsigned Integer)-see Figure 4.13
Values range from 0 to +65,535 ((2^{16}) - 1)

32-bit variable (Long)-see Figure 4.14
Values range from -2,127,483,648 (-2^{31}) to +2,127,483,647 ((2^{31}) - 1)

32-bit variable (Unsigned Long)-see Figure 4.15
Values range from 0 to +4,294,967,295 ((2^{32}) - 1)

The third consideration is the range of values that the variable needs to store. For a 16-bit memory location, the range of signed (positive and negative) numbers that you

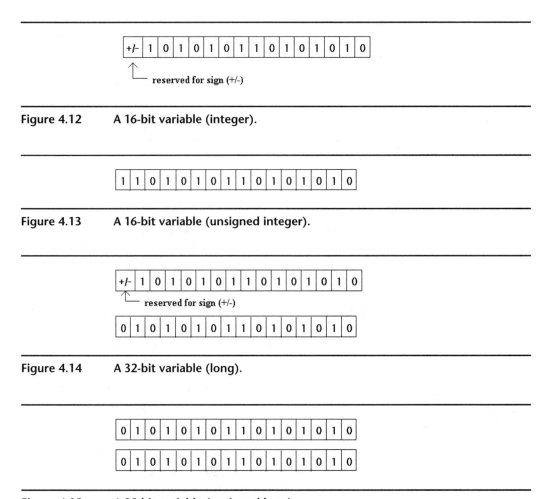

Figure 4.12   A 16-bit variable (integer).

Figure 4.13   A 16-bit variable (unsigned integer).

Figure 4.14   A 32-bit variable (long).

Figure 4.15   A 32-bit variable (unsigned long).

can store is –32,768 to +32,767. If you define the same 16-bit variable as an unsigned (positive only) number, it can store anything within the range of 0 to 65,535. Thirty-two-bit signed variables can store values ranging from –2,127,483,648 to +2,127,483,647, while a 32-bit unsigned variable can store values ranging from 0 to +4,294,967,295. So, for example, an application that needs a variable to store the numbers from 0 to 50,000 should use a 16-bit variable (unsigned integer) instead of a 32-bit variable. It is a common mistake for developers to declare a variable as a long when a 16-bit variable will suffice.

The fourth consideration is the variable's scope. The developer must determine whether the variable is for private use within the script (local), private within the window (instance), private to a window's instances (shared), or global to the entire application (global). PowerBuilder lets you declare all four types of variables. You should minimize the use of global, shared, and instance variables, when possible. When you declare a global variable, the variable remains within memory until you terminate the application. When you declare a shared or instance variable, the variable remains within memory until you close the window for the variable. Local variables are only within memory during the execution of the script within which you declared the variable, thus minimizing the overall memory your application requires.

Window Datatypes

A PowerBuilder library stores the Windows' definitions. When a window is run, Power-Builder automatically generates a variable for the window. Other than being responsible for opening and closing the window, you need not act on the window to make it open.

At times, you may need to show the same window more than once on the screen at the same time, put all the visible windows within an array, and be able to manipulate them by using an index. To do this, you must treat the window as a datatype. You can create variables as well as arrays of type windows. This is similar to the creation of string or integer type variables.

To understand how to use the window datatypes, you should first understand what really happens when PowerBuilder creates a window within the Window painter. When PowerBuilder saves a window within the Window painter, PowerBuilder generates two entities with the same name as the window: a window datatype, and a global window variable. Internally, PowerBuilder declares the window variable as being of the window datatype. If you declare a variable, the declaration resembles the following:

```
w_window1     w_window1
```

where the "w_window1" on the left specifies the window's datatype and the "w_window1" on the right specifies the window variable.

This duplicate naming of the datatype and variable provides a clever way to access the window through its variable part while ignoring the concept of datatype. At the same time, the datatype lets you create your own window variables. The datatype also supports inheritance and other object-oriented features within PowerBuilder.

Another important concept to understand is how the open function works. The open function creates a window's instance, and places a reference to that window within the supplied variable. In the default format, open(w_window1), the window variable's datatype, not the variable's name, determines which window PowerBuilder opens. Consider the following code:

```
w_window1    w_sheet
Open (w_sheet)
```

In this example, the open function determines the w_sheet variable's datatype, in this case, w_window1. The function then opens w_window1's instance and assigns a reference to the w_sheet variable. Note that the w_window1 global variable, which was part of the window definition, has not been set. In fact, variable w_window1 still contains a NULL reference.

Extending this idea, you can open windows and place their references within an array. For example:

```
w_window1 WinArray[]
For i = 1 To 5
  Open (WinArray[i])
Next
```

This code creates five instances of the window w_window1, and places them within WinArray. Creating the same window's multiple instances is not very interesting, so you can change this example to create five different types of windows and place them within the same array:

```
Window  WinArray[]
For i = 1 To 5
 Open(WinArray[i],WinName[i])
Next
```

This example introduces two new features. First, notice that the type of WinArray has changed to "Window." The Type Window is the system datatype from which Power-Builder derives all the user-defined windows. In effect, the variables of type Window can contain references to any window within the system. The other new feature is the Open function's second argument, WinName. In this form of Open, the datatype of the window to be created is taken from the string supplied within the second argument, and PowerBuilder places the resultant window reference in the window variable in the first argument. In this example, an array of window datatype names is supplied. As Power-Builder opens each window, PowerBuilder places the window within the WinArray.

Using arrays can be a very powerful way to keep track of the windows within an application, letting you access them and perform operations (such as open and close) on them as a group.

Window Controls

Table 4.2 lists the PowerBuilder window controls, their prefixes, and a description for each.

The following sections briefly discuss some of the window controls.

Table 4.2   PowerBuilder Window Controls

Control	Prefix	Description
CheckBox	cbx_	Boolean.
CommandButton	cb_	A button that lets a user perform actions or functions.
DataWindow	dw_	A window control that lets events be associated with a DataWindow object.
DropDownListBox	ddlb_	Drops down to show a list of choices for a field.
DropDownPictureListBox	ddplb_	Similar to a DropDownListBox but allows pictures.
EditMask	em_	A method of restricting data within the field.
Graph	gr_	A graphical representation of the data within a window or DataWindow.
GroupBox	gb_	A line that surrounds the controls and groups their functionality.
Hscrollbar	hsb_	Lets the user scroll horizontally.
Line	ln_	A line within a window.
ListBox	lb_	Lets multiple items be shown.
ListView	lv_	Displays a list that contains graphical information in addition to the text.
MultiLineEdit	mle_	Lets the user enter more than one line of text of information.
OLE 2	ole_	Lets the developer place an OLE object within a window.
Oval	oval_	An oval within a window.
Picture	p_	A bitmap or a graphic file.
PictureButton	pb_	A bitmap or a graphic file that contains script to perform actions or functions.
PictureListBox	plb_	Similar to the ListBox but allows pictures.
RadioButton	rb_	Lets the user choose an item.
Rectangle	r_	A rectangle within a window.
RichTextEdit	rte_	Similar to MultiLineEdit but allows formatted text.
RoundRectangle	r_	A round rectangle within a window.
SingleLineEdit	sle_	Lets the user enter only a single line of data.
StaticText	st_	Text you can use to label or describe the window.
Tab	tab_	Provides a tab-folder interface, and each tab can display other controls or a user object.
TreeView	tv_	An expanding/collapsing interface, similar to Windows Explorer.
UserObject	uo_	A developer-created object that encapsulates coded functionality.
Vscrollbar	vsb_	Lets the user scroll vertically.

DropDownListBox

The DropDownListBox (DDLB) lets you show the user a series of choices for a particular field within a window. The DropDownListBox control combines the features of a Single-LineEdit and a ListBox. There are two basic types of DDLBs—noneditable and editable.

Noneditable DDLB Noneditable DDLBs let you choose from a fixed set of choices for a field. Notice that the cursor does not appear within the SLE. Because the user does not have the opportunity to enter an incorrect response for the field, you can use the noneditable DDLB as a type of data validation. You typically use them for items with difficult spellings or for code fields.

Sometimes it is necessary to blank out a noneditable DDLB's text portion. This will be the case if the user chooses an entry from this list and then realizes the entry was not correct, nor were any of the other choices. An example of this is a window on which the user selects a salesperson's name. If the user needed to clear the field, the DDLB functionality will not allow this. If you add a Clear function, the screen will look like the one in Figure 4.16. In this example, use the following code within the command button cb_clear:

```
ddlb_salesperson.Selectitem(0)
```

By changing the DDLB's Allow Edit attribute, however, the user can edit the entry within the DDLB. You can do this for people with a higher level of security, for example. The following code within the command button cb_clear provides this functionality:

```
ddlb_salesperson.AllowEdit = True
```

The PowerBuilder Objects and Controls manual includes a complete listing of DDLB attributes and events.

The DDLB also lets the user perform a lookup on the DDLB values. When the lookup is performed, you can use the text value within the DropDownListBox to find the first entry

Figure 4.16 **Clearing the data within a DDLB.**

within the Items list. This could either be an exact match or a match of the text value with additional characters. For example, if the text value is abc and the list of items is:

```
ab
abcdefg
abc
```

The lookup will find abcdefg because it is the first entry that exactly matches the text value (even though the entry has additional characters).

Editable DDLB The editable DDLB lets the user type in data for a particular field. You can code script or call functions to validate the entry. Figure 4.17 shows a sample editable DDLB.

Radiobuttons

Radiobuttons are mutually exclusive objects. That is, within a given window, only one radiobutton can be active at a time. The exception to this is when group boxes are used with the radiobuttons. The group box frames several radiobuttons and segregates them as a unit. When an application requires that the user select a series of options and the developer chooses to use radiobuttons, it's a good idea to enclose each unique group of options (and corresponding radiobuttons) within a group box. This makes the choices more clear to the end user.

When a window has several radiobuttons that are not within a group box, the window acts as a group box and only lets one radiobutton be active at a time; that is, unless the radiobutton's Automatic attribute is False. You might do this for a radiobutton look with checkbox-like functionality. When the Automatic attribute is not checked, you must use scripts to control when the radiobutton is checked or not checked. When the Automatic attribute is False, the user can select multiple radiobuttons outside of a group. The Automatic attribute does not change how radiobuttons are processed inside a group box.

Figure 4.17   **An editable DDLB.**

SingleLineEdit, MultiLineEdit, RichTextEdit

SingleLineEdit The SingleLineEdit control lets the user enter one line of information within a field, while a MultiLineEdit control lets the user enter multiple lines of data within a field. The following example shows how you can modify an SLE programmatically to let the user overwrite an entry within the SLE, instead of the default of inserting data. The SLE looks like the one in Figure 4.18.

The first step is to define a user event, overwrite for the SLE, and map the event to the event ID pbm_char. Next, define a second user event, deltext. You need not map the deltext event to an event ID.

Next, place the following code within the SLE's overwrite event:

```
// the overwrite event
PostEvent("deltext")
```

And finally, add the following code within the deltext user event:

```
// the deltext event
Send (Handle (This),256,46,long(0,0))
```

The number 46 is the decimal equivalent of 2E hex, which is the delete key. Sending this particular handle lets the field be put into overwrite mode. After typing the text within the SLE, move the cursor to the beginning and start typing over the entry.

MultiLineEdit Tab Stops Sometimes it is necessary to place tabs within an MLE to let the data line up properly. The following example defines the tab stops within an MLE and places address information within the MLE. This code places the tab stops within the MLE as shown within the Address field in Figure 4.19.

Figure 4.18   **Overwriting the text in an SLE.**

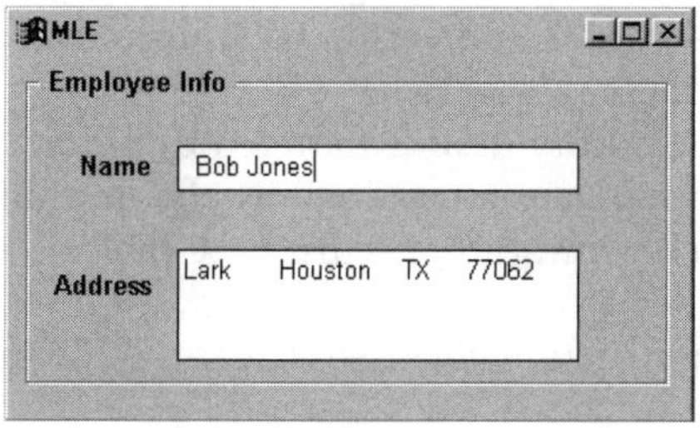

Figure 4.19   **An MLE with tab stops.**

```
// Tab stops for MLE_1
// f1, f2, f3 fields that contain strings
// define the first tabstop at position 5; define the second tabstop 10
// positions after that.
String      f1, f2, f3
mle_1.TabStop[1] = 5
mle_1.TabStop[2] = 10

f1 = "field1"
f2 = "field2"
f3 = "field3"
mle_1.Text = f1 + " ~t " + f2 + " ~t " + f3
```

TIP The ~t must have a blank space on each side, and the *t* within ~t must be lowercase.

RichTextEdit The RichTextEdit (RTE) control is a text control that provides enhanced text editing and formatting capabilities. In addition to the increased editing capabilities, an RTE control may also include input fields linked to a DataWindow, in which case an instance of the document exists within the control for each of the DataWindow's rows and any input fields whose names match the DataWindow's columns are filled with the data from the DataWindow's current row.

Tab

The tab control provides an easy way to display several pieces of data or DataWindows on one window, displayed one at a time and divided by tabs.

PowerBuilder tabs are divided into the tab control, and one or more TabPages. A tab control can contain several TabPages and each TabPage can display controls or user objects. To display the tab control's properties, select the **Properties...** option from the tab control's popup menu (obtained by clicking the right mouse button while positioned within the control's display area, i.e., anywhere within the tab control that isn't a tab). Figure 4.20 shows a tab control's Property sheet.

You can modify the properties of individual TabPages by selecting the **Properties...** option from the TabPage's popup menu (obtained by clicking the right button of your mouse while positioned on the desired tab). Figure 4.21 shows a TabPage's Property sheet.

This chapter's Window Paradigms section discusses the tab-folder interface in more detail.

PictureListBox and DropDownPictureListBox

PictureListBox and DropDownPictureListBox controls work in a similar fashion to the ListBox and DropDownListBox controls, the difference being that you may associate graphics with the list's items.

To associate a picture with a list item, you must first set up the set of pictures you want to use with the control. To do this, select the **Picture** tab from the control's Properties sheet. Within this example, seven pictures are included within the control. Each picture is associated with the index number to the left of the picture name. For example, in Figure 4.22 the Window! picture has an index of 2.

After you have defined the set of pictures, associate a picture with a list item by using the **Items** tab of the control's Property sheet, as shown in Figure 4.23. Figure 4.23 shows that the item with the text "Window" is associated with picture index 2, which is the Window! picture.

Figure 4.20   The tab control's Property sheet.

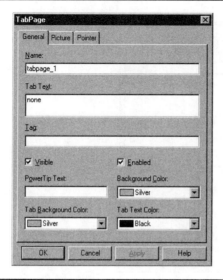

Figure 4.21   **The TabPage's Property sheet.**

Figure 4.24 shows a sample of the DropDownPictureListBox and PictureListBox controls defined with the same set of items and pictures.

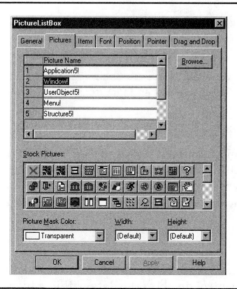

Figure 4.22   Defining the pictures for a PictureListBox control.

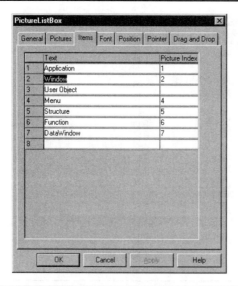

Figure 4.23 **Linking a picture with an item within a PictureListBox control.**

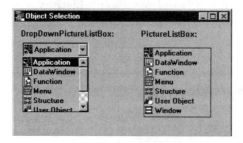

Figure 4.24 **Sample DropDownPictureListBox and PictureListBox controls.**

OLE 2

An OLE 2 control contains an object, such as a spreadsheet or word processing document, that an OLE 2–aware application created. The PowerBuilder application's user can activate and edit the object within the application within which the developer created the object (the server application). Chapter 13, "External Interfaces," discusses OLE 2 in greater detail.

TreeView

A TreeView control provides an expanding or collapsing interface that is similar to the Windows Explorer. A TreeView control displays the data within a hierarchical format. You can display master child relationships within a TreeView control.

Let's create an example of a TreeView control. Within this application, you will retrieve the associations's names from the controls.db database. When the user double-clicks on any of the associations, the TreeView displays all the committee's within that association.

Connect to the controls.db database within the application's open event by using the following code:

```
/******************************************************************************
** Connect to the database, and open the treeview window
******************************************************************************/

// Profile Controls
SQLCA.DBMS              = "ODBC"
SQLCA.AutoCommit        = False
SQLCA.DBParm            = "Connectstring='DSN=Controls'"

// Connect to the database
Connect using SQLCA;

// Check for errors when connected to the database
If SQLCA.SQLCODE <> 0 Then
    MessageBox ("Cannot Connect to the Database", sqlca.sqlerrtext)
    Halt Close
    Return
End If
Open (w_treeview)
```

Disconnect from the database within the application's **close** event by using the following code:

```
/******************************************************************************
** Disconnect from the database
******************************************************************************/

Disconnect;
```

Next, create a window w_treeview. Add a TreeView control to the window. The control will have the name tv_1. You can set the TreeView control's properties by using the control's Property sheet as shown in Figure 4.25.

Also, add a cb_close button. Within the cb_close's clicked event, add the following script:

```
/******************************************************************************
** Parameters:    long        al_parent
**                integer     ai_level
**                long        al_rows
```

continues

```
**
** Returns:      The number of rows (al_rows)
**
** Purpose:      This function calls the window function wf_set_item to set
**               the TreeView item for each record retrieved within the
**               datastore. Finally, the function adds the TreeView item to
**               the control.
*************************************************************************/
Integer         ll_count
TreeViewItem    ltvi_New

// Add each item to the TreeView
For ll_count = 1 To al_rows
     // Call a function to set the TreeView item's values from
     // the DataStore data
     wf_set_item(ai_Level, ltvi_New, ll_count)

     // Add the item after the last child
     If tv_1.InsertItemLast(al_Parent, ltvi_New) < 1 Then
          // Error
          MessageBox("Error", "Error inserting item", Exclamation!)
          Return -1
     End If
Next

Return al_Rows
```

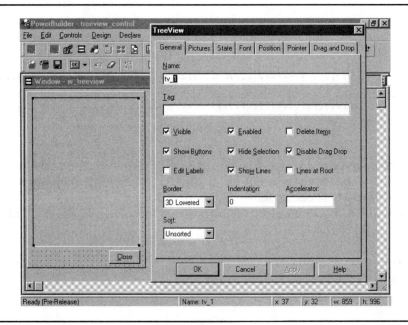

Figure 4.25   The TreeView control's Property sheet.

As you can notice, this function calls another window function wf_set_item. The code for this function is:

```
/***********************************************************************
** Parameters:    integer         ai_level
**                treeviewitem    atvi_new
**                long            al_rows
**
** Returns:       (None)
**
** Purpose:       This function sets the label, the data, and the level
**                attribute for from the values within the row. The datastore
**                to be selected depends on the level passed to it.
**                Finally, the function sets the TreeView item's children
**                attribute to True or False depending on the level.
***********************************************************************/

Integer     li_Picture

Choose Case ai_Level
    Case 1
        atvi_New.Label = ids_association.object.association_name[al_Rows]
        atvi_New.Data  = ids_association.object.association_id[al_Rows]
        atvi_New.Level  = ai_Level
    Case 2
        atvi_New.Label = ids_committee.Object.committee_name[al_Rows]
        atvi_New.Data = ids_committee.Object.committee_id[al_Rows]
        atvi_New.Level  = ai_Level
End Choose

If ai_Level = 1 Then
    atvi_New.Children = True
Else
    atvi_New.Children = False
End If

atvi_New.PictureIndex = ai_Level
atvi_New.SelectedPictureIndex = 2
```

Next, add the following PowerScript to the window's open event:

```
/***********************************************************************
** Call the window's ue_postopen event
***********************************************************************/

Post Event ue_postopen (0,0)
```

Add the following PowerScript to the window's **ue_postopen** event:

```
/**************************************************************************
** Create the datastores, and attach the dataobjects
** Call the wf_add_item to insert the associations within the treeview
**************************************************************************/
long        ll_rows

ids_association = CREATE datastore
ids_association.dataobject = "d_mnt_association_tab"
ids_association.SetTransObject (SQLCA)

ids_committee = CREATE datastore
ids_committee.dataobject = "d_mnt_committee_tab"
ids_committee.SetTransObject (SQLCA)

ll_rows = ids_association.Retrieve ()
wf_add_item(0, 1, ll_Rows)
```

When you run the application, your TreeView control will look similar to the one shown in Figure 4.26. To view an association's committees, click on that association.

ListView

A ListView control gives you a way to provide graphical information in addition to text for lists of items, such as a list of files with details and a graphical representation of the file type. You can display the items within a ListView control by using different views, and you can drag and drop the items within a ListView onto another control.

Let's create an example of the ListView control. Within this application, you will retrieve the associations's names from the controls.db database and display them within a ListView control on the window.

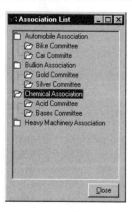

Figure 4.26   The sample TreeView control application.

Connect to the controls.db database within the application's open event by using the following code:

```
/*************************************************************************
** Connect to the database, and open the ListView window
*************************************************************************/

// Profile Controls
SQLCA.DBMS          = "ODBC"
SQLCA.AutoCommit    = False
SQLCA.DBParm        = "Connectstring='DSN=Controls'"

//Connect to the database
Connect using SQLCA;

// Check for errors when connected to the database
If SQLCA.SQLCODE <> 0 Then
    MessageBox ("Cannot Connect to the Database", sqlca.sqlerrtext)
    Halt Close
    Return
End If

Open (w_listview)
```

Disconnect from the database within the application's close event by using the following code:

```
/*************************************************************************
** Disconnect from the database
*************************************************************************/

Disconnect;
```

Next, create a window w_listview. Add a ListView control to the window, and name the control lv_association. You can set the ListView control's properties by using the control's Property sheet as shown in Figure 4.27.

Also, add two buttons, cb_retrieve and cb_close. Within cb_retrieve's clicked event, add the following script:

```
/*************************************************************************
** Call the window's ue_retrieve event
*************************************************************************/

Parent.Event  ue_retrieve (0,0)
```

Within cb_close's **clicked** event, add the following script:

```
/*************************************************************************
** Close the window
*************************************************************************/

Close (Parent)
```

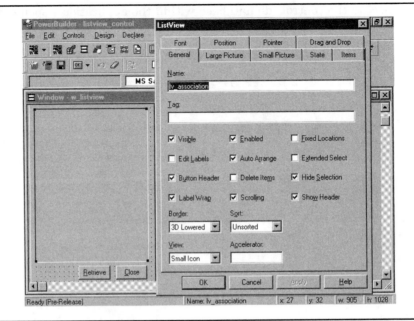

Figure 4.27 A ListView control's Property sheet.

Now, declare a datastore as an instance for the window:

```
datastore ids_association
```

Next, create a couple of user events for the window, ue_postopen and ue_retrieve. Add the following PowerScript to the window's open event:

```
/********************************************************************
** Call the window's ue_postopen event
********************************************************************/
Post Event ue_postopen (0,0)
```

Add the following PowerScript within the window's ue_postopen event:

```
/********************************************************************
** Create the datastore, and attach the dataobject
********************************************************************/

ids_association = CREATE datastore
ids_association.dataobject = "d_mnt_association_tab"
ids_association.SetTransObject (SQLCA)
```

Add the following PowerScript to the window's ue_retrieve event:

```
/*************************************************************************
** Retrieve within the datastore, and add the associations to the ListView
** Set the large, and small picture sizes
** Add a column used within the ListView
** Delete any previous items within the ListView
** Get all the rows from the datastore, and add as items to the ListView
*************************************************************************/
long            ll_row, ll_rowcount
listViewItem    llvi_Item

ll_rowcount = ids_association.Retrieve ()

// Set the large and small picture sizes
lv_association.LargePictureWidth = 48
lv_association.LargePictureHeight = 48
lv_association.SmallPictureWidth = 24
lv_association.SmallPictureHeight = 24

// Add a column used within the ListView
lv_association.AddColumn("Association_Name", Left!, 525)

// Delete any previous items within the ListView
lv_association.DeleteItems()

// Get all the rows from the datastore, and add as items to the ListView
For ll_row = 1 To ll_rowcount
    llvi_Item.PictureIndex = 1
    llvi_Item.Label = ids_association.object.association_name[ll_row]
    llvi_Item.Data  = ids_association.object.association_id[ll_row]
    lv_association.AddItem(llvi_Item)
Next
```

When you run the application, your ListView control will look similar to the one shown in Figure 4.28. To view the list of associations, click **Retrieve**.

Window Control Array

When PowerBuilder creates a window, PowerBuilder creates an internal array that stores each of the different types and values for the controls. The function within the following example accepts a window as an argument and resets the controls on that window. The function clears out the text attribute of the MultiLineEdits, SingleLineEdits, and DropDownListBoxes on that window. The function unchecks the radiobuttons and checkboxes, resets, and puts a fresh row into one DataWindow control. The function also retrieves the data into another DataWindow based on the DataWindow control's name:

```
Int    iNumControls, i
//w_control is the window passed as an argument to this function (type window)
iNumControls = UpperBound(w_control.control)
```

continues

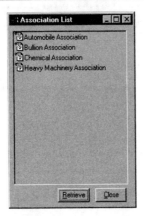

Figure 4.28   The sample ListView control application.

```
For i = 1 To iNumControls
    Choose Case Typeof(w_control.Control[i])

        Case SingleLineEdit! //clear all the SLEs' text
            SingleLineEdit my_sle
            my_sle = w_control.Control[i]
            my_sle.Text = ""

        Case MultiLineEdit! //clear all the MLEs' text
            MultiLineEdit my_mle
            my_mle = w_control.Control[i]
            my_mle.Text = ""

        Case DropDownListBox! //clear all the DDLBs' text
            DropDownListBox my_ddlb
            my_ddlb = w_control.Control[i]
            my_ddlb.SelectItem(0)

        Case EditMask!
            EditMask my_em
            my_em = w_control.Control[i]
            If my_em.MaskDataType = DateMask! Then
                my_em.Text = "01/01/93"// set the date to first of the year
            Else
                If my_em.MaskdDataType = NumericMask! Then
                    my_em.Text = ".00" // set the numeric mask .00
            Else
                    my_em.Text = "" // clear the strings' text
                End If
            End If
```

continues

```
        Case DataWindow!
            DataWindow my_dw
            my_dw = w_control.Control[i]
            If my_dw.ClassName( ) = "dw_dataentry" Then
                //set up the dw_dataentry for input
                my_dw.Reset( )
                my_dw.InsertRow(0)
            ElseIf my_dw.ClassName( ) = "dw_getinfo" Then
                // retrieve info into dw_getinfo
                my_dw.Retrieve( ) //assumes SetTransObject done
            End If

        Case Radiobutton! // uncheck all the radiobuttons
            Radiobutton my_rb
            my_rb = w_control.control[i]
            my_rb.Checked = False

        Case CheckBox! // uncheck all the checkboxes
            CheckBox my_cbx
            my_cbx = w_control.Control[i]
            my_cbx.checked = False

    End Choose
Next
```

For more information about the object class types within PowerBuilder, use the Object Browser.

Control Events

Most controls within the PowerBuilder environment have events associated with them. The only window controls that do not have events associated with them are the drawing objects (line, oval, rectangle, and round rectangle). Table 4.3 shows a list of the standard events for the window controls.

Control events are discussed in more detail throughout the book.

Window Attributes

In addition to the events, each window object has a number of different attributes the developer can change. The PowerBuilder Objects and Controls manual includes a detailed discussion of the window attributes. You can alter the Window attributes either within the Window painter or programmatically.

UnitsPerLine and LinesPerPage are examples of the window attributes. You can set these two window attributes to control the vertical window scrolling. Set the LinesPerPage attribute to 10 to give 10 pagedowns to reach the bottom of the window. Setting LinesPerPage to anything other than 10 can yield undesired results. In terms of the UnitsPerLine attribute, consider the following equation for the page:

Table 4.3   The Standard Events for the Window Controls

Window Event	Description
Clicked	Occurs when a user clicks on a window, control, or object, or when the user selects the object with the keyboard by pressing Enter.
Constructor	Occurs before the window's open event.
Destructor	Occurs immediately after the window's close event.
DragDrop	Occurs when the user drops an object on a control.
DragEnter	Occurs when the user drags an object into a control.
DragLeave	Occurs when the user drags an object out of a control.
DragWithin	Occurs when the user drags an object within a control.
GetFocus	Occurs before a control receives the focus.
LoseFocus	Occurs before the control loses focus, that is, becomes inactive.
Other	Occurs when an event other than any of the standard PowerBuilder events occur.
RButtonDown	Occurs when the user clicks the right mouse button.

```
UnitsPerLine = (<WindowHeight>-<LogicalPageHeight>)/100
```

The LogicalPageHeight is the number of PBUs the developer needs to cover when doing one pagedown. Because the LinesPerPage attribute is set to 10, calculate the LogicalPageHeight as follows:

```
<LogicalPageHeight> = <WindowHeight>/10
```

The following example shows how to control the vertical window scrolling for a window that is 6000 PBUs deep.

```
<LogicalPageHeight> = 6000/10
     = 600
UnitsPerLine  =(6000-600)/100
     =5400/100
     =54
```

In this case, LinesPerPage = 10 and UnitsPerLine = 54 lets the developer cover the 6000-PBU-deep window's entire depth.

TIP The reason you subtract the logical page height from the window height is that one page is already displayed on the screen, so 10 pagedowns cover the window height minus one page.

Horizontal Scrolling

Use the same attributes you use for vertical scrolling within a window to control the horizontal scrolling. The logic is also the same. Using the preceding example, substitute ColumnsPerPage for LinesPerPage, UnitsPerColumn for UnitsPerLine, <Logical-PageWidth> for <LogicalPageHeight>, and <WindowWidth> for <WindowHeight>.

TIP If you control the scrolling programmatically, you must always set the values for UnitsPerLine, LinesPerPage, and the like within the window's open event. Setting these values within any other event has no effect.

To provide scrolling within a window by using the PageUp and PageDown keys, add the following code to the window's open event:

```
int iLogicalPageHeight, iMaxDepth
iMaxDepth = 3000 // Assumes that maximum depth to be covered
                 // by vertical scrolling of this window is 3000 PBUs
                 // Change to whatever is appropriate
This.LinesPerPage = 10
iLogicalPageHeight = iMaxDepth/10
This.UnitsPerLine = (iMaxDepth-iLogicalPageHeight) / 100
```

Within the window's **Key** event, add the following:

```
int iCurWin

iCurWin = Handle(This)
If KeyDown(KeyPageDown!) Then
  Send(iCurWin,277,3,0)
  Return
End If

If KeyDown(KeyPageUp!) Then
  Send(iCurWin,277,2,0)
End If
```

Window Paradigms

PowerBuilder applications are a subset of the Windows applications. Within the Windows applications, there are some standard window paradigms. These paradigms are based on the user's need to view the information and the underlying datasources' relationships. Some Windows/PowerBuilder paradigms include:

- Selection dialog box
- Master/detail

- List
- Form
- Double list
- Tab-folder

The following sections discuss these paradigms.

Selection Dialog Box

A selection dialog box is a specific dialog window that lets the user select a single data object and send its key to another window on which to act. A selection dialog box commonly presents a list (or lists) of rows within a DataWindow, from which the user can choose a single row. A selection dialog box is always associated with another window, but not all the windows have selection dialog boxes associated with them.

Most selection dialog boxes contain one or more open, new, and cancel command buttons. Query selection dialog boxes, used when a high volume of data exists, include search criteria field(s) which let the user specify the first few characters of a choice; the dialog box displays only the rows that match the search pattern. (Instead of updating the list as the user keys search criteria characters, you can use a **Refresh** button to update the list with the current data.) Selection dialog boxes can contain more than one DataWindow, depending on the complexity of the data relationships.

Standard Selection Dialog Box Within a standard selection dialog box, the user can select a row and click **Open** to load the associated window with the selected data object or click **New** to invoke the window with a new, empty row. Figure 4.29 shows a list of clients from which the user could select one.

The selection dialog box has the standard control menu and a descriptive title bar that you can use to invite the user to take action on a displayed object.

Query Selection Dialog Box The query selection dialog box is similar to the standard selection dialog box except that you use a search criteria field to narrow the list of en-

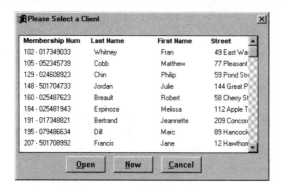

Figure 4.29   A standard selection dialog box.

tries. Use a query selection dialog box instead of a standard selection dialog box if the number of rows the standard selection dialog box returns is too large for performance or memory constraints (more than 200 rows is a good rule of thumb to use), and only one or two search criteria fields are necessary. Figure 4.30 shows an example in which the user can search on the product description.

This selection dialog box's tabular DataWindow narrows the selection set as the user keys each character into the search criteria field. If the DataWindow contains a large number of rows and the user must wait for the list to narrow after keying each character, the designer can remove this functionality and add a **Refresh** (or **Search**) button to the selection dialog box. In this scenario, the user will key the data into the search criteria field and then click **Search** to narrow the list.

Master/Detail

Use the master/detail model for master/detail maintenance (implying a one-to-many relationship between the two data entities). The master/detail model extends the basic form functionality (see Figure 4.31) to include a list of detail records that the user can open or edit depending on the required functionality. You can create the master/detail window with the window's detail portion as either a pick list or editable.

This window has a descriptive title bar that clearly shows the data object retrieved. The window should also have a standard control menu and menu bar (with the File and Help menu items at a minimum). The DataWindow dw_1 is display-only in this example, but it could be editable, if required.

List

Use the list model to display or maintain multiple rows at the same time. Figure 4.32 shows a number of products displayed within a tabular DataWindow. The user can update any of the items within the screen while being able to see the other items.

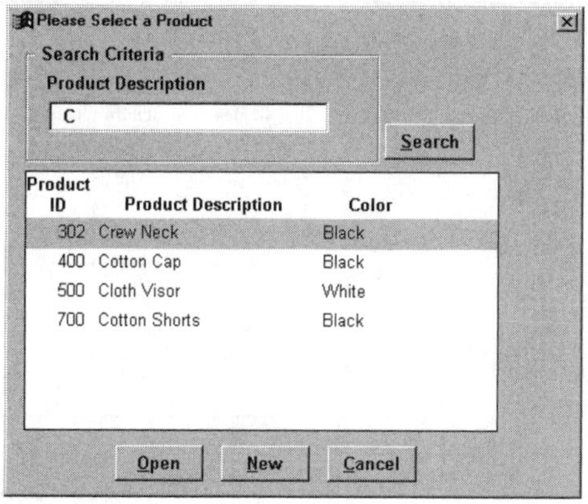

Figure 4.30   A query selection dialog box.

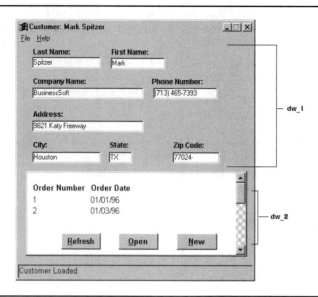

Figure 4.31   The master/detail model.

This paradigm has a descriptive title bar that clearly shows the data object retrieved, a minimize button, and a toolbar. The model should also contain a standard control menu and menu bar (with the File and Help menu items at a minimum).

Form

Use the form model paradigm for display/maintenance of a single record at a time. Figure 4.33 shows a single form that contains one product at a time.

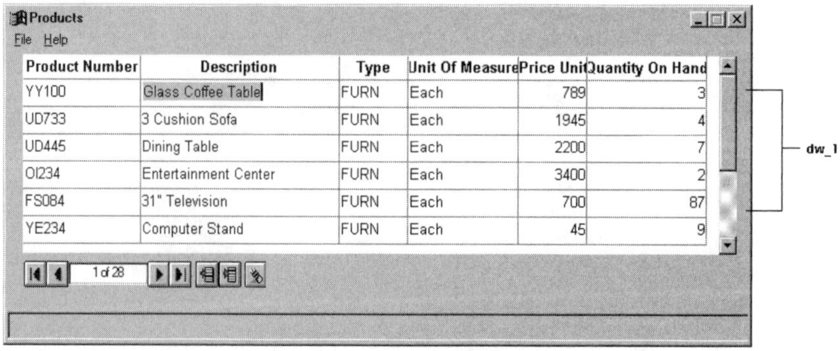

Product Number	Description	Type	Unit Of Measure	Price Unit	Quantity On Hand
YY100	Glass Coffee Table	FURN	Each	789	3
UD733	3 Cushion Sofa	FURN	Each	1945	4
UD445	Dining Table	FURN	Each	2200	7
OI234	Entertainment Center	FURN	Each	3400	2
FS084	31" Television	FURN	Each	700	87
YE234	Computer Stand	FURN	Each	45	9

Figure 4.32   The list model.

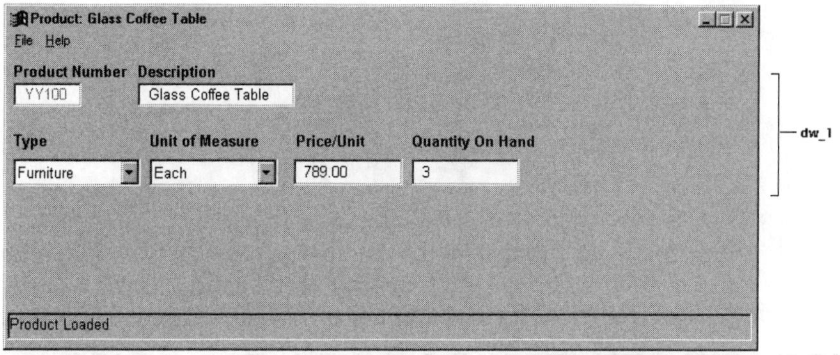

Figure 4.33   The form model.

This window has the standard control menu, and a descriptive title bar clearly shows the data object the user is currently viewing. The window also has a minimize button and a basic menu bar.

Double List

The double list paradigm lets a user choose items from one column and add them to a second column. When you add the items to the second column, they are deleted from the first column. Figure 4.34 shows a double list window that lets the values be within both DataWindows. The user can add or subtract values from either side.

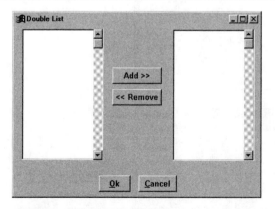

Figure 4.34   The double list model.

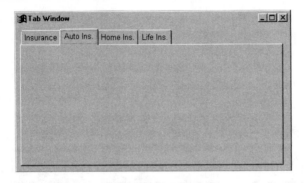

Figure 4.35   The tab folder-model.

Tab-Folder

With the introduction of the tab-folder controls with PowerBuilder 5 (see Figure 4.35), this paradigm has become increasingly popular among developers. The tab-folder interface is a window interface patterned after the tab-folder dividers found in traditional notebooks and binders.

The tab-folder interface reduces the need for multiple windows and provides a quicker interface. Traditional GUIs require users to open multiple dialog boxes to access the different information. With the tab-folder interface, you can group multiple window controls together and view them by choosing a particular tab. In the example in Figure 4.36, to view the detailed auto, home, and life insurance information from a

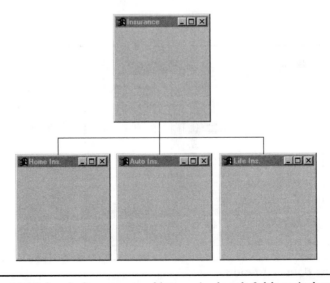

Figure 4.36   **Multiple windows grouped into a single tab-folder window.**

main insurance window already filled with the data and controls, you must open a new dialog box. By using the tab-folder interface (Figure 4.35), you can group together each type of insurance and all the information associated with it and link to the different tabs within a single window.

Traditional Look and Feel (GUI) Figure 4.36 shows multiple windows that are opened to access detailed information about an individual's home, auto, and life insurance.

The next section shows some different tab-folder interfaces, divided into single-tier and multitier tab-folder GUIs.

Single-Tier Tab-Folder Interface Figure 4.35 shows the GUI for a single-tier custom PowerBuilder tab-folder window. Each tab along the top of the container presents different information within the container. This tab-folder GUI was developed by using PowerBuilder.

You can also create multicolor tabs by using PowerBuilder. Developers can also create tabs across the top, bottom, left, right, right and left, and top and bottom of the container.

Master/Detail Tab-Folder Interface A master/detail tab interface provides a master DataWindow with the summary information combined with a tab control that displays a variety of details pertaining to the information within the master DataWindow. For example, you may want to display the name and address information within a master DataWindow for an employee, along with the salary, 401K, and job history information within three separate tabs, as shown in Figure 4.37.

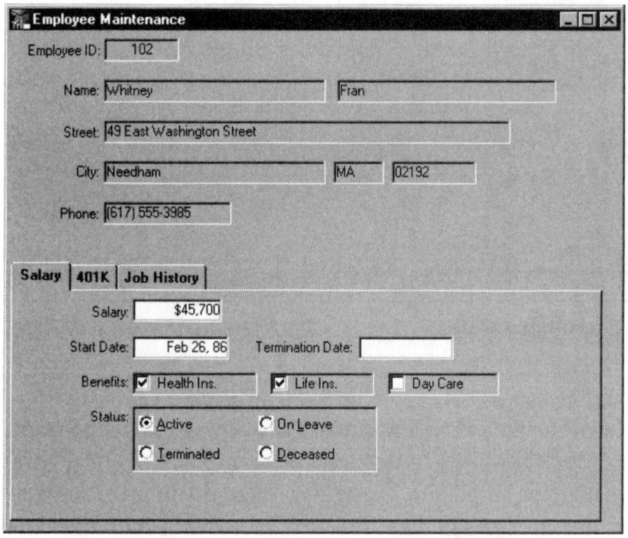

Figure 4.37   The Master/Detail tab interface.

Figure 4.38 The multitier tab folder.

Figure 4.39 The scrollable tabs.

Multitier Tab-Folder Interface The multitier tabs are a little different than the single-tier tabs in that you stack the different tiers on top of each other. PowerBuilder lets the developers create multitier tabs (see Figure 4.38) and tab folders with a scrollbar. The scrollbar appears when the tabs go beyond the container's width as seen in Figure 4.39.

CHAPTER 5

Menus

Menus are the standard method to interface between the user and the application. Menus let the user navigate through the application and perform specific tasks with a minimum amount of previous experience. PowerBuilder lets you create menus for an application by using the Menu painter. You can also use inheritance, scripts, and functions to enhance the MenuItems' functionality.

This chapter discusses the following topics:

- Types of menus
- Inheritance
- Menu events, scripts, and functions
- Menus in MDI applications
- Toolbars
- Drop-down toolbars
- Integrating with an .INI file
- Accelerator and shortcut keys
- MenuItem properties
- Design considerations

TYPES OF MENUS

Menus within PowerBuilder can be divided into two groups: menu bars and popups.

Menu Bar

The menu bar, the most common kind of menu, is a horizontal row of MenuItems that appears below the title bar. Each menu item displays either a cascading or a drop-down menu that offers the user further choices related to the MenuItem chosen. A drop-down menu displays the associated MenuItems in a drop-down menu. A cascading menu is a submenu that PowerBuilder displays to either side of a drop-down MenuItem below an item on the menu bar. PowerBuilder usually denotes the cascading menu by an arrowhead next to the associated choice within the drop-down menu bar. Typically, you use the cascading menu for multiple options (e.g., color choices).

Any window you create within an application should have a menu bar associated with it. Exceptions are the Child and Response windows. Because you always open a child window from within the parent window, and a child window is never considered active, a child window cannot have a menu. Therefore, the parent window always has the menu for the child window. Response windows cannot have menus either because they are always opened from within the parent. In addition, Response windows are application modal.

Popup Menus

The other kind of menu is a popup. You can invoke this type of menu from a MenuItem in a menu bar or when a user chooses something within the work area and clicks with either the right or left mouse button. Because you usually place them on the most frequently used areas or menu items, popup menus are sometimes referred to as *contextual menus*.

The system menu or **Control** menu is an example of a popup menu. A minus sign icon is associated with the **Control** menu at the menu bar's left end. This menu contains many of the standard system commands that PowerBuilder includes, by default, for the application. Most PowerBuilder applications do not require you to add any menu choices to the **Control** menu because you should create and place the application-specific MenuItems within the application menus, not within the **Control** menu.

To let the user use the system commands throughout the application, it is a good idea to associate a **Control** menu with all of the PowerBuilder window types except the Response window because the Response window is application modal. The Response window should let the user move the window but not to exit the window until the user responds. An example of a window without a **Control** menu is a messagebox. A messagebox does not let the user continue until the user provides a response. The default commands within a **Control** menu include **Restore**, **Move**, **Size**, **Minimize**, **Maximize**, and **Close**.

Unfortunately, PowerBuilder does not let you directly alter the **Control** menu from the Menu painter. Unlike PowerBuilder, however, the Microsoft Windows Software Devleopment Toolkit (SDK) lets you use the **GetSystemMenu( )** function to copy the default window's system menu (**Control** menu) and add menu choices. You can use the **AppendMenu( )**, **InsertMenu( )**, and **ModifyMenu( )** functions to add the menu choices to the control menu's copy. You can then associate the control menu's copy with a particular window. Because the commands in the default **Control** menu use identifier numbers greater than 0xF00, you should use identifier numbers less than 0xF000. Because the majority of the applications do not require any changes or additions to the system **Control** menu, this is typically not a problem.

Even though PowerBuilder does not explicitly let you alter the **Control** menu, there are ways to trap the Windows messages. You can accomplish this by creating a user-defined **ControlMenu( )** event. This event, which fires when the user clicks the **Control** menu, lets you trap the messages the underlying Windows functions send. Chapter 13, "External Interfaces," further discusses trapping Windows messages.

To display a popup menu that is already associated with the window, you can simply call the menu item directly with the **PopMenu( )** function. To use the PopMenu( ) function, you can either use the current cursor position or hard-code the X and Y coordinates. The example in Figure 5.1 illustrates the popup menu by placing the following code within the rbuttondown event to trigger the popup for the DataWindow control's single line edit (SLE). The menu, m_stdmnu is inherited from m_basemnu.

This statement displays the popup menu m_file at the cursor position when the user clicks within DataWindow control's single line edit (SLE) by using the right mouse button (see Figure 5.1):

```
m_stdmnu.m_file.PopMenu( xpos, ypos )
```

xpos and ypos are the arguments passed to the DataWindow control's **rbuttondown** event.

Another way to show the popup menu is to hard-code the X and Y coordinates within the **PopMenu** function. These statements display the MenuItem m_file at the location 100, 200:

```
m_stdmnu.m_file.PopMenu( 100,200 )
```

TIP If the MenuItem's Visible attribute is False, you must make the MenuItem visible before you can display it as a popup menu.

INHERITANCE

The easiest way to implement and maintain menus within an application is to use inheritance. Although inherited menus have some drawbacks, using them simplifies application maintenance.

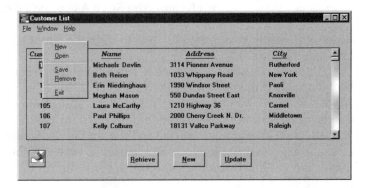

Figure 5.1   Using a popup menu.

In addition, creating menus that inherit the base functionality lets you extend the menu's functionality for specific needs at the window level. Note that within PowerBuilder scripts, you reference the ancestor menus in the same way as you do within the other painters:

```
ancestormenu::Menuitem
```

PowerBuilder's support of inheritance for the menu objects is similar to that of other PowerBuilder objects, letting the developer do the following:

- Add new MenuItems to an inherited menu
- Modify the existing MenuItems
- Build scripts
- Extend and override the ancestor scripts
- Declare functions, structures, and variables

MenuItems have an attribute called ShiftToRight. ShiftToRight lets you insert the MenuItems between the inherited MenuItems. You set the ShiftToRight attribute by selecting the **Shift Over\Down** option from the Menu painter. For example, assume you have defined the menu m_stdmnu with the MenuItems **File**, **Window**, and **Help** and that the **Window** and **Help** items have their ShiftToRight attributes set to True (see Figure 5.2).

Next, assume you inherited the menu m_editmnu from m_stdmnu, and the menu m_editmnu contains the **Edit** MenuItem. Because the **Window** and **Help** items have their ShiftToRight attributes set to True, PowerBuilder places any new MenuItems you define within m_editmnu before the **Window** and **Help** items. Figure 5.3 shows the m_editmnu's definition.

Notice that even though the Edit item is shown last in Figure 5.3, PowerBuilder displays it before any items that it shifts to the right at the time of execution, as shown in Figure 5.4.

ShiftToRight also applies to the MenuItems within a menu bar item. For example, assume the m_stdmnu's **File** MenuItem includes the **Remove, Close**, and **Exit** menu items with their ShiftToRight set to True, as shown in Figure 5.5.

ShiftToRight lets you create a **Save As** item that PowerBuilder will display below the **Save** option in m_editmnu. Figure 5.6 shows the **Save As** option's definition within m_editmnu.

Upon execution, the **Save As** option will appear after the **Save** option within the **File** menu, as shown in Figure 5.7.

Although the ShiftToRight attribute does add some flexibility, there are still some limitations when you inherit menus within PowerBuilder. First, the ShiftToRight attribute does not let you insert MenuItems between all the MenuItems of an inherited menu. PowerBuilder places all the new descendant MenuItems before all the ancestor MenuItems with the ShiftToRight attribute set to True. In the preceding example, it is not possible to create new MenuItems within m_editmnu between the **Window** and **Help** items. In addition to ShiftToRight's limitations, you cannot:

- Move or change the inherited MenuItems' order
- Delete an inherited MenuItem

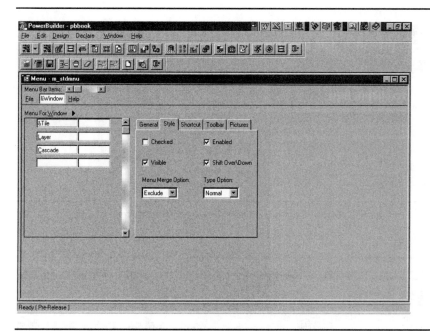

Figure 5.2   The ShiftToRight attribute in a MenuItem.

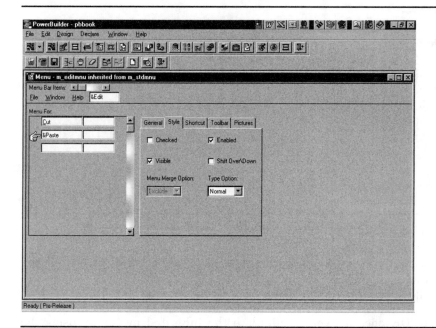

Figure 5.3   m_editmnu's definition.

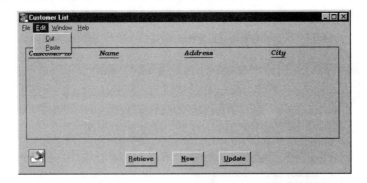

Figure 5.4 The Edit item is shown before the Window and Help items.

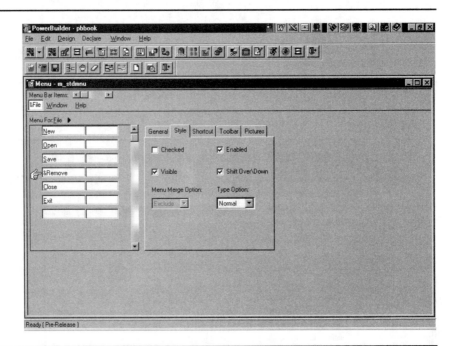

Figure 5.5 Applying ShiftToRight to the MenuItems within a menu bar item.

- Insert MenuItems between the two inherited items (other than before all the shifted MenuItems)
- Dynamically add or subtract menu items

The Windows SDK does let you manipulate the inherited menus by using the **AppendMenu( )**, **InsertMenu( )**, and **ModifyMenu( )** functions. Because of Power-

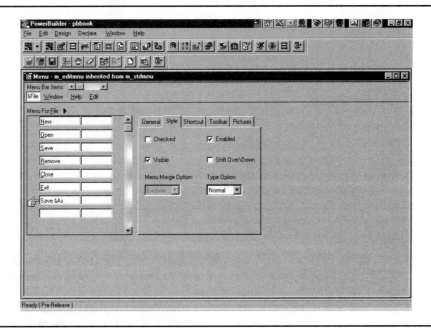

Figure 5.6   Adding the Save <u>A</u>s option.

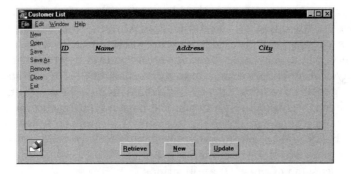

Figure 5.7   The Save <u>A</u>s option appears after the <u>S</u>ave option.

Builder's limited functionality within this area, you will not find developing complex menu inheritance structures within PowerBuilder particularly useful. Fortunately, most menus are simple in nature, and you usually do not need complex menu inheritance structures. By creating a complete inheritance tree in advance, you will not need to manipulate several of the MenuItems programmatically.

When creating an application's inheritance structure, it is good to decide if you need any Virtual Class menus (menus that you will not use but create so you can inherit from them). These menus can have the basic menu choices that all the different types of Win-

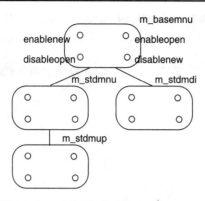

Figure 5.8   An example of menu inheritance.

dows need to use. They should have MenuItems such as **New**, **Open**, **Save**, and **Exit**. After deciding on the Virtual Class menus, you can organize the inheritance tree such that each of the other menus inherit the base functionality from the ancestor.

Figure 5.8 shows an example of menu inheritance. This tree illustrates the use of the different layers of inherited menus. The first layer is the menu m_basemnu. Because PowerBuilder does not let you save a menu without a MenuItem, it is saved with only the item Dummy (defined as invisible) within the MenuItem section. The menu m_basemnu contains all of the code for the user-defined menu functions **enableopen( )**, **enablenew( )**, **disableopen( )**, and **disablenew( )**. These four functions enable and disable the MenuItems based on the application UserId. The section covering menu functions discusses these four functions. Having such functions within the base menu level lets the descendants use these functions or override and extend them if necessary.

The next layer of inheritance, m_stdmnu, has most of the MenuItems you need for an application's generic windows. These MenuItems include **New**, **Open**, **Save**, **Print**, and **Exit**. Another menu that inherits from the base menu, m_stdmdi, contains capabilities for the MDI screens within the application. This menu includes the code to open multiple MDI sheets and to manipulate the sheets by using the **ArrangeSheets( )** function. Chapter 4, "Multiple Document Interface (MDI) and Windows," includes a more detailed discussion of the MDI applications.

The last layer of inheritance is the menu m_stdmnup. This menu, which is the menu m_stdmnu's descendant, adds print capability within a window. Chapter 8 includes a detailed discussion of printing within an application. Inheriting some menus from other menus lets you override and extend within the function script (as with other PowerBuilder objects) the code that resides within the ancestor menu.

MENU EVENTS, SCRIPTS, AND FUNCTIONS

The PowerBuilder Menu painter lets you create PowerScript for both menu events and functions. Like other PowerBuilder objects, you can also extend or override ancestor menu scripts. This section discusses the use of menu events and functions.

Menu Events

Like other PowerBuilder objects, menus have events associated with them. The two events associated with MenuItems are the clicked and selected events.

When you release the mouse button and the MenuItem's enabled and visible attributes are True, the MenuItem's clicked event is triggered. An example of the script you could include within a clicked event is a checked or unchecked bitmap. You could use such a bitmap when the MenuItem's value is True or False. This will let the user see the MenuItem's state.

An example of using the clicked event is within the menu choice for an MDI section that indicates the sheet arrangement style the user has chosen (i.e., Tile, Cascade, or Layered). You can either use the **Check( )** function or set the Check attribute to True or False (see Figure 5.9).

The code within the MenuItem Tile's clicked event is:

```
mdi_frame.ArrangeSheets(Tile!)
This.Check()
Parent.m_layer.UnCheck( )
Parent.m_cascade.UnCheck( )
```

The other event associated with a MenuItem is the **selected** event. When the user highlights the MenuItem, the selected event is triggered. Usually, you do not use this event very often because most users do not associate a MenuItem's highlighting with any action. However, you can use the selected event to show MicroHelp within an MDI application. An example of this is to use the **SetMicroHelp( )** function within the selected event of the menu m_stdmdi's **Open** MenuItem. The associated window is mdi_frame:

```
mdi_frame.SetMicroHelp("Open sheet")
```

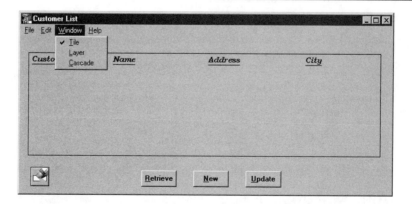

Figure 5.9   Checking a menu item.

Menu Functions

Another way to maximize the use of menus is with functions. An example using menu functions is to restrict a user's options within an application by enabling and disabling the menu options within a window. The first step is to create the four simple menu functions for public access and to set a Boolean return type. The functions are **enableopen( )**, **enablenew( )**, **disableopen( )**, and **disablenew( )**. They are object functions for the menu m_stdmdi and contain the code to enable and disable the m_stdmdi's MenuItems based on the global GroupId you set during the user's connection with the database.

The code within each of the functions is:

```
/* Function - enableOpen    enable the "open" option. */
m_file.m_open.Enable()
Return True


/* Function - enableNew    enable the "New" option. */
Enable(m_file.m_new)
Return True


/* Function - disableOpen    disable the "Open" option. */
Disable(m_file.m_open)
Return True


/* Function - disableNew    disable the "New" option. */
Disable(m_file.m_new)
Return True
```

Once you create the enable and disable menu functions, you can call the user-defined window function **Security( )** within the window mdi_frame's open event. The Security( ) function checks the GroupId and either enables or disables the menu choices of the frame's menu based on its value:

```
/* Function - Security Enable or disable menu options according to rights */
boolean bFailedOpen, bFailedNew

If G_GROUPID = "accounting" Then
  bFailedOpen = m_stdmdi.DisableOpen( )
  bFailedNew = m_stdmdi.DisableNew( )
Else
  m_stdmdi.EnableOpen( )
  m_stdmdi.EnableNew( )
End If

If (Not bFailedOpen) And (Not bFailedNew) Then
    /* to trap error*/
    MessageBox("Error","Security error",Exclamation!,OKCancel!,2)
```

```
       Return False
   End If
   Return True
```

TIP When referencing the MenuItems within a script, be sure to fully qualify the reference (e.g., m_stdmdi.m_file.m_open.Visible).

When referring to a window and its controls and attributes within a menu script, use the following notation:

```
Windowname
Windowname.Attribute
Windowname.Control.Attribute
```

It is better practice to use the ParentWindow pronoun when referring to the associated window whenever possible. You can use ParentWindow to:

- Reference the window itself
- Reference the window's attributes
- Call the window functions

For example, the following line of PowerScript will close the active window associated with the menu:

```
Close(ParentWindow)
```

To reference the controls, you must reference the window explicitly. Because a menu can be associated with several windows within an application, using Parent-Window provides a generic reference to the active window and greatly reduces the amount of code you need to accommodate multiple windows that share a menu.

You can simplify the amount of code within an application window by using the **TriggerEvent** to call the event script associated with a MenuItem. In addition to reducing the amount of code, you can use the TriggerEvent to make the code more manageable and easier to debug.

MENUS WITHIN MDI APPLICATIONS

You can easily add menus into MDI applications at the frame and sheet levels. When designing an MDI application, you can set up the menus in two ways. The first method of menu design is to have only one menu within the frame and no menus associated with the sheets. The other method is to have a menu associated with the frame as well as with all of the sheets. You should always associate a menu with the frame window.

If an MDI application only has a menu associated with the frame and no menu associated with any sheets, all of the sheets, or subapplications, use the frame's menu. The frame menu is actually acting as a menu for both the active sheet and the frame window.

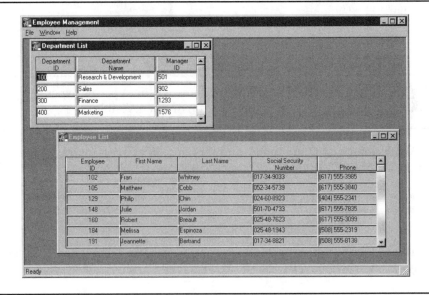

Figure 5.10   A sample MDI application with menus.

Consequently, you can associate a menu with each sheet. Because you can display only one menu bar at a time, when you open or activate a sheet that has a menu associated with it, the sheet menu appears to replace the frame menu. When you close all the sheets, PowerBuilder, in turn, redisplays the frame menu. An MDI application can have one or more sheets with the corresponding menus and one sheet without a menu. In this case, the sheet without a menu will take the frame menu.

In the example shown in Figure 5.10, the frame has a menu called m_stdmdi and sheet1 has an associated menu called m_stdmnu. Since sheet2 does not have an associated menu, sheet2 uses the last active frame menu, m_stdmdi.

TIP When creating an MDI application, you should either provide one menu that will cover all the sheets or associate a menu with each sheet.

Another feature that PowerBuilder provides for the MDI applications is the listing of open sheets within a menu. You can do this within the **OpenSheet( )** function. Open-Sheet( ) takes a parameter specifying the number of the menu item (within the menu associated with the sheet) to which you want to append the open sheets' names. If you do not provide a value, PowerBuilder will display the list of open sheets within the next-to-last menu item. This is the default because the **Window** MenuItem will be in this position within most MDI applications.

For example, the following script opens three MDI sheets and lists the sheets' names under the first menu item:

```
string     sWinName[] = {"sheet1", "sheet2", "sheet3"}
window     WinArray[]
integer    i

For i = 1 To 3
    OpenSheet(WinArray [i], sWinName[i], mdi_frame, 1)
Next
```

For simplicity, this script uses the hard-coded values of "sheet1," "sheet2," and "sheet3" to initialize the array sWinName[ ], and hard codes the value 3 into the For...Next loop.

TOOLBARS

Toolbars represent a graphical, more user-friendly interface to the application menus. Generally you use them to provide shortcuts to frequently used specific functions and features, including the external applications' execution.

PowerBuilder 6 introduces flat toolbars that are similar to the Microsoft Office 97 Suite so your applications can have the same look and feel as other Windows applications.

You create toolbars within the Menu painter by attaching bitmaps to a corresponding menu item. Because toolbar items are associated with the menu items, a menu item must exist in order to have an item within the toolbar. Table 5.1 describes some of the toolbar attributes.

Table 5.1 Toolbar Attributes

Attribute	Datatype	Uses
ToolbarItemDown	Boolean	Creates 3-D indention to show the item has been pressed.
ToolBarItemName	String	The toolbar item bitmap or default picture's name.
ToolbarItemDownName	String	Name of the toolbar bitmap referenced when the toolbar is down.
ToolbarItemOrder	Integer	The item's number within the toolbar (0–99)
ToolbarItemSpace	Integer	An integer of the amount of space in front of the toolbar item (in PB units).
ToolbarItemText	String	The text's value associated with the toolbar item.
ToolbarItemVisible	Boolean	Sets the toolbar item to visible or invisible.
ToolbarSheetTitle	String	An MDI sheet toolbar's title (when floating).
ToolbarAlignment	Enumerated	Specifies where the toolbar is located within the window.
ToolbarHeight	Integer	The toolbar's height (when floating).
ToolbarFrameTitle	String	Title of the toolbar created within an MDI floating toolbar.

You can use the toolbar attributes within scripts to manipulate a toolbar's presentation to the user. The following example uses the ToolbarItemVisible attribute. A user-defined window function **Security( )** checks the GroupId, disables the menu choice **New** and makes the related toolbar item invisible:

```
/* Enable or disable the menu options according to the rights. */
boolean bCanOpen, bCanNew
If G_GROUPID = "accounting" Then
    m_stdmdi.DisableNew( )
    m_stdmdi.m_file.m_new.ToolbarItemVisible = False
End If
If (Not bCanOpen) And (Not bCanNew) Then
  /* it makes no sense to be here if we cannot do either of these */
    Return False
End If
m_stdmdi.EnableNew( )
m_stdmdi.m_file.m_new.ToolbarItemVisible = True
Return True
```

Because toolbar items are associated with menu items, it follows that the rules for toolbars are similar to the rules for menus. When an application's MDI frame has a toolbar, and the MDI frame's sheets do not have a toolbar, each sheet uses the frame's toolbar. In addition, when each sheet has a separate toolbar associated with it, the sheet's toolbar can be visible at the same time as the frame's toolbar. This is similar to Power-Builder's implementation of the PowerBar and PainterBar. This capability lets the user of the application click the right mouse button while positioned on a toolbar and invoke a popup window that lets the user position the sheet and/or frame toolbar to the top, bottom, left, right, or create a floating toolbar.

Figure 5.11 shows the frame mdi_frame and a sheet, sheet1, each with its own menu and toolbar. By clicking on either of the toolbars with the right mouse button, a popup window that the user can use to modify the corresponding toolbar becomes visible. Within the popup menu, the user can also choose to disable either the frame toolbar or the sheet toolbar. If you choose to open the sheet and not have the frame menu toolbar visible, you can use the toolbar function **Hide( )** to make the frame menu toolbar invisible. If the toolbar needs to be visible again, you can use the **Show( )** function.

As mentioned earlier, an MDI application can have one or more sheets with a corresponding menu and one or more sheets without a menu. Again, because toolbars are associated with menus, the sheets without an associated menu will take the last active frame menu and toolbar.

Figure 5.11 shows the frame mdi_frame with a menu or toolbar associated with it and its sheet, sheet1, with its own separate menu or toolbar. However, sheet2 does not have a menu or toolbar. Sheet2 inherits the last open frame menu or toolbar when it is opened.

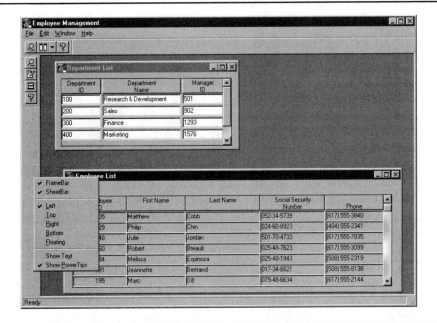

Figure 5.11   The MDI frame and sheet, each with its own menu and toolbar.

TIP If there is a menu associated with a frame and a menu associated with a sheet, the sheet menu will replace the frame menu when the user opens the sheet. However, the sheet toolbar will not replace the frame toolbar when the user opens the sheet. If you require only the sheet toolbar be visible, then hide the frame toolbar.

Many designers overuse the toolbars. You should design and implement toolbars based on user requirements and not simply to add flash and pizzazz to an application. In addition, these functions should also have simple and easy-to-understand icons that should be meaningful to most users. The icons that appear within the toolbar should be 16 pixels by 15 pixels for good visual clarity. Unfortunately, PowerBuilder does not let the user change the size of the buttons associated with the menu items. Therefore, the regular-sized icon bitmaps do not appear very well within the toolbar.

DROP-DOWN TOOLBARS

PowerBuilder provides an added capability to include drop-down toolbars as part of a menu's toolbar. You can find an example of a drop-down toolbar within the Power-Builder development environment, as shown in Figure 5.12.

You can implement the drop-down toolbars by using the new MenuCascade object type. MenuItems you define as MenuCascade objects may appear as part of a drop-down

Figure 5.12   A drop-down toolbar.

toolbar. To define a MenuItem as a MenuCascade object (rather than the normal type of Menu), select MenuCascade as the object type, located on the the MenuItem's **Toolbar** tab. For example, to create a DropDown toolbar for defining the MDI sheets' arrangement, set the object type of the Window MenuItem to MenuCascade, as shown in Figure 5.13.

Notice that when you define a MenuItem as MenuCascade, PowerBuilder enables the Columns and **DropDown** options. The Columns attribute defines the number of columns that the drop-down toolbar contains.

The drop-down toolbar in Figure 5.12 contains four columns. The DropDown attribute specifies whether the MenuItems you define as part of the MenuCascade object appear as a drop-down toolbar. If the DropDown attribute is True, the MenuItems you define as part of the MenuCascade object appear within a drop-down toolbar. If the DropDown attribute is False, PowerBuilder displays the MenuItems as normal toolbar items. The example shown in Figure 5.13 contains two columns and has its DropDown attribute set to True. Figure 5.14 shows what this example looks like when executed.

INTEGRATING WITH AN .INI FILE

Another useful function that you can integrate within menus is the ability to save the user information into an application initialization file. You can create MenuItems that will let the user save user preferences such as window position, window arrangement, toolbar position and items, and other user-specific items. PowerBuilder has three built-in functions designed to manipulate the initialization files. The **ProfileString( )** and **ProfileInt( )** functions let you read from the initialization files, and the **SetProfile-String( )** function lets you write to the initialization files.

An example of this is to use SetProfileString( ) in conjunction with the **Save** Menu-Item. This function writes the fourth parameter's value, "sheet1" in this example, into the myapp.ini's [LastSheet] section. This will let you track the last unit of work that the user saved:

```
SetProfileString("myappwin.ini","LastSheet","LastSheet1","sheet1")
```

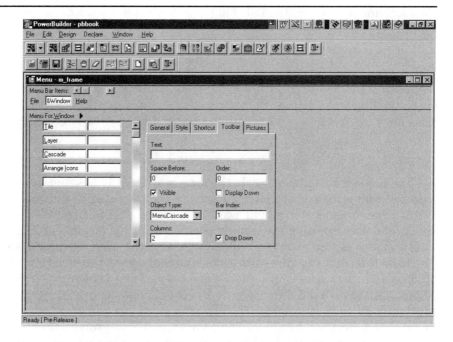

Figure 5.13   Creating a drop-down toolbar.

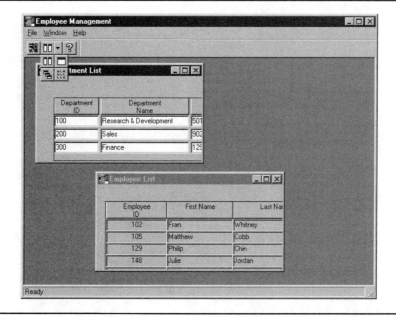

Figure 5.14   Using a drop-down toolbar to define the window arrangements.

This statement produces the following lines within myapp.ini:

```
[LastSheet]
LastSheet1=sheet1
```

You can then read this value by using ProfileString( ) to retrieve the last opened sheet within an MDI application. The ProfileString( ) function searches for the myapp.ini file, opens the file, and retrieves the LastSheet entry for LastSheet1. If no value exists for this entry, the function returns the designated default (" "). This code is:

```
string sLastFile
sLastFile = ProfileString("myappwin.ini", "LastSheet", "LastSheet1", "")
```

The ProfileInt( ) function works the same way the ProfileString( ) does, but it returns a numeric value instead of a character string and the default value must be numeric.

Another function you might want to create is one to save the application workspace. The user can save the frame's position and any sheets within an MDI application. This works similar to the Windows 3.x ability to save the user's workspace.

To do this, first save the MDI frame's state (normal, minimized, or maximized), position, width, and height into the myapp.ini variable MDIFrame (within the section MyApp). After saving the frame, save the sheet name and the same information given previously for each open sheet. The myapp.ini variable name for the sheets is *sheet* followed by the sheet number (i.e., sheet1, sheet2, . . .). This example uses instance variables to track the sheets' names (i_sOpenSheetNames) and the actual sheet windows (i_OpenSheets). Set these variables as the user opens each sheet. The code for this example is:

```
window      currentsheet
string      sWinState, sText
int         i, iSheetNum

SetPointer(HourGlass!)
/* first the frame */
/* figure out the windowState */

Choose Case This.WindowState
    Case Normal!
        sWinState = "0"
    Case Minimized!
        sWinState = "1"
    Case Maximized!
        sWinState = "2"
End Choose

SetProfileString("myappwin.ini","MyApp","MDIFrame",sWinState+&
                ","+string(This.x)+","+string(This.y)+","+&
                string(This.width)+","+string(This.height))
/* now the sheets */
currentsheet = This.GetFirstSheet( )
```

```
Do While IsValid(CurrentSheet)

    iSheetNum = iSheetNum + 1

    Choose Case CurrentSheet.WindowState
        Case Normal!
            sWinState = "0"
        Case Minimized!
            sWinState = "1"
        Case Maximized!
            sWinState = "2"
    End Choose

    SetProfileString("myappwin.ini","MyApp","Sheet"+string(iSheetNum),&
                     i_sOpenSheetNames[iSheetNum]+","+sWinState+","+&
                     string(CurrentSheet.X)+","+string(CurrentSheet.Y)+&
                     ","+string(CurrentSheet.Width)+&
                     ","+string(CurrentSheet.Height))

  currentsheet = This.GetNextSheet(CurrentSheet)

Loop

/* now blank out any previous entries */
For i = iSheetNum+1 To 20 // arbitrary maximum
    If ProfileString("myapp.ini","MyApp","Sheet"+string(i),"") <> " Then
        SetProfileString("myapp.ini","MyApp","Sheet"+string(i),"")
    End If
Next

w_mdi_frame.SetMicroHelp("Workspace Saved.")

Return True
```

The following shows how myapp.ini looks after saving the workspace in the preceding example:

```
[MyApp]
MDIFrame=0,1029,449,1581,1060
Sheet1=w_sheet1,0,343,109,1353,500
Sheet2=w_sheet2,0,558,437,1353,500
Sheet3=w_sheet3,0,188,869,1354,500
```

Once the workspace is saved, you need to write a corollary function to read the information stored in the .INI file. This function will restore the last state, the frame, and each sheet's X, Y, height, and width.

```
/* Restore the user's workspace */
int         i
string      sSheetInfo

SetPointer(hourGlass!)

/* first the sheets */
For i = 1 To 20      // arbitrary maximum
    sSheetInfo = ProfileString("myapp.ini","MyApp","Sheet"+string(i),"")
    If sSheetInfo <> "" Then
        i_sopensheetnames[i] = Nextcsv (sSheetInfo)

        /* open the sheet */
        OpenSheet(i_openSheets[i],i_sopensheetnames[i],This,2,Original!)
        If Not IsValid(i_openSheets[i]) Then
            /* could not open - display message */
            MessageBox("Open Sheet","Unable to open sheet saved"+&
                    " in workspace. Re-save workspace.")
            Continue      // go to next saved sheet
        End If

    /* next parm is window state - 0 = normal 1 = min 2 = max */
    Choose Case Nextcsv (sSheetInfo)
        Case "0" // normal
            /* move and resize the sheet with following parms */
            i_openSheets[i].Move(integer(Nextcsv(sSheetInfo)),&
                            integer(Nextcsv(sSheetInfo)))
            i_openSheets[i].Resize(integer(Nextcsv(sSheetInfo)),&
                            integer(Nextcsv(sSheetInfo)))
        Case "1" // minimized
                /* minimize the sheet */
                i_openSheets[i].WindowState = Minimized!

        Case "2" // maximized
                /* maximize the sheet */
                i_openSheets[i].WindowState = Maximized!
    End Choose

    Else
        /* done with the sheets */
        Exit
    End If
Next

i_inumopensheets = i -1

/* now the frame */
sSheetInfo = ProfileString("myapp.ini","MyApp","MDIFrame","")
If sSheetInfo <> "" Then
    Choose Case Nextcsv(sSheetInfo)
```

```
            Case "0" // normal
                  /* move and size the frame with following parms */
                  Move(integer(Nextcsv(sSheetInfo)),&
                        integer(Nextcsv(sSheetInfo)))
                  Resize(integer(Nextcsv(sSheetInfo)),&
                           integer(Nextcsv(sSheetInfo)))

            Case "1" // minimized
                  /* move and minimize the frame */
                  windowState = Minimized!

            Case "2" // maximized
                  /* maximize the frame */
                  windowState = Maximized!
      End Choose
End If

/* setFocus to the first menu */
If i_inumopensheets > 0 Then
      SetFocus(i_openSheets[1])
End If

w_mdi_frame.SetMicroHelp("Workspace Restored.")

Return True
```

Figure 5.15 shows the window function **Nextcsv( )**, which was used in the preceding example to parse the comma-separated strings.

The window function Nextcsv( )'s code is as follows:

```
/* This is used to parse a parameter string separated by commas. */
Int         iLen
string      sTmp

iLen = Pos(csvList,",")  // find end of this parm

If iLen = 0 Then
      /* no comma - must be only parm */
      sTmp = csvList
      csvList = "" // clear it out
Else
      /* remove the parm from the string */
      sTmp = Left(csvList,lng - 1)      // don't want comma
      csvList = Right(csvList,len(csvList)-iLen)  // remove from the string
End If

Return sTmp
```

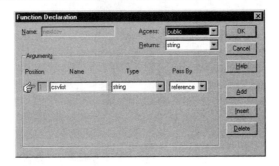

Figure 5.15   Declaring the **Nextcsv( )** function.

ACCELERATOR AND SHORTCUT KEYS

Another way that an application designer can enhance an application is to use accelerator and shortcut keys. These offer the user the ability to do the same thing that is achieved with the mouse movement by using the keyboard. PowerBuilder lets you include these keys within the menus through the Menu painter. When developing an application's menus, it is considered good practice to include accelerator keys on all the MenuItems. This lets the user access any of the MenuItems with an Alt-key. The accelerator key for each MenuItem is underlined. To create the accelerator key, include and ampersand (&) in front of the letter of choice in the MenuItem within the Menu painter.

In addition to the accelerator keys, you can use shortcut keys. These are a set of alternate keystrokes that can perform specific MenuItem tasks by using the Alt, Ctrl, or Shift keys in unison with an assigned keystroke. You denote these items to the right of the appropriate MenuItem. These keystrokes are considered to be optional, but are of help to users who have repetitious menu choices and prefer to use the keyboard for navigation. Windows has some conventions with regard to the shortcut keys (e.g., Alt-F4 = Close/Exit), but you should create and adopt an application set of keystrokes.

MENUITEM PROPERTIES

The MenuItems that determine a menu have properties and events associated with them. Both properties and events let you further customize and manipulate the menus within the application. For a complete list of the MenuItem properties, please refer to the PowerBuilder documentation.

The MenuId is a menu datatype containing a menu's identifying name (the name you use to save the menu within the Menu painter). When you change a window's menu from a script or display to a popup menu, use the MenuId attribute to identify the menu.

TIP The MenuItem name (prefix and suffix) can have up to 40 characters. If the name exceeds this size, PowerBuilder uses only the first 40 characters.

When creating scripts to manipulate the MenuItems, you can use several Power-Builder functions to hide menu items, disable (gray), check, change menus, and change the MenuItems' text within a menu bar.

One of the more popular functions is the Hide( ) function, which you can use to hide any MenuItems that you do not want the user to see. You can use this function when you inherit the menu from another menu and do not use an option.

For example, you may not always need the inherited MenuItem **Open** within an application. The converse function of Hide( ) is the Show( ) function. The syntax for these functions is:

```
m_stdmnu.m_file.m_open.Hide( )
m_stdmnu.m_file.m_open.Show( )
```

The **Enable( )** and **Disable( )** functions are useful when you want to maintain an application's security. These functions let you gray out any MenuItems that the user cannot use. This is helpful because it lets the user see that the option is within the menu, but the user cannot access or use it because of a constraint within the application. It is also useful when you want to let a user use only certain MenuItems during the flow of a unit of work.

For example, if you do not want the user to use the **Open** MenuItem because of incorrect security privileges, you can use the Disable( ) function. In addition, you can use the Enable( ) function to restore the MenuItem's use:

```
m_stdmnu.m_file.m_open.Disable( )
m_stdmnu.m_file.m_open.Enable( )
```

When you create the MenuItems with Boolean values, you can associate a checked bitmap with the appropriate MenuItems. This lets the user see that a menu choice is invoked or not invoked. You can associate the checkmark either as a default within the menu painter or associate it later via the check function.

An example is the checking of the Tile MenuItem within an MDI application to indicate that PowerBuilder will arrange the sheets in a tiled fashion:

```
m_stdmnu.m_file.m_tile.Checked( )
m_stdmnu.m_file.m_tile.UnChecked( )
```

In addition to visually showing the check and uncheck bitmap, you can change the MenuItem's text to reflect the MenuItem's state. This gives you an option when dealing with the MenuItems that do not easily work with the checked bitmap. You can do this by using the Text attribute within the MenuItem's clicked event.

An example of this is the changing of the MenuItem within m_stdmnu from **File—Open** to **File—Close** when the user clicks the MenuItem.

Sometimes, you may want to change from one menu to another during the flow of work within an application. You can do this by using the **changemenu( )** function. The changemenu( ) function handles the changing of the menu by using the MenuId and MenuName's Window attributes. PowerBuilder uses these attributes to internally track the associated menu. PowerBuilder recommends that you do not attempt to use them, but you can use the attributes, if necessary.

For example, if the window mdi_ frame needs to use a different menu, you can change the menu by using changemenu( ):

```
mdi_frame.changemenu(m_stdmdi)
```

DESIGN CONSIDERATIONS

One of the primary concerns of application design is the topic of standardization. The use of standards lets the user manipulate every application in a similar fashion and creates a cohesive flow for the users to follow. In addition, standards can also reduce the time it takes to train the users on a new system and increase user satisfaction. Unfortunately, there is no one standard type of menu system look and feel. Some application designers choose to implement the IBM CUA standards, and others create internal standards. However, most application designers choose to implement a menuing system that is similar to the Microsoft applications' current suite. Some examples include the Microsoft Word and Microsoft Excel applications.

One of the first look-and-feel standards is creating a standard menu bar. The standard menu bar includes using **File**, **Edit**, **View**, **Window**, and **Help**. Another example of a menu standard is the use of shortcut keys. The shortcut key is denoted within a menu as the series of control keys that you can use to alternately choose a menu item. Additionally, PowerBuilder lets the application designer create and use the accelerator keys. These are the underlined letters within the menu bar or menu item that allow quick access to a MenuItem. Yet another standard is the use of three dots (ellipses) following a MenuItem choice. This indicates that the user can invoke a Window or popup Window by clicking on this MenuItem. You can simplify the menu standardization through the use of inheritance, which lets you create the menu standards once at the ancestor level and extend and override at the descendant level.

The next section lists some reference materials that you will find useful for menu design in particular and application interface design in general.

Suggested Reading

Alex Calvo. *The Craft of Windows 95 Interface Design: Click Here to Begin*. New York: Springer Verlag, 1996.

Alan Cooper. *About Face: The Essentials of User Interface Design*. Foster City, CA: IDG Books Worldwide, 1995.

Virginia Howlett. *Visual Interface Design for Windows: Effective User Interfaces for Windows 95, Windows NT, and Windows 3.1*. New York: John Wiley & Sons, 1996.

Scott Isensee. *The Art of Rapid Prototyping: User Interface Design for Windows and OS/2*. New York: International Thompson Publishing, 1996.

Microsoft Press. *The Windows Interface Guidelines for Software Design: An Application Design Guide*. Redmond, WA: Microsoft Press, 1995.

CHAPTER 6

Structures, Functions, and User Objects

PowerBuilder is an object-oriented development tool. To develop object-oriented applications, PowerBuilder provides useful objects: functions, structures, and User Objects. You can use any or all of them within your applications.

This chapter discusses the following PowerBuilder objects:

- Structures
  - Creating and declaring structures
  - Types of structures
- Functions
  - Types of functions
  - Declaring external functions
  - Parameter passing
  - Object-oriented programming and functions
- User objects
  - Types of User Objects
  - Interfacing between windows and User Objects
  - Dynamic User Objects
  - Object-oriented programming and User Objects

STRUCTURES

A *structure* is a collection of one or more related variables of the same or different datatypes grouped under a single name. You generally use a structure to define the various attributes of an object, like a person. Let's define a global structure person that contains contact information such as first name, last name, street, city, state, and zip.

Creating and Declaring Structures

To create the person structure, click the **Structure** icon on the PowerBar. PowerBuilder displays the **Select Structure** window. Next, click **New**. PowerBuilder displays the **Structure** window as shown in Figure 6.1.

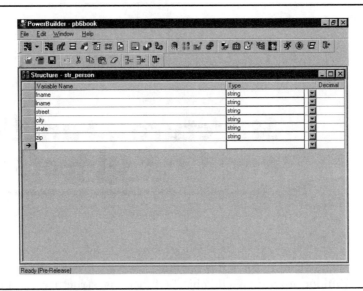

Figure 6.1   Definition of the structure str_person.

Define each of the attributes of the person as a variable name, and use string as the datatype for all the attributes.

Save the structure as str_person.

Nested Structures and Arrays.   You can define nested structures (a structure within a structure) within PowerBuilder. You can also use an array of structure within your PowerBuilder application.

Reinitializing your array.   PowerBuilder does not provide a way to reinitialize your array. However, you can reinitialize the array by defining another array of the same type and assigning the new array's value to the old array. That way, you free up the old array's values.

New Garbage Collection.   The new Garbage Collection function identifies all the unused, unreferenced, and orphaned objects within memory and immediately removes them from the memory.

Types of Structures

Structures within PowerBuilder can be divided into two groups: *global structures* and *object-level structures*.

Global Structures

Global structures are not associated with any particular object and are public in scope, meaning that you can call them from anywhere within the application.

Object-Level Structures

You can define object-level structures for windows, menus, and User Objects. Unlike global structures, object-level structures are available only to a particular object.

FUNCTIONS

Functions are a key ingredient of any PowerBuilder application. PowerBuilder provides a great deal of flexibility with regard to functions. PowerBuilder provides built-in functions that you can use as well as the flexibility to write your own functions. You can define these user functions at either the global or the object level. PowerBuilder also allows the linking of external functions written in C.

TIP You can write external functions by using languages other than C (e.g., C++, COBOL). However, for the sake of this discussion, all the references to the external functions assume the functions are written in C.

Types of Functions

You can divide functions within PowerBuilder into two groups: built-in and user-defined functions.

Built-In Functions

Built-in functions are PowerScript functions you use to obtain information about an object, change or manipulate an object's attributes, or change an object's behavior. Built-in functions include string manipulation functions, date manipulation functions, print functions, and DDE functions among others. Each PowerBuilder object has a set of built-in functions that are analogous to the set of member functions within a C++ class. For a complete list of the built-in functions, refer to the *PowerBuilder Function Reference*.

User-Defined Functions

If a built-in PowerBuilder function does not do the job or a specific task you need, you can create a user-defined function with either PowerScript code or C code written as a DLL. In either case, you can define the function to be global in scope or at the object level. If you define the function at the object level, it is valid only as long as the object for which you defined the function exists.

Global Functions

Global functions are not associated with any particular object and are public in scope, meaning that you can call them from anywhere within the application. You can write global functions by using PowerScript or C.

Object-Level Functions

You can define an object-level function for windows, menus, and User Objects. Unlike global functions, you can define an object-level function with an access level of public, private, or protected:

Public. You can call a public function from anywhere within an application.

Private. You can call a private function only from the events defined for the same object as the function. You cannot call private functions from the descendants of the object for which you defined the function.

Protected. The same as private functions, with the exception that you can call them from the descendants of the object for which you created the function.

Like the built-in functions, the object-level functions are analogous to the member functions within a C++ class.

External Functions

External functions let the developers link C functions into a PowerBuilder application. This is a very powerful feature of PowerBuilder that makes it an open and extensible development tool. You store these C functions within DLLs (by using a "far pascal" declaration) that you must declare within the application before you can call them. PowerBuilder lets external functions be either global or local in scope. You can call the global external functions from anywhere within the application, but you can call the local external functions only from the events defined for the same object as the function.

TIP Windows uses the pascal declaration because the pascal declaration is more efficient than the standard C function declaration. The pascal declaration causes the compiler to push the parameters onto the stack from left to right, while the normal C functions push the parameters onto the stack from right to left. The pascal declaration gives the responsibility for cleaning up the stack to the called function rather than the calling function.

PowerBuilder provides a set of utility functions you can use when making calls to the external C functions. These functions, which handle the communication between PowerBuilder and the Windows operating system, are:

Handle( ) returns a PowerBuilder object's handle.

IntHigh( ) returns a long value's high word returned from a C function.

IntLow( ) returns a long value's low word returned from a C function.

Long( ) combines a low and high word into a long value.

It is often necessary to obtain a PowerBuilder window's handle to pass to an external function. The following command button script, for example, maximizes the current PowerBuilder window by calling the PowerBuilder post function to post a message to the window's message queue:

```
/********************************************************************
** maximize this window by posting the message to the window's message
** queue
********************************************************************/
post(handle(parent),274,61488,0)
```

You pass the current window's handle (obtain the handle by using the **handle( )** function), the Windows message number (274 = WM_SYSCOMMAND), the message's integer value (61488 = SC_MAXIMIZE), and the message's long value (not necessary in this case) to the post function. You can obtain the Windows message numbers by referring to the Windows SDK documentation or by looking at the SDK's windows.h file.

The **IntHigh( )** and **IntLow( )** functions analyze the values returned from the external function calls or Windows messages. For example, the following script is contained within a custom user event mapped to the pbm_syscommand event ID. This script uses IntLow( ) to check the PowerBuilder message structure's wordParm element. If this value is equal to the WM_SYSCOMMAND message's (61536) SC_CLOSE value, the window is closed:

```
/**********************************************************************
** Trap the event of the user selecting the control menu options.
** Specifically, the 'close' option, which is identified by
** the WM_SYSCOMMAND message's (61536) SC_CLOSE value.
**********************************************************************/
uint uiWParm

// Check for the 'close' selection
uiWParm     = IntLow(Message.WordParm )
This.Title = "messgage number: " + string(uiWParm)
If uiWParm = 61536 Then
    Close(This)
End If
```

Declaring External Functions

To declare an external function, select the **Global External Functions...** option or the **Local External Functions...** option from an object painter or the PowerScript painter's Declare menu. For the external functions returning a value, the declaration syntax is:

```
{access} FUNCTION rtndatatype functionname ( {REF}
    {datatype1 arg1, ..., datatypen argn} ) LIBRARY libname ALIAS
      FOR extname
```

For external functions that do not return a value (e.g., C functions that have a return type of void), the declaration syntax is:

```
{access} SUBROUTINE functionname ({REF}
    {datatype1 arg1 , ..., datatypen  argn}) LIBRARY libname
      ALIAS FOR extname
```

where:

> **access** is the function's access level (local functions only): Public, Private, or Protected. The default value is Public.

> **rtndatatype** is the datatype that the function returns.

> **functionname** is the name of the function within the DLL.

datatype1, . . . , datatype*n* are the datatypes of arg1, . . . , arg*n* (optional).

arg1, . . . , arg*n* are the names of the arguments passed to the function (optional).

libname is the name of the DLL that contains the function (string). This DLL must be within the DOS path during execution.

ALIAS FOR extname is an alias for the function name. Use the alias name when you want to refer to the function by a different name or when the function's name is not a legal PowerScript name (optional).

For example, assume the developer wants to add a function to determine the user's current directory. One way to do this is by calling the Window's SDK function **GetCurrentDirectoryA( )**. This function, located within the kernel32.dll, returns an unsigned long containing the number of characters within the current directory name. Figure 6.2 shows how you can declare this function within PowerBuilder.

Once you declare an external function, you can call the function in the same fashion as any PowerScript function. The following code shows how you can call GetCurrentDirectoryA( ) from within PowerScript code:

```
/******************************************************************
** Get the current directory by using the external function
** GetCurrentDirectoryA( ), and display this value within a static text
** control.
******************************************************************/
String    sCurDir
Long      lDirLen

// Allocate space for the directory text
sCurDir = Space (80)

// Get the current directory, and display it
lDirLen = GetCurrentDirectoryA(60, sCurDir)
If lDirLen > 0 Then
     st_curDir.Text = sCurDir
End If
```

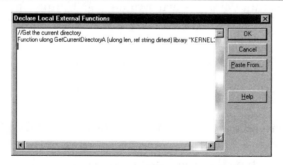

Figure 6.2   **Declaring a local external function.**

For a listing of all Windows SDK functions, refer to the *Windows SDK Programmer's Reference, Volume 1: Overview.*

Parameter Passing

You can pass parameters to a function by value, by reference, and as read-only parameters:

- Passing "by value" means you pass a copy of the argument to the function, and any changes the function makes to the copy of the argument are not reflected within the original argument.
- Passing "by reference" means you pass the argument's address, and any changes the function makes to the argument are reflected within the original argument.
- Passing by "read-only" means you pass the argument's address, but the function cannot make any changes to the argument.

However, there are some differences in parameter passing between PowerScript and external functions.

PowerScript Functions

You can define PowerScript functions to accept parameters of any standard Power-Builder datatype. This includes the basic datatypes such as integers, longs, strings, and so on. In addition, you can pass PowerBuilder objects such as windows, DataWindows, and User Objects to the PowerScript functions either by reference or by value.

PowerBuilder also lets you pass structures and arrays. You can extend this capability further by passing arrays of structures or structures of arrays. By combining arrays and structures, you can pass large amounts of data to a function in a simple manner.

To illustrate the passing of an array of structures, let's take the example of the structure str_person, which was defined earlier in this chapter.

The following code defines an array of type str_person, populates the array by selecting the data from the database, and passes the array to a function that prints the list of names to a file (note that this code is shown as a single function for simplicity; in a real application, you may find it better to use more than one function):

```
/******************************************************************
** This function declares an array of type str_person,
** populates the array by selecting the contact data from
** the database, and passes the array to a printing function.
******************************************************************/
str_person    str_contact[]
string        sFname, sLname, sStreet, sCity, sState, sZip
int           i = 1

// Declare the cursor to select contact data, and check for errors
Declare get_person Cursor For
SELECT first_name, last_name, street, city, state, zip
```

continues

```
FROM contact
Using SQLCA;

If SQLCA.SQLCode <>0 Then
  MessageBox("Cursor Error", "Unable to declare the cursor get_person")
  Return
End If

// Open the cursor, and check for errors
Open get_person;

If SQLCA.SQLCode <>0 Then
  MessageBox("Cursor Error", "Unable to open the cursor get_person")
  Return
End If

// Fetch, and load each row into the array
Do While SQLCA.SQLCode = 0
 Fetch get_person Into :sFname, :sLname, :sStreet, :sCity, :sState, :sZip;
 str_contact[i].Fname  = sFname
 str_contact[i].Lname  = sLname
 str_contact[i].Street = sStreet
 str_contact[i].City   = sCity
 str_contact[i].State  = sState
 str_contact[i].Zip    = sZip
 i+=1
Loop

// Close the cursor
Close get_person;

// Print the list of contacts to a file
print_contacts("contacts.txt", str_contact[], i-1)
```

Figure 6.3 shows the function **print_contacts( )**.

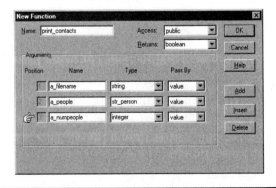

Figure 6.3   Declaration of the function print_contacts( ).

Notice the declaration of the second argument, a_people[]. The argument is declared as an array of type str_person, the structure described in Figure 6.1. The third argument, a_numpeople, represents the number of elements within the array. The code for **print_contacts( )** is:

```
/**********************************************************************
** This function takes a list of contacts passed in as the structure
** a_people[], and prints them to the file name that you pass.
**********************************************************************/
int  iFileNum, i

// Open the file
iFileNum = FileOpen(a_fileName, LineMode!, Write!, LockWrite!, Replace!)
If iFileNum = -1 Then
  MessageBox("File Error", "Error opening the Contacts file")
  Return False
End If

// Go through each item within the passed array, and print
// each structure element to the file
For i=1 To a_numPeople
  FileWrite(iFileNum, a_people[i].Fname + " " + a_people[i].Lname)
  FileWrite(iFileNum, a_people[i].Street)
  FileWrite(iFileNum, a_people[i].City + ", " + a_people[i].State + " " +
a_people[i].Zip)
  FileWrite(iFileNum, " ")
Next

// Close the file
FileClose(iFileNum)
Return True
```

To show how a structure with array elements can be handled within functions, suppose there is a window that lets the users send an email message from a PowerBuilder application (this example is intended only to demonstrate the passing of a structure with array elements; refer to Chapter 11, "Email Interfaces," for a discussion of the various email interfaces from PowerBuilder), as shown in Figure 6.4.

This window uses the structure str_email to store the email log information. This structure keeps such items as message sender, message subject, date, a list of who the message was sent to (an array), and a list of who was listed within the message's cc: field (an array). Figure 6.5 shows this structure's definition.

The window function **load_struct( )** takes the data from the screen and loads it into a structure of type str_email. This function then calls a custom DLL to send the message by using the email API. After the message is sent, the window function **log_email( )** writes the information about the message to a log file. The **Send** button's clicked event calls this function:

Figure 6.4 A sample PowerBuilder email interface.

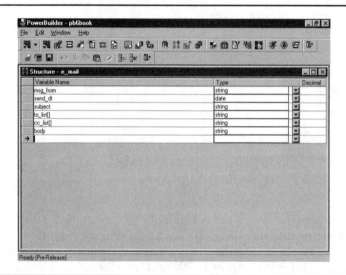

Figure 6.5 Definition of the structure str_email.

```
/********************************************************************
** This function takes the elements from the current screen,
** loads them into a structure of type str_email, calls a custom DLL
** to send an e-mail message, and calls a function to
** write information about the message to a log file.
********************************************************************/
```

continues

```
str_email     msg_struct
integer       i, iTotalTo, iTotalCC, iRet

// Load the structure from the screen
msg_struct.msg_from = sle_from.text
msg_struct.send_dt  = today()
msg_struct.subject  = sle_subject.text

// Add each item of the To: listbox to the array
For iTotalTo=1 To lb_to.totalitems()
   msg_struct.to_list[iTotalTo] = lb_to.text(iTotalTo)
Next

// Add each item of the cc: listbox to the array
For iTotalCC=1 To lb_cc.totalitems()
   msg_struct.cc_list[iTotalCC] = lb_cc.text(iTotalCC)
Next
msg_struct.Body = mle_note.text

// Call the custom DLL that will take the structure, and
// send an e-mail message based on its contents
iRet = SendMessage(msg_struct)
If iRet = 1 Then
   Beep(3)
   st_message.text = "Mailed!"
Else
   st_message.text = "Error."
End If

// Call the function to log the note information (i_sLogfile is an
// instance variable containing the log file's name)
log_email(i_sLogfile, msg_struct, iTotalTo-1, iTotalCC-1)
```

Figure 6.6 shows the function log_email( )'s definition. The arguments passed to log_email( ) are the log file's name, the structure containing all the information to be

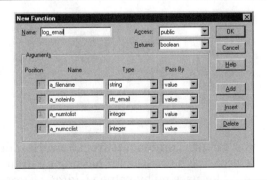

Figure 6.6   Declaration of the function log_email( ).

logged for a single message, the number of people the note was sent to, and the number of people who were on the note's cc: line.

The code for log_email( ) is:

```
/**********************************************************************
** This function takes the e-mail message information
** from the passed structure, and prints the log information to the passed **
file name.
**********************************************************************/
int  i, iFileNum

// Open the log file
iFileNum = FileOpen(a_fileName, LineMode!, Write!, LockWrite!,
Append!)
If iFileNum = -1 Then
  MessageBox("File Error", "Error opening Log file")
  Return False
End If

// Take each element from the passed structure,
// and print it to the log file
FileWrite(iFileNum, "From: " + a_noteInfo.msg_from)
FileWrite(iFileNum, "Date: " + string(a_noteInfo.send_dt))
FileWrite(iFileNum, "Subject: " + a_noteInfo.subject)
FileWrite(iFileNum, "To: ")

// Loop through the list of names on the to: line
For i=1 To a_numToList
    FileWrite(iFileNum, "  " + a_noteInfo.to_list[i])
Next
FileWrite(iFileNum, "cc: ")

// Loop through the list of names on the cc: line
For i=1 To a_numCCList
    FileWrite(iFileNum, "  " + a_noteInfo.cc_list[i])
Next
FileWrite(iFileNum, " ")

// Close the file
FileClose(iFileNum)
Return True
```

External Functions

Like PowerBuilder functions, you can pass arguments from PowerBuilder to an external C function by value or by reference. The syntax for passing an argument by reference is *ref datatype arg*; the syntax for passing by value is *datatype arg*. You can pass all the PowerBuilder datatypes, including structures, as arguments to a C function.

When passing items from PowerBuilder to the external functions by reference, the argument you pass must be a variable rather than a literal. This is because the function references this variable's address, which does not exist in the case of a literal. To illustrate this, consider the function **myfunction( )**'s definition:

```
myfunction(ref string var1)
```

Normally, you could call the function myfunction( ) by using PowerScript in one of two ways:

```
myfunction("ha ha ha")
```

or

```
string mystring = "ha ha ha"
myfunction(mystring)
```

In the first example, the pointer passed to myfunction( ) is not pointing to the correct memory location because you have not allocated any memory (see Figure 6.7).

In the second example, you declare mystring as a string and allocate memory accordingly. When you call myfunction( ) in this case, you pass a pointer to mystring's location within the memory, as Figure 6.8 shows. This illustrates that you should use the second method to avoid memory allocation problems.

Object-Oriented Programming and Functions

The concept of using functions as a method of segregating code into distinct modules is fairly straightforward. This concept is valid for both non-object-oriented environments as well as object-oriented environments. What becomes more important within an object-oriented environment such as PowerBuilder is a function's scope. With the ability to define object-level functions as public, private, and protected, it becomes important to know a function's purpose so you can define the function in a way that increases developer productivity and application performance.

Global versus Object Functions

A well-designed object class hierarchy encapsulates any action to be performed on an object into object functions. You should call these functions only from the events or

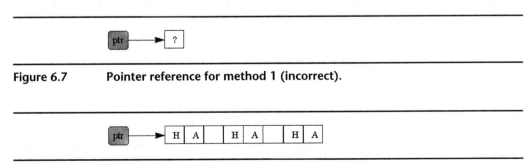

Figure 6.7   **Pointer reference for method 1 (incorrect).**

Figure 6.8   **Pointer reference for method 2 (correct).**

functions you define within the same branch of the hierarchy tree. For example, consider the following object hierarchy, shown in Figure 6.9.

You can call the functions you define for StdObject from any of the three objects within the hierarchy. However, you should only call the functions you define for ReportObj from StdObject, ReportObj, or any of ReportObj's descendants (if you have not declared the function as private). You should not call the functions you define for ReportObj from QueryObj or any of its descendants.

You can define the functions that need to be called from both ReportObj or QueryObj for StdObject or as global functions. Generally, you should define the functions that pertain to the object itself at the object level, while you should define the general purpose functions as global functions. For example, you should define the functions that perform such tasks as initializing an object, enabling or disabling an object's controls, or checking a user's rights to an object at the object level. On the other hand, you should define the functions that perform such tasks as setting up a transaction object and connecting to a database, returning values of global variables, or returning error messages as global because objects of all types use them, and they do not pertain to any single object type.

Inheritance and Functions

As stated earlier, the descendant classes may extend or override the object-level functions defined for ancestor classes. When you define the same function for the descendant, the function automatically overrides the ancestor functions. To override an ancestor function, the function declaration for the descendant must be identical to that of the ancestor, or PowerBuilder will not execute the function at the descendant level. (This is because polymorphism lets you define functions with the same name.)

You can extend an ancestor function by calling the function within the descendant function by using the **::** operator. Preceding the :: operator with the ancestor object's name executes the ancestor function or event before continuing the descendant function. PowerBuilder also lets you use the word **super** before the :: operator to execute the function or event of the object's *immediate* ancestor. For example, within a master/detail conversation, it is more efficient to initialize a detail DataWindow only if the master DataWindow is initialized without error. The following function, **initDWs( )**, calls the ancestor's initDWs( ) function before initializing the detail DataWindow:

Figure 6.9   **A sample object hierarchy.**

```
/**************************************************************************
** Extend to initialize the detail list DataWindow
**************************************************************************/

// initialize the master DataWindow before the detail
If Super::initDWs() Then
    // Initialization code for detail DataWindow
Else
    Return False
End If
```

As stated earlier, you should use inheritance whenever possible to increase code reusability and maintainability.

Polymorphism and Function Overloading

PowerBuilder supports both polymorphic functions and function overloading. While these two concepts are very similar, there is a slight difference. Polymorphism (see Chapter 2, "Application Architectures") allows for functions with the same name that behave differently depending on the context in which you call the function. A good example of using polymorphism is with the **enable( )** function. The same function when called in context with different objects behaves in a different manner. By using the object hierarchy shown earlier, the enable( ) function defined for StdObject might simply enable the object. This function (accepting no arguments) is shown below:

```
/**************************************************************************
** Enable this object
**************************************************************************/

This.Enabled = True
Return True
```

On the other hand, the enable( ) function for ReportObj might enable a DataWindow's particular column. The code for this (accepting the arguments ColName and tabOrder) is:

```
/**************************************************************************
** Enable the argument column within dw_master by setting the
** Tab Order to the argument value and changing the colors.
**************************************************************************/

dw_master.Modify(ColName+".color=~""+DATA_COLOR+ "~" " + &
    ColName+".pointer=~"iBeam!~" " + &
    ColName+".TabSequence=" + string(tabOrder) + " " + &
    ColName+".Border=5" )
Return True
```

Calling the enable( ) function from an event or function defined for StdObject (or a descendant) causes PowerBuilder to execute the first set of code. Calling the function from an event or function defined for ReportObj (or a descendant) causes PowerBuilder to execute the second set of code.

Function overloading is a form of polymorphism that lets you create two or more functions with the same name, but with a different number or type of function arguments. PowerBuilder provides the ability to overload the functions at the object level. This means that the same function name can exist multiple times for a given object. For example, you can define the function **print_error( )** for the same object in the following ways:

```
boolean print_error( integer, string)   // prints an error number & message
boolean print_error( string)            // prints a custom error message
boolean print_error( error)             // prints the PB error object's contents
```

The code for these functions is:

```
boolean print_error( integer a_errornum, string a_errortxt):

MessageBox("Application Error", "Error Number " + string(a_errornum) &
+ ": " + a_errortxt)
Return True


boolean print_error( string a_error):

MessageBox("Application Error", a_error)
Return True


boolean print_error( error a_error):

dw_master.InsertRow (1)
dw_master.object.errornum[1] = string(error.number)
dw_master.object.message[1]  = error.text
dw_master.object.where[1]    = error.windowmenu
dw_master.object.object[1]   = error.object
dw_master.object.event[1]    = error.objectevent
dw_master.object.line[1]     = string(error.line)
Return True
```

When the application calls print_error( ), the function that PowerBuilder executes depends on the value that the application passes to the function. The following three calls to print_error( ) show how PowerBuilder executes each of the three functions:

```
print_error (100, "Customer already exists.")
print_error ("Your custom error message here")
print_error (error)
```

Dynamic versus Static Binding

PowerBuilder allows two ways of making a function call. You can call a function at compile time, which is known as *static binding,* or at runtime, which is known as *dynamic binding*. Moreover, several other keywords determine the function call's nature. The syntax to declare a function is:

```
{objectname.}{type}{calltype}{when} functionname
                          ({arg1, . . . argn})
```

where:

> **objectname** is the name of the object that includes the function definition.
>
> **type** is a keyword that specifies whether you want to call an event or a function.
>
> **calltype** is a keyword that specifies when to look for the function, that is, at compile time or runtime. Calltype takes the values static (by default) for design-time binding, or dynamic for runtime binding.
>
> **when** is a keyword that specifies whether PowerBuilder should execute the function or event immediately or after executing the current script. When takes the values Trigger (by default) to fire immediately or Post to fire after executing the current script.
>
> **functionname** is the function's name.
>
> **arg1, . . ., arg*n*** are the names of arguments passed to the function (optional).

PowerBuilder supports the posting of functions. *Posting* a function means that PowerBuilder puts the function into the object's message queue and executes it after executing any previous messages within the object's queue. Posting a function means that PowerBuilder does not necessarily execute the function immediately.

Using the Any Datatype

PowerBuilder provides the Any datatype as a means for storing data of any datatype into a single variable. The datatypes you can store within an Any variable include simple datatypes (integer, string, datetime, and so on), PowerObjects, arrays, and structures. PowerBuilder assigns data to Any variables in the same way as for variables of other types. When you assign a value to an Any variable, the variable takes on the datatype's characteristics you have assigned it. For example, the following code assigns an integer, a DataWindow, and a string array to the same variable:

```
any       aAnyvar
string    months[12] = { "Jan", "Feb", "Mar", "Apr", "May", "Jun", &
                         "Jul", "Aug", "Sep", "Oct", "Nov", "Dec" }

aAnyvar = 1
aAnyvar = dw_main
aAnyvar = months
```

To use an Any variable, once you have assigned a value to the variable, you must assign the Any variable's value to a variable of the appropriate datatype. To do this, you need to know the datatype the Any variable contains. To find out the datatype an Any

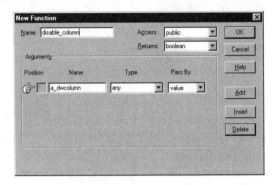

Figure 6.10   The function disable_column( )'s definition.

variable contains, call the **ClassName( )** function, passing the Any variable to the function. For example, the following function takes the Any variable passed (a_logdata) to it and uses the ClassName( ) function to determine the variable's type:

```
Choose Case ClassName(a_logdata)
Case "integer", "long", "double", "unsignedint", "unsignedlong"
    // handle numeric data
Case "string", "char"
    // handle character data
Case Else
    // handle other datatypes
End Choose
```

Any variables give the developer a great deal of power and flexibility, especially when dealing with functions. They provide a way to overload a function without creating multiple versions of it. For example, suppose you create the function **disable_column( )** to set the passed DataWindow column's Tab Order to 0. Disable_column( ) has a single argument of type Any that will either be a string containing the column name or a long containing the column number. Figure 6.10 shows disable_column( )'s definition.

Disable_column( ) calls ClassName( ) to determine the value's datatype within a_dwcolumn. If this value is a number, then the column number has been passed to the function. If the value is a string, then the column name has been passed. Once the function determines the argument's actual datatype, the function, in turn, creates the appropriate string and calls the **Modify( )** function to set the Tab Order to 0. The code for disable_column is:

```
/************************************************************************
** This function sets the Tab Order of the passed DataWindow column to 0.
** This function uses the Any datatype to pass either the column name
** (string), or number (long).
************************************************************************/
```

```
integer     iColNum
string      sColName

Choose Case ClassName( a_dwcolumn )
    Case "string", "char"
        sColName = a_dwcolumn
    Case "integer", "long", "double", "real", "decimal", &
      "unsignedinteger", "unsignedlong"
        iColNum = a_dwcolumn
        sColName = "#" + string( iColNum )
    Case Else
        sColName = ""
End Choose

// Set the column's Tab Order to 0
If dw_master.Modify( sColName + ".TabSequence=0") = "" Then
    Return True
Else
    Return False
End If
```

Taking the possibilities of the Any datatype to the extreme, you can define any function with only two arguments: an Any array passed by reference and an Any array passed by value. This will let any number of values with any datatype be passed to the function. The only reason to pass the two Any arrays is to let either array make a copy of the values passed to the function (passing by value) or to let the values of the passed items be changed within the function (passing by reference).

Doing this will eliminate the need to overload the function by creating multiple versions of the function. In essence, you are overloading the function within one place! However, doing this requires the addition of extra code within the function to parse the array and make the calls to ClassName( ) to determine the arguments' number and type. For example, you can consolidate the three print_error( ) functions into a single function defined as follows:

```
boolean print_error(any a_datalistval[], any a_datalistref[])
```

This function's code is:

```
/*************************************************************************
** This function displays an error message. The function accepts either a
** message number and text, a custom message string, or the
** PowerBuilder Error object via the Any datatype.
*************************************************************************/
string      sMsgText
any         aDatalist[]
int         iNumItems, iItem
error       myError
```

continues

```
// Check to see if the data is passed by value or reference
iNumItems = UpperBound(a_datalistval[])
aDatalist = a_datalistval[]
If iNumItems = 0 Then
    iNumItems = UpperBound(a_datalistref[])
    aDatalist = a_datalistref[]
End If

For iItem = 1 To iNumItems
Choose Case ClassName(aDatalist[iItem])
    Case "integer", "long"     // Check for message number
        sMsgText = sMsgText + string(aDatalist[iItem]) + ": "
    Case "string", "char"      // Check for message text
        sMsgText = sMsgText + aDatalist[iItem]
        a_datalistref[iItem] = "blah"
    Case Else
        // Check for Error object
        If aDatalist[iItem].typeof() = error! Then
            myError = aDatalist[iItem]
            sMsgText = sMsgText + string(myError.number) + ": " + &
            myError.text
        Else
            MessageBox("Error", "Invalid item passed to print_error()")
        End If
End Choose
Next

// Display the error message
MessageBox("Application Error", sMsgText)
Return True
```

The way PowerBuilder calls this function depends on whether you desire to pass the arguments by value or by reference. In the case of print_error( ), the data is not being changed, so the function could always pass its arguments by value, as shown for the three different scenarios:

```
any    aDatalist[]
char   cRefval[]
aDatalist[1] = 100
aDatalist[2] = "Customer already exists."
print_error(aDatalist, cRefval)

any    aDatalist[]
char   cRefval[]
aDatalist[1] = "Your custom error message here."
print_error(aDatalist, cRefval)

any    aDatalist[]
char   cRefval[]
aDatalist[1] = error
print_error(aDatalist, cRefval)
```

To call these functions by reference, simply switch the order of the two arguments.

Well, this all sounds great, right? Like all good things, there are some disadvantages to using the Any datatype. First of all, using the Any variables will slow performance due to the overhead involved in determining the variable's actual datatype. Also, you will often not find the errors you encounter when using Any variables until runtime.

In general, you should be careful when using Any variables. The best use of Any variables is as a function argument. As shown previously, it gives a great deal of flexibility to the developer with regard to the functions. A good practice is to always use the **ClassName( )** function to determine an Any variable's actual type and to cast it to a variable of that type once you know the type. In this case, the Any variable is used as an open "pipeline" into a function, but is reset to a true datatype early within the function's code.

PowerScript Functions versus External Functions

Designers and developers of PowerBuilder applications need to consider how and when to use external functions instead of PowerScript functions.

You should use external functions for one of two reasons: (1) when you cannot do a particular function by using PowerScript or (2) when performance is an issue. The ability to generate compiled machine code within PowerBuilder 6 improves the PowerBuilder applications' performance and should therefore reduce the number of cases in which you use the external functions only for performance purposes. However, there will still be situations in which you may want to develop CPU-intensive processes within a 3GL like C or C++.

In addition to developing custom DLLs, PowerBuilder can use several third-party DLLs to provide a specific set of functionality. Examples include various graphics packages, email interfaces, and network operating system interfaces.

USER OBJECTS

Another useful mechanism for developing modular and object-oriented code with PowerBuilder is the User Object. By using User Objects, PowerBuilder developers can develop reusable objects. You can develop some of the more common objects of an application as User Objects, and then share the objects throughout the application.

Types of User Objects

There are two main types of User Objects: visual and class (nonvisual, or NVO). The visual User Object includes standard, custom, and external. The class User Object includes standard and custom types.

Visual: Standard

You can use the standard User Objects to extend the standard PowerBuilder objects' functionality. For example, if a command button's functionality is repeated in different places within an application, you can create a standard command button User Object (see Figure 6.11).

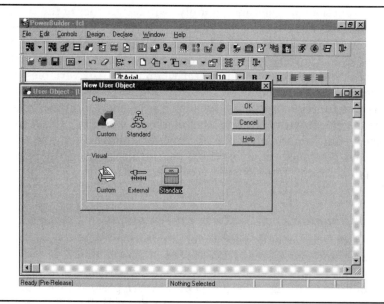

Figure 6.11   Creating a standard visual User Object.

To demonstrate, consider an application that has two unrelated windows called w_window1 and w_window2. Each window has a close button that closes the window. You can implement this by creating a close command button on each window or by having a single User Object command button and placing the button on each window. In the first case, you will have to write duplicate PowerScript within each command button's clicked event. In the case of creating a User Object, you create the command button User Object and place all the PowerScript code within the User Object. Then, you can add the User Object to any window that needs the close functionality. You can do this as follows.

Create the windows, w_window1 and w_window2. Then create a command button User Object, as shown in Figure 6.12. Within the User Object's clicked event, place the following PowerScript:

```
Close(Parent)
```

Place the User Object on both (all) the windows, as in Figure 6.13.

Close

Figure 6.12   A command button User Object.

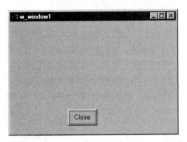

Figure 6.13   **User object placed on the window.**

TIP When you place a User Object on a window, PowerBuilder, in turn, creates an inherited instance of the original User Object. Looking more closely, the developer can see that PowerBuilder inherits the command button (User Object on the window) from the original User Object (u_close). (See Figure 6.14.)

Now that you have used the command button User Object within both the windows, if you ever wanted to change the User Object's attributes, you only need to do it at one level, that is, at the User Object level, and PowerBuilder will reflect the code within all places where you use the command button User Object.

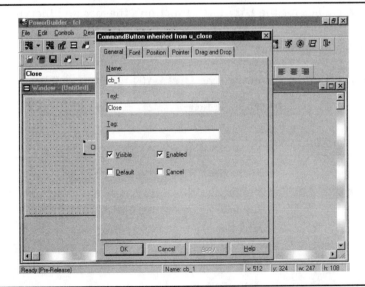

Figure 6.14   **Property Sheet showing the command button inherited from the User Object u_close.**

This is a simple example, but it demonstrates how a standard User Object can extend the base PowerBuilder objects' functionality. The example also shows how sharing code can simplify both development and maintenance.

TIP You could have achieved this functionality using inheritance by placing the User Object command button on a virtual window ancestor that both w_window1 and w_window2 were inherited from or by creating a global function that contains all the code for closing a window and calling the function from the command button. The third alternative is to create a custom class User Object with the methods for each type of command button functionality. This custom class User Object will instantiate the NVO within its constructor event. NVOs are discussed in detail later in this chapter.

You can create the standard User Objects with any of the 23 standard PowerBuilder object classes. Table 6.1 lists all the standard User Objects.

You can use a standard User Object to create several other types of objects. A few additional examples follow.

ListBox (Directory Listing Object) This example shows how you can use a ListBox User Object to encapsulate some simple functionality for a DOS directory listing. Once this is done, you can simply drop the User Object on any window and PowerBuilder empowers that window with DOS directory listing capabilities. Here's how to create this User Object.

Create a ListBox standard User Object from the User Object painter, and declare two instance variables for the **DirList( )** function's filespec and filetype parameters:

```
Uint      i_uiAllFiles    = 16400
String    i_sAllExtensions = "*.*"
```

Within PowerBuilder, prototype the **DirList( )** function as follows:

```
listboxname.DirList ( filespec, filetype {, statictext } )
```

Table 6.1   Standard User Objects

CheckBox	HScrollBar	RadioButton
CommandButton	ListBox	RichExtEdit
DataWindow	ListView	SingleLineEdit
DropDownListBox	MultiLineEdit	StaticText
DropDownPictureListBox	OleControl	Tab
EditMask	Picture	TreeView
Graph	PictureButton	VScrollBar
GroupBox	PictureListBox	

where **filetype** is an integer that represents the type of files you want to list within the ListBox:

0 indicates read/write files.

1 indicates read-only files.

2 indicates hidden files.

4 indicates system files.

16 indicates subdirectories.

32 indicates archive (modified) files.

16384 indicates drives.

32768 indicates that read/write files should be excluded from the list.

What's curious here is the recommended datatype of integer. The last **filetype** option is 32768, and the largest positive integer value (16-bit datatype) is 32767. Storing this field as an integer works, but it is quite confusing. If you would like to display only the directory names within a ListBox, pass the following filetype parameter:

```
32768 + 16 = 32784
```

PowerBuilder stores this value within memory as –32752. What happens is that PowerBuilder stores 32768 as a negative 32768, so:

```
-32768 + 16 = 32752
```

Since this parameter does not need to store negative numbers, use an unsigned integer datatype to make this less confusing. An unsigned integer datatype still allocates only a 16-bit memory address, but it uses the 16th bit, which is reserved for the sign (+/–), for the positive number. So the largest value that PowerBuilder can store within this address is 65535.

Place the following PowerScript within the **constructor** event:

```
this.DirList(i_sAllExtensions, i_uiAllFiles)
```

Place the following PowerScript within the **double-clicked** event:

```
String sItem

This.DirSelect(sItem)
This.DirList(sItem + i_sAllExtensions, i_uiAllFiles)
```

The last thing to do is to save the User Object and place it on the window (w_window1), as shown in Figure 6.15.

DataWindow You can also use the standard User Object to create the DataWindow control User Object. You can use this to code the generic DataWindow-related functionality such as drag-and-drop, error checking, and DataWindow messages. To demonstrate this concept, the following discussion presents an example of a standard DataWindow User Object.

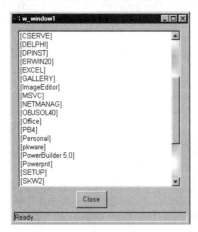

Figure 6.15 Placing the ListBox User Object on the window.

This example demonstrates how you can display all the field validation messages within a window message line as opposed to a standard message box. The message line also displays the tag messages for each column. This functionality is generic for all the editable DataWindows.

To do this, create a standard DataWindow User Object.

Place the following PowerScript within the User Object's **constructor** event:

```
/*****************************************************************************
** Insert a blank row within the DataWindow User Object. This is done only
** because you are using an external DataWindow to demonstrate the
** functionality. The actual User Object that you create does not need to
** include this line of code.
*****************************************************************************/

This.InsertRow(0)
```

Create a custom user event called Errormessage by selecting the **Declare** then **User Events...** menu options, as shown in Figure 6.16.

PowerBuilder, in turn, displays the User Events window. Create a custom event from this window, as shown in Figure 6.17.

Place the following PowerScript logic within the User Object's **ItemError** event:

```
/*****************************************************************************
** Trigger the errormessage event, set the focus to the DataWindow, and
** supress the system error screen.
*****************************************************************************/
```

```
This.Event ErrorMessage ()
SetFocus (This)

// Supress the system error message
Return 1
```

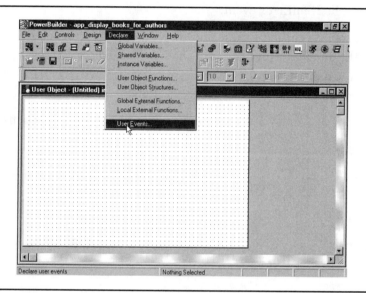

Figure 6.16 Creating the custom Errormessage user event.

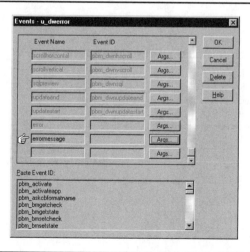

Figure 6.17 The user events window.

TIP An ItemError event occurs when a field is modified or loses focus and the current field does not pass the validation mask for its column.

With the introduction of parameterized events within PowerBuilder 5, the **Set-ActionCode( )** function became obsolete. The ItemError event now can return values which does the work for the SetActionCode( ) function. Here are some of the other return values for the ItemError event:

0 (default) rejects the data value and shows a system error screen.

1 rejects the data value but does not show a system error screen.

2 accepts the data value.

3 rejects the data value but lets the focus change.

Return to the w_window1 window and create the following functions:

```
f_DisplayErrMessage(string sErrMessage)

/*************************************************************************
** When a validation error occurs, display the validation message
** within the message line.
*************************************************************************/

st_message.text = sErrMessage
Beep(1)


f_DisplayTagMessage(string sMessage)

/*************************************************************************
** Display the sMessage string's contents within the message line
*************************************************************************/
st_message.text = sMessage
```

Place the following logic within the **Itemfocuschanged( )** event:

```
/*************************************************************************
** Retrieve the current column's tag value, and call the
** f_displayTagMessage function
*************************************************************************/
String    sMessage

// Retrieve the current column's tag value
sMessage = dwo.tag

// If no tag value is declared, PowerBuilder stores a "?" or a "!",
// then blanks out the tag message variable
If sMessage = "?" Or sMessage = "!" Then
    sMessage = ""
End If
```

```
// Call this function which should be declared within the DataWindow user
// object's parent window
Parent.DYNAMIC f_displayTagMessage(sMessage)
```

TIP For more details on the use of the DYNAMIC keyword in calling the function, refer to the function section earlier in this chapter.

Place the following code within the User Object's **Errormessage** custom event:

```
/*************************************************************************
** Obtain the validation message for the current column,
** evaluate the message for any embedded functions, and
** call the error message function to display the message.
*************************************************************************/
String     sErrMessage

// Obtain the validation message for the current column, and evaluate for
// any embedded functions
sErrMessage = dwo.validationmsg
sErrMessage = Describe(this,"evaluate("+sErrMessage+","&
             +String(GetRow(this))+")")
If sErrMessage = "!" Then
   sErrMessage = "Field is invalid (no message supplied)."
End If

// Call the following function, within the parent window, and pass
// the appropriate validation message to the function
parent.DYNAMIC f_displayErrMessage(sErrMessage)
```

Next, create a DataWindow object with the validation and tag values. Then place the User Object on w_window1 and execute the window. You will notice two things. First, when each field gets focus, PowerBuilder displays the tag message for that field within the message line, as shown in Figure 6.18. Second, when a validation rule evaluates to False, the validation message displays within the message line and a beep sounds, indicating an error.

TIP When a validation error occurs, you can choose to change the message text's color to red, to differentiate error messages from normal messages. You can do this within the w_window1 window's **f_DisplayErrMessage( )** function. Add the following line of code:

```
st_message.textColor = RGB(128,0,0)
```

Don't forget to change the text's color back to normal within the f_DisplayMessage( ) function.

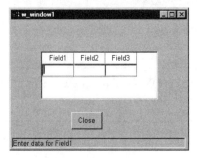

Figure 6.18   **The tag value displayed within the message line.**

Visual: Custom

The custom visual User Objects provide a level of flexibility beyond that of standard User Objects. With custom visual User Objects, you are not limited to the use of one PowerBuilder object. Rather, you can declare an object that includes multiple Power-Builder objects. This lets you create shared objects that are much more functional than the standard visual User Objects.

> **TIP** You can create custom User Objects not only with PowerBuilder objects but with other standard or custom visual User Objects.

The following examples further clarify some uses of the custom visual User Objects.

Directory Listing Object This example is an extension of the ListBox example from the standard visual User Object section, showing a more powerful use of the directory listing object. This example's directory listing object includes a more friendly interface. This object lets the user find a file by choosing the appropriate directory paths. When the user locates the file, the user can perform specific processing on the file. This is a generic object, which you can use on any window of an application by simply placing the object on the window.

To create the custom User Object, select the User Object painter. To create a new User Object, click **New**. PowerBuilder, in turn, displays the New User Object window, as shown in Figure 6.19. To create a new visual custom object, choose the **Visual Custom** option.

Next, create the controls. Place each of the objects on the User Object as shown in Figure 6.20. After placing the objects on the User Object painter, add the following Power-Script to the User Object. First, declare the following User Object instance variables:

> **TIP** This example uses the basic PowerBuilder objects, but each of the List-Boxes and DropDownListBoxes can be standard User Objects.

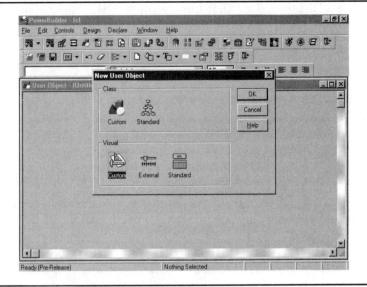

Figure 6.19   Creating a custom visual User Object.

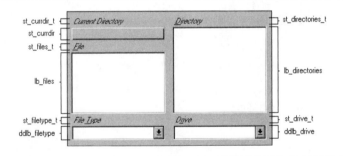

Figure 6.20   The controls that make up the custom User Object.

```
Uint       i_uiFiles = 0                    // Read/write files
Uint       i_uiDirectories = 16 + 32768    // Only subdirectories
Uint       i_uiDrives = 16384              // Drives
String     i_sExtension = "*.*"            // All files
```

Next, declare the following User Object external functions:

```
// change the directory to dirname
FUNCTION Int ChangeDir(String dirname) LIBRARY "pbdll.dll"
// get the current drive
FUNCTION String GetCurrDrive( ) LIBRARY "pbdll.dll"
```

These are two DLL functions that handle some of the application's functionality. They are explained later in conjunction with the C code for the DLL.

Place the following PowerScript within ddlb_drive's constructor event:

```
/*************************************************************************
** List the drives within the dropdown listbox, and choose the current
** drive
*************************************************************************/

This.DirList (i_sExtension,i_uiDrives,st_currdir)
This.SelectItem ("[-"+GetCurrDrive( ),1)
```

PowerBuilder does not provide a function to get the current drive's information. To set the ddlb_drive field with the current drive, write a custom DLL in C with the following code:

```
/*************************************************************************
** FUNCTION: LPSTR GetCurrDrive(void);
*************************************************************************/

LPSTR FAR PASCAL GetCurrDrive(void)
{
     int idrive = 0;
     LPSTR lpszString = "z";
     char caDrive[] = {'a', 'b', 'c', 'd', 'e', 'f', 'g', 'h', 'i',
                       'j', 'k', 'l', 'm', 'n', 'o', 'p', 'q', 'r',
                       's', 't', 'u', 'v', 'w', 'x', 'y', 'z' };
     idrive = _getdrive( );
     caDrive[idrive] = '\0';
     lpszString = &caDrive[idrive - 1];
     return (LPSTR) lpszString;
}
```

Place the following PowerScript within ddlb_drive's **SelectionChanged** event:

```
/*************************************************************************
** Get the selected directory, and call the DirList function to change the
** directory.
*************************************************************************/

String (sItem)
This.DirSelect(sItem)
lb_files.DirList (sItem+i_sExtension,i_uiFiles)
lb_directories.DirList(sItem,i_uiDirectories,st_currdir)
```

Place the following PowerScript within lb_directories's constructor event:

```
/***********************************************************************
** Call the DirList function to get the current drive's information
***********************************************************************/

This.DirList(i_sExtension,i_uiDirectories,st_currdir)
```

Place the following PowerScript within lb_directories's double-clicked event:

```
/***********************************************************************
** Get the selected directory, and call the DirList function to get
** information on the child directories.
***********************************************************************/

String     sItem

This.DirSelect(sItem)
lb_files.DirList (sItem+i_sExtension,i_uiFiles)
If sItem = "..\" Then
     sItem = "sdfsdfdsf"
Else
     ChangeDir("..")
End If

this.DirList(sItem + i_sExtension,i_uiDirectories,st_currdir)
```

Write the following function to handle the calling of the PowerBuilder **DirList( )** function twice within a script. Because the DirList( ) function actually changes the current directory to the directory selected, you must change the current directory back to the previous position before executing the DirList( ) function a second time.

```
/***********************************************************************
** FUNCTION: ChangeDir(const char *fname);
***********************************************************************/
int FAR PASCAL ChangeDir(const char *fname)
{
   return (int)_chdir(fname);
}
```

Place the following PowerScript within lb_files's constructor event:

```
This.DirList(i_sExtension,i_uiFiles)
```

Place the following PowerScript within lb_files's double-clicked event:

```
String    sPath
sPath = Trim( st_currdir.text)
If Not (Right(sPath,1) = "\") Then
     sPath = sPath + "\"
End If
Parent.DYNAMIC f_ProcessFile( sPath + This.SelectedItem( ))
```

The **f_ProcessFile( )** function is a hook to the parent window. This function is for any processing that needs to be done on the selected file. In this example, the function only displays the file within a message box. The function's prototype looks like:

```
Int f_ProcessFile(String sPathFile)
```

The PowerScript within the function looks like:

```
MessageBox("File Processing for...", sPathFile)
Return 1
```

Place the following PowerScript within ddlb_filetype's constructor event:

```
This.SelectItem(1)
```

Place the following PowerScript within ddlb_filetype's **SelectionChanged** event:

```
i_sExtension = Trim(Right(This.text,7))
lb_files.DirList (i_sextension,i_uiFiles)
```

The final step is to place the custom User Object on w_window1, and execute the window. The output should look like that shown in Figure 6.21.

When the gator.ini file is double-clicked, PowerBuilder displays the message box as shown in Figure 6.22.

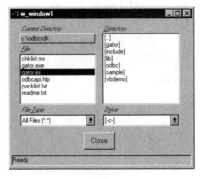

Figure 6.21   The completed window with the custom User Object.

Figure 6.22   The message box showing the complete path for the gator.ini file.

Figure 6.23   **A custom VCR control User Object.**

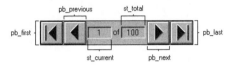

Figure 6.24   **The custom VCR User Object's controls.**

Custom VCR Controls Figure 6.23 shows a custom VCR control User Object that you can create to work with any DataWindow.

You can develop and bind this custom VCR control to any DataWindow at runtime simply by making one function call (see Figure 6.24). To create the VCR control, do the following:

1. Create a custom User Object. To create the custom User Object, select the User Object painter. To create a new User Object, click **New**. PowerBuilder, in turn, displays the New User Object window as shown in Figure 6.19. To create a new visual custom object, choose the Visual Custom option.
2. Create the controls as shown in Figure 6.24. Place each of the objects on the User Object as shown in the figure.
3. Place the following PowerScript logic within the different events of this custom User Object.
4. Declare the following two instance variables for the custom User Object:

```
// variable indicating the total number of rows
Uint            i_uiTotal
// variable pointing to the bound DataWindow control
DataWindow      i_dwControl
```

5. Within the User Object's constructor event, place the following PowerScript:

```
This.Width = 1215
This.Height = 165
```

TIP If an external object will set the User Object's width and height, create the two functions called:

```
f_SetWidth(Int iNewWidth)
f_SetHeight(Int iNewHeight)
```

---

6. Include the following five subroutines for the custom User Object:

Private Subroutine **f_nextrow ( );**

```
int     iCurrent
iCurrent = Integer(st_current.text)
If iCurrent < Integer(st_Total.text) Then
     i_dwControl.ScrollToRow(iCurrent + 1)
     st_current.text = String(iCurrent + 1)
     SetFocus(i_dwControl)
End If
```

Private Subroutine **f_previousrow( );**

```
int iCurrent
     iCurrent = Integer(st_current.text)
     If iCurrent > 1 Then
          i_dwControl.ScrollToRow(iCurrent - 1)
          st_current.text = String(iCurrent - 1)
          SetFocus(i_dwControl)
End If
```

Private Subroutine **f_lastrow( );**

```
st_current.text = st_total.text
i_dwControl.ScrollToRow(i_uitotal)
SetFocus(i_dwControl)
```

Private Subroutine **f_firstrow( );**

```
If i_uitotal > 0 Then
     st_current.text = "1"
     i_dwControl.ScrollToRow(1)
     SetFocus(i_dwControl)
End If
```

Public Subroutine **f_init** (DataWindow dwcontrol);

```
i_dwControl = dwControl
i_uiTotal = i_dwControl.RowCount( )
st_total.text = String(i_uiTotal)
```

These functions, except f_init, are called from the different PictureButtons within the VCR control:

The pb-first control's clicked event calls the **f-FirstRow( )** function.

The pb-previous control's clicked event calls the **f-PreviousRow( )** function.

The pb-next control's clicked event calls the **f-NextRow( )** function.

The pb-last control's clicked event calls the **f-LastRow( )** function.

You can now place the custom VCR User Object on a window with a DataWindow. The last step is to bind the two controls together. By calling the User Object's f_init( ) function and passing the DataWindow to the function, PowerBuilder will bind the two controls at runtime. Call the f_init( ) function after calling the bound DataWindow control's Retrieve( ) function.

For example, create a winodw w_window1, and place a DataWindow control dw_name on the window. Next, place the custom VCR control User Object. For the purposes of our discussion, let's call the User Object uo_vcr. Now, within the w_window1 window's open event, call uo_vcr's f_init( ) after you have called the Retrieve( ) function for the DataWindow. The code for the same is as follows:

```
dw_name.Retrieve( )
uo_vcr.f_init(dw_name)
```

TIP It is not necessary for the open event to call the f_init( ) function. The only requirement is that you must call the f_init( ) function only after the bound DataWindow's Retrieve( ) function.

At this point, you can now execute the window. The result looks like Figure 6.25.

CommandButton with Colored Text At times, you may want to change the text color of specific command buttons or picture buttons. Unfortunately, PowerBuilder does not permit developers to alter the standard command button or picture button controls' color. Consequently, you will have to resort to other means to accomplish this task. Here are some options:

- Use a third-party OCX or DLL that lets you change the text color.
- Write your own Custom Control DLL or OCX control.
- Create a custom User Object to accomplish this task.

If you choose to create a custom User Object, here is how you can do it.

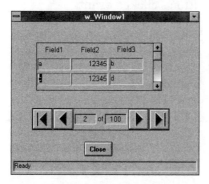

Figure 6.25   **The completed window with a DataWindow and the VCR control.**

Use a custom User Object with a command button (or picture button) and static text. Each time the user presses the command button, move the static text's X position to the right and the Y position down. Each time the user releases the command button (or presses up), move the static text back to its original position (see Figure 6.26).

When the user presses the button down, the st_text is moved X positions along the X axis and Y positions along the Y axis.

Declare two instance variables to store the st_text's initial X and Y positions:

```
UInt i_uiX
UInt i_uiY
```

Within the st_text's **Constructor** event, initialize the instance variables:

```
i_uiX = This.x
i_uiY = This.y
```

Declare the two user events for cb_button shown in Figure 6.27.

The ue_lbuttondown and ue_lbuttonup user events trap the Windows message associated with pressing the left mouse button down (on cb_button) and then releasing the left button (on cb_button), respectively.

Place the following PowerScript within the **ue_lbuttondown** event:

```
// moves the st_text 8 PowerBuilder units along the x-axis
st_text.x = st_text.x + 8
// moves the st_text 7 PowerBuilder units along the y-axis
st_text.y = st_text.y + 7
```

Place the following PowerScript within the **ue_lbuttonup** event:

```
// reset the st_text back to its original X and Y coordinates
st_text.x = i_uiX
st_text.y = i_uiY
```

Create another user event **ue_click** as shown in Figure 6.28.

Add the following code to the cb_button's clicked event:

```
// Trigger the ue_click event of the parent,
// which is the User Object itself.
Parent.Event ue_click ( )
```

Figure 6.26   The custom User Object with the CommandButton and static text controls.

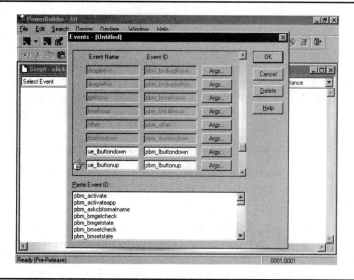

Figure 6.27   **Creating the ue_lbuttondown and ue_lbuttonup user events.**

When you place the User Object on the window, you can write code specific to your application within the object's ue_click event, from the Window painter. For this example, add the following code within the ue_click event:

```
MessageBox("Custom Command Button", "Clicked Event")
```

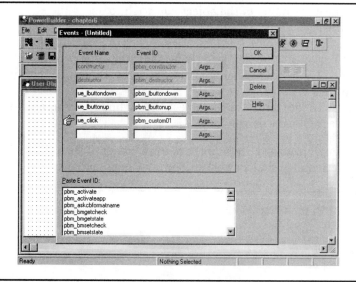

Figure 6.28   **Creating the ue_click user event.**

TIP You must create the ue_click event because you cannot access the events of each individual control that you use to build the custom control from within the User Object's instance. In short, because there is no clicked event for the User Object, you must simulate one. Within standard User Objects, the User Object's instance inherits all the original object's events. Within custom User Objects, because there can be multiple controls, the individual events are not inherited. (For further explanation and illustrations, see the *Standard and Custom User Object Class Hierarchy* section later in this chapter.)

Upon execution, PowerBuilder displays the message box shown in Figure 6.29.

Visual: External

The third type of visual User Object, the external User Object, is one of PowerBuilder's hooks to the outside world. PowerBuilder developers can either write a custom control DLL that they can use as an external User Object or use a third-party DLL. Several third-party vendors have written custom control DLLs, which you can use within Power-Builder by creating an external User Object. Blaise Computing, Inc., for example, has written a popular PowerBuilder third-party custom control DLL, the cpalette.dll. This DLL has a number of different class objects that you can declare as PowerBuilder external User Objects. PowerBuilder's earlier versions included this DLL. PowerBuilder 6's latest prerelease does not include the DLL, so we will not discuss it in detail here.

Table 6.2 shows a list of the classes within the cpalette.dll.

The steps to create an external User Object include:

1. Choose or write a custom control DLL.
2. Determine the class name of the object you wish to use.
3. Determine the style for the object.
4. Choose the external visual User Object as shown in Figure 6.30. PowerBuilder displays the User Object's property sheet as shown in Figure 6.31.
5. Provide the DLL's name, class name, and style for the control within the property sheet. Then click OK.
6. Save the User Object, and use the object throughout your application within custom visual User Objects or windows.

External User Objects are useful if there is an external DLL class of the object that provides the functionality that PowerBuilder objects do not. You can develop external

Figure 6.29   The resulting message box.

Table 6.2   Classes within the cpalette.dll

Class	Description
cpButton	Similar to a CommandButton except the text can be in different colors. The text also has a shadow.
cpCanvas	3-D background.
cpCheckBox	3-D checkbox with blue colors.
cpMeter	Meter window that monitors the progress (percent complete).
cpRadioButton	3-D radiobutton with blue colors.
cpStatic	3-D static text. This object has both a 3-D background and text.

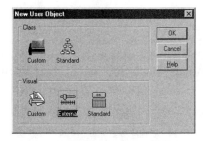

Figure 6.30   Creating an external visual User Object.

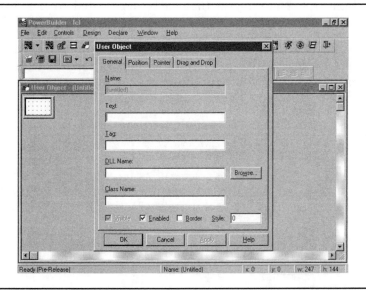

Figure 6.31   Set the external User Object's properties.

User Object DLLs, but you can achieve most of the functionality that you need from within PowerBuilder.

Class: Custom

Nonvisual objects (NVO) are objects with encapsulated functions, structures, and events that provide functionality to an application that is not visible to the user (refer to Figure 6.32). In an object-oriented environment, nonvisual User Objects are similar to classes.

General Concepts about NVOs

What Are NVOs? Custom class User Objects, better known as *nonvisual objects* (NVOs), are objects with encapsulated functionality that is not visible to the user. Each object has attributes or properties and methods or functions that perform processing related to the object and its attributes. NVOs are analogous to classes in C++ and other object-oriented programming languages. Once you have defined the processing within these classes, you can instantiate them by using the PowerBuilder CREATE statement.

NVOs versus Visual User Objects NVOs are very similar to the visual User Objects except that NVOs are not visual, which means you cannot place visual controls within an NVO.

NVOs versus Functions Several developers use global functions to write reusable, nonvisual processing. You should try to move as much of your processing from global functions to NVOs. The benefit of this is that you encapsulate all the processing into a few objects, and you can create and destroy the NVOs from the memory dynamically. Also, NVOs can take advantage of inheritance.

In PowerBuilder, the only objects that can be distributed are nonvisual objects. So by writing as much processing into NVOs as possible, your application will be scalable.

How to Build an NVO Use the User Object painter and choose the custom class. Next, you can create instance variables as Public, Private, or Protected within the NVO per your requirements. You can also create functions and events that perform different kinds of processing.

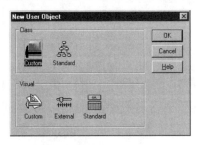

Figure 6.32   Creating a custom class User Object.

TIP You can review all the PowerBuilder objects in detail by using the Power-Builder Object Browser from the toolbar.

How to Create and Destroy NVOs When you build an NVO by using the User Object painter, you must instantiate the object within the application in one of the following ways:

Declaring a variable and creating the NVO into the variable.   Create an NVO called unv_app_service by using the User Object painter.

If this NVO's scope is global, then declare a global variable of type nonvisual object or of type fcl_unv_app_service.

```
unv_app_service gnv_asrv
```

From the application object's open event, create an instance of the object into the variable gnv_asrv.

```
gnv_asrv  = create fcl_unv_app_service
```

Once you have done this, you can call the NVO's methods. If you created a method called **myfunction( )** within fcl_unv_app_service, then you would call the method as follows:

```
gnv_asrv.myfunction ()
```

You are responsible for cleaning up the environment by calling the **destroy** statement:

```
destroy gnv_asrv
```

Creating the NVO onto itself.   In this example, follow the same rules as before, except there is no need to create a variable. The following statement will do the job:

```
unv_app_service = Create unv_app_service
unv_app_service.myfunction ()
```

The nice thing about this method is that you do not need to create any extra variables. The only problem is that you cannot debug the unv_app_service through the PowerBuilder debugger.

Again, you are responsible for cleaning up the environment by calling the destroy statement.

```
destroy unv_app_service
```

Using an NVO's AutoInstantiate attribute.   By using the NVO's autoinstantiate feature, as shown in Figure 6.33, you create the NVO before the first time PowerBuilder calls and destroys the object automatically. The nice thing about this is that you can call the myfunction( ) function from anywhere, and the first time you reference the object, PowerBuilder automatically instantiates the unv_app_service. When the user exits the application, PowerBuilder destroys the unv_app_service.

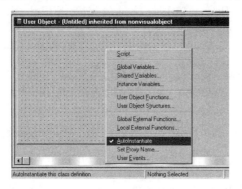

Figure 6.33   An NVO's autoinstantiate attribute.

This passes the responsibility of creating and destroying the NVO from the developer to PowerBuilder.

You can develop the NVO for different purposes. Some implementations of NVOs are:

- Application NVO
- Environment adapter NVO
- Business objects
- Multimedia NVO
- Print adapter NVO
- Email adapter NVO
- NOS adapter NVO
- SystemResource NVO

Application NVO Developers have always complained about not being able to inherit the application object or have a global variable object. Well, with NVOs, you can develop applications without having any global variables within the application painter. The advantage of doing so is that you can create your application object without the need to constantly cut and paste the global variables' latest version from the application object painter. If the application has a nonvisual User Object of type unv_app_service, you can place all the global variables and constants within this NVO with appropriate methods to set and get the variables to comply with good object-oriented programming practices. You can create an NVO with each application global variable declared as unv_app_service's instance variable. Of course, you can do this within the User Object painter. Once you do this by using the autoinstantiate method, as discussed earlier, PowerBuilder creates the object the first time your application references the object.

The other advantage of creating an unv_app_service is that you can inherit from the unv_app_service and create a descendant application object. The nice thing is that for those particular installations of the application that need some specific installation-based variables, you can instantiate the new NVO. Otherwise, you can instantiate the unv_app_service. This method minimizes the number of useless global variables within memory.

For example, you can place the following code within the application's open event:

```
If l_inifilesetting = "New York" Then
     //Create from descendant of unv_app_service
     gnv_asrv = create unv_app_service_ny
Else
     gnv_asrv = create unv_app_service
End If
```

The unv_app_service_ny is instantiated onto unv_app_service because all the global references within the application are done to the gnv_asrv. You should not use the autoinstantiate method in this case.

Let's create an application NVO with the following functionality (read *services*):

Error checking service.   Checks for application errors.

Multilingual service.   Sets the default language for the multilingual applications and gets the text for the buttons and MicroHelp from the database. You will also need to create the respective DataWindow objects for this service within your application.

Database service.   Gets the connection information from the .INI file or the registry and connects to the database.

MicroHelp service.   Sets the MicroHelp for the buttons and events.

Retrieve service.   Indicates whether PowerBuilder should display a message box when no rows are retrieved from the database.

To create the application NVO, choose the custom class User Object as shown in Figure 6.34.

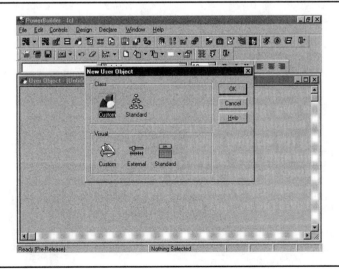

Figure 6.34   Creating a custom class nonvisual User Object.

Next, declare the following variables:

```
Instance variables
Private:
Window     iw_mdi_frame                //MDI Frame
String     is_app_reg_ini_file         //Registry or INI Information
Boolean    ib_msg_on_empty_retrieve
Boolean    ib_insertrow_on_empty_retrieve
DataStore ids_message                  // App messages
DataStore ids_microhelp                // Button Text, Microhelp
Int        ii_language_selected
Int        ii_default_language
String     is_helpfile

// Error & Message Handling
Boolean         ib_set_error

Public: //Use within the application
Int        II_NULL
String     IS_NULL
Date       ID_NULL
DateTime   IDT_NULL

Int        II_LAST_BUTTON_CLICKED

/* Constants */
constant Int II_SQL_SUCCESS       =  0
constant Int II_SQL_NOT_FOUND     =  100
constant Int II_SQL_ERROR         = -1
constant Int II_SUCCESS           =  1
constant Int II_CANCEL            =  0
constant Int II_FAILURE           = -2
constant Int II_ABORT             = -3
constant Int II_JUST              = -4 // Don't check for any changes
constant Long II_INFINITE         = 99999999

// Msg Constants
// Icon Assignments
constant Int II_NONE              = 0
constant Int II_INFORMATION       = 1
constant Int II_EXCLAMATION       = 2
constant Int II_QUESTION          = 3
constant Int II_STOPSIGN          = 4

// Button Combinations
constant Int II_WIN_OK            = 1
constant Int II_WIN_OKCANCEL      = 2
constant Int II_WIN_YESNO         = 3
constant Int II_WIN_YESNOCANCEL   = 4

// Button Clicked
constant Int II_CLICK_OK          = 1
constant Int II_CLICK_CANCEL      = 2
```

```
constant Int II_CLICK_YES       = 3
constant Int II_CLICK_NO        = 4

// Language Constants
constant Int II_ENGLISH         = 1
constant Int II_GERMAN          = 2
```

TIP The function declaration is shown next. The function's complete code is in the chapter6.pbl file on the CD-ROM that accompaines this book.

Next, declare the following functions:

```
uf_check_dberror ( )  returns boolean
uf_check_default_language ( ) returns integer
uf_close ( )
uf_db_connect ( string as_type ) returns integer
uf_decrypt ( string as_in ) returns string
uf_encrypt ( string as_in ) returns string
uf_get_insert_on_empty_retrieve ( ) returns boolean
uf_get_language ( ) returns integer
uf_get_mdiframe ( ) returns window
uf_get_msg_on_empty_retrieve ( ) returns boolean
uf_initialize ( ) returns integer
uf_load_app_from_ini ( string as_config, string as_application ) returns integer
uf_load_app_from_registry ( string as_registry_file ) returns integer
uf_profilestring ( string as_filename, string as_section, string as_key, string
     as_default ) returns string
uf_set_help_file ( string as_help_file_name )
uf_set_insert_on_empty_retrieve ( boolean ab_insert_on_empty_retrieve )
uf_set_language ( integer ai_language_id )
uf_set_language ( integer ai_language_id, integer ai_default_language_id )
uf_set_mdiframe ( readonly window aw_mdi )
uf_set_microhelp ( string as_microhelp )
uf_set_microhelp ( string as_msg_code, string as_msg )
uf_set_msg_on_empty_retrieve ( boolean ab_msg_on_empty_retrieve )
uf_show_help ( integer ai_topic ) returns integer
uf_show_help ( string as_keyword ) returns integer
uf_start_message_srv ( string as_dataobject, boolean ab_retrieve ) returns integer
uf_start_microhelp_srv ( string as_dataobject, boolean ab_retrieve )  returns integer
```

Save the User Object as unv_app_service.

TIP For more details on NVOs, refer to Chapter 22, "Distributed Application Development," Chapter 23, "Advanced Distributed Application Development," and Chapter 24, "PowerBuilder Foundation Classes."

Environment Adapter NVO You can use the environment adapter NVO to develop multiplatform applications. Before this example is explained, an explanation of the adapter concept is necessary since a number of the following examples take advantage of this concept.

The adapter concept is analogous to the plug-and-play concept that hardware vendors have made popular. This means that an object or application has a base state, and the object (or application) can adapt to any state by simply instantiating an NVO onto it. For example, a DataWindow can have several attributes such as form or list processing, updatable, or read-only, or even single- or multi-select. You can create an NVO for each of these attributes. If the DataWindow needs to have any of these attributes, you can instantiate the appropriate NVO onto the DataWindow.

In the case of the environment adapter NVO, functionality can exist for an application that is specific to an operating system. For example, you can create different NVOs for each operating system (see Figure 6.35). Within the application's startup processing or the window's open event, you can check the environment variable for the type of operating system.

```
Choose Case environment.ostype
    Case aix!
        u_osapi_nvo = create u_aix_nvo
    Case hpux!
        u_osapi_nvo = create u_hpux_nvo
    Case macintosh!
        u_osapi_nvo = create u_macintosh_nvo
    Case sol2!
        u_osapi_nvo = create u_solaris_nvo
    Case windows!
        u_osapi_nvo = create u_win16_nvo
    Case windowsnt!
        u_osapi_nvo = create u_win32_nvo
End Choose
```

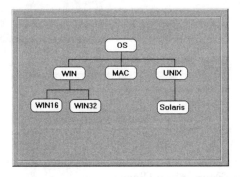

Figure 6.35 Sample environment adapter NVO hierarchy.

Business Objects This example is probably the most important of all the NVO examples. Application developers need to place much of their business rules and processing within different NVOs. The main reason is that the business rules and processes are separate from the interface logic. The GUI can call the different business object NVOs. For example, a financial application can have a series of financial NVOs. An insurance company can have a generic insurance NVO and a home insurance NVO, life insurance NVO, and auto insurance NVO inherited from the generic insurance NVO.

The discussions about business objects is deferred to Chapter 22, "Distributed Application Development," and Chapter 23, "Advanced Distributed Application Development," where the various implementations of the business objects and application partitioning in general are covered. One thing to keep in mind is that the only objects within PowerBuilder that can be distributed are the NVOs.

Multimedia Objects You can create an NVO to implement much of the functionality available through the Windows multimedia API. The main Windows multimedia API is the mmsystem.dll. (There are others, but this is the primary one.) A nonvisual User Object ancestor tree for handling several of the multimedia capabilities available by using the mmsystem API might look like the one in Figure 6.36.

The u_MMBase User Object will have generic functions such as checking for the appropriate drivers, file I/O operations, and other generic functionality that is common among the different multimedia objects.

One of the main functions within the u_MMAudio nonvisual User Object is to play a wave (.WAV) file. You can create a PowerBuilder nonvisual object that plays a wave file by doing the following:

1. Declare a local external function within the User Object:

```
Function Boolean SndPlaySound(String sWaveFile, Int iflags) &
    Library "mmsystem.dll"
```

2. Declare a local PowerScript function:

```
boolean f_PlayWave (string sWavePathFile)
Return SndPlaySound(sWavePathFile,0)
```

Simply calling the function f_PlayWave(sWavePathFile) and passing a wave file to the function plays the wave file's sound. This is just one example of a multimedia function. You can write several others and include them within nonvisual User Objects.

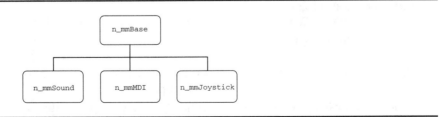

Figure 6.36   A multimedia nonvisual User Object ancestor tree.

Print Adapter NVO Table 6.3 shows a list of functions that you can include within a User Object for doing all kinds of print I/O.

Email Adapter NVO An email object could include functions to log in, validate an email address, display an address list, send mail, attach file(s), retrieve a count of the new mail, and display mail (read or unread). You can write different NVOs for the different email protocols. For example, you can write NVOs for MAPI, VIM, X.400, and PROFS. Some of the NVOs will take advantage of PowerBuilder's email capabilities (MAPI), while other NVOs will be defined with global external functions. When the application is started, based on the email connectivity for the workstation, the application will instantiate the appropriate email NVO.

NOS Adapter NVO A NOS (Network Operating System) User Object could include functions to get the network ID, the workstation ID, servers, mapped drives, mapped printers, and the like.

SystemResource NVO You can use a custom class User Object to encapsulate the system resource functionality. Within this example, you can define the Windows SDK functions as local external functions, and you can write the three PowerScript methods/functions to retrieve the GDI, memory, and resource values. What follows is an example of how you can use the system resources within a sample About dialog box.

The About box in Figure 6.37 displays the percentage of free GDI, resources, and the amount of free memory. Most About box windows display a snapshot of the free resources from when the user first opened the About box window. The About box window refreshes the values by using the window's timer event. The window in the figure gets this information by using the System Resource User Object.

You can create the Systeminfo User Object by defining a custom class User Object. A custom class User Object is actually a nonvisual object.

The first thing you must do is declare the two SDK local external functions, one from the user library and one from the kernel library, as shown in Figure 6.38.

Table 6.3 Functions for the Print Adapter NVO

Member Functions	*Description*
f_dwPrint(DataWindow dwName, Integer iCount**)**	Print from 1 to N DataWindows.
f_Print(String sFilePathName, String sFileType, Integer iCount**)**	Print from 1 to N files of type (BMP or TXT).
f_getAvailablePrinters( )	Return an array of printer info structure. This function gets the name, drive map, and device map for each printer.
f_setDefaultPrinter( )	Pass the structure of the printer that needs to be set as the default printer.
f_setPrintOrientation(Integer iStyle**)**	Dynamically change the print setup's orientation from landscape to portrait and vice versa.

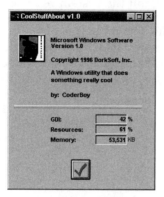

Figure 6.37   The About box with system resources.

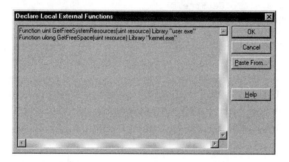

Figure 6.38   Declaring local external functions to obtain the system resources.

The next thing that you must do is declare the following two instance variables:

```
uint g_GDI = 1
uint g_USER = 2
```

Pass these variables as parameters to the **GetFreeSystemResources( )** function. If you pass G_GDI to the function, the function returns the percentage of free GDI resources. If you pass G_USER to the function, the function returns the percentage of free user resources.

Next, declare the three Resource User Object functions as follows:

```
GetFreeGDI ()
Return GetFreeSystemResources(G_GDI)
GetFreeMem ()
// returns free memory in KB
Return Truncate(GetFreeSpace(0)/1024, 0)
GetFreeUser ()
Return GetFreeSystemResources (G_USER)
```

These are the PowerScript functions that call the system resource SDK function:

- The **GetFreeMem( )** function returns the amount of free memory in kilobytes.
- The **GetFreeUser( )** function returns the percentage of free user resources.
- The **GetFreeGDI( )** function is the same as the GetFreeUser( ) function except the G_GDI variable is passed in as a parameter, and the function returns the percentage of free GDI resources.

Use the NVO's Autoinstantiate attribute. Within the About dialog box, add the following PowerScript to reuse the Systeminfo User Object. Place the following PowerScript within the window's open event:

```
Timer(.1)
```

The following PowerScript is within the window's timer event:

```
timer(5)
st_memory.text = String(u_sysinfo.GetFreeMem( ),"#,###")
st_gdi.text = String(u_sysinfo.GetFreeGDI( ))
st_resources.text = String(u_sysinfo.GetFreeUser( ))
```

The About dialog box example shows how you can reuse a custom class User Object.

Class: Standard

The latest addition to the User Object family of types is the standard class User Object. The standard class User Object permits the developers to build nonvisual User Objects of the PowerBuilder nonvisual datatypes shown in Figure 6.39.

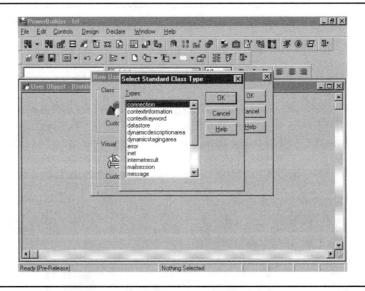

Figure 6.39 The PowerBuilder nonvisual datatypes.

You can declare a nonvisual standard User Object of the class shown in Figure 6.39 and then customize the object. Also, you can modify the default global variables, as shown in Figure 6.40.

With this feature, you can create any of the aforementioned standard class User Objects. For example, you can add extra variables to the default Message object to track additional error information. You can also create a standard transaction class User Object and define local external functions for RDBMS RPCs.

To create the standard transaction class User Object, do the following:

1. Within the User Object painter, select **New**.
2. Choose **Standard Class** from the New User Object dialog box.
3. Choose the transaction from the select standard class type dialog box.
4. Declare the following local external function:

```
function double spb8(ref double prm) rpcfunc subroutine
mypt(string prm) rpcfunc ALIAS FOR "pbdbms.put_line" subroutine
mygt(ref string prm, ref integer status) rpcfunc ALIAS FOR
    "pbdbms.get_line"
```

5. From the application painter, change the global transaction datatype to the standard transaction class User Object's name.
6. From the PowerScript painter, code the following function in PowerScript:

```
Int     myresult=5
myresult=sqlca.spm8(myresult)
If SQLCA.SQLCODE <> 0 Then
    MessageBox ("error", SQLCA.SQLERRTEXT)
End If
```

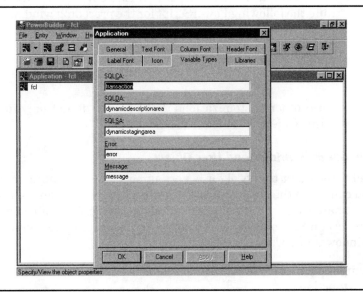

Figure 6.40   **The PowerBuilder default global variables.**

Here is another example of the transaction User Object. Create a standard trans-action class User Object with a function called **ODBCConnect( )**. The function's PowerScript should look like:

```
This.dbms = "ODBC"
This.dbparm = "ConnectString='DSN=Powersoft Demo
DB;UID=dba;PWD=sql'"
testtrans trans
trans = This
CONNECT using trans;
Return This.SQLCODE
```

This PowerScript is just an example, but you can place all the logic for the ODBC transaction processing within this function. Also, this User Object can handle the pro-cessing for obtaining the dbparm settings. Once the User Object is created, you can save the object as testtrans. Within the application window's event, you can create the fol-lowing PowerScript to connect to an ODBC data source using the developed function:

```
testtrans trans
trans = CREATE testtrans
If trans.odbcconnect( ) = -1 Then
   // Error processing
     ...
End if
```

If you change the global transaction SQLCA variable from transaction to testtrans, you need to substitute the following PowerScript for the preceding window's PowerScript:

```
If SQLCA.odbcconnect( ) = -1 Then
   // Error processing
     ...
End If
```

There are several other customizations that you can do not only to the standard transaction class User Object, but also to all the others.

Interfacing between Windows and User Objects

As mentioned throughout this book, it is very important to modularize your code into objects so you can reuse the objects within other parts of the system (or other systems). When placing shared User Objects on the windows, some form of communication be-tween the window and the objects must take place. You can implement communication between a window and a User Object by:

- Referencing the window generically
- Executing functions
- Adding User Objects to the window painter toolbar

Referencing the Window Generically

When developing the generic User Objects, it is often necessary to reference the parent window on which the User Object will reside. There are a number of ways to reference the parent window from a User Object:

- Hard-coding
- Passing the window name from the window (using this)
- Referencing the window from the constructor event (using the parent)

Hard-Coding The simplest—but worst—method of referencing the parent window from a User Object is hard-coding the window name from the User Object. The main reason this is bad is because it requires the developers either to use the User Object within windows having a standard name or to maintain the User Object's multiple instances.

If you decide to hard-code the window name, following are four different implementations.

Method 1 Reference the hard-coded window's name each time you need it. For example, create a window called w_window1 with the two standard User Objects, as shown in Figure 6.41.

From the User Object painter, place the following PowerScript within the uo_max button's clicked event:

```
w_window1.WindowState = Maximized!
```

From the User Object painter, place the following PowerScript within the uo_restore button's clicked event:

```
w_window1.WindowState = Normal!
```

Hard-coding the window name works unless you decide to place the User Objects on another window. If you would like these User Objects to be on another window, you must change the hard-coded window name and you must save each User Object under another name. Too many copies of an object can lead to resource problems. This example only has one line of PowerScript behind each User Object, but if the User Object were more complex, you would hard-code the window's name in several places (events and functions) within the User Object. This will be a maintenance nightmare.

Figure 6.41   Sample window with the two standard User Objects.

Method 2 The second method of referencing the parent window from a User Object is an extension of the first in that the window name is still hard-coded, but you hard-code the name within one location. You create an instance variable of the type Window. You then initialize the instance variable within the User Object's constructor event.

Declare an instance variable:

```
window i_wParent
```

Within the User Object's constructor event, initialize the instance variable:

```
i_wParent = w_window1
```

Throughout the User Object's events and functions, you can reference the window by using the i_wParent variable. Although this second method is inefficient, at least it binds the window name to the instance variable within a single place. This is certainly preferable to doing so within every function and event that the parent window needs to reference. This method is also a maintenance nightmare, however, because if you need to add any code to the User Object, you must add all the code to all the copies of the User Objects that are saved under another name.

Method 3 Although the third method still involves hard-coding the parent window name, all the other code is inherited. You need to initialize the parent window name by using an init function that is called from the constructor event—the Private function f_init( ):

```
i_wParent = w_window1
```

Call the f_init( ) function from the constructor event, for example:

```
f_init( )
```

The big advantage of this method over the other hard-coded methods is that when other copies of the User Object are needed for other windows, you can inherit a User Object from the base uo_max User Object. The only code you need to place within the inherited User Object will be an f_init( ) function initializing the window's other window name. Although this is still not a preferred method of referencing the parent window, it is much better than Methods 1 and 2.

Passing the Window Name from the Window (Using This) You can pass the window names to the User Object in a more generic way than hard-coding by using the reserved word, this. Similar to Method 3, you need to create a User Object function, in this case, Public Function f_init(window wParent):

```
i_wParent = wParent
```

This function is then called from the open event of the User Object's parent window:

```
uo_max1.f_init(This)
```

Once f_init( ) is called, the User Object can reference a generic instance variable. Thus you can use this User Object within several different windows.

Referencing the Window from Constructor Event (Using Parent) This method may be even more efficient because it does not require an f_init( ) function to initialize the parent window's name. The only line of code that you must add is within the User Object's constructor event:

```
// initialize the User Object's instance variable to the parent window
i_wParent = Parent
```

This is probably the most efficient of the strategies discussed within this section.

Executing Functions

Executing User Object functions from within a window is simple. For example, to execute an f_init( ) function within uo_test, write the following PowerScript:

```
uo_test.f_init( )
```

TIP You must declare the f_init( ) function as a public function if PowerBuilder must execute the function from a parent window. By parsing through the Window control[ ] array, you can reference the different controls of a window. The problem with this method is that if there is more than one User Object, it is difficult to know which one to execute. If, as part of the window's initialization, a User Object f_init( ) function must be executed within all windows, you can use the control array.

Adding User Objects to the Window Painter Toolbar

This is a simple but helpful option within the Window painter. You can define commonly used User Objects within the Window painter toolbar (PainterBar) as an icon. This is a quick way to place the User Objects on a window from the Window painter. To add an icon to the Window PainterBar, do the following:

1. Click the right button of your mouse on the Window PainterBar.
2. Choose **Customize...** from the popup menu, as shown in Figure 6.42.
3. Choose the **Custom** radiobutton.
4. Drag and drop a toolbar icon from the selected palette on the current toolbar. The window in Figure 6.43 appears.
5. Choose the **User Object...** CommandButton. The window in Figure 6.44 appears.
6. Choose a User Object, then click OK. The window in Figure 6.45 appears.
7. Fill the **Item Text** and the **Item MicroHelp** edit fields, then click OK.
8. PowerBuilder, in turn, displays the new User Object toolbar within the PainterBar.

Dynamic User Objects

You can open the PowerBuilder User Objects dynamically on a given window. You can also create, destroy, move, and hide them dynamically. This makes the PowerBuilder User Objects very powerful. Table 6.4 shows a list of functions you can use to make the User Objects operate dynamically.

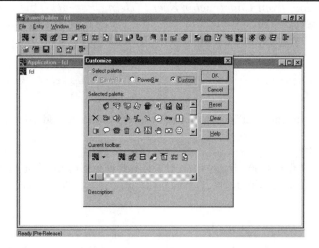

Figure 6.42 Adding a User Object to the window PainterBar.

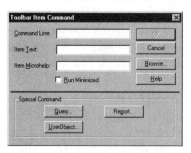

Figure 6.43 The Toolbar Item command window.

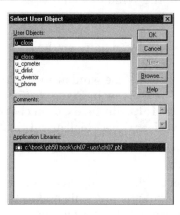

Figure 6.44 The Select User Object window.

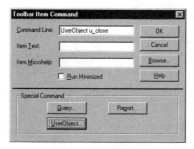

Figure 6.45   **The Toolbar Item command window after selecting a User Object.**

Table 6.4   Functions for Making the User Objects Operate Dynamically

Function Name	Description
ClassName( )	Returns an object's PowerBuilder base class. A base class could be a DataWindow, CommandButton, User Object, and so on. This function stores the result as a string.
CloseUserObject( )	Closes a User Object. In essence, this function destroys the User Object's instance.
CloseUserObjectWithParm( )	Works the same as **CloseUserObject** except the function also sets a parameter within the global message structure.
Drag( )	Starts or finishes the window control's dragging.
DraggedObject( )	Returns a reference to the object that is currently being dragged. Stores the result within a variable of type **DragObject**. This is a datatype that can store a reference to all the PowerBuilder objects.
Move( )	Moves an object to another position within the current window.
OpenUserObject( )	Opens a User Object's instance. This function basically instantiates a User Object within a window.
OpenUserObjectWithParm( )	Works the same as **OpenUserObject** except the function also sets a parameter within the global message structure.
PointerX	Returns the number of PBUs an object is located from the left of the window.
PointerY	Returns the number of PBUs an object is located from the top of the window.
SetPosition( )	Specifies a control's position in a front-to-back order.
TypeOf( )	Works the same as **ClassName** except the function returns an enumerated datatype instead of a string.

The example in Figure 6.46 shows how to open, move, and close the dynamic User Objects by simulating some features of the PowerBuilder Window painter.

Figure 6.46 Simulating some of the PowerBuilder window painter's features to open, move, and close the User Object dynamically.

First, create the standard User Objects for each of the nine controls within the toolbar (i.e., CommandButton, PictureButton, StaticText, SingleLineEdit, ListBox, CheckBox, RadioButton, DataWindow, and DropDownListBox).

Within the Window painter, create a new window, and then declare an instance variable:

```
// reference each toolbar clicked by a number
integer i_iType
```

Within each of the toolbar controls' clicked event, place the following PowerScript (with the exception of the number):

```
// the number 1 is for a command button
i_iType = 1
```

Within the toolbar items' **dragleave** event, place the following PowerScript:

```
This.TriggerEvent(Clicked!)
```

Within the window's **dragdrop** event, place the following PowerScript:

```
Choose Case i_iType
    Case 1
        OpenUserObject(u_CommandButton, PointerX( ), PointerY( ))
        p_CommandButton.Invert = True
        p_commandbutton.Enabled = False
    Case 2
        OpenUserObject(u_PictureButton, PointerX( ), PointerY( ))
        p_PictureButton.Invert = True
        p_picturebutton.Enabled = False
    Case 3
        OpenUserObject(u_StaticText, PointerX( ), PointerY( ))
        p_StaticText.Invert = True
        p_statictext.Enabled = False
```

```
    Case 4
        OpenUserObject(u_SingleLineEdit, PointerX( ), PointerY( ))
        p_SingleLineEdit.Invert = True
        p_singlelineedit.Enabled = False
    Case 5
        OpenUserObject(u_Listbox, PointerX( ), PointerY( ))
        p_Listbox.Invert = True
        p_listbox.Enabled = False
    Case 6
        OpenUserObject(u_checkbox, PointerX( ), PointerY( ))
        p_CheckBox.Invert = True
        p_checkbox.Enabled = False
    Case 7
        OpenUserObject(u_radiobutton, PointerX( ), PointerY( ))
        p_RadioButton.Invert = True
        p_radiobutton.Enabled = False
    Case 8
        OpenUserObject(u_DataWindow, PointerX( ), PointerY( ))
        p_DataWindow.Invert = True
        p_DataWindow.Enabled = False
    Case 9
        OpenUserObject(u_dropdownlistbox, PointerX( ), PointerY( ))
        p_DropDownListBox.Invert = True
        p_dropdownlistbox.Enabled = False
    Case Else
        String      sType
        DragObject  doObject
        doObject  =  DraggedObject( )
        Move(doObject, PointerX( ), PointerY( ))
        i_iType = 0
        sType ="~nMoved TypeOf = "
        Choose Case TypeOf(doObject)
            Case CommandButton!
                sType = sType + "CommandButton"
            Case PictureButton!
                sType = sType + "PictureButton"
            Case StaticText!
                sType = sType + "StaticText"
            Case SingleLineEdit!
                sType = sType + "SingleLineEdit"
            Case ListBox!
                sType = sType + "ListBox"
            Case CheckBox!
                sType = sType + "CheckBox"
            Case RadioButton!
                sType = sType + "RadioButton"
            Case DataWindow!
                sType = sType + "DataWindow"
            Case DropDownListBox!
                sType = sType + "DropDownListBox"
        End Choose

        sType = sType + "~nTo:~tX = "+String(PointerX( ))+&
            "~tY = " + String(PointerY( ))
        MessageBox("Dynamic User Objects",sType)
End Choose
```

Figure 6.47 **Adding a command button User Object to the window.**

Figure 6.47 shows the result of dragging the command button object from the toolbar onto the window's main section.

The code to delete the object is within the p_Trash control's **dragdrop** event. The code is as follows:

```
Choose Case Typeof( DraggedObject( ))
    Case CommandButton!
        CloseUserObject(u_CommandButton)
        p_CommandButton.Invert = False
        p_commandbutton.Enabled = True
    Case PictureButton!
        CloseUserObject(u_PictureButton)
        p_PictureButton.Invert = False
        p_picturebutton.Enabled = True
    Case StaticText!
        CloseUserObject(u_StaticText)
        p_StaticText.Invert = False
        p_statictext.Enabled = True
    Case SingleLineEdit!
        CloseUserObject(u_SingleLineEdit)
        p_SingleLineEdit.Invert = False
        p_singlelineedit.Enabled = True
    Case ListBox!
        CloseUserObject(u_listbox)
        p_ListBox.Invert = False
        p_listbox.Enabled = True
    Case CheckBox!
        CloseUserObject(u_checkbox)
        p_CheckBox.Invert = False
        p_checkbox.Enabled = True
    Case RadioButton!
        CloseUserObject(u_radiobutton)
        p_RadioButton.Invert = False
```

```
                p_radiobutton.Enabled = True
     Case DataWindow!
          CloseUserObject(u_DataWindow)
          p_DataWindow.Invert = False
          p_DataWindow.Enabled = True
     Case DropDownListBox!
          CloseUserObject(u_dropdownlistbox)
          p_DropDownListBox.Invert = False
          p_dropdownlistbox.Enabled = True
End Choose
```

Object-Oriented Programming and User Objects

PowerBuilder User Objects use several object-oriented techniques and concepts such as inheritance, polymorphism, encapsulation, and classes.

Inheritance and User Objects

PowerBuilder implements inheritance with User Objects in two ways:

- Object level
- Control level

Object Level To create the User Objects at the object level, you can use the User Object painter. For example, if an application uses three different implementations of DataWindows, such as a master DataWindow, a detail DataWindow, and a stand-alone list DataWindow, you can establish an inheritance tree that includes the common modules within the highest ancestor. Though these DataWindows are different, they have some basic similarities. Error checking within the DataWindow's DBError event, for example, will be similar on all the three types of DataWindows. Tag and validation message handling will also be similar among the three DataWindows. When there are similarities among the multiple User Objects, you can create a User Object hierarchy to share the common modules, such as the one in Figure 6.48. You can place this hierarchy within nonvisual User Objects and instantiate on the visual User Object based on the type of processing required.

You can develop much of the common functionality at the u_dw_ancestor level. You can declare the specific functions, events, structures, and variables that relate only to the lower-level inherited DataWindow User Objects, like u_dw_master. Inheritance within PowerBuilder can be multiple levels deep.

TIP When creating a standard User Object, all the encapsulated attributes, events, and functionality of the base PowerBuilder classes are inherited into the standard User Object. When creating a custom User Object, the events for the User Object are fixed and predetermined. They are not inherited from any base PowerBuilder class.

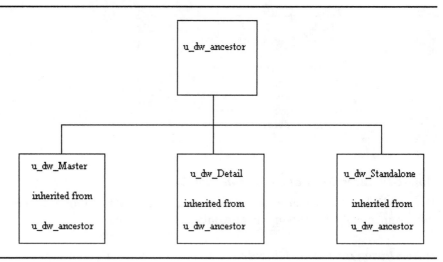

Figure 6.48   Sample User Object hierarchy.

Control Level When the developer places a normal PowerBuilder control on a window's surface from the Window painter, the developer, in essence, creates a local control that is inherited from the base classes built into PowerBuilder, as exemplified in Figure 6.49.

It works the same way with User Objects. The User Object control placed on the window is actually inherited from the User Object created within the User Object painter.

Polymorphism and User Objects

You can implement polymorphism (for definition and discussion, see Chapter 2, "Application Architectures") by using events and functions within User Objects.

Events In the last standard DataWindow example, you could implement polymorphism by placing the generic code within the DBError event and extending the processing to handle more specific error handling within the descendant events.

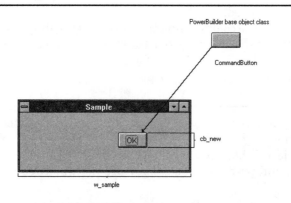

Figure 6.49   A local control inherited from the base class.

Functions You can implement polymorphism with functions in roughly the same way. The main difference is that you cannot extend the functions; you can only override them. For example, a function **f_foo( )** is declared at different places within the hierarchy, but in this case the ancestor object calls the function. Figure 6.50 shows that the f_foo( ) function is declared in two places, within u_dw_ancestor and u_dw_master. However, only the u_dw_ancestor User Object calls the f_foo( ) function.

Within this example, when you place the u_dw_master User Object on a window, upon execution, PowerBuilder executes the function at the descendant level and ignores the function at the ancestor level. When you declare either the u_dw_detail or u_dw_standalone User Object on a window, upon execution, PowerBuilder executes only the f_foo( ) function at the ancestor.

The developer should take advantage of the polymorphism's power, both by way of events and functions, to enable reusable code and minimize duplicate code.

Standard and Custom User Object Class Hierarchy

Standard User Objects and custom User Objects have different inheritance structures. You inherit the standard User Objects from the basic PowerBuilder object classes; you inherit the custom User Objects from the User Object class. Figure 6.51 clarifies this concept.

Standard User Object Class Hierarchy The standard User Objects inherit their attributes, events, and functions directly from a particular PowerBuilder object class. Inheriting directly from the base object class makes the User Object itself become an object of that particular object class, thus encapsulating all the attributes and events of that class. For example, the base object class that the standard command button User Object is inherited from is the PowerBuilder CommandButton class. This causes the User Object to inherit all the events and attributes of a command button. When the User Object is placed on a window, to the developer, it looks just like a command button.

TIP Several of the functions that are particular to the object classes are encapsulated into the PowerBuilder objects at the object base classes.

Custom User Object Class Hierarchy The custom User Objects, as opposed to standard User Objects, inherit their attributes and events from the User Object base class. The

---

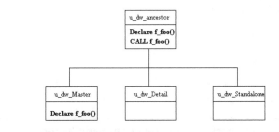

Figure 6.50   Declaring a function in multiple places within an object hierarchy.

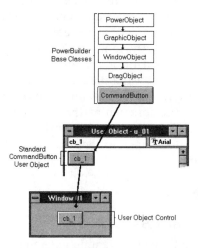

Figure 6.51   **The hierarchy of the standard CommandButton User Object.**

custom User Objects differ in this way because they can contain several different objects that are each inherited from a particular object class. Figure 6.52 shows a simple custom User Object with two command buttons. The diagram shows how the User Ob-

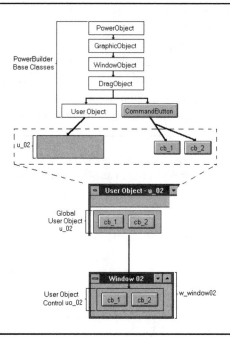

Figure 6.52   **A simple custom User Object with the two CommandButtons.**

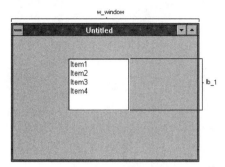

Figure 6.53   A PowerBuilder ListBox class declared on a window.

ject itself is inherited from the User Object class, while the command buttons are each inherited from the CommandButton base class. When you place a custom User Object on a window, the object inherits only the User Object's events and attributes, not those of each of the individual objects.

Encapsulation and User Objects

Some encapsulation is built into PowerBuilder by default. PowerBuilder also has built-in flexibility to extend the default functionality by using custom encapsulation. Custom encapsulation refers to the capability to extend the base classes' functionality. For the definition and further discussion of encapsulation, see Chapter 2, "Application Architectures."

Inherent Encapsulation Inherent encapsulation is a PowerBuilder feature built into the painters and objects. All PowerBuilder objects have encapsulated events, attributes, and functions. Figure 6.53 shows an example of a PowerBuilder ListBox class declared on a window.

From the export file of this window, this section declares a global standard ListBox User Object called u_listbox that is inherited, by default, from the PowerBuilder ListBox base class:

```
global type u_listbox from ListBox
end type
```

The following code, which is declared as part of the object when you create the object, shows all the encapsulated attributes and events for the u_listbox User Object:

```
global type u_listbox from listbox
int Width=494
int Height=361
int TabOrder=1
boolean DragAuto=true
BorderStyle BorderStyle=StyleLowered!
boolean VScrollBar=true
```

continues

```
long TextColor=33554432
int TextSize=-10
int Weight=400
string FaceName="Arial"
FontFamily FontFamily=Swiss!
FontPitch FontPitch=Variable!
end type
global u_listbox u_listbox
on rbuttondown;
    // place code for this event here
end on
on selectionchanged;
    // place code for this event here
end on
on constructor;
    // place code for this event here
end on
on destructor;
    // place code for this event here
end on
on doubleclicked;
    // place code for this event here
end on
on dragdrop;
    // place code for this event here
end on
on dragenter;
     // place code for this event here
end on
on dragleave;
    // place code for this event here
end on
on dragwithin;
     // place code for this event here
end on
on getfocus;
     // place code for this event here
end on
on losefocus;
     // place code for this event here
end on
on other;
     // place code for this event here
end on
```

When PowerBuilder creates the User Object, place the object on the w_window window as shown in Figure 6.53. As you drop the User Object on the window, Power-Builder defines a local listbox, called lb_1, which is inherited from u_listbox.

```
type lb_1 from u_listbox within w_window
end type
```

The following program listing shows all the descendant attributes and events for lb_1. Note that only the attributes that are changed at the descendant level are visible within the export file. Because the User Object (lb_1) is, by default, inherited from the global User Object (u_listbox), all the events of the lb_1 are extended from the corresponding u_listbox events.

When an event is extended, the ancestor event is executed before the descendant event begins execution. PowerBuilder knows to call the ancestor script because it generates the following code:

```
on selectionchanged;
    // Calls the ancestor script
    call u listbox::selectionchanged;
    // place descendant code here...
end on
```

Although the code to execute the ancestor event (call u_listbox::selectionchanged) is not visible from the painters, you can see it when you export the window.

```
type lb 1 from u listbox within w window
int X=572
int Y=237
end type
on selectionchanged;
    call u listbox::selectionchanged;
    // place descendant code here...
end on
on constructor;
    call u listbox::constructor;
    // place descendant code here...
end on
on destructor;
    call u listbox::destructor;
    // place descendant code here...
end on
on doubleclicked;
    call u listbox::doubleclicked;
    // place descendant code here...
end on
on dragdrop;
    call u listbox::dragdrop;
    // place descendant code here...
end on
on dragenter;
    call u listbox::dragenter;
    // place descendant code here...
end on
on dragleave;
    call u_listbox::dragleave;
    // place descendant code here...
end on
on dragwithin;
```

continues

```
  call u_listbox::dragwithin;
      // place descendant code here...
end on
on getfocus;
      call u_listbox::getfocus;
      // place descendant code here...
end on
on losefocus;
      call u_listbox::losefocus;
      // place descendant code here...
end on
on other;
      call u_listbox::other;
      // place descendant code here...
end on
on rbuttondown;
      call u_listbox::rbuttondown;
      // place descendant code here...
end on
```

Ancestor Events Return Value You now have a variable called AncestorReturnValue available to you within all the descendent scripts. This variable contains the ancestor script's return value. This variable is generated even when you override the ancestor script.

Custom Encapsulation The term *custom encapsulation* within User Objects merely refers to PowerBuilder's flexibility in letting the developers extend the base classes' functionality. You can extend the base classes by declaring encapsulated events, public, private, or protected object-level functions (using PowerScript or external), and variables (local and shared). You can extend or override both the standard and the custom events at any level of the visible ancestor tree. Again, all this flexibility demonstrates the tool's flexibility and object orientation.

Defining C++ Classes with User Objects

C++ developers often find it difficult to relate several of the object-oriented concepts from C++ to PowerBuilder. C++ developers will find the environment more familiar as they understand how PowerBuilder is structured. C++ developers should study some of the ways PowerBuilder implements inheritance, polymorphism, and encapsulation. The most obvious similarity between PowerBuilder and C++ is the way each defines classes.

As demonstrated throughout this chapter, PowerBuilder lets developers develop totally customizable classes (objects) through its User Object painter. When you export a User Object into an .SRU file, it becomes clear how similar the object declarations are to the C++ classes. Developers should also notice the capability to declare public, private, and protected functions. A developer should also look at the Library painter's object class browser to see the attributes and functions (methods) encapsulated within controls and objects. The object class browser, in addition to listing the application objects' ancestor structure, lists the internal ancestor structure for its object class inheritance hierarchy. As developers become familiar with the different types of User Objects (especially nonvisual User Objects), they will become very useful.

CHAPTER 7

Graphs and Reporting

Using graphs and reports to present information to the user can be an effective and important part of a PowerBuilder application. Graphs and reports let the user view data in a meaningful fashion. This chapter discusses the following topics related to graphs and reporting:

- Graphs
- Parts of a graph
- Overlays
- Using graphs
- Manipulating graphs
- Drill-down graphs
- 3-D graphs
- Reports
- Report painter/InfoMaker
- Printing reports
- Saving reports

GRAPHS

Parts of a Graph

PowerBuilder offers several types of graphs, including area, bar, column, line, pie, and scatter graphs. Each type of graph provides a different presentation of data to the user. You can find a complete description of each type of graph and its particular use within the *PowerBuilder User Guide*. PowerBuilder lets the developer change the graph type by using the Graph Object dialog box's Graph tab, shown in Figure 7.1.

Although the data presentation differs, each graph type's parts are the same. The parts of a PowerBuilder graph are:

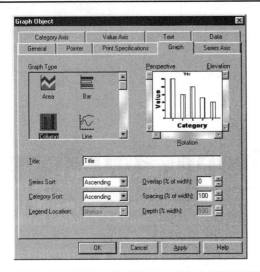

Figure 7.1   The graph object dialog box.

- Category
- Value
- Series

A discussion of each of these parts follows.

Category

The category represents a grouping of data points within a graph. A category may contain a literal, an expression, or a column. When using a literal as the category, PowerBuilder groups all the data into a single category and displays the category's value along the category axis. When using a column as the category, PowerBuilder displays the data within the graph with each unique column value representing a category. Because bar and column graphs change the orientation of the graph's axis, PowerBuilder does not always associate the category with the X axis.

   Within both the two-dimensional and three-dimensional graphs, PowerBuilder associates the category with the X axis for area, line, and column graphs and with the Y axis for bar graphs. The pie chart displays the category as a colored portion or slice of the pie. When using code tables within a DataWindow graph, you can use the **LookupDisplay( )** function to display a code table's display values, rather than the data values. For example, LookupDisplay( ) is used in Figure 7.2 to decode the value of fin_data_code, a DataWindow column that uses a code table. This function shows the code table's display value instead of the data value on the graph.

   Figure 7.2 also shows how you can assign multiple values within a category by separating the values with a comma. Each of the values then appears within the graph at the end of the category. A typical use of the multiple values within a category is the cre-

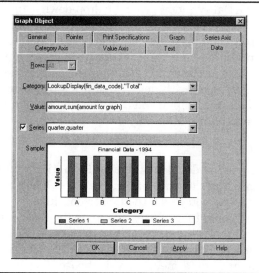

Figure 7.2   Using the LookupDisplay( ) function to return a code table's display value.

ation of a Total category that sums the categories within the graph. Figure 7.2 defines the extra text entry "Total" within the category section. This category corresponds to the sum (columnname for graph) entry within the Values section. The resulting graph in Figure 7.3 shows the total amount of expenses across all the expense types.

Value

The value is the scale that represents the category's measure within the graph. This component is associated with the Y axis within both 2-D and 3-D area, line, and column graphs, and the X axis within the bar graph. When the graph style is pie, PowerBuilder selects the data values as a percentage of the total value amount.

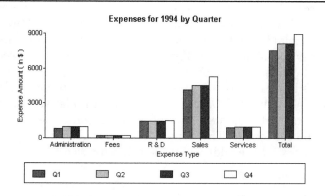

Figure 7.3   Expenses by type per quarter.

Within the value section of the DataWindow graphs, a drop-down listbox (DDLB) shows all of the columns within the DataWindow as well as the aggregate functions **Count( )** and **Sum( )**. The function Count( ) (columnname for graph) is for nonnumeric columns, and the function Sum( ) (colunmname for graph) is for numeric columns. This lets the developer choose one of these items and see the values for the entire graph. In addition, the Value item can perform any type of arithmetic calculation by specifying the operation within the Sum( ) function. For example, you can use the function Sum (amount/2 for graph) to divide an expense amount column by 2.

Series

The graph's series component lets the developer show information that relates to similar instances of categories. PowerBuilder automatically creates a legend with color-differentiated series components when you check the Series checkbox.

By indicating the series components, the user is able to display each instance side by side. A series graph might show total sales by sales representative or sales by a specific billing date. PowerBuilder will show the series value within the graph differently, depending on the graph's type and the dimension you choose. PowerBuilder will plot the 2-D area and line graph series in a different color on the same X and Y grid. Within the 2-D bar and column graph, PowerBuilder denotes the series by a different colored column within the Y and X axis, respectively.

When PowerBuilder displays a 3-D graph, PowerBuilder shows the series within the Z axis for the area, line, column, and bar graphs. If you specify a series, PowerBuilder graphs each item within the series for each category. A pie graph shows a different-sized pie segment for each series.

An example of a series is similar classes of data but a different instance, such as the Mercedes model numbers of 300, 500, or 700. Each model number has its own data point, but PowerBuilder graphs them on the same X and Y coordinates.

Overlays

You can use overlays within a graph to illustrate a trend or to call attention to a specific piece of information within a column or bar graph. The overlay functionality graphs a set of coordinates over an existing graph. You can define an overlay as a set of information from a DataWindow column or as a specified type. PowerBuilder automatically adds the overlaid item to the legend with an appropriate symbol to denote its values. The developer specifies the overlay syntax within the series section.

One type of overlay lets the developer overlay data points, and add the points to the DataWindow graph's legend. The column name you use within the overlay syntax must be a column you define within the DataWindow. PowerBuilder selects the column and graphs the data points, and then adds each of the data points associated with the column to the graph and the legend. This type of overlay is good for denoting data of special interest. The syntax for the addition of the column name is:

```
"@overlay~t" + columnName
```

The other type of overlay lets the developer specify a secondary value item and label the associated data points with a value name. In the second type of overlay, the syntax is:

```
"@overlay~tValueName"
```

PowerBuilder automatically adds the value name to the legend and shows the overlay in a different color.

Figure 7.4 shows the definition of a DataWindow graph that shows the total expenses for each quarter and overlays the sales expenses by using the value name within the series section. Figure 7.5 shows the resulting graph.

In this example, the total expenses are overlaid to illustrate how much of the total expenses are sales expenses. The overlay is useful to show a trend or relevant detail on one graph.

Using Graphs

You can use PowerBuilder graphs within a DataWindow or Window object. This section discusses both types of graphs.

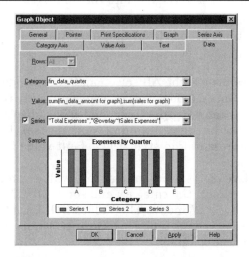

Figure 7.4   Overlaying sales expenses onto the total expenses graph.

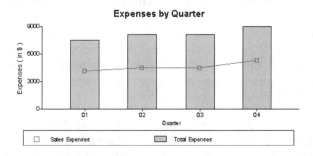

Figure 7.5   Resulting graph showing sales expenses overlaying total expenses per quarter.

Graphs in the DataWindow

The most frequent use of graphs is within a DataWindow. Because the graph is tied to the data within the database, it lets the graph change with the data rather than being static. You can create a DataWindow graph either as a separate object within a DataWindow object or define it as a DataWindow's presentation style.

Graph DataWindow Objects You can create and place a graph object within an existing or new DataWindow by entering the chosen DataWindow and clicking the graph icon. In addition to the category, values, and series parts of a graph discussed earlier in this chapter, DataWindow graphs (both graph DataWindow objects and graph presentation styles) let the developer specify the number of rows of data to use within the graph. The Rows value may contain one of the following:

All graphs all of the data that is retrieved into the DataWindow.

Page graphs all of the data that is retrieved into the displayed DataWindow by page.

Group graphs the data that has been retrieved into a DataWindow and grouped within a report.

Because most application graphs use the **All** selection, PowerBuilder chooses this as the default choice. For graph DataWindow objects, you can modify the Rows value by selecting the **Data** tab of the graph's **Properties...** dialog box (displayed when you select the graph object and click the right button of your mouse). However, for a DataWindow that uses a graph presentation style, the default value for **Rows** is **All** and you cannot change this value.

The **Data** tab also lets the developer specify the category, values, and series for the graph. For all the DataWindow graphs, the category and series DDLBs contain a list of the columns defined within the DataWindow. The Values DDLB contains the same list of columns as well as the aggregate functions **Count( )** (for all nonnumeric columns) and Sum( ) (for all numeric columns).

Graph Presentation Style Rather than creating a graph object within a DataWindow, it is often desirable to represent an entire DataWindow as a graph. You can do this by selecting the graph item when choosing a presentation style within the new DataWindow screen.

In this scenario, you can resize the graph by resizing the DataWindow control during execution. Like graph DataWindow objects, the developer defines the rows, category, values, and series for the graph by using the same methods and rules. The only difference is that the graph is saved as a DataWindow, not as an object within a DataWindow (as the DataWindow object graph is).

Graph Functions Graph functions let the developer do character manipulation or arithmetic on the graph data. For the DataWindow graphs, you can use several of the same functions used with the DataWindow with the graphs. The following lists some of the functions you can use with the DataWindow graphs:

RowCount( ) counts all of the rows that are retrieved.

Sum( ) calculates the sum of the items within the brackets.

Avg( ) computes the average of the numbers within the brackets.

LookupDisplay( ) uses the value from a DataWindow codes table to show the value's display value.

Figure 7.2 shows an example of using the **LookupDisplay( )** function.

Adding a Button Object to the Graph DataWindow With PowerBuilder 6, you can add a new control (a button object) within the graph DataWindow. With PowerBuilder's previous versions, you would add the DataWindow and button control within a window. Now you can associate a button object within the DataWindow itself. You can choose from a number of different actions to associate with the button object within the DataWindow including Query Clear, Query Mode, Query Sort, Retrieve, Save Rows As, Sort, Update, and so on. In addition, you can associate a picture bitmap with the button object it will display.

Graphs in the Window

Usually you create a graph within a DataWindow because it is easier to manipulate, and the graph ties directly to the data within the database. However, you can also create and manipulate graphs within a window. Because the window graph does not directly tie to the data within a database, the developer must create functions or scripts to create and populate the graph. You can create graphs within a window by choosing the toolbar's graph icon. When you add the graph object to the window, you can manipulate the object programmatically by using the several graph functions that PowerBuilder provides. For a complete list of the graph functions, refer to the PowerBuilder documentation.

You can create the graph in Figure 7.6 as follows.

The code behind the graph button calls the window function **graph( )**, which is defined as Boolean. The code for this function uses the **Addseries( )** and **AddData( )** functions to add the data about the series on the category line. The function's first line resets all of the graphical data by using the function **Reset( )**.

```
// Code for graphing within a window
gr_1.Reset(all!)

// create the series
int iSeries, iRtn
this.setredraw(false)

// Create the PC series
iSeries = gr_1.AddSeries("PC")
iRtn = gr_1.AddData(iSeries, 9, "Jan")
iRtn = gr_1.AddData(iSeries, 19, "Feb")
```

continues

```
iRtn = gr_1.AddData(iSeries, 22, "Mar")
iRtn = gr_1.AddData(iSeries, 25, "April")
iRtn = gr_1.AddData(iSeries, 36, "May")

// Create the Mainframe series
iSeries = gr_1.AddSeries("Mainfrm")
iRtn = gr_1.AddData(iSeries, 19, "Jan")
iRtn = gr_1.AddData(iSeries, 23, "Feb")
iRtn = gr_1.AddData(iSeries, 27, "Mar")
iRtn = gr_1.AddData(iSeries, 30, "April")
iRtn = gr_1.AddData(iSeries, 39, "May")

// Create the Mini series
iSeries = gr_1.AddSeries("Mini")
iRtn = gr_1.AddData(iSeries, 12, "Jan")
iRtn = gr_1.AddData(iSeries, 30, "Feb")
iRtn = gr_1.AddData(iSeries, 27, "Mar")
iRtn = gr_1.AddData(iSeries, 33, "April")
iRtn = gr_1.AddData(iSeries, 42, "May")

this.setredraw(true)
return true
```

The script from the graph button produces the graph in **Figure 7.6**. This graph illustrates the mainframe, mini, and PC sales for the months of January through May. You can add other functions or buttons that will manipulate or alter the graphic values.

Manipulating Graphs

Once you create a graph either within a window or DataWindow, you can alter it's attributes programmatically. Attributes include both the graph's visual and data attributes. Visual attributes include the graph type, title, axis, and legend. Data attributes

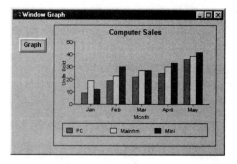

Figure 7.6   **A window graph showing computer sales.**

include such things as the number of categories and series within a graph, data values, and the style of a data point or series. This section discusses how to retrieve and modify a graph's visual and data attributes.

Visual Attributes You can change the visual attributes of a graph within a window or DataWindow simply by specifying the graph's attribute and the attribute's new value.

PowerBuilder uses an internal object called grDispAttr to maintain the graph's display attributes at runtime. PowerBuilder uses this object to maintain the display attributes of the title and legend graph components. You can alter each of these components by using the appropriate TitleDispAttr or LegendDispAttr values. You can change any of the display attributes listed in Table 7.1.

You could use these attributes, for example, to write a script for a button within a window that changes a window graph's title to "Total Sales," changes the title to italic, changes the legend's text to italic, and changes the legend's size to 20 point:

```
// Change the title and legend's attributes for a window graph
gr_1.Title = "Total Sales"
gr_1.TitleDispAttr.Italic = TRUE
gr_1.LegendDispAttr.Italic = TRUE
gr_1.LegendDispAttr.TextSize = 20
```

With this code within the Modify button's clicked event, the graph from the preceding example looks like that in Figure 7.7 after the user clicks the **Modify** button.

Table 7.1   The Display Attributes

Attribute	Description
Alignment	Graph alignment
AutoSize	To turn the Autosize for the DataWindow on or off
BackColor	The graph's background color
Escapement	The text's rotation
FaceName	The text's font
FillPattern	The object pattern to be filled with color
FontCharSet	The text's font character set
FontFamily	The group of typefaces
FontPitch	The text's horizontal spacing
Format	Value for the valid formatting
Italic	Italicize text
TextColor	Text color
TextSize	Text size
UnderLine	Underline text
Weight	Number to indicate the text's line thickness

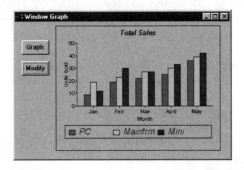

Figure 7.7   Modifying the graph title programmatically.

TIP To change the text's size within either the title or legend, be sure to disable the AutoSize attribute.

Unfortunately, when you close the graph, PowerBuilder will not save the changes with the graph. If the changes that are made to the graph need to be made before the graph is shown to the user, you can create a user-defined event and map the event to the PowerBuilder event pbm_dwngraphcreate. The section drill-down graphs later in this chapter includes an example that illustrates the user-defined event.

Data Attributes PowerBuilder provides a set of functions for retrieving and modifying a graph's data attributes. You can use the following functions to retrieve a window graph's data attributes:

CategoryCount( ) returns the number of categories within a graph.

CategoryName( ) returns the category's name and its internal number (integer).

DataCount( ) returns the number of data points within a series.

GetDataStyle( ) returns a data point's color, fill pattern, or visual property.

FindCategory( ) returns the number of a category, given its name.

FindSeries( ) returns the number of a series, given its name.

GetData( ) returns the data value, given its series and position.

SeriesCount( ) returns the number of series within a graph.

SeriesName( ) returns the name of a series, given its number.

GetSeriesStyle( ) returns the color, fill pattern, or visual property of a specified series.

With DataWindow graphs, each time the DataWindow retrieves information from a database, PowerBuilder destroys the graph and any changes that the developer made to the graph are lost. The developer can, however, place the data access code within a user event that calls the appropriate function.

The PowerBuilder event ID pbm_dwngraphcreate is triggered by a DataWindow control after it has created a graph and populated the graph with data, but before displaying the graph. The developer can create a user-defined event called pregraph, and map the event to the PowerBuilder event ID called pbm_dwngraphcreate, as shown in Figure 7.8.

A good use of this is to change a graph's title before showing the graph to the user. The next example illustrates this.

Drill-Down Graphs

A drill-down graph lets users click on the specific data that they would like to see in a more detailed (different) graph. You can achieve the capability that lets users point and click within a graph by creating a clicked script within the DataWindow control or the window control.

You enable this capability by using the data attribute **ObjectAtPointer( )** function. This function returns the object type that the user clicked on as a grObjectType enumerated datatype. In addition to returning the object type, ObjectAtPointer( ) also returns the series number and data point number that were clicked. These values are stored within the function arguments passed by reference to ObjectAtPointer( ).

TIP ObjectAtPointer( ) should be the first function you call within the clicked event's script for the graph control because you can decide about the rest of the drill-down from the values the function returns. Also, you should place any debug stops after the call to ObjectAtPointer( ) because the pointer must be on the graph, not on the debug window, when PowerBuilder executes this function.

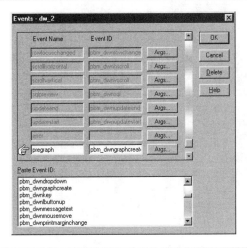

Figure 7.8   **Creating the pregraph user event.**

The following example of a drill-down graph shows the use of a user-defined event mapped to the PowerBuilder event pbm_dwngraphcreate, the use of the function ObjectAtPointer( ), and the altering of the other graphic data. In this example, the top graph in Figure 7.9 illustrates the total salaries within the company by department. When the user clicks on the column for one of the departments, the bottom graph fills with information about the choice ("Shipping" in this example). In addition, the color and the title are set from gathering the information by using the PowerBuilder Graph Functions.

First, create two graph DataWindows (dw_dept and dw_company) with a SQL Select data source. Next, create a window (w_emp_sal) that includes both of the DataWindows. Make the first DataWindow control, dw_1, visible, and make the second DataWindow, dw_2, invisible initially. When the user clicks on one of the columns in the first graph, PowerBuilder fills the second DataWindow with the appropriate data related to the department that the user clicked. The code for the open event for window w_emp_sal is:

```
// Open script for Employee Salaries window w_emp_sal
dw_1.SetTransObject(sqlca)
dw_2.SetTransObject(sqlca)
dw_1.Retrieve ()
```

This code assumes that you have set up SQLCA correctly and as the transaction object for both dw_1 and dw_2. After setting the transaction object, PowerBuilder retrieves the data for the top DataWindow and displays the department salaries graph.

The code for the clicked event for the company DataWindow dw_1 calls ObjectAtPointer( ) to gather the graph's name, series, and category. Next, the code places the category into a variable, sDept, which the code then uses to retrieve the second DataWindow, dw_2. Next, the code displays the DataWindow dw_2 to the user by using the show( ) function:

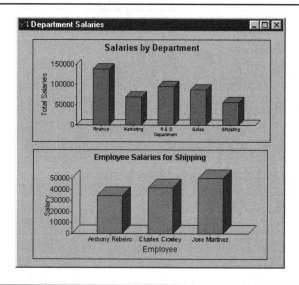

Figure 7.9   **Example of a drill-down graph.**

```
/* Clicked script for dw_1 */
grObjectType    ClickedObject
string          sDept, sGraphName="gr_1"
int             iRtn, iSeries, iCategory

/* Find out where the user clicked within the graph */
ClickedObject = this.ObjectAtPointer (sGraphName, iSeries, iCategory)

/* If the user clicked on data or category, find out which one */
if ClickedObject = TypeData! or &
    ClickedObject = TypeCategory! then
    sDept = this.CategoryName (sGraphName, &
iCategory)
    dw_2.Modify (sGraphName + ".title=" + &
"'Employee Salaries for " + sDept + "'")
    dw_2.Retrieve(sDept)
    dw_2.Show()
else
    MessageBox (Parent.Title, "Click on a department to display detailed information")
end if
```

Finally, create a user-defined event (pregraph) for the DataWindow dw_2, and map the event to the PowerBuilder event ID pbm_dwngraphcreate. This event fires before PowerBuilder draws the graph on the screen, and it will change the color of the series to purple before displaying the graph to the user:

```
/* Pregraph script for dw_2 */
string      sSeriesName
string      sGraphName = "gr_1"
int         iResult

/* Get the name of its series, and set the color of that series to purple */
sSeriesName = SeriesName (sGraphName, 1)
iResult = SetSeriesStyle (sGraphName, sSeriesName, &
    Foreground!, RGB (255, 0, 255) )
```

By using the Graph functions, you can determine the series and style from the data and then alter them programmatically by using the Set functions.

3-D Graphs

In addition to the various types of 2-D graphs that have been discussed, PowerBuilder also provides the capability to create 3-D graphs as both window and DataWindow graphs. When using 3-D graphs, the developer can alter the graph's elevation, depth, rotation, and perspective. You can do this by selecting any 3-D graph type within the graph properties dialog box (display by selecting the graph object, clicking the right button of your mouse, and selecting **Properties...**), as shown in Figure 7.10.

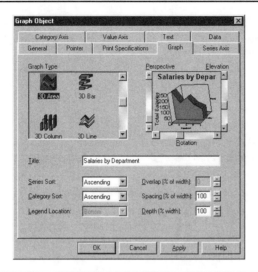

Figure 7.10 Defining a 3-D graph.

In addition to modifying a graph within the development environment, Power-Builder has the following functions, which are used to modify graphs programmatically:

GetSeriesStyle( ) returns the line's style and width for a series.

SetSeriesStyle( ) sets the style and width for a series.

GetDataStyle( ) returns the line's style and width for a series and data point.

SetDataStyle( ) sets the line's style and width for a series and data point.

GetDataPieExplode( ) returns the percentage of explosion for the pie slice specified by a series and data point.

SetDataPieExplode( ) sets the percentage of explosion into the variable for the pie slice specified by a series and data point.

As an example, you can use a 3-D pie graph to show the allocation of employee salaries among different departments. This DataWindow graph indicates the percentage of the total salaries paid to employees broken down by each department, as shown in Figure 7.11.

From this graph, the user can double-click on one of the pie sections and display a second screen to alter the graph's attributes (see Figure 7.12). This example will show how to change the graph's attributes and uses the functions for getting and setting the graph's pie explosion attributes.

First, create a structure called str_graphobjectatpoint to pass the needed information between the windows. This is similar to the structure included within the Power-Builder sample application, as shown in Figure 7.13.

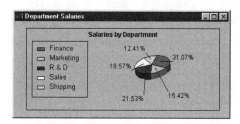

Figure 7.11   A 3-D graph showing employee salaries by department.

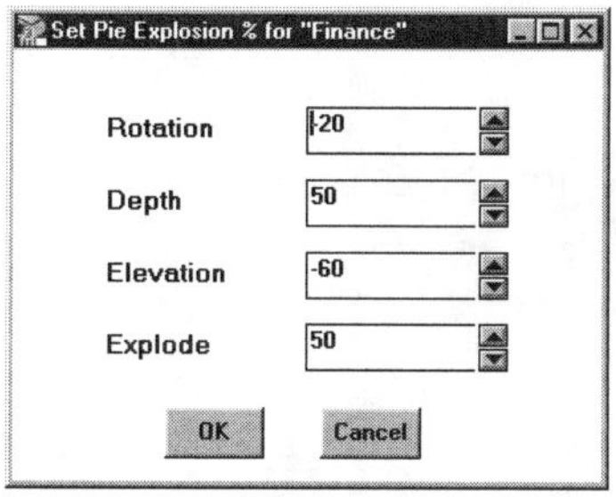

Figure 7.12   Sample screen for dynamically altering graph attributes.

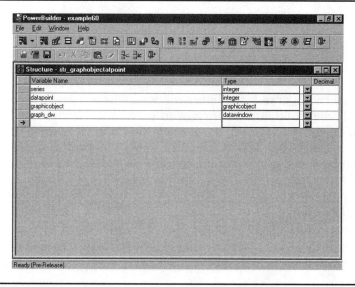

Figure 7.13   Definition of the structure str_graphobjectatpoint.

Next, create a window called w_exp_grph, and place a DataWindow control (dw_graph) within the window. Place the following code within the window's open event:

```
dw_graph.settransobject(sqlca)
dw_graph.retrieve()
```

Next, add the following code to dw_graph's double-clicked event to determine where the user clicked, and open the window to let the user modify the graph's attributes:

```
// Determine where within the DataWindow the user clicked,
// populate the structure with the current graph attributes,
// and open the window to modify the attributes
int                        iSeries, iDatapoint
grobjecttype               lgro_clickedtype
int                        iGraphType
str_graphobjectatpoint     lstr_graph

// Test for Pie (type 13) or Pie3d (type 17) graph types
iGraphType = Integer(dw_graph.object.gr_1.graphtype)
If (iGraphType <> 13) and (iGraphType <> 17) Then Return

// Get the object, series, and datapoint that was double
// clicked, save this information within the lstr_graph
// structure, and open the window
lgro_clickedtype = dw_graph.ObjectAtPointer("gr_1",iSeries,iDatapoint)
If (iSeries > 0 and iDatapoint > 0) and &
    lgro_clickedtype = TypeData! Then
        lstr_graph.graphicobject = dw_graph
        lstr_graph.graph_dw = dw_graph
        lstr_graph.series = iSeries
        lstr_graph.datapoint = iDatapoint
        OpenWithParm(w_graph_attributes,lstr_graph)
End If
```

Next, create the w_graph_attributes window. This window lets the user alter the rotation, depth, elevation, and pie explosion percentage attributes. This window includes four edit mask controls (em_rotation, em_depth, em_elevation, and em_explode), each with a range of -100 to 100. Figure 7.12 shows the window w_graph_attributes.

After creating the four edit masks, create a user-defined event (ue_enchange) for each edit mask that maps to the PowerBuilder event ID pbm_enchange. You will use this event to change the graph when the user changes one of the parameters within the edit mask. Before adding the code to each edit mask's ue_enchange event, create the following instance variables to store the graph's attributes:

```
object     io_passed
graph      igr_parm
datawindow i_dw
```

```
int          i_iOriginalExplode
int          i_iSeries
int          i_iDatapoint
int          i_iElevation
int          i_iRotation
int          i_iDepth
```

The window w_graph_attributes's open event will take the parameter passed to it from the **OpenWithParm( )** function and assign values to the instance variables listed earlier:

```
graphicobject               lgro_hold
grobjecttype                lgrot_clickedtype
str_graphobjectatpoint      lstr_graph
string                      sCategory

// Get the parameter passed to the window from the PB Message object,
// and assign values from the structure to the various instance
// variables
lstr_graph = Message.PowerObjectParm
lgro_hold = lstr_graph.graphicobject
i_iSeries = lstr_graph.series
i_iDatapoint = lstr_graph.datapoint
i_dw = lstr_graph.graph_dw
i_iElevation = Integer(i_dw.object.gr_1.elevation)
i_iDepth = Integer(i_dw.object.gr_1.depth)
i_iRotation = Integer(i_dw.object.gr_1.rotation)


// Determine the graph type (DataWindow graph or window graph),
// and get the series, data point, and original explosion percentage
If lgro_hold.TypeOf() = Graph! Then
    MessageBox("Graphs","Graph is not a datawindow", &
        Exclamation!,OKCancel!,2)
Elseif lgro_hold.TypeOf() = Datawindow! Then
    io_passed = Datawindow!
    i_dw.GetDataPieExplode("gr_1",i_iSeries,i_iDatapoint, &
        i_iOriginalExplode)
    sCategory = i_dw.categoryname("gr_1",i_iDatapoint)
End If


// Set the edit mask values to the original graph attributes, and
// trigger the user-defined event ue_enchange to explode the pie
// graph
em_elevation.text = string(i_iElevation)
em_depth.text = string(i_iDepth)
em_rotation.text = string(i_iRotation)
If i_iOriginalExplode = 0 Then
```

continues

```
        em_explode.text = "50"
        em_explode.event ue_enchange()
Else
        em_explode.text = string(i_iOriginalExplode)
End If

//set the window name to the category
this.title = "Set Pie Explosion % for ~"" + sCategory + "~""
```

After creating the instance variables, add the following code to the em_explode's ue_enchange event:

```
// Code that tests to see if the graph is a datawindow, and
// then set the variable to the value within the edit mask
If io_passed = Datawindow! Then
    i_dw.SetDataPieExplode("gr_1",i_iSeries,i_iDatapoint,&
            integer(em_explode.text))
End If
```

Add the following code to em_elevation's ue_enchange event:

```
// Code for changing the graph's elevation
If io_passed = Datawindow! Then
    i_dw.object.gr_1.elevation=em_elevation.text
End If
```

Add the following code to em_depth's ue_enchange event:

```
// Code for changing the graph's depth
If io_passed = Datawindow! Then
    i_dw.object.gr_1.depth=em_depth.text
End If
```

And finally, add the following code to em_rotation's ue_enchange event:

```
If io_passed = Datawindow! Then
    i_dw.object.gr_1.rotation=em_rotation.text
End If
```

Next, create OK and Cancel buttons. The OK button will close the parent window, and the Cancel button should ensure that the graph's attributes remain the same. The code for the Cancel button's clicked event is:

```
If io_passed = Graph! Then
    igr_parm.SetDataPieExplode(i_iSeries,i_iDatapoint, &
        i_iOriginalExplode)
Elseif io_passed = Datawindow! Then
    i_dw.SetDataPieExplode("gr_1",i_iSeries,i_iDatapoint,&
```

```
        i_iOriginalExplode)
     i_dw.object.gr_1.elevation=string(i_iElevation)
     i_dw.object.gr_1.depth=string(i_idepth)
     i_dw.object.gr_1.rotation=string(i_irotation)
  End If
  Close (parent)
```

TIP Instead of using modify( ) to change the DataWindow graph, you can use the dot notation to modify the graph directly. For more information on modifying DataWindows attributes directly, refer to Chapter 3, "DataWindows."

This example is now ready for execution. By double-clicking on one of the pie slices, the user can dynamically change the graph's attributes. This example illustrates some of PowerBuilder's 3-D graph capabilities, including the use of some of PowerBuilder's graph functions.

REPORTS

Report Painter/InfoMaker

Powersoft designed InfoMaker for end-users to create reports. The InfoMaker user can create reports and graphs that the PowerBuilder developer can use within the creation of an application.

In addition, Powersoft simplified the InfoMaker documentation to let nondevelopers create usable reports easily. The InfoMaker and the PowerBuilder development environment's reporting features are actually the same painter. Each of these painters lets developers create reports for an application. The reporting functionality within these tools creates a DataWindow, but does not let developers insert and manipulate data from the Report painter.

The primary difference between creating a DataWindow that lets the user input and edit data and a DataWindow that displays a report is that the tab order of all the controls within a DataWindow for a report is set to 0.

To specify the retrieval arguments for a report, click the right button of your mouse within the DataWindow, choose **Properties...** from the popup menu, and then click the Retrieval Arguments tab. Within the tab, you can specify the retrieval arguments and their types. If you specify the retrieval arguments, you must specify the values for the arguments within the DataWindow control's retrieve event, otherwise PowerBuilder will display a message similar to the one shown in Figure 7.14.

If the SQL for your report includes complex joins, consider writing a stored procedure and using the procedure as your report's data source. By using a stored procedure, you can significantly improve your report's performance. This is because the stored procedure executes on the server and benefits from the server's processing power.

You can also use different colors to represent the different data within a report.

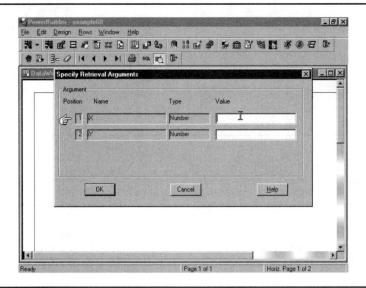

Figure 7.14 PowerBuilder displaying a message when you do not specify values for the DataWindow's retrieval arguments.

Presentation Styles

PowerBuilder's Report painter and InfoMaker let the developer show data by using the Composite, Tabular, Grid, Freeform, Crosstab, N-Up, Group, Label, Graph, OLE 2.0, and RichText formats. These formats are the same as those for the DataWindows. Chapter 3, "DataWindows," discusses them. However, this section discusses the Crosstab and the RichText report in greater detail.

Crosstab Reports

The crosstab style report lets the developer create reports that present data within a spreadsheet-like grid. This type of report performs a two-dimensional analysis of the data. The first dimension is the column, which displays data across the top of the graph. The second dimension is the row, which displays the data items down the report. Because PowerBuilder implements the crosstab style as a grid DataWindow, the user can resize and reorder the columns at runtime.

Any cell of a crosstab report can provide summary data or totals, or it can be a calculation based on the column values retrieved from the database. The crosstab style consists of the columns, rows, and values, as shown in Figure 7.15.

The following sections discuss each of these crosstab report attributes.

Columns When creating a crosstab report, the developer specifies the columns to be used in the report within the Columns drop-down listbox. You can select multiple columns by dragging them into the Column list (see Figure 7.16). If you include too many columns, however, the report expands beyond the screen and forces the user to use a horizontal scroll bar to view all of the data.

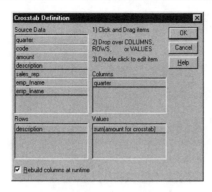

Figure 7.15   The Crosstab Definition dialog box.

In addition to simply specifying the column name, the developer can use the LookupDisplay( ) function. As mentioned earlier within this chapter, the LookupDisplay( ) function displays the display value that is stored for a column within a DataWindow code table. Another way to specify columns is by using a PowerScript function. For example, you can use the **Month( )** function to display a date's month portion only:

```
Month(OrderDate)
```

This code will display the OrderDate variable as a number (1–12) for the month value (January to December).

If the developer creates a crosstab within the DataWindow painter, the developer can save initial values, validation expressions, and validation messages within the DataWindow by using the <u>R</u>ows, **Column Specifications** MenuItem. If the developer creates a crosstab by using InfoMaker or the Report painter, the developer can only view the columns and their type, as shown in Figure 7.17.

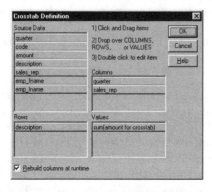

Figure 7.16   Selecting multiple columns within a Crosstab report.

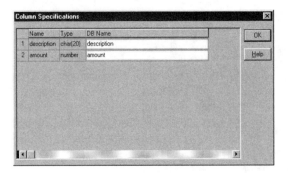

Figure 7.17   **The Column Specifications dialog box.**

Rows When creating a crosstab report, the developer should specify which rows to include in the report by using the Rows drop-down listbox (see Figure 7.15). Like columns, you can select multiple rows by dragging them into the list.

Values The crosstab value is the data that is the intersection between the row and column. The value is an aggregate data value that summarizes the data for the row and column. By default, PowerBuilder fills the DropDownListBox with the sum( ) of the column and row, and a sum of the units for the crosstab. The developer can also specify any other aggregate for the units within the crosstab, if necessary.

Crosstab Summaries Another item the user might want within a report column is a total row or column. You can compute aggregate values by columns or rows. For example, you can sum all of the values of a column together by creating a computed column or by using the summation.

In addition, you can define a summary of the values for a row by using the five predefined PowerBuilder crosstab aggregate functions. These functions are **CrosstabSum( )**, **CrosstabAvg( )**, **CrosstabCount( )**, **CrosstabMax( )**, and **CrosstabMin( )**. These functions perform the sum, average, count, max, and min, respectively, on the rows the user selects.

Figure 7.18 illustrates the summation of each of the columns and rows.

Rich Text Format (RTF)

The Rich Text Format (RTF) DataWindow style lets the user print letters or documents from PowerBuilder by using data to fill in the specific fields within the document. This functionality provides a great deal of flexibility to developers, and more power to the uses who will be printing these documents. Developers can create the RTF document within the RTF DataWindow painter or in another text editor and save the document in Rich Text Format. The developer can bring this document into the RTF DataWindow painter as the initial text. Figure 7.19 shows the options available to developers when starting the development of an RTF style DataWindow.

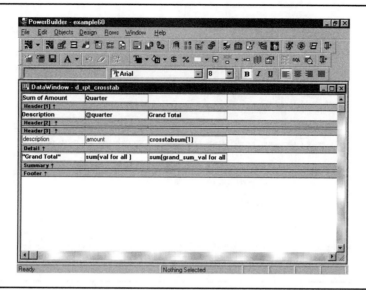

Figure 7.18   Defining a summation of each column.

Within the RTF DataWindow painter, developers can edit or add to the initial text, import additional RTF files, or change any of the DataWindow's properties. More importantly, developers can add columns from the data source directly into the text. You can do this just like you would within any other DataWindow style, by clicking on the column button on the toolbar and clicking within the DataWindow where you want to place the field. Figure 7.20 shows a short letter to be sent to all the customers of an employee. The SQL statement you use within the DataWindow selects the customer name, address information, and the employee name, and PowerBuilder places the columns throughout the text.

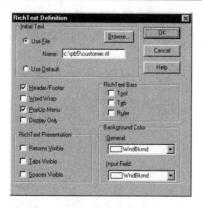

Figure 7.19   The RichText Definition dialog box.

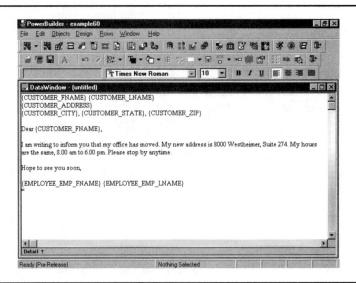

Figure 7.20 A sample letter with the data fields.

Through the attributes within the properties dialog box, you can choose how much or how little control the user has. At runtime, the DataWindow can have all of the capabilities of the RTF editor within the DataWindow painter. You can make the DataWindow "Display Only," letting the user view and print only. Or you can give the user access to the popup menu and let the user configure the editing environment. Figure 7.21 shows the DataWindow at runtime after it has been retrieved. Notice the toolbar and the ruler are added to give the user more information while editing this letter.

For every row the SQL statement returns, the DataWindow creates a separate document. Any changes the user makes to the document's text will be made to all the doc-

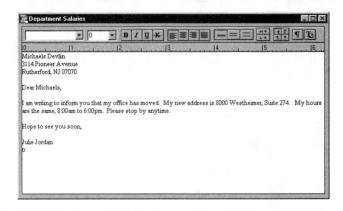

Figure 7.21 A sample letter with the data fields filled.

uments within the DataWindow. Printing the RTF DataWindow is the same as any other DataWindow, except PowerBuilder creates a new page for each row or document. In addition, you can allow access to the user to the print specifications dialog box (via the popup menu) for more printing options, such as the document's margins or orientation.

Composite Reports

The composite style report lets developers create a DataWindow that includes DataWindows nested within it. Depending on your application's reporting requirements, you can place the DataWindows side by side or one below the other. You can set each DataWindow's attributes individually by highlighting the DataWindow, clicking the right mouse button, and choosing **Properties...**.

Say you have already created a couple of reports for your users, the annual sales report and the annual revenues report. Your corporation's management would now like to see both the annual sales and annual revenues in a single report. Instead of creating a new report, you can create a composite report that uses the annual sales report and the annual revenues report as nested reports.

TIP When you create a composite style report, be sure to format and align the columns in the nested reports properly to generate a professional-looking report.

If you place the DataWindows one below the other within the composite style report and one of the DataWindows does not retrieve any data for particular cases, the composite style report will not display empty white space. This is because PowerBuilder automatically sets the DataWindow's Slide (to directly above) and AutoSize Height (on) attributes. To view these attributes, click the right mouse button on the DataWindow, choose **Properties...** from the popup menu, and then click the **Position** tab. Figure 7.22 shows the Position tab.

TIP When you choose the composite style report within the New DataWindow dialog box, PowerBuilder disables all the Data Source options. This is because the composite style report's data source will be the reports you nest within the DataWindow.

Printing Reports

PowerBuilder lets developers provide print specifications within a report or DataWindow. When you click the right mouse button, select **Properties...**, and choose the **Print Specifications** tab, the screen in Figure 7.23 appears.

The document name specifies the file's name when inserted into the print queue. In addition, if you want to prompt the user with the Printer Setup dialog box before the

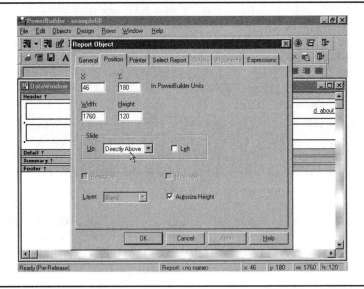

Figure 7.22   **Specifying the DataWindow's position attributes.**

report prints, check the checkbox at the bottom. PowerBuilder, in turn, invokes the standard Windows Printer Setup dialog box.

After you have defined the report's printing specifications, place the report within a window. To let the user print the report, the developer should code the script to print all of the associated DataWindows that pertain to a report. The script should include the **PrintDataWindow( )** function that prints each of the DataWindows within the

Figure 7.23   **The Print Specifications dialog box.**

window. In addition, use the **PrintOpen( )** function to name the print job, including all of the DataWindows. The PrintOpen( ) function defines a new blank page, specifies that all printing will be in the default font for the printer, and positions the cursor at the print area's upper left corner. If the developer specifies a name for the job, the Windows 95 Print Manager and the Spooler dialog boxes display the name.

For example, assume you want to print each of the two DataWindows within the window shown in Figure 7.24.

To do this, place the following code within the window's print script:

```
/* Print DataWindows dw_sales and dw_graph */
int iJob

iJob = PrintOpen("Salary Report")
PrintDataWindow(iJob, dw_salary_graph)
PrintDataWindow(iJob, dw_salary_tabular)
PrintClose(iJob)
```

The print job's name is "Salary Report." This code prints the contents of the two DataWindows dw_salary_graph and dw_salary_tabular.

TIP Before printing a DataWindow, select the DataWindow's detail band's Autosize Height. PowerBuilder, in turn, will size the DataWindow's detail band's height to the size of the largest field in the DataWindow.

In addition to printing reports, PowerBuilder has the capability to print individual objects. You can do this by using the **objectname.Print( )** function.

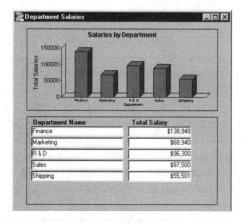

Figure 7.24   **Printing the two DataWindows.**

The **Print( )** function's format is:

```
objectname.Print (printjobnumber, x, y{, width{, height}})
```

where:

objectname is the name of the object to print.

printjobnumber is the number the **PrintOpen( )** function assigns to the print job.

x is the X coordinate of the location to print the object.

y is the Y coordinate of the location to print the object.

width (optional) is the object's printed width.

height (optional) is the object's printed height.

For example, here is the code to print the command button cb_cancel in its original size at the location 200, 400:

```
int iJob

iJob = PrintOpen()
cb_cancel.Print(iJob,200,400)
PrintClose(iJob)
```

In addition to printing individual objects, PowerBuilder provides the PrintScreen( ) function to print an entire screen. For example, the following code will print the current screen image in its original size at the location 200, 400:

```
int iJob

iJob = PrintOpen()
PrintScreen(iJob,200,400)
PrintClose(iJob)
```

Saving Reports

Another PowerBuilder feature is the **Save Rows As** menu item located on the **File** menu in Print Preview within the Report painter. When you choose this menu item, among the several options, you can direct PowerBuilder to save the definition (source and object) and the data within the report to a file with the extension .PSR. Once PowerBuilder saves the report, you can open the report from Windows Explorer, send to other users, and open from other applications. However, before you can use the .PSR file from Explorer or other applications, you must register it with the Powersoft reports in the Windows registration database (reg.dat) located within the Windows directory.

To open the report from Explorer, first associate the .PSR file with the Powersoft Report (pm050.exe). You can do this by selecting **View**, **Options...** from the Explorer Menu, and choosing the **File Types** tab.

TIP To associate .PSR files with PowerBuilder or InfoMaker reports, use Browse on the Edit Action dialog box and select the appropriate .EXE file (pb050.exe or im050.exe).

You can display reports saved as a .PSR file within a DataWindow control by assigning the .PSR file name to the DataWindow control's dataobject attribute. For example, the following code will display the report file expense.psr within the DataWindow control dw_report:

```
dw_report.dataobject=expense.psr
```

To learn how you can use .PSR files with the Internet Developer Toolkiit (IDT) within a Web environment, see Chapter 25, "Using the Internet Developer Toolkit."

TIP In addition to saving the report as a .PSR file, you can save it in a number of other formats, including HTML table, Excel, Excel with headers, dBaseII, dBaseIII, text, text with headers, comma-separated values (CSV), CSV with headers, and so on.

CHAPTER 8

Printing and File I/O

This chapter is divided into two main sections: printing and file input/output (I/O). The first section covers the various aspects of printing within PowerBuilder. The second section covers writing and reading data to and from files in PowerBuilder.

Some of the main topics this chapter covers are:

- Printing
  - How Microsoft Windows printing works
  - Printing functions
  - Print area
  - Printing single DataWindows
  - Printing multiple DataWindows
  - Printing PowerBuilder objects
  - Printing graphs
  - PrintAll capabilities
  - Changing Microsoft Windows print settings
  - Creating Print dialog boxes
- File and I/O
  - File I/O functions
  - Reading files that exceed 32,766 bytes
  - Writing a file copy function
  - ImportFile function
  - Simulating the ImportFile function
  - Environment variables
  - Directory I/O
  - Initialization (.INI) files
  - Registry functions

PRINTING

How Microsoft Windows Printing Works

Most applications provide the capability for users to print information. Traditionally (in the non-Windows days), print functions had to deal with the varied and complex capabilities and requirements of several different applications. In Windows, applications do not print by interacting directly with the printer. Instead, the application sends output to a *printer device context* (see Figure 8.1). As such, the developers need not worry about each printer's specific capabilities or requirements.

To print, the Windows applications first obtain information about the current printer. The applications obtain the printer model name, device driver, and printer port from the operating system. Applications then use this information to create a device context for the current printer. When the application sends the output to a printer device context, Windows activates the print spooler to manage the print request.

Windows applications typically use six printer functions to control print jobs. With Windows 3.1, applications had to use the printer escape sequences to communicate with the printer's device driver. (These escape sequences are available within Windows 95 for backward compatibility.) Figure 8.2 shows that a current Windows application interfaces only with a standard print interface when printing. This interface then communicates with the printer drivers to translate the printer commands and print the data.

PowerBuilder implements its print capability by interfacing with the standard Windows print interface. PowerBuilder makes life easy for the developers by providing a standard set of print functions. This chapter discusses the different methods for changing the current printer and/or settings.

You can change several of a printer's settings by calling the **ExtDeviceMode( )** function in the printer driver. This function lets the developer read and update the

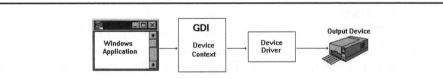

Figure 8.1   **Printing within the Windows environment.**

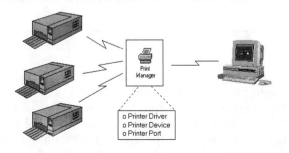

Figure 8.2   **The standard Windows printing interface.**

Table 8.1   Information from the ExtDeviceMode( ) Function

Item	Description
DeviceName	The name of the device the driver supports.
SpecVersion	The structure's version number.
DriverVersion	Printer driver version number.
Size	The structure's size (in bytes).
DriverExtra	The optional DriverData member's size, in bytes, for the device-specific data.
Fields	Specifies the DEVMODE structure's elements that are initialized.
Orientation	Specifies the paper's orientation (landscape or portrait).
PaperSize	Size of the paper to print on.
PaperLength	Paper length, in tenths of a millimeter.
PaperWidth	Paper width, in tenths of a millimeter.
Scale	Factor by which the application scales the printed output.
Copies	Number of copies to be printed.
DefaultSource	Default bin from which the paper is fed.
PrintQuality	The printer resolution.
Color	If the printer supports color or black/white output.
Duplex	Duplex printing.
YResolution	The printer's Y-resolution.
TTOption	How TrueType fonts should be printed.

printer settings. The ExtDeviceMode( ) function puts the current printer's setting information into the DEVMODE structure. Table 8.1 shows the information that a printer's driver can return by using the ExtDeviceMode( ) function.

Printing Functions

Table 8.2 shows the list of print functions and events available within PowerBuilder.

Table 8.2 lists the functions and events you can use to manipulate printing. To skip a page, for example, return 1 from a DataWindow's PrintPage event. If you do not want to skip a page, return 0.

TIP   The print functions are the same for a DataWindow or a data store.

Print Area

PowerBuilder defines printing in terms of the page area. The page area is analogous to the GDI Device Context when printing within native Windows. The print area is the physical page size less any margins. For example, if the page size is 8.5 by 11 inches, and the top, bottom, and side margins are all half an inch, the print area is 7.5 by 10 inches. All measurements within the print area are in 1/1000s of an inch. Figure 8.3 shows the relationship between the page and the print area. The figure also shows the coordinates for the print area in 1/1000s of an inch.

Table 8.2   List of Print Functions and Events

Function/Event	Description
Print	This is a generic print function. It has five different formats: one format simply prints the DataWindows; the other four print a string.
PrintOpen	This function sets up a page for printing. It returns a job ID that you can use in most of the other PowerBuilder print functions.
PrintClose	This function closes a print job. It is the last function you call within a print session, unless you call the PrintCancel function first. This function sends the current page to the printer.
PrintStart Event	This is a DataWindow event that is triggered when a DataWindow's contents begin printing.
PrintEnd Event	This is a DataWindow event that is triggered when a DataWindow's contents are finished printing.
PrintCancel	This function sends the current page's contents to the printer and cancels the print job. You can cancel a job before closing it by calling the PrintCancel function.
PrintSetSpacing	This function sets the lines' spacing within a print job. You can specify a multiplier to be used to calculate the cursor's height based on the characters' current height. This function lets you put the appropriate PowerScript in place to let the user print a document single-spaced, double-spaced, or even triple-spaced.
PrintDefineFont	This function lets you put the appropriate PowerScript in place to define a print job's fonts.
PrintSetup	This function opens the standard print setup dialog box.
PrintX	This function returns the print cursor's X coordinate.
PrintY	This function returns the print cursor's Y coordinate.
PrintSend	This function is similar to the Escape function within the Windows SDK. The function lets you send a printer escape sequence directly to a printer. The escape sequences are printer specific.
PrintWidth	This function returns a string's width in the specified print job number's current font. The width is useful in determining the next print position.
PrintDataWindow	You can use this function to print a DataWindow by using the current print job number. This function is different from the print function's DataWindow format. The print function simply sends the DataWindow printout to the default printer; the function does not need a print job.
PrintText	This function prints a string in the current font of the specified print job starting at the specified X and Y coordinates. This function's last parameter lets you specify a different font than the one assigned to the print job. You can set a different font by calling the PrintDefineFont function.
PrintBitmap	This function, which prints a bitmap by using a job number, starts printing at the specified X and Y coordinates with the specified height and width.
PrintLine	This function prints a line starting at the specified X and Y coordinates, ending at the specified X and Y coordinates, with a parameter available to set the line's thickness.
PrintOval	This function prints an oval at the specified X and Y coordinates with the parameters available for the width, height, and thickness.
PrintPage Event	This event is triggered before each print page of a DataWindow is formatted for printing. You can use this event in conjunction with the SetActionCode function, to force the printer to skip a page.

Table 8.2 *Continued*

Function/Event	Description
PrintPage	This function works similar to the PrintPage Event. You specify the event for the DataWindows whereas you use the PrintPage function for print jobs. To skip a page, you must call this function.
PrintRect	This function is identical to the PrintOval function except it prints a rectangle.
PrintRoundRect	This function is identical to the PrintRect function except the rectangle that is printed has rounded corners.

When printing, PowerBuilder uses a cursor to keep track of the print location. The cursor contains the X and Y coordinates of the upper left corner of the location at which printing will begin. The **PrintX( )** and **PrintY( )** functions return the current print cursor's X and Y coordinates. PowerBuilder updates the cursor (including the tab position, if required) after each print operation. To position the text, objects, lines, and pictures when creating complex reports, the developer specifies the cursor position as part of each print function call. All the cursor parameters (including the print cursor) within the PowerBuilder print functions are measured in 1/1000s of an inch.

Printing Single DataWindows

Simple Case

Printing a DataWindow is, in most cases, a simple process. The **Print( )** and **PrintDataWindow( )** functions provide a simple way to print the DataWindows. To print a DataWindow, execute the following code:

```
dw_name.Print( )
```

or

```
PrintDataWindow(printjobid, dw_name)
```

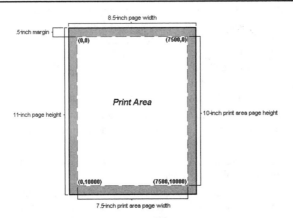

Figure 8.3 **Defining the print area.**

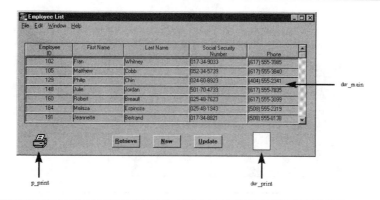

Figure 8.4   Sample DataWindow with the main controls defined.

You should use the Print( ) function if you want to display the standard Windows Print/Cancel dialog box when printing. You should use PrintDataWindow( ) if you want to print the DataWindow as part of a print job.

Case of the Hidden DataWindow (First Method) If you want to print a DataWindow in a format different from the way the DataWindow displays on the screen, the process is a little more difficult. For example, Figure 8.4 shows a display format for the DataWindow.

Table 8.3 shows the list of controls and their purpose on the window. To drag-and-drop a row onto the print icon and print its detail information as shown in Figure 8.5, do the following.

Within dw_main's **constructor** event:

```
If This.SetTransObject(SQLCA) = 1 Then
     If This.Retrieve( ) = -1 Then
          // error processing ...
     Halt Close
     End If
Else
     Halt Close
End If
```

Table 8.3   List of Controls on the Window

Controls	Purpose
dw_main	The main DataWindow. This is the DataWindow on which the user chooses an employee to print.
p_print.	This is a picture control. The user can drag an employee from the main dw_main and drop it on p_print, for printing.
dw_print	This is the print DataWindow. This DataWindow is not visible to the user. When the user drops an employee on the p_print control, the application retrieves the detail information into dw_print for printing. Instead of a DataWindow control, you can also use a datastore.

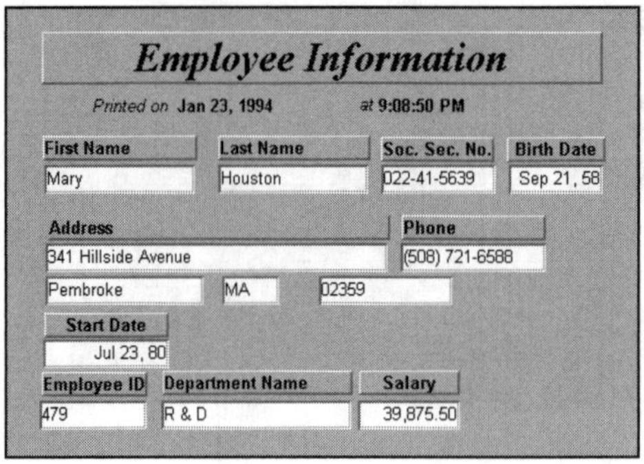

Figure 8.5 **Sample DataWindow in a printed format.**

Within dw_main's **clicked** event:

```
If row > 0 Then
    i_iempid = This.object.empid[row]
    This.SelectRow(0,False)
    This.SelectRow(row,True)
    This.Drag(Begin!)
End If
```

Within p_print's **dragdrop** event:

```
If dw_print.Retrieve(i_iEmpID) = -1 Then
    // error processing ...
ElseIf dw_print.Print( ) = -1 Then
    // error processing ...
End If
```

Within dw_print's **constructor** event:

```
If This.SetTransObject(SQLCA) = -1 Then
    // error processing . . .
    Halt Close
End If
```

That's all it takes!

Case of the Hidden DataWindow (Second Method) Another approach to meeting the previously described requirement is to use the shared result sets. This method is more efficient because it submits only one query to the database. This becomes an issue when you retrieve large result sets from a database across a network. To use this approach, do the following.

Within dw_main's constructor event:

```
This.SetTransObject(SQLCA)
This.Retrieve( )
This.ShareData(dw_print)
```

Within dw_main's clicked event:

```
If row > 0 Then
    i_iempid = This.object.empid[row]
    This.SelectRow(0,False)
    This.SelectRow(row,True)
    This.Drag(Begin!)
End If
```

Within p_print's dragdrop event:

```
dw_main.SetReDraw(False)
dw_print.SetFilter ("empid = " +String(i_iempid))
dw_print.Filter( )
If dw_print.Print( ) = -1 Then
    // error processing
End If
dw_print.SetFilter("")
dw_print.Filter( )
dw_main.SetRedraw(True)
```

TIP Since dw_main and dw_print share the result sets, when you issue a filter on dw_print, the filter affects both the DataWindows. To prevent the user from viewing the filter's effects, you can use the **SetRedraw( )** function to prevent dw_main from being repainted.

Case of the Hidden DataWindow (Third Method) The third method uses the pieces from each of the first two methods. This method retrieves the data into both dw_main and dw_print, similar to the first method. The difference here is that the method retrieves all the data from the start into both the DataWindows by using two retrieve function calls.

Add the following code to the window's open event:

```
// Error processing needs to be done
dw_main.Retrieve( )
dw_print.Retrieve( )
```

Each time the user drags an employee from dw_main into the p_print control, call the **SetFilter( )** and **Filter( )** functions for dw_print. Add the following PowerScript within p_print's dragdrop event:

```
dw_print.SetFilter ("empid = " +String(i_iempid))
dw_print.Filter( )
If dw_print.Print( ) = -1 Then
     // error processing ...
End If
```

This method's advantage over the first method is that the PowerScript in p_print's dragdrop event does not initiate a retrieve every time. All the p_print control does is set the filter and print the resulting DataWindow.

Printing Multiple DataWindows

Through the use of composite DataWindows, PowerBuilder provides a simple way to print multiple DataWindows. The following examples demonstrate some techniques to print data from multiple DataWindows without creating a separate composite DataWindow object.

This first example combines a single record from the master grid DataWindow (see Figure 8.6) with the record from the detail freeform DataWindow. The user selects the record from the master DataWindow and the detail DataWindow displays detail information about the selected record. Then the user can drag-and-drop the detail record on the print icon.

Figure 8.7 shows this example's controls.

Option 1

Create a preformatted hidden DataWindow, and let the DataWindow join the master and detail tables. When the user drops the drag icon onto the print icon, the print icon executes the PowerScript within p_print's dragdrop event:

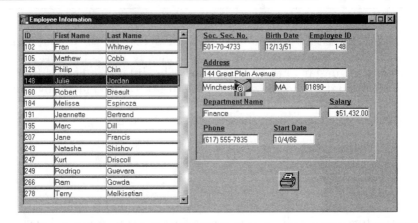

Figure 8.6   Printing the detail record by using the drag-and-drop functionality.

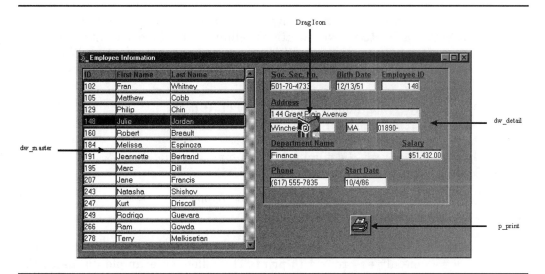

Figure 8.7   Controls defined for the drag-and-drop print window.

```
If Not dw_print.Retrieve(i_id) = -1 Then
    If dw_print.Print( ) = -1 Then
        // Error Processing ...
    End If
Else
    // Error Processing ...
End If
```

Option 2

This second example prints the same two DataWindows without submitting an additional retrieve for printing. To do this, make the hidden DataWindow the same as the detail window (but within the printed format) and add two dummy text fields to the DataWindow. When the user drops the drag icon onto the print icon, you get the selected person's first and last name from the master DataWindow. Next, you can set these values within the hidden print DataWindow. When you have done this, fire the print for the hidden DataWindow.

The PowerScript within p_print's dragdrop event is:

```
Int    iRow
iRow = dw_master.GetRow( )
dw_print.Object.dummy1[1] = dw_main.object.fname[iRow]
dw_print.Object.dummy2[1] = dw_main.object.lname[iRow]
If dw_print.Print( ) = -1 Then
    // error processing . . .
End If
```

TIP Use the **Modify( )** function with the Create and Destroy options in combination with the **SetRedraw( )** function to eliminate the hidden print DataWindow. Instead of the hidden print DataWindow, you can use the detail DataWindow. When the user drops the drag icon onto the print icon, you can do the following:

- Set Redraw to False.
- Dynamically create dummy1 and dummy2 text fields.
- Set the dummy fields with the selected person's first and last name.
- Print the detail DataWindow.
- Dynamically destroy the dummy1 and dummy2 text fields.
- Set Redraw to True.

This eliminates the need for a hidden print DataWindow.

The preceding example discusses the printing of two DataWindows when both DataWindows have only one record to print. The following example discusses the printing of two DataWindows where the detail DataWindow has multiple records to print.

Within this example, the Customer DataWindow displays the header information about a customer and the Order DataWindow lists the customer's orders. The Select a Customer window opens both the times, when the window is first opened and when the user clicks the **List-up** button next to the Customer Number field (see Figure 8.8).

The user can drag-and-drop the drag icon onto the print icon (from the Customer DataWindow) and the header information and the list of orders are printed. This example shows how a single record from one DataWindow is combined with the multiple related records from another DataWindow and printed as one report (see Figure 8.9).

You can do this by using a temporary file and a hidden print DataWindow. Also, instead of the hidden DataWindow, you can also use the DataStore object. You will then need to place the following code within p_print's **dragdrop** event:

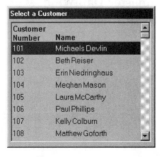

Figure 8.8   **The Select a Customer window.**

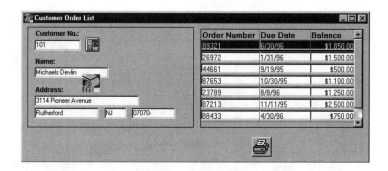

Figure 8.9   **Printing a single record combined with the multiple detail records.**

```
Long   lFileNo
String    sTemp01 = "temp01.txt"

// Clear the print DataWindow's contents
dw_print.Reset( )

// Write the titles and data for the customer DataWindow to a
// temp file, then import the file into the print DataWindow
dw_customer.SaveAs(sTemp01,Text!,True)
dw_print.ImportFile(sTemp01)

// Write the titles and data for the order DataWindow to a
// temp file, then import the file into the print DataWindow
dw_order.SaveAs(sTemp01,Text!,True)
dw_print.ImportFile(sTemp01)

// Delete the temporary file
FileDelete(sTemp01)

// Print the print DataWindow
If dw_print.Print( ) = -1 Then
     // error processing ...
End If
```

TIP If you want to print only certain fields within each DataWindow, you must programmatically get the desired fields and write them to a temporary text file. You could then import the temporary file into the print DataWindow.

Figure 8.10 shows another example in which three DataWindows need to be printed: the customer DataWindow, the order DataWindow, and the order detail

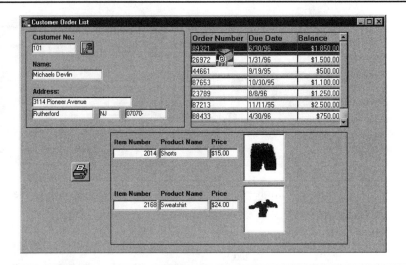

Figure 8.10 The customer, order, and order detail DataWindows.

DataWindow. The example demonstrates how to print one record from the customer DataWindow, one record from the order DataWindow, and all the order details from the order detail DataWindow. In this case, the user drags and drops a particular order, and all the items in that order are printed.

To achieve this functionality, put the following code within p_print's dragdrop event:

```
Long          lFileNo
String        sTemp01 = "temp01.txt"

// Clear the print DataWindow's contents
dw_print.Reset( )

// Write the titles and data for the customer DataWindow to a temp file,
// then import the file into the print DataWindow
dw_customer.SaveAs(sTemp01,Text!,True)
dw_print.ImportFile(sTemp01)

// Temporarily prevent repainting of the object
dw_order.SetRedraw(False)

// Only display the selected order record
dw_order.SetFilter("order_number = " + String(i_iOrderNum))
dw_order.Filter( )

// Write the titles and data for the order DataWindow to the temp file
dw_order.SaveAs(sTemp01,Text!,True)
```

```
// Import the temp file into the print DataWindow
dw_print.ImportFile(sTemp01)

// Reset the filter
dw_order.SetFilter("")
dw_order.Filter( )

// Write the titles and data for the order_detail DataWindow to a temp file,
// then import the file into the print DataWindow
dw_order_detail.SaveAs(sTemp01,Text!,True)
dw_print.ImportFile(sTemp01)

// Delete the temporary file
FileDelete(sTemp01)

// Allow repainting of the dw_order DataWindow
dw_order.SetRedraw(True)

// Print the print DataWindow
If dw_print.Print( ) = -1 Then
     // error processing ...
End If
```

Printing PowerBuilder Objects

You can print most PowerBuilder objects by using PowerScript. PowerBuilder also has functions that can print text and bitmaps. The printing of the text functions can be useful if you want to either print specific lines of the text to the printer or manually print a window's entire contents within a print job. If you want to print the data from the different non-DataWindow controls on a window, you can do this by obtaining each data value and printing it within a print job or writing it to a temporary file, which in turn, you can then import into a hidden, preformatted DataWindow.

You can also print objects such as rectangles, circles, ovals, CommandButtons, singlelineedits, static text, and windows by using the following syntax:

```
objectname.Print (printjobnumber, x, y{, width{, height}})
```

This function prints the objectname by using printjobnumber at the X and Y coordinates with the specified width and height. If the coordinates are not specified, the function prints the objectname with its original coordinates. The following PowerScript prints a CommandButton control at the position 500, 1000:

```
Int     iJob
iJob = PrintOpen( )
cb_close.Print(iJob,500,1000)
PrintClose(Job)
```

PrintScreen( ) is another print function PowerBuilder provides. This function prints the screen by using the specified screen coordinates. Following is the PrintScreen( ) function's prototype:

```
PrintScreen (printjobnumber, x, y{, width{, height}})
```

The following PowerScript prints the current screen image within its original size at the location 500, 1000:

```
int     iJob
iJob = PrintOpen( )
PrintScreen(iJob,500,1000)
PrintClose(iJob)
```

Printing Graphs

When a graph is located within a DataWindow, printing the graph is the same as printing a DataWindow. To print the DataWindow, you can call the Print( ) function. You can create graphs in four ways: as a User Object, as a window control, as a control on a DataWindow, and as a graph DataWindow. PowerBuilder only supports printing of graphs that are controls on a DataWindow or graph DataWindow objects. There are functions that can export the data for the graph and subsequently print the data, but not the graph as an image.

PowerBuilder uses the **grClipboard( )** function to a graph's copy to the clipboard. When the image is within the clipboard, you can call the Windows SDK functions to either print the image from the clipboard or just save the image as a bitmap file and print it from PowerBuilder by using the **PrintBitmap( )** function. Chapter 7, "Graphs and Reporting," includes a more detailed discussion of the PowerBuilder graphs.

Print All Capabilities

When designing MDI applications, you may want a Print All function that prints all of the open sheets. This is similar to the Close All function discussed in Chapter 4. The MDI frame maintains a global array of the open sheet handles. When the user selects the **Print All** option from the menu, the following happens:

- A FOR loop starts going through the open sheets.
- The first window is activated programmatically.
- The parent window's print event is triggered (or you can call a function within the parent window) that handles that particular window's printing.
- This process continues until all of the sheets are printed.

Changing Microsoft Windows Print Settings

PowerBuilder provides several DataWindow attributes to assist in the printing of DataWindows. The following DataWindow attributes change the Windows printer settings for DataWindows.

DataWindow Print Attributes

```
Print.Collate
Print.Color
Print.Columns
Print.Columns.Width
Print.Copies
Print.DocumentName
Print.Duplex
Print.Filename
Print.Margin.Bottom
Print.Margin.Left
Print.Margin.Right
Print.Margin.Top
Print.Orientation
Print.Page.Range
Print.Page.RangeInclude
Print.Paper.Size
Print.Paper.Source
Print.Preview
Print.Preview.Rulers
Print.Preview.Zoom
Print.Prompt
Print.Quality
Print.Scale
```

You can retrieve these attributes and modify them by using the dot notation. For example, the following code retrieves the current setting for the number of print copies for dw_custlist into the variable s_numcopies:

```
string s_numcopies
s_numcopies = dw_custlist.Object.DataWindow.Print.Copies
```

The following changes the number of copies to 5:

```
dw_custlist.Object.DataWindow.Print.Copies = 5
```

There are times when you may want to retrieve information about a printer or print driver. You can use this information to programmatically handle printing in different ways and/or to display the information on a print dialog box (see Figure 8.11).

These print attributes can enable PowerBuilder applications to interface with the Microsoft Windows print settings. These DataWindow settings interface with the print settings from the Windows SDK DEVMODE structure for a particular DataWindow.

Creating Print Dialog Boxes

Print Options Dialog Box

To create a print options dialog box, create an external DataWindow d_ext_print_options with the column specification as shown in Figure 8.12.

Create a response window w_print_options. Add a DataWindow control dw_print with d_ext_print_options as its dataobject. Add four buttons to the window viz. cb_ok, cb_cancel, cb_printer, and cb_help. Your window will look as shown in Figure 8.13.

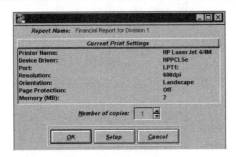

Figure 8.11   Displaying the print attributes.

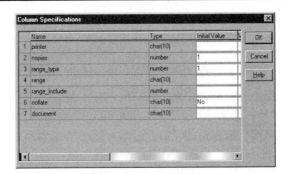

Figure 8.12   A list of columns with their datatypes and initial values for the d_ext_print_options DataWindow object.

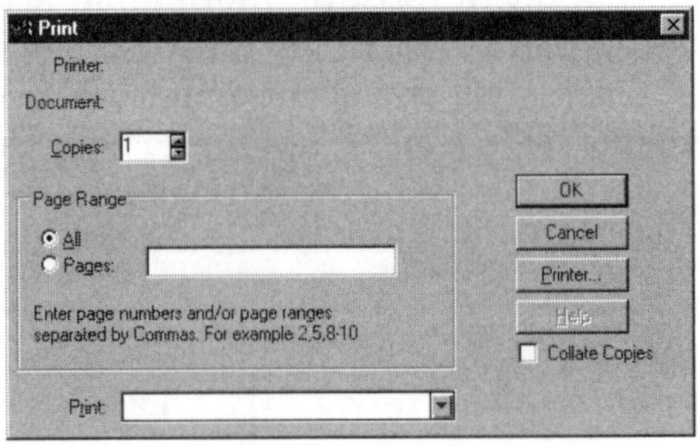

Figure 8.13   The Print dialog box window.

Create four custom events for the window control, namely, **ue_ok**, **ue_cancel**, **ue_printer**, and **ue_help**.

Create the following instance variable for the window:

```
DataWindow     idw_print
```

Next, create a window function **wf_print( )** as follows:

```
/*******************************************************************
** Set the print settings and call the print function
*******************************************************************/
string        is_collate, is_range
integer       ii_copies, ii_range_type, ii_range_include

If dw_print_options.AcceptText () = -1 Then Return
is_collate           = dw_print_options.Object.Collate[1]
ii_copies            = dw_print_options.Object.copies[1]
ii_range_type        = dw_print_options.Object.Range_Type[1]
is_range             = dw_print_options.Object.Range[1]
ii_range_include     = dw_print_options.Object.Range_Include[1]

idw_print.Object.DataWindow.Print.Collate = is_collate
If ii_copies > 0 Then
    idw_print.Object.DataWindow.Print.Copies = String(ii_copies)
End If
If ii_range_type = 2 Then
    If Not IsNull(is_range) Then
        idw_print.Object.DataWindow.Print.Page.Range = is_range
    End If
End If
If ii_range_include > 0 Then
    idw_print.Object.DataWindow.Print.Page.RangeInclude = &
                                        String(ii_range_include)
End If

idw_print.Print ()
```

Similarly, create another window function **wf_set_printer( )** as follows:

```
/*******************************************************************
** Set the printer selected to the dw_print_options DataWindow
*******************************************************************/

dw_print_options.Object.printer[1]  = idw_print.Object.DataWindow.Printer
```

Add the following code to ue_ok's clicked event:

```
Parent.Event ue_ok (0,0)
```

Add the following code to ue_cancel's clicked event:

```
Parent.Event ue_cancel (0,0)
```

Add the following code to ue_printer's clicked event:

```
Parent.Event ue_printer (0,0)
```

Next, add the following code to the window's open event:

```
/************************************************************************
** initialize the instance variable
** Insert a row and initialize the values of the columns within
** the print option DataWindow
************************************************************************/
idw_print = Message.PowerObjectParm

dw_print_options.InsertRow (0)
dw_print_options.Object.document[1] = idw_print.Object.DataWindow.Print.DocumentName
wf_set_printer ()
```

Add the following code to the window's **ue_ok** event:

```
/************************************************************************
** Call the print function to print the DataWindow & close the window
************************************************************************/
wf_print ()
Close (This)
```

Add the following code to the window's ue_cancel event:

```
/************************************************************************
** Close the window
************************************************************************/
Close (This)
```

Add the following code to the window's ue_printer event:

```
/************************************************************************
** Call the printer setup
************************************************************************/

PrintSetup ()
wf_set_printer ()
```

Print Preview/Zoom Dialog Box

Similarly, let's create another dialog box with the option to preview and zoom the output that the user may want to print. To create a print preview/zoom dialog box, create an external DataWindow d_ext_print_display_setup with the column specification as shown in Figure 8.14.

Create a response window w_display_setup. Add a DataWindow control dw_display with d_ext_print_display_setup as its dataobject.

Add three buttons to the window, namely, cb_ok, cb_cancel, and cb_apply. Your window will look as shown in Figure 8.15.

Create four custom events for the window control, namely, ue_ok, ue_cancel, **ue_apply**, and **ue_initialize**.

Create the following instance variable for the window:

```
DataWindow    idw_super
```

Next, create a window function called **wf_get_size (adw_this)**. This function takes a DataWindow as the parameter. The code for the function is:

```
/*****************************************************************
** Purpose:    Get the DataWindow's width
** Return :    DataWindow's width
*****************************************************************/
Int       li_max_xr
Long      ll_pos
String    ls_object_list, ls_this_object
```

continues

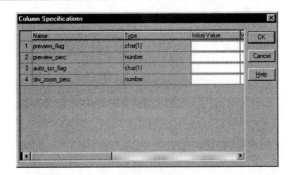

Figure 8.14   A list of columns with their datatypes and initial values for the d_ext_print_display_setup DataWindow object.

Figure 8.15   The Print Preview/Zoom dialog box window.

```
// ***** Find the farthest right any object extends *****
ls_object_list = adw_this.Object.Datawindow.Objects

li_max_xr = 0
Do While ls_object_list <> ""

    ll_pos = Pos (ls_object_list, "~t")
    If ll_pos > 1 Then
        ls_this_object     = Left (ls_object_list, ll_pos - 1)
        ls_object_list     = Mid (ls_object_list, ll_pos + 1)
Else
        ls_this_object     = ls_object_list
        ls_object_list     = ""
    End If

    li_max_xr = Max (li_max_xr, &
                     Integer (adw_this.Describe (ls_this_object &
                     + ".X" )) + Integer (adw_this.Describe     &
                     (ls_this_object + ".Width")))
Loop

//****** Ensure the distance is in PB Units *****
Choose Case adw_this.Object.Datawindow.Units
    Case "0"          // PowerBuilder Units
        li_max_xr = li_max_xr

    Case "1"          // Pixels
        li_max_xr = PixelsToUnits( li_max_xr, XPixelsToUnits! )

    Case "2"          // 1/1000 Inch
        li_max_xr = li_max_xr * 0.439

    Case "3"          // 1/1000 Centimeter
        li_max_xr = li_max_xr * 0.173

    Case Else
        li_max_xr = -1
End Choose

If li_max_xr = 0 Then li_max_xr = 1

Return li_max_xr
```

Next, add the following code to the window's open event:

```
/************************************************************************
** Purpose:     If the DataWindow is not passed to this window, shut down
**              the window
************************************************************************/
```

```
If IsValid (Message.PowerObjectParm) Then
     idw_super = Message.PowerObjectParm
Else
     Close(This)
     Return
End If

Post Event ue_initialize (0,0)
```

Add the following code to the window's ue_initialize event:

```
/*****************************************************************************
Purpose: Will initialize the DataWindow and the flags
*****************************************************************************/
String     ls_preview
Long       ll_dwzoom

ls_preview = idw_super.Object.Datawindow.Print.Preview

dw_display.InsertRow(0)

If Upper (ls_preview) = "YES" Then
     dw_display.object.preview_flag[1] = "Y"
     dw_display.object.preview_perc[1] = Integer &
                         (idw_super.Object.Datawindow.Print.Preview.Zoom)
Else
     dw_display.object.preview_flag[1] = "N"
     dw_display.object.preview_perc[1] = 100
End If

dw_display.object.dw_zoom_perc[1] = &
                         Integer(idw_super.Object.Datawindow.Zoom)
```

Add the following code to the window's ue_ok event:

```
/*****************************************************************************
Purpose: Apply the changes and close the window
*****************************************************************************/
long li_ret

li_ret = Event ue_apply (0,0)
If li_ret = -1 Then Return
Close(This)
```

Add the following code to the window's ue_cancel event:

```
/**************************************************************************
Purpose: Close the window
**************************************************************************/
Close (This)
```

Add the following code to the window's ue_apply event:

```
/**************************************************************************
Purpose: Will apply all the print settings to the passed DataWindow
**************************************************************************/
long ll_zoom, ll_dw_size, ll_ctrl_size

If dw_display.AcceptText () = -1 Then Return -1

If dw_display.object.preview_flag[1] = "Y" Then
    idw_super.Object.Datawindow.Print.Preview = "Yes"
    idw_super.Object.Datawindow.Print.Preview.Zoom = &
                        String(dw_display.object.preview_perc[1])
Else
    idw_super.Object.Datawindow.Print.Preview = "No"
    idw_super.Object.Datawindow.Print.Preview.Zoom = "100"
End If

ll_zoom = dw_display.object.dw_zoom_perc[1]

If dw_display.object.auto_scr_flag[1] = "Y" Then
    ll_dw_size = wf_get_dw_size (idw_super)
    ll_ctrl_size = idw_super.Width
    ll_zoom =        (ll_ctrl_size / ll_dw_size) * 100
    If ll_zoom > 100 Then ll_zoom = 100
    dw_display.object.dw_zoom_perc[1] = ll_zoom
End If

idw_super.Object.Datawindow.Zoom = String(ll_zoom)

Return 1
```

Plug and Play

Having created these reusable objects, let's see how you can plug them within an application. Create a window that contains a DataWindow and two command buttons, Display_Setup and Print.

Add the following code to the cb_display_setup command button's clicked event:

```
/**************************************************************
** Call the display setup window
**************************************************************/

OpenwithParm (w_display_setup, dw_association)
```

Add the following code to the cb_print command button's clicked event:

```
/*****************************************************************
** Call the print window
*****************************************************************/

OpenwithParm (w_print_options, dw_association)
```

Your application is ready to run! When you run your application and click on the **Display Setup** button, you can change the DataWindow's display with the Display Setup dialog box (see Figure 8.16).

When you click on the print button, a Print dialog box, similar to the one in Microsoft Office Suite, appears. This dialog box's functionality also works similar to the Office Print dialog box (see Figure 8.17).

FILE AND I/O

Before you take any action on a file, you must open the file. PowerBuilder uses an integer value, called a *file handle,* to keep track of the open files. Because you can open only a limited number of files at one time, you should close the files as soon as possible after use.

This section discusses the file I/O functions available within PowerBuilder and the file I/O functionality you can achieve by using PowerBuilder.

File I/O Functions

Table 8.4 shows the list of file I/O functions available within PowerBuilder.

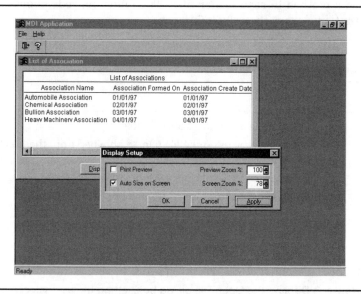

Figure 8.16   You can change the print preview and any DataWindow's size on the screen with the Display Setup dialog box.

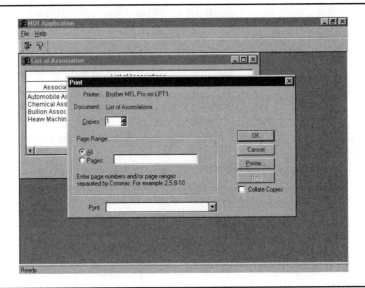

Figure 8.17 You can provide the Print dialog box facility to any DataWindow that you want to print.

Reading Files That Exceed 32,766 Bytes

Because the PowerBuilder **FileRead** function can only read 32,766 characters at a time, you need a method to read larger files. The following code shows a way of reading the files that are larger than 32,766 bytes:

Table 8.4 List of File I/O Functions

Function	Description
FileOpen( )	Opens a file and returns a file handle.
FileClose( )	Closes a file by using the file handle obtained from the FileOpen( ) function.
FileRead( )	Reads a file's contents in LineMode or StreamMode.
FileWrite( )	Writes the data to a file.
FileSeek( )	Moves the file pointer to a particular character position.
FileExists( )	Checks to see if a particular file exists.
FileDelete( )	Deletes a particular file.
FileLength( )	Determines a file's length in bytes.
GetFileOpenName( )	Displays the Open File dialog box, letting the user select a file to open.
GetFileSaveName( )	Displays the Save File dialog box, letting the user specify a filename for saving.

```
// Function int f_FileRead(String sSource)
Int    iFileHandle, iLoops, i
Long   lFileLen, lBytesRead, lNewPos
Blob   b, bTot
SetPointer(HourGlass!)
lFileLen = FileLength (sSource)
If lFileLen > 32766 Then
    If Mod(lFileLen, 32766) = 0 Then
        iLoops = lFileLen/32766
    Else
        iLoops = (lFileLen/32766) + 1
    End If
Else
    iLoops = 1
End If
iFileHandle = FileOpen (sSource,streammode!,read!,Shared!)
FOR i = 1 To iLoops
    lBytesRead = FileRead(iFileHandle, b)
    bTot = bTot + b
    lNewPos = lNewPos + lBytesRead
    FileSeek(iFileHandle,lNewPos, FromBeginning!)
Next
FileClose(iFileHandle)
```

Use the **FileLength( )** function here to determine if the file exceeds 32K.

Writing a File Copy Function

The PowerScript that follows shows how to write a file copy function within PowerBuilder:

```
int f_copyFile(string sSource, string sDest)
Int iSourceHandle, iDestHandle, iLoops, i
Long  lFileLen, lBytesRead, lNewPos
blob  b. bTot

SetPointer(HourGlass!)

// Check file length
lFileLen = FileLength (sSource)

// Determine the number of chars within the file
If lFileLen > 32766 Then
    If Mod(lFileLen, 32766) = 0 Then
        iLoops = lFileLen/32766
    Else
        iLoops = (lFileLen/32766) + 1
    End If
Else
```

continues

```
    iLoops = 1
End If

// Open the source and destination files
iSourceHandle = FileOpen (sSource,streammode!,read!,Shared!)
iDestHandle = FileOpen (sDest,streammode!,Write!,Shared!, Replace!)

// read through the source file
FOR i = 1 To iLoops
    // Read 32K buffer from the source file
    lBytesRead = FileRead(iSourceHandle, b)

    // Write 32K buffer to the destination file
    FileWrite(iDestHandle, b)

    // Point to the next 32K buffer within the destination file
    FileSeek(iDestHandle,32766 * i, FromBeginning!)

    // Calculate the next 32K file position within the source handle
    lNewPos = lNewPos + lBytesRead

    // Point to the next 32K file position within the source file
    FileSeek(iSourceHandle,lNewPos, FromBeginning!)
Next

// Close the source and destination files
FileClose( iSourceHandle)
FileClose(iDestHandle)

Return 1
```

This function copies a file from one location to another. The function is similar to using a file copy command.

ImportFile Function

The **ImportFile( )** function is useful when importing text or .DBF files into Data-Windows. When using the ImportFile( ) function to import a tab-delimited file into a DataWindow, you must create a separate column for every tab column within the file. For example, to import the following file into a DataWindow, you must set up the DataWindow as an external DataWindow with six columns.

A DataWindow you use to import such a text file could look like the one shown in Figure 8.18.

You could create a window that looks like the one in Figure 8.19 to display the imported file. To do this, place the following PowerScript within the Import Command-Button's clicked event:

```
dw_buffer.Reset( )
dw_buffer.ImportFile("sample.txt")
```

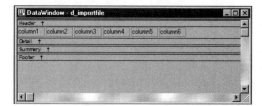

Figure 8.18   **A sample DataWindow to import a text file.**

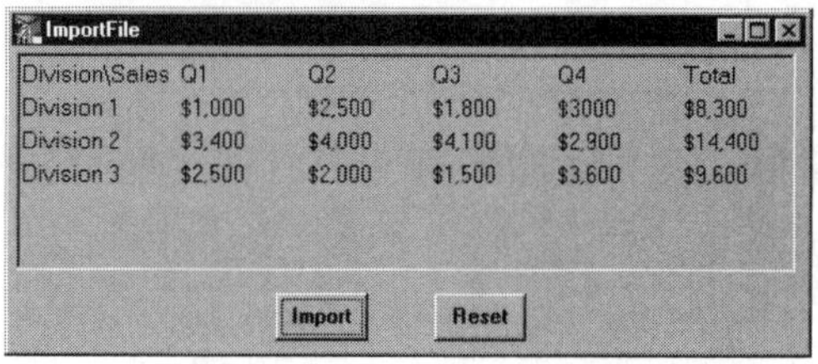

Figure 8.19   **A window displaying the imported text.**

In an application that imports data from the text files, if the column headings are constant but the data values keep changing, you can store the column headings within the DataWindow's header section and import only the row headings and the data.

TIP When trying to import large text files into a DataWindow, the ImportFile( ) function can be slow. It is much faster to import a tab-delimited file into multiple DataWindow columns than a space-delimited file into a single DataWindow column. The reason is that it requires more than one space to align the file's columns, but you need only one tab to separate the columns.

Simulating the ImportFile Function

The following PowerScript, which uses the standard PowerBuilder file I/O functions, simulates the PowerBuilder ImportFile( ) function:

```
// Function int f_ImportFile(DataWindow dwName, String sSource)
SetPointer(HourGlass!)

Integer iFNumSource

iFNumSource = FileOpen(sSource,LineMode!, Read!, Shared!)
If iFNumSource = -1 Then
    Return -10
```

continues

```
Else
    String sBuffer
    Integer iSourceRet, iCounter = 1

    Do While iSourceRet <> -100
        iSourceRet = FileRead(iFNumSource, sBuffer)
        If iSourceRet = -1 Then
            FileClose(iFNumSource)
            Return -12
        Else
            dwName.InsertRow(0)
            dwName.SetItem(iCounter, 1, sBuffer)
    End If
        iCounter = iCounter + 1
    Loop
    iSourceRet = FileClose(iFNumSource)
    If iSourceRet = -1 Then
        Return -14
    End If
    Return 1
End If
```

This function opens a text file and reads the file into a single-column external DataWindow. This function's advantage over the ImportFile( ) function is that with this function it does not matter if the source file has tabs within the records. The disadvantage is that this method is slightly slower than the ImportFile( ) function.

Environment Variables

PowerBuilder does not provide a simple function call to retrieve a particular environment variable. You can use the following custom and standard functions as the external PowerBuilder functions to enable a PowerBuilder application to retrieve the environment variables.

You can declare the following function, which you can use to retrieve any environment variable, as an external function. Declare the function within PowerBuilder as follows:

```
Function String PBGetEnv(String sEnvVar) Library "pbtools.dll"
/**************************************************
   FUNCTION: PBGetEnv(const char *fname);
**************************************************/
LPSTR FAR PASCAL PBGetEnv(LPSTR envvar)
{
    char FAR* lpszEnv;
    int icount;
    char FAR * string[1000];
    char FAR * var[1000];
    *var = NULL;

    // Return a pointer to the DOS environment
```

```
lpszEnv = GetDOSEnvironment( );

// while not end of environment
While (*lpszEnv != '\0') {
    //ascii 61 is equal to "=". Point to one position after the "="
    icount = lstrlen(lpszEnv) - lstrlen(strchr(lpszEnv,61));
    icount++;

    // return the value into string
    lstrcpyn((LPSTR) string,(LPCSTR) lpszEnv,icount);

    // null terminate the string
    string[icount] = '\0';

    // copy the environment variable into var for envvar's length
    lstrcpyn((LPSTR) var,(LPCSTR)envvar,lstrlen(envvar)+1);
    var[lstrlen(envvar)] = '\0';

    // Compare the two strings, if they are equal
    // then return the value. Else, try placing a space
    // after the variable.
    If (lstrcmpi((LPSTR) string,(LPCSTR) var) == 0)
        Return (LPSTR) lpszEnv + icount;
    Else
    lstrcat((LPSTR) var, " ");
    If (lstrcmpi((LPSTR) string, (LPCSTR) var) == 0)
        Return (LPSTR) lpszEnv + icount;

    // move to the next environment variable
    lpszEnv += lstrlen(lpszEnv) + 1;
}
Return (LPSTR) string;
}
```

The following SDK function copies the Windir environment variable's value to the lpBuffer memory location. The Windir environment variable is the directory from which the win.com file is executed:

```
WORD GetWindowsDirectoryA(LPSTR lpBuffer, WORD nSize)
```

The sBuffer variable is passed from PowerBuilder by reference. When the function is called, the sBuffer variable holds the Windir environment variable's value:

```
Function uint GetWindowsDirectoryA(Ref String sBuffer, uint iSize) Library
"kernel32.dll"
```

The following SDK function copies the Windows system directory path to the lpBuffer memory location:

```
WORD GetSystemDirectoryA(LPSTR lpBuffer, WORD nSize)
```

Declare the **GetSystemDirectoryA( )** function from PowerBuilder as an external function as follows:

```
Function uint GetSystemDirectoryA(Ref String sBuffer, uint iSize) Library
"kernel32.dll"
```

TIP This example uses the 32-bit kernel32.dll, which is part of 32-bit Windows. If you are using 16-bit Windows, the two functions described earlier are named **GetWindowsDirectory( )** and **GetSystemDirectory( )**. You will find them in the 16-bit kernel.exe.

The following PowerScript executes all three environment variable functions and stores them in three local variables:

```
String sWindowsDir, sSystemDir, sDOSPath

sWindowsDir = space(128)
sSystemDir = space(128)
GetWindowsDirectoryA(sWindowsDir, 128)
GetSystemDirectoryA(sSystemDir, 128)
sDOSPath = PBGetEnv("PATH")
```

TIP You should use the **space( )** function to preallocate memory into each variable used as a buffer for the GetWindowsDirectoryA( ) and GetSystemDirectoryA( ) functions. Because the buffer variables are passed by reference, the memory allocated for these variables must equal or be greater than the actual value stored within them by the two environment variable functions—GetWindowsDirectoryA( ) and GetSystemDirectoryA( ).

Directory I/O

The following lists the source code for a set of DLL entry functions to create, remove, and change the directories. Because these functions do not exist within PowerBuilder or within any standard Microsoft Windows DLLs, you cannot declare them directly.

TIP The following examples assume the name of the .DLL file is "pbtools.dll."

The **MakeDir( )** function shown here calls the **C_mkdir( )** function to create a DOS directory/subdirectory:

```
/********************************************************
FUNCTION: MakeDir(LPCSTR spszfname);
********************************************************/
int FAR PASCAL MakeDir(LPCSTR lpszfname)
{
Return (int)_mkdir(lpszfname);
}
```

The external function declaration for this function looks like this:

```
FUNCTION int MakeDir(String sFileName) LIBRARY "pbtools.dll"
```

This next function corresponds to the DOS **rd** command:

```
/********************************************************
FUNCTION: RemoveDir(LPCSTR lpszfname);
********************************************************/
int FAR PASCAL RemoveDir(LPCSTR lpszfname)
{
Return (int)_rmdir(lpszfname);
}
```

The external function declaration for this function looks like this:

```
FUNCTION int RemoveDir(String sFileName) LIBRARY "pbtools.dll"
```

Use the following function to change the directory:

```
/********************************************************
FUNCTION: ChangeDir(LPCSTR lpszfname);
********************************************************/
int FAR PASCAL ChangeDir(LPCSTR lpszfname)
{
Return (int)_chdir(lpszfname);
}
```

The external function declaration for this function looks like this:

```
FUNCTION int ChangeDir(String sFileName) LIBRARY "pbtools.dll"
```

To delete a file, use the following function. PowerBuilder has a **FileDelete( )** function, but if the file is a system, hidden, or read-only file then you cannot delete the file by using the FileDelete( ) function from PowerBuilder. The following function deletes a file regardless of the DOS file attribute. This function is **RemoveFile( )**:

```
/********************************************************
FUNCTION: RemoveFile(LPSTR lpszFName);
********************************************************/
```

continues

```
int FAR PASCAL RemoveFile(LPSTR lpszFName)
{
    OFSTRUCT OpenBuff;
    _dos_setfileattr (lpszFName, _A_NORMAL);
    Return OpenFile(lpszFName,&OpenBuff,OF_DELETE);
}
```

The external function declaration for this function looks like this:

```
FUNCTION int RemoveFile(String sFileName) LIBRARY "pbtools.dll"
```

Use the following function to rename a directory:

```
/*********************************************************
FUNCTION: ReName(LPCSTR lpszoldname, LPCSTR lpsznewname);
*********************************************************/
int FAR PASCAL ReName(LPCSTR lpszoldname, LPCSTR
              lpsznewname)
{
Return (int)rename(lpszoldname, lpsznewname);
}
```

The external function declaration for this function looks like this:

```
FUNCTION int Rename(String sOldName, sNewName) LIBRARY "pbtools.dll"
```

Because PowerBuilder does not have a function that returns the current drive, the **GetCurrDrive( )** function is written as a DLL. The function returns the current drive's letter to PowerBuilder:

```
/*********************************************************
FUNCTION: GetCurrDrive(unsigned *drivename);
*********************************************************/
LPSTR FAR PASCAL GetCurrDrive(void)
{
    int idrive = 0;
    LPSTR string = "z";
    char drive[] = {'a', 'b', 'c', 'd', 'e', 'f', 'g', 'h', 'i',
                    'j', 'k', 'l', 'm', 'n', 'o', 'p', 'q', 'r',
                    's', 't', 'u', 'v', 'w', 'x', 'y', 'z' };

    idrive = _getdrive( );
    drive[idrive] = '\0';
    string = &drive[idrive - 1];
    Return (LPSTR) string;
}
```

The external function declaration for this function looks like:

```
FUNCTION string GetCurrDrive( ) LIBRARY "pbtools.dll"
```

The following two functions are command line information functions. The two functions are called **f_argv(parmnumber)** and **f_argc( )**.

The f_argv(parmnumber) function retrieves the command line argument for the parmnumber command line argument.

```
/*****************************************************
** Purpose:        Return a specific command line parameter
** Arguments:      Integer iParm
*****************************************************/
sSTR =   Trim(CommandParm( ))
If sSTR = "" Or iParm = 0 Then
     Return ""
Else
     String sTmp
     Integer iPosition
     Integer iParmCounter = 0
     Integer iLength

     Do
          iLength = Len(sSTR)
          iPosition = Pos(sSTR," ")
          If iPosition = 0 Then
               iPosition = iLength
               sTmp = Left(sSTR,iPosition)
          Else
               sTmp = Left(sSTR,iPosition - 1)
          End If
          sSTR = Trim(Right(sSTR,(iLength - iPosition)))
          iParmCounter = iParmCounter + 1
     Loop Unitl iParm = iParmCounter

     If iParm > iParmCounter Then
          Return ""
     End If
     Return sTmp
End If
```

You can call this function or pass the **CommandParm( )** function into the **f_strtok( )** function illustrated here. For example:

```
f_strtok(CommandParm( ), " ", n)
```

The f_argc( ) function retrieves the number of command line parameters:

```
/********************************************************
**  Purpose: count the number of command line parameters
********************************************************/
String sParm

sParm = Trim(CommandParm( ))
If sParm = "" Then
    Return 0
Else
    Integer  iPosition
    Integer  iParmCounter = 0
    Integer  iLength

    Do
        iLength = Len(sParm)
        iPosition = Pos(sParm," ")
        If iPosition = 0 Then
            iPosition = iLength
        End If
        sParm = Trim(Right(sParm,(iLength - iPosition)))
        iParmCounter = iParmCounter + 1
    Loop Until (Len(sParm) < 1)
    Return iParmCounter
End If
```

The following function, called f_strtok( ), is a string manipulation function that processes the delimited strings:

```
/********************************************************
**  Purpose:      Parse tokens from a string
**  Arguments:    String sSTR
**                String sDelimit
**                Integer iParm
**  Call Sample:
**                String sSTR = "XXYYZZ AABBCC"
**                String sString1, sString2
**                returns XXYYZZ into sString1
**                sString1 = f_strtok(sSTR, " ", 1)
**                returns AABBCC into sString2
**                sString2 = f_strtok(sSTR, " ", 2)
********************************************************/
sSTR =  Trim(sSTR)

If sSTR = "" Or iParm = 0 Then
    Return ""
Else
    String sTmp
    Integer iPosition
```

```
        Integer iParmCounter = 0
        Integer iLength

        Do
              iLength = Len(sSTR)
              iPosition = Pos(sSTR,sDelimit)
              If iPosition = 0 Then
                    iPosition = iLength
                    sTmp = Left(sSTR,iPosition)
              Else
                    sTmp = Left(sSTR,iPosition - 1)
              End If
              sSTR = Trim(Right(sSTR,(iLength - iPosition)))
              iParmCounter = iParmCounter + 1
        Loop Unitl iParm = iParmCounter
        If iParm > iParmCounter Then
              Return ""
        End If
        Return sTmp
End If
```

These functions are an extension to the core PowerBuilder File I/O functionality.

Initialization (.INI) Files

The initialization (.INI) files are a standard means by which Windows and Windows applications configure themselves, at runtime, according to a user's needs and preferences. The two main benefits of using the .INI files are you can tailor the applications to some degree for each user and you can perform application-level configuration without creating an executable.

The discussion of initialization files can be divided into four topics:

- Standard initialization files
- Initialization file formats
- Initialization file usage
- Updating initialization files

Standard Initialization File

The standard Windows and PowerBuilder initialization files are control.ini, program.ini, system.ini, win.ini and pb.ini. Table 8.5 shows the list of the different types of INI files.

Format of Initialization Files

An initialization file is broken down into logical groups called *sections*. Each section is broken down into entries that are referred to as the *key*. The initialization file sections have the following format:

```
[section]
key=value
```

Table 8.5 The Different Types of INI Files

.INI File	Description
win.ini	This file contains entries that a user can set to alter the Windows environment according to the personal preferences.
system.ini	This file contains entries that a user can set to customize Windows to meet the system hardware needs.
control.ini	This file contains entries that describe the color schemes and patterns used in Windows and the settings for printers and installable drivers.
progman.ini	This file contains entries that define the content of program groups.
pb.ini	This file contains information about the PowerBuilder development environment.
application.ini	The application initialization files store an application's configurable information.

The section is the section's name. The brackets around the section name are required. The left bracket must be within the leftmost column on the screen. The key is the entry's name and can consist of any combination of letters and digits. For several entries, the key must be followed immediately by an equal sign. The value is the information an application uses. This can be an integer, string, or quoted string.

It is quite popular to store the value as a Boolean. You can store the Booleans as True|False, Yes|No, On|Off, or 1|0.

It is a good idea to add comments to some initialization files so users can understand each entry. To add a comment, place a semicolon at the beginning of each line of the comment.

TIP There is a 64K limit for the size of initialization files, keep your comments concise.

Initialization File Usage

Applications should create initialization files during installation or when the application cannot locate the particular initialization files. When the application creates the initialization files, the application should assign the default values. Both Windows and PowerBuilder create their initialization files during installation. The application adds or changes some entries when the user configures the application. You can use the initialization files for several different types of application-specific configurable parameters or user preferences.

User Preferences You can use the initialization files to store user-specific preferences. Examples are window position, window arrangement, automated procedure settings, colors, toolbar position and items, default template, and default font, to name a few.

The user can save the main application group's default position. This is similar to Windows' ability to save a user's workspace. When the user exits Windows, it saves the position of all the groups, icons, and other settings to the progman.ini file:

```
[Settings]
AutoArrange=1
Window=4 26 635 434 2
Order=1 4 3 2
MinOnRun=1
```

Letting the applications be configured based on each user's preferences is a desirable feature for most applications.

List Boxes You can also use the initialization files to store data for some of the application's list boxes. For example, some applications let a user search large lists of information by typing in the keywords. Storing the last two or more of the user's keywords in a DropDownListBox is often desirable, as is saving these items. So, when the user closes and reopens the application, the application fills the search DropDownListBox. You can store the search items within an initialization file, with each item separated from the other with a delimiter.

Doing this, for example, lets a generic file editor that is closed and reopened to show the last five search items used in the previous sessions in a drop-down listbox, as shown in Figure 8.20.

When the application is closed, you can save the last five items to an initialization file in either of the following formats. Method 1 has the following format:

```
[SearchItems]
ItemCount=5
SearchItem1=item1
SearchItem2=item2
SearchItem3=item3
SearchItem4=item4
SearchItem5=item5
```

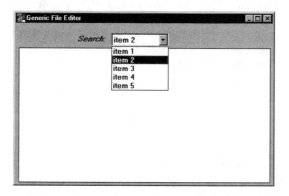

Figure 8.20   **Displaying the last five search items by using an initialization file.**

Method 2 has the following format:

```
[SearchItems]
Delimiter=";"
ItemCount=5
SearchItem1="item1;item2;item3;item4;item5"
```

The second method is a more efficient way to handle this case because, as search items increase, no additional reads to the initialization file are required.

Login Information Some applications require the user to log into an external system, such as a database or an email system. In these cases, you can store most of the user's login information within an initialization file. The user may need to enter the password or even the login ID itself for additional security. You can store these settings in an initialization file to connect a PowerBuilder user application to a popular database.

When connecting to the PowerBuilder Demo Database as the Database Administrator (DBA), you can store the following information within an initialization file:

```
[PowerBuilder Demo DB]
DBMS=ODBC
Database=PowerBuilder Demo DB
DbParm=ConnectString='DSN=PowerBuilder DemoDB;UID=dba;PWD=sql'
```

This method stores both the user id and password within the initialization file:

```
[PowerBuilder Demo DB]
DBMS=ODBC
Database=PowerBuilder Demo DB
DbParm=ConnectString='DSN=PowerBuilder Demo DB;'
```

When executing an application in production mode, the user should be required to input a password. Sometimes the user ID may also be required. In the preceding initialization file example, the user ID and password were not stored in an initialization file. The application collects that information upon startup and concatenates to the ConnectString that the application retrieves from the initialization file.

System Settings When developing an application, you need to maintain some system-wide settings that are not necessarily user-specific. In this case, it may be desirable to store the initialization files on the network rather than on each user's computer. For example, you may use a system-wide setting to enable or disable access to the email. To control this with an initialization file, you can make the following entry:

```
[email]
emailaccess=No
```

When the system comes back up, you can change the initialization file setting to "Yes." In cases like this, it is better to retrieve the setting from the initialization file each time the user wants to access email from the application. That makes the email access parameter more dynamic. When you do it this way, the users do not have to exit and restart the application every time the email access setting is changed. Application designers should think about which initialization file entries to make dynamic and which to make static based on the users' needs.

TIP One thing to remember is that a certain amount of performance degradation results if the application reads the initialization file entries dynamically.

You can store several other system settings, such as application global variables, in initialization files. Doing so makes the application more configurable.

File Path Pointers You can also use the initialization files to store the file path pointers. You can do this in Windows for several things, such as defining the location of the Program Manager group files. An example is:

```
[Groups]
Group1=C:\WINDOWS\MAIN.GRP
Group2=C:\WINDOWS\ACCESSOR.GRP
Group3=C:\WINDOWS\STARTUP.GRP
Group4=C:\WINDOWS\APPS.GRP
```

Within PowerBuilder, there are also some file path pointer settings:

```
[application]
AppName=sample50
AppLib=c:\pb50\pbsample.pbl
DefLib=c:\pb50\pbsample.pbl
$c:\pb50\pbsample.pbl(sample50)=c:\pb50\pbsample.pbl;c:
\pb50\pbsampuo.pbl;c:\pb50\pbsampfn.pbl;c:\pb50\pbsampdb.
pbl;c:\pb50\pmstyle5.pbl;
```

These examples show how both the path and filename are stored. It is important to note that you can store the path names, which you should not hard-code, within the initialization files.

Windows searches for the files in the following order: the user's current directory, the path that the windir environment variable points to, the Windows system directory, and then the directories that the path environment variable points to, from left to right. As such, rather than storing the file path names within the initialization files, you can design a system so the application can locate some files within the Windows path.

You should study the Windows initialization file settings so you don't store duplicate system information in the application-specific initialization files.

Updating Initialization Files

There are three ways to update the initialization files: manually opening the initialization file and modifying the file, developing the utilities that provide an interface for maintaining the initialization files, and letting the applications programmatically update the initialization file.

Manually Updating Initialization Files To update manually, you can read an initialization file into any text file editor. The SysEdit utility that comes with Windows lets you update the win.ini, system.ini, autoexec.bat, and config.sys files. It is very important you create a backup copy of the initialization file's before you make any changes to the file.

Programmatic Updates to Initialization Files Both PowerBuilder and the Windows SDK provide a set of functions that let developers programmatically maintain the initialization files.

PowerBuilder Functions PowerBuilder provides three functions you can use to manipulate the initialization files. The **ProfileString( )** and **ProfileInt( )** functions let the developer programmatically read from the initialization files; the **SetProfileString( )** function lets the developer write to the initialization files.

The ProfileString( ) function provides read access to the initialization file entries that are character strings. The two read functions have a default parameter that the functions use when the entry does not currently have a value specified for it. For example, to retrieve the DBMS value from the pb.ini:

```
PB.INI
[Database]
DBMS=ODBC

string s_database
s_database = &
    ProfileString("PB.INI", "Database", "DBMS", "ODBC")
```

The ProfileString( ) function searches for the pb.ini file, opens it, and retrieves the DBMS entry. If the function contains no value for this entry, the function returns the designated default (ODBC).

The ProfileInt( ) function works just as the ProfileString( ) function does except it returns a numeric value instead of a character string. The other difference is that the default value must be a numeric value.

For writing to the initialization file, use the SetProfileString( ) function. The function's fourth parameter is the value the developer wants to write to the initialization file. This function writes the value within the fourth parameter into the specified key within the specified initialization file's specified section. If the section or key is not found within the initialization file, the SetProfileString( ) function creates them:

```
SetProfileString("INIFILE.INI","Section","Key","Value")
```

This statement produces the following line in the inifile.ini when either the section or key does not exist:

```
[Section]
Key=Value
```

PowerBuilder does not provide a mechanism to delete the sections or entries by using its initialization file functions. To accomplish this, you must call the Windows SDK's **WritePrivateProfileStringA( )** or **WriteProfileStringA( )** functions.

To delete the entries by using the WritePrivateProfileStringA( ) function, you must do the following. If the entry does not exist within the specified section, create the entry. If the entry parameter is NULL, delete the entire section, including all the entries within the section. If the value parameter is NULL, delete the entry that the lpszEntry parameter specifies.

The following demonstrates how you can declare the WritePrivateProfileStringA( ) function by using C:

```
BOOL WritePrivateProfileStringA(lpszSection, lpszEntry, lpszString, lpszFilename)
LPCSTR lpszSection;      /* the section's address */
LPCSTR lpszEntry;        /* the entry's address */
LPCSTR lpszString;       /* address of the string to add   */
LPCSTR lpszFilename;     /* address of the initialization filename*/
```

To declare the function within PowerBuilder, use the following PowerScript declaration:

```
FUNCTION int WritePrivateProfileStringA(string s_section, string s_entry, string
s_value, string s_filename) LIBRARY "kernel32.dll"
```

Windows SDK Functions

The PowerBuilder functions actually call the lower-level Windows SDK functions. The Windows SDK provides developers with six initialization file functions. Table 8.6 shows the list of Windows SDK functions.

Table 8.6 A List of the Windows SDK Functions

Function	Description
GetPrivateProfileInt	Returns an integer value within a section from a specified initialization file.
GetPrivateProfileString	Returns a character string within a section from a specified initialization file.
GetProfileInt	Returns an integer value within a section from the win.ini file.
GetProfileString	Returns a character string within a section from the win.ini file.
WritePrivateProfileString	Copies a character string to a specified initialization file or deletes one or more lines from a private initialization file.
WriteProfileString	Copies a character string to the win.ini file or deletes one or more lines from win.ini.

Table 8.7   List of Registry Functions within PowerBuilder

Function	Description
RegistryDelete	Delete a key or value for an entry within the system registry.
RegistryGet	Get a value for a particular key from the system registry.
RegistryKeys	Get the subkeys available for a particular key.
RegistrySet	Set or create a value for a particular key within the system registry.
RegistryValues	Get the set of named values for a particular key.

Registry Functions

With Windows 95, Microsoft introduced PowerBuilder users to the Registry, an internal Windows database that stores the information about your machine and the Windows environment. Much of the data that you had to store in the .INI files in Windows 3.1 can now be stored in the Windows 95 or NT Registry. For example, instead of storing the registered fonts within win.ini's [fonts] section, you now find them under the HKEY_LOCAL_MACHINE key within the following folder structure:

```
\SOFTWARE\Microsoft\Windows\Currentversion\Fonts
```

You will find the System fonts under the **HKEY_CURRENT_CONFIG KEY** under \Display\Fonts.

Table 8.7 lists registry functions within PowerBuilder.

CHAPTER 9

Debugging

Unless you are the perfect programmer—and no, even *you* are not the perfect programmer!—you will need to use some form of debugging during application development. There are a number of different tools for debugging PowerBuilder applications: the Debug painter, runtime debugger, database Trace debugger, and a number of third-party debugging tools. PowerBuilder's Debug painter lets you set breakpoints and step through the application code until you find and correct the problems. You can also use PowerBuilder's just-in-time debugging to switch a running application into debug mode without terminating the application. In addition, you can use the **DebugBreak( )** function to invoke the debugger from within your application's script. The runtime debugger lets you debug a PowerBuilder executable. The database Trace debugger logs the low-level database I/O transactions in detail. In addition to the PowerBuilder debugging facilities, there are a number of Windows debugging tools you can use to assist in the debugging process. PowerBuilder 6 includes a new and improved debugging interface.

This chapter discusses each of the following debugging methods:

- Debug painter
- Just-in-time debugging
- Using the DebugBreak( ) function
- Runtime debug
- Trace debug
- Custom debug methods
- Third-party debug tools

DEBUG PAINTER

PowerBuilder lets you run the application within debug mode with the Debug painter. The application runs until it reaches a breakpoint. It then stops to let you view or change the variables within the script. The new and improved Debug painter supports a number of views including the following:

Breakpoints. The Breakpoints view displays a list of all the breakpoints (active and inactive) the developer set.

Call Stack. The Call Stack view displays the sequence of function calls leading up to the current function.

Objects In Memory. The Objects In Memory view displays an expandable list of all the current objects within memory.

Source. The Source view displays the PowerScript that the application is executing at any given point during the debugging session.

Source Browser. The Source Browser view displays a hierarchy of all the current application's objects.

Source History. The Source History view displays a list of all the scripts the debugger displayed within the Source view.

Variables. By default, the Variables view displays a list of all the variables (local, global, instance, parent, and shared) in the current application. To hide the local variables, click the right mouse button within the view and check the **Local** option from the popup menu. Similarly, you can hide or show other variables.

Watch. The Watch view displays the list of variables you have chosen to watch during the debugging session.

TIP The Source, Variables, Call Stack, and Objects in Memory views show the current context after you run the application and the application hits a breakpoint.

You can open and close any of these views at any time during the debugging session. To display a view, select the appropriate MenuItem from the View menu. To close a view, click the right button of your mouse within the view, and select **Close** from the popup menu.

In addition, you can customize the Debug painter's view. PowerBuilder automatically saves the view, so the next time you start the Debug painter, the painter displays the previously saved view. To revert to the Debug painter's default layout, select **Options** from the **Debug** menu. The Debug painter, in turn, displays the Options dialog. Within the dialog box, click **Layout**, and then click **Default**.

Figure 9.1 shows the Debug painter's default layout.

BREAKPOINTS

You can use breakpoints to stop the execution at specific places throughout the application. You can place breakpoints within any object's PowerScript. To create a breakpoint, simply click the right mouse button at the desired line of code within the Source

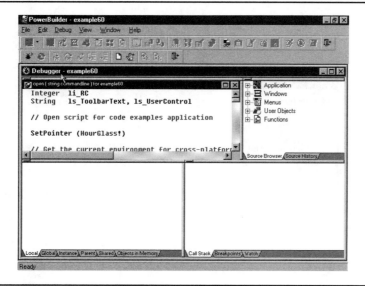

Figure 9.1   The Debug painter.

view. The PowerBuilder debugger, in turn, shows a bullet to the left of the line to denote the breakpoint. To remove breakpoints, double-click on the bullet. You can place breakpoints on any line of code within an object, with the exception of comment lines, blank lines, and variable declarations.

When the application reaches a breakpoint, PowerBuilder stops the execution, and you can view the variables and attributes' current values. You also can edit the variables.

TIP You should not place a breakpoint within the **Activate** or **Getfocus** events because it can cause recursive event-triggering that hangs the debug session.

When you place the breakpoints (also called *stops*) within a script, PowerBuilder saves the stop information within the pb.ini. In addition, you can enable and disable the breakpoints by clicking on the line with the breakpoint and selecting **Enable Breakpoint** or **Disable Breakpoint** from the popup menu. This lets you save useful breakpoints and disable them when you do not need them.

When your application hits a breakpoint, you can step into, step over, and step out of the current context within the script the application is executing. As a result, you can step through your code to examine the memory objects, variables, and expressions.

Figure 9.2 illustrates that the window w_about has an enabled breakpoint at the Open event's fourth line (you cannot actually see the line number, but its there) and a disabled breakpoint at the Open event's fifth line.

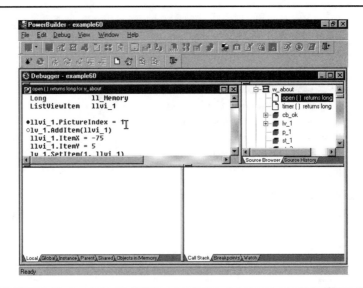

Figure 9.2   **Enabled and Disabled breakpoints.**

TIP To view all the breakpoints set for a given application, select **Breakpoints** from the **Edit** menu within the Debug painter.

Watch List

Another important feature of the Debug painter is the creation of a watch list. A watch list can "watch" singular variables or groups of variables as you step through the code. This saves you the time of going through the variable list's hierarchy to see a particular variable's value.

To place the variables within the watch list, highlight the variable(s) within the Variables view, click the right mouse button and select **Add Watch** from the popup menu. The Debug painter adds the selected variable(s) to the watch list within the Watch view, and PowerBuilder updates them as they change. Unfortunately, if you step through the code too quickly, sometimes PowerBuilder does not update the watch list correctly. To avoid this problem, you should press the step icon in a measured fashion.

One good watch variable choice is the sqlca variable sqlerrtext. Rather than having to go through the variable hierarchy each time to look at sqlerrtext, adding the variable to the watch list makes it accessible to you at all times, thus saving you a good deal of time.

Figure 9.3 shows the Debug painter's view after you add sqlerrtext to the watch list.

Variables

When running an application within debug mode, you can track the variables and their values. When you run the application from the Debug painter, you can display a list of

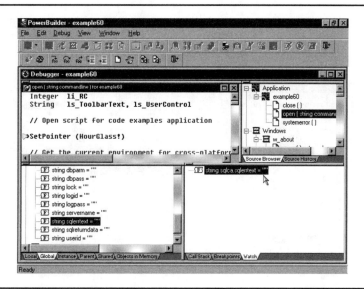

Figure 9.3   **Using the variable watch list.**

all the variables within the application by selecting **Variables** from the **View** menu. A plus sign next to the variable denotes that you can see the variables' attributes by clicking on the plus sign. The PowerBuilder debugger displays the variable's first 128 characters. If there are more than 128 characters, the debugger displays the word *more* after the string.

TIP To add a variable to the watch list, highlight the variable in the Variable view, click the right mouse button and select **Add Watch** from the popup menu.

The Debug painter shows the following types of variables:

- Instance (new to version 6)
- Parent
- Global
- Shared
- Local

The next five sections discuss the debugging of these variable types.

Instance

The instance variables are all the variables you defined for the current object. Figure 9.4 shows the variables for a window object.

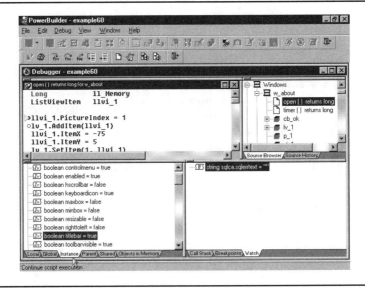

Figure 9.4   A window object's variables.

Parent

The parent variables are all the variables for the current object or control's parent object. Figure 9.5 shows the Parent variables defined for a CommandButton located on the same window as in Figure 9.4.

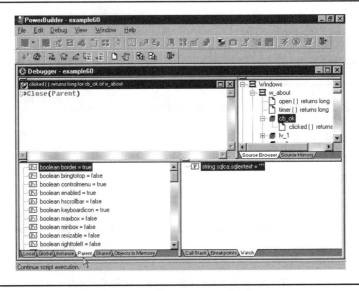

Figure 9.5   A CommandButton control's parent variables.

Global

Figure 9.6 shows a typical application's global variables. The global variables include PowerBuilder system variables such as sqlca, sqlda, sqlsa, error, and message, along with any application-specific globals. Looking at the transaction object's attributes (for sqlca or any other user-defined transaction object) can provide great assistance in debugging the database errors. In addition to the object, event, and line of a particular error, the error variable contains the error text. This information can also be extremely useful when debugging.

Shared

The shared variables are the variables shared by the windows and application being debugged. Figure 9.7 shows an example of the shared variables view.

Local

The local variables are the variables defined within the current event or function's scope. As you step from one function/event to another, the local variables' scope changes. Figure 9.8 shows an example of the local variables view.

Source

The Source View displays the PowerScript for the object you select within the Source Browser view. To view the script associated with an object, click the right mouse button on the object within the Source Browser view, and select **Source** from the popup menu. In the Source view, you can add breakpoints, view all the breakpoints that you

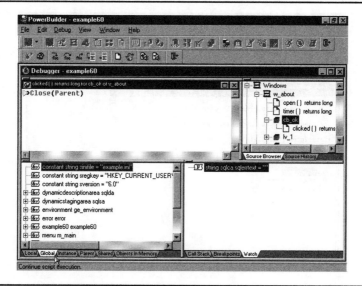

Figure 9.6   **A typical PowerBuilder application's global variables.**

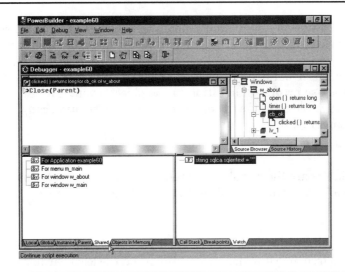

Figure 9.7   A typical PowerBuilder application's shared variables.

have defined, jump to a particular line within the script, find a particular word or string within the script, and so on. You can do so by choosing the appropriate option from the popup menu the Debug painter displays when you click the right button of your mouse within the view. Figure 9.9 shows an example of the script the Source view displays for the window w_about.

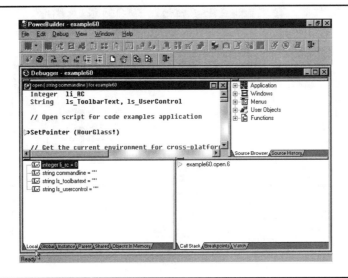

Figure 9.8   A typical PowerBuilder application's local variables.

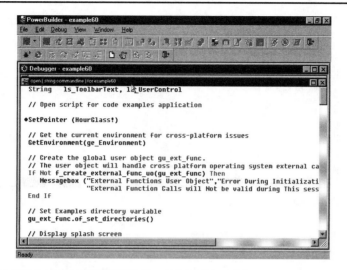

Figure 9.9   The Source view for the window w_about.

Source Browser

The Source Browser view displays a hierarchy of all the current application's objects. At the top level, the Source Browser view displays the objects: Application, Windows, Menus, User Objects, and Functions. To view the objects underneath any of these objects, double-click on the object. Figure 9.10 shows a sample Source Browser view.

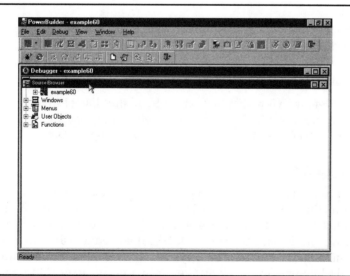

Figure 9.10   A sample Source Browser view.

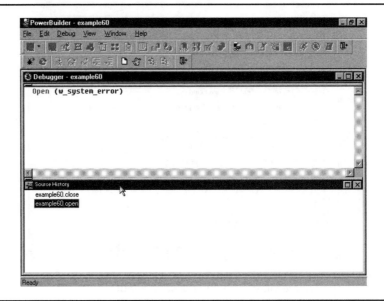

Figure 9.11 A sample Source History view.

Source History

The Source History view displays a list of all objects whose scripts the debugger displayed in the Source view. Figure 9.11 shows a sample Source History view.

Call Stack

The Call Stack view displays the sequence of function calls leading up to the current function. Figure 9.12 shows a sample Call Stack view.

Objects In Memory

The Objects In Memory view displays an expandable list of all the current objects within memory at any given point during the debugging session. Figure 9.13 shows a sample view of the objects within memory during a debugging session.

JUST IN TIME DEBUGGING

To switch a running application into debug mode without terminating the application, you can use PowerBuilder 6's new Just In Time Debugging feature. To enable Just In Time debugging, select **System Options** from the **PowerPanel**. Check the **Just In Time Debugging** checkbox, and then click OK. If you enable Just In Time debugging, when your application is running and a system error occurs, PowerBuilder automatically opens the Debug window showing the context of the error that occurred.

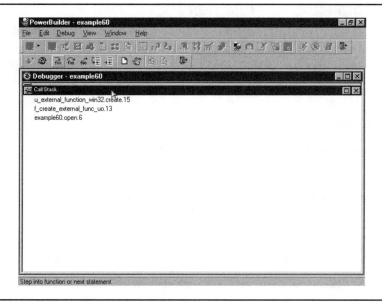

Figure 9.12   A sample Call Stack view.

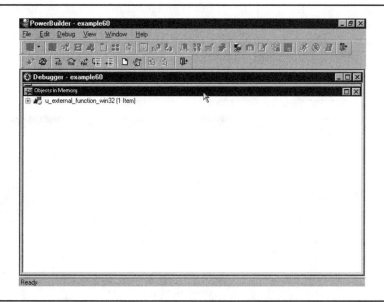

Figure 9.13   A sample view of the objects within memory after you run the PowerBuilder
application.

USING THE DEBUGBREAK( ) FUNCTION

By using the DebugBreak( ) function in your application's script, you can suspend execution and invoke the debug mode. PowerBuilder will display the debug window showing the current context. An example of using the DebugBreak( ) function is:

```
IF IsDate(sDate) THEN DebugBreak()
```

RUNTIME DEBUG

When you create an application's executable, you can run it with the PowerBuilder runtime debug setting. This setting writes every executed line of code to a trace file. Doing so is helpful to detect the errors that occur within the executable but not within the development environment. In addition, the trace file lets the developer view the order in which PowerBuilder executes the scripts and functions. For each line that Power-Builder executes, the debugger records an entry within the trace file. These entries show the objects' creation and destruction, and the scripts and functions' execution. They also show the use of the scripts line by line within the functions and events.

TIP You can perform PowerBuilder's runtime debugging only when building interpreted PowerBuilder executables and not when building machine code executables.

To create a trace file for the application executable, include the **/pbdebug** command-line switch when executing the application. Within the development environment, you can use the pbdebug setting within the pb.ini file to activate the debug trace option within the development environment. Figure 9.14 shows an example of a sim-

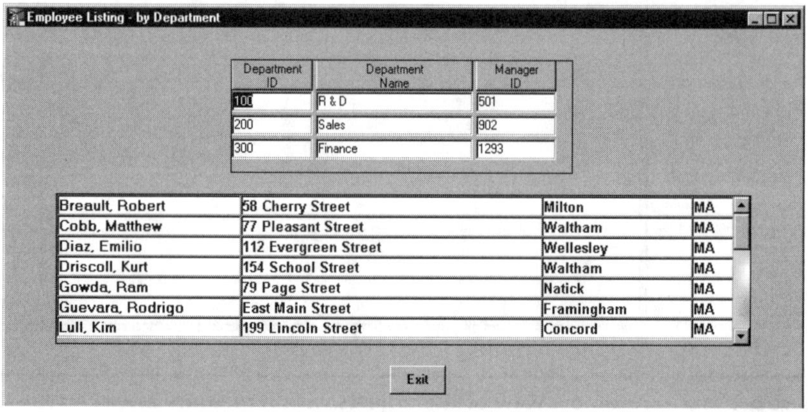

Figure 9.14   A sample trace application.

ple screen that illustrates PowerBuilder's runtime debugging. The application name is pbook.exe. The application contains one window with two DataWindows and a CommandButton. At runtime, the application retrieves data into the two DataWindows, the user clicks on the top DataWindow's second row, causing the application to retrieve new data into the bottom DataWindow. Finally, the user can close the window by clicking the **Exit** button.

TIP Alternatively, to activate the runtime debugger when you run the application from within the PowerBuilder development environment, select **Power-Panel** from the **File** menu, and then double click on **System Options** within the PowerPanel dialog box's list, check the **Enable PBDebug Tracing** checkbox, and specify the trace file's name. The runtime debugger creates the trace file within the directory where the application .PBLs reside only if a system error occurs.

Run this application with the command switch /**pbdebug**, and the application will create the following pbbook.dbg file. The file shows each event and function's creation for all of the window, menu, and user objects.

TIP PowerBuilder creates the output file with the same name as the executable, but with a .DBG file extension. PowerBuilder creates the .DBG file within the same directory as the executable.

```
Executing event +CREATE for class PBBOOK, lib entry PBBOOK
      Executing instruction at line 2
      Executing instruction at line 3
      Executing instruction at line 4
      Executing instruction at line 5
      Executing instruction at line 6
      Executing instruction at line 7
End event +CREATE for class PBBOOK, lib entry PBBOOK
Executing event +OPEN for class PBBOOK, lib entry PBBOOK
      Executing instruction at line 1
      Executing instruction at line 2
      Executing instruction at line 3
      Executing instruction at line 4
      Executing instruction at line 5
      Executing instruction at line 7
      Executing instruction at line 9
      Executing class system function FNOPENWND for class SYSTEMFUNCTIONS,lib entry
_TYPEDEF
      Executing event +CREATE for class W_EMPLIST, lib entry W_EMPLIST
          Executing instruction at line 2
```

continues

```
        Executing instruction at line 3
        Executing instruction at line 4
        Executing instruction at line 5
    End event +CREATE for class W_EMPLIST, lib entry W_EMPLIST
    Executing event +OPEN for class W_EMPLIST, lib entry W_EMPLIST
        Executing instruction at line 3
        Executing object function SETTRANSOBJECT for class DATAWINDOW,lib entry
_TYPEDEF
        End object function SETTRANSOBJECT for class DATAWINDOW,lib entry _TYPEDEF
        Executing instruction at line 4
        Executing object function SETTRANSOBJECT for class DATAWINDOW,lib entry
_TYPEDEF
        End object function SETTRANSOBJECT for class DATAWINDOW, lib entry _TYPEDEF
        Executing instruction at line 6
        Executing object function RETRIEVE for class DATAWINDOW, lib entry _TYPEDEF
            Executing event +ROWFOCUSCHANGED for class DW_DEPT, lib entry W_EMPLIST
                Executing instruction at line 3
                Executing object function GETROW for class DATAWINDOW, lib entry
_TYPEDEF
                End object function GETROW for class DATAWINDOW, lib entry
_TYPEDEF
                Executing instruction at line 5
                Executing object function GETITEMNUMBER for class DATAWINDOW, lib
entry _TYPEDEF
                End object function GETITEMNUMBER for class DATAWINDOW, lib entry
_TYPEDEF
                Executing instruction at line 7
                Executing object function RETRIEVE for class DATAWINDOW, lib entry
_TYPEDEF
                End object function RETRIEVE for class DATAWINDOW, lib entry
_TYPEDEF
                Executing instruction at line 8
            End event +ROWFOCUSCHANGED for class DW_DEPT, lib entry W_EMPLIST
        End object function RETRIEVE for class DATAWINDOW, lib entry _TYPEDEF
        Executing instruction at line 6
        Executing instruction at line 8
        Executing object function GETITEMNUMBER for class DATAWINDOW, lib entry
_TYPEDEF
        End object function GETITEMNUMBER for class DATAWINDOW, lib entry _TYPEDEF
        Executing instruction at line 10
        Executing object function RETRIEVE for class DATAWINDOW, lib entry _TYPEDEF
        End object function RETRIEVE for class DATAWINDOW, lib entry _TYPEDEF
        Executing instruction at line 11
    End event +OPEN for class W_EMPLIST, lib entry W_EMPLIST
    Executing instruction at line 9
End event +OPEN for class PBBOOK, lib entry PBBOOK
Executing event +ROWFOCUSCHANGED for class DW_DEPT, lib entry W_EMPLIST
    Executing instruction at line 3
    Executing object function GETROW for class DATAWINDOW, lib entry _TYPEDEF
    End object function GETROW for class DATAWINDOW, lib entry _TYPEDEF
```

```
     Executing instruction at line 5
     Executing object function GETITEMNUMBER for class DATAWINDOW, lib entry _TYPEDEF
     End object function GETITEMNUMBER for class DATAWINDOW, lib entry _TYPEDEF
     Executing instruction at line 7
     Executing object function RETRIEVE for class DATAWINDOW, lib entry _TYPEDEF
     End object function RETRIEVE for class DATAWINDOW, lib entry _TYPEDEF
     Executing instruction at line 8
End event +ROWFOCUSCHANGED for class DW_DEPT, lib entry W_EMPLIST
Executing event +CLICKED for class CB_1, lib entry W_EMPLIST
     Executing instruction at line 1
     Executing class system function FNCLOSEWND for class SYSTEMFUNCTIONS, lib entry
_TYPEDEF
     Executing event +DESTROY for class DWOBJECT, lib entry _TYPEDEF
          Executing instruction at line 1859
          Executing object function DESTROY_OBJECT for class DWOBJECT, lib entry
_TYPEDEF
          End object function DESTROY_OBJECT for class DWOBJECT, lib entry _TYPEDEF
     End event +DESTROY for class DWOBJECT, lib entry _TYPEDEF
     Executing event +DESTROY for class DWOBJECT, lib entry _TYPEDEF
          Executing instruction at line 1859
          Executing object function DESTROY_OBJECT for class DWOBJECT, lib entry
_TYPEDEF
          End object function DESTROY_OBJECT for class DWOBJECT, lib entry _TYPEDEF
     End event +DESTROY for class DWOBJECT, lib entry _TYPEDEF
     Executing event +DESTROY for class W_EMPLIST, lib entry W_EMPLIST
          Executing instruction at line 2
          Executing instruction at line 3
          Executing instruction at line 4
     End event +DESTROY for class W_EMPLIST, lib entry W_EMPLIST
     Executing instruction at line 1
     Executing instruction at line 2
End event +CLICKED for class CB_1, lib entry W_EMPLIST
Executing event +DESTROY for class PBBOOK, lib entry PBBOOK
     Executing instruction at line 2
     Executing instruction at line 3
     Executing instruction at line 4
     Executing instruction at line 5
     Executing instruction at line 6
End event +DESTROY for class PBBOOK, lib entry PBBOOK
```

Obviously, the debug files can become quite large. Nevertheless, they are useful when problems that do not occur within the development environment occur within the executable.

TRACE DEBUG

You can use the Trace debugger to trace the interaction between the client and the database via the PowerBuilder database interface. To start the Trace debugger, click the **Database Profile** icon on the PowerBar. PowerBuilder displays the Database Profiles

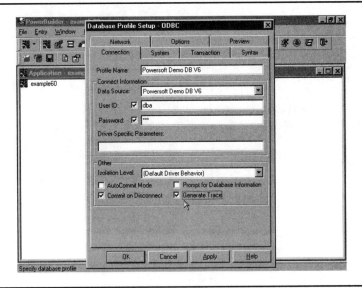

Figure 9.15   **Enabling the database Trace.**

dialog box, which displays a list of installed Powersoft Database Interfaces. Choose the database (in this example, choose the database **Powersoft Demo DB V6**), and then click **Edit**. PowerBuilder displays the Database Profile Setup dialog box. In the Other group, click the **Generate Trace** checkbox as shown in Figure 9.15. Internally, Power-Builder prepends the RDBMS value within the transaction object with the word *Trace*.

TIP Alternatively, to activate the Trace debugger when you run the application from within the PowerBuilder development environment, select **PowerPanel** from the **File** menu, and then double-click on **System Options** within the Power-Panel dialog's list, click the **Profiling** tab, check the **Enable Tracing** checkbox, and specify the trace file's name. The Trace debugger automatically creates the trace file within the directory where the application .PBLs reside. You can also check the appropriate checkboxes depending on the activities you would like the Trace debugger to trace.

Once you enable tracing, you can run the database painter to begin generating the log data. The Trace debugger writes the low-level database interface I/O information to a pbtrace.log file located within your system's Windows (windir) directory. When executing the Database painter, the messagebox in Figure 9.16 appears to show the trace file's name and location.

The database painter displays the Select Tables dialog box, as shown in Figure 9.17. Next, select the department and employee tables, as shown in Figure 9.18.

Figure 9.16   The Trace file's name and location.

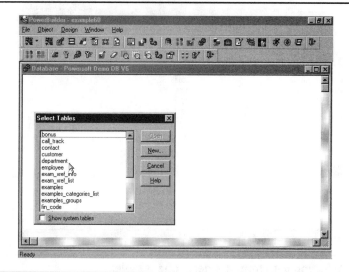

Figure 9.17   The Select Tables dialog box.

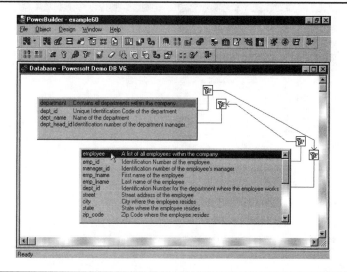

Figure 9.18   Selecting the department and employee tables.

The database painter, in turn, retrieves and displays the data from the department table, as shown in Figure 9.19.

Change the first record's department name from "R&D" to "Research & Development," and update the database, as shown in Figure 9.20.

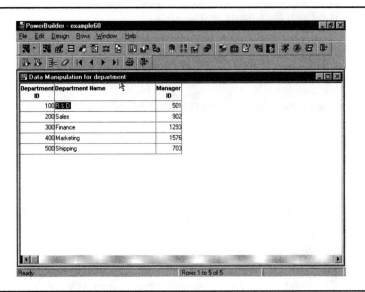

Figure 9.19   Selecting data from the department table.

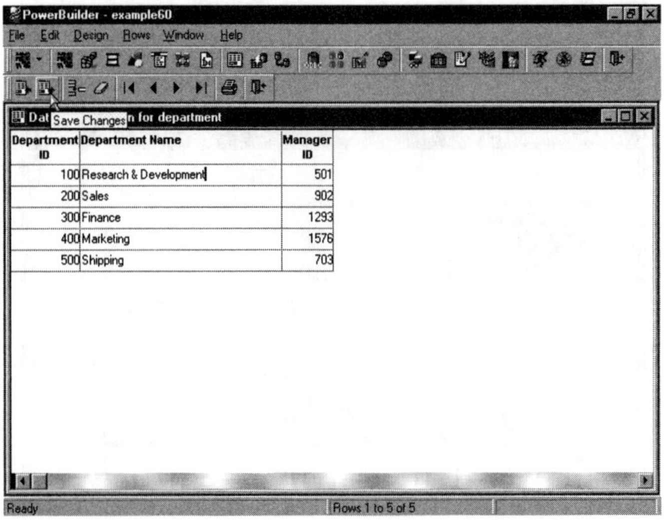

Figure 9.20   Updating the department name column.

After you complete these steps, exit the Database painter. You can now review the pbtrace.log file.

TIP The trace utility must have the pbtra050.dll file in its path.

The table shows the pbtrace.log file's contents. The file contains detail information associated with the steps taken within the database painter, as shown in Figures 9.17 through 9.20.

```
DIALOG CONNECT TO TRACE ODBC:
USERID=dba
DATA=Powersoft Demo DB V6
DBPARM=ConnectString='DSN=Powersoft Demo DB V6;UID=dba;PWD=sql' (4408 MilliSeconds)
 TABLE LIST: (73 MilliSeconds)
COLUMNS INFORMATION: TABLE=department OWNER=dba (126 MilliSeconds)
 PRIMARY KEY RETRIEVE: (23 MilliSeconds)
 FOREIGN KEY RETRIEVE: (76 MilliSeconds)
COLUMNS INFORMATION: TABLE=employee OWNER=dba (48 MilliSeconds)
 PRIMARY KEY RETRIEVE: (7 MilliSeconds)
 FOREIGN KEY RETRIEVE: (28 MilliSeconds)
 UNIQUE KEY CHECK: TABLE=department OWNER=dba USER=dba (21 MilliSeconds)
YES, unique key found
PREPARE:
  SELECT  "employee"."emp_id" ,         "employee"."emp_lname" ,
"employee"."emp_fname"    FROM "employee"   ORDER BY "employee"."emp_id"
ASC   (7 MilliSeconds)
 BIND SELECT OUTPUT BUFFER (DataWindow): (0 MilliSeconds)
,len=44,type=FLOAT,pbt3,dbt0,ct0,dec0
,len=22,type=CHAR,pbt1,dbt0,ct0,dec0
,len=22,type=CHAR,pbt1,dbt0,ct0,dec0
 EXECUTE: (0 MilliSeconds)
 FETCH NEXT: (119 MilliSeconds)
     COLUMN=      COLUMN=Whitney   COLUMN=Fran
 FETCH NEXT: (0 MilliSeconds)
     COLUMN=      COLUMN=Cobb      COLUMN=Matthew
 FETCH NEXT: (0 MilliSeconds)
     COLUMN=      COLUMN=Chin      COLUMN=Philip
 FETCH NEXT: (0 MilliSeconds)
     COLUMN=      COLUMN=Jordan    COLUMN=Julie
 FETCH NEXT: (0 MilliSeconds)
     COLUMN=      COLUMN=Breault   COLUMN=Robert
 FETCH NEXT: (0 MilliSeconds)
     COLUMN=      COLUMN=Espinoza  COLUMN=Melissa
 FETCH NEXT: (0 MilliSeconds)
```

continues

```
      COLUMN=        COLUMN=Bertrand   COLUMN=Jeannette
FETCH NEXT: (0 MilliSeconds)
      COLUMN=        COLUMN=Dill         COLUMN=Marc
FETCH NEXT: (0 MilliSeconds)
      COLUMN=        COLUMN=Francis    COLUMN=Jane
FETCH NEXT: (0 MilliSeconds)
      COLUMN=        COLUMN=Shishov    COLUMN=Natasha
FETCH NEXT: (0 MilliSeconds)
      COLUMN=        COLUMN=Driscoll   COLUMN=Kurt
FETCH NEXT: (0 MilliSeconds)
      COLUMN=        COLUMN=Guevara    COLUMN=Rodrigo
FETCH NEXT: (0 MilliSeconds)
      COLUMN=        COLUMN=Gowda        COLUMN=Ram
FETCH NEXT: (0 MilliSeconds)
      COLUMN=        COLUMN=Melkisetian      COLUMN=Terry
FETCH NEXT: (0 MilliSeconds)
      COLUMN=        COLUMN=Overbey    COLUMN=Rollin
FETCH NEXT: (0 MilliSeconds)
      COLUMN=        COLUMN=Pastor     COLUMN=Lynn
FETCH NEXT: (0 MilliSeconds)
      COLUMN=        COLUMN=Crow         COLUMN=John
FETCH NEXT: (0 MilliSeconds)
      COLUMN=        COLUMN=Davidson   COLUMN=Jo Ann
FETCH NEXT: (0 MilliSeconds)
      COLUMN=        COLUMN=Weaver     COLUMN=Bruce
FETCH NEXT: (0 MilliSeconds)
      COLUMN=        COLUMN=Lull         COLUMN=Kim
FETCH NEXT: (0 MilliSeconds)
      COLUMN=        COLUMN=Rabkin     COLUMN=Andrew
FETCH NEXT: (0 MilliSeconds)
      COLUMN=        COLUMN=Klobucher COLUMN=James
FETCH NEXT: (0 MilliSeconds)
      COLUMN=        COLUMN=Siperstein      COLUMN=Linda
FETCH NEXT: (0 MilliSeconds)
      COLUMN=        COLUMN=Scott      COLUMN=David
FETCH NEXT: (0 MilliSeconds)
      COLUMN=        COLUMN=Sullivan   COLUMN=Dorothy
FETCH NEXT: (0 MilliSeconds)
      COLUMN=        COLUMN=Samuels    COLUMN=Peter
FETCH NEXT: (0 MilliSeconds)
      COLUMN=        COLUMN=Coleman    COLUMN=James
FETCH NEXT: (0 MilliSeconds)
      COLUMN=        COLUMN=Barletta   COLUMN=Irene
FETCH NEXT: (0 MilliSeconds)
      COLUMN=        COLUMN=Wang         COLUMN=Albert
FETCH NEXT: (0 MilliSeconds)
      COLUMN=        COLUMN=Powell     COLUMN=Thomas
FETCH NEXT: (0 MilliSeconds)
      COLUMN=        COLUMN=Garcia     COLUMN=Mary
```

```
FETCH NEXT: (0 MilliSeconds)
    COLUMN=        COLUMN=Poitras   COLUMN=Kathleen
FETCH NEXT: (0 MilliSeconds)
    COLUMN=        COLUMN=Martinez COLUMN=Jose
FETCH NEXT: (0 MilliSeconds)
    COLUMN=        COLUMN=Braun     COLUMN=Jane
FETCH NEXT: (0 MilliSeconds)
    COLUMN=        COLUMN=Higgins   COLUMN=Denis
FETCH NEXT: (0 MilliSeconds)
    COLUMN=        COLUMN=Marshall  COLUMN=Dean
FETCH NEXT: (0 MilliSeconds)
    COLUMN=        COLUMN=Singer    COLUMN=Samuel
FETCH NEXT: (0 MilliSeconds)
    COLUMN=        COLUMN=Sheffield COLUMN=John
FETCH NEXT: (0 MilliSeconds)
    COLUMN=        COLUMN=Kuo       COLUMN=Felicia
FETCH NEXT: (0 MilliSeconds)
    COLUMN=        COLUMN=Coe       COLUMN=Kristen
FETCH NEXT: (0 MilliSeconds)
    COLUMN=        COLUMN=Charlton  COLUMN=Doug
FETCH NEXT: (0 MilliSeconds)
    COLUMN=        COLUMN=Kelly     COLUMN=Moira
FETCH NEXT: (0 MilliSeconds)
    COLUMN=        COLUMN=Martel    COLUMN=Ken
FETCH NEXT: (0 MilliSeconds)
    COLUMN=        COLUMN=Crowley   COLUMN=Charles
FETCH NEXT: (0 MilliSeconds)
    COLUMN=        COLUMN=Taylor    COLUMN=Ann
FETCH NEXT: (0 MilliSeconds)
    COLUMN=        COLUMN=Savarino  COLUMN=Pamela
FETCH NEXT: (0 MilliSeconds)
    COLUMN=        COLUMN=Sisson    COLUMN=Thomas
FETCH NEXT: (0 MilliSeconds)
    COLUMN=        COLUMN=Butterfield    COLUMN=Joyce
FETCH NEXT: (0 MilliSeconds)
    COLUMN=        COLUMN=Barker    COLUMN=Joseph
FETCH NEXT: (0 MilliSeconds)
    COLUMN=        COLUMN=Sterling  COLUMN=Paul
FETCH NEXT: (0 MilliSeconds)
    COLUMN=        COLUMN=Chao      COLUMN=Shih Lin
FETCH NEXT: (0 MilliSeconds)
    COLUMN=        COLUMN=Blaikie   COLUMN=Barbara
FETCH NEXT: (0 MilliSeconds)
    COLUMN=        COLUMN=Smith     COLUMN=Susan
FETCH NEXT: (0 MilliSeconds)
    COLUMN=        COLUMN=Preston   COLUMN=Mark
FETCH NEXT: (0 MilliSeconds)
    COLUMN=        COLUMN=Clark     COLUMN=Alison
FETCH NEXT: (0 MilliSeconds)
```

continues

```
    COLUMN=      COLUMN=Soo       COLUMN=Hing
FETCH NEXT: (0 MilliSeconds)
    COLUMN=      COLUMN=Goggin    COLUMN=Kevin
FETCH NEXT: (0 MilliSeconds)
    COLUMN=      COLUMN=Bucceri   COLUMN=Matthew
FETCH NEXT: (0 MilliSeconds)
    COLUMN=      COLUMN=Diaz      COLUMN=Emilio
FETCH NEXT: (0 MilliSeconds)
    COLUMN=      COLUMN=Shea      COLUMN=Mary Anne
FETCH NEXT: (0 MilliSeconds)
    COLUMN=      COLUMN=Bigelow   COLUMN=Janet
FETCH NEXT: (0 MilliSeconds)
    COLUMN=      COLUMN=Litton    COLUMN=Jennifer
FETCH NEXT: (0 MilliSeconds)
    COLUMN=      COLUMN=Yeung     COLUMN=Caroline
FETCH NEXT: (0 MilliSeconds)
    COLUMN=      COLUMN=Letiecq   COLUMN=John
FETCH NEXT: (0 MilliSeconds)
    COLUMN=      COLUMN=Wetherby  COLUMN=Ruth
FETCH NEXT: (0 MilliSeconds)
    COLUMN=      COLUMN=Rebeiro   COLUMN=Anthony
FETCH NEXT: (0 MilliSeconds)
    COLUMN=      COLUMN=Evans     COLUMN=Scott
FETCH NEXT: (0 MilliSeconds)
    COLUMN=      COLUMN=Pickett   COLUMN=Catherine
FETCH NEXT: (0 MilliSeconds)
    COLUMN=      COLUMN=Morris    COLUMN=Mark
FETCH NEXT: (0 MilliSeconds)
    COLUMN=      COLUMN=Romero    COLUMN=Sheila
FETCH NEXT: (0 MilliSeconds)
    COLUMN=      COLUMN=Lambert   COLUMN=Elizabeth
FETCH NEXT: (0 MilliSeconds)
    COLUMN=      COLUMN=Lynch     COLUMN=Michael
FETCH NEXT: (0 MilliSeconds)
    COLUMN=      COLUMN=Hildebrand    COLUMN=Janet
FETCH NEXT: (0 MilliSeconds)
    COLUMN=      COLUMN=Nielsen   COLUMN=Robert
FETCH NEXT: (0 MilliSeconds)
    COLUMN=      COLUMN=Ahmed     COLUMN=Alex
FETCH NEXT: (2 MilliSeconds)
Error 1 (rc 100)
PREPARE:
SELECT "dept_id", "dept_name", "dept_head_id" FROM "department" (6 MilliSeconds)
BIND SELECT OUTPUT BUFFER (DataWindow): (0 MilliSeconds)
,len=44,type=LONG,pbt22,dbt0,ct0,dec0
,len=42,type=CHAR,pbt1,dbt0,ct0,dec0
,len=44,type=LONG,pbt22,dbt0,ct0,dec0
EXECUTE: (0 MilliSeconds)
FETCH NEXT: (22 MilliSeconds)
```

```
      COLUMN=100      COLUMN=R & D    COLUMN=501
FETCH NEXT: (0 MilliSeconds)
      COLUMN=200      COLUMN=Sales    COLUMN=902
FETCH NEXT: (0 MilliSeconds)
      COLUMN=300      COLUMN=Finance  COLUMN=1293
FETCH NEXT: (0 MilliSeconds)
      COLUMN=400      COLUMN=MarketingCOLUMN=1576
FETCH NEXT: (0 MilliSeconds)
      COLUMN=500      COLUMN=Shipping COLUMN=703
FETCH NEXT: (2 MilliSeconds)
Error 1 (rc 100)
ROLLBACK: (0 MilliSeconds)
BEGIN TRANSACTION: (2 MilliSeconds)
PREPARE WITH BIND VARIABLES:
UPDATE "department" SET "dept_name" = ? WHERE "dept_id" = ? AND "dept_name"
= ? AND "dept_head_id" = ?  (18 MilliSeconds)
VCHAR Length22 ID:1 *Research & Development*
LONG Length0 ID:2
VCHAR Length5 ID:3 *R & D*
LONG Length0 ID:4  (2 MilliSeconds)
EXECUTE: (32 MilliSeconds)
GET AFFECTED ROWS: (33 MilliSeconds)
^  1 Rows Affected
COMMIT: (42 MilliSeconds)
```

TIP If you have any problems with a database from within the PowerBuilder development environment or a PowerBuilder application, you must generate a pbtrace.log file and send the file to Powersoft to help them debug any database interface problems.

CUSTOM DEBUG METHODS

Writing Variables to a File

Another way to debug an application is to write variables to a file. To do this, use the **FileOpen( )**, **FileWrite( )**, and **FileClose( )** functions. You can use these functions within either the development environment in debug mode or within an executable.

Unfortunately, when you run an application from the Debug painter, the application may not receive all of the Windows messages that are sent to it. Therefore, the application might run fine within the Debug painter but bomb as an executable. When you run an application as an executable, the application receives all the Windows messages, and other problems may become apparent. One way to isolate these problems is to write the parameters or variable values to a file while the executable is running. This helps you determine the exact problem or the its location.

An example of writing the values to a file during debugging is placing the

FileOpen( ) and FileWrite( ) script within a function called **custdebug( )** and referencing the function within a code segment. You define the function as a Boolean with
an argument a_sMessage of type string. The function custdebug( ) is:

```
int iFileNo

iFileNo = FileOpen("custdebug.log", LineMode!, Write!, &
    LockWrite!, Append!)
FileWrite(iFileNo, a_sMessage)
FileClose(iFileNo)
```

This function opens a debug file called custdebug.log and writes the value, a_sMessage,
passed to it from the code segment.

TIP If you open the debug file at the beginning of a program and do not close it
until the end, the writes to the file may not get flushed to the disk and the file
contents may be useless if the program blows up. You should open and close the
debug file each time a write occurs so that the file content gets flushed to the disk.

The following code shows the custdebug( ) function called at different places within
the script. The example helps detect the problem's location. If you want to write the contents of the different variables within the script, simply pass the value into the cust-
debug( ) function:

```
// dw_headcount's Clicked script
grObjectType ClickedObject
string s_company, grGraphName="gr_1", s_seriesname="Equipment"
int ret, l_series, l_category
int FileNo
string category_count

// Find out where the user clicked within the graph
ClickedObject = this.grObjectAtPointer (grGraphName, l_series, & l_category)
If g_DEBUGMODE Then
    CustDebug("1")
End If

// If the user clicked on data or a category, find out which one
if ClickedObject = TypeData!  or &
    ClickedObject = TypeCategory!  then
        If g_DEBUGMODE Then
            CustDebug("2")
        End If
        s_company = this.grCategoryName &
        (grGraphName, l_category)
```

```
            dw_2.dwModify (grGraphName + ".title=" + &
                    "'s_company " + s_company + "'")
            dw_2.Retrieve (s_company)
            If g_DEBUGMODE Then
                CustDebug("3")
            End If
            dw_2.Show()
    else
        MessageBox (Parent.Title, "To see employees, click on a department.")
    end if
```

For an explanation of the rest of this code example, see Chapter 7, "Graphs and Reporting."

In addition, for application debugging, you can create the custdebug( ) function as an external function and call the function from any script within an application. For additional information about writing to files, see Chapter 8, "Printing and File I/O."

Messages

You can also create messageboxes and beeps to denote a section of code that is being run. A messagebox can sometimes be useful to ascertain whether the application executes a loop properly or if the application sets a parameter properly. You can create the messagebox as a function, as within the file writing example, and call where you need the function within the script to display a variable or parameter.

To create a messagebox, use the preceding example. You could write a function to pass the company's name to a function that creates a messagebox like the one in Figure 9.21.

Substitute the function's write code with the following code to produce this messagebox:

```
// Function Write to create a messagebox
MessageBox("Company","Company Name is : " + s_company,Exclamation!)
Return True
```

Unfortunately, you should not use a messagebox in conjunction with a window's focus events because doing so causes PowerBuilder to become confused about which window should get the focus. In this case, you could use a PowerBuilder beep function to show whether a particular event is occurring. The event will generate an audible beep if the event is triggered.

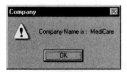

Figure 9.21   **A sample messagebox.**

TIP PowerBuilder 6 offers a couple of new functions to populate the Error object:

SignalError( ). By using the SignalError( ) function, you can populate the Error object with the specified error message and error number before the function triggers a **SystemError** event at the application level.

PopulateError( ). By using the PopulateError( ) function, you can populate the Error object with the specified error message and error number without immediately causing a SystemError event at the application level.

For more information on the syntax for these functions, refer to the PowerBuilder documentation.

THIRD-PARTY DEBUG TOOLS

Sometimes the PowerBuilder debugging facility does not provide all of the information you need to properly debug an application. The following Microsoft Windows tools let you trap the Windows messages that the PowerBuilder application sends. They also let you view the memory allocations and debug the dynamic link libraries (DLLs). The Microsoft Windows Software Development Toolkit includes most of these tools.

Spy or WinView

Spy is a Windows application that lets you view all the Windows messages sent to and from an application. Another useful tool, SPY DDE, lets you view only the DDE messages sent to and from an application.

HeapWalker

When you create an application, it is sometimes necessary to view the memory stack. HeapWalker is a Windows application that lets the developer view the entire memory stack and the modules loaded within a machine's memory. HeapWalker is very helpful for finding memory allocation problems.

For example, HeapWalker can show the PowerBuilder DLLs and their placement within the memory stack, as shown in Figure 9.22. The column OWNER lists the PowerBuilder DLLs in the sequence Windows loads them within memory. HeapWalker also shows their address, handle, and size. Within this example, the developer invoked HeapWalker and then opened PowerBuilder.

In addition to viewing the memory stack, HeapWalker also lets you sort memory items, walk the stack, and discard and allocate the memory segments.

Unload Utilities

A number of utilities let you view and unload or release modules loaded within memory. This is very useful when PowerBuilder causes a general protection fault (GPF) and does not release all the PowerBuilder DLLs. A number of utilities can do this. The CD-

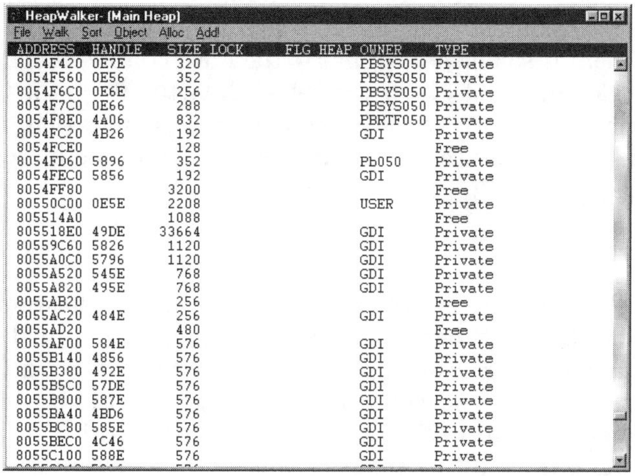

Figure 9.22   Using HeapWalker to view the memory stack.

ROM that accompanies this book includes the wrestart.exe utility. Place the utility in Program Manager, and double-click on it when you want to recycle (i.e., restart Windows) and do not want to shutdown all the other applications manually. Written in C++ for speed, this utility requires no runtimes and is totally free.

FreePower is another utility that frees you from the need to restart your Windows every time you get a GPF. FreePower cleans the computer memory and restarts Power-Builder with fresh memory. FreePower runs on Windows 3.11 and Windows 95. For more information on FreePower, contact the utility's author at 100274.1034@ compuserve.com.

TIP At the time of this writing, FreePower works with PowerBuilder versions 4 and 5. For information concerning the availability of an upgrade that will work with PowerBuilder 6, contact the author.

If you are one of those developers who design PowerBuilder applications under Windows 95 and deploy under Windows 3.1, you can use Chicago-Soft's WinMiser Pro (www.winmiser.com) utility to debug any memory leakage problems. WinMiser Pro is a memory enhancement utility for Windows 3.1, Windows 3.11, and Windows 3.11 for Workgroups. You can use the utility on a stand-alone PC or a network to analyze memory leaks that occur when you run your PowerBuilder applications (you can even recover the memory lost due to the leaks), analyze "insufficient memory" error messages, and offload portions of the GDI resource area, thus leaving more GDI space for your Power-Builder (and other Windows) applications. For more information on the product, review the product fact sheet at www.winmiser.com/wmpro/factsht.html.

Code View

CodeView is a DOS-based debugger that lets you debug C programs and DLLs. The CodeView environment is somewhat similar to the PowerBuilder debugger. For example, it includes breakpoints and watch variables. Unfortunately, the CodeView application is a character-based DOS program, not a Windows application. The *Professional Tools User's Guide* included within the Windows SDK documentation discusses the CodeView application in detail.

Windows Profiler

The Windows Profiler lets you view the statistics about an application's performance. The Windows Profiler is a DOS-based source code debugger. This tool produces statistics that show the amount of time an application spends processing different functions. These statistics let you determine which functions you can optimize and thus increase the entire application's speed. Unfortunately, you must use this tool in conjunction with the source-level code and this requires you write your own source-level breakpoints to be included within the compiled application executable. Developers who write software made up of source code (not p-code like PowerBuilder) use this tool. It is too low level for corporate software developers.

PowerBuilder gives you 90 percent of what you need to debug your applications successfully. Third-party debugging tools provide the rest. You should consider using them to debug problems like memory stack errors.

CHAPTER 10

Creating Windows Help Files

Developers do more than create programs. They create products. A software product consists of software, documentation, training, and technical support application notes.

Software in itself provides features, advantages, and benefits. A software product's features should be intuitive and obvious, but as a developer you know that an intuitive and obvious GUI is tough to achieve, particularly when both power users and novices will use the software. A software product's advantages and benefits are rarely obvious. Documentation, training, and technical support application notes can help you address these issues. Addressing these issues well can help you sell your application to internal end users, if you work in an IT organization, or to external end users if you work for a software vendor.

Help systems provide hypertext functionality. Hypertext lets the users link topics and jump from topic to topic in and between documents displayed in an online environment. You can use this basic functionality to build tutorials, online documents, online reference documents, online catalogs, and performance support systems. This basic functionality can deliver text, graphics, multimedia content, and programmed functionality in the form of macros, DLL calls, and WLL calls.

The help facility provided by Microsoft Windows 95 can perform all the functions of a hypertext system. The help facility provides several ways to access topics, including a table of contents, an index, keyword searches, and context sensitivity.

This chapter addresses how to build Microsoft Windows 95 help, how to provide context sensitivity for end users of PowerBuilder applications, and how to provide context sensitivity for PowerBuilder developers. Notice that PowerBuilder facilitates both end user and developer context sensitivity. Developer context sensitivity lets you access a help topic related to a function highlighted within PowerBuilder's Script painter. End user context sensitivity lets users press F1 to access a help topic related to the control that currently has focus.

MICROSOFT WINDOWS 95 HELP

You build a Microsoft Windows 95 help file (.HLP) from a project file, one or more topic files, and an optional contents file. A topic file contains the help system's content. The content consists of specifically formatted text. The formatting defines the topics and links that the help system displays and executes. Topic files are Rich Text Format (.RTF) files. The help compiler requires all the topic files to have an .RTF extension. A project file defines the environment within which the help system displays its content. The help compiler requires all the project files to have an .HPJ extension. Content files are new within Microsoft Windows 95 Help. A contents file defines the contents displayed on the help system's **Content** tab. Content files have a .CNT extension. Earlier versions of Windows used content topics, and you can still use them.

Topic Files

A topic file will contain RTF codes and text. It is easier to create these files by using a word processor that supports RTF than it is to work with the RTF text itself. You can save Microsoft Word source files as .RTF files. Microsoft Word can also open .RTF files as .DOC files, but Microsoft Word cannot open corrupt .RTF files. It is safer to keep two versions—a .DOC file and an .RTF file—of each file. Developers should be aware that Microsoft Windows Help does not support the RTF specification as fully as Microsoft Word does, so you cannot use some Microsoft Word formatting within help files.

Developers who want to generate help files under program control should generate RTF text directly. The *Microsoft Developer's Network* CD contains Microsoft's *Rich Text Format Specification*.

A topic file contains one or more topics. Each topic will appear on its own page. A manual page break precedes each topic. The first line of each topic will contain a heading preceded by a series of footnote references and some additional text or graphics (see Figure 10.1). This material will contain text, graphics, and links. Each footnote reference is separated by a space. These footnote references define the different attributes that the various help features use.

Help Topic Components

Figure 10.1 shows two help topics. The first is defined by using only the footnotes that are absolutely necessary to compile a topic. The second topic is defined by using all possible footnotes except "A" footnotes. "A" footnotes define secondary keyword searches.

Footnote references define a topic's context ID, topic title, keywords, browse sequence, entry macro, and build tags. A topic must have a context ID and a title. All other footnote references are optional. Context IDs define a link's target or the topic to which a reader may link. Topic titles serve as a topic's headline. In Windows 95 Help, topic titles are also used on the **Contents**, **Index**, and **Find** tabs. Keywords provide an alternative means to searching a Help file. Keywords are used on the **Index** and **Find** tabs. Browse sequence provides a way to define the sequence in which topics are displayed, or browsed, by using the **Browse** buttons. You must define the Browse button macros in the help project file before you can use the browse sequences. An *entry*

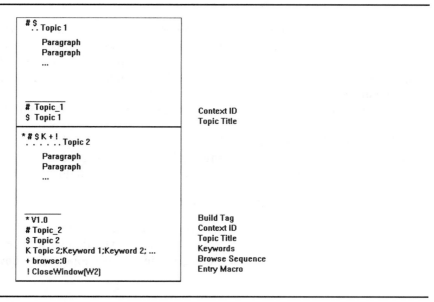

Figure 10.1   A sample topic file.

macro is a macro that will execute when you open the topic within help. Build tags let topics be marked so that they are included or omitted from the compiled help file. In addition, you must define a build expression within the help project file. The build expression determines which of the marked topics are included or excluded.

TIP Context IDs are strings that may contain the underline character, but no other special characters or spaces are allowed.

Each topic includes text, graphics, content, and links.

In text, these links may be jumps or popups. Within the help file, both jumps and popups usually appear as underlined dark green text. This formatting indicates that a context ID is associated with the text. In addition to the color, jumps have a solid underline, and popups have a dotted underline. Clicking on the jump text causes the topic with a context ID that matches the jump text's context ID to be displayed, and the reader is moved to the new topic. Clicking on the popup text causes the topic with the matching context ID to be displayed in a small window.

Define jump text as follows:

Jump Text Context_ID

Define popup text as follows:

Pop-up Text Context_ID

Graphics

Help files can include graphics in the following formats: bitmaps (.BMP, .DIB), segmented hypergraphics (.SHG), multiresolution (.MRB), and Windows metafiles (.WMF). You can also incorporate video clips (.AVI files) into help files. Multiresolution graphics are compiled graphic files that are displayed at a resolution suitable for an end user's monitor. SVGA monitors are not supported.

Segmented hypergraphics let graphics be used as links. To create these graphics, use the SHED editor.

All graphics files must be saved in the same directory as the topic file that contains the graphics. To keep the topic file small, you should reference all graphics rather than paste them into the topic file. These references appear as follows:

```
{bmx filename.extension}
```

where x can be c for centered, l for left aligned, r for right aligned.

In addition to referencing the graphics files, you should use only 16-color bitmaps. Windows 95 Help supports transparent graphics. These appear as follows:

```
{bmxt filename.extension}
```

Project File

Before you compile the topic files (.RTF) into help files (.HLP), you must define a help project file (.HPJ). Help project files contain numerous help compiler attributes, and they control the compilation of the topic files. Minimally, the [FILES] section must contain a list of the topic files to be compiled. Project files are organized into sections like an .INI file. These sections are described in Table 10.1.

The Windows Help Workshop Help covers these sections. Two sections are particularly important for the software developers: the [MAP] and the [ALIAS] sections. The [MAP] section lets you build a correspondence between the context IDs sent by the program and the context IDs used within the help topics. The [ALIAS] section lets you change a context ID into another context ID. These sections are related to the context-sensitive help.

Contents File

The contents file is new for Windows 95 Help. This file defines what appears on the **Contents** tab, which displays a hierarchically organized iconic table of contents built on a book metaphor. Users click on the book to open it and list its component books and pages. For more information, see the Windows Help Workshop help file.

CONTEXT-SENSITIVE HELP IN POWERBUILDER

PowerBuilder provides two types of context-sensitive help: keyword help and application help.

Developers are probably more familiar with keyword help. It displays the topic related to a keyword you highlight within the Script painter. Developers can document

Table 10.1   Project File Sections

Section	Description
[OPTIONS] optional section	A section to include any build options (e.g., compress = True).
[FILES]	Specifies the text file with the topics.
[BUILDTAGS] optional section	Specifies the tags for the files to be built.
[CONFIG]	Specifies the nonstandard menus or other features.
[BITMAPS]	Specifies any bitmaps to be included.
[MAP]	Specifies the context strings with optional section context numbers.
[ALIAS] optional section	Assigns different context strings to the same topic name.
[WINDOWS] optional only if no secondary windows	Specifies the primary help window's characteristics.
[BAGGAGE] optional only if no secondary windows	Specifies any additional files that are to be optional placed within the help file.

their own functions within a Help file and name that Help file usr050.hlp. When you highlight a keyword and press Shift-F1, PowerBuilder will check the USR050.hlp file before using its own help file.

The term *application help* refers to any help files that document a PowerBuilder application. These help files may be context sensitive, and you can create them like any other help files except that the [MAP] section will contain a list of context IDs that the application uses as a parameter within its **ShowHelp( )** calls.

Within the application, the developer will code the ShowHelp( ) calls for any controls or windows that may gain focus. The syntax for ShowHelp( ) call is:

```
ShowHelp ( helpfile, helpcommand{, typeid})
```

where:

> **helpfile** is the path and filename of the compiled help file that will be invoked.
>
> **helpcommand** is one of the following: Index!, Keyword!, or Topic!.
>
> **typeid** is a parameter required for Keyword! or Topic! help commands.

The preferred form is ShowHelp (helpfile, Topic!, ContextIDNumber). To use this form of ShowHelp( ), do the following:

1. Assign a ContextIDNumber to every window. If you would like context sensitivity on the controls, assign a ContextIDNumber to every control.

2. Make an entry within the help project file's [MAP] section for each ContextID-Number as follows:

```
[MAP]
TopicContextIDString   ContextIDNumber
TopicContextIDString   ContextIDNumber
...
```

3. Define any aliases for TopicContextIDStrings within the help project file as follows:

```
[ALIAS]
TopicContextIDString=TopicContextIDSting
...
```

4. Make any changes or additions to the help topic files, and recompile the help project.

Using the preferred form and this procedure lets the developers create applications without any knowledge of what will be covered within the help documentation. ContextIDNumbers should be relational rather than ordinal. This lets the interface change over time without the need to renumber existing controls, and limits the impact of interface changes. In addition, unmapped ContextIDNumbers will not have a matching topic within the help file. The help file will display its index, when no match is found for a ContextIDNumber passed to it. Further, it is recommended that you number all the controls even if you will not document them immediately, because you could need these ContextIDNumbers in the future for other purposes. By using aliases, the developer can create many-to-one correspondences between the controls and topics. For instance, you can display the OK button topic for all or some OK buttons by using aliases. Using aliases is preferred to the use of the same ContextIDNumber on each OK button, or the mapping of different ContextIDNumbers to the same TopicContextIDString. Using aliases is preferred because the correspondences are more obvious than the other methods. It is also preferred, because there may be two or more topics that contain slightly different descriptions and controls with the same name that operate in slightly different ways. Define aliases within the [ALIAS] section.

Figure 10.2 shows how a context-sensitive help topic is displayed when the ShowHelp( ) function is called by using the Topic! parameter. Within the interface, each control is assigned a ContextIDNumber. The numbers shown follow a relational scheme. The buttons **24**100 and **24**200 are part of the main window (**24**000). The tabs 24300, 24400, and 24500 are also part of the main window. The last three digits of the tab ContextIDNumbers uniquely identify the tabs: 300, 400, and 500. The field **400**1000, and the DataWindows **400**2000 and **400**3000 belong to the Products tab (24**400**). The DataWindow assigned the ContextIDNumber of 4003000 gains focus. When the user presses Shift-F1, the control with the focus executes a ShowHelp( ) function call. The function passes the ContextIDNumber 4003000 to the compiled help file. The project file maps the ContextIDNumber 4003000 to the TopicContextIDString Order_Entry_Window_Products_Tab_Subassembly. This TopicContextIDString is aliased to another TopicContextIDString Select_DataWindow within the project file's [ALIAS] section. The context IDs for all selection DataWindows map to this topic within this example. In one of the help file's original source topic files, the topic Select

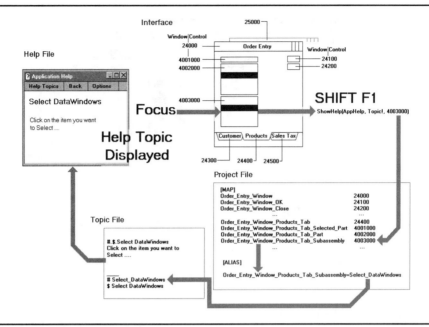

Figure 10.2   Help topic components.

DataWindows has a TopicContextIDString value of Select_DataWindows. The help file displays this help topic. The figure here shows the project and topic files for illustration purposes only. The help file (.HLP) is the only file you install with the application. If the help file finds no match for the context ID passed to the help file, the help file displays the index topic.

CREATING HELP WITH THIRD-PARTY PRODUCTS

Because creating help files with the Windows SDK is cumbersome, several third-party companies have introduced products to simplify the help creation process. Some of the more advanced tools let you create computer-based training (CBT) exercises that let the user step through a sample system, or view a video of the system. Other products simplify the creation of Microsoft Windows help files for inclusion within a PowerBuilder application. The majority of the help products let the developer create the help text by using a word processor with a specially created template. Toolbars let you select the particular features, and the product, in turn, places the correct Windows SDK syntax within the file. This lets the developer concentrate on creating the help files, and not learning the Window SDK syntax. The authors recommend any of the third-party help creation products over using the Windows SDK method.

One example of a third-party product is Blue Sky Software's RoboHelp (www.blue-sky.com). The templates for RoboHelp are automatically loaded into Microsoft Word, and you activate the application by choosing the RoboHelp help template. The application lets you create all the necessary files. In addition, the application includes a

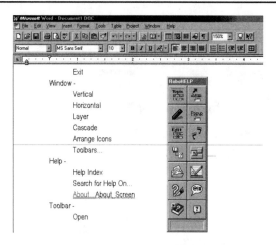

Figure 10.3 Microsoft Word with RoboHelp.

Table 10.2 Third-Party Products

Product	URL
Doc-To-Help	www.wextech.com
EasyHelp/Web	www.eon-solutions.com
ForeHelp	www.ff.com
HelpBreeze	www.solutionsoft.com
Visual Help	www.winware.com

floating toolbar for adding topics, popups, hotspots, file creation, and for help file compilation.

The example within Figure 10.3 shows a simple text file with the RoboHelp toolbar.

RoboHelp works with the Word application to add the correct SDK syntax to the text file. To create jumptext, popups, or macros, the developer simply chooses the appropriate MenuItem or toolbar selection.

Table 10.2 shows a list of other third-party products you can use to create the Windows help files for your PowerBuilder applications.

PART III

Advanced Development Concepts

CHAPTER 11

Email Interfaces

In this modern-day electronic world, email is an accepted form of communication. As developers make more and more applications mail-enabled, application development tools need to support such development.

Within the PowerBuilder environment, there are different levels at which you can integrate email into an application. These levels range from a straight Dynamic Data Exchange (DDE) connection that uses a specific email system implementing X.400 APIs to provide an interface capable of supporting a variety of different email systems.

This chapter discusses the following topics:

- Messaging standards
- PowerBuilder's DDE interface
- PowerBuilder's MAPI interface
- PowerBuilder Library for Lotus Notes
- Email APIs

MESSAGING STANDARDS

This section discusses the email messaging standards of MAPI, VIM, and X.400.

MAPI and VIM

In the Windows environment, the two dominant email API standards are Microsoft's Messaging API (MAPI) and vendor-independent messaging (VIM), a standard backed by such vendors as IBM, Apple, Borland, and Novell.

There are two versions of MAPI—simple MAPI and extended MAPI. Power-Builder's MAPI interface is based on simple MAPI, which is included with the Windows SDK, and it provides basic email services. Products such as Microsoft Mail and Windows for Workgroups use simple MAPI. Extended MAPI provides developers with a more robust API, giving them the capability to write low-level messaging services.

TIP Because MAPI is based on Microsoft technology, the MAPI functions that PowerBuilder supports work only on the Windows platform. These functions have no effect on the Mactintosh or UNIX platforms.

The two Lotus (now IBM) email systems, cc:Mail and Lotus Notes, currently support VIM. Lotus Notes version 4.0 is the first version of Notes that is fully compliant with VIM.

X.400

The OSI standard for electronic message handling is X.400. It provides the specification for such things as message structure, message enveloping, and message transfer protocol. Using X.400 lets an email system communicate with any other X.400-compatible system.

You can accomplish communication among different X.400 email systems by using an X.400 gateway that allows email to be translated from its native format to the destination email system's format. For example, in an environment in which some users use Microsoft Mail and others use Lotus Notes, you can add an X.400 gateway to allow email exchange between the two user groups (see Figure 11.1).

A true X.400 interface provides the most flexibility, but is complex to develop. Using a gateway allows the use of most email systems, while eliminating the need to develop the X.400 interface. Several third-party X.400 gateways are on the market.

POWERBUILDER'S DDE INTERFACE

Dynamic Data Exchange (DDE) is a messaging protocol that Windows applications use to exchange data with other Windows applications. The easiest way to implement an

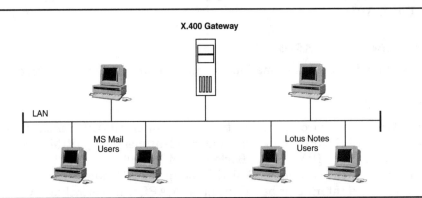

Figure 11.1   An X.400 gateway allows email exchange between the different email systems, such as Microsoft Mail and Lotus Notes.

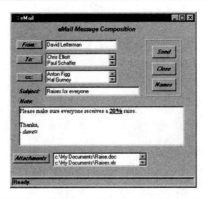

Figure 11.2   Using a PowerBuilder interface to send Lotus Notes messages.

email interface from PowerBuilder is to use DDE to communicate directly with a specific email system. For example, you could use a window like the one shown in Figure 11.2 to send Lotus Notes messages by using a PowerBuilder interface.

This window lets the user enter a list of people in the To: field, a list of people in the cc: field, a subject, the message text, and a list of attachments (as if they were within Lotus Notes). To send this by using DDE, you must add the following code to the window's **open** event:

```
/***********************************************************************
** Get the Notes program's name from WIN.INI, and
** store the name within the instance variable i_sMailExe
***********************************************************************/

// Make sure Notes is installed
If UPPER(ProfileString("Win.Ini","LotusMail", &
"Application",""))<>"NOTES" Then
     MessageBox("Error","Notes not installed.",StopSign!)
     Halt Close
End If

i_sMailExe = ProfileString("win.ini","LotusMail","Program","")

If i_sMailExe = "" Then
     MessageBox("Error","Notes not installed.",StopSign!)
     Halt Close
End If
```

This script ensures that Notes is installed, and it retrieves the Notes executable's fully qualified name into the instance variable i_sMailExe.

To send the message, add the following script to the send CommandButton's (**cb_send**) clicked event:

```
/**************************************************************************
** Send message data from the window to Notes, and send the message(s).
** i_sMailExe is an instance variable containing the Notes executable's name
**************************************************************************/
int      iRtn, iHndl, iSendCnt, iAttachCnt
time     tStartTime

SetPointer(HourGlass!)
// Open a channel with Notes
iHndl = OpenChannel("Notes","SendMail")

// If Notes is not running, start it:
If iHndl < 1 Then
    Run(i_sMailExe, Minimized!)

    // Wait up to 2 minutes for Notes to load and the user to log on
    tStartTime = Now( )
    Do
        Yield( )    // Yield control occasionally
        iHndl = OpenChannel("Notes","SendMail")
        If iHndl > 0 Then Exit    // OK, Notes is active
    Loop Until SecondsAfter(tStartTime,Now( )) > 120 // Try again
    If iHndl < 1 Then
        Messagebox("Error","Cannot start Notes.",StopSign!)
            SetPointer(Arrow!)
            Return
    End If
End If

// Notes is active, so create a new message
iRtn=ExecRemote("NewMessage", iHndl)

// Should check return code each time. If iRtn <> 1, then the function
// did not succeed.
// Send the note to everyone within the To: list
For iSendCnt = 1 To lb_to.totalitems( )
    iRtn=ExecRemote("To " + lb_to.item[iSendCnt], iHndl)
    sle_message.text = "Message sent to: " + lb_to.item[iSendCnt]
Next

// Send the note to everyone within the cc: list
For iSendCnt = 1 To lb_cc.totalitems( )
    iRtn=ExecRemote("To " + lb_cc.item[iSendCnt], iHndl)
    sle_message.text = "Message sent to: " + lb_cc.item[iSendCnt]
Next

// Send the subject, and the message text
iRtn=ExecRemote("Subject "+ sle_subject.text, iHndl)
iRtn=ExecRemote("Text " + mle_note.text, iHndl)

// Add the attachments
For iAttachCnt = 1 To lb_attach.totalitems( )
    iRtn=ExecRemote("AttachFile " + lb_attach.item[iAttachCnt], iHndl)
Next
```

```
// Send the message, and close the channel
iRtn=ExecRemote("Send",iHndl)
iRtn = CloseChannel(iHndl)
SetPointer(Arrow!)
```

This script sends the note to everyone in the To: and cc: fields, and it adds the attachments listed in the Attachments: field.

Using DDE is a fairly simple method of email integration with PowerBuilder. Providing this capability for multiple email systems, however, requires developing DDE code for each system. For more information on DDE, see Chapter 13, "External Interfaces."

TIP By using the same DDE technique, you can create mail applications within PowerBuilder to send messages to the Microsoft Exchange system. To do so, you need to send the remote commands to the exchng32.exe program. However, because PowerBuilder also supports MAPI functions, it is much more efficient to use to develop email applications with Microsoft mail programs.

POWERBUILDER'S MAPI INTERFACE

PowerBuilder provides a set of objects specifically for dealing with the simple MAPI. These objects include a system object (MailSession) and a set of functions, structures, and datatypes. These objects give you a way to interface with MAPI from PowerBuilder without writing directly to MAPI.

The PowerBuilder MailSession object has the following attributes:

SessionID is a protected long that contains the current mail session's ID.

MessageID[ ] is a string array of mail message IDs.

The following three PowerBuilder structures are specifically for use with MAPI:

mailFileDescription is a MAPI structure that identifies an attachment to a message. This structure has the following attributes:

Attribute	Datatype
FileName	String
PathName	String
FileType	mailFileType (enumerated)
Position	Unsigned Long

TIP If the position attribute is 1, the attachment is placed at the beginning of the note, preceded and followed by spaces. If the position is greater than or equal to 0, the character at the location identified by position within the note is replaced with the attachment.

mailMessage is a MAPI structure that describes a message. This structure has the following attributes:

Attribute	Datatype
ReceiptRequested	Boolean
MessageSent	Boolean
Unread	Boolean
Subject	String
NoteText	String
MessageType	String
DateReceived	String
ConversationID	String
Recipient[ ]	mailRecipient array
AttachmentFile[ ]	mailFileDescription array

mailRecipient is A MAPI structure that identifies the sender or receiver of a message. This structure has the following attributes:

Attribute	Datatype
Name	String
Address	String
mailRecipientType	mailRecipientType (enumerated)
EntryType	Protected blob

Ten functions are defined for the mailSession object:

mailAddress(mailmessage) is used to address a message or display a list of valid mail addresses. mailAddress( ) updates the mailRecipient array for the mail message. The mailRecipient structure contains information about the recipients of a mail message. An optional parameter of the mailMessage datatype (see the preceding discussion), mailmessage contains information about the message. If mailmessage is not entered, an address list is displayed.

mailAddress( ) returns one of the following enumerated datatypes:

mailReturnSuccess!
mailReturnFailure!
mailReturnInsufficientMemory!
mailReturnUserAbort!

mailDeleteMessage(messageid) is used to delete the mail message identified by messageid, which is a string that contains the ID of the message to be deleted. You can obtain this ID by using the **mailGetMessages( )** function.

mailDeleteMessage( ) returns one of the following enumerated datatypes:

mailReturnSuccess!
mailReturnFailure!
mailReturnInsufficientMemory!
mailReturnInvalidMessage!
mailReturnUserAbort!

mailGetMessages(returnunreadonly) is used to populate the messageID array of the MailSession object with message IDs. The message IDs obtained by using this function are used within other mail functions. returnunreadonly is an optional Boolean parameter that denotes whether to populate the messageID array only with the IDs of unread messages.

mailGetMessages( ) returns one of the following enumerated datatypes:

> mailReturnSuccess!
> mailReturnFailure!
> mailReturnInsufficientMemory!
> mailReturnUserAbort!
> mailReturnNoMessages!

mailHandle( ) is used to obtain the MailSession object's handle.

mailLogoff( ) is used to terminate the current mail session. It returns one of the following enumerated datatypes:

> mailReturnSuccess!
> mailReturnFailure!
> mailReturnInsufficientMemory!

mailLogon(userid, password, logonoption) is used to establish a new mail session or add the user to an existing mail session. userid and password are optional strings that contain the user's mail system logon. If the user does not enter these values, the mail system will prompt for this information. logonoption is an optional enumerated datatype that specifies one of the following logon options:

> mailNewSession!
> mailDownLoad!
> mailNewSessionWithDownLoad!

If the logonoption is not entered, the function will add the user to the existing mail session and it will not prompt the user for the user ID and password. mailLogon( ) returns one of the following enumerated datatypes:

> mailReturnSuccess!
> mailReturnFailure!
> mailReturnLoginFailure!
> mailReturnInsufficientMemory!
> mailReturnTooManySessions!
> mailReturnUserAbort!

mailReadMessage(messageid, mailmessage, mailreadoption, mark) is used to open the mail message identified by messageid as specified within mailreadoption. messageid is a string containing the ID of the message to be read. You can use the **mailGetMessages( )** function to obtain the message ID. mailmessage is of the mailMessage datatype (discussed earlier) that contains information about the message. mailreadoption is an enumerated datatype that consists of the following:

> mailEntireMessage!
> mailEnvelopeOnly!

    mailBodyAsFile!
    mailSuppressAttach!

mark is a Boolean parameter that denotes whether to mark the message as read. If it is True, the function will mark the message as read.

mailReadMessage( ) returns one of the following enumerated datatypes:

    mailReturnSuccess!
    mailReturnFailure!
    mailReturnInsufficientMemory!

TIP To read an attachment, follow the call to mailReadMessage( ) with statements that open and read the temporary file identified by the mailMessage.AttachmentFile.PathName attribute. Be sure to delete this temporary file when you no longer need it.

---

mailRecipientDetails(mailrecipient, allowupdates) is used to display details about mailrecipient by using the email system's recipient information window. mailrecipient is of the mailRecipient datatype, and it contains information about the recipient. mailrecipient must contain a recipient identifier returned by mailAddress( ), mailResolveRecipient( ), or mailReadMessage( ). allowupdates is an optional Boolean parameter that identifies whether the detail information can be modified. The default is False. mailRecipientDetails( ) returns one of the following enumerated datatypes:

    mailReturnSuccess!
    mailReturnFailure!
    mailReturnInsufficientMemory!
    mailUnknownReturnRecipient!
    mailUnknownReturnUserAbort!

mailResolveRecipient(recipientname, allowupdates) is used to resolve the name of recipientname, which is of the mailRecipient datatype, and it contains the recipient's information. allowupdates is an optional Boolean parameter that identifies whether the recipient's name can be modified. The default is False. mailResolveRecipient( ) returns one of the following enumerated datatypes:

    mailReturnSuccess!
    mailReturnFailure!
    mailReturnInsufficientMemory!
    mailReturnUserAbort!

mailSend(mailmessage) is used to send a mail message. mailmessage is an optional parameter of the mailMessage datatype, and it contains message information. If mailmessage is not entered, the function will display a Send Note dialog box for the user to enter the message. mailSend( ) returns one of the following enumerated datatypes:

mailReturnSuccess!
mailReturnFailure!
mailReturnInsufficientMemory!
mailReturnLogFailure!
mailReturnUserAbort!
mailReturnDiskFull!
mailReturnTooManySessions!
mailReturnTooManyFiles!
mailReturnTooManyRecipients!
mailReturnUnknownRecipient!
mailReturnAttachmentNotFound!

PowerBuilder has also defined five enumerated datatypes specifically for use with MAPI:

mailFileType.   Type of mail attachment. Valid values are:

mailAttach!
mailOLE!
mailOLEStatic!

mailLogonOption.   Type of logon. Valid values are:

mailNewSession!
mailDownLoad!
mailNewSessionWithDownLoad!

mailReadOption.   Portion of the message to read. Valid values are:

mailBodyAsFile!
mailEntireMessage!
mailEnvelopeOnly!
mailSuppressAttach!

mailRecipientType.   Type of the message recipient. Valid values are:

mailTo!
mailCC!
mailOriginator!
mailBCC!

mailReturnCode.   Return values from the **mailReadMessage( )** function. Valid values are:

mailReturnAccessDenied!
mailReturnAttachmentNotFound!
mailReturnAttachmentOpenFailure!
mailReturnAttachmentWriteFailure!
mailReturnDiskFull!
mailReturnFailure!
mailReturnInsufficientMemory!
mailReturnLoginFailure!

mailReturnMessageInUse!
mailReturnNoMessages!
mailReturnSuccess!
mailReturnTextTooLarge!
mailReturnTooManyFiles!
mailReturnTooManyRecipients!
mailReturnTooManySessions!
mailReturnUserAbort!

Take the preceding example using DDE, and implement it using PowerBuilder's MAPI interface. Assume the same window completed as shown in Figure 11.2.

To send this by using MAPI, replace the script **cb_send** with the following:

```
/*************************************************************************
** Obtain message information from the window, and
** send the message(s) by using MAPI
*************************************************************************/
mailSession     mSes
mailReturnCode  mRet
mailMessage     mMsg
int             iSendCnt, iAttachCnt

// Create a mail session
mSes = create mailSession

// Log on to the session
mRet = mSes.mailLogon ( mailNewSession! )
If mRet <> mailReturnSuccess! Then
   DisplayMsg ("Mail Logon Error", "Unable to Log On to Mail System")
   Return
End If

// Populate the mailMessage structure with information about the message
mMsg.Subject = sle_subject.text
mMsg.NoteText = mle_note.text
For iSendCnt = 1 To lb_to.totalitems( )
    mMsg.Recipient[iSendCnt].name = lb_to.item[iSendCnt]
    sle_message.text = "Message sent to: " + lb_to.item[iSendCnt]
Next

// Send the note to everyone within the cc: list
For iSendCnt = 1 To lb_cc.totalitems( )
    mMsg.Recipient[iSendCnt].name = lb_cc.item[iSendCnt]
    sle_message.text = "Message sent to: " + lb_cc.item[iSendCnt]
Next

// Add the attachments. Position of 1 puts the attachment at the
// beginning of the message
For iAttachCnt = 1 To lb_attach.totalitems( )
```

```
      mMsg.AttachmentFile[iAttachCnt].FileName = lb_cc.item[iSendCnt]
      mMsg.AttachmentFile[iAttachCnt].FileType = mailAttach!
      mMsg.AttachmentFile[iAttachCnt].Position = 1
Next

// Send the mail
mRet = mSes.mailSend ( mMsg )
If mRet <> mailReturnSuccess! Then
   DisplayMsg ("Send Error", "Unable to send mail message" )
   Return
End If
mSes.mailLogoff( )
destroy mSes
```

PowerBuilder's MAPI functionality also makes it easy to develop an interface for message management. For example, suppose you want to provide users with the capability to list, read, and delete messages. The PowerBuilder interface will look something like the one in Figure 11.3.

The open event contains the following script to read the list of messages for the user. This script retrieves the user's messages by using the mailGetMessages( ) function to populate the mail session's MessageID array. The date, subject, recipients, and attachment files are then read from the mailMessage structure for each message:

```
/*******************************************************************
** This script creates a mail session by using the instance variable
** i_mSes. mailGetMessages( ) retrieves the list of message IDs into
** the MessageID array of i_mSes. The script then loops through each
** message, reading the envelope information, and inserting a row into
** dw_msglist.
*******************************************************************/
int             iMsgNbr, iIDcnt
long            lCurRow
mailReturnCode  mRet
mailMessage     mMsg
```

continues

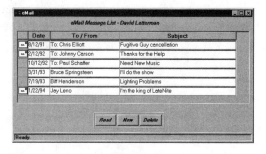

Figure 11.3   Sample PowerBuilder MAPI interface.

```
// Create the mail session
i_mSes = CREATE MailSession

// Log on to the session
mRet = i_mSes.mailLogon ( mailNewSession! )
If mRet <> mailReturnSuccess! Then
    DisplayMsg ("Mail Logon Error", "Unable to Log On to Mail System")
    Return
End If

// Call mailGetMessages to populate the MessageID attribute of
// the instance variable i_mSes of type mailSession
i_mSes.mailGetMessages(TRUE)

// Get the total number of messages
iMsgNbr = Upperbound(i_mSes.MessageID[ ])

// For each message, add a row to dw_msglist and use setItems
// to populate the messageID, message date, the first recipient, and
// the message subject. If the message has an attachment, set the
// attachment column to 1 to display the attachment bitmap
For iIDcnt = 1 To iMsgNbr
    lCurRow = dw_msglist.InsertRow(0)
    mRet = i_mSes.mailReadMessage( i_mSes.MessageID[iIDcnt], mMsg, &
        mailEnvelopeOnly!, True )
    If Not(isNull(mMsg.AttachmentFile[1].FileName)) Then
        dw_msglist.object.attachment[lCurRow] = 1
    End If
    dw_msglist.object.messageID[lCurRow] = i_mSes.MessageID[iIDcnt]
    dw_msglist.object.person[lCurRow]    = mMsg.Recipient[1].name
    dw_msglist.object.send_date[lCurRow] = date(mMsg.DateReceived)
    dw_msglist.object.subject[lCurRow]   = mMsg.Subject
Next
```

cb_read's clicked event obtains the current row's message ID and uses the ID to read the message's full text:

```
/*************************************************************************
** This script displays the message listed within dw_msglist's current row.
** It assumes that the mail session i_mSes is created, and a successful
** logon has occurred.
*************************************************************************/
int              iRowNum, iRetVal
string           sMessageID
mailMessage      mMsg
mailReturnCode   mRet

// Get the row containing the selected row
iRowNum = dw_msglist.GetRow ( )
If iRowNum > 0 Then
```

```
    // Obtain the mail Message ID to display
    sMessageID = dw_msglist.object.MessageID[iRowNum]

    // Reread this message to obtain the entire contents (because
    // previously we read only the "envelope", and not the mesaage's contents)
    // Message information goes into mMsg
    mRet = i_mSes.mailReadMessage( sMessageID, mMsg, &
              mailEntireMessage!, True )
    // Open the message display window, and get the message text
    // from mMsg.NoteText
    ....
    ....
End If
```

cb_delete's clicked event obtains the current row's message ID and deletes the message:

```
/*************************************************************************
** This script deletes the message listed within dw_msglist's current row.
** It assumes that the mail session i_mSes is created, and a successful
** logon has occurred.
*************************************************************************/
string           sMsgID
int              iRowNum
mailReturnCode   mRet

iRowNum = dw_msglist.GetRow( )
If iRowNum > 0 Then
  sMsgID = dw_msglist.object.MessageID[iRowNum]
  mRet   = i_mSes.mailDeleteMessage(sMsgID)
End If
```

Using PowerBuilder's MAPI capabilities lets you develop a PowerBuilder interface to any mail system that supports MAPI.

POWERBUILDER LIBRARY FOR LOTUS NOTES

The PowerBuilder Library for Lotus Notes provides seamless connectivity from PowerBuilder applications to the Lotus Notes database. By using the PowerBuilder library, developers can effortlessly access data from the Lotus Notes database.

The PowerBuilder Library for Lotus Notes provides a set of PowerBuilder objects designed to automate the creation of a PowerBuilder interface to Lotus Notes. This library also has the Lotus Notes Interface's samples. You can develop this interface by using either the Notes simple messaging interface (SMI) or VIM.

In addition to the object libraries, the PowerBuilder Library provides a prebuilt sample application and a set of utilities known as the PowerBuilder Library Application for Lotus Notes (PLAN) toolkit. The PLAN toolkit automates the creation of the various PowerBuilder objects you can use to access the Notes data. The PLAN toolkit includes generators that create DataWindows in the form of encapsulated user objects, which handle the interaction with the Notes API. You can then add these objects to a PowerBuilder application to provide a Notes interface with little additional code.

To implement the earlier example using the PowerBuilder Library for Lotus Notes instead of MAPI, do the following:

1. Use the PLAN toolkit to create the application DataWindows and user objects. Use PLAN's View Generator to create the message list objects and the Form Generator to create the objects for reading an individual message. After generating the objects, make any necessary changes within the DataWindow painter. The DataWindow for the message list will eventually look the same as it did in the earlier examples, as shown in Figure 11.4.

2. Add the two new user objects to the window (controls dw_list and dw_msg), and create a window instance variable named iui_db_handle to store the handle to the Notes database. The two user objects are standard user objects that contain the two respective DataWindow objects.

3. Add the following PowerScript code to the window's open event:

```
/*********************************************************************
** This script opens the notes database (*.nsf file).
** It then assigns database handles to the DataWindows.
*********************************************************************/

// Open the Notes database
If not f_database_open &
```

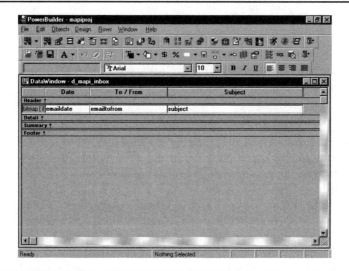

Figure 11.4   Using the PowerBuilder Library for Lotus Notes to create the DataWindow for message list.

```
    ("c:\notes\mail\dletterm.nsf", iui_db_handle) Then
    Return
End If

// Assign database handle to the DataWindow controls
dw_list.iui_db_handle = iui_db_handle
dw_msg.iui_db_handle = iui_db_handle

// Initialize list object, and retrieve the data
dw_1.TriggerEvent("ue_init")
dw_1.TriggerEvent("ue_retrieve")
```

This script first calls **f_database_open( )**, a PowerBuilder global function that is included in the PowerBuilder Library for Lotus Notes. It calls the Notes API function to open the Notes database. The code for f_database_open( ) is:

```
/*********************************************************************
** Function: f_database_open
**
** Purpose: Open a Notes database
**
** Parameters: as_database_filename  (String/Value)database filename
**             aui_db_handle         (Uint/Ref)    database handle
**
** Return: Boolean, True if successful, False if failure
*********************************************************************/
int     li_api_error // api error number

// Get the database handle
li_api_error = PB_NSFDbOpen (as_database_filename, aui_db_handle)
If (li_api_error <> API_SUCCESS) Then
    f_api_error(li_api_error)
    Return False
End if

Return True
```

The ue_init and ue_retrieve events are user-defined events that are created for the user objects generated by the PLAN toolkit generator. ue_init creates the buffer used to transfer the data from the Notes API DLL to PowerBuilder, and ue_retrieve retrieves data from the Notes database into the DataWindow. The important thing about this is that the PowerBuilder Library for Lotus Notes provides this code so you do not need to write the code.

4. Add the following code to the window's **close** event:

```
f_database_close(iui_db_handle)
```

This closes the connection to the Notes database.

5. Add the following code to the cb_read's close event to get the current row from dw_list, and read the message by retrieving the message into dw_msg:

```
long      ll_row
long      ll_note_id

ll_row               = This.getclickedrow( )
ll_note_id           = This.object.note_id[ll_row]
dw_msg.iul_note_id = ll_note_id
dw_msg.TriggerEvent("ue_init")
dw_msg.TriggerEvent("ue_retrieve")
```

6. Finally, add the following line to cb_delete's clicked event. This single line of code will mark the document within dw_list's current row for deletion and place a trash can bitmap within the DataWindow's leftmost column:

```
dw_list.TriggerEvent("ue_document_delete")
```

As you can see, you need to write very little code to implement a Notes interface from PowerBuilder by using the PowerBuilder Library for Lotus Notes.

EMAIL APIS

Another way to provide an email interface from PowerBuilder is to write directly to a specific email API. By using its external function interface, a PowerBuilder application can interface with any email system that provides an API. For an example of how to use external functions, see Chapter 6, "User Objects and Functions."

Although writing to an API is more difficult than using DDE, PowerBuilder's MAPI interface, or the PowerBuilder Library for Lotus Notes, it provides the greatest amount of flexibility and lets you to develop a more robust interface. As mentioned earlier, writing directly to X.400 provides the most flexibility and will support the most email systems, but it is the most difficult interface to write.

In conclusion, some things to consider when deciding which type of email interface to write are the number of different systems that the application must support and the amount of functionality you need within the PowerBuilder application. For example, DDE may be suitable within a single-system Windows environment in which the only requirement is to transparently send a message. However, in an environment that uses both cc:Mail and Lotus Notes, the best solution is more likely to be to write directly to the VIM API. Finally, consider the case in which the users of Microsoft Mail, Lotus Notes, and Oracle Mail must exchange messages. In this case, the best solution may be to either write directly to X.400 or to install an X.400 gateway and write to an API such as CMC. The point is that there are several ways to provide an email interface from PowerBuilder. The best answer depends on the application's requirements.

CHAPTER 12

Open Repository CASE API (ORCA)

Client/server technology has been advancing at an increasing rate, and it will continue to do so in the years to come. This rate of advancement has moved us away from the single-vendor solution of the past into a more open environment. In the client/server arena, there are a number of technologies and many vendors, each providing solutions for different parts of a system. When developing mission-critical applications or products in this environment, you must insist on an open system architecture. Powersoft has committed to an open architecture by releasing its client/server open development environment (CODE) initiative. This CODE initiative is Powersoft's way of letting vendors write interfaces between their products and PowerBuilder. This chapter discusses Powersoft's vision as it relates to the CODE initiative.

Topics addressed in this chapter include:

- CASE tools and methodology
- Powersoft's vision and the CODE initiative
- Open Repository CASE API (ORCA)
  - ORCA architecture
  - ORCA features
  - ORCA functions
  - ORCA errors
  - ORCA header file

CASE TOOLS AND METHODOLOGY

CASE (computer-aided software engineering) technology helps you analyze and design applications in a structured manner. It helps you capture business data and relationships and to enforce data integrity with business rules. CASE tools help you develop an optimized database design for enterprise-wide applications. You can design data flow diagrams, entity-relationship diagrams, as well as the physical database design with

Table 12.1   Popular CASE Tools

Company	Description
Rational Rose Rational Software Corporation 18880 Homestead Road Cupertino, CA 95014, USA Tel: 800-728-1212 Fax: 408-863-4120 Web site: www.rational.com	A graphical software engineering tool, Rational Rose uses Unified Modeling Language (UML) to help analyze and design software systems. Rational Rose can be used to model business processes as well as application logic.
ERWIN Logic Works Inc. University Square at Princeton 111 Campus Drive Princeton, New Jersey 08540, USA Tel: 609-514-1177 Fax: 609-514-1175 Web site: www.logicworks.com	ERWIN is a very popular CASE tool that works well with PowerBuilder. It uses a point-and-click graphical interface to develop an entity-relationship (ER) model for your system. ERWIN has a reverse engineering feature that will draw the ER model for your existing database system.
PowerDesigner Powersoft Inc. 561 Virginia Road Concord, MA 01742-2732 Tel: 508-287-2788 Fax: 800-SYBS-FAX Web site: www.powersoft.com	PowerDesigner comes from Powersoft itself. An extensive CASE tool, PowerDesigner includes Process Analyst, DataArchitect, AppModeler, Warehouse Architect, MetaWorks, and Viewer modules. You can use PowerDesigner for analyzing your data, drawing the data flow diagrams, moving to ER models, developing prototypes by using PowerBuilder, and more.

CASE tools. Newer CASE tools, such as PowerDesigner and ERWIN, also support reverse engineering, that is, developing entity-relationship diagrams from existing database systems.

Table 12.1 lists some popular CASE tools that can be used with PowerBuilder.

POWERSOFT'S VISION AND THE CODE INITIATIVE

There are many factors to consider when choosing an application development tool. You must have defined the major technical and functional areas of the current product/application, and you must envision the product's future direction, given the different advances in technology. Powersoft's strategy is to focus on establishing PowerBuilder as the premier graphical client/server application development environment available in the marketplace, both now and in the future. Powersoft has positioned PowerBuilder as an open development environment that is capable of tightly integrating with industry-leading, third-party software products. This enables your organization to put together a "best of breed" client/server software solution and not be locked into what may be a less than optimal solution with a competing tool.

CASE companies such as LBMS Inc., Bachman Information Systems, Inc., and Popkin Software plan to develop or already have developed PowerBuilder CASE applications. These companies plan to integrate and resell PowerBuilder with their workbenches and thus provide complete development life cycle support. Powersoft also has agreements with other CASE/methodology vendors such as Chen & Associates, Ernst and Young, Intersolv, and LogicWorks.

Powersoft requests that all vendors publish application program interfaces (APIs) for their products and stop locking users into proprietary technologies. They reinforce their commitment to open computing with their client/server open development environment (CODE). CODE is essentially a standard API that lets PowerBuilder interoperate with other vendors' products and tools. As part of its CODE strategy, Powersoft has been able to give PowerBuilder users access to third-party source control/configuration management products such as Intersolv's PVCS and Legent Corp's Endeavor. Soon a number of other version control vendors will support PowerBuilder within its own development environment.

Some vendors try to do as much as possible regardless of whether they are experts in all crafts. Similarly, some vendors want to sell you complete client/server development environments, even if they made their mark in only one area. Powersoft is not one of them. Since October 1992, Powersoft's CODE initiative has embraced a wide variety of strategic partners and products that complement PowerBuilder.

OPEN REPOSITORY CASE API (ORCA)

As part of the CODE specification, Powersoft has publicly stated it will peacefully coexist with the rest of the CASE world. Specifically, it will do whatever it takes to ensure customers that state-of-the-art CASE solutions are available to augment the suite of PowerBuilder development tools. Some customers, however, also require additional development life cycle tools that may never be offered by Powersoft or any other vendor. To address both of these requirements, Powersoft provides ORCA, an API that provides comprehensive access to all PowerBuilder library entities.

ORCA Architecture

The ORCA architecture provides vendors with a standard way to interface with PowerBuilder. Figure 12.1 shows a variety of software products communicating with PowerBuilder by using the ORCA API.

If there is also a need to communicate from PowerBuilder back to the vendor's product, Powersoft or the vendor needs to write a vendor-specific DLL. This second interface is also shown in Figure 12.1.

ORCA Features

ORCA provides developers with many features, including session management, library management, compilation, executable construction, and object query. These features are made available through standard function calls, which are listed and explained in the following sections.

Session Management

All ORCA functions operate within the context of a *session*. Before any of the ORCA functions are called, a *session handle* must be obtained. A session handle within ORCA

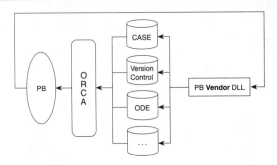

Figure 12.1   **A number of software products communicate with PowerBuilder by using the ORCA API.**

is like a file handle when opening a file. If processing is needed on a file's contents, the file is opened and a file handle is obtained; the appropriate file functions are performed on the file, and the file is closed. Using ORCA, the process is similar. If processing is needed on a set of PowerBuilder libraries, a session is opened. When the session handle is obtained, the ORCA library functions can be called. When all processing on the library is completed, the ORCA session is closed.

There are also several session service functions for setting the current library search path, setting the current application, and performing error handling. Before any setting of the current application occurs, the library search path must be set.

Library Management

ORCA also has a set of library management functions that can be called. These functions allow libraries and library entities to be manipulated outside the context of a current application or library list. That means a current application library search path does not have to be set for these library functions to work because they act on the library as a whole, not on its contents. Library functions can create libraries, delete libraries, and modify library comments. In addition, library entities can be copied, deleted, exported, and moved by using these functions.

Compilation

The ORCA compilation functions let the developer import and regenerate a single library entity or multiple library entities. All compilation must occur within the context of a current application and library list so that all library references can be resolved.

Executable Construction

These ORCA functions must also be performed within the context of a current application and library list. Application executable files and PowerBuilder dynamic libraries (PBDs) can be created by using the ORCA executable construction functions. The authors recommend calling the regeneration function before creating an executable or PowerBuilder dynamic library. The ORCA executable functions can also create compiled code.

Object Query

These ORCA functions allow querying objects for object reference explosion and object hierarchy traversal. Object querying must occur within the context of a current application and library list.

Source Management

These ORCA functions enable version control vendors to check in/out objects from the PowerBuilder applications environment.

ORCA Functions

ORCA functions are meant to be called from a custom DLL. To obtain the detail specifications of these functions and the PowerBuilder ORCA header file, contact Powersoft. Table 12.2 lists the functions.

These functions are all prototyped within the ORCA header file. A series of source management functions are also included.

Table 12.2   ORCA Functions

Function Name	Description
PBORCA_SessionOpen	Establishes an ORCA session. This call must be made before any other ORCA function calls. There are no overhead or resource issues related to keeping an ORCA session open. Therefore, once established, an ORCA session should be left open as long as it might be needed.
PBORCA_SessionClose	Terminates an ORCA session. This function frees any allocated resources related to the ORCA session. Because an ORCA session does not connect to anything, failure to execute it does not result in any loss of data.
PBORCA_SessionGetError	Gets the current error for an ORCA session. This function should be called anytime another ORCA function call has resulted in an error. If there is no current error, " " is placed within the error buffer.
PBORCA_SessionSetLibraryList	Establishes the library search path for an ORCA session. This function must be called prior to execution of any ORCA function that compiles objects, queries objects, or constructs executables. Certain library entry management functions and query functions can be called without setting the library list. Library names should be fully qualified, whenever possible.
PBORCA_SessionSet CurrentAppl	Establishes the current application for an ORCA session. This function must be called after PBORCA_SetLibraryList and prior to execution of any ORCA function that compiles objects, queries objects, or constructs executables. The application library name should be fully qualified, whenever possible.

Table 12.2 *Continued*

Function Name	Description
PBORCA_LibraryCommentModify	Modifies the comment of a PowerBuilder library.
PBORCA_LibraryCreate	Creates a new PowerBuilder library.
PBORCA_LibraryDelete	Deletes a PowerBuilder library.
PBORCA_LibraryDirectory	Explodes the directory of a PowerBuilder library.
PBORCA_LibraryEntryCopy	Copies a PowerBuilder library entry from one library to another.
PBORCA_LibraryEntryDelete	Deletes a PowerBuilder library entry.
PBORCA_LibraryEntryExport	Exports the source for a PowerBuilder library entry.
PBORCA_LibraryEntryInformation	Returns information for a PowerBuilder library entry.
PBORCA_LibraryEntryMove	Moves a PowerBuilder library entry from one library to another.
PBORCA_CompileEntryImport	Imports the source for a PowerBuilder library entry and compiles it.
PBORCA_CompileEntryImportList	Imports the source for a list of PowerBuilder library entries and compiles them. All entries are imported first, have only their type definitions compiled, and then, assuming everything works, have the entire entry list fully compiled. This call can be used to import several interrelated objects— for example, a window, its menu, and perhaps a user object that it uses. Note that ancestor objects and user objects must be imported prior to any objects that are descended from them.
PBORCA_CompileEntryRegenerate	Compiles a PowerBuilder library entry.
PBORCA_ExecutableCreate	Creates a PowerBuilder executable.
PBORCA_DynamicLibraryCreate	Creates a PowerBuilder dynamic library (PBD).
PBORCA_ObjectQueryHierarchy	Queries a PowerBuilder object for other objects within its ancestor hierarchy.
PBORCA_ObjectQueryReference	Queries a PowerBuilder object for references to other objects.

ORCA Errors

Table 12.3 lists the standard PowerBuilder ORCA errors. These error numbers are returned by the ORCA library management functions.

PowerBuilder ORCA Header File

The PowerBuilder ORCA header file is needed to write programs that communicate with ORCA. The pborca.lib file is also needed. With both 16- and 32-bit PowerBuilder code, there needs to be a different .LIB file. Powersoft provides pborca.16 and pborca.32 files for developers to download and use to create ORCA applications.

Table 12.3   Standard PowerBuilder ORCA Errors

Error Number	Error Description
-1	Invalid parameter list
-2	Duplicate operation
-3	Object not found
-4	Bad library name
-5	Library list is not set
-6	Library is not in the library list
-7	Library I/O error
-8	Object exists
-9	Invalid name
-10	Buffer size too small
-11	Compile error
-12	Link error
-13	Current application not set
-14	Object has no ancestor
-15	Object has no references
-16	Invalid Number of PBDs
-17	PBD Create Error
-18	Check out/in Error

TIP You can download the PowerBuilder ORCA documentation from the library archive at the Powersoft Website at www.powersoft.com/services/support/pbuilder/files/.

CHAPTER 13

External Interfaces

In today's world of object-oriented, component-based development, it is important for any development tool to provide a method of interfacing with the external applications or objects. PowerBuilder provides a variety of ways to incorporate external applications or objects within a PowerBuilder application.

This chapter discusses the following ways of integrating the external components into a PowerBuilder application:

- The Windows API
- DDE (Dynamic Data Exchange)
- OLE (Object Linking and Embedding)
- OLE Custom Controls (OCXs)
- Windows DLLs
- Cross-platform issues

THE WINDOWS API

An application programming interface (API) is a set of all operating system service calls for a particular product. A set of APIs lets programmers or products connect to a specified product or to the operating system. An API includes information about the internal variables and ways to link into a package. Microsoft's set of Windows APIs are known as the Microsoft Windows Software Development Kit (SDK). The SDK has more than 1000 API functions, divided into three groups: the Windows manager interface functions (User), the graphics device interface functions (GDI), and the system services interface functions (Kernel). The SDK enables programmers to interface with the Windows operating system using these APIs.

Making Windows API Calls

The GDI dynamic link library (DLL) has export functions to handle the painting, drawing, plotting, printing, and color functions of Windows. The User DLL has export functions for everything within Windows that involves window creation, communication, hardware, and messaging. The Kernel DLL has export functions for memory management, multitasking, and resources. The Kernel, GDI, and User DLLs handle most of the functionality of the Windows operating system. There are also device drivers within the Windows operating system that provide support for the different levels of Windows functionality. Device drivers are responsible for exporting the functions for Windows functionality above and beyond what the Kernel, GDI, and User DLLs can provide.

Powersoft developed more than 500 functions within PowerBuilder so application developers do not have to call the SDK functions to accomplish their tasks. There are times, however, when you need to get information from the Windows operating system and PowerBuilder does not have the functions needed to accomplish that task. In this case, you must look for the function within the SDK. Most of the functions that Power-Builder users need to call are within kernel.exe and user.exe or within the gdi.exe DLLs. Within the 32-bit Windows environments, these functions are within kernel32.dll, user32.dll, and gdi32.dll.

To determine which functions are needed for certain tasks, refer to the SDK's *Functions Manual*. When you locate the SDK function, answer the following questions:

- Can you pass the parameters from PowerBuilder by using the appropriate datatypes?
- Can PowerBuilder handle the function's return datatype?
- Can you locate the DLL that has the function?

If the answer to each of these questions is "yes," you can declare the function as an external function within the application. The external function's syntax is as follows:

```
FUNCTION Return_Data_Type &
    FunctionName ( { REF } { Data_Type1 Arg1, ..., &
                            Data_TypeN ArgN } ) &
        LIBRARY "Library Name"
```

If an external function does not return a value (for example, it has a void return type), the syntax for the external function declaration is:

```
SUBROUTINE
    FunctionName ({REF}{ Data_Type1 arg1 ,..., &
            Data_TypeN argn }) &
        LIBRARY "Library Name"
```

The following statement, for example, declares an external C function named **Is-Zoomed( )** that interfaces with the Win16 SDK and takes one argument (an integer called Handle):

```
Function Boolean IsZoomed(Int Handle) Library "User.EXE"
```

Windows Messages

Windows messaging is the most basic way for an application to communicate with itself, other applications, and the Windows operating system. Messages, which are the input to an application, represent the events to which an application may need to respond. They are basically a set of values that Windows sends to a window procedure to provide input or request the window to carry out some action.

For example, an event occurs when you press the left mouse button or a key. Upon detecting this event, Windows notifies the appropriate application by sending the messages to the application. You can associate a single message or a group of messages with an event. A message is a structure that has a message identifier and message parameters. The content of message parameters depends on the message type.

Windows collects the input messages within its message queue and places them within one of its application message queues. The application then reads the message(s) and dispatches them to the appropriate window procedure. Windows sends some messages directly to a window procedure. When this happens, it is said that Windows has *sent* a message. On the other hand, when Windows sends a message to an application message queue, it is said that Windows has *posted* a message. Figure 13.1 shows the relationship between the Windows message queues and each application's message queue.

Figure 13.2 shows a test window with a single command button in the center. The Message button's clicked event simply displays a messagebox:

```
messagebox("Message", "You just clicked this button!")
```

At runtime, when the user clicks the command button, Windows generates a series of messages that correspond to clicking the left mouse button and sends them to the PowerBuilder application message queue. The PowerBuilder application then reads the messages and sends them to the window process, which executes the line of code within the clicked event and displays the messagebox in Figure 13.3.

PowerBuilder Messages Mapped to Windows Messages

PowerBuilder has its own set of messages. These messages are mapped to one or more Windows messages. For a mapping of PowerBuilder's messages to Windows' messages, refer to the PowerBuilder documentation.

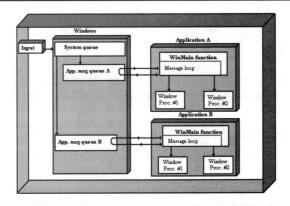

Figure 13.1   **Relationship between Windows queues and application message queues. From *Microsoft Windows 3.1 Guide to Programming.***

Figure 13.2   The test window with a single command button.

Figure 13.3   The messagebox displayed.

Trapping a Windows Message

When you need an application to respond to a specific Windows message that Power-Builder has not defined, trap the message. For example, when the user attempts to close the application by using the Control menu, a messagebox should appear asking the user to confirm his or her actions (closing the application). To do this, you must trap the appropriate Windows messages that are sent to the application. First, study the Microsoft Windows SDK documentation on messages. You will find them in the *Programmer's Reference Volume 3: Messages, Structures, and Macros*. This book lists the different types of Windows messages, their purpose, and a detailed parameter listing. You can use a number of different tools to determine which Windows messages are being generated. The example that follows uses Watcom's Spy program.

By using Spy, you can determine the Windows messages that the application generates when you close the application by using the control menu. In this case, the message generated is the WM_SYSCOMMAND. You can determine this by reviewing all the messages sent to the window and looking up what they mean (in the SDK documentation's Messages section). The WM_SYSCOMMAND Windows message is generated when a user selects a command from the control menu or when a user selects the maximize or minimize button.

After you determine the Windows message name, determine the message number. You can do this by using the wParam column within the Spy output window or by opening the Windows header. The wParam column in the Spy window shows the message number of F060 (see Figure 13.4).

A more tedious method of determining the message number is to look at the Windows header file included in the Windows SDK. The message numbers are located

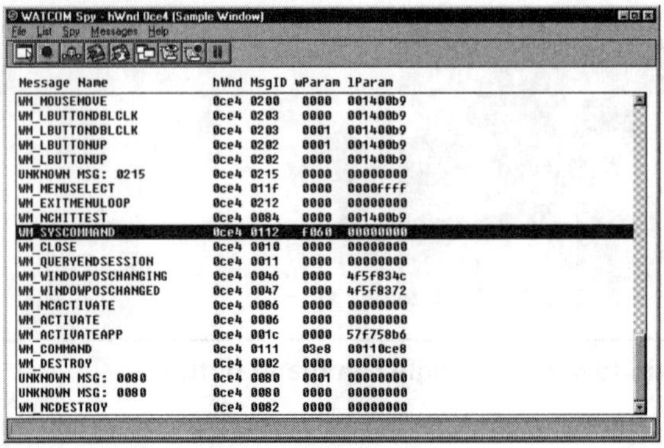

Figure 13.4 The WM_SYSCOMMAND within the Watcom Spy output window.

within the windows.h file for 16-bit Windows and in the winuser.h file for 32-bit Windows. After opening the appropriate header file, search for the line containing WM_SYSCOMMAND. This search locates the following line within both 16- and 32-bit environments:

```
#define WM_SYSCOMMAND   0x0112"
```

Next, look for the appropriate system menu command value or parameter. As mentioned before, the parameters for the Windows messages are listed in the Microsoft SDK documentation's Messages section. Because you are interested in trapping the message when trying to close the application, locate the SC_CLOSE parameter option. The following shows the portion of the Windows header file (windows.h or winuser.h) containing the SC_CLOSE's definition:

```
/*
 * System Menu Command Values
 */
#define SC_SIZE      0xF000
#define SC_MOVE      0xF010
#define SC_MINIMIZE     0xF020
#define SC_MAXIMIZE     0xF030
#define SC_NEXTWINDOW     0xF040
#define SC_PREVWINDOW     0xF050
#define SC_CLOSE     0xF060
#define SC_VSCROLL      0xF070
```

As you can see, SC_CLOSE has a message number of 0xF060, which is the same value Spy found.

The next step is to convert the message number from hexadecimal to decimal. The decimal value of F060 is 61536. For converting hexadecimal numbers to decimal numbers, the Windows scientific calculator is a good tool.

Finally, go to PowerBuilder and do several things. First, declare a user event. But before you attempt to declare the user event, map the WM_SYSCOMMAND to a Power-Builder message. The PowerBuilder message name corresponding to WM.SYSCOM-MAND is PBM_SYSCOMMAND. Open the window for which you need to trap the control menu close message. When you open the correct window, select the **Declare** and **User Events...** menu items. The Events dialog box then opens. Select any name for the event name and choose the PBM_SYSCOMMAND as the event ID. After selecting the event name and ID, click OK. Next, open the new event name from within the window and add the following PowerScript logic to the newly created event:

```
uint wParm

wParm = intLow(message.wordParm)
if wParm = 61536 then
    if (MessageBox("Exit?", "You are about to close the application, ~n"&
            + "~tAre you sure?", Question!, YesNo!, 2) ) = 1 then
        Halt Close
    else
        message.processed = true
    end if
end if
```

When the application is running and the user tries to exit the application by using the Control menu, the messagebox in Figure 13.5 appears.

If this logic must be present in other windows of the application, think about the code reusability and inheritance discussions of the earlier chapters. Either create a function and call it from the application or place the logic within the application architecture's appropriate base class.

TIP An important point to note is that you must trap the message.wordParm variable within the event mapped to the PBM_SYSCOMMAND. When you trap this parameter, you can pass the parameter to the function. If you trap the message.wordParm within another event or another function, its value may be different. This is the nature of event-driven programming.

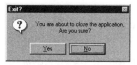

Figure 13.5 A messagebox appears when the user tries to exit the application.

User-Defined Messages

You can also define application-level messages. These messages are different from the messages that Windows and PowerBuilder defines. Windows makes a range of messages available for you to use without interfering with the messages that the operating system generates.

To help define the private messages, WM_USER is a constant used by applications. To distinguish between the message values reserved for use by Windows and the values an application can use to send messages within a private window class, use the WM_USER constant. The four ranges of message numbers are described in Table 13.1.

Message numbers within the first, third, and fourth ranges are not available to you. To send the messages within a private window class, an application can define and use the message numbers within the second range. You cannot use these values to define the messages that are meaningful throughout an application because some predefined window classes already define values within this range. For example, predefined control classes as Button, Edit, Listbox, and Combobox may use these values. You should not send messages within this range to other applications unless you design the applications to exchange messages and attach the same meaning to the message numbers. The WM_USER constant message has the following value, which you can obtain from the Windows header file:

```
#define WM_USER    0x0400
```

This message's decimal value is 1024. For private messages, this is the lower bound. The upper bound is 0x7FFF in hexadecimal, which is 524,287 in decimal. You can pass the predefined messages within applications by using **Send( )** or **Post( )**. Other useful functions for message-sending are **Handle( )**, **IntHigh( )**, and **IntLow( )**.

PowerBuilder Global Message Structure

By default, PowerBuilder declares a global message structure for all of its applications. When a Windows event occurs that is not a PowerBuilder-defined event, PowerBuilder populates the Message object with the event's information. The Message object is a PowerBuilder-defined global object (like the default transaction object SQLCA and the Error object). This message structure is based on the Windows message structure.

Table 13.1 Message Number Ranges

Range	Description
0 through WM_USER_1	Messages reserved for use by Windows
WM_USER through 0x7FFF	Integer messages for use by private window classes
0x8000 through 0xBFFF	Messages reserved for use by Windows
0xC000 through 0xFFFF	String messages reserved for the applications

Table 13.2 The Message Object's Attributes

Attribute	Datatype	Description
Handle	UnsignedInteger	The event's handle.
Number	UnsignedInteger	The number that identifies the event (this number comes from Windows).
WordParm	UnsignedInteger	The event's word parameter (this parameter comes from Windows). The event determines the parameter's value and meaning.
LongParm	Long	The event's long parameter (this number comes from Windows). The event determines the parameter's value and meaning.
Processed	Boolean	A Boolean value set within the Other event's script: True—The program processed the event. False—The default window procedure is called.
ReturnValue	Long	The value you want returned to Windows when Message.Processed is True. When Message.Processed is False, this value is ignored.
StringParm	String	A string or string variable.
DoubleParm	Double	A numeric or numeric variable.
PowerObjectParm	PowerObject	Any PowerBuilder object type including the structures.

The PowerBuilder Message Structure's Attributes Table 13.2 describes the Message object's attributes. The first four attributes correspond to the Windows message structure's first four attributes.

Windows Message Structure Every message consists of four values: a handle that identifies the window, a message identifier, a 16-bit message-specified value, and a 32-bit message-specified value. Pass these values as individual parameters to the window procedure. The window procedure then examines the message identifier to determine the response and how to interpret the 16- and 32-bit values. Table 13.3 defines the Windows message structure.

Table 13.3 The Windows Message Structure

Attribute	Datatype	Description
hwnd	HWND	The handle to the window receiving the message.
Message	UINT	The message identifier.
wParm	WPARAM	16 bits of additional message-specific information.
LParam	LPARAM	32 bits of additional message-specific information.
time	DWORD	The time the message occurred.
pt	POINT	Points to a structure that contains the mouse pointer's X and Y position.

DDE (DYNAMIC DATA EXCHANGE)

DDE is a messaging protocol you can use to exchange data between the Windows applications. As a message-based protocol, DDE employs no special Windows functions or libraries. You can perform all the DDE transactions by passing certain defined DDE messages between the client and server windows. Table 13.4 describes these messages.

PowerBuilder DDE Functions/Attributes

Although DDE is a message-based protocol, PowerBuilder has certain functions to make things simpler for you. You can use these functions for something as simple as calling the Windows **SendMessage( )** or **PostMessage( )** functions and passing the appropriate message(s). Table 13.5 lists the PowerBuilder DDE client functions and their descriptions.

Table 13.6 lists the DDE server functions and their descriptions. Examples of these functions are shown throughout this section.

DDE to Microsoft Word and Microsoft Excel

There are times when an application may need to establish a DDE link to a word processor or spreadsheet simply to take advantage of particular features. You can es-

Table 13.4 The DDE Messages

Windows Message Name	Description
WM_DDE_ACK	This message notifies the application of the receipt and processing of (acknowledges) most of the other messages.
WM_DDE_ADVISE	The listener on the server end that responds to a DDE client's request to start a hot link or permanent data link.
WM_DDE_DATA	This message is fired off on the client when the DDE server sends new data to the client.
WM_DDE_EXECUTE	This message is fired off on the DDE server when the server receives a request to execute a command from the client.
WM_DDE_INITIATE	This server message is fired off when the client requests to start/initiate a conversation on the server.
WM_DDE_POKE	This server message is fired off when a remote or client application sends data.
WM_DDE_REQUEST	This server message is fired off when a remote or client application requests data.
WM_DDE_TERMINATE	This message is fired off when either the client or server makes a request to terminate a conversation.
WM_DDE_UNADVISE	The listener on the server end that responds to a DDE client's request to stop a hot link or permanent data link.

Table 13.5   PowerBuilder DDE Client Functions

PowerBuilder DDE Client Function	Description
OpenChannel( )	Open a channel to a DDE server application.
CloseChannel( )	Close a channel to a DDE server application.
ExecRemote( )	Request a specific command to be executed on the DDE server application.
GetDataDDE( )	Get the new data from a server application by using a hot link channel.
GetDataDDEOrigin( )	Get the origin of the data that has arrived from a server application by using a hot link channel.
GetRemote( )	Request the data from a server application.
RespondRemote( )	Send an acknowledgment to the server application.
SetRemote( )	Request the server application to set one of its properties to a specific value.
StartHotLink( )	Initiate a hot link to a server application.
StopHotLink( )	Terminate a hot link channel with a DDE server application.

tablish a DDE link to Microsoft Word, pass some information by using the link, and display a form or newsletter with the formatting and presentation only a word processor could do. You can do the same thing with a spreadsheet. The application may pass certain financial information to a spreadsheet and let the spreadsheet perform all the calculations. An example of how you can make a DDE link to Microsoft Word (a word processor) or Microsoft Excel (a spreadsheet) follows.

Table 13.6   PowerBuilder DDE Server Functions

PowerBuilder DDE Server Function	Description
StartServerDDE( )	Cause a PowerBuilder application to start acting as a DDE server.
StopServerDDE( )	Cause a PowerBuilder application to stop acting as a DDE server.
GetCommandDDE( )	Get a command that the client application sends.
GetCommandDDEOrigin( )	Get the application name used by the DDE client sending the command.
GetDataDDE( )	Get the data that the client sent.
GetDataDDEOrigin( )	Determines the origin of data from a hot-linked DDE server application or a DDE client application, and if successful, stores the application's DDE identifiers in the specified strings.
SetDataDDE( )	Send data to the client application.

Maximizing Word and Excel

There are times when you need to call an external application by using the PowerBuilder **Run( )** function. Simply calling the Run( ) function does not always yield the same results.

For example, assume an application needs to start Microsoft Word when the user presses the **Word Processing** icon. If Microsoft Word is not already running, invoke the application by using the PowerBuilder Run( ) function. If, however, a Microsoft Word's instance is already running, open and maximize the instance for the user. If you choose to use the run command, the application opens a new instance of Microsoft Word, even if an instance of Microsoft Word is already opened. To build the intelligence into the application such that if Microsoft Word's instance is already running when the user clicks the word processing button, open and maximize the instance; otherwise, the application starts Microsoft Word. To accomplish this, declare the local external function (unless other objects call the function) as shown in Figure 13.6.

Also, place a picture button on a window (see Figure 13.7) or add the functionality to a toolbar. Within the clicked event, pb_winword, add the following PowerScript:

```
string ModuleName
uint hWnd
// This function checks to see if Word's instance is already running
hWnd = GetModuleHandleW("winword.exe")
if hWnd = 0 then
     Run("winword.exe", Maximized!)
else
     hWnd = OpenChannel("WinWord","System")
     ExecRemote("[AppMaximize]",hWnd)
     CloseChannel(hWnd)
end if
```

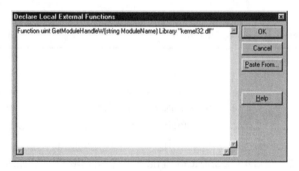

Figure 13.6   Declaring a local external function.

   pb_WinWord

Figure 13.7   The Microsoft Word picture button.

To do the same thing with Microsoft Excel, place the following PowerScript within the pb_Excel PictureButton:

```
string ModuleName
uint hWnd

hWnd = GetModuleHandle("excel.exe")
If hWnd = 0 Then
    Run("excel.exe", Maximized!)
Else
    hWnd = OpenChannel("Excel","System")
    ExecRemote("[App.Maximize]",hWnd)
    CloseChannel(hWnd)
end if
```

Use the Microsoft Excel picture button instead of the Microsoft Word picture button, as shown in Figure 13.8.

Passing Data from PowerBuilder to Microsoft Word

This example sends the data from a PowerBuilder application to Microsoft Word. The user enters the name and address data into the fields of the following window and clicks **Print**. This transfers the entered data to a predefined standard form within Microsoft Word for printing, as shown in Figure 13.9.

```
string sFname, sMI, sLname, sStAddress, sCity, sState, sZip
integer iDDEHandle

sFname = dw_main.Object.Fname.[1]
sMI = dw_main.Object.MI[1]
sLname = dw_main.Object.Lname[1]
sStAddress = dw_main.Object.StAddress[1]
sCity = dw_main.Object.City[1]
sState = dw_main.Object.State[1]
sZip = dw_main.Object.Zip.[1]


if f_StartWord( ) then
    iDDEHandle = OpenChannel("WinWord", "System")

    // open the document
    ExecRemote("[FileOpen.Name = ~"form.doc~"]", iDDEHandle)
```

continues

 pb_Excel

Figure 13.8   The Microsoft Excel picture button.

Figure 13.9   Data transferred to Microsoft Word.

```
      // Send data to Microsoft Word, and set it to the appropriate bookmark
      SetRemote("Fname",sFname,iDDEHandle)
      SetRemote("MI",sMI,iDDEHandle)
      SetRemote("Lname",sLname,iDDEHandle)
      SetRemote("StAddress",sStAddress,iDDEHandle)
      SetRemote("City",sCity,iDDEHandle)
      SetRemote("State",sState,iDDEHandle)
      SetRemote("Zip",sZip,iDDEHandle)
      ExecRemote("[FilePrint]",DDEHandle)
   end if
```

In Microsoft Word, the form could look like the one in Figure 13.10.

To select the appropriate bookmarks within Microsoft Word, click on the **Insert** and **Bookmark** menu items. The dialog box shown in Figure 13.11 appears.

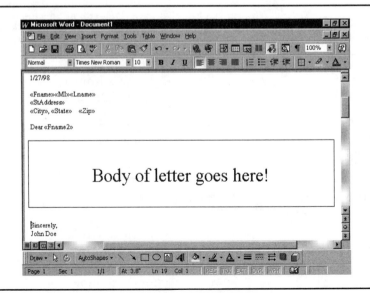

Figure 13.10   The data's format within Microsoft Word.

Figure 13.11   The Bookmark dialog box.

Bookmarks are a reference to the actual locations within a Word document. To set the values from PowerBuilder, you can use the bookmark names with the **SetRemote( )** function.

DDE Client/Server

Two applications participating within a dynamic data exchange are said to be engaged in a "DDE conversation." The application initiating the request is the client, and the application responding to the request is the server. The terms *client* and *server* are not used in the same way here as in a discussion about client/server architecture, where a workstation (client) makes requests of the database or file server(s). Although they are similar in theory, in that the client requests data/information from the server and the server responds, the major difference is that, with DDE, the client/server relationship is happening on one workstation.

A DDE conversation takes place between two windows, one for each of the applications that are exchanging the data. The windows may be the application's main window, a window associated with a specific document, as within an MDI application, or a hidden window, whose only purpose is to process the DDE messages.

TIP A pair of client and server windows can never be involved in more than one DDE conversation at any time.

OLE (OBJECT LINKING AND EMBEDDING)

OLE is the standard method of object communication within the Windows environment. PowerBuilder provides extensive support for OLE 2 in the form of OLE controls and OLE control containers. In addition to the support for OLE controls and control containers, PowerBuilder also provides support for OLE automation, meaning that you can automate the OLE 2 servers from within a PowerBuilder application.

You can add OLE controls to the PowerBuilder Windows, DataWindows, and User Objects. There is also a set of PowerScript functions for manipulating the OLE controls at runtime.

This section discusses the following OLE topics:

- Microsoft OLE 2 features
- PowerBuilder OLE 2 control properties
- PowerBuilder OLE 2 functions
- PowerBuilder OLE 2 container application support
- PowerBuilder OLE 2 sample code

Microsoft OLE 2 Features

The primary feature of OLE that lets software components communicate is the OLE Component Object Model (COM). Several other OLE features, however, directly benefit both users and developers. Some of the major features of OLE are discussed next.

OLE Component Object Model

COM provides all of the interface standards and handles all the intercomponent communication that lets you integrate the software components. Because it is a binary standard, you can write the OLE software components in any language and any software vendor can supply them, yet still you can seamlessly integrate them within a single application.

OLE Automation

OLE Automation lets applications expose the command sets that operate within and across applications. For example, a user can invoke a command from a word processing program that sorts a range of cells within a spreadsheet that a different application created.

OLE Controls

OLE Controls are OLE-enabled software components you can purchase to extend and enhance an application's functionality. You can use the OLE Controls within custom or off-the-shelf OLE-enabled applications. OLE Custom Controls (OCX) are discussed later in this chapter.

OLE Drag-and-Drop

Users can drag the objects from one application to be autonomously upgraded without affecting the component-based solution's operation.

OLE Documents

OLE documents are a kind of compound document that can incorporate the data you create within any OLE-enabled application. For example, an OLE-enabled word processor can accept tables and charts from an OLE-enabled spreadsheet. OLE documents let users convey their ideas more effectively by incorporating any type of information into their documents. In addition to incorporating static information like charts and tables, OLE documents can also incorporate live data such as sound, video, and animation.

OLE documents also make the users more productive by improving the process of creating compound documents. The following features are specific to OLE documents.

OLE (Object Linking and Embedding) Through object linking, you can link the applications to the data objects in other applications. For example, you can link a spreadsheet table to multiple custom business reports. As you make changes to the table in the spreadsheet application, all the report documents are automatically updated. Object embedding is the ability to embed an object within another document without maintaining a link to the object's data source. Within both object linking and object embedding, the applications supplying the objects are called *OLE servers*, while the applications containing the objects are called *OLE containers*. An application can be both an OLE container and an OLE server.

OLE Visual Editing Visual editing lets users create rich, compound documents easily, incorporating text, graphics, sound, video, and other diverse object types. Instead of switching between applications to create parts of the compound document, users can work within a document's context. As the user begins to edit an object that originated within another application, such as a spreadsheet or image, the container application's menus and tools automatically change to that object's native (server) application's menus and tools. The user can then edit the object within the document's context without worrying about activating and switching to another application.

Nested Object Support You can nest the objects within multiple layers within other objects. Users can directly manipulate the objects nested within other objects and establish links to the nested objects.

Object Conversion You can convert the objects to different types so you can use different applications with the same object. For example, you can convert an object that you created with one brand of spreadsheet so that a different spreadsheet application can interpret the object for editing.

Optimized Object Storage The objects remain on disk until they are needed, and they are not loaded into memory each time you open the container application. Also, OLE has complete transacted object storage, supporting commits and rollbacks of objects to the disk. This ensures that data integrity is maintained as the objects are stored within the file system.

PowerBuilder OLE 2 Control Properties

PowerBuilder provides 30 different properties for OLE controls. Table 13.7 lists some of these properties. For a complete list of the OLE control properties, refer to the PowerBuilder documentation.

PowerBuilder OLE 2 Functions

PowerBuilder provides a set of functions for OLE Controls and OLE Automation. Some of these functions are described next. For a complete list of functions, refer to the PowerBuilder documentation.

Table 13.7   Some PowerBuilder OLE Control Properties

Attribute	Datatype	Description
Activation	omActivation	Specifies how the OLE object is activated.
ClassLongName	String	The long name for the server application associated with the OLE object within the control.
ClassShortName	String	The short name for the server application associated with the OLE object within the control.
ContentsAllowed	omContentsAllowed	Specifies whether the OLE objects within the control must be embedded or linked or whether either method is allowed.
DisplayName	String	User-readable name for the OLE control. This name is displayed within the OLE dialog boxes and windows that show the object's name. If this value is not specified, the control's name (such as ole_1) is the DisplayName.
DisplayType	omDisplayType	Specifies how the OLE object is displayed within the control. To represent the object, the control can display the actual contents or an icon.
DocFileName	String	The name of an OLE storage file or a data file of the server application that is opened for the control.
IsDragTarget	Boolean	Specifies whether you can drop an OLE object on the control.
LinkItem	String	The name of an item within the server application's data file to which the control is linked.
LinkUpdateOptions	omLinkUpdateOptions	Specifies how a linked object within the control is updated. If it is automatic, the link is updated when the object is opened and whenever the object changes within the server application. If it is manual, the link is not updated.
Object	omObject	The link information connecting the control to the server's data.
ObjectData	Blob	If the object is embedded, the object itself is stored as a blob within the ObjectData attribute.
ParentStorage	omStorage	Specifies the parent storage.

OLE 2 Control Functions

InsertFile( ) inserts a new object into the OLE control with a default template.

InsertClass( ) inserts a new object of a certain class. Some classes include "Excel.Sheet," "Excel.Chart," or "Word.Document."

InsertObject( ) prompts the user with the standard InsertObject dialog box and inserts an object based on the user's selection.

LinkTo( ) links an OLE control with a file or a portion of a file.

Activate( ) activates the object within the control. If InPlace! is specified, Activate activates the object in place. If OffSite! is specified, the object becomes active within the server application.

Save( ) saves the object within the control to the storage from which it was loaded or to the storage specified by a previous **SaveAs( )** function.

SaveAs( ) saves the object within the control to a specified storage file.

Open( ) opens the file specified and loads the object into the control. The control "owns" the file.

Clear( ) releases the object within the control and deletes the references to the object without updating the storage.

Copy( ) copies the control's contents to the Clipboard.

Cut( ) copies the control's contents to the Clipboard and clears the control.

Paste( ) pastes the Clipboard's contents into the control.

PasteLink( ) pastes a link to the Clipboard's contents into the control.

PasteSpecial( ) presents the users with a dialog box that lets them select **Paste** or **PasteLink**.

DoVerb( ) executes the verb specified for the control.

Drag( ) puts the control within drag mode.

OLE 2 Automation Functions

ConnectToObject( ) associates an OLE object with a PowerBuilder OLEObject variable and starts the server application.

ConnectToNewObject( ) creates a new instance of the class specified and connects to the instance.

DisconnectObject( ) releases any object previously connected to the control.

PowerBuilder OLE 2 Container Application Support

You can link or embed OLE objects into a PowerBuilder Window, DataWindow, or User Object. To add an OLE Control to a PowerBuilder User Object, select **OLE** from the **Controls** menu or choose the OLE icon from the control toolbar, as shown in Figure 13.12.

When you place an OLE 2 control on an object, PowerBuilder prompts you with the standard Insert Object dialog box (shown in Figure 13.13), which lets you embed an object, embed a file, or link to a file. If you do not want to assign an object to the control, click **Cancel**. You can assign an object at runtime by using PowerScript.

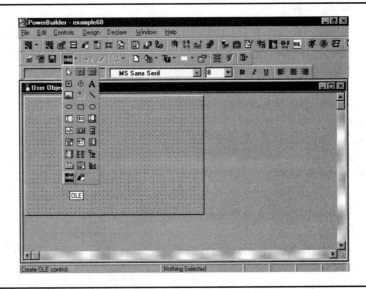

Figure 13.12   Adding an OLE control to a PowerBuilder object.

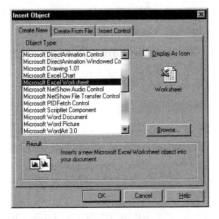

Figure 13.13   The Insert Object dialog box.

If you select the **Create New** tab, you can choose from a list of applications regis-tered as OLE 2 servers. If you choose one of these applications, PowerBuilder starts a new instance of the application, and you can use the application as desired. For exam-ple, if you choose a Microsoft Excel worksheet, the object's image appears within the OLE 2 control on the object when you exit the application (see Figure 13.14).

Once you click OK, PowerBuilder opens the OLE server application, and you can enter data. As you type the data into each cell, PowerBuilder automatically updates the corresponding OLE control. To exit the server application and update the OLE control, select **Update** from the server application's **File** menu, as shown in Figure 13.15.

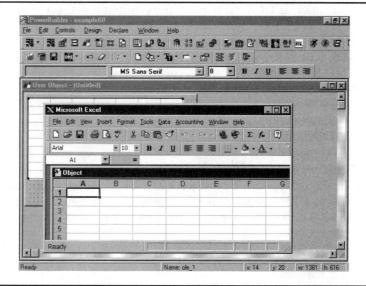

Figure 13.14   The Excel OLE object on a PowerBuilder object.

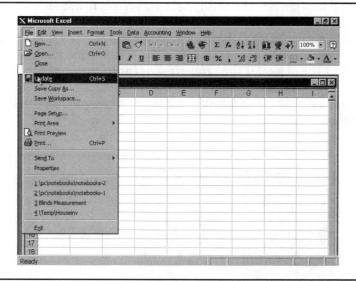

Figure 13.15   Updating an OLE control.

If you select the **Create From File** tab, PowerBuilder prompts you for a filename. After you select a file, PowerBuilder starts the application associated with that file's extension within the Windows registry, and that file is active. For instance, if you choose readme.doc, PowerBuilder starts Microsoft Word and opens the file readme.doc. The readme.doc file is active. After you exit the application, PowerBuilder copies the file's contents into the object and embeds the object into the OLE 2 control.

If you want to link this OLE 2 control to the original file, thereby sharing the data, check the **Link** checkbox (see Figure 13.16).

The following PowerScript functions let you insert or link to the objects at runtime. Details of these functions are given in the PowerBuilder documentation:

- InsertObject( )
- InsertClass(string class)
- InsertFile(string filename)
- LinkTo(string filename)

Saving Embedded or Linked Objects

You can save the embedded or linked objects as files, blobs, or OLE Storages. To save the objects as files or OLE Storages, use the SaveAs( ) function. To save the object as a blob, use the ObjectData's OLE 2 control attribute, which is of type blob. For example:

```
blob myblob

myblob = ole_1.ObjectData
```

PowerScript Automation Facilities

PowerScript functions provide the ability to write scripts to automate the OLE 2 server applications and OLE 2 controls.

For OLE automation support, use the dynamic object type OLEObject. The Power-Builder compiler accepts property names, function names, and parameter lists that are not yet defined for the object. If the properties or functions do not exist during execution, a runtime error occurs.

The following shows the OLE 2 server application's automation (in this case, Excel) from PowerBuilder:

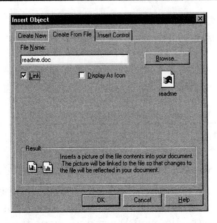

Figure 13.16   Linking an OLE control.

```
OLEObject MyOLEObject

MyOLEObject = Create OLEObject
MyOLEObject.ConnectToNewObject("excel.application")
MyOLEObject.Application.Visible = True
MyOLEObject.Application.Cells(1,1).Value = 14
Destroy MyOLEObject
```

If you want to use automation for an OLE 2 control, a simple call to the server's methods prefacing it with the OLE 2 control's Object attribute will suffice. Note that you do not need to do any of the steps listed earlier:

```
controlname.object.application.cells(1,1).value = 14
```

where controlname is the OLE 2 control's name.

PowerBuilder OLE 2 Sample Code

The following examples show how you can accomplish some of the OLE functionality by using PowerScript.

Loading a File

```
string ls_path,ls_filename

GetFileOpenName("Select file to open",ls_path,ls_filename)
If ls_filename ="" Then Return
ole_1.Insertfile(ls_path)
st_type.Text = ole_1.Classlongname
```

Loading an Object

```
ole_1.Insertobject( )
st_type.Text = ole_1.Classlongname
```

Paste Special

```
int li_rc

li_rc = ole_1.Pastespecial( )
If li_rc <> 0 Then Return -1
st_type.Text = ole_1.Classlongname
```

Paste

```
int li_rc

li_rc = ole_1.Paste( )
If li_rc <> 0 Then Return -1
st_type.Text = ole_1.Classlongname
```

Activate in Place

```
ole_1.Activate(Inplace!)
```

Activate Off Site

```
ole_1.Activate(Offsite!)
```

Copy

```
int li_rc

li_rc = ole_1.Copy( )
If li_rc <> 0 Then Return -1
```

Updating a Table

In this example, we are updating a table called "ole" from an OLE control, a static text, and a MultiLineEdit:

```
blob lb_object

lb_object = ole_1.Objectdata
INSERT INTO "ole"( "id", "object", "description" )
VALUES ( :sle_title.text,' ", :mle_desc.text );
If SQLCA.SQLCode = -1 Then
    MessageBox("SQL error",SQLCA.SQLErrText,Information!)
    Return -1
End If
UpdateBlob "ole" set "object" = :lb_object
    where "id" = :sle_title.text;
If SQLCA.SQLCode = -1 Then
    MessageBox("SQL error",SQLCA.SQLErrText,Information!)
    Return -1
End If
Commit;
```

Retrieving into an OLE Control

In this example, we are retrieving data into an OLE control from a database table called "ole":

```
string ls_index
blob ole_blob

SELECT "ole"."id", "ole"."description"
    INTO :sle_title.text, :mle_desc.text
    FROM "ole"
    WHERE "ole"."id" = :ls_index ;
```

```
If SQLCA.SQLCode = -1 Then
     MessageBox("SQL error",SQLCA.SQLErrText,Information!)
End If
selectblob "object" into :ole_blob from "ole"
     where "id" = :ls_title;
If SQLCA.SQLCode <> 0 Then
     MessageBox("SQL error",SQLCA.SQLErrText,Information!)
End If
ole_1.Objectdata = ole_blob
st_type.Text = ole_1.Classlongname
```

Inbound OLE Automation

With the release of PowerBuilder 5, PowerBuilder enhanced its OLE Automation by letting other applications (such as Visual Basic or Delphi) drive PowerBuilder nonvisual objects. That means that any client program that handles OLE automation can create a PowerBuilder object's instance and invoke the object's methods. The following example shows how to create a PowerBuilder object's instance within Visual Basic and call the object's methods.

What is unique about PowerBuilder's OLE automation technique is that the technique lets the client applications access the nonvisual objects. You can deploy these nonvisual objects as In-Process OLE automation servers. To accomplish this, create a registry entry for OLE to find the appropriate PowerBuilder object. The entry creates a global unique identifier from the Programmatic identifier. To find the appropriate PowerBuilder DLL, use the global identifier:

```
Private Sub Command1_Click()
     Dim MyPBObject As Object

     Set MyPBObject = CreateObject("uo_message")
     If MyPBObject Is Nothing Then
          Rem Put in error handling routine to trap any problems
     Else
          MyPBObject.log_message()
     End If
End Sub
```

As the preceding example shows, first create a variable of type Object. Next, set that variable equal to the PowerBuilder object that you want to use. Remember to make sure that you created a registry entry for the object. If you are able to create the object, you can reference the object's methods and attributes. One thing to remember when creating the PowerBuilder object is to make sure that the functions and attributes the OLE clients have access to are declared as Public. Figure 13.17 shows the entry within the registry.

You can see there is an entry for the uo_message object that we created within PowerBuilder. Figure 13.17 shows the information contained within the registry for the

Figure 13.17 The Registry entry for uo_message.

CLSID number assigned to uo_message. It contains the classname uo_message and the library where the DLL that contains the object can be found.

A more advanced way to access the PowerBuilder objects uses the programmatic identifier PowerBuilder.Application. Using PowerBuilder.Application lets you connect an OLE client to a PowerBuilder nonvisual object without creating an entry in the registry. The following code shows how you can do this:

```
Dim MyPBObject as Object
Dim PBAppObject as Object

SET PBAppObject = CreateObject("PowerBuilder.Application")
If PBAppObject Is NOTHING Then
     REM Put in your error handling routine here
Else
     PBAppObject.LibraryList = "c:\apps\myapp.dll"
     SET MyPBObject = PBAppObject.CreateObject("uo_message")
     If MyPBObject Is NOTHING Then
          REM Put in your error handling routine
     Else
          MyPBObject.log_message()
          MyPBObject = nothing
     End If
     PBAppObject = nothing
End if
```

This example also uses Visual Basic. First, create the PowerBuilder.Application object's instance. (Be sure the file pbappl.reg is registered with OLE.) You need to set a few properties for this object. The first is the LibraryList. In the last example, we set the path to point to where the DLL containing the desired object is located. Set this property before creating the object's instance. The other property is MachineCode. This property lets you instantiate pCode instead of machine code. The MachineCode property (Boolean) defaults to True so it is not explicitly set within the example.

Once you create the PowerBuilder.Application's instance, you can use one of its methods to create the instances of objects contained within the LibraryList. Within the previous example, you can do this by calling:

```
PBAppObject.CreateObject("uo_message")
```

Two other methods are associated with the PowerBuilder.Application object: GenerateGUID( ) and GenerateRegFile( ). These two methods let you create an instance of PowerBuilder.Application within a script and then, by using the two methods in conjunction with the LibraryList property, create a registry file based on the information given. The following code is an example of this script:

```
oleObject    PBObject
string       GUID
long         result


PBObject = Create OleObject

// Establish a connection with PowerBuilder.Application
result = PBObject.ConnectToNewObject("PowerBuilder.Application")

If result < 0 Then
    // handle the error
Else
    PBObject.LibraryList = "c:\myappl\mylibrary.dll"// Set the library list
    result = PBObject.GenerateGUID(REF GUID)

    If (result < 0) Then
        // handle the error
    Else
        result = PBObject.GenerateRegFile(GUID, "nvo_myuo", &
            "My Object",1, 0, "My nvo description", &
            "C:\myproj\mynvo.reg")
    End If // GUID created successfully
End If // Successfully established a connection to PowerBuilder.Application
```

PowerBuilder also provides a companion application that does the same thing, thus eliminating the need to create this script. For every PowerBuilder nonvisual object created for use with OLE Automation, you must create an entry within the registry. Otherwise, OLE clients do not know how to find the particular object they want to use.

There are a few issues to consider when deploying a PowerBuilder application for use as an OLE Automation server. First, the files pbroi050.dll and pbaen050.tlb should be in the deployment directory along with the appropriate DLLs that go along with the PowerBuilder application. Second, make sure you have an entry in the registration files.

Creating OLE Automation Server

This section discusses how to create and use a simple OLE Automation server with Power-Builder. The calc.dll is a PowerBuilder PBL (calc.pbl) converted to a dynamic link library. The calc.dll represents the OLE Automation server and contains a single, nonvisual User Object: nvo_myobject. The nonvisual User Object includes the following functions. The last argument for each of the functions is of type long that you pass by reference:

```
uf_multiply (long argument_a, long argument_b, ref long result)
uf_add (long argument_a, long argument_b, ref long result)
uf_divide (long argument_a, long argument_b, ref long result)
uf_subtract (long argument_a, long argument_b, ref long result)
```

Create a PowerBuilder application that will create a PowerBuilder application server and an object that is contained within the object calc.dll. Based on the user selection, you can then call the respective function within the DLL to calculate the values.

Running the Application

To run the application, use the following steps. Within the window w_ole_test:

1. Type a number within the Number 1 edit mask.
2. Choose an Operator from the Operation drop-down list box.
3. Type a number within the Number2 edit mask.
4. Click **Start the calculator**.
5. Click **Calculate**.
6. Click **Stop**.

When you click **Start the calculator**, the application creates a remote Power-Builder OLE object on the server. The server is the calc.dll, and the application creates the nvo_myobject from the calc.dll.

When you click **Calculate**, the application calls the necessary function from the calc.dll to perform the calculation.

When you click **Stop**, the application stops the OLE automation server.

Designing the Application

First, create a custom user object, and then add the four methods uf_multiply, uf_add, uf_divide, and uf_subtract.

To add the method uf_multiply, do the following:

1. Select **User Object Functions** from the **Declare** menu. PowerBuilder will display the Select Function in User Object dialog box.
2. To add a new function, click **New**. PowerBuilder displays the New Function dialog box.
3. In the New Function dialog box, type the function's name uf_multiply, and specify the three arguments: argument_a passed by value of type long, argument_b passed by value of type long, and result passed by reference of type long. Click OK. PowerBuilder returns you to the script window. In the script window, type the following lines of code:

```
result = argument_a * argument_b
Return 1
```

Similarly, add the remaining three functions to the user object nvo_myobject :

```
uf_add (long argument_a, long argument_b, ref long result)
result = argument_a + argument_b
Return 1


uf_divide (long argument_a, long argument_b, ref long result)
result = argument_a / argument_b
Return 1


uf_subtract (long argument_a, long argument_b, ref long result)
result = argument_a - argument_b
Return 1
```

Next, create a DLL (calc.dll) from the PBL (calc.pbl). To create the DLL:

1. Click the right mouse button on the calc.pbl within the library painter.
2. Select **Build Runtime Library** from the popup menu. PowerBuilder will display the Build Runtime Library dialog box.
3. Choose **Full** from the Build Type drop-down list box.
4. Choose **No optimization** from the Optimization drop-down list box.
5. To create the calc.dll, click OK.

Next, create a calculator application that accepts the values from the two edit masks. Perform a mathematical operation on the values by calling the appropriate function from the calc.dll.

To create the calculator application, add three events to the window w_ole_object as follows:

1. Open the window w_ole_object within PowerBuilder.
2. Select **User Events** from the **Declare** menu. PowerBuilder, in turn, displays the Events - w_ole_object dialog box. Type ue_start_calculator, ue_calculate, and ue_stop_calculator within the Event Name column. Assign pbm_custom01, pbm_custom02, and pbm_custom03 event IDs to the three events, respectively. To close the Events - w_ole_object dialog box, click OK.
3. Open the script window and add code for the three events: ue_start_calculator, ue_calculate, and ue_stop_calculator as shown next.
4. Within the ue_start_calculator event:
   1. Start the automation server and check if the connection is established. A status of 0 indicates success.
   2. Retrieve the name of the DLL that contains the calculation functions.
   3. Create the appropriate user object on the OLE automation server. The following is the code:

```
long      li_status

// Start the automation server and check that the connection is //
established. A status of 0 indicates success.
ole_pba = CREATE OLEObject

li_status = ole_pba.ConnectToNewObject ("PowerBuilder.Application")

If li_status < 0 Then
    MessageBox(This.Title, "No server exists! Can not connect to the &
       remote PowerBuilder application server.")
   Return
Else
    st_display.Text = "Connection to the remote PowerBuilder application &
       server successful"
End If

// Get the name of the DLL that contains the calculation functions
string docname, named
integer value

MessageBox (This.Title, "Please locate the calc.dll :")
value = GetFileOpenName ("Choose the DLL", docname, named, "DLL",  "DLL &
       Files (*.DLL),*.DLL")

If value = 1 Then
    ole_pba.LibraryList =  docname
Else
    MessageBox (This.Title, "Error! Could not find the DLL")
    Return
End If

// We assume here that the DLL is built with machine code
ole_pba.MachineCode = TRUE

// Create the first object you want to use and check for
// success. Specify the object's name as defined within the
// library.
ole_analyze = ole_pba.CreateObject("nvo_myobject")

If IsNull(ole_analyze) Then
      MessageBox(This.Title,  "No object! Could not create the object &
         nvo_myobject.")
   Return
Else
    st_display.Text = "Created the remote object successfully"
End If

// Enable and disable the appropriate buttons
cb_2.Enabled = True
cb_3.Enabled = True
cb_1.Enabled = False
```

5. Within the ue_calculate event:
   1. Perform error checking.
   2. Access the object's functions or properties by using the OLE automation syntax.
   3. Display the result. The following is the code:

```
long      ld_result

// Error checking
If em_1.Text   = "" Then
MessageBox (This.Title, "Please specify Number 1")
     Return
End If


If ddlb_1.Text = "" Then
     MessageBox (This.Title, "Please choose an operator")
     Return
End If


If em_2.Text   = "" Then
     MessageBox (This.Title, "Please specify Number 2")
     Return
End If


//Check for Divide by Zero
If ddlb_1.Text = "Divide" and Long(em_2.Text) = 0 Then
     MessageBox (This.Title, "Cannot divide by zero")
     Return
End If


// Access the object's functions or properties by using the OLE automation syntax

CHOOSE CASE ddlb_1.Text
     CASE "Add"
          ole_analyze.uf_add (Long(em_1.Text), Long(em_2.Text), REF ld_result )
          st_display.Text = "Calling the remote object function to Add data"
     CASE "Subtract"
          ole_analyze.uf_subtract (Long(em_1.Text), Long(em_2.Text), REF &
            ld_result )
          st_display.Text = "Calling the remote object function to Subtract data"
     CASE "Multiply"
          ole_analyze.uf_multiply (Long(em_1.Text), Long(em_2.Text), REF ld_result )
          st_display.Text = "Calling the remote object function to Multiply data"
     CASE "Divide"
          ole_analyze.uf_divide (Long(em_1.Text), Long(em_2.Text), REF ld_result )
          st_display.Text = "Calling the remote object function to Divide data"
END CHOOSE

// Display the result
sle_1.Text = String (ld_result)
```

6. Within the ue_stop_calculator event:
   1. Destroy the objects.
   2. Disable the appropriate buttons. The following is the code:

```
// Destroy the objects
DESTROY ole_analyze
ole_pba.DisconnectObject( )
DESTROY ole_pba

st_display.Text = "Disconnected from the remote PowerBuilder application server"

// Enable and disable the appropriate buttons
cb_2.Enabled = False
cb_3.Enabled = False
cb_1.Enabled = True
```

OLE CUSTOM CONTROLS (OCX)

In addition to the OLE 2 support described earlier, PowerBuilder also includes support for OLE custom controls (OCX). As part of its Component Gallery, PowerBuilder 6 includes a set of OLE custom controls (OCX) for use within the PowerBuilder development environment. The Component Gallery provides a collection of custom controls that encapsulate specific functionality that you can use within PowerBuilder applications or as part of an application architecture. Several third-party OCX controls are also available to accomplish a wide variety of tasks, including graphics, multimedia, and network access, among others. Any OLE custom control's (not just those included within the Component Gallery) properties, events, and methods become an extension of the standard PowerBuilder OLE control's properties, events, and functions.

   To add an OCX to a PowerBuilder application, do the following:

1. Register the OCX with the Windows registry. You can do this from the Power-Builder development environment or by running the regsvr32.exe program.
2. Choose the OCX to place on the PowerBuilder object by selecting the OLE control type and selecting the particular OCX from the Insert Object dialog box's **Insert Control** tab.

   For example, to place the calendar OCX included within the PowerBuilder Component Gallery on a User Object, select the calendar control from the list of OCX controls on the Insert Object dialog box as shown in Figure 13.18.

   To register a new OCX from the PowerBuilder development environment, click the **Register New...** button on the **Insert Control** tab. This lets you choose the OCX file to be registered. Once registered, the OCX appears in the list of controls. After choosing the calendar control, PowerBuilder displays the control on the PowerBuilder User Object, as shown in Figure 13.19.

   This control has two sets of properties. One set pertains to the generic Power-Builder OLE control, and the other pertains to the OCX control's properties itself. To

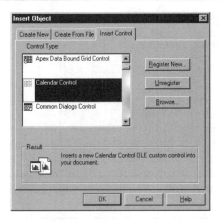

Figure 13.18   The calendar OCX.

modify the set of OCX properties, select the **OCX Properties...** option from the control's popup menu (obtained by right-clicking on the control). Each OCX has a specific set of properties. Figure 13.20 shows the calendar OCX's properties.

To view the list of attributes for an OCX, select the OLE Custom Control item from the PowerBuilder Object Browser's **OLE** tab. An OCX's attributes are divided into the following four areas: Class Information, Properties, Events, and Functions, as shown in Figure 13.21 for the calendar OCX.

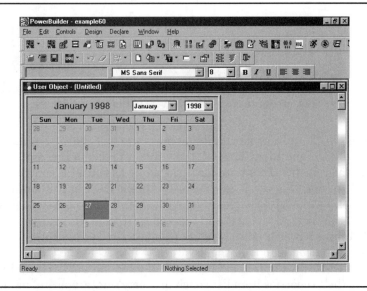

Figure 13.19   The calendar OCX on a PowerBuilder User Object.

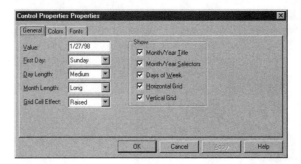

Figure 13.20   The calendar OCX's properties.

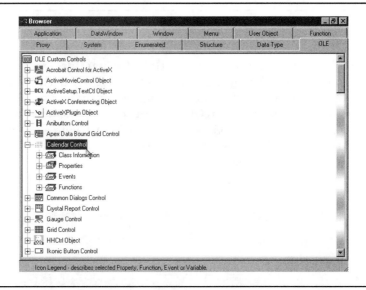

Figure 13.21   The OCX attributes from the PowerBuilder Object Browser.

Expanding the Class Information item shows some of the OCX's class characteristics. The Globally Unique Identifier (GUID) value represents the control's 32-byte ID, obtained from the registry. This number is the same as the OLE control's Class Identifier (CLSID). The InprocServer32 value represents the OCX implementation's full path name. The TypeLib value also represents the OCX's full path name and designates from where the OCX's properties, events, and functions are read. It is important to note that because both InprocServer32 and TypeLib (along with ToolboxBitmap32) specify the OCX's location, you need to modify these values to represent the OCX's correct location if you move the OCX file. Figure 13.22 shows the calendar OCX's Class Information.

Expanding the Properties item lists each property's datatype and name, or instance variable, of the OCX. Figure 13.23 shows the calendar OCX's list of properties.

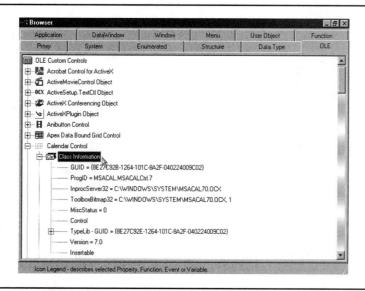

Figure 13.22   The Calendar OCX Class Information.

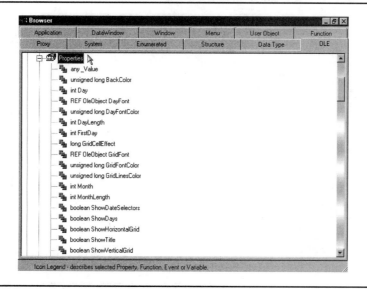

Figure 13.23   The Calendar OCX Properties.

Expanding the Events item lists all of the OCX's events, as shown in Figure 13.24 for the calendar OCX.

Finally, expanding the Functions item lists all of the OCX's functions, as shown in Figure 13.25 for the calendar OCX.

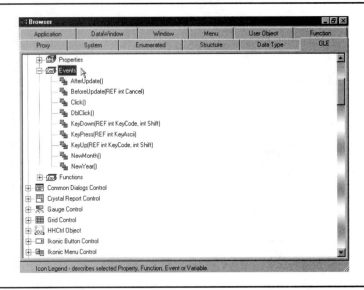

Figure 13.24   The Calendar OCX Events.

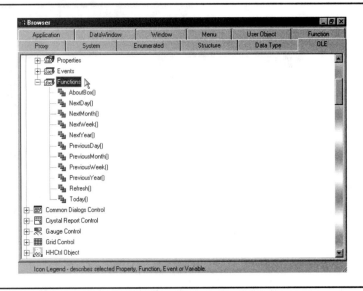

Figure 13.25   The Calendar OCX Functions.

When adding an OCX to a PowerBuilder application, the properties, events, and functions accessible to you are a combination of the OCX's set of properties, events, and methods, and the PowerBuilder OLE control's properties, events, and functions. Figure 13.26 shows the PowerBuilder olecustomcontrol events.

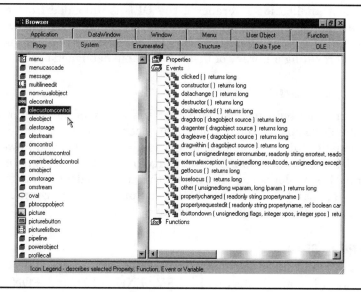

Figure 13.26   The olecustomcontrol events.

The OCX's properties, events, and methods work in the same way as the Power-Builder OLE control properties, events, and functions, with one exception: you must reference the OCX's properties and functions by using the dot notation with the keyword *object* placed before the property or function name, as shown:

```
controlname.object.property = value
controlname.object.function()
```

where controlname is the PowerBuilder OLE control's name and property/function is the OCX's property or function's name.

For example, calling the calendar OCX's **NextDay( )** function (PowerBuilder control name ole_1) uses the following syntax:

```
ole_1.object.NextDay()
```

On the other hand, you can call the show( ) function, which is not a method of the calendar OCX but a PowerBuilder OLE control function, by using the following syntax:

```
ole_1.show()
```

WINDOWS DLLS

A Dynamic Link Library (DLL) is a special library that lets applications share code and resources. A DLL is an executable module with export functions that an application calls to do certain tasks. An application links the DLLs at runtime. This lets a Power-Builder application and the Windows environment share code and resources. A DLL's main purpose is to provide a library of callable functions or resources. To call the DLL's functions, the application must load the DLL into memory. The DLL remains in memory until the last application referencing the DLL is unloaded from memory. DLLs have several uses, some of which are registering and storing the global window classes, writing device drivers, housing large quantities of resources (e.g., bitmaps, icons, dialog boxes), and providing a library of instantly usable debugged code.

Why Write Your Own DLLs?

PowerBuilder provides built-in capabilities to handle most of the functionality typically found in the Windows application development. There are times when you need to build certain functionality into an application that is above and beyond PowerBuilder's inherent capabilities. This functionality can range from using a DLL to interfacing with other vendors' APIs, to doing complicated mathematical calculations within computation-intensive applications (which are better compiled in C or Assembler). When you need this type of functionality, you must write a DLL.

DLLs and Applications

The Windows environment works with two fundamental program units: applications (.EXE executable files) and DLLs (.DLL, .DRV, .EXE, .VXD, and .FON files). Both applications and DLLs are referred to as *loadable*, or *executable*, modules. Applications are different from DLLs in that applications can have multiple copies or instances executed. An instance handle maintains and references each copy of an application. The reason for this is that Windows shares code and resource segments, so an application's data segment is the only part of it that is unique; it is what the instance handle references.

DLLs function differently within 16- and 32-bit environments. In the Win16 environment, only one copy of the DLL is loaded into memory. This DLL module does not have its own stack so it uses the stack, of the task that has called the DLL. In the Win32 environment, each DLL is mapped into the calling application's address space. Each process that calls the DLL has its own copy of that DLL's data.

When you execute an application, it actively processes messages, creates windows, interacts with the user, and generates output. In contrast, a DLL library function is passive. The DLL library function serves only as a function that an active application can call to perform some operation. With very few exceptions, DLL modules are as passive as any other library function.

When an application or a DLL is first loaded into memory, Windows creates a data structure known as a *module database*. A module database, like all the other program segments (i.e., code, data, and resources), is stored within the global heap. A module database has information found within the applications and DLLs' header portions. This header has a wealth of information regarding all the program's exported functions, resources, and other unique, unchangeable information. Under Windows, a module handle maintains a module database.

DLLs have different file extensions, depending on their particular function, such as font resources (.FON), device drivers (.DRV), virtual device drivers (.VXD), or operating system files (.EXE). All operate on the same basic principle, but there are some differences among them. The device-driver DLLs are always loaded into the DOS conventional memory's lower portion, and their segments are marked as fixed and page-locked so that memory cannot move or be paged to disk. This is because the device-driver code interfaces with interrupts and must always be within the same position within the memory each time it is called. The font DLLs also have some unique properties. The font DLLs do not have any code or data segments, only resource segments that contain fonts. Only font DLLs can house the resource segments. If you wrote a Win16 DLL to house resources such as icons and bitmaps, the DLL must have at least one code segment holding the DLL's entry point (LibEntry) and exit point (WEP).

A DLL's Assembly-language-defined entry point is called when it is first loaded into memory. In 16-bit Windows, the first piece of a DLL, which is optional, is the **LibEntry( )**. The LibEntry( ), when included, can initialize the DLL's local heap, link in C startup code, and make a call to **LibMain( )**. LibMain( ) is the main initialization for the Win16 DLLs. In 32-bit Windows, this main initialization is **DLLMain( )** (Microsoft) or **DLLEntry-Point( )** (Borland). DLLMain( ) and DLLEntrypoint( ) are only for Win32 and do not compile within WIN16. When the initialization is complete, Windows gets the control back and the DLL is ready for access. Before a DLL is unloaded from memory, Windows calls either **WEP( )** (Win16) or DLLMain( ) (Win32). Borland includes a WEP( ) in all of its DLLs. These are the places that should handle any final cleanup of memory that the DLL used. The WEP( ) (Win16) is often referred to as the DLL's *exit procedure* (see Figure 13.27).

How to Write a DLL

Generally, you write DLLs in the C programming language, so you need a C compiler. The C examples in this section and throughout the book are written and compiled with Microsoft's Visual C++, but most C/C++ compilers such as the Borland C++ compiler version 5.02 or above, the Microsoft Visual C++ version 5.0, and the Microsoft Quick C compiler should work with minimal modifications (see the following Tip). As described earlier, a DLL has an initialization procedure LibMain( ) (Win16) or DLLMain( ) (Win32) and an exit procedure WEP( ) (Win16). Win32 DLLs do not require the WEP( ) exit procedure. Instead, Win32 DLLs make another call to DLLMain( ), passing it a special parameter for exit processing (DLL_PROCESS_DETACH). The DLL's remaining portions have all the DLL's functions. You can call these export functions directly from Power-Builder or other C modules. A DLL has a number of different files. In writing a simple DLL, you may need a module definition file, a source file, a make file, and some header files, as Table 13.8 shows.

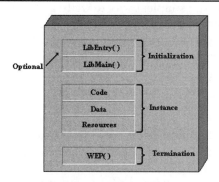

Figure 13.27   A Win16 DLL's components.

Table 13.8   Files for Writing a Simple DLL

Files	Description
sample.def	Module definition file
sample.c	C source file
sample.h	Header file
sample.mak	Make file

TIP Depending on which compiler you are using, you need to consider different things when writing the DLLs. Here are a few pointers (no pun intended). Using Visual C++ for this is really easy. For Win16 DLLs, write the functions in a .c file with **FAR PASCAL _export( )** function attributes/calling conventions. The compiler and linker handle everything from there if you specify the appropriate project template. This assumes that no initialization or cleanup is needed. For Win32 DLLs, declare the export functions with **__declspec(dllexport)**.

If you are using the Borland C++ compiler 3.1 or above, add a DLLMain( ) (Win32), DLLEntryPoint( ) (Win32), LibMain( ) (Win16), and a WEP( ) (Win16) function to the .c file, as explained before. LibMain( ) allows for any global initialization such as grabbing the DLL's instance handle. This is required if you need to get a resource. An explanation of LibMain( ) and WEP( ) was given earlier, but because most simple DLLs don't do anything special within their LibMain( ) and WEP( ) functions, Microsoft added default LibMain( ) and WEP( ) functions to Visual C++. DLLEntryPoint( ) and DLLMain( ) are both called whenever a DLL is loaded or unloaded, a process detaches or attaches to a DLL, or each time a thread is created or destroyed within the process.

If the compiler you use is Microsoft C/C++ 7 or earlier versions of Quick C for Windows, be sure to link with the libentry.lib library. The documentation explains this fairly well. Basically, the library adds some code to initialize the DLL's data segment. The older compiler versions also require that there be an EXPORT section within the .DEF file. Basically, the simplest way to write a DLL is to get an existing DLL from the SAMPLES that come with the compiler, compile, and link the DLL. Examining the output gives you an understanding of what is needed. Then all you need to do is to modify the code, compile, and link again.

Module Definition File

To establish certain unchangeable program-wide characteristics, use the Module definition file. These include giving the module a name, declaring the heap and stack sizes, exporting the functions, and establishing attributes for the code and data segments. The Module definition file greatly affects a completed module's organization and structure.

The Module definition file, Module database, and .EXE header have much in common. Each of these structures contains program-wide information. For example, when a program is compiled and linked, the information from the module definition file is placed near the beginning of the module's binary image. This block of memory, present for every application and DLL, is referred to as the *new-style* .EXE header. Like the .DEF file, the new-style .EXE header contains the module-wide information that the program instances can share between them. When Windows loads a program into memory, Windows creates a global heap entry called a Module database, which contains much of the information you find in the .EXE header.

The Module definition file's format for a Win16 DLL is:

```
LIBRARY  Sample
DESCRIPTION  'SampleßSample DLL'
EXETYPE  WINDOWS
STUB  'WINSTUB.EXE'
CODE MOVEABLE DISCARDABLE
DATA MOVEABLE SINGLE
HEAPSIZE 0
EXPORTS
WEP      @1   RESIDENTNAME
Sample   @2
```

Source File

A Win16 source file contains the LibMain( ) and WEP( ) functions as well as all the exported functions. The following shows a sample Win16 source file:

```
#include <windows.h>
/********************************************************
    FUNCTION: LibMain(HINSTANCE, WORD, WORD, LPSTR)
    PURPOSE: The initialization function for a DLL calls this function.
        Windows requires this function.
    COMMENTS: The entry routine within LIBENTRY.LIB calls this function.
        The routine is responsible for initializing the DLL. Because
        this DLL requires no initialization, the DLL simply returns 1.
********************************************************/
int FAR PASCAL LibMain (HINSTANCE hInstance, WORD wDataSeg,
WORD cbHeapSize, LPSTR lpCmdLine)
{
    if (cbHeapSize !=0)
        UnlockData(0); /* The entry function called LocalInit( ) */
            /* Because this call locked the DataSegment, */
            /* UnlockData(0) is required to unlock it. */
        return 1; /* 1 => successful, 0 => unsuccessful */
}
```

continues

```
/********************************************************
     FUNCTION:     Sample(int)
     PURPOSE:      Sample Export Function for this example
     COMMENTS:     The export function sample( ) is listed
 ********************************************************/
int FAR PASCAL _export Sample(int nParameter)
{
     Return nParameter++;
}
/********************************************************
     FUNCTION:     WEP(int)
     PURPOSE:      Windows requires and calls this function
     COMMENTS:     This function processes the messages that Windows sends to
the DLL. This function is used to properly close the DLL and simply
return 1.
 ********************************************************/
int FAR PASCAL WEP(int nParameter)
{
     /* This function is necessary but all it does is return a 1
         regardless of the message sent to this function. */
     if (nParameter == WEP_SYSTEM_EXIT)
     {
         return 1;
     }
     else if (nParameter == WEP_FREE_DLL)
     {
         return 1;
     }
     else
     {
         return 1;
     }
}
```

The same function as part of a Win32 DLL is shown:

```
BOOL WINAPI DLLMain (HANDLE hModule, DWORD fdwReason, LPVOID lpReserved)
{
  switch (fdwReason)
     {
    case DLL_PROCESS_ATTACH:
        ...
      break;
    case DLL_THREAD_ATTACH:
        ...
      break;
    case DLL_THREAD_DETACH:
        ...
```

```
        break;
     case DLL_PROCESS_DETACH:
         ...
        break;
   }

        return TRUE;    // successful DLL_PROCESS_ATTACH
   }
   /**********************************************************
        FUNCTION:        Sample(int)
        PURPOSE:         Sample Export Function for this example
        COMMENTS:        The export function sample( ) is listed
   **********************************************************/
   __declspec (dllexport) FAR PASCAL Sample(int nParameter)
   {
        Return nParameter++;
   }
```

The **sample( )** export function does not have any application functionality. It mainly shows an export function's structure. If you need to add more export functions to the DLL, both the Module definition and the source files should reflect the changes for the new functions. Within PowerBuilder, Figure 13.28 shows the sample function's declaration.

The declaration for DLLMain (Win32) is:

```
   BOOL  WINAPI  DLLMain (hModule, DWORD fdwReason, LPVOID lpReserved)
```

You can call DLLMain( ) multiple times while the DLL is within memory, but you can call LibMain( ) only once. The reason for this is the second parameter within the declaration. DLLMain is called when an application is loading the DLL, a thread from a process is accessing the DLL, a process is detaching from the DLL, and a thread is detaching from a DLL. If DLLMain( ) receives a fdwReason parameter value of DLL_PROCESS_DETACH, then you would do the same thing that you did within the Win16 world's WEP( ) function. To process the second parameter, just set up a CASE statement to handle the different values that DLLMain receives.

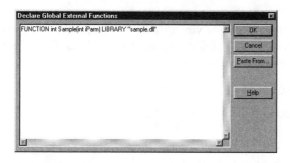

Figure 13.28   **A sample DLL function declaration.**

The DllEntryPoint's definition (Borland's equivelant to DLLMain) is:

```
INT WINAPI DllEntryPoint(Hinstance hinst, DWORD reason, LPVOID)
```

TIP From the PowerBuilder documentation:

```
FUNCTION [returntype] MyFunction( [ [ref] datatype MyArg
[, ...] ] ) LIBRARY "mylib.dll"
```

The C counterpart must be declared as FAR PASCAL.

You can pass back the values from an external DLL call by using one of the following two methods:

1. Pass the result back with a return.

From the Win16 C DLL:

```
LPSTR FAR PASCAL _export f_foo(void)
    {
        return "Hello";
    }
```

From the Win32 C DLL:

```
__declspec(dllexport) LPSTR FAR PASCAL f_foo(void)
    {
        return "Hello";
    }
```

From PowerBuilder:

```
FUNCTION string f_foo( ) LIBRARY "mydll.dll"

String sSTR
sSTR = f_foo( )
// process sSTR
```

2. Use the parameter list and pass a variable by reference. When you declare an external function in the PowerBuilder External Functions dialog box, use the Ref modifier on the parameter's type.

From the Win16 C DLL:

```
void FAR PASCAL _export f_foo(LPSTR lpszSTR)
{
    strcpy(lpszSTR, "Hello");
}
```

From the Win32 C DLL:

```
__declspec(dllexport) void FAR PASCAL f_foo(LPSTR lpszSTR)
{
    strcpy(lpszSTR, "Hello");
}
```

From PowerBuilder:

```
SUBROUTINE f_foo(ref string sSTR) LIBRARY "mydll.dll"

String sSTR

sSTR = Space(10);
f_foo(sSTR)
// process sSTR
```

This method lets the C function update a string variable called sSTR that you should declare within the PowerScript code. Without the Ref modifier, PowerBuilder ignores any changes made to the pointer or the value PowerBuilder passes to the external function. It is *very* important when passing the strings by reference that you allocate sufficient space for the return buffer *before* you make the external call. If you do not preallocate the space, a General Protection fault occurs within pbshare.dll. This is why the preceding example uses the PowerBuilder **Space(...)** function.

PowerBuilder and C SDK Datatype Mapping

The *PowerScript Language Reference* includes a list of supported and unsupported datatypes and their mappings between PowerBuilder and the Windows SDK. The most common ones are as shown in Table 13.9. When using this chart, it is important to remember that while PowerBuilder is not case-sensitive, C is.

Table 13.9   PowerBuilder and C SDK Datatype Mapping

PowerBuilder	C Windows SDK
string	LPSTR
integer	int
uint	UINT
word	UINT
long	long
ulong	DWORD/ULONG
uint	HANDLE
char	BYTE
boolean	BOOL

Table 13.10   The Environment Object's Attributes and Values

Attribute	Value
CPUType	The CPU type. For a complete list of the CPUTypes values, select the Object Browser's **Enumerated** tab.
MachineCode	Specifies whether the application executable is machine code (compiled). Values are: True—Executable is machine code. False—Executable is not machine code (pseudo-code).
OSFixesRevision	The operating system's maintenance version.
OSMajorRevision	The operating system's major version. For example, this value is 3 for Windows 3.x and 4 for 32-bit Windows 95 and 16-bit applications under Windows 95. If you are running a 16-bit application under Windows 95, OSMajorRevision is 3, not 4, and OSMinorRevision is 95.
OSMinorRevision	The operating system's point release. For example, this value is 10 for Windows 3.10.
PBFixesRevision	PowerBuilder's maintenance version.
PBMajorRevision	PowerBuilder's major version.
PBMinorRevision	PowerBuilder's point release.
NumberOfColors	Number of colors on the screen.
ScreenHeight	The screen's height in pixels.
ScreenWidth	The screen's width in pixels.
OSType	The operating system or environment. For a complete list of OSType values, select the PowerBuilder Object Browser's **Enumerated** tab.
PBType	PowerBuilder product's version. For a complete list of PBType values, select the PowerBuilder Object Browser's **Enumerated** tab.
Win16	Indicates the type of the operating system on which the application executable is running. Values are: True—Executable is running under a 16-bit operating system. False—Executable is running under a 32-bit operating system.

CROSS-PLATFORM ISSUES

In addition to the various Windows platforms, PowerBuilder also supports the Macintosh and UNIX operating systems. To obtain information about the platform PowerBuilder is running, along with other environment characteristics, use the PowerBuilder global Environment object. Table 13.10 describes the PowerBuilder Environment object's attributes and values. For example, if you are running PowerBuilder Enterprise 5 under Windows 3.1 on an Intel 486 computer with Super VGA, the Environment object includes the values shown in Table 13.10.

CHAPTER 14

Network Considerations

One of the advantages of client/server systems is you can run them on top of a wide variety of networks by using several different communication protocols to communicate between clients and servers. This capability lets you distribute data throughout a network on different machines by using different operating systems, providing a great deal of scalability and flexibility. This capability is even more evident with PowerBuilder 6, where you can distribute PowerBuilder objects themselves across a network.

In the simplest type of PowerBuilder application, PowerBuilder communicates with a single database by using either a direct database interface or ODBC. However, things are not always this simple. In several cases, PowerBuilder must retrieve data from a variety of data sources, including those on mainframes within both relational and non-relational formats.

This chapter is not intended to discuss the basic concepts of LANs and WANs, but rather to discuss some of the network and communication issues encountered when developing PowerBuilder applications. The chapter covers the following topics:

- The OSI model
- Supporting multiple protocols
- Interfacing with a network operating system (NOS)
- Networking with Distributed PowerBuilder
- Middleware

THE OSI MODEL

To accommodate the wide range of network architectures used within client/server systems, the International Standards Organization (ISO) developed the Open Systems Interconnect (OSI) model. The OSI model is a seven-layer structure the ISO designed to break down the communication of data from the hardware to the user interface. Each

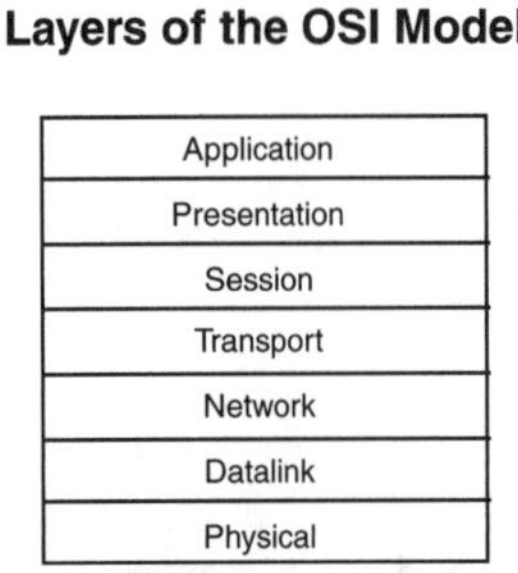

Layers of the OSI Model

Application
Presentation
Session
Transport
Network
Datalink
Physical

Figure 14.1   The OSI model's seven layers.

of the seven OSI layers provides services to the layer immediately above it within the model. All data communication products fall into one or more of the OSI layers, depending on the roles they play. Figure 14.1 shows the OSI model's seven layers.

Application Layer

The application layer is the layer with which an application communicates directly. The network operating system (NOS) and its applications make themselves available to the user at this layer.

Presentation Layer

The presentation layer supplies an application with the information it needs to read and understand the data it receives. This layer resolves the differences between data representation from one computer to another. An example of this is the translation of data from the ASCII character set on the PCs to the EBCDIC character set on the mainframes.

Session Layer

The session layer establishes and maintains communication between the applications. This layer gets its name from the communication session that it establishes and terminates. Coordination is required if one system is slower than the other, or if packet transfer is not orderly. This layer adds the beginning and the ending brackets plus information about the communication protocol in use, and it sends the message to the transport layer.

Transport Layer

The transport layer controls the flow of data between the applications, handling transmission errors and ensuring reliable data delivery. *Reliable* in this instance means that delivery is either confirmed or denied. If the product operating at the transport layer determines that delivery has failed, it notifies the layers above it so that the application can handle the failure.

Network Layer

The network layer breaks the data into packets and directs these packets to their intended destination. The cable access method or the operating system determines each packet's size. In sending the packets, the network layer is also responsible for matching the names and addresses of the destinations on the network. At the receiving end, the network layer is responsible for reassembling the data packets into complete messages. Routing software, for example, operates at the network level.

Datalink Layer

The datalink layer consists of the specific protocols for accessing a network and creating packets. Within a multiprotocol setting, the datalink layer is responsible for directing the packets to the appropriate network adapter or protocol stack.

Physical Layer

The physical layer is the lowest level of connectivity. The physical layer defines the physical and electrical characteristics of the connections that make up the network. The physical layer consists of the actual hardware you use to connect the computers on a network and transfer data. Standards are well-defined at this layer, and include IEEE 802.3 (Ethernet) and 802.5 (Token Ring).

SUPPORTING MULTIPLE PROTOCOLS

Often PC clients must support more than one protocol type. In several cases, the NOS requires one type of protocol, while communications with a database server or remote host requires another type of protocol. For example, an application may need to communicate with a UNIX database server through TCP/IP, the de facto industry standard for communication with UNIX servers. Therefore, to communicate with both the NOS and the database server, a client workstation must support at least two protocol stacks, the NOS stack and TCP/IP.

The key to supporting multiple protocols is device driver standards. The two prominent standards are Novell's Open Datalink Interface (ODI) and Microsoft/3Com's Network Driver Interface Specification (NDIS). Each of these standards establishes a layer of software between the NIC (network interface card) driver and the network protocol. This software is responsible for directing the data packets to the appropriate protocol stack or adapter. Figure 14.2 shows where ODI and NDIS fit into the OSI model within a typical NetWare and TCP/IP environment.

Considering the example in Figure 14.2, assume the user must also communicate with an IBM mainframe by using the LU6.2 protocol. You can do this by using IBM's LAN Support. LAN Support is a set of drivers that, like ODI, lets a single network adapter support multiple protocol stacks. You can use LAN Support in combination with the ODI to let a client communicate with an IBM mainframe, a UNIX server, and a NOS. Figure 14.3 shows where the ODI/NDIS and LAN Support drivers fit into the OSI model.

As Figure 14.3 indicates, the NOS-specific protocols exist at the layers above the ODI or NDIS drivers. Because of this, and the fact that the major NOSs (NetWare,

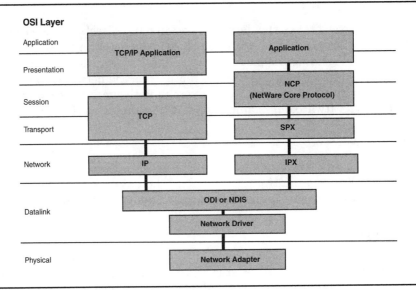

Figure 14.2   **Multiprotocol support with ODI/NDIS.**

Microsoft Network, and VINES) all support either ODI or NDIS, you can use any of the major NOSs without significant impact to the technical architecture. This provides an open solution that allows the use of any of the major NOSs.

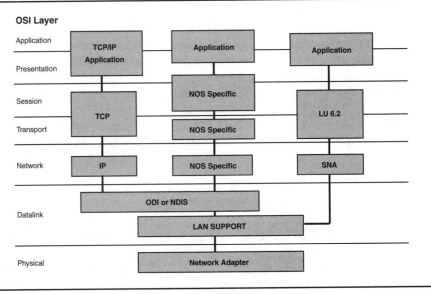

Figure 14.3   **Multiprotocol support with ODI/NDIS and LAN Support.**

INTERFACING WITH A NETWORK OPERATING SYSTEM (NOS)

Applications sometimes need to access such data as network login IDs, node IDs, network printers, and server names. To obtain this data, the application must interface with the NOS at some level.

Within a NetWare environment, you can interface with the NOS by using the NetWare C API. The NetWare API is a set of functions that provides information on such things as network file servers, diagnostics, and connection information. You can use these functions within a PowerBuilder application by declaring them as either global or object-level external functions (see Chapter 6, "User Objects and Functions").

The following example shows how you can use the NetWare API to log a user into a NetWare network and map a drive used for storing user reports.

```
/*************************************************************
** This function logs the user into the network and maps a drive.
** The user name and password are global variables previously set at
** login time. The directory and drive letter of the new drive mapping
** are read from the user's application INI file—MYAPP.INI. If there are no
** values within MYAPP.INI, the report is put within the user's root
** directory and the letter R is assigned as the new drive mapping.
*************************************************************/
string      sRptPath, sRptDrive
int         iRtn


If LoginToFileServer(name, 1, password) <> 0 Then
        DisplayMsg("Network Login Error", "The login to NetWare " &
    + "failed. Please contact the system administrator.")
    Return False
End If


sRptPath = ProfileString ( "MYAPP.INI, "REPORTS", "DIRECTORY", "C:\" )
sRptDrive = ProfileString ( "MYAPP.INI, "REPORTS", "DRIVE", "R" )


// Map a network drive that corresponds to the user's report directory
iRtn = MapDrive(0, 255, sRptPath, 1, 0, sRptDrive)
If iRtn <> 0 Then
    DisplayMsg("Drive Mapping Error", "Drive mapping for the " &
    + "reports directory " + sRptPath + " failed with return code "
    + string(iRtn) &
    + ". Please contact the system administrator.")
        Return False
End If
```

The PowerBuilder external function declarations for the **LoginToFileServer( )** and **MapDrive( )** functions are:

```
/* NetWare interface DLL functions */
function int LoginToFileServer(ref string username, int objtype, ref string
password) library "nwconn.dll"
function int MapDrive(int ConnectionID, int baseDriveNumber, ref string
directoryPath, int flag, int SearchOrder, ref string DriveLetter) library
"nwdir.dll"
```

You can also use the PowerBuilder Library for NetWare to provide NetWare network information to a PowerBuilder application. Powersoft developed this product to provide a simple interface between a PowerBuilder application and the NetWare API. The PowerBuilder Library for NetWare contains a set of functions and structures designed to shield developers from some of the complexities of dealing with low-level NetWare API functions. The library also contains a sample application that developers can use to further reduce the amount of code required to interface with NetWare. For more information on the PowerBuilder Library for NetWare, contact Powersoft.

There are also APIs for other network environments. For example, several of the TCP/IP products provide an API you can use for such tasks as FTP file transfers, remote logins, or obtaining IP addresses.

NETWORKING WITH DISTRIBUTED POWERBUILDER

With the added capability provided within PowerBuilder 6 to distribute PowerBuilder objects, it becomes more important for the designers and developers to understand the networking issues in general, and specifically the networking issues involved in developing a distributed PowerBuilder application.

PowerBuilder 6 uses the following network drivers to support distributed applications:

Named Pipes is a generic IPC mechanism.

Winsock is used to communicate via TCP/IP. Winsock is usually the communication driver of choice when communicating between PowerBuilder clients and UNIX servers, although you can use Winsock for any server platform that supports TCP/IP.

Open Client is used to communicate with a Sybase Open Server application. For more information on Open Server applications, please refer to the Sybase documentation.

To learn about developing distributed applications by using PowerBuilder 6, see Chapter 22, "Distributed Application Development," and Chapter 23, "Advanced Distributed Application Development."

MIDDLEWARE

Middleware is a type of software that provides a seamless method of network communication and data access across multiple platforms by using different protocols. As distributed computing continues to grow, applications are evolving from the traditional two-tiered "client/database server" architecture to an n-tiered services-based architecture. Middleware serves as the glue that lets the variety of platforms and protocols that make up this type of architecture work together as a single system.

Middleware is designed to decrease the development time by eliminating the need for developers to know a network protocol or database interface's specifics. Because middleware supports a large variety of network types and protocols, you eliminate the need to choose a single protocol on which to run an application.

In its most basic form, middleware works by translating the client requests into the appropriate protocol and sending the requests to a server. In case of data access, middleware also translates data requests and data to and from the client and the appropriate database server. This translation adds another layer to the normal client/server communication model. The trade-off of using middleware is the flexibility and reduced development time compared to the performance degradation the required protocol causes, and data translation as well as the management of an additional system component.

There are several middleware products on the market. The most common one is Microsoft's ODBC. ODBC provides a standard data access method to a large number of data sources. For a detailed discussion of ODBC, refer to Chapter 15, "Open Database Connectivity (ODBC)."

In addition, Sybase provides a number of middleware products including Open Server, OmniCONNECT, Open Client, and Replication Server. The Open Server is a server-side API. By using Open Server, you can implement a custom server for a client/server application. By using OmniCONNECT, you can implement connections between a wide range of relational and nonrelational databases. For example, you can perform a cross-platform table join between the three different databases, say, Sybase Adaptive Server, Oracle, and VSAM. By using the Open Client client library, your PowerBuilder applications can access data from Sybase Adaptive Server and other Sybase servers. By using the Sybase Replication Server, a distributed client/server application can support data replication across multiple sites. For more information on these products, visit Sybase's Web site at www.sybase.com.

This section provides an overview of the two types of middleware architectures: remote procedure calls (RPCs) and message passing. This section also discusses the two emerging standards within the area of middleware and distributed computing: DCE and CORBA. Finally, the section discusses database gateways and transaction processing (TP) monitors. Database gateways and TP monitors take advantage of middleware to provide distributed data access and other capabilities to the client/server applications.

RPCs and Message-Passing

Within traditional, nonclient/server applications, a single machine handles all the process-to-process communication. In this environment, all the data and programs that access the data are kept together, as shown in Figure 14.4.

In today's client/server applications, however, you usually separate the data from the machine running the application that accesses the data. RPCs and message-pass-

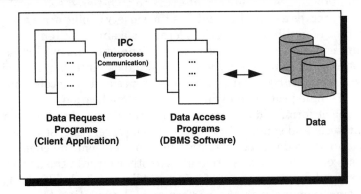

Figure 14.4   Process-to-process communication within traditional applications.

ing systems provide the two methods of communicating within this type of distributed environment.

RPCs function the same way as a normal function call does, but the function executes on a different machine from which it is called. For example, when retrieving the data by using an RPC, the application makes the function call on the machine requesting the data and the function executes on the "remote" machine. The server then sends the retrieved data to the requesting client, as shown in Figure 14.5.

RPCs provide a direct synchronous connection between the two machines. Although some RPCs support asynchronous communication, the majority support synchronous communication only.

Like RPCs, message passing provides a means of communication among the different machines on a network. However, instead of one machine calling a procedure located on another machine, message-passing systems communicate by placing messages into an application's message queue.

Figure 14.6 shows an example of a message-passing system. When retrieving the data on a message-passing system, the application requesting the data places a "data request"

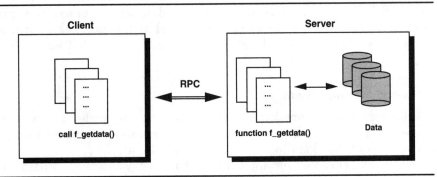

Figure 14.5   Using an RPC to send retrieved data from server to client.

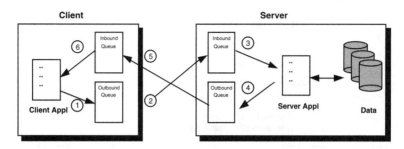

① The requesting application puts "get data" message in its outbound queue.

② The message is sent to the inbound queue of the server application.

③ The server application processes the message.

④ The server application retrieves the data and puts the "data message" into its outbound queue.

⑤ The message is sent to the inbound queue of the client application.

⑥ The client application retrieves the "data message" from its inbound queue.

Figure 14.6   Sample message-passing system.

message into its outbound queue. This message is then sent to the receiving application's inbound queue, which answers the request by placing the requested data within its outbound queue in the form of a message. This message is then sent to the requesting application's inbound queue, where the requesting application retrieves the data.

Message-passing systems are considered to be more flexible than RPCs because instead of relying on the existence of a direct connection between the two machines, a message-passing system asynchronously moves a message through the network until the message reaches its final destination.

One drawback of message-passing systems is the lack of a direct connection makes them less reliable than RPCs. Email systems commonly use message-passing systems.

The preceding examples represent a simplified view of how RPCs and message-passing systems work. The implementation of these systems varies depending on the specific product you use. For more details, refer to the RPC or message-passing product's documentation.

There are several third-party tools available to help developers easily build applications that use an RPC or message-passing architecture. These tools shield you from the underlying network protocols and require the development of only the business functionality. Several of these tools also provide a program generator that provides you with a way to use the underlying communication protocols such as TCP/IP, IPX/SPX, and LU 6.2 without having to know each protocol's details (see Figure 14.7).

Another benefit of this type of architecture is that because the application interfaces with the RPC or message API and not the network, any changes to the underlying network do not impact the application.

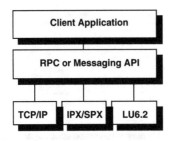

Figure 14.7   Using an RPC or message-passing architecture.

You can retrieve data for a PowerBuilder application by using both RPC and message-passing APIs. Like other third-party DLLs, you link the API functions to a PowerBuilder application by declaring external functions.

DCE and CORBA

In an effort to establish a standard for the development of client/server applications within a distributed heterogeneous environment, the Open Software Foundation (OSF) developed the Distributed Computing Environment (DCE) standard. DCE provides a standard set of services for such things as data representation, directory services, distributed security, and RPCs, among others. Several vendors, including IBM, Hewlett-Packard, Open Environment Corporation, and Digital Equipment Corporation, have developed (or are developing) DCE products.

Another effort is under way to address the growing acceptance of object technology into mainstream computing. This effort involves a large group of vendors who are attempting to develop a standard specification for supporting multivendor distributed object-oriented systems. The result of this effort is the formation of the Object Management Group (OMG), a nonprofit international corporation comprising more than 300 vendors, developers, and users.

OMG has developed the Object Management Architecture (OMA) to provide a foundation for the development of distributed object-oriented systems. The Object Request Broker (ORB) is at the heart of the OMA.

An ORB is the mechanism by which application objects interface with service objects to transparently send and receive messages within a distributed environment. Application objects in this case refer to the application-specific objects and to the objects common to multiple applications; service objects refer to the set of objects designed to provide various services to the application objects such as communication, data access, printing, and the like.

To provide a standard interface between the objects, OMG has developed the Common Object Request Broker Architecture (CORBA) as its ORB standard. CORBA specifies for how objects make requests and receive responses by using ORBs within a distributed environment across multiple platforms. Several vendors, including IBM, Hewlett-Packard, Digital Equipment Corporation, and AT&T Corp., have already developed CORBA-compliant products, and a number of corporations have implemented the CORBA standard. The CORBA 2 standard has led to greater acceptance and wider use of the CORBA standard.

The main challenger to CORBA 2 is Microsoft's Distributed Common Object Model (DCOM). DCOM expands upon Microsoft's ActiveX technology by letting the objects distributed across a network communicate via ActiveX.

The development of standards such as DCE, CORBA, and DCOM will help developers quickly produce object-oriented systems that are capable of running within a distributed heterogeneous environment by using a variety of protocols.

For more information on OMG and CORBA, visit the following Web sites:

www.corba.org/

www.omg.org/index.html

www.omg.org/about/wicorba.htm

For more information on ActiveX and DCOM, visit Microsoft's Web site at www .microsoft.com.

DRDA

The Distributed Relational Database Architecture (DRDA) is IBM's solution for communication among distributed databases. Access to the DRDA databases is accomplished by using IBM's Distributed Database Connection Services/2 (DDCS/2). DDCS/2 provides an API that lets applications access any DRDA-compliant database, including DB2/MVS, SQL/DS, DB2/2, and OS/2 Database Manager (DBM), among others.

Although PowerBuilder supports such DRDA-compliant databases as DB2/2 and OS/2 DBM, it currently does not provide an interface to all DRDA-compliant databases. For example, there is not currently a direct PowerBuilder interface to DB2/MVS. The reason for this is that although the DDCS/2 API provides the necessary interface to any DRDA database, the SQL dialect and system tables of each database are different.

DRDA provides a good solution within an all-IBM environment, for example, a distributed environment with DB2/MVS running on a mainframe, DB2/6000 on an RS/6000 running AIX, and DB2/2 running under OS/2. However, even with such vendors as Oracle, Sybase, and Informix providing DRDA support within their products, it is yet to be widely accepted as a complete solution within a multivendor environment.

Database Gateways

You often use database gateways in situations where a direct database interface is not possible or efficient. Several gateways on the market today are designed to provide access to the mainframe-based data sources within a client/server environment. PowerBuilder currently provides a direct interface to several database gateway products, including Sybase (MDI) Database Gateway for DB2, Sybase's Net-Gateway for DB2, and Oracle's Transparent and Procedural gateway products.

Database gateways let a client application transparently retrieve data from a variety of data sources through a single interface. For example, the MDI DB2 gateway provides access not only to DB2 but to other mainframe data sources (relational and nonrelational) such as SQL/DS, VSAM, IMS, and IDMS, among others. Figure 14.8 shows the generic network topology when using a gateway to access the mainframe data sources.

As Figure 14.8 shows, you can access any mainframe data source by using a single interface from the client application to the database gateway. You can then access all the required data sources transparently from the gateway.

While a gateway provides transparent access to the distributed data sources, it does so at a performance cost. Part of the performance impact of using a gateway arises from the fact that the gateway must translate the data from its native format to the format the gateway uses and finally to the format the client uses. The gateway must also perform any protocol translation required between the gateway environment and the data source's environment. Dealing with mainframe data sources usually involves translation to or from the protocol used between the gateway protocol and a systems network architecture (SNA) protocol such as LU 6.2. In addition, because the gateway adds another layer between the client and the data source, network delay and latency can also slow performance.

Most of the major RDBMS vendors (including Oracle, Sybase, and Informix) offer gateway products that are available as extensions to their RDBMs. These gateways provide access to both mainframe data sources and data from other server databases.

Transaction Processing Monitors

Like database gateways, you can use transaction processing (TP) monitors to provide transparent access to a variety of data sources. However, you generally use TP monitors to increase performance within high-volume OLTP applications. TP monitors provide a way of increasing the system performance by managing the processes in a way that makes efficient use of system resources. For client/server database applications, you can use a TP monitor to manage the number of connections to a database and control access to the distributed data sources. For example, database applications without a TP monitor require at least one database connection per user process. These connections remain active throughout the entire user session, as shown in Figure 14.9.

This type of architecture is adequate within most small- to medium-scale applica-

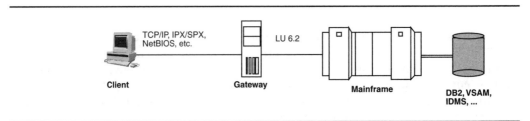

Figure 14.8   Generic network topology when using a gateway to access mainframe data source.

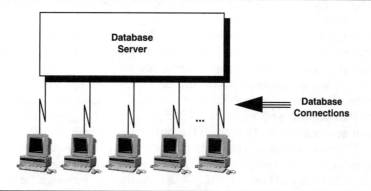

Figure 14.9   Database connections without a TP monitor.

tions. However, within a large-scale OLTP application, the system resources required to manage each user connection can drastically impact the system performance.

A TP monitor can manage the database connections such that a database connection is established only when necessary, as shown in Figure 14.10. Because the number of connections is reduced, the database can support several more users.

A TP monitor can act as a transaction manager, scheduling and controlling trans-

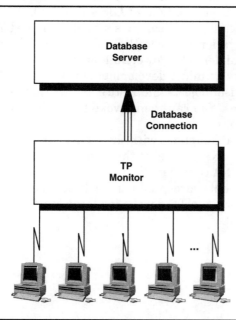

Figure 14.10   Using a TP monitor to manage the database connections.

actions so that it does not overload the system. TP monitors can also provide load balancing across multiple processors.

In addition to the performance benefits, a TP monitor also provides the capability to access the multiple data sources by using a single API. Much like a database gateway, a TP monitor can serve as a single interface from an application to the data distributed across multiple heterogeneous databases and servers. This capability provides a level of data abstraction such that you can distribute data across multiple RDBMSs and servers. The machine on which the TP monitor resides generally executes the distributed data access services that the TP monitor provides.

While a TP monitor can increase the performance of large-scale applications, there are some disadvantages to using one. First, the services a TP monitor provides are developed in a 3GL such as C or COBOL. This usually requires significant development effort and increases application maintenance responsibilities.

Second, a TP monitor adds some performance overhead. It is, therefore, important to make sure the performance gains outweigh the overhead of using the TP monitor. In applications with few users and low transaction volumes, performance may actually degrade because the application uses a TP monitor. For these reasons, you should use a TP monitor only for large-scale applications with several users and a high volume of transactions.

Within the IBM world, CICS is the most prominent TP monitor. In the past, CICS only existed within mainframe environments. However, IBM has ported CICS to different platforms, including AIX. For more information on IBM's CICS, visit the Web site at www.software.ibm.com/ts/cics.

The three leading UNIX TP monitors are Novell's Tuxedo (www.novell.com), Transarc's Encina (www.transarc.com), and AT&T GIS's TOP END (www.att.com). Of these, only Encina is DCE-based. Also, Transarc has a product named EncinaBuilder, which provides a seamless integration between PowerBuilder and Transarc's Encina for Windows product. EncinaBuilder lets PowerBuilder developers develop Encina client applications within the PowerBuilder development environment. EncinaBuilder does this by generating a set of user objects and DataWindows that represent the different Encina application services. You can then invoke the Encina services from the PowerBuilder application via RPCs.

Many DBMS products are also compliant with the X/Open's standard interface between TP monitors and databases (XA), meaning that the DBMS can interface directly with any TP monitor that is also XA compliant.

With direct interfaces to middleware products such as EncinaBuilder, PowerBuilder becomes a much more viable tool for developing large-scale applications within multitier distributed environments.

PART IV

Database Connectivity

CHAPTER 15

Open Database Connectivity (ODBC)

On November 14, 1991, Microsoft Corporation introduced open database connectivity (ODBC), a database connectivity API that lets applications communicate with various RDBMSs (see Figure 15.1).

ODBC is based on the SQL Access Group's call level interface (CLI) specification, which uses SQL to access database environments. ODBC supports access to both SQL and non-SQL data. The ODBC layer provides a transparent mechanism for the applications to communicate with various RDBMSs. Traditionally, applications could connect to different RDBMSs only by interfacing with each RDBMS's proprietary CLI. Although the method of communicating with a RDBMS's CLI has some advantages (performance is better, for example), it typically binds the applications to a specific RDBMS's CLI. Binding the applications to a specific RDBMS CLI makes switching from one RDBMS

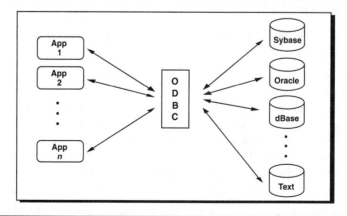

Figure 15.1   ODBC lets applications communicate with various RDBMSs.

to another difficult. With ODBC, switching from one RDBMS to another requires little or no program modification.

This chapter discusses some of the following topics:

- Advantages of ODBC
- Disadvantages of ODBC
- ODBC SQL processing
- ODBC conformance levels
- PowerBuilder's support for ODBC
- .INI file settings
- Registry settings
- Connecting to ODBC from PowerBuilder
- Setting up ODBC on the client

ADVANTAGES OF ODBC

ODBC's several advantages include:

- Developers and independent software vendors (ISVs) use a single set of function calls within all the applications to access the multiple RDBMSs. The burden of writing code for a particular database is gone, as is the need to update the code for the new releases of RDBMSs.
- RDBMS vendors have a more streamlined way to provide end-user connections to their data. By writing a single driver that supports ODBC, the database vendor can, in a sense, "plug into" an ODBC "socket" that the front-end ISV creates.
- Customers gain transparent access to several data sources, accessing multiple databases with equal ease from their front-end applications.
- Because you can use several front-ends, ODBC offers the potential for a wider selection of applications to give users access to the database they need.

DISADVANTAGES OF ODBC

ODBC's two major drawbacks are:

- Performance can be slow because an additional layer is added between the RDBMS and the client.

> **TIP** There are different schools of thought when it comes to ODBC performance. Some developers do not consider performance to be a problem. There are comparisons of ODBC and DB-Lib; test results show that ODBC yielded faster performance than DB-Lib. On the other hand, there are developers who claim that ODBC is having a hard time living up to its reputation when it comes to functionality, performance, or stability.

- You may not always be able to use the specific features of a RDBMS because ODBC does not support all the features of all RDBMSs. This may limit a developer's use of an RDBMS's functionality.

ODBC SQL PROCESSING

To truly understand how ODBC works, it is best to learn how ODBC executes a SQL query and returns the result set. When a SQL query is executed, ODBC allocates the memory for the ODBC environment and an environment handle points to the memory. Only one environment handle per application is possible. After creating an environment handle, ODBC obtains a connection handle. This handle points to a memory location containing the information about a particular connection. There can be multiple connection handles for each environment handle. ODBC then creates a lower-level handle. This third type of handle, a statement handle, processes a query within a connection. There can be multiple statement handles for each connection. Figure 15.2 shows this process, as well as the relationship between the different ODBC handles. Figure 15.3 de-

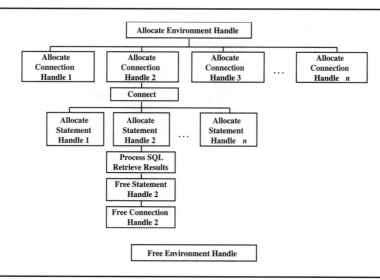

Figure 15.2   The process involved when ODBC executes a SQL query.

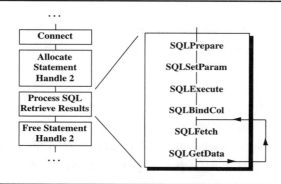

Figure 15.3   The flow within the Process SQL/Retrieve Results box.

tails the flow within the Process SQL/Retrieve Results box, along with the ODBC functions that are called to process a SQL query and retrieve the results.

ODBC CONFORMANCE LEVELS

SQL Access Group (SAG) is a consortium of vendors with a mission to provide a standard for the language of relational databases, SQL. Despite SAG's efforts, vendors have produced variants within their implementations of SQL. ODBC is structured around the work of SAG. A conformance level establishes the amount of interoperability a driver has with its corresponding data source. ODBC defines the conformance levels for the drivers within two areas: the ODBC API and the ODBC SQL grammar (which includes the ODBC SQL datatypes). The conformance levels help both the application and driver developers to establish the standard sets of functionality.

API Conformance Levels

The ODBC API defines a set of core functions that correspond to the functions within the X/Open and SQL Access Group Call Level Interface specification. ODBC also defines two extended sets of functionality, Level 1 and Level 2. The API calls at each level are closely tied to the class of ODBC functions the RDBMS's ODBC driver supports, which is closely tied to the data source's functional capability. The following sections summarize the functionality included within each conformance level.

Core API

- Allocate and free environment, connection, and statement handles.
- Connect to the data sources. Use multiple statement handles on a connection.
- Prepare and execute the SQL statements. Execute the SQL statements immediately.
- Assign storage for the parameters within a SQL statement and the result columns.
- Retrieve the data from a result set. Retrieve information about a result set.
- Commit or roll back the transactions.
- Retrieve the error information.

You can implement this functionality by using the functions in the following section.

Core Functions

SQLAllocConnect( ) obtains a connection handle.

SQLAllocEnv( ) obtains an environment handle. One environment handle is used for one or more connections.

SQLAllocStmt( ) allocates a statement handle.

SQLBindCol( ) assigns storage for a result column and specifies the datatype.

SQLCancel( ) cancels a SQL statement.

SQLColAttributes( ) describes a column's attributes within the result set.

SQLConnect( ) connects to a specific driver by the data source name, user ID, and password.

SQLDescribeCol( ) describes a column within the result set.

SQLDisconnect( ) closes the connection.

SQLError( ) returns additional error or status information.

SQLExecDirect( ) executes a statement.

SQLExecute( ) executes a prepared statement.

SQLFetch( ) returns a result row.

SQLFreeConnect( ) releases the connection handle.

SQLFreeEnv( ) releases the environment handle.

SQLFreeStmt( ) ends statement processing and closes the associated cursor, discards pending results, and, optionally, frees all resources associated with the statement handle.

SQLGetCursorName( ) returns the cursor name associated with a statement handle.

SQLNumResultCols( ) returns the number of columns within the result set.

SQLPrepare( ) prepares a SQL statement for later execution.

SQLRowCount( ) returns the number of rows affected by an insert, update, or delete request.

SQLSetCursorName( ) specifies a cursor name.

SQLSetParam( ) assigns storage for a parameter within a SQL statement.

SQLTransact( ) commits or rolls back a transaction.

Level 1 API

- Meet the core API functionality conformance level.
- Connect to the data sources with the driver-specific dialog boxes.
- Set and inquire about the values of statement and connection options.
- Send part or all of a parameter value (useful for long data).
- Retrieve all or part of a result column value (useful for long data).
- Retrieve the catalog information (columns, special columns, statistics, and tables).
- Retrieve the information about driver and data source capabilities, such as supported datatypes.
- Supports both scalar and ODBC functions.

You can implement this functionality by using the functions in the following section.

Level 1 Functions

SQLColumns( ) returns the list of column names within the specified tables.

SQLDriverConnect( ) connects to a specific driver by connection string or requests that the Driver Manager and driver display the connection dialog boxes for the user.

SQLGetConnectOption( ) returns the connection option's value.

SQLGetData( ) returns part or all of one column of one row of a result set (useful for long data values).

SQLGetFunctions( ) returns the supported driver functions.

SQLGetInfo( ) returns the information about a specific driver and data source.

SQLGetStmtOption( ) returns a statement option's value.

SQLGetTypeInfo( ) returns the information about the supported datatypes.

SQLParamData( ) returns the storage value assigned to a parameter for which data is sent at execution time (useful for long data values).

SQLPutData( ) sends part or all of a data value for a parameter (useful for long data values).

SQLSetConnectOption( ) sets a particular connection's transaction isolation level (a more detailed discussion of this function follows).

SQLSetStmtOption( ) sets a statement option.

SQLSpecialColumns( ) retrieves information about the optimal set of columns that uniquely identifies a row within a specified table and the columns that are automatically updated when a transaction updates any value within the row.

SQLStatistics( ) retrieves the statistics about a single table and the list of indexes associated with the table.

SQLTables( ) returns the list of table names stored within a specific data source.

Level 2 API

- Meet the core and Level 1 API functionality conformance level.
- Browse the available connections and list the available data sources.
- Send the arrays of parameter values. Retrieve the arrays of result column values.
- Retrieve the number of parameters and describe individual parameters.
- Use a scrollable cursor.
- Retrieve the SQL statement's native form.
- Retrieve the catalog information (privileges, keys, and procedures).
- Call the translation DLL.

You can implement this functionality by using the functions in the following section.

Level 2 Functions

SQLBrowseConnect( ) returns the successive levels of connection attributes and valid attribute values. When a value is specified for each connection attribute, it connects to the data source.

SQLColumnPrivileges( ) returns a list of columns and associated privileges for one or more tables.

SQLDataSources( ) returns a list of available data sources.

SQLDescribeParam( ) returns the description for a specific parameter within a statement.

SQLExtendedFetch( ) returns the multiple result rows.

SQLForeignKeys( ) returns a list of column names that comprise foreign keys, if they exist for a specified table.

SQLMoreResults( ) determines whether there are more result sets available and, if so, initializes processing for the next result set.

SQLNativeSql( ) returns a SQL statement's text as translated by the driver.

SQLNumParams( ) returns the number of parameters within a statement.

SQLParamOptions( ) specifies the use of multiple values for the parameters.

SQLPrimaryKeys( ) returns the list of column name(s) that comprise a table's primary key.

SQLProcedureColumns( ) returns the list of input and output parameters as well as the columns that make up the result set for the specified procedures.

SQLProcedures( ) returns the list of procedure names stored within a specific data source.

SQLSetPos( ) positions a cursor within a fetched block of data.

SQLSetScrollOptions( ) sets the options that control the cursor behavior.

SQLTablePrivileges( ) returns a list of tables and the privileges associated with each table.

SQL Conformance Levels

ODBC defines a core grammar that corresponds to the X/Open and SQL Access Group CAE draft specification (1991). ODBC also defines a minimum grammar to meet a basic ODBC conformance level and an extended grammar to provide for the common RDBMS extensions to SQL. The following sections summarize the grammar included within each conformance level.

Minimum SQL Grammar

- Data definition language (DDL): CREATE TABLE and DROP TABLE
- Data manipulation language (DML): SELECT, INSERT, UPDATE, DELETE
- Expressions: simple (such as A > B + C)
- Datatypes: CHAR

Core SQL Grammar

- Minimum SQL grammar
- DDL: ALTER TABLE, CREATE INDEX, DROP INDEX, CREATE VIEW, DROP VIEW, GRANT, and REVOKE
- DML: full SELECT, positioned UPDATE, and positioned DELETE
- Expressions: subquery and set functions such as SUM and MIN
- Datatypes: VARCHAR, DECIMAL, NUMERIC, SMALLINT, INTEGER, REAL, FLOAT, DOUBLE PRECISION

Extended SQL Grammar

- Minimum and core SQL grammar
- DML: outer joins
- Expressions: scalar functions such as SUBSTRING and ABS; date, time, and time-stamp literals

- Datatypes: LONG VARCHAR, BIT, TINYINT, BIGINT, BINARY, VARBINARY, LONG VARBINARY, DATE, TIME, and TIMESTAMP
- Batch SQL statements
- Procedure calls

Although a RDBMS does not support all the three levels, it is ideal if your RDBMS conforms to all the three levels. Both API and SQL conformance should be a consideration when you select a RDBMS.

POWERBUILDER'S SUPPORT FOR ODBC

With the release of PowerBuilder 6, PowerBuilder now supports ODBC 3. The ODBC 3 supports access through any Level 1 or higher 32-bit ODBC 1.x, 2.x, or 3 driver that you can obtain from Powersoft or another vendor.

.INI FILE SETTINGS

This section discusses the three .INI files that you use to provide ODBC connectivity from a PowerBuilder application: odbc.ini, odbcinst.ini, and pbodb60.ini.

ODBC Driver Manager Initialization File (odbc.ini)

The odbc.ini file is the main ODBC initialization file (see Figure 15.4). The ODBC Driver Manager uses this file to get a unique data source name's detail information to connect to the RDBMS. This file includes all the ODBC RDBMSs and their corresponding drivers, the RDBMS ODBC driver and data source name mappings, and a data source's detail information.

ODBC Installation Initialization File (odbcinst.ini)

To install the ODBC drivers, the ODBC installation programs mainly use this file (see Figure 15.5). When troubleshooting, you can look at this .INI file to verify the installed data sources' driver information.

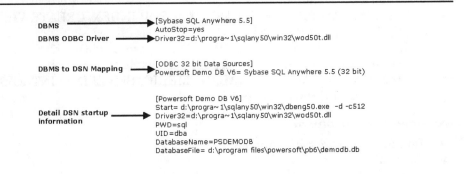

Figure 15.4   The odbc.ini file.

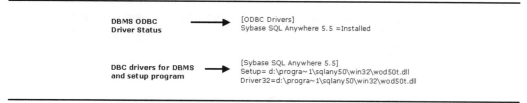

Figure 15.5   The odbcinst.ini file.

PowerBuilder ODBC Configuration File (pbodb60.ini)

PowerBuilder takes advantage of the extended capabilities of ODBC drivers and navigates around the shortcomings by using the pbodb60.ini file entries within the data source, RDBMS driver, or RDBMS section. If no sections exist for a particular connection, PowerBuilder runs as an ODBC-compliant client, and you cannot use the extensions that might be available.

The search algorithm for the entries is:

```
IF section and entry are present for the current datasource THEN
    use entry value
ELSE IF section corresponding to the RDBMS_Name Driver_Name exists THEN
    use entry value if it exists
ELSE IF section corresponding to the RDBMS_Name exists THEN
    use entry value if it exists
END IF
```

If PowerBuilder searches for the SQL syntax and finds no entry with this search criteria, PowerBuilder searches the syntax section that corresponds to the current data source's SQL grammar conformance level.

If you want to override the more general settings of RDBMS_Driver or RDBMS_Name, create a data source–specific section.

REGISTRY SETTINGS

With Windows 95 and the registration database, the role of configuration or initialization files has changed. Developers should take advantage of the registration database in place of the initialization files. Figures 15.6 and 15.7 show how the registry stores the odbc.ini and the odbcinst.ini file information.

In fact, the power of the registry is such that the environment path that Windows searches for application-related files were traditionally stored within the DOS environment variable called PATH. When you or the application made changes to this file, you had to reboot the PC for the changes to take effect. With the registry, you can set the path for PowerBuilder without rebooting the machine by simply adding the path to the path statement within the registry as Figure 15.8 shows.

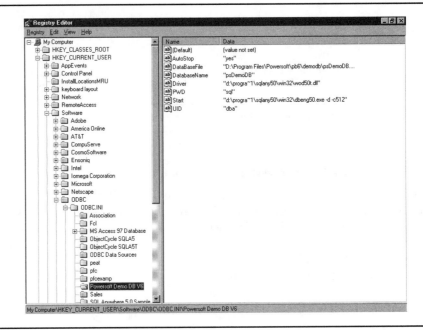

Figure 15.6   The odbc.ini information within the Windows Registry.

Figure 15.7   The odbcinst.ini information within the Windows Registry.

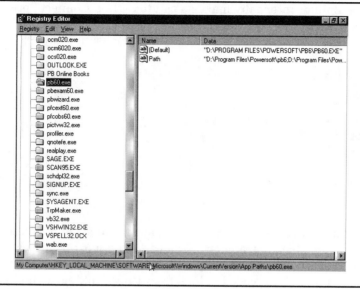

Figure 15.8   Setting the PowerBuilder path by using the Windows Registry.

CONNECTING TO ODBC FROM POWERBUILDER

With ODBC, an application connects to the data source by specifying the data source name and any additional information needed to complete the connection.

The following list shows the database variables within the PowerBuilder initialization file (pb.ini). You can set these parameters by either editing the pb.ini file or using the preferences icon on the power panel:

Vendor. ODBC.

DBMS. ODBC.

LogID. Developer's log ID (used only if the ODBC SQL driver CONNECT call is not supported).

UserID. Developer's user ID (optional; use with caution because it overrides the connection's UserName attribute that the ODBC SQLGetInfo call returns).

AutoCommit. If set to True; you cannot roll back the data updates. If set to False (default); you can roll back the data updates if the back-end data source supports transaction processing.

Lock. Lock value.

DBParm. PowerBuilder uses the DBParm variable for a connect string.

The lock variable is used for the ODBC transaction isolation levels. When the developer sets the Lock parameter to either RV (Uncommitted read), RC (Committed read), RR (Repeatable read), TS (Serializable transactions), or TV (Transaction versioning), PowerBuilder internally makes a call to SQLSetConnectOption and sets the isolation level. Following is an example of connecting to a SQL Anywhere local database through ODBC, by using the default SQLCA transaction object:

```
SQLCA.DBMS = sDBMS
SQLCA.dbparm =      &
     "ConnectString='DSN=" + sDataSourceName + ";UID=" &
          + sUserId + ";PWD=" + sPassword + "'"
Connect;
If SQLCA.SQLCODE = -1 Then
     MessageBox ("Error Connecting to Database", SQLCA.SQLERRTEXT)
     // error proccessing code ...
End If
```

Note there is no hard-coding in this case. You should avoid hard-coding, especially with the transaction object parameters. You can store most of the parameters in initialization files, encrypted files, security tables, or enter them at runtime. If you fill the transaction object with hard-coded values from the script, each time you add a new user, the database name is changed, or passwords are changed, you would have to modify the code. It is better to have the configurable parameters and user-specific parameters separate from the code.

Database Profile Painter and DBParm Settings

With PowerBuilder 6, the Database Profile Painter is revamped (see Figure 15.9). With the Database Profile Painter, you can define a database profile to access a data source within PowerBuilder.

The Database Profile Setup dialog box lets you create or edit a database profile (see Figure 15.10). Further, you can also set the data source's DBParm parameters.

TIP When you define the data source by using the Configure ODBC painter, PowerBuilder creates the database profile for you.

If you change the data source's name through the Database Profile Painter, the existing profile cannot connect to the data source. To access the data source, you must edit the database profile and choose the correct data source name from the Data Source drop-down listbox.

The DBParm parameter has several attributes you can set, either within the preferences or within the application script, by using the transaction object that the previous sample code shows.

You can set asynchronous operations, delimited SQL syntax, scrolling and locking options for cursors, the list of displayed tables, and the PowerBuilder catalog owner by using the DBParm parameter.

Table 15.1 lists the connection options on the Database Profile Painter's each tab.

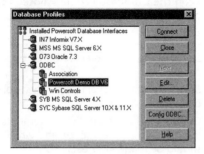

Figure 15.9   **The Database Profile dialog box.**

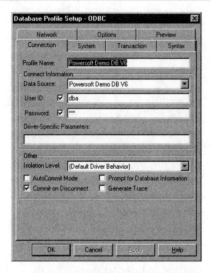

Figure 15.10   **Click on the New or Edit command button to display the Database Profile Setup dialog box.**

TIP The Database Profile Painter also has a **Preview** tab. This tab generates the correct PowerScript connection syntax that you can use within your Power-Builder application script.

As you complete the Database Profile Setup dialog box within PowerBuilder, PowerBuilder builds the correct PowerScript connection syntax for each selected option on the **Preview** tab. You can then copy the syntax you want from the **Preview** tab into your PowerBuilder application script by using the **Copy** button provided on the tab.

Table 15.1   List of the Connection Options on the Database Profile Painter's Each Tab

Tab	Option	Description
Connection	Driver-Specific Parameters	Specifies the parameters required to connect to a data source.
	Isolation Level	Sets the isolation level to use when connecting to the database.
	AutoCommit Mode	Controls the issuing of SQL statements outside or inside a transaction's scope and whether a commit should be made after each SQL.
	Commit on Disconnect	Specifies whether the transactions should be committed to the database or rolled back before disconnecting from a data source.
System	Display Terse Error Messages	Specifies whether terse error messages for the ODBC data source drivers should be displayed. A terse ODBC error message is one without the SQLSTATE = x prefix, where x is the error message's number.
	PowerBuilder Catalog Table Owner	Specifies a nondefault owner for the tables within the repository.
	Table Criteria	Enables you to specify the criteria (search conditions) to limit the list of tables and views that displays within the Select Tables list.
Transaction	Asynchronous	Lets you perform asynchronous operations on your database.
	Number of Seconds to Wait	When you enable asynchronous operations on your database, you can further specify the number of seconds to wait for a response from the database with the DBGetTime parameter.
	Retrieve Blocking Factor	Specifies the cursor blocking factor when connecting to a data source.
	Insert Blocking Factor	Specifies the number of rows you want the Data Pipeline to insert at one time into a table within the destination database.
	Number of SQL Statements Cached	Specifies the number of SQL statements PowerBuilder should cache. By default, SQLCache is set to 0, indicating an empty SQL cache.
	Cursor Library	Specifies the cursor library to use when connecting to a data source.
	Locking	When used with the CursorScroll parameter, specifies the locking options for the cursors within a data source.
	Scrolling Options	When used with the CursorLock parameter, specifies the scrolling options for the cursors within a data source.
	Qualify Stored Procedures with Owner Name	Specifies if there is a need to qualify the stored procedure with the owner name within the SQL EXECUTE statement that the DataWindow builds and passes to the database driver.

Table 15.1 *Continued*

Tab	Option	Description
Transaction	DisableBind	The DisableBind parameter lets you specify whether you want to disable the binds on the input parameters to a compiled SQL statement.
	Static Bind	Specifies whether to get a result set description to validate the SELECT statement against the database server before retrieving the data.
Syntax	Enclose Table and Column Names in Quotes	Specifies whether to enclose the names of tables, columns, indexes, and constraints within double quotes when generating the SQL statements.
	Identifier Quote Character	Specifies the single quote character you want to use to delimit the names of identifiers (tables, columns, indexes, and constraints) when generating the SQL statements.
	Date Format	Specifies a date datatype when PowerBuilder builds the SQL UPDATE statement.
	DateTime Format	Specifies a datetime datatype when PowerBuilder builds the SQL UPDATE statement.
	Time Format	Specifies a time datatype when PowerBuilder builds the SQL UPDATE statement.
	Decimal Separator	Specifies the decimal separator setting the database uses.
	Numeric Format	Specifies the NumericFormat when formatting the numeric portion of the SQL syntax string.
	Format Arguments in Scientific Notation	Controls whether to convert a DataWindow retrieval argument of decimal datatype to a scientific (exponential) notation if the argument exceeds 12 digits.
Network	Packet Size	Specifies the network packet size in bytes when accessing a data source.
	Login Timeout	Specifies the number of seconds the database driver should wait for a login request to the database.
Options	Connect Type	Specifies how the database driver prompts for the additional connection information.
	Trace ODBC API Calls	Specifies whether the Driver Manager Trace is on or off.
	Trace File	Specifies the trace file to use.
	Integrated Security	Specifies the security options.
	Preserve Cursors	Specifies whether cursors are closed or left open on a SQLTransact call.
	Use Procedures for Prepare	Specifies how the temporary stored procedures are treated for a SQLPrepare call.

SETTING UP ODBC ON THE CLIENT

To execute the ODBC applications, you must install the ODBC administrator and drivers and configure the data sources. The ODBC installation kit adds an ODBC Administrator icon to the Windows Control Panel. Before an application can access the data, you must create a data source.

The ODBC Administrator's main purpose is to create and manage the data sources. A unique name identifies each data source. To add a new data source for a SQL Anywhere database, for example, select the SQL Anywhere ODBC driver from the ODBC Administrator and click **Add**, as Figure 15.11 shows. The screen in Figure 15.12 will then be displayed.

Figure 15.11   Creating a new data source by using the ODBC Administrator.

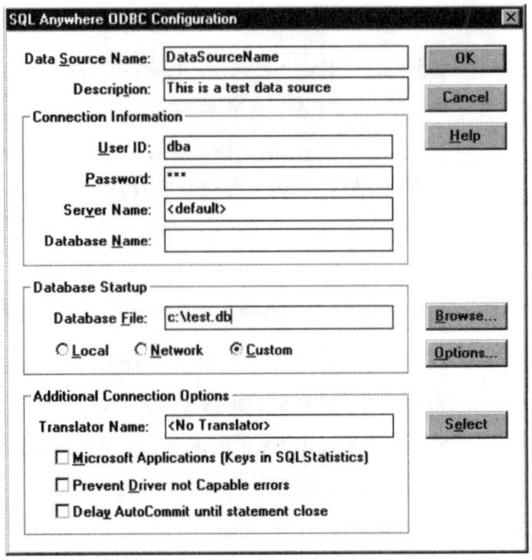

Figure 15.12   Adding a new SQL Anywhere ODBC data source.

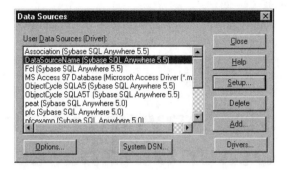

Figure 15.13   The newly installed ODBC data source.

You must assign a unique data source name and a database file. When you have entered the two fields, clicking OK installs the data source (see Figure 15.13).

After you define the data source, the program makes the following changes to the odbc.ini file:

```
[ODBC 32 bit Data Sources]
DataSourceName=Sybase SQL Anywhere 5.0 (32 bit)


[DataSourceName]
Driver32=c:\SQLANY50\win32\WOD50T.DLL
```

You could have also done this process from the Database painter's Configure ODBC menu option, from the ODBC Administrator painter, or programmatically during installation or at runtime.

The following functions are ODBC Installer (odbcinst.dll) API calls you can use within an application to set up an ODBC application:

SQLConfigDataSource( ) adds, modifies, or deletes data sources.

SQLGetAvailableDrivers( ) reads the odbc.ini file's "[ODBC Drivers]" section and returns the descriptions of the drivers that the user may install.

SQLGetInstalledDrivers( ) reads the odbc.ini file's "[ODBC Drivers]" section and returns the installed drivers descriptions.

SQLInstallDriver( ) adds information about the driver to the odbcinst.ini file and returns the target directory's path for the installation.

SQLInstallDriverManager( ) returns the target directory's path for the installation. The caller must actually copy the driver manager's files to the target directory.

SQLRemoveDefaultDataSource( ) removes the default data source specification section from the odbc.ini file. It also removes the default driver specification section from the odbcinst.ini file.

SQLRemoveDSNFromIni( ) removes a data source from the odbc.ini file.

SQLWriteDSNToIni( ) adds a data source to the odbc.ini file.

CHAPTER 16

SQL Anywhere and Other Databases

PowerBuilder provides connectivity to a variety of databases. Combining the native database interfaces with ODBC lets PowerBuilder communicate with just about any database on the market today (see Chapter 15, "Open Database Connectivity"). These databases range from small xBase systems to large server database systems.

This chapter focuses on four of the more popular server databases:

- SQL Anywhere
- Oracle
- SQL Server (Microsoft and Sybase)
- Informix

These databases were chosen simply because of their large market share. While it is beyond the scope of this book to discuss all the features of each of these databases, this chapter focuses specifically on the areas relevant to a PowerBuilder developer. These areas include:

- Database architecture and features
- Connecting from PowerBuilder
- The PowerBuilder System tables
- Datatypes

SQL ANYWHERE

SQL Anywhere is a full-featured relational database that comes packaged with the PowerBuilder development environment. SQL Anywhere can run as either a local PC database or on a network file server accessible to several users. It can run on a variety of 16- and 32-bit operating systems.

Database Architecture and Features

The following section discusses the database architecture and some of the SQL Anywhere's features.

Database Architecture

The SQL Anywhere database engine conforms to the SQL 89 standard and has several features defined in IBM's DB2 and SAA specifications, as well as in the ISO/ANSI SQL/92. The SQL Anywhere database engine runs as a single process by using a relatively small amount of system memory. Each version of the SQL Anywhere database engine is a different executable depending on the platform. Accordingly, PowerBuilder uniquely named them among the platforms with all non-Windows 3.x platforms garnering the name dbeng50.exe. The 16-bit Windows 3.x engine is dbeng50w.exe, while the 32-bit is dbeng50s.exe.

A SQL Anywhere database comprises of one or more database files and, except within the runtime version, a single transaction log file. SQL Anywhere also uses checkpoint logs and rollback logs to provide recovery from the system errors. Figure 16.1 shows the SQL Anywhere architecture.

SQL Anywhere reads or caches the data in the form of pages from a database file on the disk drive into the cache within the computer's memory. This lets the application access the data much faster (60 to 70 nanoseconds for memory versus 9 to 11 milliseconds for the hard drive). When a particular data page is changed, SQL Anywhere

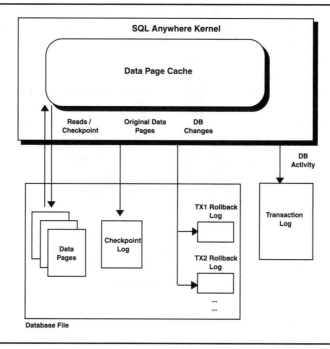

Figure 16.1   The SQL Anywhere architecture.

copies the original page to the checkpoint log. For performance reasons, SQL Anywhere does not copy the updated pages immediately back to the database file but keeps them in memory within the data page cache.

SQL Anywhere copies the data pages to the disk when either the data page cache becomes full or a checkpoint occurs. A checkpoint occurs in the following instances:

- A **Checkpoint** command is issued explicitly.
- The server is idle for a long enough period of time to write all the updated data pages to the disk.
- A transaction is committed and no transaction log is being used.
- The database engine is shut down.
- The amount of time since the last checkpoint is greater than the value contained within the CHECKPOINT_TIME configuration parameter.
- The estimated time to perform a recovery is greater than the value within the RECOVERY_TIME configuration parameter.

When a checkpoint occurs, SQL Anywhere copies all the updated pages within the page cache to the disk and clears the checkpoint log. Remembering the cache concepts just mentioned will help you create a system that offers maximum performance while ensuring data integrity.

SQL Anywhere maintains a rollback log for each transaction. This log contains any changes to the database that the application made within the given transaction. SQL Anywhere uses rollback logs only for recovery purposes.

As mentioned earlier, with the exception of the runtime version, each SQL Anywhere database can also have a transaction log, which maintains information for all the activity performed against a database. Without a transaction log, SQL Anywhere issues a checkpoint every time it executes a **Commit** command. This slows performance because SQL Anywhere copies the updated data pages to the disk after each transaction. It is recommended that you use a transaction log for both performance and recovery purposes.

The SQL Anywhere Optimizer

SQL Anywhere uses a cost-based query optimizer to improve database query performance. The optimizer attempts to pick the best execution path for a query based on a guess of the percentage of rows returned by using the different operators. For example, SQL Anywhere might assume that the following operators return the percentage of rows shown in Table 16.1.

Table 16.1   Operators and Percentage of Rows Returned

Operator	Percentage Rows Returned
=	5
< >	95
<, <=, >, >=	25

Each of the other operators, such as LIKE, BETWEEN, and EXISTS, also has arbitrary values for the estimated percentage of rows returned from a query.

When SQL Anywhere executes a query, it derives estimates for each possible execution path and uses the quickest estimated execution path. The estimates are based on such variables as the size of the tables, indexes, and the query's Where clause.

If an estimate is known to be incorrect, you can include your own estimate within a query by putting the criteria in parentheses and adding the estimated percentage of rows returned to the Where clause. For example, if you estimated that sales commissions over $10,000 occur only in 3 percent of sales (rather than the default estimate of 25 percent), you could write the SELECT statement as follows:

```
SELECT cust_id, sales_date
FROM sales
WHERE ( commission >= 10000, 3);
```

This capability provides you with a way to override the default estimates of SQL Anywhere and choose a more efficient query execution path.

SQL Central Database Administrator

SQL Central is a tool you can use as the primary interface to administer SQL Anywhere (see Figure 16.2). This tool can connect to and manage multiple databases, as well as the objects within those databases. With this familiar, easy-to-use interface, which is similiar to Windows 95 Explorer, tasks are no longer cumbersome command-line arguments or confusing scripts. For more complicated tasks, the utility wizard interface guides each step, gathering the required parameters along the way. SQL Central supports the full repertoire of the Windows GUI interface, including drop-down menus, popup menus, toolbars, keyboard shortcuts, and drag-and-drop. Backup and recovery are two of most important aspects of managing a database. The SQL Central interface makes both easier.

Figure 16.2   **The SQL Central Database Administrator.**

Backup and Recovery

Through SQL Central, SQL Anywhere provides the utilities for doing either a full database or an incremental backup. Full database backups involve backing up only the database file(s); incremental backups involve an initial backup of the database file(s), backing up only the transaction logs thereafter.

A recommended approach is to back up database file(s) weekly and the transaction log daily, as shown in Figure 16.3.

If a large amount of database activity results in a large transaction log file, you may need full database backups more frequently.

TIP It is a good idea to check database file(s) for corruption. You can do this by selecting the database to be checked from the left panel of SQL Central, and then selecting **Validate** from the **File** menu.

Backing up a Database You may back up the databases while they are running or when the database is off-line. To back up any database, running or not, use the Backup Database wizard in the Database Utilities folder. To back up a database that is connected to SQL Central, select the database to be backed up from the left panel of SQL Central, and then select **Backup** from the **File** menu. In either case, follow the instructions on each page of the wizard.

Recovery The method you use for SQL Anywhere database recovery depends on the type of error that has occurred. When the database is restarted, SQL Anywhere auto-

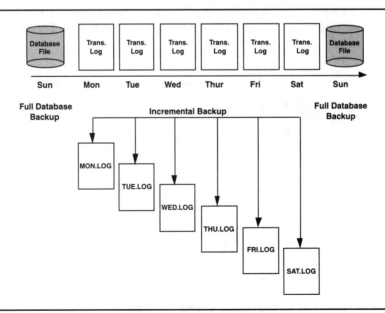

Figure 16.3 **Weekly database backups with daily transaction log backups.**

matically corrects system failures, such as power outages, in which the database and transaction files are still intact. In this case, all the committed transactions remain intact, and any pending transactions are rolled back. SQL Anywhere's automatic recovery involves three steps:

1. Using the checkpoint log to restore all the pages to the most recent checkpoint.
2. Using the transaction log to apply any pending changes after the last checkpoint. This step is executed only when using a transaction log.
3. Using the rollback log to roll back any uncommitted transactions.

If media failure has occurred or a file is corrupted, the recovery action to take depends on which files need to be recovered. In each case, the database engine for the particular platform on which the failed database resides must be started from outside of SQL Central. If, for example, both the database and transaction log files are no longer usable, use the following steps to completely restore the database:

1. Restore the database file(s) from the most recent full database backup.
2. Restore, in the correct order, each transaction log created after you made the most recent database backup. To apply the transaction log to the database, start the database with the -a switch. For example, to restore the transaction logs mon.log, tue.log, and the current transaction log pbdemo.log against the database POWER-SOFT DEMO DB (V6), SQL Anywhere recovers the files:

```
<engine name> PSDEMODB.DB -a MON.LOG
<engine name> PSDEMODB.DB -a TUE.LOG
<engine name> PSDEMODB.DB -a PBDEMO.LOG
```

3. Start the database.

If the transaction log is usable, but the database file(s) is not, use the following steps:

1. Back up the transaction log.
2. Restore the database file(s) from the most recent full database backup.
3. Restore, in the correct order, each transaction log created after you made the most recent database backup. To apply the transaction log to the database, start the database with the -a switch. For example, to restore the transaction logs mon.log, tue.log, and the current transaction log pbdemo.log against the database POWER-SOFT DEMO DB (V6), SQL Anywhere recovers the files:

```
<engine name> PSDEMODB.DB -a MON.LOG
<engine name> PSDEMODB.DB -a TUE.LOG
<engine name> PSDEMODB.DB -a PSDEMODB.LOG
```

4. Start the database.

Notice that the only difference between recovering from the loss of a database file and recovering the loss of both a database file and the transaction log is that if the log exists, you should back up the log first because it is the only record of any database changes.

If the database files are usable but the transaction log is not, do the following:

1. Back up the database file.

2. Start the database with the -f switch. This starts the database without a transaction log:

```
<engine name> PSDEMODB.DB -f
```

This creates a new transaction log.

It is best to keep the database files and transaction log files on separate devices, if possible. If there is more than one disk controller, keeping the database and log files on disks controlled by the different controllers can reduce problems. You should also use disk mirroring, if possible, to provide a second copy of the files in the case of media failure.

As mentioned earlier, SQL Anywhere uses three different types of logs: checkpoint, rollback, and transaction. Each log provides a different level of recovery.

Stored Procedures and Triggers

Stored procedures and triggers are SQL statements that reside on SQL Anywhere and are independent of any single application. You can use them to provide standardization, increased efficiency, and greater security. You achieve standardization by providing a single place to create and update the code. You increase the efficiency by offloading the processing from the client and reducing the network traffic. You can also enhance security by specifying the security for the procedures apart from the tables that they access.

By using the new procedure method from SQL Central, the following template generates a stored procedure:

```
CREATE PROCEDURE [creator].name ( [parameters,...] )
[ RESULT ( column-name,... ) ]
BEGIN
  ;
END
CREATE PROCEDURE dba.sum_all_items ( )
```

For example, the task of summing all the item quantities from a table with hundreds of thousands of rows might be resource-intensive. Also, you might not want all the users to see the individual items, just the summed quantities. You could achieve this by creating the following procedure:

```
BEGIN
  select sum(sales_order_items.quantity) from sales_order_items;
END
DECLARE sum_all_items PROCEDURE FOR my_proc USING SQLCA;
EXECUTE sum_all_items
```

Triggers differ from stored procedures in that they are associated with an action to a specified table. You often use triggers whenever referential integrity and other declarative constraints are not sufficient. SQL Central provides a utility wizard interface to guide you through creating triggers and ultimately generating a template as SQL

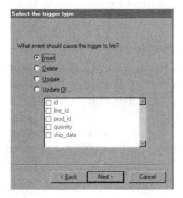

Figure 16.4   SQL Central's Trigger Creation wizard.

Central does for the stored procedure. Figure 16.4 demonstrates the wizard step in which the chosen action will activate the trigger. The final generated script results in a trigger template for the sales_order_items table which is executed on the insert of a row:

```
CREATE TRIGGER "tr_insert" BEFORE INSERT
  ORDER 1 ON "DBA"."sales_order_items"
    [ REFERENCING [ OLD AS old_name ][ NEW AS new_name ] ]
    FOR EACH ROW
    [ WHEN( search_condition ) ]
BEGIN
  ;
END
```

Database Security

SQL Anywhere lets you create users and groups, each of which can have either CON-NECT, RESOURCE, or DBA privileges. The CONNECT privilege is the lowest level of rights and only lets users or groups connect to the database and perform data manipulation language (DML) commands, if they also have that privilege. The RESOURCE privilege lets the users or groups create tables and views. The DBA privilege is the highest level of rights and lets users or groups do anything with the database.

Like other databases, you can grant SELECT, INSERT, UPDATE, and DELETE privileges to the users or groups to let them perform various DML commands against a table or view. You can give the UPDATE privilege to the entire table or only to specific columns within a table. SQL Anywhere also lets you specify the WITH GRANT OP-TION to let users or groups grant the same privilege to the other users. For example, the grant command to give user BMarley the UPDATE privilege to the Songs table and let him give other users the privilege to update the Songs table looks like:

```
GRANT UPDATE ON songs to BMARLEY
WITH GRANT OPTION;
```

To revoke the database privileges, use the **Revoke** command. You can also perform this through SQL Central.

Connecting to SQL Anywhere From PowerBuilder

This section describes how to connect to a SQL Anywhere database from PowerBuilder.

Connecting to a SQL Anywhere database from PowerBuilder first requires configuring a SQL Anywhere ODBC data source. For more details on ODBC connection, refer to Chapter 15, "Open Database Connectivity."

To connect to the database from an application, you must create a transaction object (unless you are using SQLCA). Set the transaction object's attributes according to those in Table 16.2.

TIP If the ODBC SQL driver CONNECT call is supported, PowerBuilder uses the value within DBParm to connect to the database. Otherwise, PowerBuilder uses the connect string's DSN value along with the LogID and LogPassword values to connect by using the ODBC SQL CONNECT call.

When using ODBC, you can set the parameters within DBParm to specify the following.

Asynchronous Operation

This option allows the setting of asynchronous operation. Although most ODBC data sources do not allow asynchronous operation, PowerBuilder does. To change from synchronous operation (the default) to asynchronous operation, add the following to the transaction object's DBParm parameter:

```
transobj.DBParm="Async = 1"
```

Table 16.2   Transaction Objects Attributes and Their Values

Attribute	Value
Vendor	ODBC
DBMS	ODBC
LogID	Database Login ID
UserID	Database Login ID
AutoCommit	If set to True, you cannot roll back the updates (if the DBMS supports transaction processing)
LogPassword	Database login password
Lock	Lock Value: RU indicates uncommited read; RC, commited read; RR, repeatable read; TS, serializable transactions; TV, transaction versioning
DBParm	ConnectString='DSN=ODBC datasource name, UID = userID, PWD = password, any other required datasource specific parameters'

When using asynchronous operation, PowerBuilder waits for an ODBC driver response to be set by using the dbgettime parameter. For example, to set the operation mode to asynchronous and the wait time from the default time of 0 to 10 seconds, add the following to the transaction object's DBParm parameter:

```
transobj.DBParm="Async=1,dbgettime=10"
```

Identifier Delimiters in SQL Syntax

This option lets you turn the delimit identifiers feature on and off. To change from the default value of Yes to No, add the following to the transaction object's DBParm parameter:

```
transobj.DBParm="delimitidentifiers=No"
```

This parameter is used when importing SQL into the PowerBuilder objects, for example, to obviate the need for delimiters.

Cursor Scrolling and Locking Options

This option lets you set the cursor scrolling and locking options for databases that support these features. The options available for scrolling are:

Forward.　The cursor acts as a forward-only cursor.

Keyset.　The ODBC driver keeps the key for every row retrieved.

Dynamic.　The cursor is keyset-driven to a certain point, after which it is dynamic.

The locking options are:

Lock.　The cursor uses the intent-to-update locks.

Opt.　The cursor uses the optimistic concurrency control to compare timestamps.

Opt Value.　The cursor uses the optimistic concurrency control to compare values.

To set the scrolling option to **Forward** and the locking option to **Opt**, for example, add the following to the transaction object's DBParm parameter:

```
transobj.DBParm="CursorScroll='Forward', CursorLock='Opt'"
```

Tables Displayed within the Database Painter

This option lets you restrict the list of tables that the Database painter displays. Set this value, which is used only within the development environment, by using the TableCriteria attribute. You can use the TableCriteria attribute to restrict the table list based on table name, owner, and/or table qualifier criteria. For example, to restrict the list of tables to those beginning with EMP that the user DRM owns, set the TableCriteria as follows:

```
TableCriteria = 'EMP%, DRM'
```

TIP　To keep the table list from displaying altogether, set the TableDir attribute to 0.

The PowerBuilder Catalog Owner

This option lets you set the PowerBuilder catalog tables' owner. Setting this value overrides what is within the pbodb60.ini file. Set this value by using the PBCatalogOwner attribute. For example, to set the catalog owner to DRM, add the following to the transaction object's DBParm parameter:

```
transobj.DBParm-"PBCatalogOwner='DRM'"
```

To set the SQLCA transaction object's attributes to connect to a SQL Anywhere data source Mydata with the User ID "syslogin" and the password "bigdog," execute the following script:

```
SQLCA.DBMS = "ODBC"
SQLCA.LogID = "syslogin"
SQLCA.LogPass = "bigdog"
SQLCA.UserID = "sysusr"
SQLCA.DBParm = "ConnectString = "DSN=mydata, UID=sysusr, PWD = bigdog'"
```

This sets up SQLCA with all the data necessary to connect a SQL Anywhere data source. When this is done, set each DataWindow to use SQLCA by calling the **SetTrans( )** or **SetTransObject( )** functions.

The PowerBuilder System Tables

PowerBuilder uses the tables listed in Table 16.3 to store the extended table and column information. These tables are created the first time someone connects to the database from the PowerBuilder Database painter. The DataWindow painter uses the data stored within these tables when referencing a table or view within a DataWindow's SELECT statement.

TIP It is important that a database's owner be the first to connect to the database by using PowerBuilder. This lets all of the database users access the database.

Table 16.3 PowerBuilder Tables

Information	Table Name	Description
Table level	PBCATTBL	The default fonts for the columns within a table or view.
Column level	PBCATCOL	Formats, validation rules, headers, labels, case, initial value, and justification for the particular columns.
Display format	PBCATFMT	Column formatting (output) information. Some formats are defined automatically when this table is created. You can create additional formats.
Validation rules	PBCATVLD	Column validation (input) information. You can define all the validation rules.
Edit styles	PBCATEDT	Column edit style information. You can define the edit styles.

Datatypes

SQL Anywhere supports the following datatypes:

- Character datatypes
- Numeric datatypes
- Date and time datatypes
- Binary datatypes
- User-defined datatypes

Character Datatypes

CHARACTER VARYING/VARCHAR/CHARACTER/CHAR [(size)] is used for character data of maximum length size. If size is omitted, the default is 1. The maximum size allowed is 32,767.

LONG VARCHAR is used for arbitrary length character data. The maximum size is limited by the database file's maximum size (currently 2 gigabytes).

Numeric Datatypes

INTEGER/INT is a signed integer of maximum value 2,147,483,647, requiring 4 bytes of storage.

SMALLINT is a signed integer of maximum value 32,767, requiring 2 bytes of storage.

NUMERIC/DECIMAL [(precision[,scale])] is a decimal number with precision total digits and with scale of the digits after the decimal point. You can compute the storage required for a decimal number as:

```
2 + int( (digits before decimal+1) / 2 ) + int( (after +1)/2 )
```

DOUBLE is a double precision floating-point number stored in 8 bytes. The range of values is 2.22507385850720160e-308 to 1.79769313486231560e+308.

FLOAT/REAL is a single precision floating-point number stored in 4 bytes. The range of values is 1.175494351e-38 to 3.402823466e+38. Values held as REAL are accurate to 6 significant digits but may be subject to the round-off error beyond the sixth digit.

Date and Time Datatypes

DATE is a calendar date, such as a year, month, and day. The year can be from the year 0001 to 9999. For historical reasons, a DATE column can also contain an hour and minute, but the TIMESTAMP datatype is now recommended for anything with hours and minutes. A DATE value requires 4 bytes of storage.

TIMESTAMP is a point in time, containing year, month, day, hour, minute, second, and fraction of a second. The fraction is stored to 6 decimal places. A TIMESTAMP value requires 8 bytes of storage. It is the recommended date time datatype for use with PowerBuilder.

TIME is a time of day, containing hour, minute, second, and fraction of a second. The fraction is stored to 6 decimal places. A TIME value requires 8 bytes of storage. It is not recommended because of ODBC limitations.

Binary Datatypes

BINARY [(size)] is used for binary data of maximum length size (in bytes). If size is omitted, the default is 1. The maximum size allowed is 32,767. The BINARY datatype is identical to the CHAR datatype except when used in comparisons. BINARY values are compared exactly, while CHAR values are compared without respect to case (depending on the database's case sensitivity) or accented characters.

LONG BINARY is used for arbitrary length binary data. The maximum size is limited by the database file's maximum size (currently 2 gigabytes).

User-Defined Datatypes

SQL Anywhere lets you create user-defined datatypes by using the CREATE DATATYPE statement. For example:

```
CREATE DATATYPE email_address CHAR( 35 )
CREATE TABLE part_vendor (
   id INT,
   email email_address
);
```

ORACLE

As this book went to press, PowerBuilder supported Oracle version 7.3 and Oracle8 Beta. Hence, this book covers Oracle7.

Database Architecture and Features

Database Architecture

Oracle7 employs a multiprocess architecture comprising memory structures, system and user processes, and disk structures. The system global area (SGA) is a shared memory area that contains data and control information for a single Oracle instance. An Oracle instance is defined as the SGA plus the set of Oracle background processes discussed later within this section. Figure 16.5 illustrates the Oracle architecture.

There are two types of processes within an Oracle instance: user processes and system processes. User processes, spawned from application programs such as PowerBuilder, communicate with a server process through the Oracle program interface. System processes are responsible for the database's overall operation. They are divided into server processes and background processes.

Oracle creates server processes to handle the requests from user processes. Server processes may either be dedicated or shared. Dedicated server processes operate in a one-to-one relationship with a user process; Oracle uses the shared server processes within a multithreaded architecture to provide a set of server processes available to be shared among all the user processes. Shared server processes can communicate directly with the user process or can use the dispatcher process to communicate indirectly with a user process.

The Oracle background processes are a set of system processes for such tasks as disk I/O and user process cleanup. The background processes are:

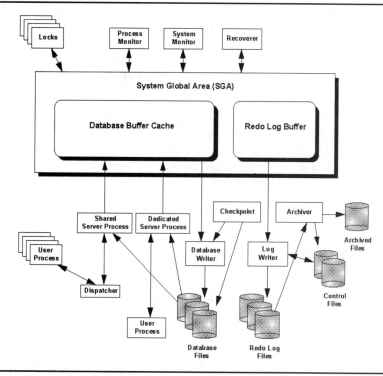

Figure 16.5   The Oracle architecture.

Printed with permission from the Oracle7™ Server Concepts Manual.

Database Writer (DBWR) writes modified data pages from the SGA's Database Buffer Cache to the disk.

Log Writer (LGWR) writes pages from the SGA's Redo Log Buffer to the disk.

Checkpoint (CKPT) an optional process that signals the DBWR process when a checkpoint occurs and writes a checkpoint record to all the data files and control files. If CKPT is not used, LGWR handles this task.

Recoverer (RECO) resolves the pending distributed transactions.

System Monitor (SMON) performs instance recovery.

Process Monitor (PMON) performs user-process recovery.

Archiver (ARCH) archives Redo log files.

Locks (LCKn) handles inter-instance locking within parallel server systems. n ranges from 0 to 9.

Dispatcher (Dnnn) routes user-process requests to a shared server process within a multithreaded architecture.

During processing, database pages are read from the disk into the database buffer cache of the SGA. As the data changes, Oracle copies the original data into the rollback segment records in the SGA, and the Oracle server process for the current user process writes the activity to the Redo log buffer.

Meanwhile, the DBWR and LGWR periodically copy data from the Database Cache Buffer and Redo Log Buffers to the disk. This process continues until either a COMMIT or ROLLBACK is executed for the current transaction. When a COMMIT is issued, Oracle performs the following:

- Generate a system change number (SCN) for the transaction.
- LGWR copies the data from the Redo Log Buffers into a Redo log file. The SCN is also written, indicating that the transaction is committed.
- Release all the locks on the affected rows.
- Mark the transaction complete.

When a transaction is rolled back, Oracle performs the following:

- Undo all the changes by using the rollback segments.
- Release all the locks on the affected rows.
- End the transaction.

For more information, refer to the Oracle system documentation.

PL/SQL

This is Oracle's Procedural Language extension to SQL. All Oracle triggers and stored procedures are written in PL/SQL. PL/SQL combines SQL with procedural constructs such as IF THEN statements and looping. For information on PL/SQL, refer to the Oracle documentation.

SQL Optimization

Oracle7 supports both cost- and rules-based SQL optimization. A cost-based optimizer uses statistics within the data dictionary to determine a SQL statement's execution path. A rules-based optimizer uses a predefined ranking of access paths to determine a SQL statement's access path. A rules-based optimizer lets the developers structure a SQL statement in a way that takes advantage of a more efficient execution path.

Triggers

Oracle supports the use of triggers and stored procedures. There are four types of Oracle triggers, each of which may have three trigger events associated with it (INSERT, UPDATE, and DELETE). The four trigger types are:

BEFORE statement.   Executes the trigger once, before executing the triggering statement.

AFTER statement.   Executes the trigger once, after executing the triggering statement.

BEFORE row.   Executes the trigger once for each row affected by the triggering statement, before executing the triggering statement.

AFTER row. Executes the trigger once for each row that the triggering statement affects, after executing the triggering statement.

Oracle Stored Procedures

Calling Stored Procedures as Embedded SQL You can execute an Oracle stored procedure via embedded SQL from PowerBuilder in one of two methods.

The first method requires the PowerBuilder DECLARE statement to assign a logical name to the stored procedure. To execute the procedure, use this logical name within the EXECUTE statement. For example, to execute the stored procedure my_proc from PowerBuilder by using the SQLCA transaction object, the script looks like this:

```
DECLARE proc1 PROCEDURE FOR my_proc USING SQLCA;
EXECUTE proc1;
```

The second method involves embedding the stored procedure call within a PL/SQL block. PL/SQL blocks start with a BEGIN statement and end with an END statement. You can copy the PL/SQL block to a PowerBuilder string variable. To execute the stored procedure, you can then use the string variable with the **Execute Immediate** command. For example, the script to call the stored procedure my_proc using a PL/SQL block looks like this:

```
string s_plsql
s_plsql = "BEGIN MY_PROC; END"
EXECUTE IMMEDIATE :s_plsql USING SQLCA;
```

Calling Stored Procedures as a DataWindow Source Using Oracle stored procedures as a DataWindow data source works a little differently than for other databases because Oracle's stored procedures do not return result sets. There are two ways to achieve this objective.

The first method obtains the result set within a PowerBuilder DataWindow by using the modified version of the Oracle system package DBMS_OUTPUT. This package, named PBDBMS, uses the **Put_Line( )** function to store the SQL Select statement's text. After the complete SQL statement is stored in a buffer, the procedure is executed. Upon execution, PowerBuilder executes the package function **Get_Line( )** to retrieve the SQL statement text from the buffer and execute the query to return the results into the DataWindow.

Using this approach requires you to modify the stored procedure code to add the Put_Line( ) function calls. The following example shows what a stored procedure looks like with the addition of Put_Line( ) statements to build the query:

```
CREATE PROCEDURE selectcust (custname varchar2)
BEGIN
//
PBDBMS.Put_Line("SELECT custnum, custssn');
PBDBMS.Put_Line("FROM customer');
END;
```

The generated SELECT statement is:

```
SELECT custnum, custssn FROM customer
```

Any DataWindow using this stored procedure as its data source requires one retrieval argument representing the customer name (custname). After creating the stored procedure, set PBDBMS DBParm to 1 so you can use the PBDBMS stored procedure as a data source.

Using this method is slower than a standard SQL SELECT statement because of the time required to obtain the SQL statement text before actually executing the query. Also, this method prevents the use of bind variables or cached statements, and you cannot use the method within embedded SQL (only as a DataWindow data source). Clearly, this is not the best way to obtain the result sets.

There is yet another method. It requires you to create some objects on the server side and some on the client side. In this method, you create a global package procedure that all the stored procedures can call within your Oracle database. The package procedure has a global variable that stores the results of the stored procedure you execute. On the client side, create a PowerBuilder function that imports the data stored within this global variable into the DataWindow by using the ImportString function. The following example builds a sample application based on this approach.

First, create a package pb_result_set and the following procedures. This will help to use the Oracle stored procedures as the DataWindows' data source. The basic idea is to create a buffer that will hold all the values from the procedures and then to populate the DataWindow with this buffer. The buffer, g_s_lines, is an array of string type in which no element can be greater than 2000 characters. Table 16.4 lists the stored procedures you need to create in the pb_result_set package procedure.

The code for the package procedure pb_result_set is:

Table 16.4   List of Stored Procedures in the pb_result_set Package Procedure

Procedure	Description
initialize	Initializes package variables.
put_data	Appends the column passed to the procedure to the buffer g_s_lines.
put_item	Appends the column passed to the procedure to the buffer g_s_lines. This procedure is overloaded to include the string, numeric, and datetype of columns passed.
put_line	Appends the column passed along with line feed carriage return characters to the buffer g_s_lines.
next_line	Appends line feed carriage return characters to the buffer g_s_lines.
get_data	Returns the buffer g_s_lines. Returns the result set of the procedure in the form of a string *not* more than 2000 characters. The string is passed by reference.

```
CREATE OR REPLACE PACKAGE pb_result_set AS
    TYPE string_array IS TABLE OF VARCHAR2(2000) INDEX BY BINARY_INTEGER;
    PROCEDURE initialize(dummy VARCHAR2);
    PROCEDURE put_data(a_s_data VARCHAR2);
    PROCEDURE get_data(a_s_data IN OUT VARCHAR2);
    PROCEDURE put_item(a_item VARCHAR2);
    PROCEDURE put_item(a_item NUMBER);
    PROCEDURE put_item(a_item DATE);
    PROCEDURE put_line(a_s_line VARCHAR2);
    PROCEDURE next_line;
END;

CREATE OR REPLACE PACKAGE BODY pb_result_set AS
    g_s_lines          string_array;
    g_s_lines_init     string_array;
    g_s_line           VARCHAR2(2000);
    g_l_out            NUMBER;
    g_l_in             NUMBER;
    g_s_tab            VARCHAR2(1);

PROCEDURE initialize(dummy VARCHAR2) AS
BEGIN
    g_s_lines          := g_s_lines_init;
    g_s_lines(1)       := NULL;
    g_s_line           := NULL;
    g_l_out            := 1;
    g_l_in             := 1;
    g_s_tab            := NULL;
END;

PROCEDURE put_data(a_s_data VARCHAR2) AS
BEGIN
    IF (Nvl(Length(g_s_line), 0) + Nvl(Length(a_s_data), 0)) > 2000 THEN
        g_l_in             := g_l_in + 1;
        g_s_lines(g_l_in)  := NULL;
        g_s_line           := NULL;
    END IF;
    g_s_line               := g_s_line || a_s_data;
    g_s_lines(g_l_in)      := g_s_line;
END;

PROCEDURE get_data(a_s_data IN OUT VARCHAR2) AS
BEGIN
    a_s_data        := NULL;
    IF g_l_out <= g_l_in THEN
        a_s_data    := g_s_lines(g_l_out);
        g_l_out     := g_l_out + 1;
    END IF;
END;
```

continues

```
PROCEDURE put_item(a_item VARCHAR2) AS
BEGIN
    put_data(g_s_tab || a_item);
    g_s_tab := CHR(9);
END;

PROCEDURE put_item(a_item NUMBER) AS
BEGIN
    put_data(g_s_tab || To_Char(a_item));
    g_s_tab := CHR(9);
END;

PROCEDURE put_item(a_item DATE) AS
BEGIN
    put_data(g_s_tab || To_Char(a_item, "yyyy-mm-dd hh:mi:ss'));
    g_s_tab := CHR(9);
END;

PROCEDURE put_line(a_s_line VARCHAR2) AS
BEGIN
    put_data(a_s_line ||  CHR(13) || CHR(10));
    g_s_tab := NULL;
END;

PROCEDURE next_line AS
BEGIN
    put_data(CHR(13) || CHR(10));
    g_s_tab := NULL;
END;

END;
```

Next, grant execute rights to everyone. You can do this in Oracle by using the following command:

```
Grant Execute On pb_result_set To Public;
```

Next, create a public synonym for the package. You can do this in Oracle by using the following command:

```
Create Public synonym pb_result_set For pb_result_set;
```

Now create your own custom procedures within Oracle, and dump the results of your custom stored procedure to this publicly accessible pakcage procedure, pb_result_set. In the following example, you create a stored procedure **my_procedure( )** that retrieves the product name and quantity from the inventory table. The procedure stores these values as well as the total quantity retrieved into the pb_result_set variables.

```
CREATE OR REPLACE PROCEDURE MY_PROCEDURE () IS
    ll_qty         Number := 0   ;

BEGIN
    -- One must initialize the pb_result_set in his procedure
    pb_result_set.Initialize ("X')  ;

FOR C1 IN (SELECT product.name, product.quantity FROM inventory)

LOOP
    pb_result_set.put_line (To_char (c1.quantity)) ;
    ll_qty := ll_qty + c1.quantity
END LOOP ;

    pb_result_set.put_line ("TOTAL QTY' || chr (9) || to_char (ll_qty)) ;

END;
```

Next, you need to create a couple of custom objects on the client side, that is, with PowerBuilder, to extract this data into the DataWindow.

First, create a nonvisual object uo_trans of type transaction. This is an extension of the default transaction object where you make the remote procedure calls (read declare local external functions) as follows:

```
Subroutine initialize(string dummy) rpcfunc alias for "PB_RESULT_SET.INITIALIZE"
Subroutine get_data(ref string a_s_data) rpcfunc alias for "PB_RESULT_SET.GET_DATA"
Subroutine debug_initialize(string dummy) rpcfunc alias for "PB_DEBUG_SET.INITIALIZE"
Subroutine debug_get_data(ref string a_s_data)  rpcfunc alias for "PB_DEBUG_SET.GET_DATA"
```

Similarly, declare **my_procedure( )** within this object as a local external function as follows (see Figure 16.6):

```
Subroutine MY_PROCEDURE () rpcfunc alias for "MY_PROCEDURE"
```

TIP For guidance in creating user objects and declaring external functions, refer to Chapter 6, "Structures, User Objects, and Functions."

Next, change the transaction object for the application from SQLCA to uo_trans. To do this, select the application icon. Next, select the properties icon. This will bring up the Application dialog box. Select the **Variable Types** tab. Change the value for SQLCA to uo_trans (see Figure 16.7).

Based on the stored procedure you call, you need to design a DataWindow with an external datasource. In my_procedure( ), you need two columns: product name and

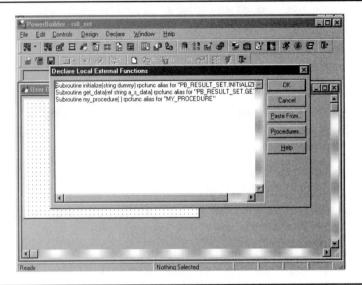

Figure 16.6 Declaring the local external functions within the uo_trans nonvisual object of type transaction.

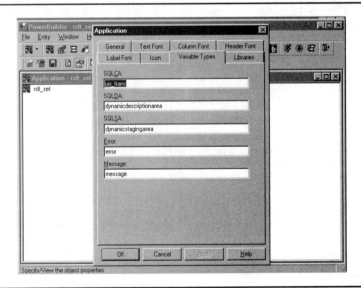

Figure 16.7 Changing the application's transaction object from SQLCA to uo_trans.

quantity. Create an external DataWindow with the two fields, and save it as **d_rslt_set** (see Figure 16.8).

Next, create a global PowerBuilder function **f_sp_ora_retrieve( )** that takes a DataWindow as an argument and retrieves the values from the global package proce-

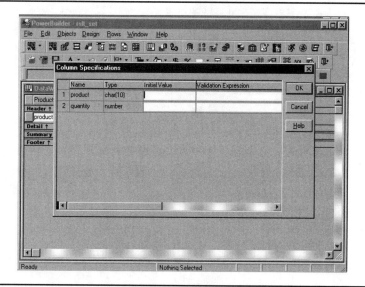

Figure 16.8   **The DataWindow with the external data source.**

dure pb_result_set into this DataWindow by using the Import function. The code for the f_sp_ora_retrieve( ) is as follows:

```
/***********************************************************************
** Purpose:      To import data into the DataWindow using Oracle
**               package procedure pb_result_set/get_data
**
** Parameters:   DataWindow a_dw (The DataWindow in which to retrieve data)
**
** Returns:      True  - Success
**               False - Failure
**
***********************************************************************/
String     ls_import, ls_data, ls_temp
Long       ll_string_limit
Long       ll_pos, ll_pos1

//Set Wait Cursor
SetPointer (HourGlass!)

//Initialize variables
ll_string_limit = 10000
ls_import = "'
a_dw.Reset ()
```

continues

```
//Get the result set from package procedure pb_result_set/get_data
Do While True
    ls_data = Space (2000)

    //Get the result set in sets of 2000 characters at a time
    SQLCA.get_data (ls_data)
    If SQLCA.SqlCode <> 0 Then
        MessageBox ("SQLCA.GET_DATA", String(SQLCA.SqlCode) &
                        + SQLCA.SqlErrText)
        Return False
    End If

    //Exit of loop if there is nothing is retrieved from the procedure
    If ls_data = "' Or IsNull(ls_data) Then Exit
    ls_import += ls_data

    //Get the data in parts if the data is longer than limit set
    //Get the last line feed carriage return & import only till that
    //part. The remaining portion shall be imported the next time.
    If Len(ls_import) > ll_string_limit Then
        ll_pos = 1
        ll_pos1 = 1
        Do While True
            ll_pos1 = Pos(ls_import, "~r~n", ll_pos+1)

            If ll_pos1 > 0 Then
                ll_pos = ll_pos1
            Else
                Exit
            End If

        Loop

        a_dw.ImportString (Left(ls_import, ll_pos))
        ls_temp = Mid(ls_import, ll_pos + 2)
        ls_import = ls_temp

    End If

Loop

//Import the remaining portion, if any
If ls_import <> "' Then a_dw.ImportString (ls_import)

//reinitialize the package
SQLCA.initialize("x')
If SQLCA.SqlCode <> 0 Then
    MessageBox("SQLCA.INITIALIZE", String(SQLCA.SqlCode) &
                + SQLCA.SqlErrText)
    Return False
End If

Return True
```

Next, create a window w_rslt_set and place a DataWindow control dw_result_set on the window. Add two buttons, cb_retireve and cb_close, to it. Also, create two custom events for the window: ue_retrieve and ue_close.

In the window's **open** event, add the following code:

```
/**********************************************************************
** Set the Transaction Object for the DataWindow
**********************************************************************/

dw_result_set.SetTransObject(sqlca)
```

In the window's **ue_retrieve** event, add the following code:

```
/**********************************************************************
** Trigger the Oracle Stored Procedure
** Call the f_ora_sp_retrieve function to import the data into the
** DataWindow
**********************************************************************/
SetPointer(HourGlass!)

SQLCA.my_procedure ()

If sqlca.sqlcode <> 0 Then
    MessageBox(This.Title, string(SQLCA.SQLCODE) + SQLCA.SQLERRTEXT)
End If;

If f_ora_sp_retrieve(dw_result_set) = False Then Return

SetPointer(Arrow!)
```

Within the window's **ue_close** event, add the following code:

```
/**********************************************************************
** Close the Window
**********************************************************************/

Close (This)
```

Next, add the following code to cb_retrieve's **clicked** event:

```
/**********************************************************************
** Call the ue_retrieve event of the window
**********************************************************************/

Parent.Event ue_retrieve (0,0)
```

Next, add the following code to cb_close's clicked event:

```
/**********************************************************************
** Call the ue_close event of the window
**********************************************************************/

Parent.Event ue_close (0,0)
```

You are all set. When you run the application (see Figure 16.9) and click on the window's **Retrieve** button, the application fires the stored procedure **my_procedure( )** on the database, which in turn, gets the names and quantity of products from the inventory table and stores them in the pb_result_set package procedure's global variables. Next, the f_sp_ora_retrieve( ) function retrieves all these values from the package procedure and imports them into your DataWindow.

Sequences

A sequence is a special Oracle database object you can use to automatically generate the sequential numbers. This feature is extremely useful within multiuser environments using system-generated sequential values. Multiple sequences can exist within a database. When referencing a sequence within a Select statement, developers can retrieve either the sequence's current value or increment the sequence and use the new value. For example, the following script retrieves the current value from the sequence object employee_num:

```
SELECT employee_num.CURRVAL from dual;
```

To increment the sequence and use the new value, the script is:

```
SELECT employee_num.NEXTVAL from dual;
```

TIP Dual is a special Oracle system table that has a single row and column. It is used to guarantee a known result.

Using sequences eliminates the need for you to programmatically determine the sequential values.

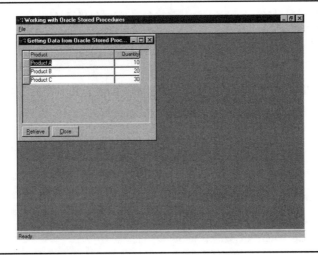

Figure 16.9   **Getting data from Oracle stored procedures.**

Select For Update

To lock the selected rows, Oracle supports the For Update clause within Select statements. Oracle locks all the rows selected with the For Update clause until it receives a COMMIT or ROLLBACK command. To avoid data contention problems, rows selected with the For Update clause should only be held for short periods of time.

Connecting to Oracle from PowerBuilder

PowerBuilder communicates with an Oracle7.3 database by using PowerBuilder's pbo7360.dll in conjunction with Oracle's ora7win.dll and corewin.dll. These DLLs then communicate with Oracle's SQL*Net, which accesses the data by using the underlying network protocol.

TIP As this book went to press, PowerBuilder included support for Oracle7 and Oracle8 Beta. For all practical purposes, this section covers Oracle7.

SQL*Net provides a common interface for Oracle applications that makes the underlying network transparent to the application. SQL*Net supports most network and transport layer protocols, including TCP/IP and IPX/SPX.

The connection from PowerBuilder to an Oracle7 database running on a UNIX server within a TCP/IP environment looks something like that in Figure 16.10. The same connection within an IPX/SPX environment looks like the one in Figure 16.11.

Notice that the only difference between these two examples is the underlying transport/network protocols and the SQL*Net driver used on both the client and the server.

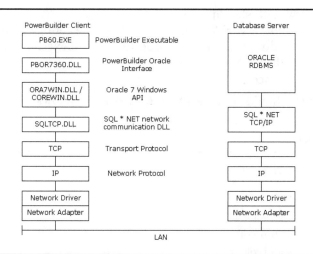

Figure 16.10   Connecting to an Oracle7 database from PowerBuilder within a TCP/IP environment.

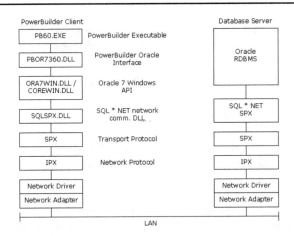

Figure 16.11   Connecting to an Oracle7 database from PowerBuilder within a IPX/SPX environment.

The SQL*Net driver is dependent on the network protocol in use. Table 16.5 lists the SQL*Net DLL required for some of the more common network protocols.

The following sections describe a couple of the more common problems encountered when connecting to an Oracle7 database.

The Oracle Configuration Is Not Set Up Correctly

Installing SQL*Net should handle setting up the client Oracle environment. Check the following when a problem occurs:

- ora7win.dll and corwin.dll should be within the DOS path.
- The CONFIG environment variable should be set to the config.ora file's full path. You can do this by adding the following line to the autoexec.bat (assuming config.ora is within the ORAWIN directory):

  ```
  SET CONFIG=C:\ORAWIN\CONFIG.ORA
  ```

- The SQL*Net driver should be loaded before starting Windows.

Table 16.5   SQL*Net DLLs

Network Protocol	SQL*Net Driver
TCP/IP	sqltcp.dll
IPX/SPX	sqlspx.dll
Named Pipes	sqlnmp.dll
NetBIOS	sqlntb.dll
Vines	sqlvin.dll
DECNet	sqldnt.dll

There Is an Invalid Connect String

The connect string specifies the network protocol, database server name, and possibly a database name. The Oracle APIs use the connect string to establish a database connection. The connect string's format is:

```
@identifer:LogicalServerName:DatabaseName
```

where identifier is a one-letter abbreviation for the network protocol. Valid identifiers are:

T TCP/IP, SQLTCP

X Novell, SQLSPX

P named pipes, SQLNMP

B NetBIOS, SQLNTB

V Vines, SQLVIN

D DECNet, SQLDNT

LogicalServerName is the database server's logical name, and DatabaseName is the database's name. The DatabaseName is optional; you need it only if more than one database is running on a single server. For example, the connect string to connect to an Oracle database DB1 running on the server ARUBA by using IPX/SPX is:

```
@X:ARUBA:DB1
```

TIP You can store a default connect string in config.ora by using the LOCAL parameter. This prevents a developer from entering the connect string when connecting to a database.

Transaction Object Attributes

Table 16.6 shows the list of attributes necessary to use a transaction object to connect to Oracle7.

Note that a database parameter is not required because it is part of the connect string. Also note that Oracle does not support AutoCommit.

Use the transaction object's DBParm attribute to control a variety of different

Table 16.6 Attributes Necessary to Use a Transaction Object to Connect to an Oracle Database

Attribute	Value
DBMS	OR7 / O73
Servername	Server Connect String
LogID	Server Login ID
LogPass	Server Login Password

things about a database connection. The following sections describe the DBParm attributes you can use when connecting to an Oracle7 database.

Set the Blocking Factor The blocking factor refers to the number of rows fetched from a database at one time. Because of Oracle's array processing capabilities, the server can return multiple rows within a single fetch. Oracle recommends a blocking factor of 100 (the default), although you may use any value from 1 to 500. For example, to set the blocking factor to 150, add the following to the transaction object's DBParm parameter:

```
transobj.DBParm="BLOCK=150"
```

Specify Date, Time, and DateTime Formats PowerBuilder can either use its own format or the Oracle format to handle these datatypes. The Oracle format is the default. To change the format of all three of these datatypes to the PowerBuilder format, add the following to the transaction object's DBParm parameter:

```
transobj.DBParm="Date=PB_date_format,
Time=PB_time_format, DateTime=PB_datetime_format"
```

Disable Binding The input parameters to a select statement are, by default, bound by using the Oracle Call interface (OCI). You can disable this binding by setting the DBParm's DisableBind attribute to 1:

```
transobj.DBParm="DisableBind=1"
```

Specify Mixed Case You can make Oracle case-sensitive by setting the DBParm's MixedCase attribute to 1:

```
transobj.DBParm="MixedCase=1"
```

Set Delimiter You can specify whether you want PowerBuilder to enclose the names of tables, columns, indexes, and constraints within double quotes when PowerBuilder generates the SQL statements. In Oracle, this value is YES by default. To prevent the use of double quotes with these items, set this attribute to NO:

```
transobj.DBParm="DelimitIdentifier=NO"
```

Using Stored Procedures as a Data Source By default, PowerBuilder lets you create a DataWindow object or report that uses an ORACLE7 stored procedure as its data source (as discussed previously). If you do not want to be able to use ORACLE7 stored procedures with PBDBMS.Put_Line calls as a data source, set PBDBMS to 0:

```
transobj.DBParm="PBDBMS=0"
```

Static Binding You can specify whether PowerBuilder obtains a result set description before retrieving data from a database into a DataWindow, report, or form. By default, PowerBuilder does not obtain a result set description before retrieving the data, which results in better performance. To have PowerBuilder obtain a result set description before retrieving the data, add the following to the transaction object's DBParm attribute:

```
transobj.DBParm="StaticBind='No'"
```

Set Table Criteria This option lets you specify the criteria to limit the list of tables and views that the Select Tables list within PowerBuilder displays. In Oracle, you can limit the table list by table name, owner name, and object type (table, view, or synonym). The TableCriteria attribute's format is:

```
TableCriteria = "{table_name_criteria},{table_owner_criteria},{table_qualifier_criteria}'
```

For example, to display only the tables that the user joeuser owns that begin with "mktg," the TableCriteria attribute contains:

```
transobj.DBParm="TableCriteria=mktg%,joeuser,''TABLE''"
```

Set SQL Cache Size To set the SQL cache size, set SQLCache to a value that is less than the maximum number of cursors that the client can open. To determine this number, use the following formula:

```
transobj.DBParm="SQLCache=n"
```

where

n is <= open_cursors - 5 - declare_cursor_space.

open–cursors is the server setting for the number of cursors that a process may have open.

5 is the number of reserved cursors. Reserve five cursors for use by the Power-Builder Oracle interface.

declare_cursor_space is the maximum number of cursors you expect to open from within the PowerBuilder environment per connection.

The PowerBuilder System Tables

Table 16.7 shows the tables that PowerBuilder uses to store the extended table and column information. To ensure that these tables have the correct owner, the first user to

Table 16.7 PowerBuilder System Tables for the Oracle Database

Information	Table Name	Description
Table level	system.pbcattbl	Default fonts for the columns within a table or view.
Column level	system.pbcatcol	Formats, validation rules, headers, labels, case, initial value, and justification for the particular columns.
Display format	system.pbcatfmt	Column formatting (output) information. Some formats are defined automatically when this table is created. You can create additional formats.
Validation rules	system.pbcatvld	Column validation (input) information. You can define all the validation rules.
Edit styles	system.pbcatedt	Column edit style information. You can define the edit styles.

connect to an Oracle database should log in as the Oracle user SYSTEM. The DataWindow painter uses the data stored within these tables when referencing a table or view within a DataWindow's Select statement.

To ensure developers have proper access to these tables, the first user should be the Oracle7 SYSTEM user.

Datatypes

Oracle7 supports the following datatypes:

CHAR (size) is used for fixed-length character data of length size. Maximum length of 255.

VARCHAR2 (size) is used for variable-length character data of length size. Maximum length of 2000 bytes.

DATE is used for date and time data. Values range from January 1, 4712 B.C. to December 31, 4712 A.D. Default format of DD-MON-YY. Fixed length of 7 bytes.

NUMBER(p,s) is used for variable-length numeric data. Maximum precision p and/or scale s is 38. Maximum length of 21 bytes.

LONG is used for variable-length character data. Maximum length of 2 gigabytes.

RAW (size) is used for variable-length raw binary data of length size. Maximum length of 2000 bytes.

LONG RAW is used for variable-length raw binary data. Maximum length of 2 gigabytes.

ROWID is used for binary data representing a row address. Fixed length of 6 bytes.

MLSLABEL is used for variable-length binary data representing OS labels. Size ranges from 2 to 5 bytes.

Of these datatypes, PowerBuilder supports all except the ROWID and MLSLABEL types. Oracle uses these types internally. When data is selected or updated, PowerBuilder automatically converts between the Oracle datatypes and corresponding PowerBuilder datatypes.

TIP Oracle8 supports user-defined datatypes, but PowerBuilder is yet to announce support to this datatype.

SQL SERVER

PowerBuilder provides an interface to both the Microsoft and Sybase versions of SQL Server. While these systems differ somewhat within their features and implementation, they share several similarities with the interface from PowerBuilder to these databases. This section briefly discusses the SQL Server architecture, followed by a more detailed discussion of the PowerBuilder interface and some of the differences between Microsoft and Sybase SQL Server as they relate to the PowerBuilder interface.

Database Architecture

While Oracle employs a multiprocess architecture, all versions of the SQL Server use a single-process, multithreaded architecture. Within this type of architecture, all database tasks, including user connections, are handled as threads of a single process. This has the advantage of being able to switch among tasks more quickly because a single process handles everything. Handling everything within one process also means that the architecture does not have to rely on the underlying operating system to perform several of its tasks. This architecture is generally considered more efficient than a multiprocess architecture because of the cost involved in managing the multiple processes within the multiprocess architecture.

This architecture does have some disadvantages, however. First, because each user connection uses a single thread, that thread must handle all the user requests within a single user connection. The inability to distribute the requests of a single user connection among multiple threads can slow performance. In addition, because everything is done within a single process, any problems within a process's thread are more likely to impact the RDBMS engine. Figure 16.12 shows the SQL Server architecture.

The SQL Server kernel performs several of the tasks that the operating system generally performs, such as task switching and caching. As mentioned earlier, this makes the SQL Server more efficient because it does not have to go to the operating system

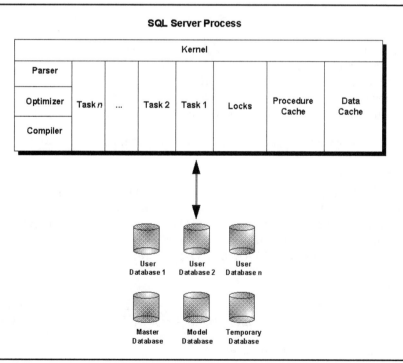

Figure 16.12   The SQL Server architecture.

for these services. Each task shown in Figure 16.12 (Task 1 through n) can be either a SQL Server system task or a user database connection.

SQL Server uses multiple databases within its operation. These databases are divided into system databases and user databases. The SQL Server system databases are the Master, Model, and Temporary databases (Microsoft SQL Server 6 also contains a database called msdb to handle task scheduling and replication). The Master database maintains system-related information such as logins, devices, and lock information. The Model database provides a template from which you can create all the new databases. Any modifications to the Model database are reflected in all databases created after the time of modification. The system uses the Temporary database for such things as sorting or grouping a result set. You can also use the Temporary database as a temporary storage location.

User databases are all nonsystem databases used within an application. The user databases are created from the Master database and contain a subset of the system tables from the Master database.

During execution, a SQL Server user must connect to a single database. All SQL is then executed against that database. As the data is requested, it is read from the disk into the data cache. The date cache contains both data pages and log pages. As the data changes, transactions are written to the transaction log (the Syslogs System table) for the current database. This process continues until a checkpoint occurs. Either the server automatically performs a checkpoint after a preset time interval has expired, or it is done explicitly by the database owner (DBO).

When a checkpoint occurs, the Server executes the following events:

- All the transactions updating the database are frozen.
- Transaction log pages are written to the database file.
- All modified data pages are written to the database file.
- A checkpoint record is written to the transaction log.
- All the frozen transactions are allowed to continue.

For more information, refer to the SQL Server system documentation.

TRANSACT-SQL

TRANSACT-SQL is SQL Server's extension to SQL. TRANSACT-SQL is compatible with both ANSI SQL and IBM's SAA SQL standards. All SQL Server triggers and stored procedures are written in TRANSACT-SQL. TRANSACT-SQL combines SQL with the procedural constructs such as IF statements and looping.

For more information on TRANSACT-SQL, refer to SQL Server documentation.

SQL Optimization

SQL Server supports only cost-based SQL optimization. A cost-based optimizer uses statistics within the data dictionary to determine a SQL statement's execution path.

Triggers and Stored Procedures

SQL Server supports the use of triggers and stored procedures. As mentioned earlier, all the SQL Server triggers and stored procedures are written in TRANSACT-SQL.

SQL Server triggers are executed only once for each triggering statement (Insert, Update, or Delete), not once for each row the triggering statement affects.

PowerBuilder supports SQL Server stored procedures and triggers. Executing a SQL Server stored procedure from PowerBuilder requires the PowerBuilder Declare statement to assign a logical name to the stored procedure. PowerBuilder then uses this logical name within the Execute statement to execute the procedure. For example, to execute the stored procedure get_cust from PowerBuilder by using the SQLCA transaction object, the script looks like this:

```
DECLARE get_customer PROCEDURE FOR get_cust;
EXECUTE get_customer;
```

If the stored procedure requires two arguments, the Execute statement looks like this:

```
DECLARE get_customer PROCEDURE FOR getcust
  @custlname = :cust_lname, @custfname = :cust_fname;
// get cust_lname and cust_fname
EXECUTE get_customer;
```

The result sets from a stored procedure are handled much like a cursor in that the **Fetch** command is used to obtain each row of the result set. Because SQL Server stored procedures return result sets, you can use them as a DataWindow object's data source.

Connecting to SQL Server from PowerBuilder

PowerBuilder communicates with all the versions of SQL Server by using its database interface file (pbsty60.dll for Sybase System 10/11 using DB-Library, PBSYC60 for Sybase System 10 using CTLIB, and pbmss60.dll for Microsoft SQL Server 6.0) in conjunction with the appropriate DB-Library API DLL. The DB-Library DLL varies depending on the version of SQL Server in use and the client operating system. For Microsoft SQL Server 6 running under Windows 95 or Windows NT, the DB-Library API is ntwdblib.dll. For Windows 3.x, the DB-Library API is w3dblib.dll. One important thing to remember is that the DB-Library DLL used for Microsoft and Sybase SQL Server is different, and you should obtain the library from the database vendor.

PowerBuilder applications send all the data requests to PowerBuilder's SQL Server interface file, pb??60.dll (?? varies depending on the version of SQL Server in use). pb??60.dll then passes the request to the SQL Server DB-Library (or CTLIB) programs located within the DB-Library DLL. When the request passes from PowerBuilder to the DB-Library DLL, PowerBuilder waits for a response while the SQL Server programs process the request.

The requests to the DB-Library DLL are passed to the network library DLL and finally on to the server that processes the request. The network library DLL varies depending on the network protocol over which SQL Server is running. Figures 16.13, 16.14, and 16.15 show the files used for communicating from PowerBuilder running on a Windows 95 client to Microsoft SQL Server 6.0 running over IPX/SPX, TCP/IP, and Named Pipes, respectively.

Several problems involved with connecting to a SQL Server have to do with mismatched communication files or bad versions of the various DLLs used for data access.

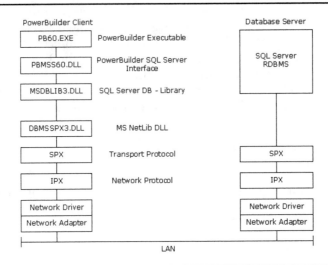

Figure 16.13   **Connecting to a Microsoft SQL Server 6 database from PowerBuilder within an IPX/SPX environment.**

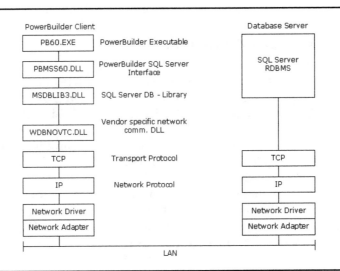

Figure 16.14   **Connecting to a Microsoft SQL Server 6 database from PowerBuilder within a TCP/IP environment.**

It is important to know the network environment and to make sure you use the correct version of each of the several programs involved.

Transaction Object Attributes

Table 16.8 shows a list of attributes necessary to use a transaction object to connect to the SQL Server database.

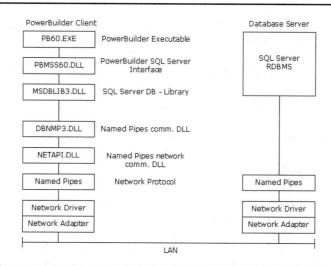

Figure 16.15   **Connecting to a Microsoft SQL Server 6 database from PowerBuilder within a Named Pipes environment.**

Table 16.8   A List of Attributes Necessary to Use a Transaction Object to Connect to a SQL Server Database

Attribute	Value
DBMS	Sybase / MSS SQL Server 6
Servername	Database server name
LogID	Server Login ID
LogPass	Server Login Password
Database	Name of the database to which the transaction is connecting
AutoCommit	Commits after each Insert, Update, or Delete if True (= 1)

Using AutoCommit

As mentioned earlier, the AutoCommit setting determines whether PowerBuilder automatically issues a Commit after each Insert, Update, or Delete. When set to True, SQL Server treats the SQL Statements (including DataWindow updates) as "implicit transactions." This means that the statement is not associated with a user-defined transaction (no BEGIN TRANSACTION), and its changes to the database are committed as they successfully occur. This is the same as going into ISQL and entering an Update statement. If the update is successful, the change is made and you cannot roll back the change. When AutoCommit is True, you cannot execute any ROLLBACK TRANSACTION or COMMIT TRANSACTION statement, because there is no BEGIN TRANSACTION to associate the transaction with.

This will not work in situations where multiple DataWindow updates occur and the updates must be committed or rolled back as a single logical unit of work. For example, in a master/detail conversation, changes should not be made to the database unless the update of both the master and detail DataWindows is successful. With AutoCommit set to True, if the first update is successful and the second update fails, there is no way to roll back the changes made to the first DataWindow because the DataWindow's changes are already committed. Another example is making multiple updates to a single list DataWindow. If two rows are updated and an **update( )** is executed, two separate SQL statements are sent to the SQL Server. The first row could be updated successfully while the second row has an error. In this case, there is no way to roll back the first update. Not good!

When AutoCommit is set to False, use "explicit transactions." This means that transactions are user-defined and use a BEGIN TRANSACTION in conjunction with a COMMIT TRANSACTION or ROLLBACK TRANSACTION. The way PowerBuilder handles this is by issuing a BEGIN TRANSACTION when the application makes a connection to the database and issuing a COMMIT TRANSACTION followed by a new BEGIN TRANSACTION when the application executes the PB commit command (same thing for rollbacks). This allows for commits and rollbacks with the PowerBuilder code and therefore solves the multiupdate problems encountered when using AutoCommit set to True, but there's still a problem.

By automatically issuing a BEGIN TRANSACTION, there is always a transaction open when the PowerBuilder application is connected to the database. The problem with this is that it is possible to have a long running transaction that may eventually cause the transaction log to fill and possibly prevent the log from being dumped. In general, transactions should be short and sweet. At save time, begin the transaction, do the updates, and either commit or rollback to end the transaction. Avoid long-running transactions and situations where a transaction is opened while the user is entering the data or staring at a messagebox or online help.

The following example uses PowerBuilder trace files to illustrate the differences between setting AutoCommit to True and setting it to False. In this example, data is retrieved into a DataWindow, modified, and updated. The following shows the trace file when AutoCommit is set to False:

```
LOGIN: (2380 MilliSeconds)
CONNECT TO TRACE SYB SQL Server v4.x:
USERID=dmosley
DATA=dev01
LOGID=dmosley
SERVER=CJ (1002 MilliSeconds)
PREPARE: (0 MilliSeconds)
BEGIN TRANSACTION: (1002 MilliSeconds) begin trans caused by AC = False
PREPARE:
SELECT dbo.customer.cust_id , dbo.customer.cust_name  FROM dbo.customer     (1017
MilliSeconds)
DESCRIBE: (76 MilliSeconds)
//... retrieve logic continued...
```

```
FETCH NEXT: (0 MilliSeconds)
Error 1 (rc 100)
COMMIT: (1003 MilliSeconds) commit explicitly called after the retrieve
GET AFFECTED ROWS: (0 MilliSeconds)
^ 0 Rows Affected
BEGIN TRANSACTION: (1002 MilliSeconds) corresponding begin trans due to AC=FALSE
PREPARE:
INSERT INTO dbo.customer ( cust_id, cust_name ) VALUES ( 3, "Smith" ) (1014 MilliSeconds)
EXECUTE: (0 MilliSeconds)
COMMIT: (1000 MilliSeconds) commit explicitly called following DW update( )
GET AFFECTED ROWS: (0 MilliSeconds)
^ 0 Rows Affected
BEGIN TRANSACTION: (1003 MilliSeconds) corresponding begin trans due to AC=FALSE
COMMIT: (1008 MilliSeconds) commit explicitly called in the app close event
DISCONNECT: (62 MilliSeconds)
SHUTDOWN DATABASE INTERFACE: (0 MilliSeconds)
```

Notice how PowerBuilder automatically issues a BEGIN TRANSACTION at the beginning of the application and again after each COMMIT. The next example shows the database trace file for the same example with AutoCommit set to True:

```
// retrieve logic continued...
FETCH NEXT: (0 MilliSeconds)
Error 1 (rc 100)
EXECUTE:
BEGIN TRANSACTION (1015 MilliSeconds) explicit begin trans called from the app
GET AFFECTED ROWS: (0 MilliSeconds)
^ 0 Rows Affected
CANCEL: (0 MilliSeconds)
PREPARE:
INSERT INTO dbo.customer ( cust_id, cust_name ) VALUES ( 3, "Smith" ) (1014 MilliSeconds)
EXECUTE: (0 MilliSeconds)
GET AFFECTED ROWS: (0 MilliSeconds)
^ 0 Rows Affected
COMMIT TRANSACTION (1003 MilliSeconds) commit called from the app after DW update( )
GET AFFECTED ROWS: (0 MilliSeconds) notice no begin trans after this commit
^ 0 Rows Affected
CANCEL: (0 MilliSeconds)
COMMIT: (1013 MilliSeconds) commit explicitly called in the app close event
Error 3902 (rc -1) : The commit transaction request has no corresponding BEGIN TRANSACTION.
DISCONNECT: (0 MilliSeconds)
SHUTDOWN DATABASE INTERFACE: (0 MilliSeconds)
eof
```

Notice that with AutoCommit set to True, there is no call to BEGIN TRANSACTION at the beginning of the application. Also notice that an error occurs when a COMMIT is executed without a corresponding BEGIN TRANSACTION. While this does cause an error condition, it is relatively harmless in cases where the COMMIT is executed without any database updates having occurred. However, it is good practice to always have a corresponding BEGIN TRANSACTION for any COMMIT or ROLLBACK when manually controlling the transactions.

There are different DBParm attributes for Microsoft SQL Server 6 and Sybase System 10 and 11. The following are all the DBParm attributes for SQL Server with a designation for which version of SQL Server applies:

Release 4.2.   When using SQL Server version 4.x, you should set the release attribute to 4.2. This specifies that you want to use SQL Server DB-Library cursor processing instead of the default PowerBuilder cursor processing. To do this, add the following to the transaction object's DBParm parameter:

```
transobj.DBParm="Release='4.2'"
```

Asynchronous Operation.   To change from the default of synchronous operation to asynchronous operation, add the following to the transaction object's DBParm parameter:

```
transobj.DBParm="Async = 1"
```

When using asynchronous operation, set the time DB-Library waits for a SQL Server response by using the dbgettime parameter. For example, to set the operation mode to asynchronous and the wait time from the default time of 0 to 10 seconds, add the following to the transaction object's DBParm parameter:

```
transobj.DBParm="Async = 1, dbgettime = 10"
```

This attribute is valid for Microsoft SQL Server 6 and for Sybase System 10 and 11.

Cursor Scrolling and Locking Options.   The options available for scrolling are:

Forward.   The cursor acts as a forward-only cursor.

Keyset.   The ODBC driver keeps the key for every row retrieved.

Dynamic.   The cursor is keyset-driven to a certain point, after which it is dynamic.

The locking options are:

Lock.   The cursor uses intent-to-update locks.

Opt.   The cursor uses optimistic concurrency control to compare the timestamps.

Opt Value.   The cursor uses optimistic concurrency control to compare the values.

When setting these options, the release attribute should be set to 4.2. For example, to set the scrolling option to Forward and the locking option to Opt, add the following to the transaction object's DBParm parameter:

```
transobj.DBParm="Release='4.2', CursorScroll='Forward', CursorLock='Opt'"
```

This attribute is valid for Microsoft SQL Servers 4.x and 6.

AppName and Host.   The setting of an application name and host server lets you use the SQL Server tools to view the database users. To set the application name to "myapp" and the host name to "MAUI," add the following to the transaction object's DBParm parameter:

```
transobj.DBParm="Appname='myapp', Host='Maui'"
```

This attribute is valid for Microsoft SQL Server 6 and Sybase System 10 and 11.

Set the blocking factor.   Specifies the internal blocking factor the Sybase Client Library (CT-Lib) interface uses when declaring a cursor. The blocking factor determines the number of rows fetched from the database at one time when CT-Lib makes a physical request for the data. To set the blocking factor to 150, for example, add the following to the transaction object's DBParm parameter:

```
transobj.DBParm="BLOCK=150"
```

This attribute is valid for Sybase System 10 and 11.

Set the character set.   Specifies the character set you want the Sybase Open Client software to use when connecting to a Sybase SQL Server database from PowerBuilder. For example, to set the character set to iso_1 within a Sybase SQL Server or Sybase System 10 connection, add the following to the transaction object's DBParm parameter:

```
transobj.DBParm="CharSet='iso_1'"
```

This attribute is valid for SQL Server 4.x (Windows NT only), Sybase System 10 and 11.

Set the text limit.   Specifies the maximum length of a text field that the DB-Library returns when you include the text field within a SQL SELECT statement. The valid values for this attribute are 1–32K. The DBTextLimit's default value is the default that the SQL Server specifies for the DBTEXTLIMIT DB-Library option (maintained within the SQL Server global variable @@textsize). For example, to set the text limit to 32,000, add the following to the transaction object's DBParm parameter:

```
transobj.DBParm="DBTextLimit='32000'"
```

This attribute is valid for SQL Server 4.x and Microsoft SQL Server 6.

Set delimiter.   Same as that defined for Oracle.

Language.   Specifies the language to use when connecting to a SQL Server database. For example, to set the language to French, add the following to the transaction object's DBParm parameter:

```
transobj.DBParm="Language='French'"
```

This attribute is valid for Microsoft SQL Server 6 and for Sybase System 10 and 11.

Locale.   Specifies the locale name that the Sybase Open Client software uses when connecting to a Sybase System 10 or System 11 database. For example, to set the language to French and the character set to cp850, add the following to the transaction object's DBParm parameter:

```
transobj.DBParm="Locale='fra'"
```

This attribute is valid for Sybase System 10 and 11.

Log. Specifies whether the database server should log the updates of text and image data within the SQL Server transaction log. By default, the server logs the updates of text and image data. To disable the logging of text and image updates, add the following to the transaction object's DBParm parameter:

```
transobj.DBParm="Log=0"
```

This attribute is valid for Microsoft SQL Server 6 and for Sybase System 10 and 11.

PowerBuilder Catalog Owner. Specifies a nondefault owner of the Power-Builder system catalog tables. By default, the owner of these tables is 'DBO'. To specify a different owner, add the following to the transaction object's DBParm parameter:

```
transobj.DBParm="PBCatalogOwner='JADMIN'"
```

This attribute is valid for Microsoft SQL Server 6 and for Sybase System 10 and 11.

Password Encryption. Specifies whether to automatically encrypt the password when connecting to a Sybase SQL Server System 10 or System 11 database when using Sybase Open Client software. By default, the password is encrypted. To prevent the encryption, add the following to the transaction object's DBParm parameter:

```
transobj.DBParm="PWEncrypt='No'"
```

This attribute is valid for Sybase System 10 and 11.

Secured Connection. Specifies whether to use the Windows NT integrated login security and a secure (trusted) connection when connecting to a Microsoft SQL Server 6 database. By default, the standard login security (nontrusted) is used. To use a secured connection, add the following to the transaction object's DB-Parm parameter:

```
transobj.DBParm="Secure='Yes'"
```

This attribute is valid for Microsoft SQL Server 6.

Static Binding. Same as that defined for Oracle.

Display System Stored Procedures. Specifies whether PowerBuilder displays both system stored procedures and user-defined stored procedures within the connected SQL Server database when a list of stored procedures is requested. By default, PowerBuilder displays both. To prevent PowerBuilder from displaying the system stored procedures, add the following to the transaction object's DBParm parameter:

```
transobj.DBParm="SystemProcs='No'"
```

This attribute is valid for Microsoft SQL Server 6 and for Sybase System 10 and 11.

Set Table Criteria. Specifies the criteria to limit the list of tables and views that the Select Tables list displays within PowerBuilder. With SQL Server, you can limit the table list by the table name, owner name, and object type (table, view, system table, alias, or synonym). The TableCriteria attribute's format is:

```
TableCriteria = "{table_name},{table_owner},{table_qualifier},{"table_type"}'
```

So, for example, to display only the tables that the user joeuser owns and that begin with "mktg," the TableCriteria attribute contains:

```
transobj.DBParm="TableCriteria='mktg%','joeuser','',''TABLE''"
```

This attribute is valid for Sybase System 10 and 11.

Updatable cursors. Specifies whether cursors within a Sybase SQL Server System 10 or System 11 database are declared read-only or updatable. By default, the cursors are declared read-only. To make the cursors updatable, add the following to the transaction object's DBParm parameter:

```
transobj.DBParm="CursorUpdate=1"
```

This attribute is valid for Sybase System 10 and 11.

The PowerBuilder System Tables

PowerBuilder uses the tables that Table 16.9 lists to store the extended table and column information. PowerBuilder creates these tables the first time the database owner connects to the database from the PowerBuilder Database painter. The DataWindow painter uses the data stored within these tables when referencing a table or view within a DataWindow's select statement.

To ensure that developers have proper access to these tables, the first user should be a user with database administrator privileges.

Datatypes

Both Sybase SQL Server and Microsoft SQL Server 6 support the following datatypes:

BINARY (size) is used for binary data of length size. Maximum length of 255.

VARBINARY (size) is used for variable-length binary data of length size. Maximum length of 255.

Table 16.9   PowerBuilder System Tables for the SQL Server Database

Information	Table Name	Description
Table level	DBO.PBCATTBL	Default fonts for the columns within a table or view.
Column level	DBO.PBCATCOL	Formats, validation rules, headers, labels, case, initial value, and justification for the particular columns.
Display format	DBO.PBCATFMT	Column formatting (output) information. Some formats are defined automatically when this table is created. You can create additional formats.
Validation rules	DBO.PBCATVLD	Column validation (input) information. You define all the validation rules.
Edit styles	DBO.PBCATEDT	Column edit style information. You can define the edit styles.

CHAR (size) is used for fixed-length character data of length size. Maximum length of 255.

VARCHAR (size) is used for variable-length character data of length size. Maximum length of 255.

DATETIME is used for date and time data. Fixed length of 8 bytes. Values are any date greater than January 1, 1753.

SMALLDATETIME is used for date and time data. Fixed length of 4 bytes. Values are any date from January 1, 1900 to June 6, 2079.

INT is used for integer values ranging from -2^{31} to $2^{31}-1$ ($-2,147,438,648$ and $2,147,483,647$). Fixed length of 4 bytes.

SMALLINT is used for integer values ranging from $-32,768$ to $32,767$. Fixed length of 2 bytes.

TINYINT is used for positive integer values ranging from 0 to 255. Fixed length of 1 byte.

FLOAT/REAL is used for floating-point numbers. Range and precision are machine-dependent. Fixed length of 8 bytes.

DECIMAL/NUMERIC is used for exact numeric data. Length ranges from 2 to 17 bytes, depending on the desired precision.

BIT is used for binary digits, either 0 or 1. Fixed length of 1 byte, with 8 bit datatypes per byte.

MONEY is used for money data. Fixed length of 8 bytes, with values ranging from $-922,337,203,685,447.5808$ to $922,337,203,685,447.5807$.

SMALLMONEY is used for money data. Fixed length = 4 bytes, with values ranging from $-214,748.3649$ to $214,748.3648$.

TEXT is used for large text data. Minimum length of 2000 bytes; maximum length of 2 gigabytes.

IMAGE is used for large binary data. Minimum length of 2000 bytes; maximum length of 2 gigabytes.

TIMESTAMP is used exclusively to maintain the timestamps for browse mode.

Of these datatypes, PowerBuilder supports all except TIMESTAMP. The SQL Server uses this type internally. When data is selected or updated, PowerBuilder automatically converts between the SQL Server datatypes and the corresponding PowerBuilder datatypes.

One other item to note concerning the SQL Server datatypes is the fact that a column defined as CHAR(xx) lets Nulls be treated the same way as a VARCHAR(xx) column. This means that not all CHAR(xx) columns are necessarily fixed length.

INFORMIX

PowerBuilder supports the following Informix database products:

- INFORMIX-SE v 5.x, and 6.x
- INFORMIX-OnLine v5.x, 6.x, and 7.x

This section provides a brief description of the INFORMIX-OnLine architecture, followed by a more detailed discussion of the PowerBuilder interface to all the supported versions of informix.

Database Architecture and Features

Database Architecture

Like Oracle, the INFORMIX-OnLine architecture is a multiprocess architecture composed of a shared memory area, system and user processes, and disk structures. Currently, INFORMIX-OnLine runs on NetWare, Windows NT, and most UNIX platforms. Figure 16.16 shows the OnLine architecture.

As Figure 16.16 shows, the OnLine shared memory area is divided into three areas: the header, the OnLine internal tables, and the buffer pool. The header has pointers to all the other shared memory structures (i.e., the internal tables and buffer pool). The OnLine internal tables track the shared memory resources. The buffer pool is composed of four types of buffers:

Regular buffers is used to store the data pages from the disk. Each regular buffer is the size of one page (page sizes are platform-dependent).

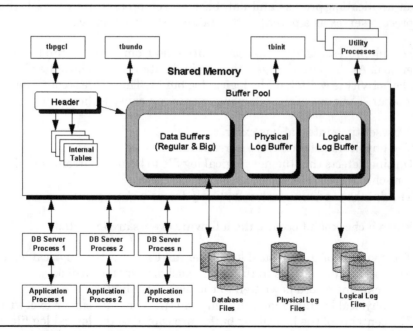

Figure 16.16   The INFORMIX-OnLine architecture.

Big buffers is used to increase the performance of large disk reads/writes. Big buffers are the size of eight pages. One big buffer exists for every 100 regular buffers.

Physical log buffers is used to store Before images of data pages. Physical log buffers are written to the physical log files when a checkpoint occurs.

Logical log buffers is used to track database changes. Logical log buffers are written to the logical log files when a checkpoint occurs.

OnLine user processes are divided into three types:

Daemon processes.   Used to perform system-wide tasks. The three daemon processes are:

> **tbinit** is the main OnLine daemon, responsible for disk and memory initialization.

> **tbundo** performs cleanup of the "hanging" processes.

> **tbpgcl** is the "page cleaner" daemon. It is used to write the pages from shared memory to disk.

Utility processes.   Used to perform the utility tasks such as database monitoring and tape archiving.

Database server processes.   Used to manage database access. Database server processes are used in a one-to-one relationship in which parent application processes provide a database connection. When a database connection is requested, an application process and database server process are created; the application process serves as a parent to the database server process.

During processing, database pages are read from the disk into the shared memory buffer pool. As the data changes, the original data is copied into the physical log buffer and the activity is written to the logical log buffer. This process continues until a checkpoint occurs. Any one of the following events can cause a checkpoint:

- A preset time interval has expired.
- The physical log becomes 75 percent full.
- OnLine detects that the next logical log file to become current contains the most recent checkpoint record.
- The database administrator explicitly forces a checkpoint.

When a checkpoint occurs, the following events are executed:

- The contents of the physical log buffer are copied to the physical log file.
- All modified data pages in the buffer pool are written to disk.
- A checkpoint record is written to the logical log buffer.
- The physical log file is logically emptied (the contents can be overwritten).
- The contents of the logical log buffer are copied to the logical log file.

For more information, refer to the INFORMIX-OnLine system documentation.

SPL

SPL is Informix's stored procedure language (SPL) extension to SQL. All OnLine stored procedures are written in SPL. SPL combines SQL with procedural constructs such as IF statements and looping. For more information on SPL, refer to the Informix documentation.

SQL Optimization

OnLine supports both cost- and syntax-based SQL optimization. A cost-based optimizer uses statistics within the data dictionary to determine a SQL statement's execution path; a syntax-based optimizer lets you structure the SQL code in a way to take advantage of a faster execution path. OnLine also lets the optimization level be set explicitly to high or low. Setting the optimization level to high (the default) causes the server to examine and select the best of all the possible optimization strategies. This can slow performance because of the increased time needed to choose the execution path. To set the optimization level, use the Set Optimization statement.

Triggers and Stored Procedures

OnLine supports the use of triggers and stored procedures. You can execute the OnLine triggers once before or after (using the Before or After clause) the triggering statement, or once for each row that the triggering statement (by using the For Each Row clause) affects.

As mentioned earlier, the OnLine stored procedures are written in Informix's SPL. PowerBuilder supports OnLine stored procedures. Executing an OnLine stored procedure from PowerBuilder requires the PowerBuilder Declare statement to assign a logical name to the stored procedure. PowerBuilder then uses this logical name within the Execute statement to execute the procedure. For example, to execute the stored procedure get_cust from PowerBuilder by using the SQLCA transaction object, the script looks like this:

```
DECLARE get_customer PROCEDURE FOR get_cust ();
EXECUTE get_customer;
```

If the stored procedure requires two arguments, the Execute statement looks like this:

```
DECLARE get_customer PROCEDURE FOR getcust
   (:cust_lname, :cust_fname);

// get cust_lname and cust_fname
EXECUTE get_customer;
```

PowerBuilder handles the result sets from a stored procedure much like a cursor in that PowerBuilder uses the Fetch command to obtain each row of the result set. Because the OnLine stored procedures return result sets, you can use them as a DataWindow object's data source.

Connecting to Informix from PowerBuilder

Powersoft provides two interfaces to the Informix databases, depending on the version of INFORMIX-NET (I-NET) client software in use. The pbin560.dll and pbin660.dll files provide these two interfaces and you may use either to connect to any of the versions of INFORMIX that PowerBuilder supports.

PowerBuilder communicates with an INFORMIX-OnLine database by using either the pbin560.dll or pbin660.dll in conjunction with Informix's ldllsqlw.dll. The interface from ldllsqlw.dll differs depending on the version of I-NET in use.

If version 5.x of I-NET is in use, ldllsqlw.dll is all that you need to provide the interface (you do not need remsql.exe with I-NET 5.x). Make sure you are using ldllsqlw.dll's 5.x (version 4.x is dated before 1994, and version 5.x is dated 1994 or later). The connection from PowerBuilder to an OnLine database running on a UNIX server in a TCP/IP environment by using I-NET 5.x is the same as shown in Figure 16.17.

Transaction Object Attributes

Table 16.10 shows a list of attributes necessary to use a transaction object to connect to the INFORMIX-OnLine database.

Note also that AutoCommit has no effect within an INFORMIX database.

When using INFORMIX, you can use a transaction object's DBParm attribute to set the following connection attributes:

Disable binding. Same as that defined for Oracle.

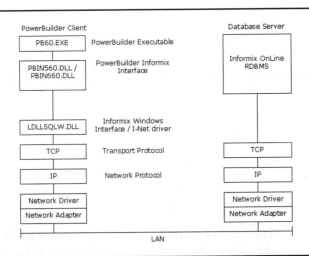

Figure 16.17 Connecting to a INFORMIX-OnLine database from PowerBuilder by using I-Net 5.x within a TCP/IP environment.

Table 16.10   List of Attributes Necessary to Use a Transaction Object to Connect to the INFORMIX-OnLine Database

Attribute	Value
DBMS	INFORMIX.
Database	Name of the database to which the transaction is connecting.
LockValues	Used to set the isolation level for record locking. The valid values are Dirty Read, Committed Read, Cursor Stability, and Repeatable Read.
SQLReturnData	The row's serial number is stored within this variable after an Insert statement executes.

Scrollable cursors. A scrollable cursor allows the fetching of rows from the active result set in any sequence. To specify a scrollable cursor, add the following to the transaction object's DBParm parameter:

```
transobj.DBParm="scroll=1"
```

I-NET Database path. Specifies the INFORMIX DBPATH setting. The DBPATH environment variable identifies a list of directories that contain the INFORMIX databases. To specify a database path, add the following to the transaction object's DBParm parameter:

```
transobj.DBParm="INET_DBPATH='server_dbpath'"
```

I-NET protocol. Specifies the network protocol that the I-NET 5.x client software uses to communicate with a remote INFORMIX version 5.x, 6.x, or 7.x database server. To specify a protocol, add the following to the transaction object's DBParm parameter:

```
transobj.DBParm="INET_PROTOCOL='protocol_name'"
```

I-NET service. Specifies the name of the service that a remote INFORMIX version 5.x, 6.x, or 7.x database server uses to listen to all the incoming requests from the client applications. To specify a service, add the following to the transaction object's DBParm parameter:

```
transobj.DBParm="INET_SERVICE='service_name'"
```

The PowerBuilder System Tables

PowerBuilder uses the tables listed in Table 16.11 to store the extended table and column information. PowerBuilder creates these tables the first time the database owner connects to the database from the PowerBuilder Database painter. The DataWindow painter uses the data stored within these tables when referencing a table or view within a DataWindow's select statement.

To ensure that developers have proper access to these tables, the first user to access them should have database administrator privileges.

Table 16.11   PowerBuilder System Tables

Information	Table Name	Description
Table level	INFORMIX.PBCATTBL	Default fonts for the columns within a table or view.
Column level	INFORMIX.PBCATCOL	Formats, validation rules, headers, labels, case, initial value, and justification for particular columns.
Display format	INFORMIX.PBCATFMT	Column formatting (output) information. Some formats are defined automatically when PowerBuilder creates this table. You can create additional formats.
Validation rules	INFORMIX.PBCATVLD	Column validation (input) information. You define all the validation rules.
Edit styles	INFORMIX.PBCATEDT	Column edit style information. You can define the edit styles.

Datatypes

INFORMIX-OnLine supports the following datatypes:

BYTE is used for binary data. Theoretical limit of 2^{31} bytes. The available disk storage determines the actual limit.

CHARACTER/CHAR (size) is used for fixed-length character data of length size. Maximum length of 32,767.

VARCHAR (m,r) is used for variable-length character data with a maximum length of m. r is the minimum amount of space reserved for the column.

DATE is used to store calendar dates as integers equal to the number of days since 12/31/1899. Fixed length of 4 bytes.

DATETIME is used for calendar date and time of day. To determine the number of bytes required for storage, use the following formula:

```
total # of digits for all fields/2 + 1
```

DECIMAL/DEC/NUMERIC (p,s) is used for decimal floating-point numbers up to a maximum of 32 significant digits, where p is the precision and s is the scale. To determine the number of bytes required for storage, use the following formula:

```
precision/2 + 1
```

INTEGER/INT is used for integer values ranging from -2^{31} to $2^{31}-1$ ($-2,147,483,647$ to $2,147,483,647$). Fixed length of 4 bytes.

INTERVAL is used for a span of time value in either a year-month format or a day-time format. To determine the number of bytes required for storage, use the following formula:

```
total # of digits for all fields/2 + 1
```

SMALLINT is used for integer values ranging from $-32,767$ to 32,767. Fixed length of 2 bytes.

FLOAT/DOUBLE PRECISION (n) is used for double-precision floating-point numbers with up to 16 significant digits. The range is machine-dependent. n specifies the precision.

SMALLFLOAT/REAL is used for single-precision floating-point numbers with approximately eight significant digits. The range is machine-dependent. SMALLFLOAT types usually require 4 bytes.

SERIAL (n) is used for sequential integers assigned automatically by OnLine when a row is inserted. Only one serial column is allowed per table. Maximum number is 2,147,483,647. Fixed length of 4 bytes.

MONEY (p,s) is used for money data. Stores fixed-point numbers up to a maximum of 32 significant digits, where p is the precision and s is the scale. To determine the number of bytes required for storage, use the following formula:

```
precision/2 + 1
```

TEXT is used for large text data. Theoretical limit of 2^{31} bytes. The available disk storage determines the actual limit.

PowerBuilder supports all the datatypes just listed. When data is selected or updated, PowerBuilder automatically converts between the Informix datatypes and the corresponding PowerBuilder datatypes.

PART V

Administration

CHAPTER 17

Project Standards and Naming Conventions

Programming standards can be one of the most important parts of building and maintaining an application. You should establish standards before development begins. Standards let teams of developers, even large teams, create applications that they can easily maintain.

This chapter discusses the following topics:

- Programming standards
- Naming conventions
- Window type standards
- GUI standards
- Error handling

Most programming standards are based on common sense. Still, if a project begins without them, you should determine and retrofit them. A little perseverance in this area pays off grandly when you need system modification or maintenance.

When developing large applications, creating and using programming standards is imperative. Although it is not one of the most exciting aspects of application design, overlooking standards can be financially draining and time-consuming. Regardless of the conventions you use, you should enforce and document standards for both client and server components.

PROGRAMMING STANDARDS

In a multiple-developer environment, programming standards become the thread of similarity among the developers. Standards also provide new developers with an easier transition into the development environment and thus increase the project team productivity. Within the PowerBuilder environment, programming standards should address the following areas:

- Hard-coded references
- Code modularization

- Encapsulation
- Comments
- Function visibility

The following sections discuss each of these types of standards.

Hard-Coded References

One of the most important programming standards is to avoid using hard-coded references. To maximize the use of the object-oriented principles of polymorphism and overloading, you should code with generic references. Table 17.1 shows the PowerBuilder keywords you can use to reference the objects generically.

By using the references of This, Parent, and ParentWindow, you can create reusable generic scripts within windows, menus, and user objects. These references let the script determine and use the correct object, even if the object's name changes.

This

Most commonly, PowerBuilder uses the generic reference of This to create an implied reference for the object attributes. As an illustration, export a simple window, sheet1, from an MDI application and view the resulting .SRW file's create and destroy sections. The example illustrates how PowerBuilder creates all of the objects (e.g., CommandButtons and radiobuttons) by referring to each of the object's controls as this.controlname instead of using the hard-coded object name (sheet1).

```
On Sheet1.Create
If This.MenuName = "m_stdmdi" Then This.MenuID = Create m_stdmdi
This.cb_1=Create cb_1
This.rb_2=Create rb_2
This.rb_1=Create rb_1
This.sle_1=Create sle_1
This.st_1=Create st_1
This.gb_1=Create gb_1
This.Control[]={ This.cb_1,&
This.rb_2,&
This.rb_1,&
This.sle_1,&
This.st_1,&
This.gb_1}
End On

On Sheet1.Destroy
If IsValid(MenuID) Then Destroy(MenuID)
Destroy(this.cb_1)
Destroy(this.rb_2)
Destroy(this.rb_1)
Destroy(this.sle_1)
Destroy(this.st_1)
Destroy(this.gb_1)
End On
```

Table 17.1   PowerBuilder Keywords to Reference Objects

Convention	Type of Script	Object Type
This	Window, User Object, Control	Reference that indicates the object or control.
Parent	MenuItem, Window, User Object	The object that contains the control.
ParentWindow	MenuItem	The window that is associated with the MenuItem at runtime.

The window function **titlebar( )** shows another example using This within a script. This function sets the window's windowtitle attribute to the person's name within the instance variables i_sFirstName, i_sMiddleName, and i_sLastName. You can place the window function titlebar( ) within a virtual class window for use by the descendant windows. Because the script uses This as a window reference, any window can use the attribute windowtitle.

```
/*************************************************************************
** Set the title bar with some descriptive information about this
** customer.
*************************************************************************/
This.WindowTitle = i_sFirstName + " " + i_sMiddleName + " " + i_sLastName
Return True
```

Parent

Window controls, user objects, or menu items can use the keyword Parent. Using Parent within a window control's script refers to the window that contains the control. Using Parent within a user object control's script refers to the user object. Using Parent with menu items refers to the menu item for which you have written the script.

Figure 17.1 shows how to use the keyword Parent within a window control. This example uses a CommandButton, cb_exit, to close an MDI application's active sheet. Using Parent lets you use the same CommandButton for closing any of the MDI sheets:

```
Close(Parent)
```

Now take this example a step further: Assume cb_exit is a standard user object rather than a window control. Replacing the user object's clicked event with the **hide( )** function hides the button itself, rather than the window that has the user object control:

```
Parent.Hide()
```

Because the user object control's script uses Parent, the script hides the related object (cb_exit), not the related window (sheet1).

The third use of Parent is within the MenuItem scripts. In this case, Parent refers to the MenuItem for which you have written the script. An example is a script to disable the MenuItem **<u>S</u>ave** within a sub-MenuItem script **<u>D</u>isable:**

```
Parent.Disable()
```

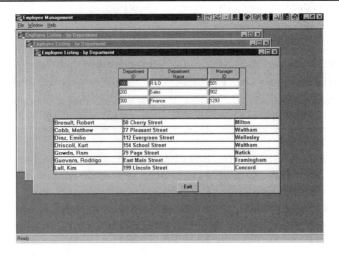

Figure 17.1   Using Parent within a window's control.

ParentWindow

Usually, developers do not use the keyword ParentWindow as frequently as Parent or This, but you can use the keyword within the MenuItem scripts. For example, you can use ParentWindow within the following script of the MenuItem **File, Close.** The script closes the window that is associated with the menu at runtime. This reference lets you use the menu with any window:

```
Close(ParentWindow)
```

Code Modularization

Another important programming standard is code modularization. Whenever possible, you should break common or frequently used code into separate modules that you can use throughout an application. Modularization, combined with the identification of common application functionality, can yield code reusability, which results in simplified debugging and maintenance. Application functions such as displaying messages and error handling are good candidates for modularization because you generally use them throughout an application. Within the following example, **Applicationinit( )**, a function that executes at login time, sets a global variable to a value within an application.ini file. You can achieve this by using the PowerBuilder function **ProfileString( )**. You can break this functionality into three functions to modularize certain code segments that you may use repeatedly within the application.

Because ProfileString( ) is a function you will use throughout the application, you can modularize the function's use by creating a new function, **appProfile( )**. AppProfile( ) calls ProfileString( ) and passes the section and key values that ProfileString( ) requires. This puts the calls to ProfileString( ) within a single location and, because you

Figure 17.2   The appProfile( ) function declaration.

do not hard-code these values within the call to ProfileString( ), provides greater flexibility. Figure 17.2 shows appProfile( )'s definition.

You can use the appProfile( ) function to retrieve the values from myapp.ini. The code for appProfile( ) is as follows:

```
/******************************************************************
** Return the value associated with the argument section and key in
** myapp.ini. If none exists, return an empty string.
******************************************************************/

Return ProfileString("myapp.ini",a_sSection,a_sKey,"")
```

When you call this function, the function takes the value from the myapp.ini file within the passed section and key. Assume myapp.ini looks like this:

```
[Servers]
dev_server=devserv
test_server=testserv
prod_server=corpserv1

[Preferences]
ReportDir=c:\rpts\
ReportName=myrpt.txt
```

Create a second function, **setDBServer( )**, to take the value from myapp.ini and assign it to the global variable g_sDBServer (see Figure 17.3). Use this value within the application to set up the different transaction objects. With this code within a separate function, g_sDBServer is set within a single place rather than having the same code within a number of places throughout the application.

```
/******************************************************************
** Set the global variable value
******************************************************************/

g_sDBServer = a_sValue
Return g_sDBServer
```

Figure 17.3   The setDBServer( ) function definition.

The final step in this example is to create the function **applicationInit( )**. This function sets the global variable for the default database server name. Getting the server name from the .INI file and setting the name equal to a global variable, you can set up the necessary transaction objects for connecting to a development, testing, or production database server:

```
/******************************************************************
** Set the System User value
******************************************************************/

SetPointer(hourGlass!)
SetDBServer(appProfile("Servers","dev_server"))
Return True
```

This example shows how to modularize the code instead of putting it all into one larger function.

Encapsulation

Another programming technique that you should incorporate into your programming standards is encapsulation (see Chapter 2, "Application Architectures"). You can use encapsulation both to hide complexity from other developers and to simplify the code maintenance. By encapsulating the code into functions that reference nonlocal variables instead of calling them directly, you can make changes within one function only, instead of having to change the code throughout an application.

TIP You should try to avoid referencing nonlocal variables directly. Instead, you should call a function to get the value.

Comments

Several developers preach about the merits of well-commented code. Unfortunately, while frequently preached, it is often not practiced. The rules for commenting Power-Script (or any other 4GL) are no different from those for any other programming language. You should use a small section at the top of a script to explain the script's functionality, noting when you wrote (and modified) the code. If a script is complex or calls other functions, it is a good idea to briefly describe what is going on within the script. You should also write comments to help those who will maintain the code. Comments are not intended to be a narrative of the script. The golden rule is to say what you do within the script rather than how you have done it!

PowerBuilder gives you the choice of using C++-style comments.

```
// Comments
```

or C-style comments:

```
/* comment */
```

Either set of characters is acceptable to set off the comments. However, you should stick to the one you decide to implement.

Function Visibility

You can control the object-level function's visibility within PowerScript by designating one of the access levels that Table 17.2 describes.

The Function painter defaults the access level to public. The use of private and public access lets you create truly encapsulated scripts. Tightening the access ensures that you (or another developer) can never inadvertently call the function from another script. Using public access is different from using a global function because the public access function is bound to the object and is accessible only as long as you have instantiated the object. (For a further discussion of this subject, see Chapter 6, "User Objects and Functions.")

NAMING CONVENTIONS

Naming conventions, which are often overlooked because they do not seem to be important, do not become an issue until they are not implemented. A lack of naming conventions causes the developers to spend more of their valuable time trying to debug and maintain the application code. You should implement naming conventions for objects, variables, datatypes, controls, and database objects.

Objects

The naming convention for objects is fairly straightforward. You can mimic the Power-Builder's own naming scheme by designating the first letter(s) as the object's type, as Table 17.3 shows.

Table 17.2 The Function Access Levels

Access Level	Description
Private	Visible to the window instances within the class but not descendants.
Protected	Visible to the instances and descendants.
Public	Visible to any code.

Table 17.3 The Object Naming Conventions

Convention	Object Type	Convention	Object Type
none	Application	str_	Structure
w_	Window	q_	Query
m_	Menu	f_	Function
u_	User Oject	p_	Pipeline
d_	DataWindow		

Variables

Table 17.4 shows the widely used abbreviations for naming the variables.

Using a variable-naming convention helps you recognize a variable's scope within a script.

Datatypes

Table 17.5 shows the widely used abbreviations to designate a variable's datatype.

The following illustrates the combination of abbreviations used for a variable Var's variable and datatypes:

```
Local:
      Integer
            iVar
      UnsignedLong
            ulVar
      String
            sVar
Shared:
      Integer
            s_iVar
```

continues

Table 17.4 The Variable Naming Conventions

Convention	Variable Type	Description
none	Local	Declare within a script. The variable exists as long as PowerBuilder processes the script. No other script can access this variable.
i_	Instance	Declare at the object level. Only a single instance of a window can access this variable.
s_	Shared	Declare at the object level. Only the scripts within any instance of an object can access this variable.
g_	Global	Declare at the application level. All objects (windows, functions, menus, and so on) can access this variable.

```
          UnsignedLong
                s_ulVar
          UnsignedInt
                s_uiVar
   Instance:
          Integer
                i_iVar
          UnsignedLong
                i_ulVar
          UnsignedInt
                i_uiVar
   Global:
          Integer
                g_iVar
          UnsignedLong
                g_ulVar
          UnsignedInt
                g_uiVar
```

To distinguish the variable names from the datatype abbreviation, the authors recommend using underscores or capitalization.

Another approach to variable naming is to specify only the variable's scope, with no designation of the datatype. For example, you can define the string variable fname as fname, i_fname, s_fname, or g_fname depending on the variable's scope (local, instance, shared, or global), rather than sFname, i_sFname, s_sFname, or g_sFname. While this method makes it more difficult to determine the variable's datatype, it simplifies maintenance in situations where you want to change a variable's datatype. Again, the particular standard you use may vary, as long as you use some sort of standard.

Controls

PowerBuilder controls also follow a naming convention, which consists of a prefix representing the control type, followed by an underscore and the control's number within the object. You can change the name's numeric portion to represent a name that has

Table 17.5 The Datatype Naming Conventions

Convention	Datatype	Convention	Datatype
_a	Any	_i	Integer
_bl	Blob	_l	Long
_b	Boolean	_r	Real
_c	Character	_s	String
_d	Date	_t	Time
_dt	DateTime	_ui	UnSignedInteger
_dec	Decimal	_ul	UnsignedLong
_dbl	Double		

some meaning to the control's function. Table 17.6 shows the prefixes PowerBuilder uses for some of the more popular control types.

For example, the default names PowerBuilder assigns to the CommandButtons that open and close a window are cb_1 and cb_2. You should change these names to something more descriptive such as cb_open and cb_close.

You should also change the name assigned to the DataWindow controls from dw_1 and dw_2 to something more descriptive, such as dw_master and dw_detail within a master/detail relationship window.

Database Objects

To eliminate confusion and ease database maintenance, you should develop some form of naming convention for database objects. Again, the actual standard you use is not as important as simply having a standard in place. Table 17.7 shows a suggested naming convention for database objects.

WINDOW TYPE STANDARDS

When developing an application, one of the key decisions is whether the application will adhere to Microsoft Windows standards or some other standard. If the application follows Microsoft Windows standards, there are some window types that let you create an application that is consistent with other Microsoft Windows applications. Each of the PowerBuilder window types (i.e., Main, Response, Child, and Popup) has a specific use within an application. They should adhere to a set of standards depending on the type of application you create—MDI (see Chapter 4, "Multiple Document Interface (MDI) and Windows") or SDI (Single Document Interface).

SDI

The SDI, which interfaces with one instance of a document at a time, uses the Power-Builder Window types described in the following sections.

Table 17.6   Control Naming Conventions

Convention	Control Type	Convention	Control Type
cb_	CommandButton	em_	EditMask
pb_	PictureButton	rb_	RadioButton
sle_	SingleLineEdit	cbx_	CheckBox
st_	Static Text	ole_	OLE control
mle_	Multi-Line Edit	tv_	TreeView
lb_	List Box	lv_	ListView
dw_	DataWindow	plb_	PictureListBox
ddlb_	DropDownListBox	tab_	Tab

Table 17.7   Database Objects Naming Conventions

Convention	Database Object
[application_code]_tablename	Table
[application_code]_viewname	View
tablename_ndx#	Index
[application code]_spname	Stored Procedure
ins_tablename	Insert Trigger
upd_tablename	Update Trigger
del_tablename	Delete Trigger
pk_tablename_keyname	Primary Key
fk_tablename_keyname	Foreign Key

Main

The Main window is a stand-alone window that is considered to be an SDI application's base. The Main window is thus considered the Parent window; all other windows within the application should be subordinate to the Main window. The Main window should have a title bar and a menu associated with it. The user should be able to be minimize and maximize the window, and the window's icon should appear within the Microsoft Windows desktop.

Child

The Child window is always subordinate to the Parent window. PowerBuilder closes the Child window when the user closes the associated Parent window. The Child window is similar to the MDI sheet, with the parent as the Main window. The Child window usually does not have a menu, but it can have a title bar. The user can minimize the Child window, and the window will display as an icon inside the Parent window.

Popup

Although you may not use them frequently, Popup windows can have a title bar and a menu. The user can minimize and maximize them, and an icon appears on the Microsoft Windows desktop.

Response

The Response window is application modal, and it provides the user with information. The user cannot minimize this type of window. In addition, this type of window does not have a menu. You can use the Response window for messages, printing, or opening files.

TIP If you have not explicitly named a Parent window for a Child or Popup window, the last active Main window becomes the Parent window.

MDI

The MDI application, which interfaces with multiple instances or sheets at the same time, uses the PowerBuilder Window types described in the following sections.

MDI Frame (with Microhelp)

The MDI frame window is an MDI application's base window. The MDI frame is the Parent window for the other sheet windows even though they are the Main window types. Because the MDI frame is the Parent window, when the user closes the frame, PowerBuilder, in turn, closes all of the related sheets. The MDI frame window should have a menu or toolbar associated with it, and each sheet's menu passes through the frame's menu. For further explanation of menus, see Chapter 5, "Menus."

Main

You use the Main window primarily within MDI as the main frame's sheet. The sheet is always the frame's child, and the user sees the sheet only within the frame. Each of the sheet windows should have a title bar and a menu associated with it. The user can minimize and maximize the sheets. PowerBuilder iconizes the sheets within the frame window. In addition, PowerBuilder closes any open sheets when the user closes the MDI frame window.

Child

The Child window is always subordinate to the Parent window. PowerBuilder closes the Child window when the user closes the associated Parent window. Within an MDI application, the sheet (Main), which is the Parent window, closes any Child windows if the sheet closes.

Popup

Within MDI applications, the sheet (Main) window's functionality replaces the use of the Popup windows.

Response

MDI applications use Response windows the same way SDI applications do. Response windows are application modal and provide the user with information pertaining to a particular sheet. Usually, you do not invoke a Response window directly from the MDI frame. A Response window does not have a menu, and the user cannot minimize this type of window. You can use the Response window for messages, printing, or opening files.

For a further discussion of MDI applications, see Chapter 4, "Multiple Document Interface (MDI) and Windows."

GUI STANDARDS

Another area where you should apply standards is within an application's graphical interface. This is very important in terms of how a user reacts to a new system, and therefore the user's acceptance of a system. It is important that a consistent look and feel exist for all the parts of an application or suite of applications.

Different vendors have published different sets of GUI standards (IBM's CUA and Microsoft's Windows Interface Guidelines are two of the more popular). These documents contain a robust set of standards for all aspects of GUI design, but they do not contain everything you need when designing PowerBuilder applications. One area specific to the PowerBuilder development concerns DataWindows. It is important that you establish GUI standards for DataWindow design. Table 17.8 provides a sample set of GUI standards for DataWindows.

In addition to the items listed in Table 17.8, you should establish standards for such things as edit and display masks, video resolution, and error message format. Once again, the specific standard is not as important, as long as you apply a standard.

ERROR HANDLING

Error handling is critical within any application, and some level of error handling must exist within every application. In general, the more error-handling logic you build into an application, the more solid that application will be. The errors an application detects may be of several different severity levels. The actions an application takes when the

Table 17.8   Sample GUI Standards for PowerBuilder DataWindows

Control	Font	Color/ Background	Border	Justification	Other
Checkbox	MS Sans Serif 8 point	Dark Blue/ Light Gray	None	Right Text	Box itself is 3D-Lowered
Picture Button	Not Bold	N/A	N/A	N/A	(Never use Command buttons.)
Tabular and grid DWs	N/A	Background– Gray	3D-Lowered	Centered on the window	
Labels on tabular and grid DWs	Bold first letter of each word in uppercase Height = 53	Enabled– Blue/Gray Disabled– Dark gray/gray	3D-Raised	Centered	
Columns on tabular and grid DWs	Not bold Height = 57	Enabled– Black/White Disabled– Black/Gray	3D-Lowered	Numerics– Right Text–Left Dates–Center	
Form DWs	N/A	Background– Gray	None	Centered on the window	
Labels on form DWs	First letter of each word in uppercase	Enabled– Blue on Gray Disabled– Dark Gray on Gray		Left	Flush left with column. There should not be a colon ":" at the end of each label.

continues

Table 17.8 *Continued*

Control	Font	Color/ Background	Border	Justification	Other
Columns on form DWs	Not bold	Enabled– Black/White Disabled– Black/Dark Gray	3D-Lowered	Numerics–Right Text–Left Dates–Center	
ListBox		Black Text on White	3D-Lowered	Left	
DDDW/DDLB		Black Text on White	No border on the columns	Left	"Always Show Arrow" en- abled for the form style DWs. "Always Show Arrow" disabled for the list style DWs.
GroupBox Label	Bold	Blue Text/ Gray Back- ground	Dark gray and white lines in DW	Left	
Radio Buttons	Not bold	Black Text/ Gray	No border	Right Text	3D on button itself.
MLE	Not bold	Black Text/Gray	3D-Lowered	Left	

application encounters an error can range from informational messages, warning messages, or serious error messages, to doing some critical secondary processing. For example, if an application is trying to connect to a server and the server is down, you could give the user a message, try a few more times, or try to connect to another server. There are several ways to handle errors. A common misconception is that error handling is not necessary in all situations. This opinion is incorrect, and it can cause developers, end users, and support personnel headaches.

Error handling is critical for every part of an application, but it is especially important when interfacing with an application's external pieces. These pieces can be database servers, file servers, other applications, external libraries, or application programming interfaces (APIs). Following are some examples of error handling for an application's external pieces.

Database Error Handling

PowerBuilder has powerful built-in capabilities to handle the errors from database transaction activities. PowerBuilder has functions, events, and structure fields specifically for handling database errors. The PowerBuilder transaction object, through which all the database communication takes place, has three error-trapping entries. These entries are SQLCode, SQLDBCode, and SQLErrText. The latter two are especially useful because they store the particular database vendor's error code and message, respectively. On the other hand, SQLCode is a PowerBuilder generic error entry. SQLCode's value can be 0, which yields a successful transaction, 100, which means the database returned no result set for that particular transaction, or –1, which means an error occurred. To determine the error, you can either use the vendor entries within the transaction object or use the DBError event's arguments (sqldbcode and sqlerrtext).

Handling Deadlocks within SQL Server

Within both Microsoft and Sybase SQL Server, problems with deadlocks have occurred. The infamous database error number 1205 has frustrated many database administrators and developers. A deadlock occurs when two users have a lock on a separate object, and each user wants to acquire an additional lock on the other user's object. When this happens, the first user is waiting for the second to let go of the lock, but the second user will not let go until the lock on the first user's object is freed.

SQL Server detects this situation and chooses one of the users, rolls back that user's transaction, notifies the application of this action with message number 1205, and lets the users' processes move forward. SQL Server cancels the first user's process and displays an unfriendly and wordy message to the user. You can trap the deadlock error number (1205) from within PowerBuilder. You can then choose to either display or suppress the error message, or send the SQL through again. Within the DataWindow's dberror event, you should use the following logic to trap the deadlock error and resend the SQL:

```
If sqldbcode = 1205 Then
      // Code to resend the SQL
Else
      MessageBox("DB Error","Error Code="+sqldbcode+&
                    "~nError Message="+sqlerrtext)
End If
Return 1
```

This is a simple yet graceful way of providing a user-friendly solution to the deadlock error within SQL Server.

Dynamic Load-Balancing of Database Servers

Error handling can be a very powerful feature if you use it effectively. You can write dynamic load-balancing routines to manage multiple databases from within PowerBuilder. If multiple database servers are available to an application at startup, the system can connect the user to the one that is least busy. With good error-handling routines, if a database server fails when a user issues a query, the system can transparently connect the user to a different server and execute the query again.

The Error and ExternalException Events

PowerBuilder provides two special events for trapping errors within DataWindows, OLE 2, and OLEObjects: the Error and ExternalException events. Both events help you trap runtime errors that may not occur within all instances but only when certain runtime conditions exist. For example, the dot notation you use to refer to certain DataWindows may be valid under some runtime conditions but not others.

The Error event occurs when PowerBuilder finds an error within an external object or DataWindow object's data or property expression. This event gives an opportunity to handle the error without triggering the SystemError event. The Error event's arguments are:

errornumber is the PowerBuilder error number.

errortext is the PowerBuilder error message.

errorwindowmenu is the name of the window or menu that is the parent of the object whose script caused the error.

errorobject is the name of the object whose script caused the error.

errorscript is the full text of the script in which the error occurred.

errorline is the line in the script where the error occurred.

action is a value of type ExceptionAction that lets you control the error handling. Valid values are:

ExceptionFail! Fail as if PowerBuilder did not implement this script. The error condition triggers the SystemError event.

ExceptionIgnore! Ignore this error and return as if no error occurred.

ExceptionRetry! Execute the function or evaluate the expression again in case the OLE server was not ready. This option is not valid for the DataWindows.

ExceptionSubstituteReturnValue! Use the value specified within the returnvalue argument instead of the value the OLE server or DataWindow returns, and cancel the error condition.

returnvalue is a value whose datatype matches the expected value that the OLE server or DataWindow would have returned. This value is used when the action's value is ExceptionSubstituteReturnValue!.

The Error event gives you a chance to substitute a default value when the error is not critical to the application. The Error event's arguments also provide information that is helpful in debugging expressions that you can check only at runtime. With the Error event, the DataWindow error processing now occurs as shown below:

1. The error occurs, triggering the Error event.
2. If the Error event has no script or its action argument is set to ExceptionFail!, the SystemError event occurs.
3. If the SystemError event has no script, an application error occurs and PowerBuilder terminates the application.

The ExternalException event is used only with OLE 2 and OLEObjects objects, and it is triggered when an expression's evaluation involving an external object's properties causes an error. The ExternalException event occurs before the Error event. The ExternalException event's arguments are:

Resultcode is the PowerBuilder number that identifies the exception that occurred on the server.

Exceptioncode is the number that identifies the error that occurred on the server.

Source is the server's name.

Description is the exception's description.

Helpfile is the name of a help file containing information about the exception.

Helpcontext is the help topic's context ID within the help file that contains information about the exception (that the server provides).

Action is a value of type ExceptionAction that lets you control the error handling. Valid values are:

ExceptionFail! Fail as if PowerBuilder did not implement this script. The error condition triggers the SystemError event.

ExceptionIgnore! Ignore this error and return as if no error occurred.

ExceptionRetry! Execute the function or evaluate the expression again, in case the OLE server was not ready.

ExceptionSubstituteReturnValue! Use the value specified within the returnvalue argument instead of the value the OLE server returns, and cancel the error condition.

returnvalue A value whose datatype matches the expected value that the OLE server would have returned. This value is used when the action's value is ExceptionSubstituteReturnValue!.

The ExternalException event gives information about the error that occurred on an OLE server. Like the Error event, the ExternalException's arguments provide information that is helpful in debugging situations that occur at runtime. With the ExternalException event, error processing when communicating with an OLE server now occurs as follows:

1. The error occurs, triggering the ExternalException event.
2. If the ExternalException event has no script or its action argument is set to ExceptionFail!, the Error event occurs.
3. If the Error event has no script or its action argument is set to ExceptionFail!, the SystemError event occurs.
4. If the SystemEvent has no script, an application error occurs and PowerBuilder terminates the application.

System Error Handling

PowerBuilder has objects and events to handle system errors that occur at runtime. If a serious error occurs when executing an application (e.g., failure loading a dynamic library for one of the application external functions), PowerBuilder halts the application abnormally and displays a very unfriendly message to the user. (Windows sends the message to PowerBuilder, and PowerBuilder, in turn, displays the message.) A way to avoid issuing an unfriendly message is to use PowerBuilder's system event and error structure to trap the system errors and do some custom processing.

Within the application object, PowerBuilder has defined a SystemError event. When an execution error occurs, PowerBuilder automatically triggers this event (with the exception of the situations mentioned earlier, where the SystemError event does not occur until after the ExternalException and/or the Error event). If the SystemError event has a script, PowerBuilder executes the script and does not display a messagebox. From within the SystemError event, you can access the data within the message structure. Table 17.9 provides information about the message structure.

The structure lets you trap any of the PowerBuilder errors by using the error structure from within the SystemError event, and then you can provide custom processing.

You can test the script within the SystemError event by using the **SignalError( )** function. This function simply causes a SystemError event at the application level. Powersoft has made available a list of execution error numbers. You can trap these error numbers, as well as any others that you come up with, from within the SystemError event. Table 17.10 provides information about the execution error messages.

You may want to trap two of the error numbers and display a friendlier message to the user. The following script is an example of the code you could add to the application object's SystemError event:

```
Choose Case Error.Number
     Case 3 // Array boundary exceeded
         MessageBox("Oooops","The application accidentally burped, "&
                  +"please call the application "&
                  +"administrator.~nSee you soon!")
Case 14 // Error opening DLL library for external function
     MessageBox("Don't worry","The application has some minor "&
              +"problems. We are currently hunting "&
              +"down the developer.")
End Choose
Halt
```

Table 17.9   Information about the Message Structure

Item	Description
Number	An integer identifying the PowerBuilder error.
Text	A string containing the error message's text.
WindowMenu	A string containing the name of the Window or Menu object within which the error occurred.
Object	A string containing the name of the object within which the error occurred. If the error occurred within a window or menu, Object will be the same as WindowMenu.
ObjectEvent	A string containing the event for which the error occurred.
Line	An integer identifying the line on the script at which the error occurred.

Table 17.10   Information about the Execution Error Messages

Number	Description
1	Divide by zero.
2	Null object reference.
3	Array boundary exceeded.
4	Enumerated value is out of range for function.
5	Negative value encountered in function.
6	Invalid DataWindow row/column specified.
7	Unresolved external when linking reference.
8	Reference of array with NULL subscript.
9	DLL function not found in current application.
10	Unsupported argument type in DLL function.
12	DataWindow column type does not match GetItem type.
13	Unresolved attribute reference.
14	Error opening DLL library for external function.
15	Error calling external function.
16	Maximum string size exceeded.
17	DataWindow referenced in DataWindow object does not exist.
50	Application reference could not be resolved.
51	Failure loading dynamic library.

You may also choose to write the additional information that the error structure provides (e.g., the error text, window or menu name, object/control name, object event name, and line number) into an error log. You could use such a log as an audit trail for the person responsible for fixing the problem.

Error Handling When Calling Dynamic Link Libraries

When calling Dynamic Link Libraries (DLLs) or any other external library function, it is critical to do error checking. When calling the published APIs, it is important to study the return codes for each function and handle the errors accordingly. You can implement error handling in this situation by logging the errors in detail, so that the person responsible for correcting them can determine exactly what went wrong.

Nested Error Handling

There are several different ways to handle error messages programmatically. One method is to nest the code within the error-handling logic. The following example shows how to accomplish nested error handling:

```
If Not Function() Then
    If Not Function2() Then
        If Not Function3() Then
            Return Success
```

continues

```
            Else
                    Return Error
            End If
        Else
            Return Error
        End If
    Else
        Return Error
    End If
```

ImportFile Error Messages

You can use PowerBuilder's **ImportFile( )** function to demonstrate how PowerBuilder can display the error messages. To do this, you should write a function (**f_ImportFileMsg(l_error)**) that returns the error message's text as a string:

```
Choose Case l_error
    Case -3
            Return "Invalid argument"
    Case -4
            Return "Invalid input"
    Case -5
            Return "Could not open the file"
    Case -6
            Return "Could not close the file"
    Case -7
            Return "Error reading the text"
    Case -8
            Return "Not a .TXT file"
    Case Else
            Return ""
End Choose
```

A function like f_ImportFileMsg( ) can reduce the duplicate code within an application. The following code demonstrates how to use the f_ImportFileMsg( ) function:

```
Long     lError
lError = dw_1.ImportFile("textfile.TXT")
If lError < 0 Then
    MessageBox("ImportFile Error",f_ImportFileMsg(lError))
End If
```

You can create f_ImportFileMsg( ) within an ancestor object so all the descendant objects have access to it. This way, every time you call the ImportFile( ) function, the application simply calls f_ImportFileMsg( ) to handle the error messages.

Location of Error Logs

When an error occurs, the support person must be able to locate the exact line where the error occurred. Sometimes this is difficult, but you should give as much information as possible to the person responsible for resolving the error. One option is to display detailed information (including information similar to that provided within the error object) about a particular error to the user. However, this information may seem somewhat cryptic and unfriendly to the user. Writing this information to an error log is often a better alternative. Such an error log can be a file on the user's computer or on the network. Other options include printing to the closest printer or updating an application-specific error log table within the database.

A key thing to remember when designing an error log mechanism is how to handle the errors within the mechanism itself. For example, if the application writes an error log to a file on a network drive, and the drive suddenly becomes full, the error handling mechanism must detect this and act accordingly. The best way to approach this is to have some type of contingency plan in place for error logging.

Error Actions

It is often a good idea to centralize error processing by calling a series of generic error functions. There can be error functions that write detailed information in a log file, display error or warning messages, or return message numbers, for example. It is often a good idea to use a generic error-display function. You can use such a function to display all application errors, regardless of where the message text comes from.

Another issue concerns storing of the messages. You should store the error messages in a central location rather than hard-coding them within the application code. This simplifies maintenance and provides a way to access all the possible error messages from a single location.

Usually, you store the messages in a file or a database. Storing the messages in a database involves a risk because if an application cannot connect to the database, it cannot retrieve the error message. You can minimize the performance sacrifice of storing the error messages in a centralized location by loading the error messages into memory at login time. Although this increases the amount of time needed to log in, it eliminates the delay of retrieving a message every time the application needs it.

Action functions are an important aspect of error handling. You can divide application error messages into categories based on their severity level. It makes sense to have one category for each type of action. For example, you can group together errors for which you would want someone paged immediately. That way, when those actions take place, a specific category of error occurs. The types of error action functions an application can perform include dialing a pager number, leaving voice mail, sending an email message, writing to an error log, broadcasting a systemwide message, shutting down the system, and displaying an error message, to name a few. The application can handle all of these programmatically.

There are a number of ways to accomplish proper error handling. However to implement error handling, the important thing is that you must implement it throughout the application.

CHAPTER 18

Creating an Executable and Testing PowerBuilder Applications

The final step in putting together an application is creating an executable file. Power-Builder provides the options of compiling executables into either machine code or p-code when developing in a 32-bit environment (Windows 95 and Windows NT). Both options involve creating an .EXE file and building the external runtime libraries. When PowerBuilder compiles the executable into machine code, it creates Dynamic Link Library files (.DLLs). When PowerBuilder compiles the executable into p-code, Power-Builder generates Dynamic Library files (.PBDs). This is also the point at which Power-Builder binds all the external resources (bitmaps, icons, cursors, etc.).

This chapter discusses the following topics related to building an application executable:

- What happens when building the .EXE
- Using .PBDs or .DLLs
- The library search path
- Resource files
- Optimizing .PBLS
- The PowerBuilder Project painter
- Windows 95 considerations

This chapter will provide you with a good understanding of the issues and techniques related to creating executables in the PowerBuilder environment.

WHAT HAPPENS WHEN BUILDING THE .EXE

PowerBuilder 6 provides two ways to compile PowerBuilder source code when creating an executable: as machine code or as p-code. When PowerBuilder compiles the source code into machine code, PowerBuilder creates .DLLs and when PowerBuilder compiles the source code into p-code, PowerBuilder generates .PBDs.

When you build the executable code for an application, the compiled PowerBuilder objects can be a part of the .EXE file itself or part of a .PBD or .DLL file (depending on the code generation option you choose). PowerBuilder uses a PowerBuilder Resource (.PBR) file to include any dynamically referenced objects or any objects that are not automatically included by PowerBuilder into the .EXE, .PBD, or .DLL files.

When building the .EXE, PowerBuilder copies all the referenced compiled objects from the .PBLs listed within the application's library search path that are *not* declared to be external libraries (.PBDs or .DLLs). By default, PowerBuilder creates the .EXE in the directory where the .PBLS containing the application object resides. You can change this location by selecting a different directory when building the executable. The .EXE contains the following:

- A Windows bootstrap routine
- Compiled code for all the referenced objects in the .PBLs listed in the application's library search path
- The application icon (optional)
- All the external resources listed in the .EXE's .PBR file

Machine Code versus P-Code

PowerBuilder 6 comes bundled with the Watcom C++ compiler. This gives you the option of generating either 16- or 32-bit machine code. However, you can still choose to generate the executable in p-code as with PowerBuilder's previous versions. One of the benefits of being able to compile the executable directly into machine code is that it lets the executable run faster since the computer can execute machine code directly. On the other hand, the computer cannot execute the p-code directly but requires a runtime interpreter, which is a small program incorporated into the executable file. Programs compiled into p-code are slower than the programs compiled into machine code.

In addition to speed considerations, the executable's size depends on whether you generate machine code or p-code. Machine code executables can be much larger than their p-code equivalents.

Using .PBDs or .DLLs

.PBDs function in much the same way as Windows .DLL files, that is, they allow the dynamic linking of the code into an application at runtime. The main difference between them is that the .DLL is compiled machine code. During the generation of the executable, PowerBuilder converts the .PBDs into .DLLs. A .PBD contains the compiled PowerBuilder objects plus any resources specified within the application's .PBR file. Like an .EXE, the compiled objects within a .PBD are copied from the .PBLS listed in the application's library search path. At runtime, PowerBuilder loads the individual objects from a .PBD or .EXE into memory only as they are needed.

The ability to distribute the objects among the .EXE and .PBDs or .DLLs provides some flexibility with regard to memory usage and other performance considerations. For example, within a simple application, you could increase performance by including all the objects and resources within the .EXE and not using any .PBDs or .DLLs. Obviously, performance depends on such things as the client workstation's configuration and network and the .EXE file's size. As a general guideline, Powersoft recommends that an .EXE file be no larger than 1.5 MB and that a .PBL be smaller than 800K and contain no more than 60 objects.

For most medium- to large-scale applications, it is recommended that you use .PBDs or .DLLs. In addition to the benefits of dynamic linking, .PBDs and .DLLs reduce the .EXE file's size and break an application down into smaller, more manageable parts. The authors have found it best to group objects into .PBLs (and subsequently into .PBDs and .DLLs) based on their functionality. This allows objects that are often used together to exist within a common file, which makes bug fixes and upgrades easier to manage and distribute. This is true because the changes made to an object within a .PBD or .DLL require only the rebuilding of the .PBD or .DLL file, not the complete rebuilding of the .EXE. A rebuilding of the .EXE usually takes more time and resources. When you make the change and rebuild the .PBD or .DLL, you need to deliver only this file to users. Different PowerBuilder applications can also share the .PBDs and .DLLs, which provides code reusability.

Another consideration to keep in mind when generating executables that use .DLLs is that you will still need to have the PowerBuilder runtime environment installed on the client for these executables to run. Also, other external applications cannot call the PowerBuilder-generated .DLLs.

TIP Because global variables and external function calls in an application object can change, including the application object in a .PBD or .DLL can reduce the number of times you need to rebuild an .EXE.

The Library Search Path

An application's library search path is very important, and it is often overlooked when building a PowerBuilder application. It is important because it dictates the path Power-Builder follows when searching for objects during execution. When retrieving an object, PowerBuilder first looks in the .EXE file. If the object is not found there, PowerBuilder searches each .PBD or .DLL in the order they are listed in the application's library search path. As such, the order of the .PBLs within the library search path becomes a significant factor in application performance. To enhance the performance, the .PBLs containing the most often used objects should be put at the top of the library search list.

TIP PowerBuilder caches the location of the objects. The next time the application uses an object, PowerBuilder knows exactly where to get the object from.

Resource Files

You can include resources such as bitmaps, compressed bitmaps, icons, and cursors as part of the .EXE file or as part of any application's .PBD or .DLL. Including these files prevents the developers and system administrators from having to distribute these files separately. To specify which files PowerBuilder will include as part of an .EXE, .PBD, or .DLL, create an ASCII file (usually with a .PBR extension) with each resource listed on a separate line. For example, the .PBR file to include the two bitmaps insert.bmp and delete.bmp looks like this:

```
C:\BMP\INSERT.BMP
C:\BMP\DELETE.BMP
```

One important thing to note is the way the resource is referenced within the .PBR file is the exact way you must reference the resource throughout the application. In the preceding example, you must reference the resource listed as C:\BMP\INSERT.BMP as C:\BMP\INSERT.BMP within the application.

TIP A good way to avoid problems and confusion when creating the .PBR file is to keep all the resource files in a single directory. You can use this directory when referencing the resources.

A .PBR file can also include PowerBuilder DataWindow objects. To specify the Data-Window, list its .PBL's name followed by the DataWindow's name within parentheses:

```
C:\PB\COMMON.PBL(d_clock)
```

TIP To dynamically change a DataWindow control's DataWindow object, the DataWindow object must exist within a .PBD, .DLL, or .PBR file.

If you create an executable with no .PBDs and your application associates a DataWindow object to a DataWindow control dynamically (e.g., dw_1.dataobject = 'd_loan'), you must include the DataWindow object's name within a .PBR file. Since the DataWindow's name is enclosed in quotes, the PowerBuilder compiler does not know to include the DataWindow within the executable. On the other hand, if you create an executable and .PBDs for your application and your application associates a DataWindow object to a DataWindow control dynamically, you do not need to include the DataWindow object's name in a .PBR file.

After creating the .PBR file, you can link the file to the .EXE or to a .PBD by specifying the file in the Project painter window, as shown in Figure 18.1.

TIP To avoid rebuilding the .EXE file to accommodate a change within a .PBR file, bind the .PBR file to a .PBD rather than the .EXE. When done this way, PowerBuilder treats a change within the .PBR file the same as a change to an object of the .PBD. You need to rebuild only the .PBD file to which you have bound the .PBR file.

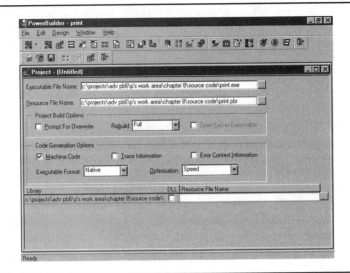

Figure 18.1   Linking a .PBR file to an .EXE by using the Project painter.

Optimizing .PBLs

.PBLs are linked lists containing both source code and compiled code for each of the PowerBuilder object types. During the course of development, as you create, modify, and delete objects, the object data's storage and indexes can become inefficient and disorganized. For example, when you delete an object from a .PBL, PowerBuilder removes the *references* to the object from the .PBL, but the code for the object still exists.

Optimizing cleans up the .PBL by removing the code for any deleted objects and reorganizing the object storage and indexes within the .PBL. You should optimize at regular intervals throughout the development cycle and immediately before building an executable. To optimize a .PBL, highlight the .PBL and then select the **Optimize** option from the **Library** menu in the Library painter.

THE POWERBUILDER PROJECT PAINTER

To create PowerBuilder executables, use the Project painter. This section discusses the Project painter's options. Before building an executable, there are certain variables you may want to consider:

- You can reduce the time it takes to build the .EXE by increasing the amount of memory on the machine where you the build the .EXE. The larger the application, the more memory is needed. If a great deal of disk activity occurs while building the .EXE or it takes a particularly long time to build the .EXE, consider adding more memory to the machine.
- Copy all the .PBLs to your hard disk. This speeds up the building of the .EXE by eliminating network delays. In addition, be sure to modify the library search path to point to the .PBLs on the local disk.

- Based on the authors' experience, it is best if all of the application objects go through at least two regeneration cycles prior to building the executable. You can use the library painter for the first regeneration. To do this, select **Design, Full Rebuild** from the Library painter's menu. The Project painter automatically performs the second regeneration of the application objects prior to building the executable. This two-cycle regeneration of the application objects resolves any pointer inconsistencies between them. Such inconsistencies can exist between objects that reference each other, such as ancestor and descendant objects in an application that uses inheritance.
- Optimize all the .PBLs. You can do this within the Library painter by selecting **Library, Optimize** from the menu.

Building the Executable

PowerBuilder 6's Project painter consolidates creating the executables into one screen. To create a project for an application, click on the **Project** icon on the PowerBar and select the **New** option. PowerBuilder prompts you to select an executable file to work with. The default is the current PowerBuilder application name. You can overwrite this with a new name if you want your executable file's name to be different from your PowerBuilder application name. After choosing the appropriate directory and executable file name, click on the **Save** option. You will now be in the Project painter (see Figure 18.1).

Executable and Resource Filenames

The Project painter's first section lets you change the executable file's name and the directory into which PowerBuilder will place the .EXE and the accompanying .PBDs (or .DLLs). This first section also lets you associate a .PBR file with the .EXE (see the section "Resource Files" later in this chapter).

Project Build Options

The Project painter gives you the ability to provide notification that you are overwriting the existing .EXE or .PBDs. There is also now an option to perform full or incremental builds of your executables (see Figure 18.2). Choosing the full option will generate a completely new .EXE and .PBDs associated with the executable. The incremental option will build a new .EXE, but it will only build the new .PBDs if you have changed the source within the corresponding .PBLs. To create a Sybase Open Server application, you can use the **Open Server Executable** option. This lets the application communicate with one or more Sybase database systems. For more information on Sybase Open Server, see Chapter 2, "Application Architectures."

Figure 18.2   Specifying a full or incremental build by using the Project painter.

Code Generation Options

As discussed earlier, you can generate machine code executables by using Power-Builder 6. All of the options in this section deal mainly with this feature. If you do not choose the machine code option, PowerBuilder generates the traditional p-code and .PBDs for any libraries you choose. When you choose the machine code option, there is some flexibility with how you can build your executables. You can choose the trace and error context information as part of your code generation options. When developing in a 32-bit environment (Windows 95 and Windows NT), you also have the ability to generate either 16- or 32-bit executables (see Figure 18.3). Options are also available for optimizing your executable for speed and size (see Figure 18.4).

Libraries

The Project painter's final section lets you choose the libraries to compile into .PBDs or .DLLs. PowerBuilder displays all the libraries defined within the current application path. You can choose a library by checking its corresponding .PBD column. Also at this point, you can associate a .PBR file with a particular .PBD. Note that for any library you do not choose within this section, PowerBuilder will bind all the objects within that library to the .EXE file (see the section *Using .PBDs or .DLLs* later in this chapter).

Windows 95 Considerations

This section discusses some considerations when developing in a Windows 95 environment.

Autoexec.bat and the Windows 95 Registry The PowerBuilder installation process no longer supports updating the autoexec.bat file with the path information. If you choose the 32-bit installation option that supports long file names, you will need to create or modify the path information for your executable that is recorded in the Registry. You can find this information by using the regedit.exe utility and drilling down the following directory structure:

```
HKEY_LOCAL_MACHINE
    SOFTWARE
        MICROSOFT
            WINDOWS
                CURRENT VERSION
                    APPPATHS
```

Figure 18.3   **Generating the 16-bit or 32-bit executables.**

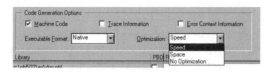

Figure 18.4   Optimizing an executable for speed or size.

If you choose the 32-bit installation option that supports short filenames (the 8.3 naming convention), you can edit your autoexec.bat and add the relevant PowerBuilder directories to your path.

16-bit Executables and Windows 95 PowerBuilder 6's 32-bit version lets you create 16-bit executables. Be aware that these executables will not run unless you install the 16-bit PowerBuilder runtime .DLLs on the client.

In conclusion, an executable PowerBuilder application will usually be a combination of an .EXE file and one or more .PBD files (.DLLs if you choose the machine code option). This method lets you distribute the objects among the different files, providing a degree of modularity, flexibility, and tuning capability. You should determine an application's size and nature before deciding the best method of distributing the Power-Builder objects and external resources among the .EXE and .PBDs or .DLLs. These decisions can affect your application's performance and maintainability.

TIP You can also generate proxy objects by using PowerBuilder 6's Project painter. To learn more about proxy objects and how to create them, see Chapter 22, "Distributed Application Development," and Chapter 23, "Advanced Distributed Application Development."

The PowerBuilder Virtual Machine

With PowerBuilder 6, Powersoft has renamed the PowerBuilder runtime environment the *PowerBuilder Virtual Machine* (PVM). Just as you need the Java Virtual Machine (JVM) to run Java applications on the client, you need the PVM on the client to run PowerBuilder applications. With PowerBuilder 6, Powersoft has reduced the number of runtime files your PowerBuilder application needs on the client machine. Note that Powersoft has reduced the number of files needed, not the total size. A small number of runtime files makes the distribution environment easier and manageable. In addition, the 16-bit runtime files have different names than the 32-bit runtime files. This helps reduce or eliminate the confusion involved with distributing 16-bit and 32-bit versions of the same application.

Component Generators

PowerBuilder 6 supports component generators. You can use the component generators to create components such as C++ classes, ActiveX controls, and so on from the custom class user objects. The C++ class generator comes with the PowerBuilder 6 Enterprise Edition. To generate ActiveX controls, you must buy and install the appropriate component generator from Powersoft. Similarly, to generate Java components, you must buy and install the appropriate component generator from Powersoft. Depending on the component generators installed on your machine, the Project painter displays the appropriate choices. You can also use the Project painter to generate proxy objects for your application.

PowerBuilder Synchronization Tool

In addition, PowerBuilder 6 includes a new synchronization tool called PBSync. By using and configuring PBSync on the client, you can synchronize the PVM files on the client automatically with the patch upgrades. PBSync can synchronize the files from the following three locations:

FTP.   ftp://ftp.powersoft.com

Local drive.   c:\directory\filename

Server on the network.   \\panther\common\filename

You can synchronize the PVM upon startup (by using the PowerBuilder Synchronization executable, pbsyncrt.exe) or from within the application when the user starts the application (by using the PowerBuilder Synchronization ActiveX control, pbsync.ocx). You can pass a synchronization data file to the synchronization executable. PBSync includes both the 16-bit and 32-bit versions of the executable and ActiveX control. In addition, PBSync includes a synchronization editor (pbpbsync.exe) you can use to create the synchronization data file.

TESTING POWERBUILDER APPLICATIONS

This section provides a sample testing methodology for PowerBuilder client/server applications. The development of increasingly complex PowerBuilder applications is bringing to light the need for more effective software testing and quality assurance (QA). Among the several challenges we face in developing client/server applications are new GUIs (graphical user interfaces), which replace the traditional character-based nonmodal interfaces; a wider variety of development tools and platforms; multiuser systems across heterogeneous networks; multiprocessor systems connected through highly layered communications protocols; distributed processing on a central database; and concurrent processing on client workstations. When confronted with application testing, developers must meet the challenges of test design for adequate testing coverage, a central testing repository, and management and control of the testing process. Some testing tools currently exist to assist in this effort, but overall, the problem being faced in testing requires an entirely new approach to the testing process. This section covers the following topics:

- Testing relative to the system development life cycle (SDLC)
- Application test stages
- Unit test
- Integration test

- External interface test
- Security/error test
- System test
- Performance test
- Documentation test
- User Acceptance test
- Regression test
- Testing tools
- Stress/performance test plan

You will find sample testing forms at the end of the chapter.

Testing Relative to the Systems Development Life Cycle (SDLC)

The testing effort is as important as the systems development life cycle (SDLC). That's why you must fully integrate the testing effort with the entire SDLC. Testing should parallel the design and development process. You should not isolate testing within one phase of development as a step that occurs after programming.

Testing has its own life cycle. Figure 18.5 shows the systems development life cycle (SDLC) relative to the systems testing life cycle's (STLC) phases. Systems testing begins when you deliver the system requirements document, and it continues for the life of the system.

The STLC phases are as follows:

Planning.   The test planning phase begins when you deliver the system requirements document. This phase establishes the test strategy.

Design.   The test design phase overlaps with the planning phase. It begins during the SDLC's design phase, after you have defined the system's test objectives and approaches.

Execution.   The testing execution phase begins when you complete the programming of the individual code modules. At this point, you must have completed both the SDLC and STLC design phases.

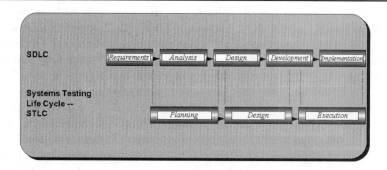

Figure 18.5   **Integration of testing within the SDLC.**

Reprinted by permission from *Testing Client/Server Applications*, Patricia Goglia, QED, 1993.

At times, you can address testing during design and even during the later stages of the system requirements phase. To ensure you can adequately test an application, a PowerBuilder application's design should take into account the complexities of testing across multiple platforms, the variety of communications protocols the application uses, and the mixture of development tools you use. You should also consider the other characteristics peculiar to the way you have implemented the client/server system.

Additional considerations that have not changed with the introduction of client/server but are essential to a successful testing effort are avoiding the last-minute crunch to get an application tested, the scheduling of adequate resources, the development of test data that fully exercises all the business scenarios (before you release the application), and managing the integration of the different testing phases (to avoid schedule dependencies).

Taking all of this into account and dividing systems testing into phases, with the planning and design phases beginning well before programming starts, achieves several goals:

- Allocate adequate time for planning, design, and documenting test criteria and results.
- Allocate sufficient lead time and knowledge to write or acquire testing tools.
- Design the test conditions from the system requirements document, not the program specifications or the code itself.

The last item is key. Design the test conditions early within the SDLC. You can use them as examples during design reviews. Users can use them to verify that the requirements definition is complete, and developers can use them to verify that the design supports the identified requirements.

Application Test Stages

Application test means an application's testing in its entirety. The application test includes a number of different stages. This chapter uses the terms *application test* and *test* interchangeably. Figure 18.6 shows how the different application test stages relate to each other. The application testing's first stage is the unit test, which the developer performs as the developer completes each module. As the developer successfully unit tests the additional modules, the integration test stage can begin. This stage tests the different modules of the system working together. Because you often perform the integration test only with the system's internal pieces, you must perform an external interface test. Perform the external interface test to test the PowerBuilder application's links with the system's different external pieces such as email, fax, and imaging. In addition, use this stage to test the interface between the new application and existing applications.

The application testing's next phase includes testing the system's security and error handling. Consider these two pieces as a separate stage within the testing process because of their importance and scope. The next stage is the system test, which is the first time you test the application as a whole. When you complete the system testing (or during its later stages), implement the performance and stress testing. During this phase, examine the system's performance and each individual module to make sure everything is running at optimal speed. The performance testing stage applies not only to the PowerBuilder application but to the system's other components, including the application servers and RDBMS.

At this point, you must perform documentation testing. This testing stage checks for appropriate online and hard-copy documentation. This testing stage also examines the system's user-friendliness. The less friendly the system is, the more documentation you will require. Alternatively, you can modify the system to provide a friendlier interface.

The application testing's last stage is the user acceptance test. During this testing stage, the system's end users test the system to make sure it meets their requirements and that it presents the correct data/information. You should use the user acceptance testing stage to get the user group(s)'s sign-off (final system approval).

During the testing process, if you make any modifications to the system's pieces that you have already tested, you must perform a regression test. The STLC's regression test stage can occur at any time during the testing process. As Figure 18.6 shows, regression testing may be necessary during any or all of the testing stages.

The sections that follow discuss the application testing's different stages in detail.

Unit Test

The client/server world defines a *unit* as a logical unit of work. You should develop test cases for all the logical units based on all the functional and performance requirements. Design documentation provides a good framework to begin building the unit test cases. You should develop and test the critical units first. When you have developed a test unit, you can add the additional test cases and testing can begin. Add additional white and black box test cases to the test plan during the design and development phases as they arise.

Unit testing is an iterative process that is not complete until you have tested all the test cases with perfect results. Although you cannot be absolutely certain that software will never fail, by using statistical methods, you can determine when you have completed sufficient testing. Numerous units undergo unit testing in parallel. Identifying the units that closely interact helps determine the scheduling dependencies. To facilitate integration testing, manage the unit testing closely.

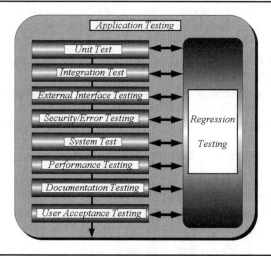

Figure 18.6   Relationship of the application test stages.

White box testing uses the knowledge of the unit's internal design to develop the test cases, and it is generally done for the following:

Interfaces.   Ensure information properly flows into and out of the unit.

Logical paths.   Ensure you have tested all the logical paths, including error trapping.

Local data structures.   Ensure the data you store temporarily maintains its integrity.

Boundary conditions.   Ensure proper operation at the boundaries established to limit or restrict processing.

Black box testing assumes no knowledge of a unit's internal design and focuses on testing the functional and performance requirements.

During both white and black box testing, document the test cases with a set of expected results. Because a unit is not a stand-alone program, you need to create drivers and stubs. Drivers emulate the higher-level program structures that invoke a unit. Stubs emulate any subroutines that a unit invokes. Creating drivers and stubs represents an overhead, so you should manage them judiciously.

Integration Test

Integration testing is a systematic technique for combining the unit-tested modules and building the program structure according to the system design while conducting tests to uncover errors associated with combining these units. Use the string testing methods to combine the tested units into the system structure. The string testing combines the units that have directly related inputs and outputs. After successful testing of the interfaces between the two related units, add the third and test it, then a fourth, and so on. This iterative approach creates clusters of related units that you then integrate into the entire system's structure.

Use simulated inputs and environmental conditions to perform integrated units' volume and stress tests. Limit the integration testing to internal interfaces. If external interfaces are necessary for data inputs or environmental conditions, simulate them carefully to adequately control the testing environment.

The proper approach and timing of integration testing depends both on the kind of system you build and the nature of your development project. Enhancements to existing systems and entirely new systems have very different requirements related to integration testing. In addition, very large systems generally have several relatively large components that you can build and integrate separately before combining them into a full system.

The two main types of integration testing that help dictate when you should perform integration testing are nonincremental and incremental.

Nonincremental.   Combine all the units at once, and test the entire system as a whole. This is usually referred to as the "big bang approach."

Incremental.   Link together the related units, and test them in small segments or clusters. After all the interfaces and functional tests are passed for the tested segments, add new units. Modify the test cases, test scripts, control drivers, and test stubs, and perform all the interfaces and functional tests again. Repeat this iterative process until you have combined all the units. You can conduct incremental testing in parallel with the unit testing and development as soon as you have successfully tested some related units.

Perform nonincremental integration testing on small or simple systems or on simple enhancement projects.

External Interface Test

Perform external interface testing to ensure that the interfaces to other systems function properly. Some applications interface with other applications by using DDE, OLE, the Clipboard, and/or Windows messages. There are also times when an application simply executes other applications. Other major areas that you must include within the external interface test are the external interfaces that extend beyond the user's workstation, that is, when there are applications running on the remote servers or other workstations. These include the links between the applications—to make sure the two applications connect without timing out and to test the time it takes for one application to connect to the other. Other areas that you must test vary based on the specific external application interfaces.

Security/Error Test

Because it is best to isolate security and error-checking into separate modules within a PowerBuilder system, give special attention to the security and error-checking modules when testing. That is why they are a separate testing phase within the STLC. Perform security testing to ensure that the system is protected from improper penetration. You must perform error testing for a number of reasons.

Error Messages Must Read Properly   It is important that error messages display a descriptive, friendly message. The error message in Figure 18.7, for example, should not be considered acceptable.

Substitute a message, such as the one in Figure 18.8, for this unfriendly message. Write any detailed information about the error that the system administrator needs to resolve the problem to a log file.

Error messages can include more specific information than the message Figure 18.8 shows, but they should be friendly to the user. During the error testing process, review all the error messages to ensure they read properly and align correctly.

Display Error Messages When a Particular Error Occurs   The next thing you must test is that the application displays the correct message when a particular error occurs.

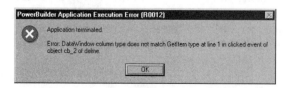

Figure 18.7   An unacceptable error message.

Figure 18.8   An acceptable error message.

Generate Error Logs Properly Sometimes developers choose to create error logs or dumps when an error occurs. Error logs should specifically detail the exact nature of the error encountered. The error log must show the details that will be helpful to the system administrator, who must understand and then fix the problem.

Error Actions Must Work Correctly When an error occurs, several different things could happen: display a message for the user, create or update an error log, send an email message to the appropriate support person automatically, page or call a support person immediately. Depending on the error's severity, different combinations can occur. In any case, perform the appropriate tests to ensure all the error actions work as planned.

System Test

Execute the system test after completing the integration testing and before starting the acceptance testing. System testing is critical because you test and review the entire system as an entity. Test the client workstation, the LAN, the WAN, the gateway(s), the file and application server(s), the RDBMS server(s), and all the other components that make up the system for the intended functionality. This testing stage ensures not only that the system functions correctly but that the system functions based on the requirements the system's users supplied. Test the functional requirements before handing the system over to users for acceptance testing to detect any obvious problems that could embarrass the development team.

Performance Test

Performance testing is an entire integrated system's runtime test. During this stage, perform a series of stress tests. Test the system's various pieces for performance and stress.

Each piece of a system typically has its own unique tools for testing or monitoring activity. The network, for example, has LAN analyzers you can use to monitor data, stress, usage, and the like. The RDBMS engine has different tools for monitoring activity within the engine during testing.

To monitor a system's performance, it is useful to simulate the absolute maximum number of users that could potentially be using the system at one time. You can do this by using a workstation for each potential user and running through the application manually or by using a recording tool. If the number of workstations or people to execute the application are not available for testing, write simulation applications to assist in the process. To simulate 40 users with only 8 workstations, for example, run 5 instances of the simulation application on each of the 8 workstations.

To test a PowerBuilder application's performance, you can do a number of things. Identify the major parts of the system where performance could be an issue. Some of those areas can be:

- The login process
- Security verification
- Window creation and display
- Retrieving the data
- Updating the data
- Interfacing with the external modules (e.g., email, word processor, fax, etc.)
- Printing

To test a PowerBuilder application's performance, it is helpful to have a function that tracks a particular action's execution time. Call this function before and after the action occurs in the application. Calling this function before and after an action provides the developer with the elapsed time the tested action takes to execute. For example, the following PowerBuilder function, **f_timestamp( )**, writes the system time to a log file.

The PowerScript for an f_timestamp(String sMSG) function is as follows:

```
integer iFileHandle

// open the error log file
iFileHandle = FileOpen(g_sLogFile, LineMode!, Write!)

// perform error checking
FileWrite(iFileHandle, sMSG + "~t" + String(Today()) + "-" + &
    String(Now()))

// close the error log file
FileClose(iFileHandle)
```

To use f_timestamp( ) to track the time required to retrieve the data into a DataWindow, place a call before and after the **retrieve( )** function:

```
f_timestamp("Start Retrieve dw_Persons")
dw_persons.Retrieve()
f_timestamp("End Retrieve dw_Persons")
```

When you execute this program, use an error log file that the tester has created to analyze the performance statistics. The tester can modify f_timestamp( ) to gather other information such as the system resources, memory, and GDI count. You can do this by calling the Windows SDK **GetFreeSystemResources( )** function. Alternatively, or in addition, you can call the **GetFreeSpace( )** function for other system information.

For an example of a stress and performance test plan, see the test plan provided later in this chapter.

Documentation Test

This may seem to be a trivial test stage, but it is not. This test assesses the written documentation and online help's user-friendliness to facilitate the system operation. To do this test, choose random users who do not have any experience with the application. Ask them to use the system and see if the interface is intuitive enough for them to be productive. If they have difficulty, they should refer to the online and written documentation to figure out how to use the application. Assess their ease and success with the documentation, and change the parts they have difficulty with.

User Acceptance Test

User acceptance testing is the validation of all the system requirements. Normally, users perform the user acceptance test within their environment. If it is not practical to have the end users perform this function, as with packaged software, you can test it in-house within an internal application environment or substitute the alpha and beta testing for user acceptance testing (users usually conduct alpha testing at the developer's site; users usually conduct beta testing at their site). User acceptance testing is usually the final test.

Create a user acceptance, alpha, or beta test plan. Test all aspects of the system for ease of use and functionality. Users should systematically execute the tests and document the results.

Regression Testing

Application testing is both progressive and regressive. The progressive phase introduces and tests the new functions, uncovering problems within or related to the recently added modules. The regressive phase concerns the effects of the changes you recently introduced into a module, on all the previously integrated (and tested) code. Problems arise when errors made in incorporating the new functions have an effect on the previously tested functions. Regression testing is particularly important in software maintenance, where it is not uncommon for bug fixes within one module to disrupt seemingly unrelated functions. The process of regression testing often uncovers new functional problems as well. Regression testing is impossible unless you have kept detailed records of past testing and you have structured all the software maintenance efforts. Focus your attention on a system's critical modules when performing regression testing.

You can perform the regression testing at any level (unit, integration, or system). What makes a test a *regression test* is that you have introduced changes or new modules or functions to previously tested areas. You can either run the groups of regression tests periodically or after you have made a change.

The integration test plan is invaluable during software maintenance when regression tests are necessary. A detailed history of all tests, bugs found and fixed, and expected and actual results reduces the effort required for regression testing and enhances a change or correction's overall quality. The following is an effective approach to regression testing you can use during production as well as for long-term maintenance:

1. Identify both a comprehensive set of regression tests for the entire system and two kinds of subsets for every module. The first subset for each module is a collection of tests for the new units or functions you introduced; the other is a sample set from the full set of regression tests for the system, selected with this module's functionality in mind. Base your selection of these subsets on the complexity of the individual areas you will test and on the success history of the test cases themselves. Keep in mind that regression problems often stem from rare business cases that you may have overlooked during the functional testing.

2. Run the comprehensive regression bucket periodically.
3. Run the subsets after you make every change.
4. It is important to remember that you may need new test cases when system maintenance adds functionality to a system.

Testing Tools

This section discusses the use of testing tools within the testing process.

Automated Testing Tool(s) for Unit Testing

Using an automated testing tool, even if the developers and testers have experience with the tool, actually increases the amount of time it takes to test a unit. Therefore, within initial unit testing, there is no time savings in using a testing tool. You can test a unit against the requirements documentation manually in much less time than it would take to "capture" a test script of a finished unit that you have already manually checked, and then execute and debug the test script to capture all the actual results. You will not recognize any time savings until later within integration and regression testing.

For reasons noted, however, the use of automated testing tools is recommended at this stage if you will also use the selected automated test tool for integration and system testing. If this is the case, write the unit test scripts with later testing phase needs in mind.

Automated Testing Tool(s) for Integration and System Testing

This is where you can recognize the benefits of using automated testing tools. The accuracy and efficiency of having a tool execute a long series of test steps and record the actual results is where you can realize the time savings with testing tools. However, testing the integration of a number of units by using an automated testing tool is effective only if you have developed test scripts for those units. Of course, you cannot use the scripts used for unit testing for integration testing, you can use only parts of them. In addition, if it becomes necessary to test a unit that you had to modify as a result of integration testing, you can reexecute the old unit test scripts. Therefore, using a testing tool within integration and system testing has benefits, but if you don't have the complete unit test scripts, the time savings start to slip away.

Time Savings

As just mentioned, the accuracy and efficiency of having an automated test tool results in several benefits. Manual testers get tired, bored, and do not execute the tests exactly the same way each time. Therefore, you can significantly enhance the testing's quality within any development effort by using the testing tools. This is most dramatic within regression testing. For example, if a developer implemented an order entry system with the assumption that the "unit of measure" is dozen and the company later changes its policy to a new unit of measure (eaches), what will the system impact be? The developer makes the necessary database and programming changes, but now there are approximately 20 different windows and reports that use the unit of measure. The dream is to have a repository of test scripts that take the developer and tester all the way through the unit tests, and on through to the system tests. Only then will the developer and tester feel comfortable that the impact of that change is fully tested.

Third-Party Testing Tools

A number of vendors offer automated testing tools you can use to test PowerBuilder client/server and Web applications. Table 18.1 lists some of these tools. The tools from Rational Corporation and Mercury Interactive are quite popular in the PowerBuilder developer community.

Implementing a Testing Tool

It is important to capitalize on any and all time savings and quality enhancements by testing with an automated tool. The problem is that developers get frustrated with having to develop the system and then develop all the test scripts. You can avoid this frustration by including the test script development in the project plan and schedule. Note that as soon as you have climbed the testing tool learning curve, you have completed the hard work. Including the testing tool in subsequent testing phases and projects has less and less impact on the project time.

One way to start using the testing tools is to take the following steps:

1. Staff a development effort with consideration of rolling some of the developers (the ones that usually roll off the project early) into a testing team.
2. Test all the modules to the requirements manually.
3. Give the tested modules to the testing team. They then develop the complete module unit test scripts, begin putting together the required test data, and begin developing the integration and system test plans and associated test scripts.

Having done this, the test team has familiarity with the project and the relevant business needs. In addition, the test scripts tend to depersonalize the testing, thus avoiding the pride-of-authorship problems that sometimes result in testers going easy on their own code.

The testing team wraps up after the system's full testing and implementation. As the final deliverable, they produce the regression testing approach, complete with a repository of test scripts from unit to full system test.

This or a similar approach takes advantage of the automated testing tools while minimizing the investment in time and resources. The obvious benefit is that a group

Table 18.1   Automated Testing Tools

Vendor	URL
Rational	www.rational.com/products/sqasuite/
Mercury Interactive	www.merc-int.com/products/
Segue Software	www.segue.com/
Cyrano	www.cyrano.com
McCabe & Associates	www.mccabe.com/

of people develop a new set of skills, not only in testing in general but with using an automated testing tool(s).

Sample Stress/Performance Test Plan

This test plan was originally written for a real-world PowerBuilder development project for a real business.

Stress tests attempt to determine an application's performance thresholds. Performance tests emulate a production environment (before the new application is put into production) to ascertain if the new system's performance is acceptable. The information you collect from these tests will help reduce the risk associated with implementing the new application.

Stress Test

The stress test helps avoid unforeseen performance problems within the existing LAN architecture that could occur when the new application goes into production. The stress test's goal is to quantify the new application's incremental impact on the LAN architecture. The stress test attempts to define performance thresholds for application usage on the current LAN. Measure the following stress points as part of the stress test:

- RDBMS server/application server usage
- Network horizontal and vertical ring traffic
- Network bridging traffic
- File server performance
- Workstation performance

Approach The stress test should focus on creating stress on the network by systematically increasing the load placed on the network. To accomplish this, you can use application simulation programs to collect most of the stress test statistics. Because you execute the application simulation programs on workstations, this approach generates network traffic beyond the normal network load, or the steady-state load. You must attempt to quantify the incremental load placed on the network.

The application simulation approach simplifies the stress test's setup and execution. By using the application simulation approach, you can achieve more uniformity within the test results across test cycles. The application simulation program should use carefully selected excerpts of code from different parts of the real application. To simulate the new system's rapid and concurrent use, execute these code excerpts within a loop.

To the extent possible, collect and record electronically all the times you gather from the simulation application. The application simulator should also have the following features:

- A time interface to allow for execution synchronization across machines
- Programmatic collection of the runtime statistics (to the extent possible)
- A process to write the workstation execution statistics to a file

For the stress test cycles, eliminate the workstation configuration's variability. This will let you collect results that are more directly correlated to the tested stress points.

TIP You may need to conduct some stress test cycles outside of normal business hours. If you do this, you will need some way to generate a steady-state load on the network.

High-level Test Conditions The variables you should manipulate to stress the application are:

- Number of workstations simulating the application usage
- Number of database connections
- Number of concurrent database accesses

By increasing the values of these three conditions, measurable increases within the overall network traffic will occur.

Test Cycles For the stress test, a test cycle defines the number of times you need to execute the application simulation program to collect the desired information. This stress test has the following test cycles, as shown in Table 18.2.

Table 18.2   Stress Test Cycles

Cycle Number	Workstations	Database Connections	Maximum Concurrent Connections	Active Number of Executions
1	1	1	1	5
2	1	3	1	5
3	1	5	1	5
4	3	11	3	1
5	3	13	3	1
6	3	15	3	1
7	5	21	5	1
8	5	23	5	1
9	5	25	5	5
10	7	31	7	1
11	7	33	7	1
12	7	35	7	1
13	9	41	9	1
14	9	43	9	1
15	9	45	9	1
16	10	46	10	1
17	10	48	10	1
18	10	50	10	5
19	10	75	10	1
20	10	100	10	1

> **T**IP In the event that a test cycle fails to execute because a performance threshold is met, reexecute the test cycle up to five times. If the test cycle cannot be passed, reexecute the test cycle by using staggered execution times. Execute the remaining test cycles to the extent possible. Document all the configuration changes on a cycle-by-cycle basis.

The approach for increasing the number of database connections is to execute multiple instances of the application simulation program. Design the application simulation program to maintain the database connections until you have completed the entire test cycle.

Monitored Variables The variables you collect from each test cycle within the Stress Test will include those listed in Table 18.3.

Performance Test

The performance test measures the new system's user-perceived and actual performance. This test helps establish user expectations and helps drive the future workstation purchase decisions. You can measure performance by varying workstation configurations and recording the variations in execution times within the application. Also, you can evaluate the impact of increasing the number of users.

Approach The application performance test evaluates the application's performance from the user's perspective. This test collects the statistics as users proceed through the application. In addition, this test takes the workstation configuration variations into consideration. Unlike the stress test, you execute the application performance test by using the actual application (not a simulation). To collect the most significant results, configure the application as it will be within production. The only exception will be the minor modifications you have made to programmatically collect the required performance statistics (through file I/O).

High-Level Test Conditions The variables this test will manipulate are:

- Number of workstations using the application
- Workstation configuration variations

Test Cycles for Performance For the performance test, a test cycle is defined by the number of times the execution script is run. These test cycles vary the workstation configuration and the number of concurrent workstations using the application. Table 18.4 shows the planned test cycle.

Monitored Variables Determine the results from this portion of the test from the information in Table 18.5 collected from each application performance test cycle.

Application Simulation Program The stress test application simulation program should attempt to simulate the stress the new application will put on the LAN, appli-

Table 18.3 Variables for Each Test Cycle

Monitored Variable	Variable Tests	Collection Source	Calculation Method
Workstation throughput	Workstation configuration	Application simulator	Aggregate data throughput to workstation (kb) divided by total test cycle execution time
Server CPU usage (%)	RDBMS server configuration	Stored procedure executed at the end of each cycle	CPU utilization divided by total test cycle execution time
Server I/O usage (%)	RDBMS server configuration	Stored procedure executed at the end of each cycle	CPU I/O divided by total test cycle execution time
Server packets (packets/sec)	RDBMS server configuration	Stored procedure executed at the end of each cycle	Total packets (received + sent) divided by total test cycle execution time
Disk device utilization (%)	RDBMS server configuration	LAN administration	N/A
Network interface utilization (%)	RDBMS server configuration	LAN administration	N/A
Backbone utilization (%)	LAN architecture: utility ring	LAN administration	Bandwidth utilization as a percent of theoretical maximum (4 Mbs)
Bridge utilization (%)	LAN architecture: bridge utilization	LAN administration	Packets per second as a percent of theoretical maximum (14,000 pps)
Horizontal ring utilization (%)	LAN architecture: workstation ring	LAN administration	Bandwidth utilization as a percent of theoretical maximum (16M bps)
Server CPU usage (%)	File server configuration	LAN administration	Bandwidth utilization as a percent of theoretical maximum (16M bps)
Server I/O usage (%)	File server configuration	LAN administration	CPU I/O divided by total test cycle execution time
Server packets (packets/sec)	File server configuration	LAN administration	Total packet (received + send) divided by total test cycle execution time
Disk device utilization (%)	File server configuration	LAN administration	N/A
Network interface utilization (%)	File server configuration	LAN administration	N/A
File server configuration: OS/2	LAN administration	N/A	
Server response time	File server	LAN administration	Periodic snapshots of server response time
Server response time	RDBMS server	LAN administration	Periodic snapshots of server response time

Table 18.4 Test Cycles for Performance Test

Cycle Number	Number of Workstations	Workstation Configuration	Number of Executions
1	1	High	5
2	1	Medium	5
3	1	Low	5
4	3	High	5
5	3	Medium	5
6	3	Low	5
7	5	Mixed	5
8	7	Mixed	5
9	10	Mixed	5

Table 18.5 Information from Each Performance Test Cycle

Monitored Variable	Variable Tests	Collection Source	Calculation Method
Workstation throughput (kb/sec)	Workstation configuration	Application modification	Aggregate data throughput to workstation (kb) divided by total test cycle execution time
Workstation user resource usage (%)	User resource space used by the application	Application modification (call to Windows SDK)	N/A
Workstation GDI resources (%)	GDI resources used by the application	Application modification (call to Windows SDK)	N/A
Workstation memory (%)	Amount of global memory used by the application	Application modification (call to Windows SDK)	N/A

cation and database servers, and the RDBMS. The following section provides an example of the application flow.

Application Flow

1. The application starts execution when the workstation time is equal to or greater than the execution time SingleLineEdit.
2. The application establishes one connection.

3. The application executes the stored procedures against the database and records the time.

4. There will be some application input parameters. You must enter the following parameters on the front-end screen before the execution commences:

```
Workstation:      workstation type
RAM:              amount of workstation RAM
Loop Counter:     Max # of times to execute the loop
DB ID:            database login ID
Cycle #:          01
Workstation #:    01
Execution #:      01
Instance:         01
Time:             Execution time
```

Figure 18.9 shows the application's front-end screen.

Application Output The application simulation program creates an output file for each application within a test directory called outXXYY.txt, where:

```
XX = Workstation number, and
YY = Instance
```

Each file will look like the one in Figure 18.10.

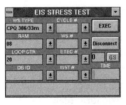

Figure 18.9   **The Stress Test simulation screen.**

	DATABASE ID : DEYHID01		
WORKSTATION: CPQ386-33M		WORKSTATION # : 1	
RAM: 12		INSTANCE: 1	
DATE: date|time		COUNTER : 10	
Loop Counter	**Task**	**Start Time**	**End Time**
01	RUNRATES	starttime	endtime
01	RUNRATES	starttime	endtime
01	RUNRATES	starttime	endtime
...	...	...	...
01	RUNRATES	starttime	endtime

Figure 18.10   **The simulation application's output file.**

SAMPLE TESTING FORMS

Following is a multi-unit testing form the authors have found useful:

APPLICATION NAME
MODULE UNIT TEST

Created By:
Date:
Modified By:
Date:
Status:
Conversation:
Developer:
Reviewer:
Date Performed:
Tested by:
Date:
Approved by:
Date:

Components Developed:

Name	Type

Reused Components:

Name	Type

Note to Tester:

Windows Used:

Main Window	PB Component Names

SECTION 1—STANDARDS

Test/Expected results *Selection Dialogs*	Actual Results	Initials	Date
Background is white			
Title should read "Please Select a [Object Name]"			

Test/Expected results *Windows*	Actual Results	Initials	Date
Background is white			
System menu			
Menu bar			
Minimize button			
Message line			

Test/Expected results *Scrolling DataWindows*	Actual Results	Initials	Date
Background is white			
Vertical scroll bar			

Test/Expected results *Non-Scrolling DataWindows*	Actual Results	Initials	Date
Background is white			
Fields are white with no border			

Test/Expected results *Group Boxes*	Actual Results	Initials	Date
Dark blue background with black border			
Heading text is white			

Test/Expected results *Buttons*	Actual Results	Initials	Date
Text is 13pt MS Sans Serif			
Text is black and bold			
Buttons are aligned and spaced evenly			

Test/Expected results *Background Text/Labels*	Actual Results	Initials	Date
Text is 13pt MS Sans Serif—**bold**			
Text is black (background should be the color of the DataWindow)			
No border			
Left position above and one character to the left of its entry field if associated w/ a field on a free form based DataWindow; centered if associated w/ a column of a tabular grid DataWindow			

Test/Expected results *Non-Editable Fields*	Actual Results	Initials	Date
Text is 13pt MS Sans Serif			
Text is black (background should be the color of the DataWindow)			
No border			
Left position for alphanumeric; Right positioned for numeric or fields validated to be numbers only			

Test/Expected results *Editable Fields*	Actual Results	Initials	Date
Text is 13pt MS Sans Serif			
Text is black on white background			
Use black border			
Left position for alphanumeric; Right positioned for numeric or fields validated to be numbers only			

Test/Expected results	Actual Results	Initials	Date
DropDownListBoxes			
Text is 13pt MS Sans Serif			
Text is black on white background			
No border			
Uneditable and use vertical scroll bar when all options aren't visible			

Test/Expected results	Actual Results	Initials	Date
Boolean or Single-Character Flag Fields			
Text is 13pt MS Sans Serif—**bold**			
Text is black on white			
No border			
CheckBox with values of Y = ON and N = OFF, and left justify			

Test/Expected results	Actual Results	Initials	Date
Mutually Exclusive Options			
Text is 13pt MS Sans Serif—**bold**			
Text is dark blue on white			
No border			
Radiobuttons and left justify			

Errors Found/Comments:

Sign-Off Initials/Date:

SECTION 2—FUNCTIONALITY

Part 1—Menu Options:

Test/Expected results—Menu Option	Actual Results	Initials	Date
File/New/Business Associate—Clears out Business Associate Window and puts user in "New" mode			
File/New/BA Address—Inserts new row into dw_all_addresses			
File/New/BA Contact—Inserts new row into dw_all_contacts			
File/Open—Clears out Business Associate Window and puts user in "Open" mode			
File/Save—Save changes to the database			
File/Remove/BA Deactivate—Sets current date into Deactivated Date column and saves changes to the database			
File/Remove/BA Address—Removes currently selected address			
File/Remove/BA Contact—Removes currently selected contact			
File/Exit—Close Business Associate Window			
Help/Context—Displays help specific to the module			
Help/General—Displays help specific to the module			
Help/Index—Displays the help index for ABC			
Help/About—Displays the System About box			

Part 2—Controls:

Test/Expected Results—Controls	Actual Results	Initials	Date

Errors Found/Comments:

Sign-Off Initials/Date:

SECTION 3—PROCESSING

Part 1—Error Processing—Validation/Required Fields

For required-fields testing, required columns should be left blank in the Data Entered section to ensure correct error messages are given. Each required field should be tested separately.

Description	Data Entered	Expected Error Message	Date/Initials
BA class is required	dw_main BA Number: 13 BA Class: BA Type: Corporate BA Name: A NEW BA	"Please select a BA class"	
Social Security number must be 9 digits	dw_main BA Number: 13 BA Class: Vendor BA Type: Corporate BA Name: A NEW BA SSN: 123456789	"Please enter a 9-digit social security number with no delimiters"	

Errors Found/Comments:

Sign-Off Initials/Date:

Part 2—Normal Processing

1) Data Retrieval—If fields are formatted differently for different conditions during data retrieval, each case must be tested separately.

Table Data	Expected Data Displayed on Window	Expected Formatting—Tab Orders, Menu Options, etc.	Date/Initials

Errors Found/Comments:

Sign-Off Initials/Date:

2) Data Update—Creating, modifying, and deleting a retrieved record should be tested separately.

Data Entered	Expected Database Results	Expected Formatting—Tab Orders, Menu Options, etc. after update	Date/Initials
New Record:			
Modified Record:			

Errors Found/Comments:

Sign-Off Initials/Date:

Part 3—Special Processing

Description	Data Entered	Expected Result	Date/Initials

Errors Found/Comments:

Sign-Off Initials/Date:

CHAPTER 19

PowerBuilder
Software Migration

When building applications, whether corporate systems or packaged software, the integrity of the code as it evolves from development to production is important. Because of the many components within a client/server environment, software migration is an important issue. This chapter explains a software migration life cycle, especially as it pertains to PowerBuilder. It is important to note that the life cycle/methodology discussed in this chapter is only one option. You must choose a software management methodology that best suits your needs. In addition, the tools mentioned in this chapter are not the only ones available. Again, you must choose the appropriate tool(s) that match your specific requirements.

This chapter discusses the following topics:

- Software development life cycle
- File types and locations
- Directory structure
- An example of a typical software management environment
- Version control interface
- Migration forms

SOFTWARE DEVELOPMENT LIFE CYCLE

Software migration is a process in which you save the individual code modules (to document the iterations of effort), and the code modules provide a framework from which you can assemble a release from all of its component parts. The software migration process begins after you have successfully unit tested the programs. Because the programs in production occasionally require maintenance, the migration process does not end until you no longer use the code. At every stage in between, the programmers must use the code's latest version.

As you develop an application, the application evolves. Each new version has more features and functionality. Before a software product becomes a fully released version, it goes through various stages of development and testing. A software package may go through various stages of release. At each stage, a controlled migration must occur.

When you have system tested an application (especially a software package), it typically migrates from the alpha to the beta testing stage, and then to the different release stages. PowerBuilder itself usually goes through a number of different release stages, which Powersoft calls *candidates,* and then on to final release, which Powersoft calls the *gold disk.* Alpha and beta are the stages during which you make the product available to a select few for review and testing. All the stages prior to the gold disk stage are usually not available to the general user community.

Each stage of development, testing, and release may be iterative. Normally, a developer checks out the object into his or her local development directory. When the developer completes and tests the code changes, the code is submitted to the object manager for review. When the object manager has tested the module(s), he or she checks the code into a shared area. After the modifications are complete for this phase, release, or version of the software, the code is submitted for system test. After system testing is successful, the code is moved into a staging area and the user test area. When the users sign off on the system, the application is moved to the production environment. This process is called the *software migration life cycle* (see Figure 19.1).

During the development's alpha stage, a number of iterations and/or steps must occur before a product is available as an alpha release, as depicted in Figure 19.2. The steps may include migration from a developer's local work area, obtaining the object manager's approval, system testing, user testing, and release.

Since a number of developers generally work on the different pieces of an application concurrently, it is imperative that each developer always work on the program's newest version. The common phraseology used within version control is *check in / check out.* Before working on a particular program, a developer must check the program out

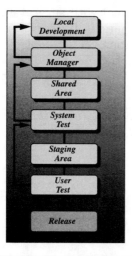

Figure 19.1   **The software migration life cycle.**

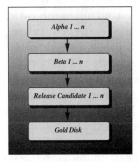

Figure 19.2   The development's alpha stage.

to his or her own work area. Ideally, this work area is a separate drive on the development network, but it can also be a local drive on the developer's workstation. When the developer has finished creating or fixing the code and it has been tested, he or she checks the code in. While a programmer has a piece of code checked out, no other programmer can work on it. A software management tool that helps manage the versions of each type of program is vital.

Applications within production and released software packages may go through a number of releases, as depicted in Figure 19.3.

Typically, when a version number changes to the next whole number, major changes have been made to the application. Putting all of the steps and iterations of software migration together, the process looks something like Figure 19.4. Success is guaranteed only through diligent tracking of each component within an application or software package.

File Types and Locations

When you build a client/server application, you deal with several different types of files. You can locate these files on individual workstations, file servers, and/or database servers. The person responsible for software migration/version control must be very familiar with all the different files that the application needs and where they reside. Table 19.1 lists some file types that may be part of a PowerBuilder application.

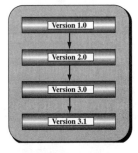

Figure 19.3   The software releases.

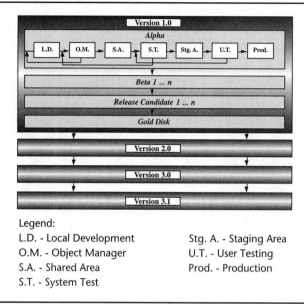

Legend:
L.D. - Local Development
O.M. - Object Manager
S.A. - Shared Area
S.T. - System Test

Stg. A. - Staging Area
U.T. - User Testing
Prod. - Production

Figure 19.4   The software migration's process.

Table 19.1   PowerBuilder File Types

File Type	Description	File Type	Description
.PBL	PowerBuilder Library	.EXE	Executable
.PBD	PowerBuilder Dynamic Library	.TXT	Text file
.DLL	Dynamic Linked Library	.INI	Windows or application initialization file
.SQL	Query, table schema script		
.DOC	Application documentation, migration form, design spec	.HLP	Help file
		.PRJ	Help project file
.C	C source program	.RTF	Rich Text Format file (for help file creation)
.H	C header file	.A	UNIX static library
.DEF	C module definition file	.AWK	UNIX AWK Script file
.RES	C resource file	.BMP	Bitmap
.MAK	C make file	.ICO	Icon
.LIB	Windows/DOS static library	.BAT	Batch file
.PBR	PowerBuilder resource file		

You must manage these file types—and possibly several more, depending on the particular environment—with release or configuration control software. You must manage them in such a way that if you need a file from a previous version, you could easily retrieve it.

A number of version control software products communicate with PowerBuilder. These products use various mechanisms to help developers manage files that are located on different servers or platforms. Being able to do this from a single server, as depicted in Figure 19.5, is the most complex release management issue.

Directory Structure

Before you begin the application development process, it is important to set up a directory structure that supports not only the current application development effort but the entire application environment. This will take into account a set of common modules that all the applications can share, common modules that one or more applications share, and the other applications themselves (see Figure 19.6).

Having a standard directory structure in place prior to beginning a development effort makes code management easier. This way, the developers spend a minimal amount of time looking for a specific piece of code. When it is time to create the application executable, all the files (of similar type) that you include within the executable are in the same place. You should compile only production-ready code into the executable.

Figure 19.6 and Table 19.2 represent one way you could organize a PowerBuilder directory structure. You should alter this structure depending on the number of servers and applications involved. If a particular environment has a large number of other types of files, you could create a subdirectory for each.

If you develop multiple applications on the same server, there should be an entire **\dev** structure under a directory name denoting the application, as shown in Figure 19.6. In addition, under **\app1,** there should be the following directories parallel to the **..\dev** directory:

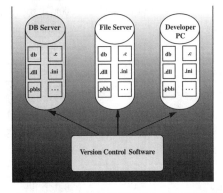

Figure 19.5   Cross-platform software version control.

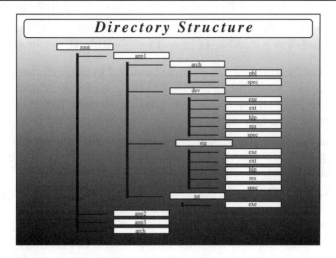

Figure 19.6   The directory structure.

..\tst is a testing area, where you perform the unit testing. Only the executables should be here.

..\stg is a staging area, where the unit-tested software is a frozen copy of the **..\dev** directory, for later system testing.

..\arch is where you store the application's common modules.

TIP There should be both an **\arch** directory under the root directory to store the common modules for all the applications, and an **\arch** directory under the specific **\app** directory for more application-specific common modules.

Table 19.2   The Directory Structure's Organization

Location	Extension	Nature	Description
\DEV\	N/A	N/A	Source directory (contains no files).
\DEV\EXT	.C, .H, .RC, .RES	External	Use to store the files used to create external objects (e.g., DLLs).
DEV\PBL	.PBL	Libraries	Use to store the PBL-related files that the application uses.
\DEV\RES	.BMP, .ICO, .PBR	Resources	Use to store the application resources.
\DEV\HLP	.HLP	Help	Use to store the application help files.
\DEV\SPEC	.DOC	Specifications	Use to store the files related to specifications (e.g., pre- and post-design documents).
\DEV\EXE	.EXE, .PBD, .DLL	Executable	Use to store the files necessary to execute the application.

AN EXAMPLE OF A TYPICAL SOFTWARE MANAGEMENT ENVIRONMENT

The following setup provides for multiple layers of security within an application development cycle. There are a number of logical roles within this scenario, as follows:

Version Control Manager. The version control manager is responsible for the version control repository's integrity. He or she typically interfaces with the object manager to store and release the source from the version control repository. Only the version control manager has access to the version control repository.

Object Manager. The object manager is responsible for the integrity of all the code that is on the application server, and it interfaces with both the version control manager and each application lead.

Application Lead. The application lead is responsible for the integrity of an application module's code and for interfacing with the object manager, and all the developers for the particular application module under the lead's responsibility.

Developer. The developer is responsible for the pieces of code assigned to him or her and for interfacing with the application lead.

Figure 19.7 shows the interaction among all the different people within a multiple application software development environment.

The different source code locations are:

Version control repository is the repository that holds all the source code.

Application server is where the version control manager places the code recently taken from the repository.

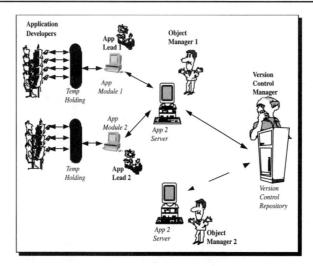

Figure 19.7   The interaction among the different roles within a multiapplication software development environment.

Application module directory tree is where the code for each application module that needs to be modified resides.

Temporary holding area is used to prevent the developer from having write access to the application module directory tree. When the developer is ready to check in some code, he or she checks the code into the holding area, and the application lead immediately moves the code into the application module directory tree.

Table 19.3 shows who has what level of access to each server or directory tree.

This configuration is only a suggestion. There are a number of different ways to set up a software management environment.

Version Control within PowerBuilder

PowerBuilder has version control capabilities that you can use in different ways. The first method is the standard library check-in\check-out process. This process is simple, but it works. PowerBuilder 5 introduced version control software called ObjectCycle, which is much more feature-rich than the basic version control traditionally available within PowerBuilder. ObjectCycle (www.sybase.com/products/objectcycle/) can be the second alternative to version control within PowerBuilder. The third method is to use an external vendor's version control product. Such vendor products include PVCS (www.intersolv.com/index.html) and CCC (www.platinum.com/index.html).

Source Code Control API

The PowerBuilder Source Code Control API is based on the Microsoft Common Source Code Control Interface Specification, version 0.00.0823. You can use the PowerBuilder Source Code Control API to achieve the following:

- Synchronize the object in the library
- Better registration and reporting facility with the ability to add check-in comments as well as compare objects in the library with objects in the archive
- New tracing and profiling capabilities

Table 19.3   Access Levels

	Version Control Repository	Application Server	Application Module directory tree	Temporary holding area	Developers hard disk
Version Control Manager	W	W	R	R	N
Object Manager	R	W	W	W	N
Application Lead	N	R	W	W	N
Application Developer	N	N	R	W	W

*R—Read Access; W—Write Access; N—No Access

Default Version Control

PowerBuilder's default version control capabilities include check-in and check-out functionality. The toolbar you can use to perform these operations is available from the Library painter (see Figure 19.8).

Version control functionality is also available from the **Source** menu, as shown in Figure 19.9.

When the developer attempts to check out an object for the first time, PowerBuilder prompts with the dialog box shown in Figure 19.10.

PowerBuilder keeps track of the checkout based on the user ID parameter the developer enters here. The developer should key in his or her user ID and click OK, as shown in Figure 19.11.

When the developer does this, PowerBuilder modifies the user preferences within the pb.ini file's Library section, as shown in Figure 19.12.

After the developer enters the user ID information, PowerBuilder prompts with a dialog box (see Figure 19.13) for the destination library, usually the developer's local library.

This is the extent of PowerBuilder's built-in version control capabilities. The default process is deficient, especially for large development projects. Consequently, Powersoft provided a mechanism for vendors to link their version control software to PowerBuilder. The next section discusses how PowerBuilder's architecture is set up to communicate with version control software.

ObjectCycle

Powersoft bundles ObjectCycle, a client/server version control software, with PowerBuilder 6's Enterprise Edition. If you purchase PowerBuilder 6's Professional Edition,

Figure 19.8   The toolbar for check in and check out.

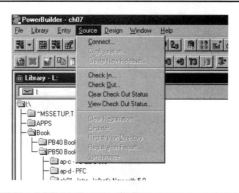

Figure 19.9   The version control items from the Library painter's <u>S</u>ource menu.

Figure 19.10   The PowerBuilder object check-out dialog.

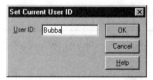

Figure 19.11   Entering the User ID to check out an object.

Figure 19.12   The Library section's User ID value within pb.ini.

you can purchase ObjectCycle as an add-on. Powersoft also bundles ObjectCycle within the Enterprise Editions of PowerJ, PowerDesigner, Power++, and PowerSite. In addition to PowerBuilder and these other products, ObjectCycle also supports other development environments including Microsoft Developer Studio and Microsoft Visual Basic. ObjectCycle includes the following components:

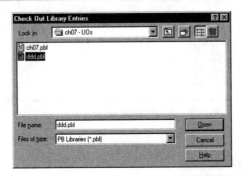

Figure 19.13   Specifying the destination library when checking out an object.

ObjectCycle Client Library. The ObjectCycle client library provides interface hooks that PowerBuilder needs to connect to the ObjectCycle Server and share objects.

ObjectCycle Server. The ObjectCycle Server is a 32-bit multithreaded application that handles the client requests from the ObjectCycle Manager and PowerBuilder. When you start the server, it starts the ObjectCycle Database by using an ODBC connection.

ObjectCycle Manager. The ObjectCycle Manager is a PowerBuilder client application you can use to access the PowerBuilder objects and project information stored within the ObjectCycle Database. By using the ObjectCycle Manager, you can add new projects and delete or modify existing ones. You can also add new users and delete or modify existing users.

ObjectCycle Database. The ObjectCycle Database is a SQL Anywhere database (Sa50oc.db) that stores the PowerBuilder objects you register. In addition, you can store other objects, such as data models, project plans, spreadsheets, and so on within the ObjectCycle Database. When you start the ObjectCycle Server, it automatically starts the ObjectCycle Database.

ObjectCycle Software Development Kit (SDK). You can use the ObjectCycle SDK to write code to access the ObjectCycle Server objects and version control services.

TIP ObjectCycle supports Windows 95 and Windows NT platforms only. You can install both the ObjectCycle Manager and ObjectCycle Server on a single machine, although Powersoft recommends installing the server on a high-performance Windows NT machine to derive the best performance from the product. The more powerful the server is, the more developers it can support.

Using ObjectCycle

To use ObjectCycle with PowerBuilder, first configure ObjectCycle with your PowerBuilder development environment and then register your PowerBuilder application objects with ObjectCycle. Start the ObjectCycle Server. The server, in turn, starts the ObjectCycle Database. The server includes a default project called system. Next, start the ObjectCycle Manager. To open an existing project, select **Open Project** from the **File** menu. The ObjectCycle Manager, in turn, displays the Open Project dialog box, shown in Figure 19.14.

The default login parameters are:

User: admin

Password: camus

Server: <provide the ObjectCycle server name or your machine name>

Project: system

Upon successful login, the ObjectCycle Manager displays the ObjectCycle Manager dialog box, shown in Figure 19.15.

To create a new project, select **New...Project** from the **File** menu. To add a new user or edit an existing user and his/her role, select **Server Options** from the **Configure** menu. The ObjectCycle Manager, in turn, displays the Server Options dialog. Click the **Users** tab. To add a new user, click **Add**. To edit an existing user, click **Edit**. The three types of users you can add are: Administrators (who can perform all the ObjectCycle actions), Users (who can perform the version control operations but no administration actions), and Inactive (who can only view the objects registered within ObjectCycle).

At this point, you can register your PowerBuilder application objects within ObjectCycle. Note that you cannot use the ObjectCycle's version control capabilities with-

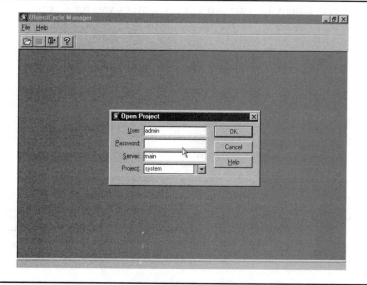

Figure 19.14   The ObjectCycle Manager's Open Project dialog box.

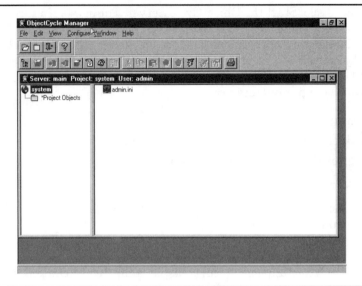

Figure 19.15   The ObjectCycle Manager environment.

out registering your application objects. To register the objects, use the Library painter in the PowerBuilder development environment.

Within the Library painter, select **Connect** from the **Source** menu, and choose **ObjectCycle** within the Vendors drop-down listbox. Then, click OK. The ObjectCycle client library now needs the login information to connect to the ObjectCycle Server. As a result, you see the ObjectCycle Connect dialog box. Enter the login information as shown in Figure 19.16.

The ObjectCycle Client Library, in turn, prompts you for a configuration file. The Library painter will use the configuration file to automatically log into the ObjectCycle Server the next time you open the painter.

Now, you are ready to register your application objects with ObjectCycle. To register a single object, highlight it and select **Register** from the **Source** menu. To register all the objects within a .PBL, highlight the .PBL, click the right mouse button, and then choose **Select All**. Now, select **Register** from the **Source** menu. Unfortunately, Power-Builder prompts you with a confirmation dialog box (the ObjectCycle Registration dialog box) for every object, as shown in Figure 19.17. There is no OK (or Yes) to All button in the dialog box. You can also register the starting revision number for the object.

TIP To unregister your application object(s) from ObjectCycle, highlight the object(s) and then select **Clear Registration** from the **Source** menu in the Library painter. To synchronize an application object(s) with its repository image(s), highlight the object(s) and then select **Synchronize** from the **Source** menu in the Library painter.

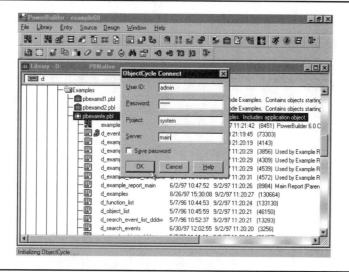

Figure 19.16   Logging into the ObjectCycle Server.

Figure 19.18 shows the registered objects within the ObjectCycle Manager.

TIP PowerBuilder shows a small can next to the registered object in the Library painter.

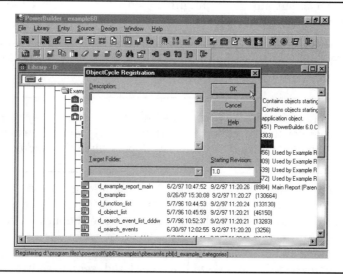

Figure 19.17   Registering your application objects with ObjectCycle.

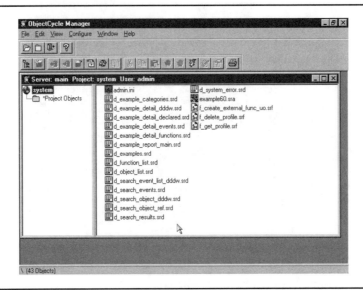

Figure 19.18 Viewing the registered objects within the ObjectCycle Manager.

After you register your application objects, you can check in and check out the objects. To check out an object, highlight the object within the Library painter and select **Check Out...** from the **Source** menu. The ObjectCycle client interface prompts you for a user ID when you check an object out for the first time. This user ID is different from the user ID you entered to log into the ObjectCycle Server. The ObjectCycle client interface uses this user ID to indicate the person's ID who has checked the object out. To clear an object's check out status, highlight the object and select **Clear Check Out Status** from the **Source** menu.

TIP PowerBuilder shows a small lock next to the checked out object within the Library painter.

To check the object back in, highlight the object, and select **Check In...** from the **Source** menu. Other developers cannot modify the objects you have checked out. Similarly, you cannot modify objects that other developers have checked out.

TIP A primary difference between using PowerBuilder and a version control software like ObjectCycle for source code control is that PowerBuilder does not natively enforce checking an object out before you can make changes to the object. As a result, you may be editing an object directly within PowerBuilder and another developer may come along and check the object out. As a result, PowerBuilder will not let you save your changes to the object. On the other hand, version control software like ObjectCycle forces you to check an object out before you can make any changes to it.

External Version Control Software

When you install a vendor's version control product, you must set the SourceVendor entry in the Connect dialog box from the Library painter's **Source** menu (e.g., to PVCS for PVCS; see Figure 19.19). To display the Connect dialog box, select **Connect...** from the **Source** menu within the Library painter.

Figure 19.20 shows how PowerBuilder communicates with a version control software product. The vendor provides a specific DLL to link the check-in and check-out process directly with the vendor's repository. The figure also shows that the version control software must communicate through the PowerBuilder Open Repository CASE API (ORCA) to provide the information to PowerBuilder.

Figure 19.19   The SourceVendor value of the Library section within pb.ini.

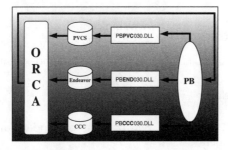

Figure 19.20   PowerBuilder communicates with a version control software product through ORCA.

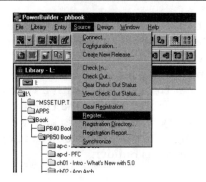

Figure 19.21 Enabled MenuItems for third-party version control.

When you install the third-party version control software on a workstation and establish the link to PowerBuilder, the menu items that PowerBuilder had grayed out become available (see Figure 19.21). Note that before you can check objects in and out, you must register the PowerBuilder objects (see the menu in Figure 19.21).

Table 19.4 lists of some popular version control products. They are not necessarily PowerBuilder-enabled, but more and more vendors are releasing links to PowerBuilder every day.

Table 19.4   Version Control Products

Company	Product	URL
Rational Software Corporation	ClearCase	www.rational.com
Burton Systems	TLIB	www.burtonsys.com
Computer Associates International, Inc.	CA-PAN/LCM	www.cai.com
Computer Associates International, Inc.	CA-Librarian	www.cai.com
Computer Associates International, Inc.	CA-PANVALET	www.cai.com
IBM	CMVC	www.ibm.com
Intersolv, Inc.	PVCS	www.intersolv.com/index.html
Intersolv, Inc.	Configuration Builder	www.intersolv.com/index.html
Mortice Kern Systems, Inc.	MKS RCS	www.mks.com
Object Technology International, Inc.	ENVY/Developer	www.oti.com
Platinum Technology	Platinum CCC/Life Cycle Manager	www.platinum.com/index.html
Sun Microsystems, Inc.	TeamWare	www.sun.com/software/Developer-products/literature/ProductGuide/SWP.SW/SWTW.html

The following section discusses some procedures PVCS users can use.

PVCS Procedures

Creating Initial Source Files When you assign a task or process to a programmer, he or she should inform the PVCS administrator and provide the following information:

- The programmer's name
- The program file's name, including extension (e.g., rass1002.pco)
- A short description of the program's purpose or function

Upon receiving this information, the PVCS administrator creates the initial archive file. Then the programmer can check the files in and out, as necessary.

Source Migration When a developer thinks that a program is functioning according to the requirements, he or she is permitted to "promote" the source code to "test" status. After achieving test status, the program is further tested against other called or calling procedures. This environment uses its own data set and looks at the system-wide functionality. To simplify this process, you can create a UNIX script file. You can call the script file as follows:

```
promote <filename.ext>
```

Upon successful completion of system-wide testing, the code administrator promotes the program through the following levels by using PVCS:

Simulation test. Test the programs in a realistic setting.

Acceptance test. A select group of users test the programs.

Retrieving a Source File To shield the developers from the PVCS syntax to retrieve the source code files, a UNIX script file simplifies the process. To check out a program, use the following command:

```
checkout <filename.ext>
```

PVCS retrieves and places the file within the directory from which you invoke the retrieval script. Retrieve all the files into your development subdirectory.

Returning a Source File Upon a program's completion or at the end of the day, archive the source files back to the PVCS. Again, a UNIX script file simplifies this process. To return a program, use the following command:

```
checkin <filename.ext>
```

When you check a program in, PVCS places the program in the version manager's archive directory. The file's most recent read-only version is maintained in the /development/ras/ref subdirectory. You can use the files in this location for viewing, printing, or compiling.

TIP Making copies of these files, modifying the copies, and then attempting to check them in will result in a PVCS error. You must use the **checkout** command to retrieve a writeable source file. For more information, see "Retrieving a Source File."

MIGRATION FORMS

It is critical that you have a well-documented process for migrating from one development or testing stage to the next. The project team can develop standard migration forms or use products such as Lotus Notes to set up a migration database. A simple migration form might look as follows:

CODE MIGRATION REQUEST FORM

Requested By _____ Date Requested _____

Reason for Change

_____

_____

Application; __Batch, __Contract, __Corp., __Credit, __Discount, __EBB, __Noms, __Plmaps, __Rates, __Sched

Mgr. Approval _____ Explain SQL Required :   Y/N   Entry

Type: (PB, SQR, etc.) _____

636 SE Notify _____ Curr to: UnitTest Y/N, UserAccep Y/N, Prod Y/N.

SQR MIGRATIONS

Program Name	Source Directory on LAN	Destination Server (Production/Development)			Program Type *	
		Development	SystemTest	Prod	Report	Update

*Report programs should only read from the database. Programs that change the database are Updates.

New SQR Program Migration (this section only required for new SQR programs)

Program Name: _____

Description: _____

Input Parameters:

Description/Prompt	Type	Required

POWERBUILDER OBJECT MIGRATIONS

Object Name	Type	Source PBL	Destination Server (Production/Enhancement)		
			Development	System Test	Production

ADMINISTRATOR USE ONLY

Completed By _____ Date Completed _____

CHAPTER 20

Performance Considerations

Even in the simplest client/server application, several elements must work together to form the application system, as shown in Figure 20.1.

As this figure shows, these elements include the client workstation, network architecture, database design, and the application itself. Each element has an impact on overall application performance, and you should address them individually to provide the best possible performance.

While briefly discussing the other performance-related issues of client/server applications, this chapter focuses primarily on the performance issues regarding a Power-Builder application's design and development. *Application performance* refers to both the actual performance and perceived performance. *Perceived performance* is the user's view of application performance, which may be better than the actual performance.

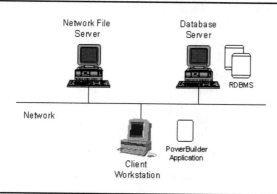

Figure 20.1   A typical client/server application.

The other topics this chapter discusses include:

- Client configuration
- Network architecture
- Database design
- PowerBuilder application design issues
- PowerBuilder application development

CLIENT CONFIGURATION

You can do several things on the client workstation to increase application performance, including:

- Increase the workstation memory. Memory is often the limiting factor in Windows, largely because of its capability to run several applications simultaneously.
- Because Windows does not use expanded memory, using extended memory can increase application performance.
- For Windows 3.x, load as many programs as possible in the high memory because this leaves more of the 640K base memory available for DOS applications. Items that you should load in high memory include device drivers, network drivers, and any terminate-and-stay-resident (TSR) programs.
- Use a disk-caching program, such as smartdrv.exe, and allocate as much memory as possible. This can provide a big performance improvement within Windows.
- Do not use a wallpaper as the background in Windows. To save memory, use a color or pattern rather than a wallpaper for a background.
- For Windows 3.x, use a permanent swap file, rather than a temporary swap file. This increases performance because Windows stores virtual memory in contiguous blocks on the hard disk. To create a swap file, click the **Virtual Memory** button of the 386 Enhanced window from the Windows 3.x Control Panel, as shown in Figure 20.2.

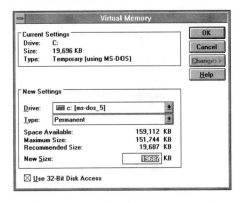

Figure 20.2   Configuring the Windows 3.x virtual memory.

TIP The space available for creating a permanent swap file is only as large as the largest contiguous block available on the hard disk. Windows cannot create a permanent swap file if Stacker is running.

If using a temporary swap file, do not store it on a network drive. Network delays and contention with other users can significantly decrease performance.

For Windows 95, configure the system so it manages the virtual memory itself. This lets Windows decide how it should handle the memory for optimal performance. To check this setting, click the **Virtual Memory** button on the **Performance** tab of the System Properties window from the Windows 95 Control Panel, as shown in Figure 20.3.

- Defragment the hard drive regularly.

In addition, refer to DOS and Windows documentation in an effort to completely understand each item's effect in the config.sys, autoexec.bat, win.ini, and system.ini files on performance.

NETWORK ARCHITECTURE

An application's network architecture includes such items as the network type (e.g., Ethernet, Token Ring, ArcNet), the network operating system (e.g., NetWare, Windows NT, VINES, LAN Manager), and the protocols to communicate between different systems (e.g., TCP/IP, IPX/SPX, NetBIOS, SNA).

Today's systems can run on several combinations of network type, network operating system, and protocols. While network performance tuning differs among the various combinations, there are some general areas that, regardless of the combination of network type, NOS, and protocol, you should look at when addressing the network performance. They include:

Number of peak users.   When designing a network, the architect needs to know the approximate number of peak users to make such decisions as the required

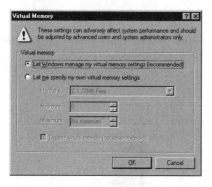

Figure 20.3   Configuring Windows 95 virtual memory.

bandwidth, the access media (e.g., fiber optic, coaxial cable, twisted pair), the number of segments or rings, and the number of servers required. Consider the number of peak users for the entire network as well as for each network segment or ring.

Type of applications. To estimate the type, frequency, and volume of data the network must support, the network designer needs to know the type(s) of applications that will run on the network. For example, an imaging system usually requires more network resources than a word processing application.

Placement of network file servers. The number of hops between the user workstation and the server users are accessing impact a network file server. *Hops* refers to the number of bridges, switches, and so forth, that lie between the network segment or ring of the user's workstation and the network segment or ring of the server. For example, consider the Ethernet network architecture shown in Figure 20.4. Within this network, all the communications between the client and network server must go across two routers to get from Segment A to Segment C. This obviously slows performance. If possible, the frequently accessed servers should be on the same segment or ring as the client(s), as shown in Figure 20.5. While it is not always possible to have the client and server on the same network segment or ring, analyze when designing the network architecture to minimize the number of hops between the user workstations and servers.

Network packet size. The packet size is each data packet's size sent across the network. The smaller the packet size, the more packets that must be sent across the network. A large number of packets can adversely affect performance. On the other hand, packets that are too large may clutter a network when only a few users or processes are running. For recommended packet size, refer to the network operating system documentation.

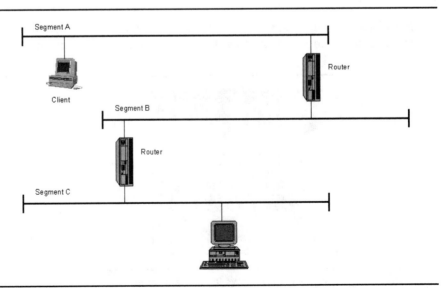

Figure 20.4 **A network architecture requiring two "hops" from the client to the server.**

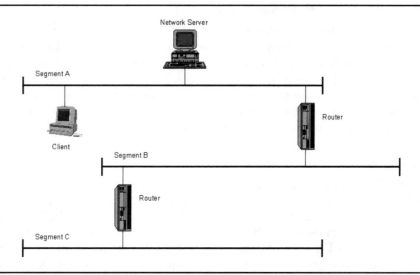

Figure 20.5   **Minimizing the number of "hops" between the client and the server by placing both on the same network segment.**

DATABASE DESIGN

At the database level, there are several things you can do to increase system performance. These range from design decisions to tuning the database when the application goes into production. Design time considerations include:

- Number of concurrent users
- Number of database connections per user
- The types of transactions to be performed (query versus update)
- Proper database sizing
- Choosing the proper platform
- The data model's normalization

Things that you can do to fine-tune RDBMS and application performance include:

- Proper use of indexes
- Optimization of the SQL
- Tweaking the RDBMS configuration parameters
- Data distribution

While the methods for dealing with these issues differ among RDBMS products, you should address them when considering performance.

POWERBUILDER APPLICATION DESIGN ISSUES

Before beginning to develop a PowerBuilder application, you need to make several design decisions. In addition to improving the productivity during the development cycle, these design decisions can impact the application performance. This section addresses some of the design issues that you should consider before starting the development.

Partitioning Application Components

A client/server application may consist of several pieces of code distributed among the architecture's various components. For example, a single PowerBuilder application can consist of PowerScript and C code on the client side, along with triggers, stored procedures, and other 3GL code on the server side. With the introduction of distributed computing, things get more complex. However, making the right decision about which component should reside where can make or break your application's efficiency. The following sections discuss some of the important issues.

When to Use Database Triggers

Most relational databases support the use of triggers. A trigger is a set of code that the database performs automatically in response to a specific database action. Although RDBMS vendors implement the triggers differently (for a detailed description of how triggers are implemented within the different RDBMSs, see Chapter 16, "SQL Anywhere and Other Databases"), the basic RDBMS approach remains the same; that is, the database may fire them in response to an INSERT, UPDATE, or DELETE SQL statement that your application performs against the database.

Because of this, you should use triggers whenever you must perform a specific action in response to the changes the application makes to the database. It is much more efficient to use triggers for this purpose rather than for performing such a function at the client workstation. Performing this action at the client workstation requires another call to the database, thus increasing the network traffic and decreasing the performance. You can usually optimize the SQL that makes up a trigger, which results in more efficient execution of the SQL than if the client submitted the SQL.

TIP Within the databases that support declarative referential integrity, it is best to enforce referential integrity declaratively rather than by using triggers.

When to Use Stored Procedures

Although not all the relational databases support stored procedures, taking advantage of them within those databases that do can significantly impact the application design and performance. A stored procedure, like a trigger, is a collection of SQL code. However, unlike a trigger, the database does not execute a stored procedure automatically based on the database activity. You must explicitly call a stored procedure from within an application, trigger, or another procedure.

Use stored procedures to execute commonly used SQL (or vendor-specific SQL extensions) in a database. Although a stored procedure is nothing more than SQL, there are advantages to using stored procedures instead of SQL scripts. Because the database stores the stored procedures in a compiled form, their performance is generally better than that of native SQL. Stored procedures can also provide a level of application security in that a user allowed to execute a procedure does not need access to the data the procedure uses.

As mentioned earlier, you can usually use stored procedures to increase performance over the standard SQL queries. Figure 20.6 illustrates the performance advantage of stored procedures over standard SQL queries in Microsoft's SQL Server.

The database does not need to parse the stored procedure's syntax every time it executes the procedure as a standard SQL query does. Also, because the database already compiles the stored procedures, this step is not required each time the database executes the procedure. However, it is important to recompile the stored procedures periodically to update the execution path and ensure optimum performance.

PowerBuilder 6 has enhanced the features of distributed computing. If you would like to create monthly or annual reports that take a lot of time to create because the system has to process a lot of data, you can provide a neat solution by converting those reports to stored procedures. Whenever the user wants to create the report, the client makes an asynchronous call to the distributed application server, which in turn, calls the stored procedure that processes the report on the database server. Upon the report's completion, the distributed server pushes the report to the client machine that requests this information. This way, the client machine is not tied up waiting for the database stored procedure to compile the report. For more details on Distributed PowerBuilder, see Chapter 22, "Distributed Application Development," and Chapter 23, "Advanced Distributed Application Development."

When to Perform Validation

Data validation time and location is another design issue that you need to consider. Should the application validate the data as the user enters the data or at save time? Should validation occur on the client or at the server by using a trigger or stored procedure?

The answers to these questions depend on the type of validation and whether database access is required to validate the data. Validating such things as the format of the data that the user enters within a field or the length of the data entered should be done on the client as the user attempts to leave the field, usually through the edit mask or validation code defined for the column within the DataWindow painter. The reason for

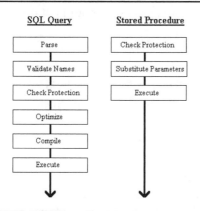

Figure 20.6   Executing a SQL query versus a stored procedure.

doing this type of validation immediately is that it is better to present users with a problem as they attempt to leave a field rather than notifying them of the problem after they have spent time entering data in all of the fields on the screen.

To reduce the number of database queries, you should do any validation that requires database access at save time. Doing this for several fields as the user attempts to leave each one can greatly reduce performance.

Whether to perform validation on the client or server is a decision that you should make based on the validation code's nature. If the validation code requires a great deal of processing or involves some complicated SQL, it is usually best to perform the validation on the server. As mentioned earlier, you can optimize this code to improve the performance. Note that when performing the validation on the server, it is important that the PowerBuilder application handles the trigger or stored procedure's return code and displays an appropriate message to the user.

PowerScript Functions versus External Functions

As mentioned in the discussion of functions in Chapter 6, "Structures, User Objects, and Functions," you can use external C functions to improve a PowerBuilder application's performance if the application is not compiled into machine code. This is because PowerBuilder compiles the PowerScript code that is not compiled into machine code into p-code, interprets the p-code at runtime, and executes more slowly than the compiled code. With PowerBuilder's ability to produce compiled code, this becomes less of an issue, but it is still something that you should consider for any CPU-intensive processes.

One EXE versus Several EXEs

You can increase the performance of a large application by breaking it into a series of smaller EXEs rather than one large one. Divide the application into portions (EXEs) that can run in stand-alone mode, independent of the application's other parts.

For example, you could more than likely divide an application with functions for both a company's marketing division and its research and development division into two smaller EXEs, one for each division. Because you can keep PowerBuilder EXEs relatively small by using PBD or DLL and PBR files, this problem should not occur frequently.

Building PBLs into Both EXE and the PBDs or DLLs

For best performance, bind all the PBLs into the executable. If the application is too large for a single executable, you can increase the performance by doing one of two things:

- Creating an executable with all the application PBLs within their respective PBDs or DLLs
- Creating an executable with some PBLs within the executable and some as PBDs or DLLs

The advantage in creating one executable with all the PBLs as PBDs or DLLs is that the executable is small and the memory usage is minimal. If you do this, however, it is critical to place the objects in the PBLs with respect to the usage. This is because opening and closing the application PBDs can net a performance decrease. If you ignore the placement of objects within PBLs with respect to the usage, you end up with the following type of situation.

The application executes the command to open window1, but because the controls on window1 are inherited from the objects that physically reside in different PBDs or DLLs, PowerBuilder must open each PBD or DLL to display window1. Figure 20.7 shows the problem. To open window1, PowerBuilder must also open PBD1 or DLL1, PBD2 or DLL2, and PBD3 or DLL3.

To improve the performance, it is better to combine the objects used together within one PBD or DLL. In this example, place objects A, E, and F in the same PBD or DLL, as shown in Figure 20.8. That way, PowerBuilder must open only PBD1 or DLL1 to open the window.

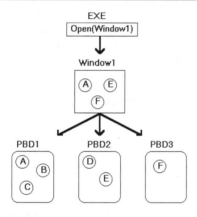

Figure 20.7   **Opening Window1 requires opening 3 PBDs or DLLs, thus slowing performance.**

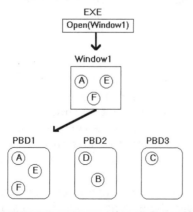

Figure 20.8   **Improving the performance by grouping the objects used together into a single PBD or DLL.**

Sometimes it is best to combine some of the application PBLs with the executable and compile some into PBDs or DLLs. Bind the objects within the application that are used most often into the executable; compile the less frequently accessed objects into PBDs or DLLs.

A significant performance improvement within PowerBuilder is the introduction of native code generation. PowerBuilder now uses the Watcom C compiler to produce optimized compiled code. Mathematical expressions, function calls, integer and floating point arithmetic, arrays, and loops are several times faster when using compiled code. When generating the compiled code within PowerBuilder, PowerBuilder creates a DLL for every PBD.

Distribution of Application Components

In a client/server environment, there are several places to store application components. You can store client components on the user workstation or a network file server. Server components can reside on a database server or another application server. Application components include the following:

- PowerBuilder runtime DLLs (including the PowerBuilder interface to the RDBMS)
- PowerBuilder application dynamic libraries (PBDs or DLLs)
- Additional application DLLs
- Any external client-side software packages (e.g., word processing, spreadsheet, or reporting tools)
- PowerBuilder distributed server executables and dynamic libraries
- Additional server-side application programs

Two things you should consider when determining where to store the application components are performance and application maintenance.

PowerBuilder now offers a solution that lets nonvisual objects be both distributed and run on any server platform such as Windows 95, Windows NT, and UNIX. Distributed PowerBuilder lets you compile these objects into native code for even faster execution. By porting the CPU-intensive routines to the server, the client machines benefit with a reduced workload. You could supply these same performance advantages by using a C routine, but now you need not be hindered by C's learning curve. You can now accomplish the same task by using PowerScript.

Although storing the components on a server accessible to several users may decrease maintenance efforts, it usually hinders performance because files must be transferred across the network from the server to the target machine.

Another issue is the medium on which you store the components. Options include hard disk, tape, and optical disk. The storage medium has an impact on system performance. In most cases, hard disk access is faster than optical disk, which is faster than tape.

Yet another issue is the amount of storage space available on the target machine. Obviously, if a workstation or server lacks the disk space needed to store the application components, you must keep the components on another server.

The approach to distributing the application components should be to provide a system within which you reduce maintenance as much as possible without decreasing performance to an unacceptable level. For example, if you need to update a particular PowerBuilder application every month, it is easier (from a maintenance perspective) to store the application libraries on a network file server rather than trying to maintain the application's releases on each user's workstation.

PowerBuilder 6 introduces a synchronizer that can take care of all the above issues. You can read about the synchronizer in Chapter 25, "Using Internet Tools."

Preloading Objects

Preloading application objects refers to loading objects into the memory of the client workstation at the application login time. At login time, if you preload an object, you open it and then hide it. Any calls to open the object result in displaying the hidden object rather than reopening it, which is slower. When you close a preloaded object, you actually hide it instead of close it. Preloading the objects slows the login procedure, but provides faster access to the object at any point after login. This increases the overall application performance if you open and close an object frequently.

The price of preloading an object is sacrificing available memory on the client workstation because the object remains resident within memory even after you "close" it. The number of objects that you can preload is limited by the amount of available memory on the client workstation and depends on the objects' size.

You can either determine which objects are to be preloaded at development time and build them into the application or determine this dynamically based on user profiles. For example, system administrators may use screen 1 more often than they use screen 2, while clerks use screen 2 more than screen 1. Without dynamic preloading, if you preload screen 1, all the users incur a longer login caused by preloading screen 1. For users who do not regularly access this screen and therefore do not benefit from preloading's performance gain, this is inefficient. With dynamic preloading, you can configure the system to preload screen 1 only for system administrators and screen 2 only for clerks.

In either case, to obtain the greatest benefit of preloading, you should preload only the objects that the user opens and closes frequently within a user session.

Without preloading, the application opens all the objects each time when displaying them. This can be slow and inefficient, depending on such things as the object's size and the number of database requests when opening an object.

You can put all the objects that you decide to preload on the application server. That way you can save valuable client workstation memory usage. Also, you can create these objects as shared objects on the distributed application server. To learn more about distributed computing, refer to Chapter 22, "Distributed Application Development," and Chapter 23, "Advanced Distributed Application Development."

Choosing PowerBuilder Controls

Understanding the set of PowerBuilder controls and their intended use can keep you from writing unnecessary code that can decrease performance and lead to inconsistency among the application components.

PowerBuilder controls are an extended set of the standard Windows controls. Each control has a set of built-in capabilities that let you interface with an application by either entering the data, initiating an action, or choosing an option. Each control on a window uses part of the Windows User Heap. The Windows User Heap is a 64K region of memory that Windows uses to store the handles, controls, resources, and other objects that Windows applications use.

There is no limit to the number of controls that you can place on a window, however, the time required to open a window increases as the number of controls on the window increases. Powersoft recommends that the number of controls (visible and hidden) on a single window be less than 20.

TIP It is important to remember that each user object counts toward the number of controls that make up the user object. PowerBuilder does not view them as a single control.

DataWindows

In addition to all the advantages the DataWindow object provides you with regard to database access and validation, the DataWindow object can also enhance performance because Windows treats a DataWindow control as a single control rather than multiple standard controls. Assume, for example, you want to enter an employee's ID, first name, last name, status, and salary. Doing this without using a DataWindow requires placing 12 controls onto the window, as shown in Figure 20.9.

When PowerBuilder opens this window, PowerBuilder must paint each of the 12 controls separately. Doing this with a DataWindow results in only a single control, the DataWindow control, on the window, as shown in Figure 20.10.

You can treat the DataWindow as a single control because PowerBuilder, rather than Windows, manages the control. Treating the DataWindow as a single control reduces the amount of the Windows User Heap required because PowerBuilder needs to paint only one control when the window is opened. This results in better performance. Regardless of the number of items within a DataWindow, Windows still treats the

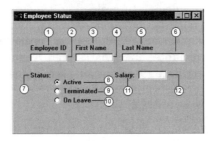

Figure 20.9   **A window with 12 controls.**

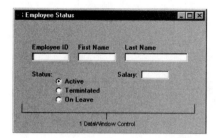

Figure 20.10   **Using a DataWindow, the same window now has only one control.**

DataWindow as only one control. Therefore, the more complex the DataWindow, the greater the performance gain of using the DataWindow control instead of the standard controls.

DataWindows versus DropDownListBoxes

You may often be faced with the question of whether to use a DataWindow or Drop-DownListBox to list a set of options available to the user. The answer to this question depends on the data within the list. If the data is static and does not reside within a database, it is more efficient and easier for you to use a DropDownListBox window control. You can then hard-code the values coded into the control with no other changes required to display the set of values.

If the data is retrieved from the database, however, it is more efficient to use a DataWindow. Otherwise, you would have to write the code to retrieve the data from the database and add the retrieved data to the DropDownListBox control.

Static versus Dynamic Interfaces

A static interface is one that remains unchanged during an application's execution. Most simple applications have a static interface.

A dynamic interface, on the other hand, is one that can change at runtime. You can implement a dynamic interface within PowerBuilder by such measures as hiding and displaying the controls, dynamically creating the objects, changing a DataWindow control's DataWindow object, changing the pictures on a PictureButton or Picture object, or enabling and disabling the controls on a window. While application requirements may dictate a dynamic interface, keep in mind that the more dynamic the interface, the worse an application performs.

Inheritance and Performance

Several people mistakenly believe that while inheritance provides several benefits within the development of PowerBuilder applications, it does so at the expense of performance. Not only is this an incorrect assumption, but if implemented correctly, inheritance can actually increase performance. The best way to show this is through an example. Suppose the following inheritance hierarchy in Figure 20.11 is in place.

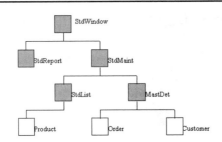

Figure 20.11   A sample object hierarchy.

The shaded boxes are virtual classes while the Product, Order, and Customer windows are actual application windows. Using this hierarchy, all the three windows share code within the StdMaint and StdWindow classes, while the Order and Customer windows share code within the MastDet, StdMaint, and StdWindow classes. When opening the Customer window for the first time, PowerBuilder does the following:

1. Searches the library search list for Customer.
2. Sees that Customer is inherited from MastDet. Searches for MastDet.
3. Sees that MastDet is inherited from StdMaint. Searches for StdMaint.
4. Sees that StdMaint is inherited from StdWindow. Searches for StdWindow.
5. Loads StdWindow.
6. Searches for and loads the objects contained within StdWindow.
7. Loads StdMaint.
8. Searches for and loads the objects contained within StdMaint.
9. Loads MastDet.
10. Searches for and loads the objects contained within MastDet.
11. Loads Customer.
12. Searches for and loads all the objects within Customer.
13. Executes Customer's open event.

Once PowerBuilder loads Customer into memory, loading Order is done much more quickly because the code contained in the virtual classes is already resident in memory, and thus PowerBuilder does not need to load the code. To open Order when Customer is open, PowerBuilder:

1. Searches the library search list for Order.
2. Sees that Order is inherited from MastDet, which is already resident in memory.
3. Loads Order.
4. Searches for and loads all the objects within Order.
5. Executes Order's open event.

Because much of the code that the application windows use is contained within the virtual classes, the application windows' size is smaller than it is without using inheritance. This makes the opening of the application windows much faster.

TIP To enhance performance, moving as much of the processing to nonvisual user object services helps.

POWERBUILDER APPLICATION DEVELOPMENT

You can do a lot to increase the application performance. You can divide a Power-Builder application's performance into three areas: object creation, script execution, and data retrieval. You can do specific things within each of these areas to increase performance. This section lists some of the things you should be aware of when developing PowerBuilder applications.

Scope of Variables and Functions

Declare variables and functions only within the scope for which you need them. Global variables remain within memory throughout the application's execution, while local and instance variables remain within memory only as long as the object(s) for which you define them exist. Thus you should use global variables and functions only when necessary. Global functions are slower than object-level functions.

Managing the PowerBuilder Libraries

Although there is no physical limitation on a .PBL's size, Powersoft recommends that .PBLs be smaller than 800K. A .PBL file is nothing more than a linked list of objects. Knowing this, it is easy to see why a large .PBL could decrease performance. The larger the .PBL, the more time PowerBuilder may require to access an object at runtime. PowerBuilder also takes longer to open or save an object in the development environment with a large .PBL.

Powersoft also recommends that the number of objects within a single .PBL be limited to approximately 50. This is primarily to simplify the Library painter's use within the development environment. While it is important to keep the .PBLs from becoming too large or cluttered, using a large number of smaller .PBLs can also negatively impact performance because you must add each new library to the application's library search list. Increasing the number of libraries within the search list can decrease performance by forcing PowerBuilder to search through more files to access an object.

An application's library search path plays an important role in an application's performance. The library search path is important because it dictates the path that Power-Builder follows when searching for the objects during execution. When retrieving an object, PowerBuilder first looks within the .EXE file. If the object is not found within the .EXE file, PowerBuilder searches each .PBD file in the order the .PBD is listed in the application's library search path. This makes the order of the .PBLs within the library search path a significant factor in application performance. To achieve better performance, place the .PBLs containing the most frequently used objects at the top of the library search list. It is also recommended that you list the .PBLs that contain the ancestor objects before the .PBLs that contain the descendant objects.

Optimize the PowerBuilder libraries often and regenerate them before creating an .EXE. Optimizing the library removes any unused space in the .PBL. Unused space in a .PBL increases as you update and delete the objects during the development cycle. Regenerating the objects within a .PBL cleans up any pointer references among the objects within the .PBL that may have been corrupted during the development. For more information, refer to Chapter 18, "Creating an Executable and Testing PowerBuilder Applications."

PowerScript Coding Considerations

Following are some useful coding tips you should be aware of while coding with Power-Builder.

Direct Data Access within DataWindows

The DataWindow control's Object property lets you specify the expressions that refer directly to the DataWindow object's data within the control. This direct data manipulation lets you access small and large amounts of data within a single statement, without calling the functions. For more details on direct data access, refer to Chapter 3, "DataWindows."

Restrict the Function Calls in Loop Control Statements

Although it may reduce the number of lines of code, placing a call to a function that returns a constant value within a loop control statement can greatly reduce performance. The degree to which performance is reduced depends on the function called and the number of times the loop executes. For example, when initializing an array's elements, instead of the following:

```
// This function initializes the passed array
integer li_ArrayCount


For li_ArrayCount = passedArray.UpperBound() To 1 Step -1
    passedArray[li_ArrayCount] = li_ArrayCount * .05
Next
```

Load the value that the function returns into a variable, and use the variable within the loop as follows:

```
// This function initializes the passed array
integer li_ArrayCount, li_ArrayLength


li_ArrayLength = passedArray.UpperBound()
For li_ArrayCount = li_ArrayLength To 1 Step -1
    passedArray[li_ArrayCount] = li_ArrayCount * .05
Next
```

Use Object-Level Functions

In addition to the benefits of using object-level functions with regard to data encapsulation, object-level functions also improve performance when compared to global functions.

When you call a global function, PowerBuilder locates it by searching through the .EXE file and all the application .PBD files until it is found. After locating the function, PowerBuilder executes it and removes it from memory. PowerBuilder repeats this process every time the function is called.

PowerBuilder loads the object-level functions, on the other hand, into memory at the same time as the parent object. When PowerBuilder calls an object-level function, execution is much faster because the object is already in memory.

Minimize the Use of UpperBound( ) and LowerBound( )

Because the **upperBound( )** and **lowerBound( )** functions are relatively slow, try to minimize the number of times your application must call them. One way to do this is by storing the return values of these functions in variables and referencing these variables throughout the application.

Use Compound Commands for Describe( ) and Modify( )

Take advantage of PowerBuilder's ability to pass multiple commands to the **describe( )** and **modify( )** functions. This improves performance by reducing the number of function calls and by reducing the number of calls to Windows to repaint the screen.

Use SetRedraw( )

When making the several changes to the controls within a window, use the **SetRedraw( )** function to turn off the screen painting until all the changes are made. Leaving redraw on while making the changes slows performance and causes the screen to flicker as the changes are made. It is important that you call SetRedraw( ) after making the changes to turn the drawing back on again. The following example shows how to use SetRedraw( ) when changing every row in a DataWindow:

```
// Change the account status of all the accounts within the DataWindow to "CLOSED"
LONG ll_Row, ll_RowCount

ll_RowCount = dw_accounts.RowCount ()
dw_accounts.SetRedraw(False)

For ll_Row = 1 To ll_RowCount
     dw_accounts.Object.account_status[ll_Row] = "CLOSED"
Next

dw_accounts.SetRedraw(True)
Return True
```

TIP In certain instances, turning redraw on again by calling SetRedraw(True) may not cause the screen to be repainted. Within these situations, force the redraw by sending the WM_PAINT message to the window.

Use Static Arrays Instead of Dynamic Arrays

While dynamic arrays provide a great deal of flexibility in coding, this flexibility is at the cost of performance. Performance decreases when the application creates a dynamic array and each time the array must grow to accommodate new data elements. This performance decrease occurs because of the way PowerBuilder handles an array's growth. When a dynamic array needs to grow, the following events occur:

1. PowerBuilder requests additional memory from Windows.
2. Windows allocates the new memory. The amount of memory that Windows allocates is the existing array's size plus the next array element's size.
3. The existing array is copied to the new memory location.
4. PowerBuilder releases the old memory back to Windows.

Performing this sequence of events each time the dynamic array grows has obvious performance implications. One approach to reduce the number of times these steps need to be performed is to start from an array's last element and work back toward the beginning. For example, when initializing a dynamic array's elements, looping from the last element to the first is more efficient than the traditional looping from first to last:

```
// This function initializes the passed array
integer li_ArrayCount, li_ArrayLength

li_ArrayLength = passedArray.UpperBound()
For li_ArrayCount = li_ArrayLength To 1 Step -1
    passedArray[li_ArrayCount] = li_ArrayCount * .05
Next
```

With static arrays, the amount of memory required is known when you declare the array, and it can be allocated at this time with no additional overhead required.

Pass Arguments to the Functions by Reference

Passing arguments by reference is more efficient than passing by value because passing an argument by value causes a copy of the argument to be made by PowerBuilder for use by the function. This increases the amount of memory used, and it increases the time required to execute the function. When passing by reference, on the other hand, a pointer to the argument is passed, and no additional memory is required to execute the function.

No Long-Running Events within Open and Activate Events

Because PowerBuilder does not display a window until it has finished executing the open and activate events, try to limit the amount of code within these events. Instead, create a user event such as ue_postopen or ue_initialize and post this event from the open event.

Post to a User-Defined Event to Perform Retrieval

Posting to a user-defined event to perform long-running tasks such as data retrieval can improve perceived performance because posting to a user-defined event lets the processing continue before the process is complete.

RetrieveRow Decreases Performance

Any code (even a comment) within a DataWindow's RetrieveRow event decreases performance because PowerBuilder performs a Yield after each row returned to the DataWindow.

Limit the Code within ItemChanged and ItemFocusChanged Events

Too much code within the ItemChanged or ItemFocusChanged events causes delays in moving from column to column within a DataWindow.

Limit the Code within a Clicked Event if a Double-Clicked Event Exists

Within situations where there are both a clicked and a double-clicked event, too much code within the clicked event may keep a second click from getting registered. This effectively prevents the code within the double-clicked event from getting triggered.

Do Not Use the Other Event

The Other event is designed to handle a Windows event that does not correspond to a PowerBuilder event. The Other event is a holdover from PowerBuilder's previous versions, and you should not use it. Instead, create a user-defined event or use the PowerBuilder message object to handle the Windows events.

Database Connectivity Considerations

Use SetTransObject( ) instead of SetTrans( ) To minimize the number of times an application connects to the database, use **SetTransObject( )** rather than **SetTrans( )**. Using SetTrans( ), the application connects to the database, performs an action, and disconnects from the database for each database transaction. This decreases performance because of the added time to connect to the database.

Using SetTransObject( ) makes you responsible for connecting to the database from within a script. This lets you perform multiple database transactions during a single connection with the database. With SetTransObject( ), you are also responsible for committing or rolling back any data as well as explicitly disconnecting from the database.

The following example shows how you can update a master and detail DataWindow within a single database connection by using SetTransObject( ):

```
/**************************************************************************
** Insert a row into dw_master and three rows into dw_detail
** Update our DataWindows-maintain transaction appropriately
** Update the transaction from top down-from parent to child to
** ensure the data's integrity. This assumes that myTrans is
** already created, set up correctly, and f_getNextID returns
** the next available key.
**************************************************************************/
long      ll_newrow, ll_keyid, ll_row

dw_master.SetTransObject(myTrans)
dw_detail.SetTransObject(myTrans)
Connect Using myTrans ;

ll_keyid = f_GetNextId ()

ll_newrow = dw_master.InsertRow (0)

// Insert within Master
dw_master.object.id[ll_newrow]         = lKeyID
dw_master.object.cust_id[ll_newrow]    = 10
dw_master.object.order_date[ll_newrow] = today()
dw_master.object.sales_rep[ll_newrow]  = 5

// Insert within Detail
For ll_row = 1 to 3
    ll_newrow = dw_detail.InsertRow(0)
    dw_detail.object.id[ll_newrow] = lKeyID
    dw_detail.object.line_id[ll_newrow] = ll_row
Next

// Update the DataWindows
IF dw_master.Update() = 1 Then
    If dw_detail.Update() = 1 Then
        dw_detail.ResetUpdate ()
        dw_master.ResetUpdate ()
        Commit Using myTrans;
        Disconnect Using myTrans;
        Return True
    End If
End If

// Error within update. The DataWindow handles the error.
Rollback Using myTrans;
Disconnect Using myTrans;
Return False
```

Using Retrieve As Needed

Retrieve As Needed provides the ability to return a result set from the server to the client only as the rows are needed for displaying within a DataWindow. For example, if you size a DataWindow control to show only three rows at a time, Retrieve As Needed initially returns only enough data from the server to show the first three rows. As the user pages down through the data, PowerBuilder continues to return the data from the server to display within the DataWindow. The user may or may not continue to page down until all the data within the result set is returned to the client. The diagram in Figure 20.12 illustrates how Retrieve As Needed differs from the traditional data retrieval.

PowerBuilder implements Retrieve As Needed by opening a cursor and maintaining the cursor as it retrieves the rows from the server. When data is needed on the client, PowerBuilder simply fetches enough rows from the server (in two-page increments) to update the DataWindow's display (see Figure 20.13).

You must use Retrieve As Needed properly to achieve performance gains. If the

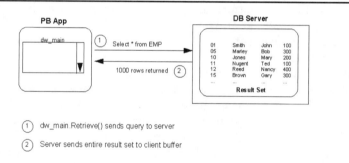

Figure 20.12   **Data retrieval without Retrieve As Needed.**

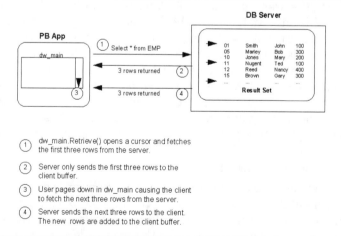

Figure 20.13   **Data retrieval with Retrieve As Needed.**

user pages through a large percentage of the result set, Retrieve As Needed decreases the perceived performance because PowerBuilder retrieves the data each time the user scrolls. In this situation, you should not use Retrieve As Needed. However, if a large result set is retrieved and the user usually does not page through the result set, Retrieve As Needed can provide a significant gain in the perceived performance.

Using Retrieve Rows to Disk

Retrieve Rows to Disk provides the ability to return large result sets from the server to the client and instead of keeping them within memory, PowerBuilder stores the data on the client machine. Whenever needed, PowerBuilder automatically displays in the DataWindow.

Preloading the Data

The preloading of data refers to loading database values into the client workstation's memory at application login time. This reduces the number of database queries and thus improves the application performance. Preloading data slows the login procedure but provides faster data access at any point after login. The price paid for preloading is the available memory on the client workstation. You should determine data preloading on a per-application basis.

The amount of data that you can preload is limited to the amount of available memory on the client workstation. You can preload data by retrieving it from the database at application login time and storing these values in a global array. After the data is loaded into the array, all subsequent requests for this data access the array rather than the database. This reduces the network traffic and increases performance.

There are some drawbacks to preloading data, however. With the data within memory, any changes made to the data in the database are not reflected immediately to the user. Because the application reads the data from the database at login time only, the user must exit the system and login again to see any changes. For this reason, if the data is fairly dynamic and the user must see the updates in a relatively short time frame, you should not preload this data. If, however, the data is accessed in a read-only mode or is fairly static, you should consider preloading as a way of increasing the performance. As mentioned earlier, preloading the data slows the login procedure, but it increases overall performance if the data is referenced several times throughout an application.

Analyze to determine which data the application should preload. Codes tables are good candidates for data preloading, because this data is usually fairly static and is used several times throughout an application. Without preloading, data referenced multiple times throughout an application requires a separate database query for each reference.

Minimize the Number of Connections

The number of connections to a database can impact performance on both the client and database server. All databases have a limit on the number of concurrent connections they allow. While this value varies among different platforms and RDBMS products, each connection consumes server resources. On the client side, each connection requires a separate PowerBuilder transaction object.

Commit Often

Because committing the changes to the database removes any pending locks and frees the server resources, issue a commit statement as often as possible within the logical unit of work.

Tune SQL Statements

Tuning the SQL sent to the server reduces the time and resources needed to process the statement. Most databases have either a rule- or cost-based optimizer that lets you structure a SQL statement in a way that achieves the best performance. To take advantage of them, it is important for you to know how these optimizers work.

Garbage Collection

Garbage collection involves freeing up memory from objects that are no longer accessible. PowerBuilder counts the references on each application object and marks as garbage those objects and object classes that have no references. The default garbage collection interval is 0.5 seconds. However, you can control the garbage collection by forcing immediate garbage collection with the **GarbageCollect( )** function or change the default interval for garbage collection with the **GarbageCollectSetTimeLimit( )** function.

Tracing and Profiling

PowerBuilder 6 provides three ways to collect and analyze the information about your PowerBuilder application's execution. This information helps you identify areas where you may want to rectify your code to enhance your application's performance. You can collect trace data in the following three ways:

- Use the tracing options on the Profiling page of the Systems Option dialog box. For details, refer to Chapter 9, "Debugging."
- Mark the scripts that you want to trace by using the trace functions. Refer to PowerBuilder's online documentation for a list of trace functions. All trace functions begin with the word *trace*.
- Add a window to your application that lets you turn tracing on and off as you run the application (the Profile.pbl provides w_starttrace).

After collecting the trace information, you can analyze it from a sample Power-Builder application Profiler (see Figure 20.14). PowerBuilder also provides you with the source code for this application. You can quickly modify the application to meet your needs.

New Features in PowerBuilder 6
New Timing Object

PowerBuilder also includes a new nonvisual timing object, similar to the window's timer event without you having to associate the event with a window.

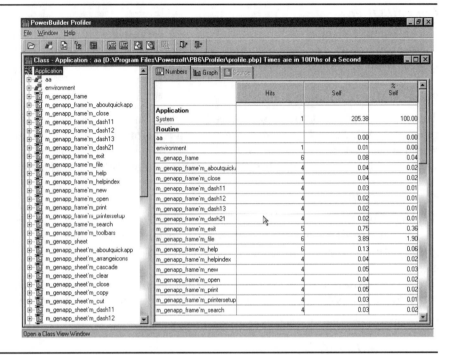

Figure 20.14 Analyze your application with the Profiler application.

New AncestorReturnValue Variable

When you extend a script within a descendent object, PowerBuilder 6 creates a local variable AncestorReturnValue that you can use to check the ancestor script's return value. The variable is also generated if you override the ancestor script and use the CALL syntax to call the ancestor event script.

PowerBuilder Browser

The PowerBuilder browser is nonmodel. The new browser lets you keep information available in the browser in the background while you move between the painters.

Improved Library Painter

The Library painter displays a last modified as well as last complied time stamp for every object. If the object is not yet compiled, the Library painter does not display the compile date. This helps you identify which objects were modified but not compiled.

IntelliMouse Support

PowerBuilder now supports the IntelliMouse pointing device.

CHAPTER 21

The Data Pipeline

The Data Pipeline object lets you transfer data between data objects in a database. These data objects may be database tables, PowerBuilder Query objects, or stored procedures. You may transfer data between objects in the same database or different databases—including databases from different RDBMSs.

The Data Pipeline is a very powerful feature. In the development environment, the Data Pipeline provides an easy way to make a local copy of the data for you to use during the development. Within a production environment, you can use the Data Pipeline to simplify the data distribution or synchronization of data among the different databases within a distributed environment. While you can perform these functions without the Data Pipeline, using the Data Pipeline eases the job of the developer and data administrator.

This chapter discusses the following:

- Creating a Data Pipeline object
- Executing a Data Pipeline object
- Data Pipeline object attributes, events, and functions

CREATING A DATA PIPELINE OBJECT

You can create the Data Pipeline objects by using the Data Pipeline painter. For example, assume we want to transfer data from a customer table on a production SQL Server database to a customer table on a local SQL Anywhere database.

When creating a new pipeline object, PowerBuilder prompts you for the source and destination database connections as shown in Figure 21.1.

Valid data sources include Quick Select, SQL Select, queries, and stored procedures. Figures 24.2 through 24.4 show examples of these interfaces.

For this example, select the SQL Select data source. Once you choose the source and the destination database connection profiles, PowerBuilder displays a table listing from the source database profile, as shown in Figure 21.5.

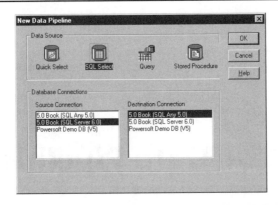

Figure 21.1 Choosing the source and destination database connections.

The Select Tables dialog box works the same way as for the other PowerBuilder painters, letting you select one or more tables to build the query. For this example, you require only the customer table. After making the table(s) selection, build the query by using the PowerBuilder SQL painter. Select all of the columns within the customer table and sort the results by the customer's identification number. Figure 21.6 shows the SQL painter for this query.

After building the query, return to the Data Pipeline workspace by clicking the **Design** icon on the painter toolbar. Figure 21.7 shows the Data Pipeline workspace.

The following sections describe the fields contained in Data Pipeline painter.

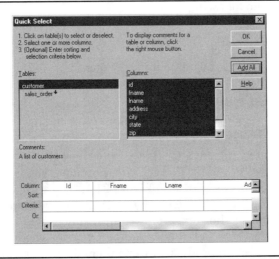

Figure 21.2 Using a Quick Select data source.

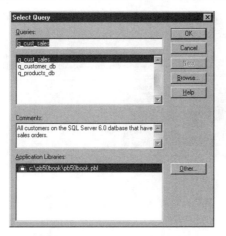

Figure 21.3   Using a query data source.

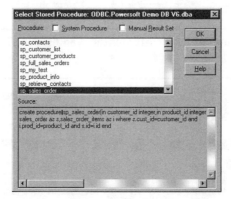

Figure 21.4   Using a stored procedure data source.

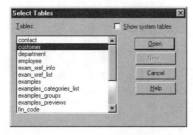

Figure 21.5   The table listing for a SQL Select data source.

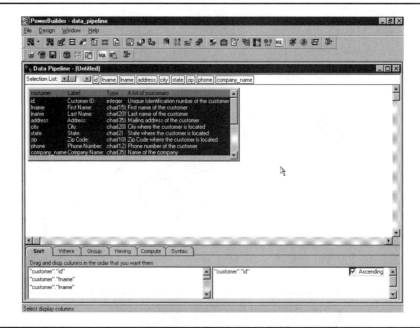

Figure 21.6 Selecting all the columns of the customer table and sorting by ID.

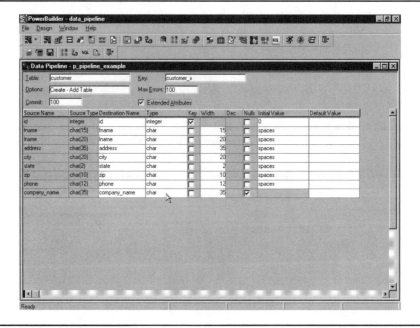

Figure 21.7 The Data Pipeline workspace.

Table

This field is the table's name within the destination database. The default is the source table's name, but you can change this. This field dynamically changes to an editable DropDownListBox that displays the available tables in the destination database, for the Refresh–Delete/Insert Rows, Append–Insert Rows, and Update–Update/Insert Rows options.

Options

This field designates the data transfer method. The choices are:

Create–Add Table. Creates a new table within the destination database and copies the data from the source data object to the newly created table. If the destination table already exists, an error occurs.

Replace–Drop/Add Table. Drops and recreates the table within the destination database and copies the data from the source data object to the newly created table. No error occurs if the destination table already exists.

When using either the Create–Add Table or Replace–Drop /Add Table options, you can modify the destination table's table definition. All modifications must follow the destination database's rules. Also, if you enter a value in the Key field, you must specify a key column for the destination table (and vice versa). PowerBuilder creates a primary key or index (whichever is supported by that RDBMS) for the table within the destination database.

Refresh–Delete/Insert Rows. Adds data to the destination table by first deleting all the data from the table and then copying the data from the source data object to the destination table. When using this option, the destination table must exist.

Append–Insert Rows. Appends the data from the source object to the destination table. PowerBuilder does not delete data from the destination table before inserting the source data. When using this option, the destination table must exist.

Update–Update/Insert Rows. Updates the data within the destination table by using data from the source data object. PowerBuilder inserts any new rows from the source data object into the destination table, while updating the rows from the source data object that already exist within the destination table. When using this option, the destination table must exist and you must specify the Key field.

Commit

Specifies the number of rows copied through the pipeline to the destination database before the changes are committed. This field's default value is 100. In this case, 100 rows are copied to the destination table before a Commit statement is issued. If Commit is set to 0, PowerBuilder issues a Commit only after reading all the rows. In this case, either PowerBuilder makes all the changes to the destination database or makes no changes. If Commit is less than 100, PowerBuilder uses it as the blocking factor. For example, if the Commit field is 10, PowerBuilder reads 10 rows and then writes them at once.

Key

This is the primary key's name for the table within the destination database. When using the Create–Add Table or Replace–Drop/Add Table options, PowerBuilder creates the primary key by using the name specified in this field.

Max Errors

This is the maximum number of errors allowed before stopping the pipeline. This field's default value is 100, which means that when the 100th error occurs during a pipeline execution, PowerBuilder stops the pipeline. PowerBuilder displays all the pipeline errors within a DataWindow that lets the user manually correct the errors and update the destination database with the corrected values. Correcting pipeline errors is discussed later in this chapter.

Extended Attributes

The extended attributes let you copy any extended attributes (validation rules, edit masks, or display formats) from the source data object to the destination table. The columns within the source table with the extended attributes should have the extended attributes copied to the new table to use them in the destination table.

Column Definition

This defines each column's name and type from the source data object along with the following information for each column within the destination table:

Destination Name.   Column's name in the destination table.

Type.   Column's datatype in the destination table.

Key.   Specifies if the column is a key column in the destination table.

Width.   Specifies the column's precision.

Dec.   Specifies the column's scale.

Nulls.   Specifies whether the column allows nulls values.

Initial Value.   Specifies the column's initial value if the column is not allowed to store null values.

Default Value.   Specifies the column's default value if no value exists for the column in the source data object.

PowerBuilder obtains the initial column information from the Select statement used to retrieve the data from the source database. When using the Create–Add Table or Replace–Drop/Add Table options, you may change this information. However, when using any of the other options, you may change only the Initial Value information.

Once you enter the column information, save the Data Pipeline object by selecting the **Save As...** option from the **File** menu and assigning the object a name (p_customer_example in our example).

A new data pipeline feature within PowerBuilder is the ability to transfer Binary/

Figure 21.8   Transferring a blob column by using the Pipeline painter.

Text Large Object datatypes. To transfer the data from a column of type blob, choose the **Database Blob...** menu item from the **Options** menu. Next, name the destination column and select the source database table and column, as shown in Figure 21.8.

EXECUTING A DATA PIPELINE

You can execute data pipelines within the development environment or add to an application and execute at runtime. This section discusses executing data pipeline in both the environments.

Using Pipelines within the Development Environment

To execute a pipeline within the development environment, simply click the **Execute Pipeline** icon from the Data Pipeline painter, as shown in Figure 21.9, or select **Execute** from the **Options** menu.

During pipeline execution, PowerBuilder displays the number of rows read, the number of rows written, the elapsed time, and the number of errors within MicroHelp.

TIP To change a pipeline object's source or destination database, select **Source Connect** or **Destination Connect** from the **File** menu and choose the new database.

A special Error DataWindow displays the errors encountered when executing a pipeline from the development environment. The Error DataWindow displays the table's name in the destination database in which the errors occur and the option that you select in the Data Pipeline painter. The Error DataWindow also displays each error message and the values in the row in which each error occurs.

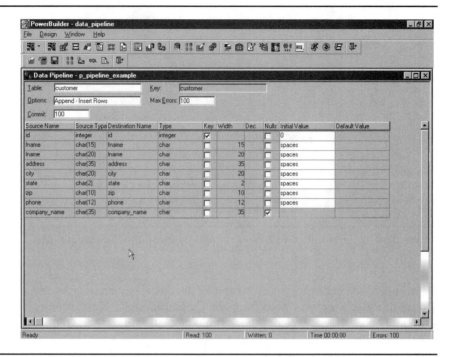

Figure 21.9 Executing a Data Pipeline within the development environment.

You may correct the errors by changing the values within the Error DataWindow and clicking the **Update Database** icon. When correcting the errors, PowerBuilder updates the database and displays any remaining errors within the Error DataWindow. For example, within the preceding example, change the option to Append–Insert Rows. Because data is already in the destination table, a duplicate key error occurs for each row. When executing the pipeline, PowerBuilder displays the Error DataWindow, as shown in Figure 21.10.

When all the errors are corrected, PowerBuilder returns the to the Data Pipeline Design dialog box. The user may also return to the Design dialog box without correcting the errors by clicking the **Design** icon.

TIP You may print or save the Pipeline errors to a file by selecting **Print** or **Save Row As...** from the **File** menu.

Using Pipelines within an Application

Using a data pipeline within an application requires creating a Data Pipeline object as well as creating a standard nonvisual user object of the pipeline type. Using the preceding example, create a user object as shown in Figure 21.11.

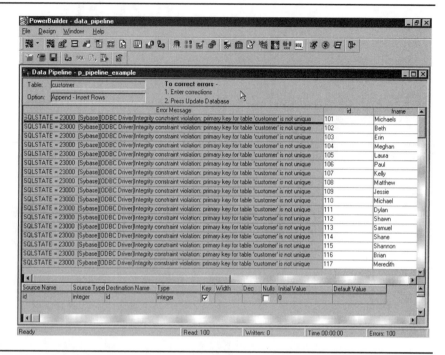

Figure 21.10   The Error DataWindow.

Select the standard class user object of type pipeline, as shown in Figure 21.12. This user object has special attributes, events, and functions. The next section describes the pipeline user object's attributes, events, and functions.

After saving the new user object (named u_pipeline_control), you can create the object dynamically within the application. For example, assume there is a window designed to use the Data Pipeline object that you created earlier in the chapter. This window contains a DataWindow for the customer table on the production SQL Server database, a DataWindow for the customer table on the local SQL Anywhere database, and a DataWindow as the Error DataWindow for the pipeline. In addition to these con-

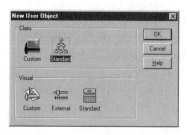

Figure 21.11   Creating a Pipeline User Object.

Figure 21.12 A nonvisual User Object inherited from the PowerBuilder Pipeline object.

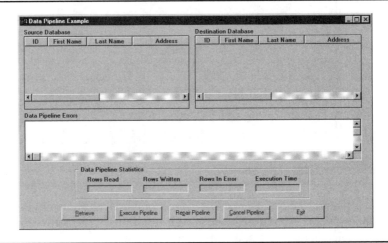

Figure 21.13 A sample window for executing a Data Pipeline within an application.

trols, the window contains four single-line edit controls to display the pipeline statistics and a set of commandbuttons to retrieve the data into the DataWindows, execute, and repair the pipeline. Figure 21.13 shows this window.

The window's open event calls a function to set up and connect the source and destination transaction objects, create the instance variable i_DataPipeline of type u_pipeline_control. i_DataPipeline is used throughout the application to refer to the Data Pipeline nonvisual user object. The first thing done after creating i_DataPipeline is to set its DataObject attribute to p_customer_pipeline, the Data Pipeline object you created earlier in the chapter. The window open event's code is:

```
SetPointer (Hourglass!)

// Connect to the Source and Destination Databases
Connect_DBs ( )
```

```
// Create the u_pipeline_control's instance and assign the
// p_customer_pipeline to it's DataObject
i_DataPipeline              = Create u_pipeline_control
i_DataPipeline.DataObject      = "p_customer_pipeline "
```

The window function **ConnectDBs( )** reads the connection information from example.ini and creates a separate Transaction object for the source and destination transactions. After connecting to each database, call the SetTransObject( ) function for the two main application DataWindows:

```
// Create the Source Transaction and Connect to the Source Database
i_SourceTrans = Create Transaction
i_SourceTrans.RDBMS = ProfileString ( "example.ini", "SQLServer", "RDBMS", "" )
i_SourceTrans.Database = ProfileString ( "example.ini", "SQLServer", "Database", "" )
i_SourceTrans.UserId = ProfileString ( "example.ini", "SQLServer", "UserId", "" )
i_SourceTrans.DBPass = ProfileString ( "example.ini", " SQLServer", "DatabasePassword", "" )
i_SourceTrans.LogId = ProfileString ( "example.ini", "SQLServer", &
"LogId", "" )
i_SourceTrans.LogPass = ProfileString ( "example.ini", "SQLServer", "LogPassword", "" )
i_SourceTrans.ServerName = ProfileString ( "example.ini","SQLServer", "ServerName", "" )
i_SourceTrans.DBParm = ProfileString ( "example.ini", "SQLServer", "DBParm", "" )

Connect Using i_SourceTrans;

If i_SourceTrans.SQLCode <> 0 Then
    MessageBox ( "Source Connect Error", i_SourceTrans.SQLErrText )
    Return
End If

// Create the Destination Transaction and Connect to the Destination
// Database
i_DestinationTrans = Create Transaction
i_DestinationTrans.RDBMS = ProfileString ( "example.ini", "SQLAnywhere", "RDBMS", "" )
i_DestinationTrans.Database = ProfileString ( "example.ini", & "SQLAnywhere",&
"Database", "" )
i_DestinationTrans.UserId = ProfileString ( "example.ini", "SQLAnywhere", "UserId", "" )
i_DestinationTrans.DBPass = ProfileString ( "example.ini", "SQLAnywhere", &
"DatabasePassword", "" )
i_DestinationTrans.LogPass = ProfileString ( "example.ini", "SQLAnywhere", &
"LogPassword", "" )
i_DestinationTrans.ServerName = ProfileString ( "example.ini", "SQLAnywhere", &
"ServerName", "" )
i_DestinationTrans.LogId = ProfileString ( "example.ini", "SQLAnywhere", & "LogId", "" )
i_DestinationTrans.DBParm = ProfileString ( "example.ini", "SQLAnywhere", & "DbParm", "" )
```

continues

```
Connect Using i_DestinationTrans;

If i_DestinationTrans.SQLCode <> 0 Then
    MessageBox ( "Destination Connect Error", &
        i_DestinationTrans.SQLErrText )
    Return
End If

// Assign the Transaction Objects to the Source and Destination DataWindows
dw_customer_source.SetTransObject ( i_SourceTrans )
dw_customer_destination.SetTransObject ( i_DestinationTrans )
```

The example.ini's [SQLServer] and [SQLAnywhere] sections are:

```
[SQLServer]
RDBMS=MSS
Database=PB60BookDB
UserId=joeuser
DatabasePassword=
LogPassword=
ServerName=prod_dev_01
LogId=joeuser
Lock=
DbParm=
Prompt=0
AutoCommit=0

[SQLAnywhere]
RDBMS=ODBC
Database=PB60Book
UserId=dba
DatabasePassword=sql
LogPassword=sql
ServerName=
LogId=dba
Lock=
DbParm=ConnectString='DSN=PB60Book;UID=dba;PWD=sql'
Prompt=0
AutoCommit=0
```

Initially, there are 110 rows in the customer table on SQL Server and only 16 rows in the customer table on SQL Anywhere. The window looks like Figure 21.14 after clicking **Retrieve**.

When you click **Execute**, PowerBuilder executes the pipeline as shown in the button's clicked event:

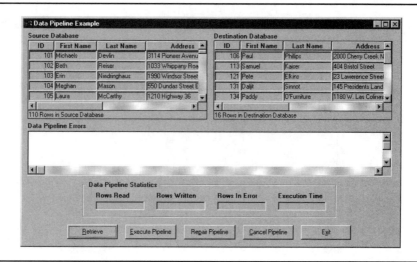

Figure 21.14   The sample window after retrieving.

```
Int       i_ReturnCode
Long      l_StartTime, l_EndTime

// Get the Transfer's Start Time
l_StartTime = CPU ( )

// Execute the Pipeline
i_ReturnCode = i_DataPipeline.Start ( i_SourceTrans, i_DestinationTrans, & dw_pipline_errors )

// Get the Transfer's End Time
l_EndTime = CPU ( )

// Display the Data Pipeline Statistics
sle_rows_read.Text = String ( i_DataPipeline.RowsRead )
sle_rows_written.Text = String ( i_DataPipeline.RowsWritten )
sle_rows_in_error.Text = String ( i_DataPipeline.RowsInError )
sle_execution_time.Text = String ( ( l_EndTime¤l_StartTime ) / 1000, & "##0.0" ) + " sec."

// Display the Results within the Destination DataWindow
dw_customer_destination.SetRedraw (False)
dw_customer_destination.Retrieve ( )
dw_customer_destination.Sort ( )
dw_customer_destination.SetRedraw (True)
```

This example assumes that the Data Pipeline object is using the Append–Insert Rows option in which PowerBuilder inserts the data into the destination database table when executing the pipeline. Figure 21.15 shows the results of executing the pipeline.

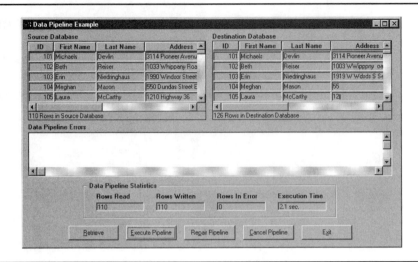

Figure 21.15   A sample window after executing the pipeline.

If we execute the pipeline again, we receive a duplicate key error for each row. The Error DataWindow displays each row that contains an error (in this case, all the rows), as shown in Figure 21.16.

At this point, there is freedom to make any corrections within the Error DataWindow and update the destination database by clicking **Repair Pipeline**. If you were to change the key value (customer ID) of the first two rows and click **Repair Pipeline**, PowerBuilder copies the two corrected rows to the destination database and the window looks like the one in Figure 21.17.

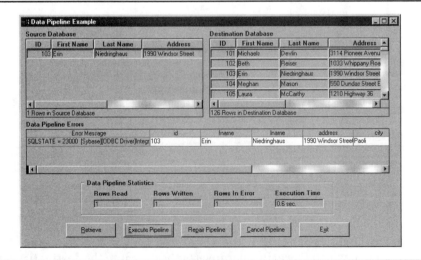

Figure 21.16   A sample window with the pipeline errors.

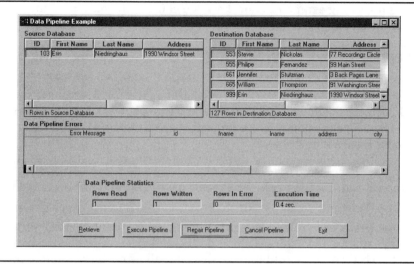

Figure 21.17   A sample window after correcting the errors and clicking Repair Pipeline.

Notice that the Rows Read, Rows Written, and Error values are changed from the original pipeline execution to correspond to the two corrected records. The **Repair Pipeline** button's code is:

```
Int      i_ReturnCode
Long     l_StartTime, l_EndTime

// Get the Transfer's Start Time
l_StartTime = CPU ( )

// Repair the Pipeline
i_ReturnCode = i_DataPipeline.Repair ( i_DestinationTrans )

// Get the Transfer's End Time
l_EndTime = CPU ( )

// Display the Data Pipeline Statistics
sle_rows_read.Text = String ( i_DataPipeline.RowsRead )
sle_rows_written.Text = String ( i_DataPipeline.RowsWritten )
sle_rows_in_error.Text = String ( i_DataPipeline.RowsInError )
sle_execution_time.Text = String ( ( l_EndTime§l_StartTime ) / 1000, &
"##0.0" ) + " sec."

// Display the Results within the Destination DataWindow
dw_customer_destination.SetRedraw (False)
dw_customer_destination.Retrieve ( )
dw_customer_destination.Sort ( )
dw_customer_destination.SetRedraw (True)
```

The preceding examples show how you can use the data pipelines from the Power-Builder development environment as well as within a PowerBuilder application.

DATA PIPELINE OBJECT ATTRIBUTES, EVENTS, AND FUNCTIONS

This section lists the Data Pipeline object's attributes, events, and functions. Note that these are associated with the nonvisual Data Pipeline user object and not the Data Pipeline object itself. The relationship between the Data Pipeline user object and the actual Data Pipeline object is the same as the relationship between a DataWindow control and a DataWindow object.

Data Pipeline objects have the following attributes:

RowsRead.   A long value that contains the number of rows read by the pipeline.

RowsWritten.   A long value that contains the number of rows read by the pipeline.

RowsInError.   A long value that contains the number of rows the pipeline found in error. Possible errors include duplicate keys within the destination table, null values copied into a column that does not allow nulls, or an invalid datatype.

DataObject.   A string value that contains the pipeline object's name.

Syntax.   A string value that contains the pipeline object's syntax.

The following events are associated with Data Pipeline objects:

PipeEnd.   Fired when the **Start( )** or **Repair( )** functions are completed.

PipeMeter.   Fired after the Data Pipeline object reads or writes each block of rows during a pipeline execution. The Commit setting you specified when creating the Data Pipeline object determines each block's size.

PipeStart.   Fired when the Start( ) or Repair( ) function is started.

The following functions exist for the Data Pipeline objects:

Start( ).   Executes a defined Data Pipeline object. The Start( ) function's format is:

```
pipelineobject.Start (sourcetransaction, destinationtransaction,
errordatawindow {,arg1, arg2,..., argn })
```

where:

> **pipelineobject.**   The name of the pipeline object to be executed.
>
> **sourcetransaction.**   The Source transaction object's name.
>
> **destinationtransaction.**   The Destination transaction object's name.
>
> **errodatawindow.**   The DataWindow control containing the pipeline Error DataWindow.
>
> **argn (optional).**   Retrieval arguments that you can specify within the Select painter.

The Start( ) function returns a 1 if successful and a –1 if an error occurs.

Repair( ).   Executes a defined Data Pipeline object to update the destination database with the corrections contained in the pipeline's Error DataWindow. The Repair( ) function's format is:

```
pipelineobject.Repair (destinationtransaction)
```

where:

> **pipelineobject.**   The name of the pipeline object to be repaired.

> **destinationtransaction.**   The Destination transaction object's name.

The Repair( ) function returns a 1 if successful and a −1 if an error occurs.

> **Cancel( ).**   Stops the execution of a Data Pipeline object. Call this function when a Data Pipeline is being executed or repaired. The **Cancel( )** function's format is:

```
pipelineobject.Cancel( )
```

where:

> **pipelineobject.**   The name of the pipeline object you want to cancel.

The Cancel( ) function returns a 1 if successful and a −1 if an error occurs.

In conclusion, the Data Pipeline object provides a simple way to transfer data between data objects in the same database or among different databases in a distributed data environment. This is a very powerful feature that you may use within the PowerBuilder development environment or within an application by using the PowerBuilder nonvisual pipeline user object. This user object type encapsulates the attributes, events, and functions necessary to dynamically transfer the data among the databases from a PowerBuilder application.

PART VI

Distributed Application and Internet Development

CHAPTER 22

Distributed Application Development

Distributed PowerBuilder (DPB) introduces a new way of architecting PowerBuilder applications. The traditional approach was based on a classic two-tier approach. This two-tier approach involved a client module, which included the PowerBuilder application and any business logic that you developed on the client side, and a server module, which included the database server. (The database server sometimes resided on the client machine, as in the case of stand-alone applications). PowerBuilder 5 introduced a mechanism for partitioning PowerBuilder applications into a logical three-tier, distributed solution. As you plan, design, and develop these applications, keep in mind that at this time the only objects that you can partition as a remote distributed object are the nonvisual user objects. Therefore, you should develop any modules that you plan for distribution as nonvisual user objects.

OVERVIEW OF DISTRIBUTED POWERBUILDER

The addition of DPB provides several new benefits to the classic PowerBuilder application design. Some of the major benefits include:

Centralized control. With an application's reusable components, such as business logic, deployed on the server, there are several maintenance and security benefits associated with the application's modules. It is much simpler to maintain or provide security for an application's modules on a few application servers rather than on hundreds of client machines.

Thinner client applications. Partitioning the application's parts off the client and moving them to the server results in a thinner client, therefore reducing the resource and system requirements on the client PC.

Enhanced scalability. With the application's modules deployed to the server, the processing required of a client application workstation is reduced. For example, if an application must perform processor-intensive mathematical calculations, moving that processing to execute on an application server reduces the client workstation's load requirements. This reduces the need to upgrade the several client workstations to higher processors and additional memory. Instead, you have to upgrade only a few application servers, which, in most cases, proves to be more cost effective. These are the main benefits of the DPB functionality.

With the release of PowerBuilder 6 comes a number of exciting new features that you can use to build applications by developing components and scaling your applications across multi-tiered, often a three-tiered, architecture. In particular, PowerBuilder 6 includes support for:

- Transaction servers, including Microsoft and Sybase transaction servers.
- Open technology standards, including extended UNIX platform support and extended database connectivity that includes support for Informix 7.2, Sybase SQL 11.1, ODBC 3, and more.
- Server push technology.
- Creation of shared objects that reside on the application server within a three- (or *n*-) tier architecture.
- Asynchronous application server processing.
- DataWindow synchronization.

This chapter discusses PowerBuilder 6's support for transaction servers and open technology standards. For more information on PowerBuilder 6's other distributed application development capabilities, such as server push technology, creating shared objects, asynchronous application server processing, and DataWindow synchronization, refer to Chapter 23, "Advanced Distributed Application Development."

This chapter covers the following:

- DPB classes and concepts
- Some uses of DPB
- Distributed PowerBuilder drivers and configuration
- Transaction server support
- Open technology support

A discussion of the DPB components within PowerBuilder follows.

DPB CLASSES AND CONCEPTS

Figure 22.1 shows the communication infrastructure for DPB and the role each of the new PowerBuilder objects play. This section explains these objects.

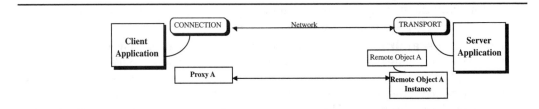

Figure 22.1   **The Distributed PowerBuilder communication infrastructure.**

DPB Classes

Figure 22.2 shows the DPB classes' object hierarchy.

Connection Object

To establish a connection and then send messages to the server application based on the specific driver information, use the connection object.

Declare a global connection variable within the application:

```
connection myconnect
```

Next, instantiate the global connection object by using the create statement and reference it by using the variable myconnect. Define the connection's properties based on the application's environment. The client application can now connect to the server via the connection object's **ConnectToServer( )** method:

```
myconnect = create connection
myconnect.driver = "namedpipes"
myconnect.location = "nt_houfs01"
myconnect.application = "dist_server"
myconnect.ConnectToServer()
```

You can implement this only if the server application is running and set up to listen. To set up the server application to listen, set up the transport object on the application server side. Table 22.1 describes the connection object's methods, Table 22.2 describes the connection object's properties, and Table 22.3 describes the connection object's events.

Transport Object

The transport object is the connection's server side. The object listens for the incoming client requests. Create the transport object on the server application. The first step is to declare a global variable as follows:

```
transport mytransport
```

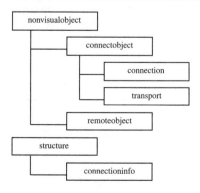

Figure 22.2   The DPB object hierarchy.

Table 22.1 The Connection Object's Methods

Method	Definition
ConnectToServer	Connects a client application to a server application.
DisconnectServer	Disconnects a client application from a server application.
GetServerInfo	Lets a client application retrieve the information about its connection to a server.
RemoteStopConnection	Lets a client application disconnect another client from a server application.
RemoteStopListening	Lets a client application instruct a server application to stop listening for the client requests.

Table 22.2 The Connection Object's Properties

Property	Definition
Application	Specifies the server application that a client application wants to connect to.
ConnectString	The text passed to the server's Application object's ConnectionBegin event at connection time. The text can include application-specific information, such as the database connection parameters.
Driver	The communications driver for the connection. Values are: WinSock, NamedPipes, OpenClientServer, Local.
ErrCode	The code indicating the most recent operation's success or failure.
ErrText	The text indicating the most recent operation's success or failure.
Location	Specifies the server application's location.
Options	Specifies one or more communications options.
Password	The password for connecting to the server.
Trace	Specifies one or more trace options.
UserID	The name or ID of the user connecting to the server. This value is application-specific. PowerBuilder does not evaluate this value.

Table 22.3 The Connection Object's Events

Event	Definition
Constructor	When the connection object is created.
Destructor	When the connection object is destroyed.
Error	When a client request cannot be satisfied.

A transport object variable called mytransport is created. Next, create the transport object's instance and reference the instance by this variable. Define properties such as driver information for the transport object. Call the transport object's **Listen( )** function so the transport application can listen for the client requests:

```
mytransport = create transport
mytransport.driver = "namedpipes"
mytransport.application = "dist_server"
mytransport.listen()
```

Once you have the connection and transport objects set up to send and receive, create the remote and proxy objects to perform the distributed processing. Table 22.4 describes the transport object's methods and Table 22.5 describes the transport object's properties.

Remote User Object

The remote object is simply a nonvisual user object. As mentioned in Chapter 7, "Graphs and Reporting," and throughout the book, you should develop the reusable components and application processing within nonvisual user objects whenever possible. The remote object discussed here is different from the remote object, which is a standard object shipped with PowerBuilder. To develop a remote sser object, simply create a nonvisual user object and declare the appropriate functions. Then, create a proxy name for the object. This proxy is simply the client reference to the remote user object. To create the proxy object, inherit from the PowerBuilder remote object as shown in

Table 22.4   The Transport Object's Methods

Method	Definition
Listen	Instructs a server application to begin listening for the client connections.
StopListening	Instructs a server application to stop listening for the client connections.

Table 22.5   The Transport Object's Properties

Property	Definition
Application	Identifies the server application.
Driver	The communications driver used to listen for the client connections. Values are WinSock, NamedPipes, OpenClientServer, and Local.
ErrCode	The code indicating the most recent operation's success or failure.
ErrText	The text indicating the most recent operation's success or failure.
Location	Specifies the pipe name's machine name portion for the NamedPipes driver.
Options	Specifies one or more communications options.
Trace	Specifies one or more trace options.

Figure 22.2. Move the remote user object that you developed with the application functionality to the remote application server. The proxy for that object resides on the application's client side.

Proxy Object

As the preceding section discussed, the proxy object is inherited from the PowerBuilder remote object class. Create one proxy object per remote object. The proxy object has the communication code to execute the methods within the remote user object on the server application. It is not visible from within PowerBuilder. To view the code in the proxy object, first export the object and view by using a text editor. The code for a proxy object source file for a proxy named bubba for a remote user object with one function called **gettest( )** that simply returns a string is shown next. Much of the other processing is already generated as part of naming the proxy from within the nonvisual remote User Object. Each time the nonvisual remote User Object is updated, a new proxy is generated.

```
$PBExportHeader$bubba.srx
forward
global type bubba from remoteobject
end type
end forward
global type bubba from remoteobject
end type
global bubba bubba
type variables
end variables
forward prototypes
public function string classname ()
public function boolean postevent (string e)
public function boolean postevent (string e,long w,long l)
public function boolean postevent (string e,long w,string l)
public function int triggerevent (string e)
public function int triggerevent (string e,long w,long l)
public function int triggerevent (string e,long w,string l)
public function string gettest ()
end prototypes
public function string classname ();
any __aapbpm__[]
return invoke_method("classname@rsp0",0,__aapbpm__)
end function
public function boolean postevent (string e);
any __aapbpm__[1]
__aapbpm__[1]=e
return invoke_method("postevent@rtp1s",1,__aapbpm__)
end function
public function boolean postevent (string e,long w,long l);
any __aapbpm__[3]
__aapbpm__[1]=e
```

```
__aapbpm__[2]=w
__aapbpm__[3]=l
return invoke_method("postevent@rtp3sll",3,__aapbpm__)
end function
public function boolean postevent (string e,long w,string l);
any __aapbpm__[3]
__aapbpm__[1]=e
__aapbpm__[2]=w
__aapbpm__[3]=l
return invoke_method("postevent@rtp3sls",3,__aapbpm__)
end function
public function int triggerevent (string e);
any __aapbpm__[1]
__aapbpm__[1]=e
return invoke_method("triggerevent@rip1s",1,__aapbpm__)
end function
public function int triggerevent (string e,long w,long l);
any __aapbpm__[3]
__aapbpm__[1]=e
__aapbpm__[2]=w
__aapbpm__[3]=l
return invoke_method("triggerevent@rip3sll",3,__aapbpm__)
end function
public function int triggerevent (string e,long w,string l);
any __aapbpm__[3]
__aapbpm__[1]=e
__aapbpm__[2]=w
__aapbpm__[3]=l
return invoke_method("triggerevent@rip3sls",3,__aapbpm__)
end function
public function string gettest ();
any __aapbpm__[]
return invoke_method("gettest@rsp0",0,__aapbpm__)
end function
on bubba.create
remoteobject::create_object("remoteobject1")
end on
on bubba.destroy
remoteobject::destroy_object()
end on
```

Client Application

Traditionally, the application's PowerBuilder side is the client application. This is still true except that it does not include the application processing that is distributed.

Server Application

With DPB, a new tier houses the remote applications, which are simply remote object managers. The server application can reside on a completely different machine or on a multithreaded server with the client application. Typically, the server application is located on a different computer.

SOME USES OF DPB

The many uses of DPB include executing remote programs from the server. For example, if there is a batch report or process that needs to execute on the server and the client must trigger the report, DPB can provide a simple interface for this to take place. DPB also is a good choice if you need to remove some of the processing from the client application due to its high processor or resource requirements. If you develop an application with some business logic that is shareable among multiple applications, if application scalability is or may become an issue, or if you need to minimize an application's maintenance requirements, DPB is a good choice.

DISTRIBUTED POWERBUILDER DRIVERS AND CONFIGURATION

Table 22.6 lists the various combinations of the operating platforms and drivers you can use with distributed PowerBuilder.

Communication Driver Platform Requirements and Usage

- Named Pipes Server, pbnps050.dll
  - Windows NT.
- Named Pipes Client, pbnpc050.dll
  - Windows NT.
  - Windows 95.
- Winsock Server, pbwss050.dll
  - Windows NT—Requires TCP/IP to be installed and configured.
  - Windows 95—Requires TCP/IP to be installed and configured.
- Winsock Client, pbwsc050.dll
  - Windows NT—Requires TCP/IP to be installed and configured.
  - Windows 95—Requires TCP/IP to be installed and configured.
  - Windows WFW 3.11—Requires Microsoft TCP/IP 32 for WFW.
- Open Client/Server Server, pboss050.dll, pbosrv050.exe
  - Windows NT—Requires Sybase Open Server to be installed and configured.

Table 22.6   Application Platforms and Drivers

Platform	Communication Driver	Server?	Client?
Windows 3.x	Sockets	No	Yes
	OpenClientServer	No	Yes
Windows NT 3.51	NamedPipes	Yes	Yes
	Sockets	Yes	Yes
	OpenClientServer	Yes	Yes
Windows95	NamedPipes	No	Yes
	Sockets	Yes	Yes
	OpenClientServer	No	Yes

Limitations

- Cannot generate an .EXE for a server.
- Server application cannot function as a client to itself but can be a client to other servers.
- Only one OpenClientServer transport object can listen at a time in a server application.
- The last two are limitations of CSLIB/CTLIB. Note, however, that one Open-ClientServer transport object can listen on multiple protocols simultaneously (Named Pipes, Winsock, IPX).

- Open Client/Server Client, pbosc050.dll.
  - Windows NT—Requires Sybase Open Client for Windows NT to be installed and configured.
  - Windows 95—Requires Sybase Open Client to be installed and configured.
  - Windows 3.x—Requires Sybase Open Client for Windows to be installed and configured.

Limitations

- Cannot send more than 64k data to server but can receive more than 64k.
- Local driver pbdpb050.dll.
  - Windows NT—No additional software is required.
  - Windows 95—No additional software is required.
  - Windows 3.x—No additional software is required.

TIP Powersoft continues to use *050* in its naming convention for these DLLs: pbnps050.dll, pbnpc050.dll, pbwss050.dll, pbwsc050.dll, pboss050.dll, pbosrv050 .exe, and pbdpb050.dll.

TRANSACTION SERVER SUPPORT

By using a transaction server, your application benefits from improved and enhanced transaction control and management services. Say your application uses multiple databases, and a number of users access the application. Without a transaction server, you must explicitly code the transaction management routines to handle the calls and commands to the different databases. By using a transaction server, you can save yourself a good deal of time and effort and focus more on your application's business logic. The transaction server handles transaction management effectively and efficiently. In particular, a transaction server performs the following services:

- Connectivity to the multiple databases
- Transaction, session, and connection management
- Threading, locking, and memory management
- Easy administration

A couple of prominent transaction servers are the Microsoft and Sybase transaction servers.

Sybase Transaction Server (Jaguar CTS)

Jaguar CTS is a new Sybase product that works well with Sybase's other products, including PowerBuilder and Adaptive server. Jaguar CTS is a component-based transaction server that supports hosting of multiple technology components, including JavaBeans, Java, C++, and ActiveX. As a result, you are not restricted to a particular component technology, and you can use the technology that best suits your application. In addition, Jaguar CTS is a highly scalable transaction server ideal for high-performance, multitier WebOLTP (Online Transaction Processing) applications. Jaguar CTS transaction server includes two components: a Transaction Processing (TP) monitor and an Object Request Broker (ORB).

To develop Jaguar CTS applets and servlets, you can choose from a number of standard development tools, including PowerBuilder, Power++, PowerJ, Visual Basic, Visual C++, and Visual J++.

In addition, Jaguar CTS supports a number of back end databases, including Sybase Adaptive Server, Sybase SQL Anywhere, Microsoft SQL Server, and Oracle 7.x. Jaguar CTS connects and communicates with these databases through a number of connection protocols, including ODBC, JDBC, Sybase Open Client, and CTLib.

TIP To get more information about Jaguar CTS, visit Sybase's Web site at www.powersoft.com/products/jaguar/prodinfo.html.

To download an evaluation copy of Jaguar CTS, visit Sybase's Web site at www.powersoft.com/products/jaguar/protected/betasrc.html.

To participate in technical discussion forums on Jaguar CTS, connect to the server forums.powersoft.com and subscribe to the newsgroup powersoft.public .jaguar.cts.

Microsoft Transaction Server

The Microsoft Transaction Server (MTS) is part of Microsoft's Active Platform Internet model. The Active Platform is a suite of technologies you can use to design intranet and Internet applications based on Microsoft's ActiveX technology.

The MTS is tightly integrated with Windows NT and the Microsoft BackOffice family of products. As a result, if you would like to use MTS, ideally you must use Windows NT as your application server's operating system. Like Jaguar CTS, MTS also supports hosting components that you create by using Java, ActiveX, and C++.

To develop MTS applets and servlets, you can choose from a number of industry standard development tools, including Visual Basic, Visual C++, and Visual J++.

Like Jaguar CTS, MTS also supports a number of back-end databases, including Sybase Adaptive Server, Sybase SQL Anywhere, Microsoft SQL Server, and Oracle 7.x. The MTS connects and communicates with these databases through a number of connection protocols, including ODBC and JDBC.

TIP To get more information on MTS, visit the Web site at www.microsoft
.com/ntserver/guide/trans_intro.asp.

   To download an evaluation copy of MTS, visit the Web site at www
.backoffice.microsoft.com/downtrial.

When Should You Use a Transaction Server?

If your application retrieves and updates data within multiple databases and a number of users access the application at any given time, you should consider using a transaction server. If your application retrieves and updates the data within a single
database, using a transaction server is not necessary. As your application grows and
you add access to multiple databases, you can introduce a transaction server.

OPEN TECHNOLOGY SUPPORT

PowerBuilder 6 includes support for the following technologies that make designing
your PowerBuilder 6 applications as open as possible:

Support for UNIX platform.   You can design and deploy your PowerBuilder 6
applications on the UNIX platform, including Sun's Solaris, IBM's AIX, and HP's
UX UNIX versions. In addition, PowerBuilder supports both Windows and Macintosh platforms. Several corporations use UNIX as the Web server or middle tier in
a three-tier client/server deployment. PowerBuilder's support for the UNIX platform is an important factor in increasing PowerBuilder's market share as the application development tool of choice within the industry.

Multiple platform support.   PowerBuilder's support for multiple platforms
helps you deploy the PowerBuilder PBLs you develop on one platform to other platforms with no recoding as long as the PowerBuilder objects do not make platform-
specific function calls. For example, if a PowerBuilder object calls the functions in
a Windows DLL, the PowerBuilder object works only on the Windows platform.
This is because only the Windows platform supports dynamic link library technology, unless you make the DLL available on the other platforms in a form that these
platforms support.

Database support.   PowerBuilder 6 also supports Informix 7.2, Sybase SQL 11.1
and Adaptive Server, ODBC 3, and more. This means your PowerBuilder 6 applications benefit from the latest versions of Informix, Sybase, and ODBC, and the features they offer.

UNICODE support.   PowerBuilder 6 provides extended language support with
UNICODE. You can design an application in one language and port the application
to another language very easily.

Third-party interface support.   PowerBuilder 6 includes expanded support for
third-party application interfaces. You can call the 32-bit Windows Application Programming Interface (API) functions within your PowerBuilder 6 applications. Before using an API function, include the function's prototype declaration within your

PowerBuilder application. The function's prototype declaration should reference the appropriate Windows DLL(s).

Source control management. You can integrate such version control environments as ObjectCycle and PVCS within PowerBuilder 6's development environment. ObjectCycle comes bundled within PowerBuilder 6's Enterprise Edition. Multiple developers working on a large PowerBuilder 6 project should use a version control system to enable easy team development, source code maintenance, and tracking. By using a version control environment, you can check objects in and out of an application, thus providing better control over the changes you and the other developers on your team make.

CHAPTER 23

Advanced Distributed Application Development

One interesting PowerBuilder feature is its support for building n-tier, distributed client/server applications. By distributing your application's functionality across several tiers, your application benefits from improved performance and easy maintainability.

The most commonly used n-tier architecture is the three-tier architecture. In a three-tier architecture, the client performs the presentation logic, the application server contains the business rule components (typically, in the form of nonvisual user objects), and the database server processes the SQL requests.

An n-tier (or three-tier) architecture also simplifies an application's distribution. For example, you can use a browser client to handle the presentation logic. The browser sends a request to the Web server, which connects to the application server to process the request.

The application server, in turn, hosts the business rule components. If your application's business requirements change, you need to update only the application server with the new business rule components. A change made at the application server is automatically reflected in all the clients. Your application's client machines may be geographically dispersed, yet they all see the changes almost instantaneously.

TIP The client can be a normal PowerBuilder application or an HTML form within a browser.

In Chapter 22, "Distributed Application Development," you learned about the distributed architecutre within PowerBuilder 6 and the different objects available within PowerBuilder to build an application server.

This chapter discusses the following topics related to distributed application development:

- Development methodology
- Creating shared objects
- Server push
- Asynchronous processing
- DataWindow synchronization

DEVELOPMENT METHODOLOGY

To develop an *n*-tier distributed application by using PowerBuilder 6, use the following steps:

1. Create the application server.
2. Create the client application.

> **TIP** You can run multiple instances of PowerBuilder 6 on the same machine. This way you can test your application on a single machine.

3. Deploy your application's database access logic on the application server. As a result, your application's database connections, commits, and rollbacks reside in a central location.
4. Multiple clients can access the business logic through the user objects residing on the application server. To do so, use PowerBuilder 6's ability to create proxy objects.
5. During design, consider whether your application needs DataWindow synchronization, asynchronous processing, or the server's ability to push information to the client. To learn more about writing PowerBuilder 6 applications that take advantage of DataWindow synchronization, asynchronous processing, and server push, refer to the sections "DataWindow Synchronization," "Asynchronous Processing," and "Server Push" later in this chapter.

> **TIP** You can design *n*-tier applications by using PowerBuilder 6 in two ways:
>
> 1. Browser-based thin client, where the Web server accesses the application server. This is the web.pb architecture. For more details on web.pb, refer to Chapter 25, "Using Internet Tools."
> 2. You can use the normal PowerBuilder client as your client, but the need for PowerBuilder 6's runtime files on the client machine basically defeats the purpose of building a thin-client application.

CREATING SHARED OBJECTS

This example demonstrates creating a nonvisual, shared object on the application server. Since the shared object resides on the application server, all clients accessing the application server can access the shared object's instance. As a result, there is no need to create separate instances of the object for each client connection.

By using shared objects, you can improve your application's performance. For example, you can use a datastore as a shared object and retrieve data from the database into the datastore only once (or at regular intervals). Thereafter, all the client connections use the shared object datastore, thus reducing network traffic and the number of hits on the database.

This example uses the agent table from the sales.db database. The agent table includes information about sales agents. Create a datastore shared object on the application server, retrieve the agents information into the shared object, and then use the shared object to return the number of agents retrieved.

Running the Application

Before running the application, add the following line of code to the c:\windows\services file:

```
pbserver            10091/tcp
```

This line of code specifies the port number the application server uses and the protocol the client and server use to interact and communicate with each other. In this case, the port number is 10091 and the protocol is TCP/IP.

Configure the ODBC for the Sales Profile through the ODBC painter, as shown in Figure 23.1. For more details on configuring your ODBC settings, refer to Chapter 15, "Open Database Connectivity."

TIP The Sales Profile points to the sales.db SQL Anywhere database.

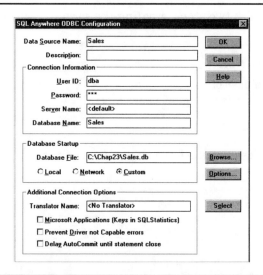

Figure 23.1   Creating a sales profile within the ODBC painter.

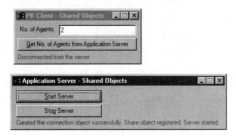

Figure 23.2 **Example of using shared objects on the application server.**

The server.pbl represents the application server. The client.pbl represents the client that connects to the application server.

Start an instance of PowerBuilder with the server.pbl, and run the application server. To start the application server, click **Start Server**.

Start another instance of PowerBuilder with the client.pbl this time, and run the application. To connect the client PowerBuilder application to the application server and retrieve the number of agents, click **Get No. of Agents from Application Server**. The user object function returns the total number of sales agents: 2.

Start a third instance of PowerBuilder with the client.pbl. Connect this instance to the application server and retrieve the number of agents. The server does not retrieve the number of sales agents. Instead, making use of the shared object, the server returns the same number of sales agents as was retrieved earlier for client 1.

Figure 23.2 shows an example of using shared objects on the server.

Designing the Application

The application's design includes two steps, creating the server application and creating the client application.

Creating the Server Application

On the server side, create the user object uo_agent.

Add an instance variable to the uo_agent user object:

```
datastore        ids_agent
```

Add the following PowerScript to the User Object's **constructor** event:

```
///////////////////////////////////////////////////////////////////////////////
// This script will connect to the database, and set the dataobject and
// transaction object to the datastore to be used within the functions.
///////////////////////////////////////////////////////////////////////////////
// Profile Sales
SQLCA.DBMS       = "ODBC"
SQLCA.AutoCommit = False
SQLCA.DBParm     = "Connectstring='DSN=Sales'"
```

```
// Connect to the database
Connect using SQLCA;

// Check for errors when connecting to the database
If sqlca.sqlcode <> 0 Then
MessageBox ("Cannot Connect to the Database", sqlca.sqlerrtext)
End If

// Set the transaction object, and dataobject for the datastore
ids_agent = Create datastore
ids_agent.dataobject = "d_agent_tab"
ids_agent.SetTransObject (SQLCA)
```

This script attaches the d_agent_tab dataobject to the datastore. You need to create this dataobject.

Add the following code to the user object's **destructor** event:

```
//////////////////////////////////////////////////////////////////////////////
// Destroy the datastore, and disconnect from database
//////////////////////////////////////////////////////////////////////////////
DESTROY ids_agent

Disconnect using SQLCA;
```

Add a method (read function) uf_refresh_agents to the User Object uo_agent. The method uf_refresh_agents refreshes the datastore by retrieving the information from the database and returns the total number of agents retrieved:

```
//////////////////////////////////////////////////////////////////////////////
// Retrieve the datastore, and return the no of agents
//////////////////////////////////////////////////////////////////////////////
long      ll_rowcount

ll_rowcount = ids_agent.Retrieve ()

Return ll_rowcount
```

Create another User Object, uo_agent_list, an object on the server that you create as a proxy object on the client. Create the proxy object on the server and then move the object to the client.pbl. To create a proxy object, use the following steps:

1. Open the user object uo_agent.
2. Click the right mouse button in the User Object painter. Select **Set Proxy Name** from the popup menu, as shown in Figure 23.3.
3. PowerBuilder displays the Save Proxy dialog box. Specify the proxy object's name uo_agent_list in the Proxy text box. You can add comments or a description of the proxy object within the Comments text box. To create the proxy object, click OK.
4. PowerBuilder, in turn, returns you to the user object painter. Save the User Object.

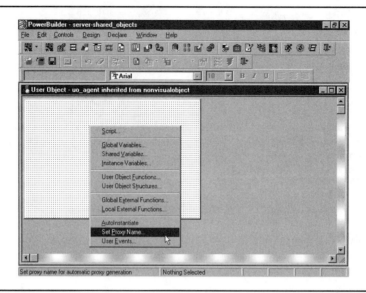

Figure 23.3 Set the proxy name.

5. You now see the library painter displaying a new user object with the name you specified in the Save Proxy dialog box (uo_agent_list). This new user object (see Figure 23.4) represents the proxy object. Move the proxy object from the server to the client.

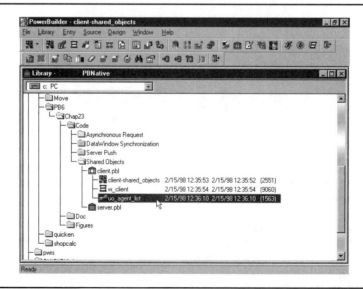

Figure 23.4 The proxy object—uo_agent_list.

Declare the following instance variables for uo_agent_list:

```
uo_agent     shared_object
long         il_rowcount
boolean      ib_retrieved
```

Within the user object uo_agent_list's constructor event, create an instance of the shared object and obtain a reference to the shared object as shown:

```
/////////////////////////////////////////////////////////////////////////////
// Instantiate the shared object, and get a reference to the object
/////////////////////////////////////////////////////////////////////////////
SharedObjectGet ("share1", shared_object)
```

Add the function uf_get_no_of_agents to the proxy user object uo_agent_list. The function uf_get_no_of_agents retrieves the number of agents from the database, if the information is not already retrieved. If the information is already retrieved, the function simply returns the number of agents:

```
/////////////////////////////////////////////////////////////////////////////
// If you have not yet retrieved the no of agents from the database,
// retrieve from the database, get the no of agents and return.
// In all other cases, just return the no of agents from the instance
// variable
/////////////////////////////////////////////////////////////////////////////

If ib_retrieved = FALSE Then
    ib_retrieved = TRUE
    il_rowcount = shared_object.uf_refresh_agents()
End If

Return il_rowcount
```

Start and Stop the Server Create and open a window w_server within PowerBuilder. Declare a couple of instance variables:

```
transport       mytransport
uo_agent        iuo_shared_object
```

Add a couple of user events, ue_start_server and ue_stop_server. To learn how to define a user event, refer to Chapter 4, "Multiple Document Interface (MDI) and Windows." Within the ue_start_server event:

1. Create the transport object.
2. Check the error code and verify if creating the transport object is successful.
3. Create an instance of the shared object and register the instance. The following is the **ue_start_server** event's code:

```
///////////////////////////////////////////////////////////////////
// Create the transport object, and initialize it
// Check for error codes on creation of the transport object
// Register, and instantiate the shared object
// Check for errors on registration of the shared object
///////////////////////////////////////////////////////////////////
string          ErrText, ErrNo
ErrorReturn     result

// configure the connection information
mytransport                 = CREATE transport
mytransport.driver          = "winsock"
mytransport.location        = "localhost"
mytransport.application     = "pbserver"

// start listening for client connections
mytransport.Listen ()

// Check for errors
If (mytransport.ErrCode <> 0) Then
    ErrText = mytransport.ErrText
    ErrNo = string(mytransport.ErrCode)
    MessageBox (This.Title , "Could not start 'Listener'.~r~n" + ErrNo &
                + ": " + ErrText )
    Close (This)
    Return
End If

st_display.Text = "Created the connection object successfully. Registering Shared
Object ..."

result = SharedObjectRegister ("uo_agent", "share1")

// Check for errors when registering the shared object
Choose Case result

    Case SharedObjectCreateInstanceError!
        MessageBox (This.Title, "Registering shared object—the &
                                specified object could not be created")
        Close (This)
        Return

    Case SharedObjectCreatePBSessionError!
        MessageBox (This.Title, "Registering shared object —A &
                    PowerBuilder context session could not be &
                    created for the object")
        Close (This)
        Return
```

```
      Case FeatureNotSupportedError!
          MessageBox (This.Title, "Registering shared object—This &
                     function is not supported on the Windows 3.x &
                     and Macintosh platforms ")
          Close (This)
          Return

      Case SharedObjectExistsError!
          MessageBox (This.Title, "Registering shared object—The &
                     shared object instance name has already been used")
          Close (This)
          Return
      Case MutexCreateError!
          MessageBox (This.Title, "Registering shared object— An &
                     operating system locking mechanism could not be &
                     obtained")
          Close (This)
          Return

      Case Success!
          //Nothing to do
End Choose

//Get the shared object registerd into the instance variable
SharedObjectGet ("share1", iuo_shared_object)

st_display.Text = "Created the connection object successfully. Share object
registered. Server started."
```

Within the ue_stop_server event:

1. Unregister the shared object's instance.
2. Stop the server.
3. Destroy the transport object. The following is the code for the ue_stop_server event:

```
/////////////////////////////////////////////////////////////////////////
// Unregister the Shared Object.
// Stop the Server.
// Destroy the Transport Object
/////////////////////////////////////////////////////////////////////////
ErrorReturn result

result = SharedObjectUnRegister ("share1")

// Check for errors on unregistering the shared object
Choose Case result
```

continues

```
        Case SharedObjectNotExistsError!
            MessageBox (This.Title, "UnRegistering Shared Object-&
                                    The shared object instance name &
                                    has not been registered")
            Close (This)
            Return

        Case FeatureNotSupportedError!
            MessageBox (This.Title, "Registering Shared Object-This &
                                    function is not supported on the &
                                    Windows 3.x and Macintosh platforms ")
            Close (This)
            Return

        Case Success!
            // Nothing to do
    End Choose

mytransport.stopListening()

DESTROY mytransport

st_display.Text = "Server Stopped. Press the Start Button to Start the
PowerBuilder Application Server"
```

Creating the Client Application

Create the client application by using the following steps:

1. Create the connection object. By using the connection object, you can connect to the application server.
2. Check for errors connecting to the server. If no error occurs, create the remote object.
3. Check for errors creating the remote object.
4. If no error occurs, call the remote user object's function to retrieve the number of sales agents.
5. Display the number.
6. Destroy the remote and connection objects.

The code for the client application is shown next. Within the application object's **open** event for the client.pbl, add the following code:

```
//////////////////////////////////////////////////////////////////////
// Open the client window
//////////////////////////////////////////////////////////////////////
Open (w_client)
```

Create a window w_client. Declare the following instance variables for the window:

```
connection              myconnect
```

Declare a user event **ue_get_agents**. Add the following code to this event:

```
////////////////////////////////////////////////////////////////////
// Create the connection object and connect to the server
// Check for errors upon connecting to the server
// Create the remote object
// Check for errors upon creating the remote object
// Call the remote object function and retrieve the no of agents on
// the server
// Destroy the remote and connection objects
////////////////////////////////////////////////////////////////////
connection        myconnect
uo_agent_list     iou_agent

// Create the connection object and connect to the server
myconnect              = create connection
myconnect.driver       = "winsock"
myconnect.application   = "pbserver"
myconnect.location     = "localhost"

// Check for errors upon connecting to the server
If myconnect.ConnectToServer () <> 0 Then
    MessageBox ("Connect to Server", "Failed")
End If

// Create the remote object
// Check for errors upon creating the remote object
If myconnect.CreateInstance (iou_agent) <> 0 Then
    MessageBox ("Create Instance",  "Failed")
End If

// Call the remote object function and get the no of agents on the server
If isValid(iou_agent) Then
    sle_1.text = String(iou_agent.uf_get_no_of_agents())
Else
    MessageBox ("Agents", "Error in Instantiating Remote Object")
End If

// Destroy the remote object
Destroy iou_agent

// Destroy the connection object
myconnect.DisconnectServer ()
```

The next section discusses implementing server push by using PowerBuilder 6.

SERVER PUSH

PointCast Network is an excellent example of push technology. You can configure PointCast Network to download and display the specific information you are interested in at regular intervals. As a result, you need not search the Internet for information. PointCast searches the Internet for you and displays the information you want in the format you specify. The PointCast server searches and *pushes* the information on to your desktop. This is a very helpful technology as it frees up the client machine so you can use it to perform other tasks. With PowerBuilder 6, you can design *n*-tier client/server applications that take advantage of server push technology.

In this example, you learn about implementing server push by using PowerBuilder 6. The client application establishes a connection with the application server. You develop both the client and application server by using PowerBuilder 6. The server hosts the datastores that you populate with the stock price information from the stocks.db database. The user specifies the stock symbol through the client front end. The server, in turn, retrieves the stock price information from the datastores and pushes the data to the client. To push the data to the client, the server calls a function of the remote object and displays the stock price on the client.

TIP The examples discussed in this chapter are for demonstration purposes only. The intent is to demonstrate how you can use PowerBuilder 6 to implement a number of different things. Real-world production examples may be more complex.

Running the Application

Before running the application, add the following line of code to the c:\windows\services file:

```
pbserver          10091/tcp
```

Configure the ODBC for the Stocks Profile through the ODBC painter, as shown in Figure 23.5.

TIP The Stocks Profile points to the stocks.db SQL Anywhere database.

Start an instance of PowerBuilder with the server.pbl and run the application server. To start the application server, click **Start Server**. Start another instance of PowerBuilder with the client.pbl this time, and run the application. To connect to the application server, click **Connect to Server**.

When you click **Get Stock Price**, the client validates the filter DataWindow and sends the stock symbol to the server. Upon receiving the stock symbol, the server finds

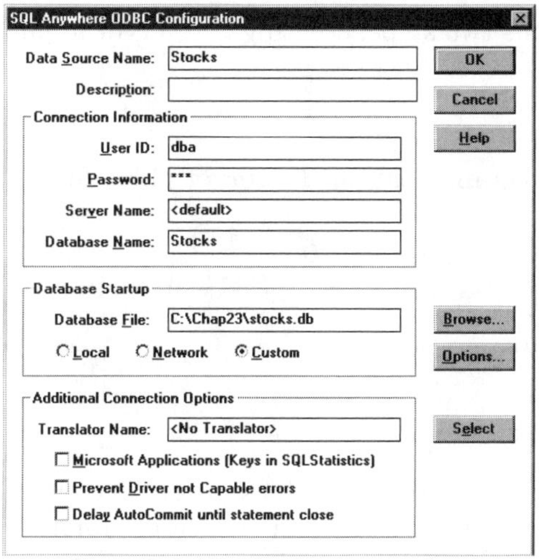

Figure 23.5   Configuring your ODBC for the Stocks Profile.

the stock symbol within the database (read datastore), retrieves the stock price and pushes the data back to the client. To push the data back to the client, the server calls a function of the client with the results of its processing. In this case, the server finds the stock price on the server in the datastore and calls a function of the client with the stock price. The client-side function, in turn, displays the stock price.

The client sends the stock symbol every nth second, as specified by the user in the filter DataWindow. The server, in turn, processes the information at its end, retrieves the stock quote, and pushes the data back to the client. The client, in turn, displays the stock price within the DataWindow's Share Price column. This is an example of implementing server push with PowerBuilder 6 (see Figure 23.6).

To disconnect from the server, click **Disconnect From Server**.

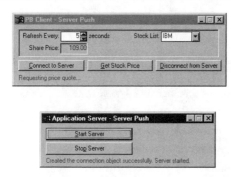

Figure 23.6   Example of Server Push.

Designing the Application

The application's design includes two steps, creating the server application and creating the client application.

Creating the Server Application

Within the application object's **open** event for the server.pbl, add the following code:

```
//////////////////////////////////////////////////////////////////////
// Open the server window that will create this application as a server,
// and listen to client requests
//////////////////////////////////////////////////////////////////////

open(w_server)
```

Create a nonvisual user object uo_retrieve_stock_price. The object connects to the database, retrieves all the stock prices, and provides another user object—uo_get_stock_price—with the stock price the client requests. For more details on creating a nonvisual object, refer to Chapter 6, "Structures, User Objects, and Functions."

Create an instance variable for uo_retrieve_stock_price as follows:

```
datastore      ids_stocks
```

Add the following PowerScript to the uo_retrieve_stock_price User Object's constructor event:

```
//////////////////////////////////////////////////////////////////////
// This script will connect to the database, set the dataobject and
// transaction object to the datastore to be used within the functions.
//////////////////////////////////////////////////////////////////////

// Profile Stocks
SQLCA.DBMS           = "ODBC"
SQLCA.AutoCommit     = False
SQLCA.DBParm         = "Connectstring='DSN=Stocks'"

// Connect to the database
Connect using SQLCA;

// Check for errors when connecting to the database
If SQLCA.sqlcode <> 0 Then
    MessageBox ("Cannot Connect to the Database", sqlca.sqlerrtext)
End If

// Set the transaction object, and dataobject for the datastore
ids_stocks = CREATE datastore
ids_stocks.dataobject = "d_stock_tab"
ids_stocks.SetTransObject (SQLCA)
ids_stocks.Retrieve ()
```

This script attaches the d_stock_tab dataobject to the datastore. You need to create this dataobject.

Add the following PowerScript to the uo_retrieve_stock_price user object's **destructor** event:

```
//////////////////////////////////////////////////////////////////////////////
Destroy the datastore, and disconnect from the database
//////////////////////////////////////////////////////////////////////////////
DESTROY ids_stocks

Disconnect Using SQLCA;
```

Add a method uf_get_stock_price to the uo_retrieve_stock_price user object. The uf_get_stock_price function retrieves the price quote through the datastore. The uf_get_stock_price function's code is:

```
////////////////////////////////////////////////////////////////////////
// Find the stock symbol in the datastore, and retrieve the stock price
////////////////////////////////////////////////////////////////////////
double     idb_stock_price
long       ll_row

ll_row = ids_stocks.Find ("stock_symbol ='"+as_stock_symbol+"'", &
                                    1, ids_stocks.RowCount())
If ll_row > 0 Then
     idb_stock_price = ids_stocks.object.stock_price[ll_row]
Else
     idb_stock_price = 0
End If

Return idb_stock_price
```

Similarly, create the user object uo_get_stock_price. Create an instance variable for uo_get_stock_price as follows:

```
uo_retrieve_stock_price     iuo_retrieve_stock_price
```

Add the following PowerScript to the uo_get_stock_price User Object's **constructor** event:

```
//////////////////////////////////////////////////////////////////////////////
// Create the user object for retrieving the stock price
//////////////////////////////////////////////////////////////////////////////
iuo_retrieve_stock_price = CREATE uo_retrieve_stock_price
```

Add the following PowerScript to the uo_get_stock_price User Object's **destructor** event:

```
//////////////////////////////////////////////////////////////////////////////
// Destroy the datastore
//////////////////////////////////////////////////////////////////////////////
DESTROY iuo_retrieve_stock_price
```

Add a method uf_send_price_quote to the uo_get_stock_price user object. The uf_send_price_quote function's code is:

```
//////////////////////////////////////////////////////////////////////////
// Get the stock price from the user object, and push it back to the client
//////////////////////////////////////////////////////////////////////////
double idb_stock_price

idb_stock_price = iuo_retrieve_stock_price.uf_get_stock_price (as_company_symbol)

auo_response_object.uf_set_stock_price (idb_stock_price)

Return
```

The uo_get_stock_price user object is an object on the server. The object contains the uo_retrieve_stock_price as an instance variable to obtain a particular stock's price. Create a proxy from this user object on the server, and then move the proxy to the client.

Start and Stop the Server Write code to start and stop the application server within the window object w_server. Open the window w_server within PowerBuilder and declare an instance variable:

```
transport      mytransport
```

Define a couple of user events: ue_start_server and ue_stop_server. Within the ue_start_server event:

1. Create the transport object.
2. Check the error code and verify if creating the transport object is successful.
3. Create and register an instance of the shared object. The following is the ue_start_server event's code:

```
//////////////////////////////////////////////////////////////////////////
// Create the transport object, and initialize it
// Check for error codes on creation of the transport object
//////////////////////////////////////////////////////////////////////////
string          ErrText, ErrNo

// configure connection information
mytransport                = CREATE transport
mytransport.driver         = "winsock"
mytransport.location       = "localhost"
mytransport.application    = "pbserver"

// start listening for client connections
mytransport.Listen()

// Check for errors
```

```
If (mytransport.ErrCode <> 0) Then
    ErrText = mytransport.ErrText
    ErrNo = string(mytransport.ErrCode)
    MessageBox (This.Title , "Could not start 'Listener'.~r~n" + ErrNo &
 + ": " + ErrText )
    Close (This)
    Return
End If


st_display.Text = "Created the connection object successfully. Server started."
```

Within the ue_stop_server event:

1. Stop the server.
2. Destroy the transport object. The following is the ue_stop_server event's code:

```
//////////////////////////////////////////////////////////////////////////
// Stop the server, and destroy the transport object
//////////////////////////////////////////////////////////////////////////
mytransport.stopListening()

DESTROY mytransport

st_display.Text = "Server stopped. To restart the application server, click Start
Server."
```

Creating the Client Application

To create the client application, use the following steps:

1. Open a new window, w_client.
2. Insert a blank row into the filter DataWindow within the window's open event.
3. Add an event to the window, ue_connect_to_server.
4. Within the event, create the connection object. To connect to the application server, use the connection object.
5. Check for errors connecting to the server. If no errors occur, create the remote object.
6. Check for errors when creating the remote object.
7. Add another window event, ue_get_price_quote. In the event, get the timer and price symbol from the DataWindow. Set the timer to call this event periodically and refresh the stock price. Call the remote object's function and pass the stock symbol to this function. Upon processing, the server returns the stock price to the client by calling the client's function.
8. Call the ue_get_price_quote event in the window's timer event.
9. Add another window event, ue_disconnect_from_server. In the event, destroy the remote and connection objects.
10. Create a user object uo_response_object and add the function uf_set_stock_price to

the user object. This is a remote object the server uses to return the stock quotes. This object is an important part of the server push technology where you can create proxy objects from the client to the server, thereby enabling server push.

The code for the client application is shown next. Within the application object's open event for the client.pbl, add the following code:

```
/////////////////////////////////////////////////////////////////////
// Open the client window
/////////////////////////////////////////////////////////////////////
Open (w_client)
```

Create a window w_client. Declare the following instance variables for the window:

```
connection           myconnect
uo_get_stock_price    iou_get_stock_price
```

Add the following code to the window's **timer** event:

```
This.Event ue_get_price_quote (0,0)
```

Add the following code to the window's open event:

```
/////////////////////////////////////////////////////////////////////////
// Insert a blank row within the external datawindow
/////////////////////////////////////////////////////////////////////////
dw_stock_price.ScrolltoRow (dw_stock_price.InsertRow (0))
```

Declare the following user events:

- ue_connect_to_server
- ue_get_price_quote
- ue_disconnect_from_server

The code for the ue_connect_to_server user event is:

```
///////////////////////////////////////////////////////////////////////////
// Create the connection object, and connect to the server.
// Check for errors when connecting to the server
// Create the remote object
// Check for errors when creating the remote object
///////////////////////////////////////////////////////////////////////////

// Create the connection object, and connect to the server
myconnect                = CREATE connection
myconnect.driver         = "winsock"
myconnect.application     = "pbserver"
myconnect.location        = "localhost"

st_display.Text = "Connecting to the PowerBuilder application server..."
// Check for errors when connecting to the server
```

```
If myconnect.ConnectToServer () <> 0 Then
    MessageBox (This.Title, "Connection to the application server failed!")
Else
    st_display.Text = "Connection to the application server successful"
End If


// Create the remote object
// Check for errors when creating the remote object
If myconnect.CreateInstance (iou_get_stock_price) <> 0 Then
    MessageBox (This.Title, "Creating instance of the remote object failed")
Else
    st_display.Text = "Creation of the remote object successful"
End If
```

The code for the ue_get_price_quote user event is:

```
///////////////////////////////////////////////////////////////////////////////
// Get the timer, and price symbol from the datawindow
// Set the timer to call this event periodically
// Call the remote object function, and obtain the share price
///////////////////////////////////////////////////////////////////////////////
uo_response_object    iou_response_object
integer               ii_timer
string                is_stock_symbol

// Get the timer, and price symbol from the datawindow
If dw_stock_price.AcceptText () = -1 Then Return

ii_timer        = dw_stock_price.object.timer_set[1]
is_stock_symbol = dw_stock_price.object.share_list[1]

// Set the timer to call this event periodically
If ii_timer > 65 Then ii_timer = 65
If ii_timer < 0  Then ii_timer = 0
Timer (ii_timer)

// Create the response object
iou_response_object = CREATE uo_response_object

// Call the remote object function, and obtain the share price
If IsValid(iou_get_stock_price) And IsValid(iou_response_object) Then
    iou_response_object.uf_initialize (dw_stock_price)
    iou_get_stock_price.uf_send_price_quote (is_stock_symbol, iou_response_object)
    st_display.Text = "Requesting price quote..."
Else
    MessageBox (This.Title, "Error in instantiating the remote object")
End If

DESTROY iou_response_object
```

The code for the ue_disconnect_from_server user event is:

```
///////////////////////////////////////////////////////////////////////
// Reset the timer
// Destory the remote, and the connection objects
///////////////////////////////////////////////////////////////////////
Timer (0)

// Destroy the remote object
If IsValid (iou_get_stock_price) Then
     DESTROY iou_get_stock_price
End If

// Destroy the connection object
If IsValid (myconnect) Then
     myconnect.DisconnectServer ()
End If
st_display.Text = "Disconnected from the application server"
```

Create a nonvisual user object called uo_response_object. This is an object on the client. The object has a datastore as an instance variable that shares data with the DataWindow within the w_client window. Create a proxy of this object, move the proxy to the server. The server uses the object's uf_set_stock_price function to push the data back to the client.

Create an instance variable for uo_response_object as follows:

```
datastore    ids_stock_price
```

Add the following PowerScript to the uo_response_object User Object's constructor event:

```
///////////////////////////////////////////////////////////////////////
// Create the datastore
///////////////////////////////////////////////////////////////////////
ids_stock_price = CREATE datastore

ids_stock_price.dataobject = "d_display_stock_price"
```

This script attaches the d_display_stock_price dataobject to the datastore. You need to create this dataobject.

Add the following PowerScript to the uo_response_object User Object's destructor event:

```
//////////////////////////////////////////////////////////////////
// Destroy the data store
//////////////////////////////////////////////////////////////////
DESTROY ids_stock_price
```

Add the methods uf_initialize and uf_set_stock_price to the uo_response_object user object.

The uf_initialize function's code is:

```
///////////////////////////////////////////////////////////////////////////////
// Share the data
///////////////////////////////////////////////////////////////////////////////
adw_stock_price.ShareData (ids_stock_price)

Return
```

The uf_set_stock_price function's code is:

```
///////////////////////////////////////////////////////////////////////////////
// Display the stock price
///////////////////////////////////////////////////////////////////////////////
ids_stock_price.object.share_price[1] = al_stock_price
Beep (2)
Return
```

You have now created a distributed PowerBuilder application by using server push technology.

The next section helps you develop another interesting application by using asynchronous processing.

ASYNCHRONOUS PROCESSING

In this section, you implement asynchronous requests by using PowerBuilder 6's distributed application development capabilities. The example uses the books.db database. The database includes information about publishers, authors, and books. A user object containing a datastore resides on the server. The client front end includes drop-down listboxes that you populate asynchronously with the data from the datastore. You can then execute SQL requests. For example, you can find books published by a particular publisher.

To implement asynchronous processing, use the POST method. When a client application sends a message to the server by using the POST method, the server stores the method within its queue. At this point, the client application is free to perform other tasks. In other words, the client application need not wait for the server to complete processing the request the client sends by using the POST method.

TIP When you implement asynchronous processing, note that you cannot use server push to push the data back to the client.

Running the Application

Before you run the application, add the following line of code to the c:\windows\services file:

```
pbserver          10091/tcp
```

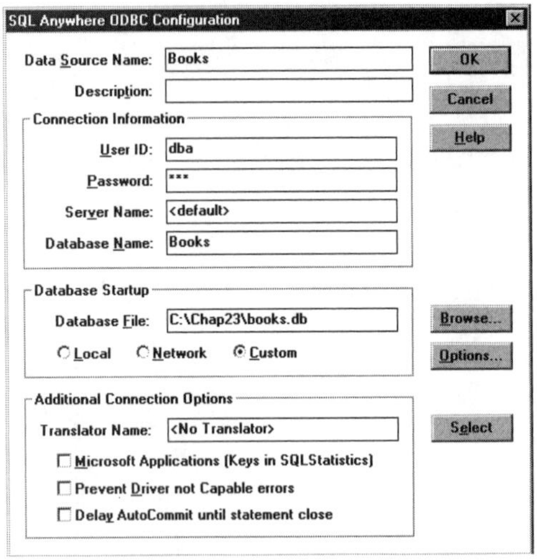

Figure 23.7 Configuring your ODBC for the Books Profile.

Configure the ODBC for the Books Profile through the ODBC painter, as shown in Figure 23.7.

TIP The Books Profile points to the books.db SQL Anywhere database.

Start an instance of PowerBuilder with the server.pbl, and run the application. To start the application server, click **Start Server**.

Start another instance of PowerBuilder by using the client.pbl. Run the client.pbl application. To connect to the server, click **Connect to Server**. Click **Fill Drop Downs**, and the client sends asynchronous requests to the server to populate the datastores on the server. In addition, the client also populates the drop-down filters for the publishers and authors. Choose a publisher, an author, or both, and click **Get Book Names**. The client application displays a list of books in the DataWindow (see Figure 23.8).

To disconnect from the server, click **Disconnect from Server**.

Designing the Application

The application's design includes two steps, creating the server application and creating the client application.

Creating the Server Application

Within the application object's open event for the server.pbl, add the following code:

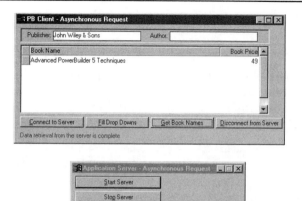

Figure 23.8   Example of asynchronous processing.

```
/////////////////////////////////////////////////////////////////////////
// Open the server window that will create the application as a server,
// and listen to client requests
/////////////////////////////////////////////////////////////////////////

open(w_server)
```

Create a structure str_name with the elements as shown in Figure 23.9.

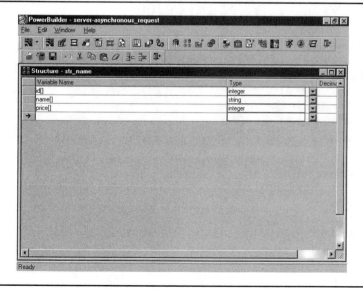

Figure 23.9   Elements of the str_name structure.

TIP You need this structure on the client side, too. You may copy the structure to the client.pbl.

Create a nonvisual user object called uo_data. The uo_data resides on the application server. The object connects to the database and uses the datastores as instance variables to store the list of authors, publishers, and books.

Create instance variables for uo_data as follows:

```
datastore    ids_books, ids_authors, ids_publishers
str_name     istr_publishers, istr_authors
boolean      ib_connected
```

Add the following PowerScript to uo_data User Object's constructor event:

```
//////////////////////////////////////////////////////////////////////////
// Create the datastore
//////////////////////////////////////////////////////////////////////////
ids_stock_price = CREATE datastore

ids_stock_price.dataobject = "d_display_stock_price"
```

Add the following PowerScript to uo_data User Object's destructor event:

```
//////////////////////////////////////////////////////////////////////////
// Destroy the datastores, if created
// Disconnect from database, if connected
//////////////////////////////////////////////////////////////////////////

If IsValid (ids_books)      Then DESTROY ids_books
If IsValid (ids_authors)    Then DESTROY ids_authors
If IsValid (ids_publishers) Then DESTROY ids_publishers

If ib_connected Then
    disconnect using sqlca;
End If
```

Add the following methods:

- uf_get_publishers
- uf_connect_to_database
- uf_populate_publishers
- uf_get_authors
- uf_populate_authors
- uf_get_books
- uf_populate_books

The PowerScript for uf_get_publishers is:

```
//////////////////////////////////////////////////////////////////////
// Return the publishers
//////////////////////////////////////////////////////////////////////
Return istr_publishers
```

The PowerScript for uf_connect_to_database is:

```
//////////////////////////////////////////////////////////////////////////
// This script will connect to the database
//////////////////////////////////////////////////////////////////////////
// Profile Books
SQLCA.DBMS       = "ODBC"
SQLCA.AutoCommit = False
SQLCA.DBParm     = "Connectstring='DSN=Books'"

// Connect to the database
Connect using SQLCA;

// Check for errors when connected to the database
If sqlca.sqlcode <> 0 Then
    MessageBox ("Cannot Connect to the Database", sqlca.sqlerrtext)
    Return -1
End if

Return 1
```

The PowerScript for uf_populate_publishers is:

```
//////////////////////////////////////////////////////////////////////////
// Retrieve all the publishers
//////////////////////////////////////////////////////////////////////////
long          ll_row, ll_rowcount

// Check for database connection. If there is no prior connection,
// connect to the database
If Not ib_connected Then
    If uf_connect_to_database () = 1 Then ib_connected = True
End If

// Set the transaction object, and dataobject for the datastore
If Not IsValid(ids_publishers) Then
    ids_publishers = CREATE datastore
    ids_publishers.dataobject = "d_publisher_tab"
    ids_publishers.SetTransObject (sqlca)
End If

ll_rowcount = ids_publishers.Retrieve ()
```

continues

```
For ll_row = 1 to ll_rowcount
    istr_publishers.id[ll_row] = &
        ids_publishers.object.publisher_id[ll_row]
    istr_publishers.name[ll_row] = &
        ids_publishers.object.company_name[ll_row]
Next

Return
```

This script attaches the d_publisher_tab dataobject to the datastore. You need to create this dataobject.

The PowerScript for uf_get_authors is:

```
////////////////////////////////////////////////////////////////////////
// Return the authors
////////////////////////////////////////////////////////////////////////
Return istr_authors
```

The PowerScript for uf_populate_authors is:

```
////////////////////////////////////////////////////////////////////////
// Retrieve all the authors
////////////////////////////////////////////////////////////////////////
long          ll_row, ll_rowcount

// Check for database connection. If there is no prior connection,
// connect to the database
If Not ib_connected Then
    If uf_connect_to_database () = 1 Then ib_connected = True
End If

// Set the transaction object, and dataobject for the datastore
If Not IsValid(ids_authors) Then
    ids_authors = CREATE datastore
    ids_authors.dataobject = "d_author_tab"
    ids_authors.SetTransObject (sqlca)
End If

ll_rowcount = ids_authors.Retrieve ()

For ll_row = 1 to ll_rowcount
    istr_authors.id[ll_row] = ids_authors.object.author_id[ll_row]
    istr_authors.name[ll_row] = ids_authors.object.author_name[ll_row]
Next

Return
```

This script attaches the d_author_tab dataobject to the datastore. You need to create this dataobject.

The PowerScript for uf_get_books is:

```
/////////////////////////////////////////////////////////////////////////
// Return the books
/////////////////////////////////////////////////////////////////////////
string      ls_filter
integer     il_filter
long        ll_row, ll_rowcount
str_name    istr_books

// Construct the filter
If ail_publisher > 0 Then
    ls_filter = " publisher_id = "+string(ail_publisher)+" "
    il_filter++
End If

If ail_author > 0 Then
    If il_filter > 0 Then
        ls_filter += " and author_id = "+string(ail_author)+" "
    Else
        ls_filter += " author_id = "+string(ail_author)+" "
    End If
    il_filter++
End If

If il_filter < 1 Then ls_filter = ""

// Set the Filter
ids_books.SetFilter (ls_filter)
ids_books.Filter ()

ll_rowcount = ids_books.RowCount ()

For ll_row = 1 to ll_rowcount
    istr_books.id[ll_row]    = ids_books.object.book_id[ll_row]
    istr_books.name[ll_row]  = ids_books.object.book_name[ll_row]
    istr_books.price[ll_row] = ids_books.object.price[ll_row]
Next

Return istr_books
```

The PowerScript for uf_populate_books is:

```
/////////////////////////////////////////////////////////////////////////
// Retrieve all the books
/////////////////////////////////////////////////////////////////////////
long        ll_row, ll_rowcount

// Check for database connection. If there is no prior connection,
// connect to the database
If Not ib_connected Then
```

continues

```
     If uf_connect_to_database () = 1 Then ib_connected = True
End If

// Set the transaction object, and dataobject for the datastore
If Not IsValid(ids_books) Then
    ids_books = CREATE datastore
    ids_books.dataobject = "d_book_tab"
    ids_books.SetTransObject (sqlca)
    ids_books.Retrieve ()
End If

Return
```

This script attaches the d_book_tab dataobject to the datastore. You need to create this dataobject.

Create another user object called uo_publishing_service on the application server. The user object acts as a proxy on the client. Create the proxy object on the server, and then move the proxy to the client.

Create the following instance variable for uo_publishing_service:

```
uo_data    iuo_data
```

Add the following PowerScript to the uo_publishing_service User Object's constructor event:

```
///////////////////////////////////////////////////////////////////////////
// Create the non visual data object
///////////////////////////////////////////////////////////////////////////

iuo_data = CREATE uo_data
```

Add the following PowerScript to the uo_publishing_service user object's destructor event:

```
///////////////////////////////////////////////////////////////////////////
// Destroy the non visual data object
///////////////////////////////////////////////////////////////////////////

DESTROY iuo_data
```

Next, add the following methods:

- uf_populate_publishers
- uf_get_publishers
- uf_get_authors
- uf_populate_authors
- uf_get_books
- uf_populate_books

The PowerScript for uf_populate_publishers is:

```
////////////////////////////////////////////////////////////////////////
// Call the function from the non visual data object to populate the
// datastore for publishers
////////////////////////////////////////////////////////////////////////

iuo_data.uf_populate_publishers ()
```

The PowerScript for uf_get_publishers is:

```
////////////////////////////////////////////////////////////////////////
// Get the publisher names
////////////////////////////////////////////////////////////////////////
Return iuo_data.uf_get_publishers()
```

The PowerScript for uf_get_authors is:

```
////////////////////////////////////////////////////////////////////////
// Get the author names
////////////////////////////////////////////////////////////////////////
Return iuo_data.uf_get_authors()
```

The PowerScript for uf_populate_authors is:

```
////////////////////////////////////////////////////////////////////////
// Call the function from the non visual data object to populate the
// datastore for authors
////////////////////////////////////////////////////////////////////////

iuo_data.uf_populate_authors ()
```

The PowerScript for uf_get_books is:

```
////////////////////////////////////////////////////////////////////////
// Get the books
////////////////////////////////////////////////////////////////////////
Return iuo_data.uf_get_books(ail_publisher_id, ail_author_id)
```

The PowerScript for uf_populate_books is:

```
////////////////////////////////////////////////////////////////////////
// Call the function from the non visual data object to populate the
// datastore for books
////////////////////////////////////////////////////////////////////////

iuo_data.uf_populate_books ()
```

Next, add the events ue_start_server and ue_stop_server to the window w_server. The code for these events is exactly similar to the ones shown for the example discussed in the "Server Push" section. Refer to the "Start and Stop Server" section for the code listing.

Creating the Client Application

To create the client application, use the following steps:

1. Declare a structure str_name similar to the one declared for the server. For more details, refer to the section "Creating the Server Application."
2. Open a new window, w_client, and add an event to the window, ue_connect_to_server.
3. In the event, create the connection object. By using the connection object, you can connect to the application server.
4. Check for errors connecting to the server. If no error occurs, create the remote object.
5. Check for errors creating the remote object.
6. Add another window event, ue_fill_drop_downs. Within the event, call the remote object's method asynchronously to populate the information on the server into the datastores. Call the methods from the remote object to populate the filter DataWindow's drop-down columns.
7. Add another window event, ue_show_books. Within the event, send the filter items (publisher and author that the user selects) to the remote object function. The function, in turn, returns the books and displays them within the client DataWindow.
8. Finally, add another window event, ue_disconnect_from_server. Within the event, destroy the remote and connection objects.

The code for the client application is shown next. Within the application object's open event for the client.pbl, add the following code:

```
////////////////////////////////////////////////////////////////////////
// Open the client window
////////////////////////////////////////////////////////////////////////
Open (w_client)
```

Create a window w_client. Declare the following instance variables for the window:

```
connection              myconnect
uo_publishing_service   iuo_publishing_service
```

Add the following code to the window's open event:

```
////////////////////////////////////////////////////////////////////////
// Insert a blank row in the filter datawindow
////////////////////////////////////////////////////////////////////////
dw_filter.ScrolltoRow (dw_filter.InsertRow (0))
```

Declare the following user events:

- ue_connect_to_server
- ue_fill_drop_downs
- ue_show_books
- ue_disconnect_to_server

The code for ue_connect_to_server event is:

```
//////////////////////////////////////////////////////////////////////
// Create the connection object, and connect to the server
// Check for errors when connecting to the server
// Create the remote object
// Check for errors when creating the remote object
//////////////////////////////////////////////////////////////////////
// Create the connection object, and connect to the server
myconnect                = CREATE connection
myconnect.driver         = "winsock"
myconnect.application    = "pbserver"
myconnect.location       = "localhost"

st_display.Text = "Connecting to the PowerBuilder application server..."

// Check for errors when connecting to the server
If myconnect.ConnectToServer () <> 0 Then
    MessageBox (This.Title, "Connection to the application server &
                            failed!")
Else
    st_display.Text = "Connection to the application server successful"
End If


// Create the remote object
// Check for errors when creating the remote object
If myconnect.CreateInstance (iuo_publishing_service) <> 0 Then
    MessageBox (This.Title, "Creating instance of the remote object &
                            failed")
Else
    st_display.Text = "Creation of the remote object successful"
End If
```

The code for ue_fill_drop_downs event is:

```
//////////////////////////////////////////////////////////////////////
// Call the remote object functions to populate the
// drop down columns within the filter datawindow
//////////////////////////////////////////////////////////////////////
datawindowchild    idw_child
str_name           istr_publishers, istr_authors
long               ll_row, ll_insertrow

// Call the remote object function, and populate the drop downs
If IsValid(iuo_publishing_service) Then
    iuo_publishing_service.post uf_populate_publishers ()
    iuo_publishing_service.post uf_populate_authors ()
    iuo_publishing_service.post uf_populate_books ()
    st_display.Text = "Populating data stores on the server..."
```

continues

```
Else
    MessageBox (This.Title, "Error in instantiating the remote object")
End If

If IsValid(iuo_publishing_service) Then

    // For Publisher
    dw_filter.GetChild ("publisher_id", idw_child)
    idw_child.Reset ()
    istr_publishers = iuo_publishing_service.uf_get_publishers ()
    st_display.Text = "Getting publisher data from the data stores on the server..."
    For ll_row = 1 to UpperBound(istr_publishers.id)
        ll_insertrow = idw_child.InsertRow (0)
        idw_child.SetItem (ll_insertrow, "id", &
                            istr_publishers.id[ll_row])
        idw_child.SetItem (ll_insertrow, "name", &
                            istr_publishers.name[ll_row])
    Next

    // For Author
    dw_filter.GetChild ("author_id", idw_child)
    idw_child.Reset ()
    istr_publishers = iuo_publishing_service.uf_get_authors ()
    st_display.Text = "Getting author data from the data stores on the server..."
    For ll_row = 1 to UpperBound(istr_publishers.id)
        ll_insertrow = idw_child.InsertRow (0)
        idw_child.SetItem (ll_insertrow, "id", &
                            istr_publishers.id[ll_row])
        idw_child.SetItem (ll_insertrow, "name", &
                            istr_publishers.name[ll_row])
    Next
    st_display.Text = "Data retrieval from the server is complete"
Else
    MessageBox (This.Title, "Error in instantiating the remote object")
End If
```

The code for ue_show_books event is:

```
//////////////////////////////////////////////////////////////////////////
// Send the filter items to the remote object function, and retrieve the
// book details
//////////////////////////////////////////////////////////////////////////
integer     il_publisher, il_author, il_filter
str_name    istr_books
long        ll_row, ll_insertrow

If dw_filter.AcceptText () = -1 Then Return
```

```
il_publisher = dw_filter.object.publisher_id[1]
il_author   = dw_filter.object.author_id[1]

If IsNull(il_publisher) Then il_publisher = 0
If IsNull(il_author)    Then il_author    = 0

If IsValid(iuo_publishing_service) Then
    istr_books = iuo_publishing_service.uf_get_books (il_publisher, &
                                             il_author)
    dw_books.Reset ()
    st_display.Text = "Getting data from the object on the server..."
    For ll_row = 1 To UpperBound(istr_books.id)
        ll_insertrow = dw_books.InsertRow (0)
        dw_books.object.book_id[ll_insertrow] = istr_books.id[ll_row]
        dw_books.object.book_name[ll_insertrow] = & istr_books.name[ll_row]
        dw_books.object.book_price[ll_insertrow] = &
istr_books.price[ll_row]
    Next
    st_display.Text = "Data retrieval from the server is complete"
End If
```

The code for ue_disconnect_to_server event is:

```
///////////////////////////////////////////////////////////////////////////
// Destroy the remote, and connection objects
///////////////////////////////////////////////////////////////////////////
// Destroy the remote object
If IsValid (iuo_publishing_service) Then
    DESTROY iuo_publishing_service
End If

// Destroy the connection object
If IsValid (myconnect) Then
    myconnect.DisconnectServer ()
End If

st_display.Text = "Disconnected from the application server"
```

Your client is all set!

The next section discusses DataWindow synchronization.

DATAWINDOW SYNCHRONIZATION

At some point, everyone who develops distributed applications with PowerBuilder 5 has felt that there should be some way to automatically manage the DataWindow data buffers and status flags within distributed applications.

PowerBuilder 6 introduces DataWindow synchronization, which lets you synchronize a DataWindow control on the client with a datastore on the application server.

No longer do you need to write logic to ensure the data buffers and status flags for the DataWindow control on the client are synchronized with those for the DataStore on the server. You can now achieve this functionality by using the following four DataWindow control functions:

GetFullState( ). Captures the DataWindow's current state.

GetChanges( ). Captures the changes from the source DataWindow.

SetChanges( ). Applies the changes from the source DataWindow to the target.

SetFullState( ). Applies the source DataWindow's state to the target.

In this section, you learn how to easily embed DataWindow synchronization within your application. This example uses the same books.db database you used for the Asynchronous Processing application discussed earlier. In this example, you can retrieve, add, delete, and modify the list of authors on the client side, and the application updates the same on the server side when you save the information. You can do this now without writing the cumbersome logic to keep track of the data buffers and status flags for the DataWindow control on the client.

TIP Although the four DataWindow control functions are best used for distributed applications, you can use these functions in normal client/server applications to update data.

Running the Application

Before running the application, add the following line of code within the c:\windows\services file:

```
pbserver        10092/tcp
```

Configure the ODBC for the Books Profile through the ODBC painter, as shown in Figure 23.7.

TIP The Books Profile points to the books.db SQL Anywhere database. You may already have configured this while trying out the asynchronous processing example in the preceding section.

Start an instance of PowerBuilder with the server.pbl and run the application. To start the application server, click **Start Server**.

Start another instance of PowerBuilder by using the client.pbl. Run the client.pbl application. You can now perform the tasks listed below with your distributed application:

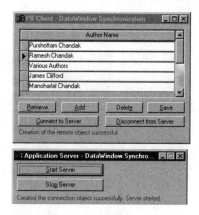

Figure 23.10   Example of DataWindow synchronization.

- To connect to the server, click **Connect to Server**.
- To retrieve a list of all the existing authors within the database, click **Retrieve**.
- To add a new author, click **Add**.
- To delete an author, click **Delete**.
- To modify any rows, change the information in the Author grid.
- Upon completing all the changes to the list, click **Save** to save the information.
- To disconnect from the server, click **Disconnect from Server**.

Figure 23.10 displays the DataWindow synchronization example.

Designing the Application

The application's design includes two steps, creating the server application and creating the client application.

Creating the Server Application

Within the application object's open event for the server.pbl, add the following code:

```
///////////////////////////////////////////////////////////////////////
// Open the server window that will create the application as a server,
// and listen to client requests
///////////////////////////////////////////////////////////////////////

open(w_server)
```

Create a nonvisual user object called uo_data. The uo_data resides on the application server. The object connects to the database and uses the datastores as instance variables to store the list of authors.

Create the following instance variable for uo_data:

```
datastore      ids_authors
boolean        ib_connected
long           il_author_count
```

Add the following PowerScript to the uo_data User Object's destructor event:

```
///////////////////////////////////////////////////////////////////////////
// Destroy the datastores, if created
// Disconnect from database, if connected
///////////////////////////////////////////////////////////////////////////

If IsValid (ids_authors)    Then DESTROY ids_authors

If ib_connected Then
    disconnect using sqlca;
End If
```

Add the following methods to the uo_data user object:

- uf_populate_authors
- uf_update_authors
- uf_get_max_authors
- uf_get_authors
- uf_fill_author_id
- uf_connect_to_database

The PowerScript for uf_populate_authors is:

```
///////////////////////////////////////////////////////////////////////////
// Retrieve all the authors
///////////////////////////////////////////////////////////////////////////
// Check for database connection. If there is no prior connection,
// connect to the database
If Not ib_connected Then
    If uf_connect_to_database () = 1 Then ib_connected = True
End If

// Set the transaction object, and dataobject for the datastore
If Not IsValid(ids_authors) Then
    ids_authors = CREATE datastore
    ids_authors.dataobject = "d_author_display_grid"
    ids_authors.SetTransObject (sqlca)
End If

//Retrieve for the datastore
ids_authors.Retrieve ()

//Fill the instance variable for the total number of authors in the
//database
uf_get_max_authors ()

Return
```

This script attaches the d_author_display_grid dataobject to the datastore. You will need to create this dataobject.

The PowerScript for uf_update_authors is:

```
//////////////////////////////////////////////////////////////////////////////
// Update the authors datastore through the blob object passed
// by the client
//////////////////////////////////////////////////////////////////////////////
long ll_return

//Set the datastore with the blob object and update it
If ids_authors.SetChanges(ablb_authors) = 1 Then
    //Before updating, make sure all new author rows have a valid
    //author id
    uf_fill_author_id_for_new_authors ()
    ll_return = ids_authors.Update()
End If

//Commit the changes and get the new datawindow state to be passed back
//to the client
If ll_return = 1 Then
    Commit;
    ids_authors.GetChanges(ablb_authors)
Else
    Rollback;
End If

Return ll_return
```

The PowerScript for uf_get_max_authors is:

```
//////////////////////////////////////////////////////////////////////////////
// Store the highest author id from the database to the instance variable
//////////////////////////////////////////////////////////////////////////////
SELECT Max(Author_id) INTO :il_author_count FROM AUTHOR;

// Check for errors when connected to the database
If sqlca.sqlcode <> 0 Then
    MessageBox ("Database Error", sqlca.sqlerrtext)
    Return -1
End if

Return 1
```

The PowerScript for uf_get_authors is:

```
//////////////////////////////////////////////////////////////////////////
// Return the authors retrieved in a blob object to be passed
// over to the client
//////////////////////////////////////////////////////////////////////////
long  ll_return

//Pass the datawindow to the blob object
ll_return = ids_authors.GetFullState(ablb_authors)

Return ll_return
```

The PowerScript for uf_fill_author_id is:

```
//////////////////////////////////////////////////////////////////////////
// This script will loop through the datawindow and put the
// author ids for all the new rows. The maximum number of authors
// has already been stored in the instance variable il_author_count
//////////////////////////////////////////////////////////////////////////
long ll_row, ll_rowcount

ll_rowcount = ids_authors.RowCount ()

For ll_row = 1 to ll_rowcount
    If ids_authors.GetItemStatus (ll_row, 0, Primary!) = NewModified! Then
        il_author_count ++
        ids_authors.object.author_id[ll_row] = il_author_count
    End If
Next

Return
```

The PowerScript for uf_connect_to_database is:

```
//////////////////////////////////////////////////////////////////////////
// This script will connect to the database
//////////////////////////////////////////////////////////////////////////

// Profile Books
SQLCA.DBMS       = "ODBC"
SQLCA.AutoCommit = False
SQLCA.DBParm     = "Connectstring='DSN=Books'"

// Connect to the database
Connect using sqlca;

// Check for errors when connected to the database
```

```
If sqlca.sqlcode <> 0 Then
    MessageBox ("Cannot Connect to the Database", sqlca.sqlerrtext)
    Return -1
End if

Return 1
```

Create another user object uo_publishing_service on the application server. The user object acts as a proxy on the client. Create the proxy object on the server, and then move the proxy to the client.

Create the following instance variable for uo_publishing_service:

```
uo_data    iuo_data
```

Add the following PowerScript to the uo_publishing_service User Object's constructor event:

```
//////////////////////////////////////////////////////////////////////////
// Create the non visual data object & populate the datastores of the nvo
//////////////////////////////////////////////////////////////////////////

iuo_data = CREATE uo_data

iuo_data.uf_populate_authors ()
```

Add the following PowerScript to the uo_publishing_service User Object's destructor event:

```
//////////////////////////////////////////////////////////////////////////
// Destroy the non visual data object
//////////////////////////////////////////////////////////////////////////

DESTROY iuo_data
```

Add the following methods to the uo_publishing_service user object:

- uf_get_authors
- uf_save_authors

The PowerScript for uf_get_authors is:

```
//////////////////////////////////////////////////////////////////////////
// Get authors from the datastore and pass the blob
//////////////////////////////////////////////////////////////////////////
long ll_return

ll_return = iuo_data.uf_get_authors(ablb_authors)

Return ll_return
```

The PowerScript for uf_save_authors is:

```
///////////////////////////////////////////////////////////////////////////
// Update the authors on the server
///////////////////////////////////////////////////////////////////////////
long     ll_return

ll_return = iuo_data.uf_update_authors(ablb_authors)

Return ll_return
```

Add the events ue_start_server and ue_stop_server to the window w_server. The code for these events is exactly similar to the ones shown for the example discussed in the "Server Push" section. Refer to the "Start and Stop Server" section for the code listing.

Creating the Client Application

To create the client application, use the following steps:

1. Open a new window, w_client. Add an event to the window, ue_connect_to_server.
2. In the event, create the connection object. By using the connection object, you can connect to the application server.
3. Check for errors connecting to the server. If no error occurs, create the remote object.
4. Check for errors creating the remote object.
5. Add another window event, ue_retrieve. In the event, call the remote object's method to call the function to retrieve on the database. Apply the contents of a DataWindow blob retrieved to the DataWindow on the w_client window.
6. Add another window event, ue_add. This event adds a row to the DataWindow.
7. Add another window event, ue_delete. This event deletes the current row from the DataWindow.
8. Add another window event, ue_save. Within the event, capture the changes to the client DataWindow within a blob and pass the DataWindow blob to save to the server for saving the data through the datastore on the server.
9. Finally, add another window event, ue_disconnect_from_server. In the event, destroy the remote and connection objects.

The code for the client application is shown next. In the application object's open event for the client.pbl, add the following code:

```
///////////////////////////////////////////////////////////////////
// Open the client window
///////////////////////////////////////////////////////////////////
Open (w_client)
```

Create a window w_client. Declare the following instance variables for the window:

```
connection                myconnect
uo_publishing_service     iuo_publishing_service
```

Declare the following user events:

- ue_connect_to_server
- ue_retrieve
- ue_add
- ue_delete
- ue_save
- ue_disconnect_from_server

The code for the ue_connect_to_server event is:

```
///////////////////////////////////////////////////////////////////////////////
// Create the connection object, and connect to the server
// Check for errors when connecting to the server
// Create the remote object
// Check for errors when creating the remote object
///////////////////////////////////////////////////////////////////////////////
// Create the connection object, and connect to the server
myconnect                   = CREATE connection
myconnect.driver            = "winsock"
myconnect.application       = "pbserver"
myconnect.location          = "localhost"

st_display.Text = "Connecting to the PowerBuilder application server..."

// Check for errors when connecting to the server
If myconnect.ConnectToServer () <> 0 Then
    MessageBox (This.Title, "Connection to the application server &
                            failed!")
Else
    st_display.Text = "Connection to the application server successful"
End If


// Create the remote object
// Check for errors when creating the remote object
If myconnect.CreateInstance (iuo_publishing_service) <> 0 Then
    MessageBox (This.Title, "Creating instance of the remote object &
                            failed")
Else
    st_display.Text = "Creation of the remote object successful"
End If
```

The code for the ue_retrieve event is:

```
///////////////////////////////////////////////////////////////////////////////
// Make sure the remote object is created. If the object is created,
// call the function to retrieve on the database.
// Apply the contents of a DataWindow blob retrieved.
///////////////////////////////////////////////////////////////////////////////
```

continues

```
blob lblb_authors
long ll_returncode

If IsValid (iuo_publishing_service) Then
     iuo_publishing_service.uf_get_authors (lblb_authors)
Else
     MessageBox ("Error", "Please connect to server")
     Return
End If

//Synchronize the datawindow on the client
ll_returncode = dw_authors.SetFullState(lblb_authors)

If ll_returncode  < 0 Then
     MessageBox("Error", "Failed to Synchronize the datawindow")
End If
```

The code for the ue_add event is:

```
////////////////////////////////////////////////////////////////////////
// Add a row to the datawindow
////////////////////////////////////////////////////////////////////////
dw_authors.ScrolltoRow (dw_authors.InsertRow (0))
```

The code for the ue_delete event is:

```
////////////////////////////////////////////////////////////////////////
// Delete the current row
////////////////////////////////////////////////////////////////////////
dw_authors.DeleteRow (0)
```

The code for the ue_save event is:

```
////////////////////////////////////////////////////////////////////////
// Make sure the remote object is created. If the object is created,
// pass the DataWindow blob to save the object on the server.
////////////////////////////////////////////////////////////////////////
blob lblb_authors
long ll_returncode

//Check for server connection
If IsValid (iuo_publishing_service) Then
     iuo_publishing_service.uf_get_authors (lblb_authors)
Else
     MessageBox ("Error", "Please connect to server")
     Return
End If
```

```
//Make sure the DataWindow passes all validations on the client side
If dw_authors.AcceptText () = -1 Then Return

//Get all the changes into a blob object
ll_returncode = dw_authors.GetChanges(lblb_authors)

//Check for error on getting the blob object
If ll_returncode < 0 Then
        MessageBox("Error", "GetChanges call failed!")
End If

//Pass the blob to the server for saving on the server side
ll_returncode = iuo_publishing_service.uf_save_authors (lblb_authors)

//Check for any error that may be returned by the server
If ll_returncode < 0 Then
    MessageBox ("Update on Server Failed", ll_returncode)
Else
    dw_authors.SetChanges(lblb_authors)
End If

//Call the retrieve to sync back the datawindow with author_ids for
//new authors
This.Event ue_retrieve (0,0)
```

The code for the ue_disconnect_from_server event is:

```
///////////////////////////////////////////////////////////////////////////
// Destroy the remote, and connection objects
///////////////////////////////////////////////////////////////////////////
// Destroy the remote object
If IsValid (iuo_publishing_service) Then
    DESTROY iuo_publishing_service
End If

// Destroy the connection object
If IsValid (myconnect) Then
    myconnect.DisconnectServer ()
End If

st_display.Text = "Disconnected from the application server"
```

Your client is all set!

As you have seen, PowerBuilder 6 includes a number of features you can use to develop and deploy *n*-tier distributed applications. The features Powersoft enhanced within PowerBuilder 6 include the ability to create all the proxy objects for your project at once by using the project painter, application partitioning, server push technology, creating and deploying shared objects on the application server, asynchronous processing, DataWindow synchronization, transaction server support, support for open technology standards (including extended UNIX platform support), and expanded database connectivity (including support for Informix 7.2, Sybase SQL 11.1, ODBC 3, and more). In addition, PowerBuilder 6 offers expanded language support with UNICODE and expanded support for third-party application interfaces such as API calls, source code control management, and IntelliMouse support for DataWindows. In addition, Riverton Software's HOW is a complete, visual integrated system you can use for requirements analysis, business and data modeling, application development, application and use case analysis, and maintaining a repository of reusable PowerBuilder objects—all within a single IDE. To learn more about HOW, refer to Chapter 26, "Learning HOW to Build PowerBuilder Applications."

CHAPTER 24

PowerBuilder Foundation Class (PFC) Library

WHAT IS PFC?

Powersoft released a new addition to PowerBuilder 5 called the PowerBuilder Foundation Class (PFC) library. The library's purpose is to provide a foundation for developers to build their applications. PowerBuilder customers asked Powersoft for a class library, and Powersoft delivered. Powersoft designed this library with several of the advanced PowerBuilder object-oriented concepts in mind. You can use the PFC to replace the custom class libraries several companies have developed, and you can also use the PFC in place of any third-party class library. Developers can build the business templates (e.g., master detail, form maintenance) to extend the functionality that PFC delivers out of the box. PFC provides several loosely coupled objects that constitute a services-based nonvisual object framework. The rest of this chapter describes the PFC architecture and provides examples of how to develop an application by using PFC. In addition, wherever applicable, the chapter identifies the new and enhanced PFC services that Powersoft introduced within PowerBuilder 6:

- PFC services architecture
- PFC process flows
- Third-party PFC-based products
- Third-party class libraries

PFC SERVICES ARCHITECTURE

Traditionally, PowerBuilder applications were developed one window at a time. Powersoft did not introduce the concept of inheritance until PowerBuilder 2. In the early days, there was little code modularity and reusability. PowerBuilder 2's implementation of several object-oriented concepts such as inheritance and polymorphism enabled a new way of developing the applications. This new method was based on a window inheritance model that provided much of the application's basic functionality within a hierarchical template-based window architecture. PowerBuilder's later versions, especially PowerBuilder 5, gave birth to a new way of building modularity and reusability within applications. This new approach implements a plug-and-play method of developing the applications and application components. You can implement this plug-and-play approach by taking advantage of PowerBuilder's class objects or nonvisual objects. The new approach is a services-based architecture. A services-based framework like the PFC provides much of the functionality and processing in nonvisual objects. An overview of the different PFC services follows.

TIP If your application does not require certain PFC services, disable them. This will reduce your application's overhead and improve your application's overall performance.

PFC Libraries

pfemain.pbl includes the extension class objects for a variety of services including calendar, calculator, split bar, progress bar, and so on.

pfeapsrv.pbl includes the extension class objects for the application services.

pfewinsrv.pbl includes the extension class objects for the Window services.

pfedwsrv.pbl includes the extension class objects for the DataWindow services.

pfeutil.pbl includes the extension class objects for the utilities.

pfcmain.pbl includes the foundation class objects for a variety of services such as calendar, calculator, split bar, progress bar, and so on.

pfcapsrv.pbl includes the foundation class objects for application services.

pfcwinsrv.pbl includes the foundation class objects for Window services.

pfcdwsrv.pbl includes the foundation class objects for DataWindow services.

pfcutil.pbl includes the foundation class objects for utilities.

TIP You will find the PFC PBLs in the \adk\pfc directory of the PowerBuilder 6 installation.

PFC Extension Layers

Within PFC, the libraries are named with PFC and PFE prefixes. These prefixes differentiate between the main PFC modules (PFCxxxx.PBL) and the extension PFC modules (PFExxxx.PBL).

In the PFC-prefixed libraries, you can inherit the objects such as user objects and windows that are prefixed with a pfc_n_, pfc_u_, or pfc_w_. In the PFE-prefixed libraries, the pfc_extensions are eliminated for each inheritable object. The extension layer's main benefit is that it allows developers to customize any aspect of the PFC framework at any level without the code being overwritten when a new version of PFC is released. When Powersoft releases a new version, the extension layers located in the PFE*.PBL libraries will remain, while the upgrade replaces the PFC*.PBL libraries with the new version. This is a very powerful implementation within the PFC framework.

You may need to build a common layer of PFC objects that meet the specific requirements of the applications within your corporation. You must build such a *corporate* layer by inheriting from the PFC layer. The corporate layer thus resides between the PFC and PFE layers. You may also need to build a *department* layer of PFC objects that meet the specific requirements of the applications within each of the departments in your corporation. You must build such department layers by inheriting from the corporate layer. The department layers thus reside between the corporate and PFE layers.

Adding corporate and departmental extensions to intermediate extension levels lets you make full use of the extension level. To automatically create and populate an intermediate extension level, such as the corporate and department layers between two existing levels (the PFC and PFE ancestor levels), you can use the PFC Library Extender.

Application Services

The PFC framework's application services provide several different application level services such as:

- About dialog service.
- SQL spy service.
- Application security service (enhanced).
- Splash screen service.
- File services for 16- and 32-bit operating systems.
- Application manager service.
- Conversion service.
- Find/replace service.
- .INI file service.
- Cross-platform services.
- Transaction registration service.
- String service.
- Caching service (enhanced).
- Application preference service.
- Most recently used service (new). To display the most recently used windows or sheets within the File menu, enable the most recently used (mru) service.
- Linked list service (new). To implement linked list processing, enable the linked list service.
- Balanced binary tree list service (new). To implement list processing within a balanced binary tree, enable the binary tree list service.
- Metaclass service (new).

The core application services and objects are located in the pfcapsrv.pbl library. Figures 24.1 through 24.8 show the object breakdown by object type.

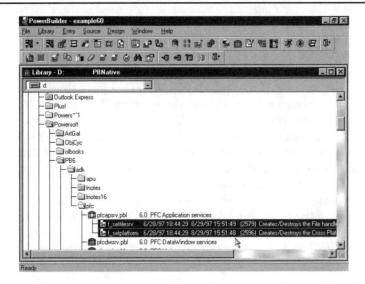

Figure 24.1   PFC application service function objects.

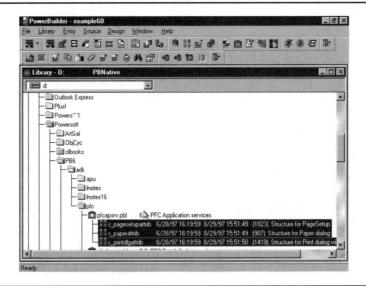

Figure 24.2   PFC application service structure objects.

One of the most critical objects within the application services is the application manager services. This service handles several of the PFC application-wide components such as startup processing, shutdown processing, transaction registration, splash window pro-

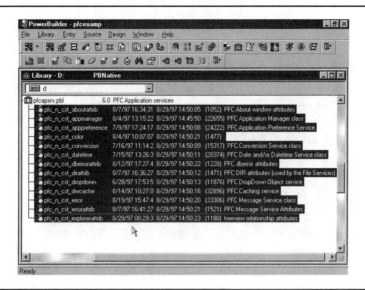

Figure 24.3   **PFC application service nonvisual user objects (a–e).**

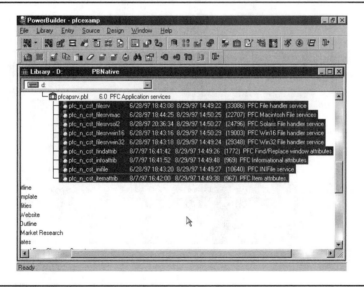

Figure 24.4   **PFC application service nonvisual user objects (f–i).**

cessing, debug processing, user and application information, microhelp processing, .INI file and registry information and login processing. This object also holds the application objects, environment object, transaction object, caching object, and error object.

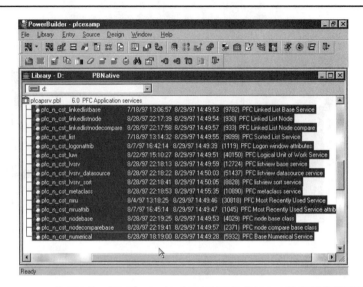

Figure 24.5 PFC application service nonvisual user objects (j–n).

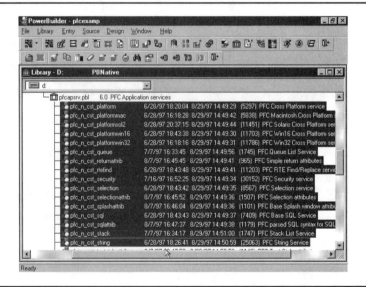

Figure 24.6 PFC application service nonvisual user objects (o–p).

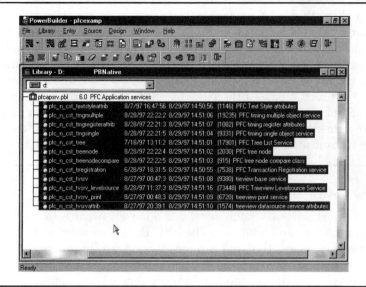

Figure 24.7   PFC application service nonvisual user objects (q–z).

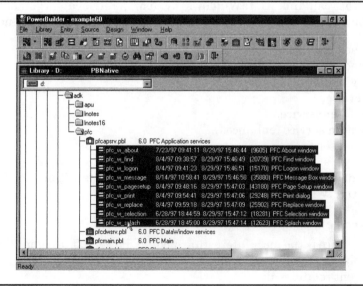

Figure 24.8   PFC application service window objects.

> **TIP** One thing that is true for most PFC services is that they are not always enabled or created the same way they were in earlier versions of PowerBuilder. PowerBuilder 5 introduced an autoinstantiate attribute within the nonvisual user object property. If you choose this attribute, PowerBuilder instantiates the object as soon as the application references the object, such as when calling a member function. This process passes the responsibility of cleaning up to PowerBuilder, and you need not create and destroy the objects. There are instances where you need not implement the autoinstantiate attribute, such as when different nonvisual objects are instantiated into a single variable based on runtime options.

DataWindow Service

The PFC framework's DataWindow service is a loosely architected series of nonvisual and visual user objects and windows. The PFC DataWindow objects come together to provide a series of services that you can incorporate within an application. These services include: search service, linkage service, filter service, sort service, multiple table update service, print preview service, querymode service, row manager service, and row selection service. The search service provides four different options: using DDLB/DDPB, using DDDW, find and replace DW, and find and replace rich text format. The linkage service links the DataWindows together in a master/detail or one-to-many relationship. You can link DataWindows by using retrieval arguments, filters, or scrolling. The services built within the global DataWindow service include:

- Linkage service.
- Query mode service.
- Reporting and printing service.
- Resize service.
- Sort and filter service.
- Row selection service (enhanced).
- Verification service.
- Search, find, and selection service.
- DataWindow resize service (new). To resize the objects within a DataWindow, enable the DataWindow resize service.

Linkage Service

The linkage service is the most interesting module. Powersoft designed the linkage service with a plug-and-play approach. This service links the DataWindows together in several different relationships.

To build a master detail window within PFC, you must do the following (see Figure 24.9 for an example). This example emphasizes the linkage service, not the entire master detail window.

Within the master DataWindow's constructor event, write the following lines of PowerScript. The first line is the more important of the two because it turns on the linkage service for the master DataWindow:

Figure 24.9   Example of a master detail window.

```
of _SetLinkage ( TRUE )
this.SetRowFocusIndicator(Hand!)
```

In the detail DataWindow's constructor event, write the following code. The first line turns on the linkage service for the detail DataWindow, the second line links the current DataWindow (detail DataWindow) to the master DataWindow or the DataWindow passed in as the **of_linkto( )** function's parameter, the next line of code initiates how PowerBuilder links the master and detail DataWindows (e.g., filter, scrolling, retrieve), in this case via scrolling, and the last line of code specifies the columns that link the master and the detail:

```
of_SetLinkage ( TRUE )
inv_Linkage.of_LinkTo ( DataWindow_emp )
inv_Linkage.of_setUseColLinks ( 3 )
inv_Linkage.of_SetArguments ( "emp_id", "emp_id" )
```

Finally, in the window's open event, write the following code. The first line sets the transaction object for both the DataWindows. The second line retrieves the DataWindows:

```
DataWindow_cust.inv_Linkage.of_SetTransObject (SQLCA)
DataWindow_cust.inv_Linkage.of_Retrieve
```

The pfcdwsrv.pbl includes the PFC DataWindow services. Figures 24.10 through 24.13 show all of the DataWindow objects and services by object type.

Window Services

The window service is also a very important part of the PFC framework. The window service includes several different kinds of services that you can enable, such as:

- Menu service
- Resize service
- Toolbar service
- Base window service
- Window preference service
- Sheet manager service (enhanced)

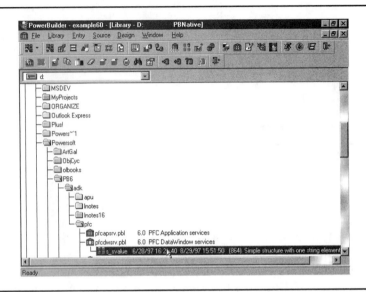

Figure 24.10   PFC DataWindow service structure objects.

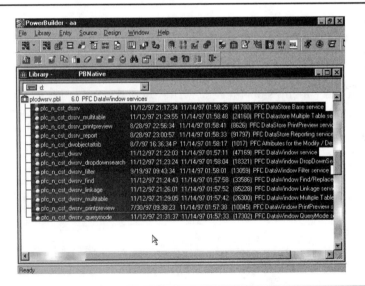

Figure 24.11   PFC DataWindow service nonvisual user objects (a–q).

- Statusbar service (enhanced)
- Message manager service
- Timer service (new)

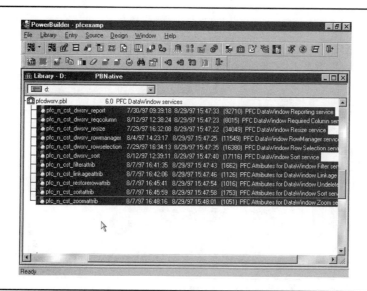

Figure 24.12   PFC DataWindow service nonvisual user objects (r–z).

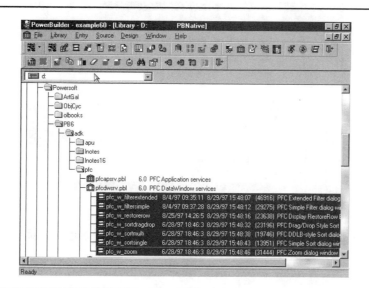

Figure 24.13   PFC DataWindow service window objects.

Figures 24.14 through 24.17 list all of the objects in the PFC window service library by object type. The pfcwnsrv.pbl includes all the objects and services that belong to the window service.

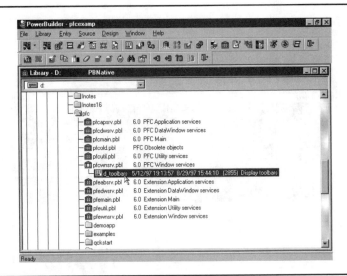

Figure 24.14   PFC Window service DataWindow objects.

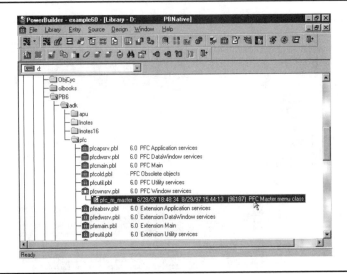

Figure 24.15   PFC Window service menu objects.

TIP If you are not already familiar with PFC, there is a learning curve. However, it is well worth the time and effort needed to learn and use the PFC. You can expect Powersoft to continually expand and enhance the PFC in PowerBuilder's future releases.

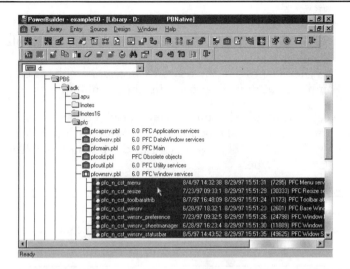

Figure 24.16   PFC Window service nonvisual user objects.

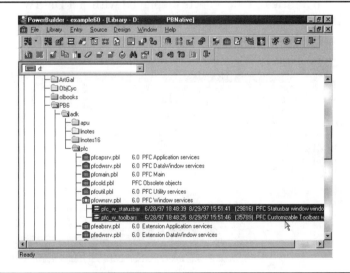

Figure 24.17   PFC Window service window objects.

PFC Objects

The PFC Main objects library includes the core visual objects within the PFC framework. Powersoft has extended all the PowerBuilder controls to become PFC controls. This module also includes the base window types that PFC is based on. In addition, the PFC Main objects library includes PFC objects for the following new services:

- Calculator service.
- Calendar service.
- Splitbar service. To add splitbar functionality to two or more controls within a window, enable the splitbar service.
- Progress bar service. To provide the users with visual feedback on the percentage of operation completed at any given point in time, enable the progress bar service.

The PFC Main objects library also includes an enhanced pfc_save service. The next section shows the hierarchical breakdown of the objects within PFC. Figures 24.18 through 24.24 show all the PFC objects located in the pfcmain.pbl. These objects are listed based on their object type.

TIP In PowerBuilder 6's PFC, most objects use constants as typical return codes. By using constants instead of the actual return code values, the code you write will be more readable and easily maintenable.

TIP In PowerBuilder 6's PFC, you can use the DataWindow resize object to provide resize capabilities to the objects displayed within a DataWindow.

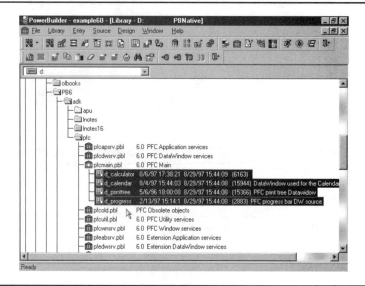

Figure 24.18 PFC Objects service DataWindow objects.

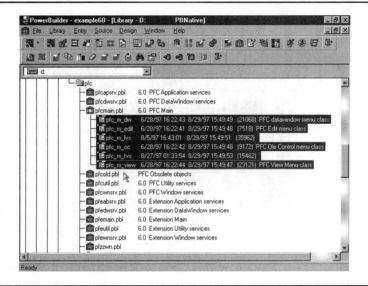

Figure 24.19   PFC Objects service menu objects.

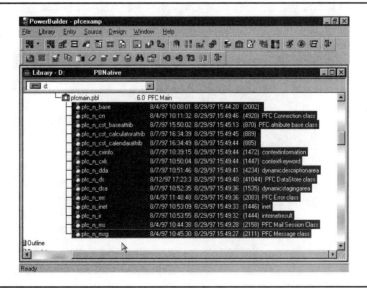

Figure 24.20   PFC Objects service user objects (a–m).

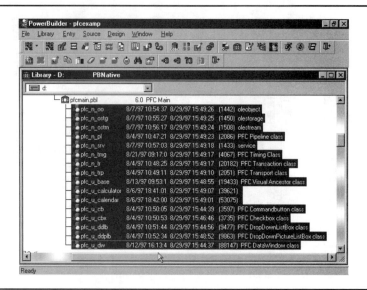

Figure 24.21 PFC Objects service user objects (n–u).

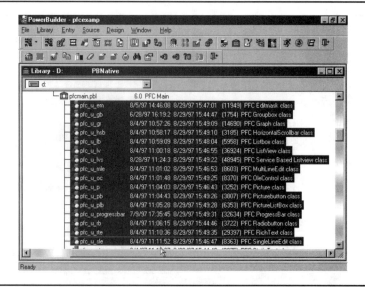

Figure 24.22 PFC Objects service user objects (u continued).

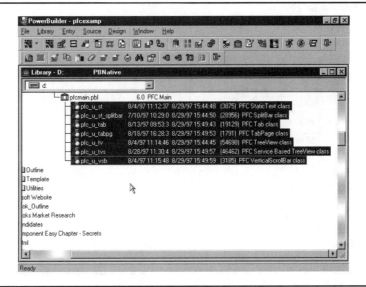

Figure 24.23   PFC Objects service user objects (u continued).

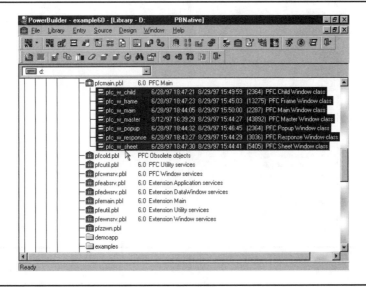

Figure 24.24   PFC Objects service window objects.

PFC OBJECT HIERARCHY

Figures 24.25 and 24.26 do not show the extension layer.

Figure 24.25   PFC window object hierarchy list.

Figure 24.26   PFC nonvisual user object hierarchy list.

PFC PROCESS FLOWS

Application startup process:
1. Application open event:
   1.1 Create the application manager's instance.
   1.2 Call the application manager's open event (PFC_OPEN).
   1.3 Call the **of_init( )** function within the transaction NVO.
      1.3.1 Check the .INI file.
      1.3.2 Check the .INI file selection.
      1.3.3 Get the transaction data from the .INI file.
   1.4 Connect by using SQLCA.
   1.5 Open the application main menu.

PFC DataWindow Linkage Startup and Retrieve:
1. The window's Open event:
   1.1 Call **of_settransobject( )** in the first DataWindow's linkage NVO. (This is done to set the transaction object.)
   1.2 Call **of_retrieve( )** in the first DataWindow's linkage service.
2. First DataWindow's constructor:
   2.1 Call of_setlinkage(true).
3. Second DataWindow's constructor (do the same processing for all the subsequent child DataWindow processing).
   3.1 Call of_setlinkage(true).
   3.2 Within the current DataWindow's linkage service, call the **of_linkto-(dsw_link1)** function and link this DataWindow to its immediate master DataWindow.
   3.3 Linkage **of_setarguments( )** specify the columns that will link the two DataWindows.
   3.4 Call the linkage.**of_setusercollinks( )** to set if retrieval arguments, filters, or cursors will be used.
   3.5 Continue this process until more children DataWindows exist:
      3.5.1 Call the **of_retrieve( )** function in the first DataWindow's linkage service:
         3.5.1.1 Call the **pfc_retrieve( )** event within the requestor DataWindow:
            3.5.1.1.1 This event simply calls the PowerBuilder retrieve event.
         3.5.1.2 Call the **of_retrieve( )** function in each child DataWindow's linkage NVO.

The idw_details instance variable contains the number of detail DataWindows.

Update Process (pfc_w_master):

1. Window event pfc_save( ):
   1.1 Call the function of_update_checks (checks the update status):
      1.1.1 Call the pfc_accepttext event.
      1.1.2 Call the pfc_updatespending event.
      1.1.3 Call the pfc_validation event.
   1.2 Call the pfc_preupdate event:
      1.2.1 You can override/extend this event.

1.3 Call the event pfc_begintrans:
    1.3.1 You can extend this event.
1.4 Call the pfc_update event:
    1.4.1 Call of_getdwType( ).
1.5 Call the pfc_endtrans event:
    1.5.1 You can extend this event.
1.6 Call the pfc_postupdate event:
    1.6.1 To reset the update flag upon successful update, call the **of_resetupdate( )** function.

THIRD-PARTY PFC-BASED PRODUCTS

BusinessSoft's ObjectComposer is a PFC application generator that accelerates the development of PFC applications. ObjectComposer is not a class library. The tool generates applications by using PFC and other class libraries such as Cornerstone, Financial Dynamics' PFC-based class library. If you use PFC as your base class library, ObjectComposer generates objects based on PFC's extension layer. You can then generate applications created by ObjectComposer in other class libraries without writing a line of code. By using ObjectComposer, you can enable and set up the PFC application, window, and DataWindow services. However, ObjectComposer does not currently support generation of DataWindows.

You can download a demo of ObjectComposer from BusinessSoft's Web site (www.bsisoft.com).

THIRD-PARTY CLASS LIBRARIES

The question everyone asks is: Do you need a third-party class library when you already got the PFC? Typically, the answer is no. However, if you invested in a third-party class library before the PowerBuilder 5 release and are now quite familiar with it, you may want to upgrade to a version that works with PowerBuilder's PFC. This saves you time by leveraging from your investment in learning the third-party class library.

If you did not use a third-party class library before the PowerBuilder 5 release, you should learn PFC and then determine whether a third-party class library offers anything significant over and above the PFC that might expedite your application development. Keep in mind, though, there is a learning curve, especially if you have no prior experience using a class library.

Table 24.1 lists third-party class libraries that work with PowerBuilder's PFC.

Table 24.1   Third-Party Class Libraries

Library	URL
CornerStone	www.findyn.com
APOL	www.janiff.com/docs/softw.htm
	www.janiff.com/docs/pfc.htm
PFCtool	www.powercerv.com/Tools/PFCtool/index.htm
PowerClass	www.serverlogic.com/tools.htm

CHAPTER 25

Using Internet Tools

After Powersoft released PowerBuilder 5, it released the Internet Developer Toolkit (IDT) as an add-on. The IDT included tools and utilities that you could use to Web-enable your PowerBuilder applications. With PowerBuilder 6, all these tools and utilities were enhanced and come integrated within the development environment. In addition, there are a few new features such as the synchronizer and customizable Web jumps.

This chapter covers the following:

- DataWindow plug-in
- Window plug-in
- Window ActiveX control
- Web.pb
- DataWindow HTML generation
- Customizable Web jumps
- Synchronizer
- Secure mode

DATAWINDOW PLUG-IN

By using the DataWindow plug-in, you can display PowerBuilder DataWindows in .PSR (Powersoft Reports) in a browser. Note that users can only view the data in the .PSR file. Users cannot edit or update the data. Since you can present read-only data by using the DataWindow plug-in, you will find limited use for it. You can use the plug-in to let managers in your organization view existing reports that are updated on a regular basis, for example. Say you designed a client/server application with PowerBuilder, and a number of users at the officer level in your organization use the application on a day-to-day basis. The managers are interested in reviewing monthly reports that the officers generate for them. There are two ways you can make the reports available to the managers. You can install the application on the workstations the managers use, and the managers can use the Reports menu in the application to generate the reports. An alternative approach is to configure the workstations the managers use so they can view the Powersoft reports that the officers generate in a browser. The following steps outline the procedure:

- Install and configure the Web server. In addition, you must register the appropriate content (MIME) types with the Web server. That is, you must register the DataWindow plug-in with the Web server. To register the DataWindow plug-in, use the following steps:

    1. Start the WebSite Server Administration program (i.e., Server Admin). The Server Admin program displays the Web Site Server Properties dialog box.
    2. Click the **Mapping** tab, and then click the **Content Types** radiobutton.
    3. Type **.PSR** in the File Extension (class) field. Then type **application/ datawindow** within the MIME content type field, as shown in Figure 25.1.
    4. Click **Add**, then click OK, then click **Yes** within the Immediate Reset message box.

TIP O'Reilley's Web site server comes with PowerBuilder 6 Enterprise Edition.

- The officers use the PowerBuilder application to generate the monthly reports and save them as .PSR files.
- Configure the workstations the managers use so they can use the browser to view the .PSR files. Copy the DataWindow plug-in (npdwe60.dll) to the \plugins directory of Internet Explorer (or Netscape Communicator) on the workstations.

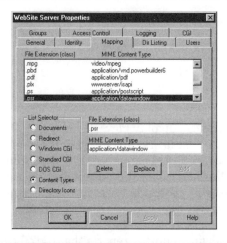

Figure 25.1   **Specifying the MIME type.**

- Copy the .PSR file(s) to the Web server's \htdocs directory.
- Create and copy the HTML file (dwplug.htm) to the Web server's \htdocs directory. To embed the .PSR file within the HTML file (for example, custlist.psr), use the <EMBED/> tag as shown. The <EMBED/> tag takes a number of parameters. For the SRC parameter, specify the .PSR. Specify the display area's width and height (by using the WIDTH and HEIGHT parameters) within which the browser displays the PowerBuilder window:

```
<!DOCTYPE HTML PUBLIC "-//W3C//DTD HTML 3.2//EN">
<HTML>
<HEAD>
   <TITLE>PowerBuilder DataWindow Plugin Example</TITLE>
   <META NAME="GENERATOR" CONTENT="Mozilla/3.0Gold (Win95; I) [Netscape]">
</HEAD>
<BODY BGCOLOR="#FFFFFF">

<H2>PowerBuilder DataWindow Plugin Example</H2>

<P>
<HR></P>

<P><EMBED SRC="custlist.psr" WIDTH=550 HEIGHT=300></P>

<P>
<HR></P>

</BODY>
</HTML>
```

- The managers can now view the reports within their browser. Figure 25.2 shows a sample .PSR file in Internet Explorer.

TIP The DataWindow plug-in does not require the PowerBuilder runtime files. The DataWindow plug-in is supported only on Windows 95, Windows NT, and Power Macintosh. As a result, the Windows-based DataWindow plug-in does not work on other platforms, such as UNIX. You must keep in mind that the solution you create by using the Windows-based DataWindow plug-in only works for Windows and Power Macintosh clients. The PowerBuilder DataWindow plug-in requires a browser that supports plug-ins such as Netscape Navigator 3.x or higher or Microsoft Internet Explorer 3.x or higher.

WINDOW PLUG-IN

By using the Window plug-in, you can display PowerBuilder windows within a browser. The following steps outline the procedure:

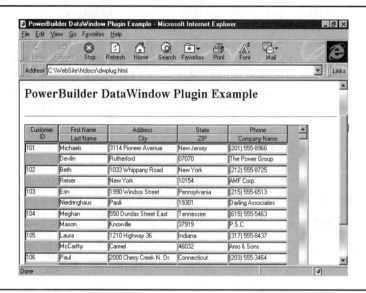

Figure 25.2   **Viewing a .PSR report in Internet Explorer.**

- Install and configure the Web server. Register the appropriate content (MIME) types with the Web server. That is, register the Window plug-in with the Web server. To register the Window plug-in, use the following steps:
    1. Start the WebSite Server Administration program (i.e., Server Admin). The Server Admin program displays the Web Site Server Properties dialog box.
    2. Click the **Mapping** tab, and then click the **Content Types** radiobutton.
    3. Type **.PBD** in the File Extension (class) field. Then type **application/vnd .powerbuilder6** in the MIME content type field, as shown in Figure 25.3.

TIP To deploy an application in secure mode, type **application/ vnd.powerbuilder6-s** in the MIME content type field.

---

     4. Click **Add**, then click OK, and click **Yes** in the Immediate Reset message box.

- Create the PowerBuilder window(s) and save the window(s) within a .PBD (mytest.pbd). There are some restrictions on the type of PowerBuilder window(s) you can display within a browser. These restrictions include:
    1. The PowerBuilder window must be a child window. This is because the browser is the main window and every PowerBuilder window that displays within the browser must be a child window.
    2. Check off the PowerBuilder window's Control menu maximize box, minimize box, and resizable checkboxes.

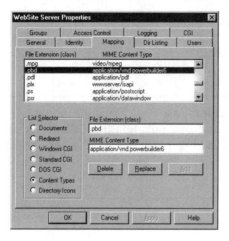

Figure 25.3   Establishing the mappings.

- Create the HTML file (winplug2.htm). To embed the .PBD within the HTML file (e.g., mytest.pbd), use the <EMBED/> tag as shown. The <EMBED/> tag takes a number of parameters. For the SRC parameter, specify the .PBD. Specify the display area's width and height (by using the WIDTH and HEIGHT parameters) within which the browser displays the PowerBuilder window. For the WINDOW parameter, specify the child PowerBuilder window's name:

```
<!DOCTYPE HTML PUBLIC "-//W3C//DTD HTML 3.2//EN">
<HTML>
<HEAD>
   <TITLE>PowerBuilder Window Plug-in Example</TITLE>
   <META NAME="GENERATOR" CONTENT="Mozilla/3.0Gold (Win95; I) [Netscape]">
</HEAD>
<BODY BGCOLOR="#FFFFFF">

<H2>PowerBuilder Window Plug-in Example</H2>

<P>
<HR></P>

<P><EMBED SRC="mytest.pbd" WIDTH=550 HEIGHT=400 WINDOW=w_child ></P>

<P>
<HR></P>

</BODY>
</HTML>
```

- Configure the client workstations by copying the Window plug-in (nppba60.dll) to the \plugins directory of Internet Explorer (or Netscape Communicator) on the client workstations.
- Copy the HTML file (winplug2.htm) to the Web site server's \htdocs directory. You can now view the HTML file in Internet Explorer (see Figure 25.4).

TIP The Window plug-in requires the PowerBuilder runtime files. Also, the Window plug-in is implemented by nppba60.dll on Windows and the Power-Builder Window Plug-in shared library on Power Macintosh. The PowerBuilder Window plug-in requires a browser that supports plug-ins such as Netscape Navigator 3.x or higher or Microsoft Internet Explorer 3.x or higher.

WINDOW ACTIVEX CONTROL

The Window ActiveX control provides an alternative way to deploy your application's PowerBuilder windows in a browser. The control has properties, methods, and events. As a result, you can write JavaScript or VBScript code to configure the control's behavior per your application's requirements. In addition, you can invoke the PowerBuilder window's methods in the Window ActiveX control. When an event associated with the control is triggered, the browser executes the PowerBuilder script associated with the event. The browser then executes the JavaScript or VBScript code associated with the event, if any. You cannot do all this with the Window plug-in.

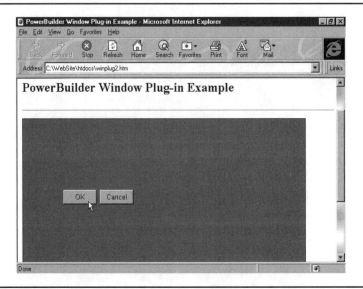

Figure 25.4   **Viewing a PowerBuilder window in Internet Explorer.**

Use the following steps to integrate your application's PowerBuilder windows in a Web application:

- Create and save the PowerBuilder window(s) within a .PBD (mytest.pbd). The Window ActiveX control includes certain characteristics and features you should be aware of. Similar to the Window plug-in, the control supports child windows only. This is because the browser is the main window, and every PowerBuilder window that displays within the browser must be a child window. The child window may contain other controls, including DataWindows, OLE objects, treeview, and other ActiveX controls. In the child window, you can also invoke popup and response windows. You can save your application's objects within one or more .PBDs. The database access in the window occurs locally via the client's database connections.
- Create the HTML file (mytest2.htm). To integrate the control within the HTML file, use the <OBJECT/> tag as shown. The <OBJECT/> tag takes a number of parameters. For the LIB parameter, specify the .PBD's location. For the PBWINDOW parameter, specify the child PowerBuilder window's name. For the PBAPPLICATION parameter, specify the PowerBuilder application's name as shown:

```
<!DOCTYPE HTML PUBLIC "-//W3C//DTD HTML 3.2//EN">
<HTML>
<HEAD>
   <TITLE>PowerBuilder Window ActiveX Control Example</TITLE>
   <META NAME="GENERATOR" CONTENT="Mozilla/3.0Gold (Win95; I) [Netscape]">
</HEAD>
<BODY BGCOLOR="#FFFFFF">

<H2>PowerBuilder Window ActiveX Control Example</H2>

<P>
<HR></P>

<OBJECT NAME="PBRX1" WIDTH=400 HEIGHT=400

CLASSID="CLSID:CEC58653-C842-11CF-A6FB-00805FA8669E">
     <PARAM NAME="_Version" VALUE="65536">
     <PARAM NAME="_ExtentX" VALUE="5962">
     <PARAM NAME="_ExtentY" VALUE="2164">
     <PARAM NAME="_StockProps" VALUE="0">
     <PARAM NAME="PBWindow" VALUE="w_child">
     <PARAM NAME="LibList" VALUE="http://localhost/mytest.pbd;">
     <PARAM NAME="PBApplication" VALUE="mytest">
</OBJECT>

<P>
<HR></P>

</BODY>
</HTML>
```

- Configure the client workstations by registering the PowerBuilder Window ActiveX control (pbrx60.ocx). To register the control, use the Registration Server (regsvr32) program. In addition, install the PowerBuilder runtime DLLs on the client workstations.

> **TIP** To deploy an application in secure mode, use the secure mode ActiveX control (pbrxs60.ocx).

- Copy the HTML file (mytest2.htm) and the .PBD to the Web site server's \htdocs directory. You can now view the HTML file in Internet Explorer (see Figure 25.5).

> **TIP** The Window ActiveX control requires the PowerBuilder runtime files. The PowerBuilder Window ActiveX control is supported only on Windows 95 and Windows NT 4.0 platforms. The control does not work on other platforms such as Macintosh and UNIX. Keep in mind that the solution you create by using the Window ActiveX control only works for Windows clients.

To view the HTML pages enhanced by the Window ActiveX control, you can use any browser that supports ActiveX technology, such as Microsoft Internet Explorer 3.x or higher. You can also use Netscape Navigator version 3.x or higher to view the pages enhanced by the Window ActiveX control, provided you use NCompassLabs' (www.ncompasslabs.com) ScriptActive plug-in.

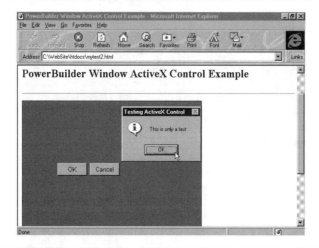

Figure 25.5   **Viewing a PowerBuilder window in Internet Explorer by using the Window ActiveX control.**

CUSTOMIZABLE WEB JUMPS

PowerBuilder provides four customizable Web jumps in the development environment. To view them, select the **Help** menu from within the development environment. The defaults are Powersoft Web Site, Web Express Web Site, Powersoft Online Books Site, and PB Application Gallery Site. You can use Web jumps to connect to four of your most frequently visited Web sites. This feature provides an easy way for you to connect to a Web site directly from within your PowerBuilder development environment.

To change the default URLs, open pb.ini Provide the alternate site names and URLs in the [PB] section of the .INI file for WebLink1, WebLink2, WebLink3, and WebLink4. The following shows the default [PB] section within the pb.ini file:

```
[PB]
CompilerWarnings=1
DashesInIdentifiers=1
DatabaseWarnings=1
Maximized=1
PromptOnExit=0
StripComments=0
WebLink1=&Powersoft Web Site,http://www.sybase.com/powersoft
WebLink2=&Web Express Web
Site,http://etsprod.powersoft.com/scripts/pbisa050.dll/ptrackt/u_logon/f_entry?[Help]
WebLink3=&Powersoft Online Books Site,http://calas.sybase.com/
WebLink4=&PB Application Gallery Site,http://www.sybase.com/powerbuilder/appgal/
ToolbarText=1
ToolbarTips=1
OleGenReg=pbgenreg,C:\Program Files\Powersoft\shared\pbgenreg.pbd
UserHelpFile=pbusr60.hlp
UserHelpPrefix=uf_
WebPBWizard=html_webpb,C:\Program Files\Powersoft\pb6\IT\wizard.pbd
Synchronizer=C:\Program Files\Powersoft\pb6\sync\sync.exe
Object1=/p Window /l c:\work\mytest.pbl /o w_test
Object2=/p DataWindow /l c:\work\mytest.pbl /o test
Object3=/p UserObject /l c:\work\mytest.pbl /o mytest
Object4=/p Window /l c:\work\mytest.pbl /o w_child
```

TIP The maximum number of customizable Web jumps you can set is four.

SECURE MODE

You can run a PowerBuilder application in secure mode. Running an application in secure mode means the application cannot access information on the client workstation. There are flip sides to using the secure approach. Although the client workstation is secure because the application cannot harm the system, the application cannot offer much in terms of functionality. For example, a secure application cannot perform any kind of I/O with the client workstation. As a result, the application cannot cache information on the client workstation, read from or write to the cookie files on the client workstation, and so on.

Restricted PowerBuilder Functions

A number of activities are restricted within the secure mode.

DDE Functions

You cannot call the PowerScript DDE functions in an application running in secure mode. Doing so causes an execution error. As a result, the following PowerScript functions are restricted within the secure mode: **CloseChannel( )**, **GetDataDDE( )**, **GetDataDDEOrigin( )**, **GetFileOpenName( )**, **GetRemote( )**, **Send( )**, **SetDataDDE( )**, **StartHotLink( )**, **StartServerDDE( )**, and **StopServerDDE( )**.

Mail Functions

You cannot call the PowerScript mail functions in an application running in secure mode. Doing so causes an execution error. The following functions are restricted in secure mode: **mailAddress( )**, **mailDeleteMessage( )**, **mailGetMessages( )**, **mailHandle( )**, **mailLogoff( )**, **mailLogon( )**, **mailReadMessage( )**, **mailRecipientDetails( )**, **mailResolveRecipient( )**, **mailSaveMessage( )**, and **mailSend( )**.

OLE Functions

You cannot call the PowerScript OLE functions either: **InsertObject( )**, **InsertClass( )**, **InsertFile( )**, and **LinkTo( )**.

Database Functions

In addition, you cannot call the PowerScript database functions: **SetTrans( )**, **SetTransObject( )**, and **Update( )**.

Library Functions

A number of library functions are also restricted within the secure mode: **LibraryCreate( )**, **LibraryDirectory( )**, **LibraryExport( )**, **LibraryImport( )**, and **SetLibraryList( )**.

File Functions

You got it! You cannot call the PowerScript I/O functions either: **DirList( )**, **DirSelect( )**, **DoScript( )**, **FileClose( )**, **FileExists( )**, **FileLength( )**, **FileRead( )**, **FileSeek( )**, **ImportFile( )**, **SaveAs( )**, and **ShowHelp( )**.

Registry Functions

A number of Registry functions are restricted in secure mode: **RegistryDelete( )**, **RegistryGet( )**, **RegistryKeys( )**, and **RegistryValues( )**.

Distributed Computing Functions

You cannot connect to a PowerBuilder application server in the secure mode. A number of PowerScript functions you use for distributed application development are restricted within the secure mode, including **ConncetToServer( )** and **DisconnectServer( )**.

.INI Functions

The INI functions restricted within the secure mode are **ProfileInt( )** and **SetProfileString( )**.

Running the Window ActiveX Control in Secure Mode

To run the Window ActiveX control within secure mode, use the Window ActiveX control's secure version (pbrxs60.ocx) and perform the following steps:

1. Create and save the PowerBuilder window(s) within a .PBD.
2. Create the HTML file.
3. Configure the client workstations by registering the PowerBuilder Window ActiveX control's secure version (pbrxs60.ocx).
4. Copy the HTML file and the .PBD to the Web site server's \htdocs directory. You can now view the HTML file in Internet Explorer.

Running the Window Plug-In in Secure Mode

To run the Window plug-in in secure mode, use the plug-in's secure version (nppbs60.dll) and perform the following steps:

- Install and configure the Web server. Register the secure Window plug-in with the Web server. To register the secure Window plug-in, use the following steps:

  1. Start the WebSite Server Administration program (i.e., Server Admin). The Server Admin program displays the Web Site Server Properties dialog box.
  2. Click the **Mapping** tab, then click the **Content Types** radiobutton.
  3. Type **.PBD** in the File Extension (class) field. Then, type **application/vnd.powerbuilder6-s** in the MIME content type field.
  4. Click **Add**, then click OK, and click **Yes** within the Immediate Reset message box.

- Create the PowerBuilder window(s) and save the window(s) within a .PBD. For the restrictions on the type of PowerBuilder window(s) you can create, see the *Window Plug-In* section.
- Create the HTML file. For information on creating the HTML file, see the *Window Plug-In* section.
- Configure the client workstations by copying the secure Window plug-in (nppbs60.dll) to the \plugins directory of Internet Explorer (or Netscape Communicator) on the client workstations.
- Copy the HTML file to the Web site server's \htdocs directory. You can view the HTML file in your browser.

Running the DataWindow Plug-In in Secure Mode

There is no separate secure version of the DataWindow plug-in because the DataWindow plug-in only reads and displays information; the plug-in does not write information on the client workstation.

SYNCHRONIZER

How many times in the past did you upgrade the client workstations with a maintenance release of your application? If the client workstations are geographically dispersed and the client base is not very experienced with computers and software upgrades, how many times did you have to physically travel to the client site and upgrade the application manually with the new maintenance release? Wouldn't it be wonderful if the application automatically upgraded itself with the new set of files within the maintenance release when the user starts the application? Well, PowerBuilder 6 provides a way for you to do this. It is called the *synchronizer*. The synchronizer's basic function is to update the target set of files with the files from the master set. In essence, the synchronizer makes the target and master one and the same.

There are a couple of ways to use and deploy the synchronizer. You can either run the synchronizer as a stand-alone application (syncrt.exe or syncrt16.exe) or from within a PowerBuilder application. To run the synchronizer from within a Power-Builder application, use the Sync ActiveX control (sync.ocx). You can use the Sync ActiveX control with a PowerBuilder or Web application.

Building the Synchronization Data File

The synchronization data file contains the instructions for synchronizing the files within the target set from the files within the master set.

To build the synchronization data file (.SYC), use the Sync Builder that comes with PowerBuilder 6. To start the Sync Builder, run sync.exe. The Sync Builder, in turn, displays the window, as shown in Figure 25.6.

To create a new sync data file and add a new task, click the right mouse button in the Sync Builder window and select **New... Sync Command** from the popup menu. The Sync Builder displays the Command Properties dialog box, as shown in Figure 25.7.

In the Command Properties dialog box, specify the master set's location in the Source File text box. The master set's location can be a valid local or network drive or a valid FTP site. Similarly, specify the target set's location within the Destination File text box. Similar to the master set's location, the target set's location can be a valid local or network drive or a valid FTP site.

If the date and time of the files within the target set are different from the files within the master set, and you would like the synchronizer to synchronize the target set files based on this verification, check the File/Date Time Check checkbox.

If the size of the files within the target set is different from the files within the master set, and you would like the synchronizer to synchronize the target set files based on this verification, check the Size Check checkbox.

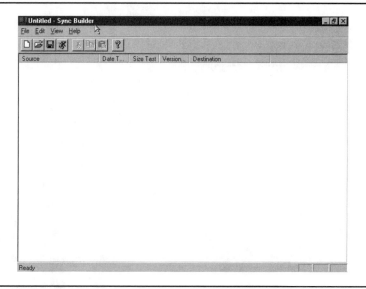

Figure 25.6   Running the Sync Builder.

If the version of the files within the target set is different from the files within the master set, and you would like the synchronizer to synchronize the target set files based on this verification, check the File Version Check checkbox.

To close the Command Properties dialog box, click OK. The Sync Builder window now looks like the one shown in Figure 25.8.

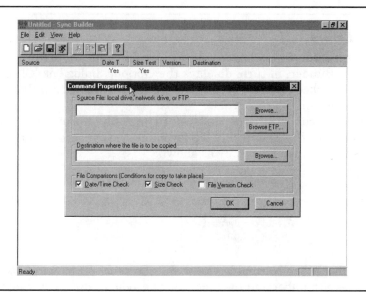

Figure 25.7   The Command Properties dialog box.

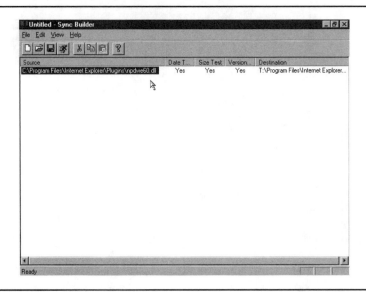

Figure 25.8 **Building the Sync data file.**

Similarly, you can add other tasks to the data sync file. To save the file, select **Save As** from the **File** menu.

TIP If you choose to install Sync Builder when you install PowerBuilder, you can also run Sync Builder from within the PowerBuilder development environment.

Logging the Errors

To direct the synchronizer to log errors to a log file, select **Options** from the **View** menu. The Sync Builder, in turn, displays the Options dialog box. Check the Log Actions to a Log File checkbox and specify the log file's name within the Log File Name dialog box as shown in Figure 25.9.

In addition, you can choose the log level: Errors only, Normal, or Verbose.

When you choose the Errors only log level and the synchronization fails, the synchronizer logs the error number only as shown:

```
02/03/1998 11:56:59       *****LOG FILE CREATED*****
02/03/1998 11:56:59       FindFirst error:   error 21

02/03/1998 11:56:59       File copy failed
02/03/1998 11:56:59       *****END OF LOG*****
```

When you choose the Normal log level and the synchronization fails, the synchronizer logs the error number and the task that the synchronizer is trying to accomplish as shown:

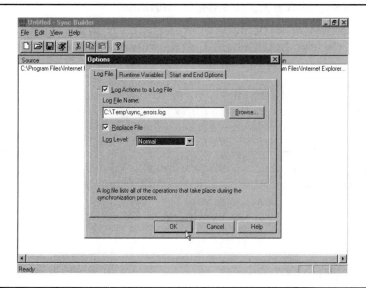

Figure 25.9   Enabling logging of the errors.

```
02/03/1998 11:59:16      *****LOG FILE CREATED*****
02/03/1998 11:59:16      FindFirst error:  error 21

02/03/1998 11:59:16      Copying: C:\loantrak\loan.pbd to e:\loantrak
02/03/1998 11:59:16      File copy failed
02/03/1998 11:59:16      *****END OF LOG*****
```

When you choose the Verbose log level and the synchronization fails, the synchronizer logs the most detailed information about the failed synchronization process as shown:

```
02/03/1998 12:01:23      *****LOG FILE CREATED*****
02/03/1998 12:01:23      *Command: Copy C:\loantrak\loan.pbd to e:\loantrak w/date
check w/size check
02/03/1998 12:01:23      Comparing File Sizes
02/03/1998 12:01:23          Reading attributes of file: C:\loantrak\loan.pbd
02/03/1998 12:01:23          Reading attributes of file: e:\loantrak
02/03/1998 12:01:23      FindFirst error:  error 21

02/03/1998 12:01:23          Source and Destination files are different sizes
02/03/1998 12:01:23      Copying: C:\loantrak\loan.pbd to e:\loantrak
02/03/1998 12:01:23      File copy failed
02/03/1998 12:01:23      Copying Completed
02/03/1998 12:01:23      *****END OF LOG*****
```

Running Synchronizer as a Stand-Alone Application

Pass the synchronization data file as a parameter to the synchronizer executable (syncrt.exe or syncrt16.exe). For example, the following executes the loan.syc data file:

```
SYNCRT loan.syc
```

The executable executes the instructions within the loan.syc data file and displays a status screen. The status screen indicates the synchronization process's progress. If an error occurs, the executable logs them to a log file.

TIP You must pass the synchronization data file as a parameter to the synchronizer executable, otherwise the executable will not run. Also, note that the synchronizer executable that comes with the PowerBuilder Windows version works only on Windows platforms. The synchronizer ActiveX control also works only on Windows platforms.

Using the Sync ActiveX Control

By using the Sync ActiveX control (sync.ocx), you can integrate the file synchronization process within a PowerBuilder application or HTML page. Integrating the Sync ActiveX control within a PowerBuilder application is similar to integrating any other ActiveX control.

Integrating the Sync Control in a PowerBuilder Application

The following are the steps to add the control to a PowerBuilder window:

1. Open the window. Select **OLE** from the Controls menu. PowerBuilder displays the Insert Object dialog box. Click the **Insert Control** tab.
2. If the Sync ActiveX control is not already registered on your system, you can register the control by clicking **Register New**. Choose **sync.ocx** from the \Ddk6\Synchronizer directory of your PowerBuilder 6 installation. Upon registration, choose **Synchronizer Control** from the list of controls, as shown in Figure 25.10 and click OK. Then click your mouse in the window space. PowerBuilder adds the control to the window.
3. To set the control's properties, click the right mouse button on the control and select **Properties** from the popup menu. PowerBuilder displays the OLE Custom Control dialog box. Within the dialog box, click **OLE Control Properties**. PowerBuilder, in turn, displays the Control Properties dialog box. In this dialog box, you can specify the sync data file's location. To direct the control to display the status dialog box, check the **Show Status Dialog** checkbox, as shown in Figure 25.11.
4. Next, you can write scripts for the control.

Integrating the Sync Control in a Web page

You can embed the Sync ActiveX control within an HTML file by using the <OBJECT> tag. To view the control's properties and methods, use the browser in the PowerBuilder development environment.

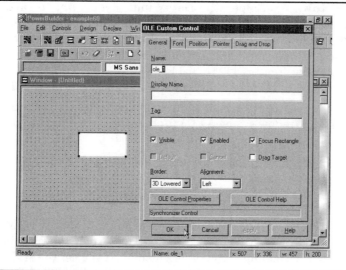

Figure 25.10   Adding the Synchronizer control to the PowerBuilder window.

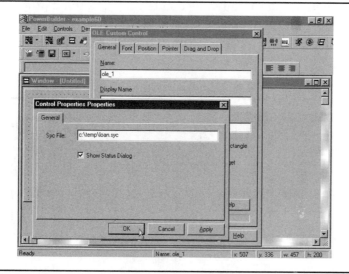

Figure 25.11   Setting the Synchronizer control's properties.

HTML TABLE GENERATION

The HTML table you generate with PowerBuilder 6 now supports cascading style sheets (CSS). The CSS include additional formatting and font information for displaying the HTML tables that you generate by using PowerBuilder 6. The following are the couple of ways you can generate the HTML tables:

Using Save Rows As. Open the DataWindow you want to save as an HTML table in the DataWindow painter and select **Preview** from the **Design** menu. In the Preview window, select **Save Rows As...** from the **File** menu and choose **HTML Table** as the format. PowerBuilder 6 creates an HTML file that includes the DataWindow within an HTML Table format. Figure 25.12 shows an example DataWindow saved in HTML table format and viewed in Internet Explorer.

Using the SaveAs function. Within your application's PowerScript code, you can use the DataWindow's SaveAs ( ) function to save a DataWindow in HTML table format as shown:

```
dw_1.SaveAs("c:\loantrak\reports\loanstat.htm", HTMLTable!, TRUE)
```

For more information on the SaveAs ( ) function and its parameters, see the PowerBuilder documentation.

PowerBuilder 6's DataWindow object supports a new property: HTMLTable. If you set the HTMLTable's GenerateCSS property to True, PowerBuilder uses the HTMLTable property to customize the table's display. If you set the HTMLTable's GenerateCSS property to False, PowerBuilder does not use the HTMLTable property to customize the table's display. In addition to the GenerateCSS property, you can configure the following HTMLTable properties: NoWrap, width, border, CellSpacing, and CellPadding. You can use the Modify function to configure these properties as shown:

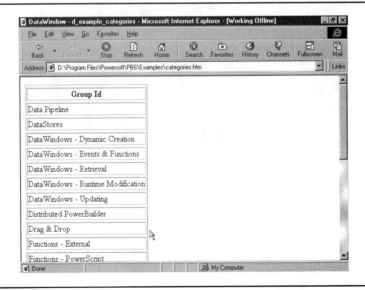

Figure 25.12 **Viewing the DataWindow within HTML Table format.**

```
dw_1.Modify("datawindow.HTMLTable.GenerateCSS='yes'")
dw_1.Modify("datawindow.HTMLTable.NoWrap='yes'")
dw_1.Modify("datawindow.HTMLTable.width=5")
dw_1.Modify("datawindow.HTMLTable.border=5")
dw_1.Modify("datawindow.HTMLTable.CellSpacing=2")
dw_1.Modify("datawindow.HTMLTable.CellPadding=2")
```

WEB.PB

PowerBuilder's distributed capabilities are brought to the World Wide Web by web.pb. In the web.pb architecture, you use PowerScript, nonvisual user objects, and datastores to generate the client-side HTML. A web.pb application includes the following four components:

Browser.   The browser's function is to serve HTML to the end user. The web.pb application responds to a couple of HTML elements: form (<FORM></FORM>) and anchor (<A></A>).

Web server.   The Web server's function is to convey the browser's request to the application server and return the results from the application server to the browser.

Application server.   This is the heart and soul of distributed Web application with PowerBuilder. Typically, the application server includes nonvisual Power-Builder business objects. The Web server and application server communicate with each other by using Common Gateway Interface (CGI; pbcgi060.exe), Microsoft Internet Server Application Programming Interface (ISAPI; pbisa60.dll), or Netscape ISAPI (pbns160.dll or pbns260.dll).

Database server.   The database server processes the database requests that the application server sends.

Figure 25.13 shows a distributed Web application's architecture.

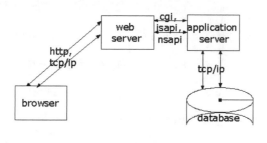

web.pb architecture

Figure 25.13   **A distributed Web application's architecture by using PowerBuilder.**

The following steps outline the procedure for creating a web.pb application:

1. Install, configure, and start the Web server. To configure the Web server, use the Web server's administration tool and map the /SCRIPTS/URL path to \CGI-SHL.
2. Edit the HOSTS and SERVICES files. Within the HOSTS files, associate IP addresses with the host names. The entry looks like this:

```
127.0.0.1    localhost
```

Within the SERVICES files, associate port numbers with the application names. The entry looks like this (your port number may be different):

```
pbserver     10013/tcp
```

3. Develop and run the PowerBuilder application server. The application server listens for the incoming client requests. For more information on creating a PowerBuilder application server, see Chapter 23, "Advanced Distributed Application Development."
4. Create the client-side HTML by using web.pb wizard and the server's nonvisual user objects.
5. Run the web.pb application.

web.pb Wizard

PowerBuilder 6 comes with an integrated web.pb wizard. By using this wizard, you can generate the HTML that invokes the nonvisual user object's functions. Note the web.pb wizard generates one HTML page per function.

The following is a sample HTML page that invokes the uo_webpbdemo user object's uf_retrieve-list function:

```
<form action="/cgi-shl/pbcgi060.exe/pbexamples/uo_webpbdemo/uf_retrieve_list"
method="POST" name="Login">
<p align="center">Last Name: <input type="text" size="25" maxlength="256"
name="as_lastname">
<p align="center">First Name: <input type="text" size="25" maxlength="256"
name="as_firstname">
<p align="center">SSN: <input type="text" size="25" maxlength="256"
name="as_ssn">
<p align="center"><input type="submit" name="insert_btn" value="Insert">
</form>
```

The following is the uf_retrieve_list function's code:

```
Function:  uf_retrieve_list
Arguments: as_lastname String
           as_firstname String
           as_ssn string
```

```
// The function takes the customer's last name, first name, and ssn as
// arguments and returns the HTML that displays a list of products the
// customer ordered

string        ls_html
DataStore     ldst_products_table

SQLCA.userid = "Admin"
SQLCA.dbpass = "Admin"
SQLCA.database = "Products"
connect;

ldst_products_table = Create DataStore
ldst_ products _table = "d_products"
ldst_customer.SetTransObject(SQLCA)
ldst_products_table.retrieve(as_lastname, as_firstname, as_ssn)
ls_html = ldst_products_table.Object.DataWindow.Data.HTMLTable

DESTROY ldst_products_table
RETURN ls_html
```

Using the GenerateHTMLForm Function

Within a web.pb application, you can also use the GenerateHTMLForm function to generate the client-side HTML form dynamically. Note that you can generate the HTML form for free-form or tabular DataWindows only.

The following is the uf_retrieve_list function's code that uses the GenerateHTML-Form function:

```
Function:     uf_retrieve_list
Arguments:    as_lastname String
              as_firstname String
              as_ssn string

// The function takes the customer's last name, first name, and ssn as
// arguments and returns the HTML that displays a list of products the
// customer ordered

string        ls_html, ls_style
string        ls_syntax, ls_action
long          ll_return
DataStore     ldst_products_table

SQLCA.userid = "Admin"
SQLCA.dbpass = "Admin"
SQLCA.database = "Products"
connect;
```

continues

```
ldst_products_table = Create DataStore
ldst_ products _table = "d_products"
ldst_customer.SetTransObject(SQLCA)
ll_return = ldst_products_table.retrieve(as_lastname, as_firstname, as_ssn)
If ll_return = -1 then
     RETURN("Retrieval error")
End If
ll_return = ldst_products_table.GenerateHTMLForm(ls_syntax, ls_style, ls_action)

ls_html = "<HTML>"
ls_html += ls_style
ls_html += "<BODY>"

ls_html += "<H1>Products</H1>"
ls_html += "<HR>"
ls_html += ls_syntax
ls_html += "</BODY></HTML>"

DESTROY ldst_products_table
RETURN ls_html
```

TIP In addition to the Windows 95 and Windows NT platforms, the web.pb wizard supports the Power Macintosh, Sun Solaris, HP UX, and IBM AIX platforms.

web.pb Class Library

By using the web.pb class library (webpb.pbl), you can develop PowerBuilder server applications. The web.pb class library includes custom nonvisual user objects you can use to generate the client-side HTML and manage the browser's session with the server.

The web.pb class library also helps you to:

- Build html pages programmatically
- Provide session and transaction management
- Develop "shopping cart" applications

TIP The web.pb class library that comes with PowerBuilder 6 supports only the Windows 95 and Windows NT platforms.

CHAPTER 26

Learning HOW to Build PowerBuilder Applications

This chapter covers the following:

- An introduction to HOW
- Steps to building PowerBuilder applications by using HOW
- Building a PowerBuilder application by using HOW

INTRODUCTION

To build *n*-tier distributed client/server PowerBuilder applications, you can use River-ton Software's new product called HOW. HOW is a complete visual integrated system you can use for requirements analysis, business and data modeling, application development, application and use case analysis, and maintaining a repository of reusable PowerBuilder objects—all within a single IDE. HOW stores the repository within an object database. By using HOW, you can:

- Gather user requirements and define business objects.
- Perform use case and business analysis on your application.
- Generate data models from the definitions of business objects. Alternatively, you can import and use the existing data models within HOW. HOW works with data models from Erwin/ERX and PowerDesigner.
- Use HOW to generate the PowerBuilder user objects, DataWindows, windows, and other objects from the business objects.
- Generate PowerBuilder code based on the PFC ancestors.
- Maintain a central repository of the objects. Over time, the repository will contain several objects that you can use as the building blocks for your next application. You may need to write very little or no new code. This is one of the biggest advantages of using HOW.
- Support both individual and team development.

Installing HOW

To install and use HOW, you need a Pentium 100 MHz (or higher) running Windows 95 (or Windows NT) with at least 24 Mb RAM and 30 Mb of free hard disk space. In addition, you need PowerBuilder 6 and ERwin 2.6, ERwin 3, or PowerDesigner 4.3, 5, or 5.1. You can visit Riverton's Web site at www.riverton.com.

Editions and Components

Riverton Software distributes Professional and Enterprise editions of HOW. There are two types of Professional and Enterprise editions, those with and without team development support. The Enterprise Edition includes everything the Professional Edition offers and more. The Enterprise Edition adds a variety of analysis tools. To gather and organize user requirements, you can use the Use-Case analysis tool. To derive the business rules from the use cases, link the business objects to the business rules, track implementation and business rules to the requirements, and so on, you can use the Business Rule analysis tool. To design your application's workflow, you can use HOW's integrated Workflow Builder.

To build an application by using HOW's integrated development environment, use the Use Case Builder and Use Case View Builder to define, gather, and view the user requirements. Next, use the integrated Domain Builder to define, create, and group the class objects. For each object, define the object's properties, methods, events, and queries. In addition, you can define the relationships between the different class objects. Within HOW, you can define two types of objects: business and technology objects. Business and technology objects constitute your application's building blocks. Business objects define the application's business requirements. To define your application's business objects, use HOW's integrated Business Rule Builder. Technology objects constitute the application's user interface and navigational components. To assemble and storyboard the business and technology objects together to build n-tier, distributed client/server applications, use HOW's integrated Task Builder. As you define and create new objects, HOW maintains a central repository of the objects. The repository is extremely useful when you build your next PowerBuilder application with HOW because you can build the next application simply by gluing together the objects from the repository. As you might expect, you can use Sybase's SQL Anywhere database with HOW to create reports based on the information contained in HOW's object repository.

Within HOW, you can generate a new data model for ERwin/ERX or PowerDesigner from the business rule objects. Alternatively, you can import your application's existing data models into HOW and synchronize the model with the object repository. Not only that, you can use HOW to create the database access and DataWindow objects within PowerBuilder from the data model.

You can run HOW from within PowerBuilder. You can also incorporate your existing PowerBuilder objects into HOW. In addition, you can synchronize HOW with your PowerBuilder libraries in the following manner:

- Generate PowerBuilder objects for a new HOW object
- Import a PowerBuilder object into HOW
- Synchronize a PowerBuilder object with the object's HOW counterpart

USING HOW TO BUILD POWERBUILDER APPLICATIONS

To build PowerBuilder applications by using HOW, use the following steps:

1. Create a project and library. Each HOW project consists of one or more libraries. Each library consists of one or more HOW objects. Examples of HOW objects include window, data control, task, query, association, and data model map.
2. Create a domain with class objects. Creating a domain means outlining the application's business components. You can define a number of objects within a domain. You can define class objects and associations between the class objects. You can also define business rules and use cases. In this example, you define a couple of class objects (authors and books) and an association between them (an author *has* books).
3. Create attributes for the class objects. Define attributes for each class object. For example, author_id and author_name are the attributes for the Authors class object.
4. Establish an association between the class objects. An association between the class objects indicates the relationship between the class objects.
5. Create a data model based on the domain. After defining your application's business components within HOW, you are ready to generate the logical and physical data model. This is one of HOW's biggest advantages. HOW provides an IDE (integrated development environment) within which you can define your application's business domain by using HOW and then generate logical and physical data models based on the domain you define.
6. Synchronize the data model and bring the physical data model information into HOW. You can use HOW to synchronize the logical and physical data models with the business domain you define. You can then bring the physical data model information into HOW.
7. Create the windows and controls. To define your application's interface, you can define windows and data controls. You can associate the data controls with the windows. Note that HOW stores the windows and controls you create within its object repository. When you define the windows and controls, try to define them as generically as possible so you can reuse them.
8. Create the queries. In addition, you can define queries and associate them with the appropriate data controls. Note that HOW stores the queries you create within its object repository. When you define the queries, try to define them as generically as possible so you can reuse them.
9. Create the tasks that use the windows, controls, queries, and the given navigations between the windows. After defining the windows, controls, and queries, define the tasks. Each task consists of the windows, controls, queries, and navigations between the windows.
10. Specify the navigations between the windows to establish the program's flow. The navigation between the windows establishes the program's flow.
11. Create the parameters and links. Keep a window independent of the other windows by defining parameters for the window. By defining a link between a window object and a data control, for example, you can specify the retrieval argument(s) for

the query. As a result, you can define queries that are independent of the data controls you associate them with. The queries thus become reusable.

12. Generate the PowerBuilder application. You are now ready to generate the PowerBuilder application from the HOW objects.

13. Run the application. Create the database, establish the data connection, and run the application.

14. Examine the objects that HOW generates. HOW generates a partitioned, *n*-tier application that takes advantage of the PFC services. The presentation logic is different from the data access and business logic.

15. Generate documentation for the project by using HOW. To generate the project documentation, use Microsoft Word and HOW.

In this example, you will build a PowerBuilder application using HOW. The application uses a database containing a couple of tables: authors and books. The relationship between the tables is that an author has one or more books. The fields for the authors table are listed in Table 26.1 and the fields for the books table are listed in Table 26.2.

Create a Project and Library

To create a project and add a library to the project, use the following steps:

1. Start HOW. Select **New...Project** from the **File** menu. HOW, in turn, displays the Project Properties dialog box.

2. Type the project's name, **AuthorTrak**, in the Name field as shown in Figure 26.1. In addition, you can type the project's description in the Description field.

3. To view the library name that HOW automatically assigns to the project, click the **Libraries** tab. Make a note of this library's name (in this case, the name is Library1) because you will change the name to something more meaningful shortly. To close the dialog box, click OK.

Table 26.1   Authors Table

Field	Datatype	Primary Key?
author_id	smallint	Yes
author_name	string varchar(18)	No

Table 26.2   Books Table

Field	Datatype	Primary Key?
book_id	smallint	Yes
author_id	smallint	Yes
book_name	string varchar(18)	No

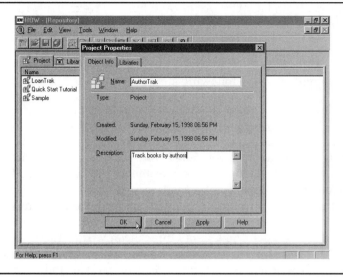

Figure 26.1   **Creating a HOW project.**

4. Click the **Library** tab in the HOW–[Repository] window. HOW displays the list of available libraries. Click the right mouse button on **Library1** and select **Properties** from the popup menu. HOW, in turn, displays the Library Properties dialog box.
5. Change the library's name to **AuthorTrak** within the Name field as shown in Figure 26.2. In addition, you can type the library's description within the Description field. To close the dialog box, click OK.

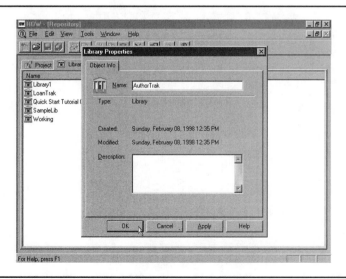

Figure 26.2   **Changing the name of HOW project's library.**

In this step, you created a HOW project and library. Next, you will create a domain with class objects.

Create a Domain with Class Objects

To create a new domain, use the following steps:

1. To open the AuthorTrak project, double-click **AuthorTrak**. To add a domain to the project, select **New Object** from the **File** menu. HOW, in turn, displays the New Object dialog box.

2. Type the domain's name, say, **AuthorTrak**, within the Name field. Choose **Domain** from the Type drop-down listbox as shown in Figure 26.3. In addition, you can type the domain's description in the Description field.

3. HOW opens the Domain Builder for the **AuthorTrak domain,** as shown in Figure 26.4.

4. To add a class object, click the **Class Object** icon within the floating toolbar and click once anywhere within the Domain Builder space. To add another class object, click the **Class Object** icon again in the floating toolbar and click once anywhere in the Domain Builder space. HOW adds two class objects, Class1 and Class2, to the AuthorTrak domain, as shown in Figure 26.5.

5. To rename Class1, double-click **Class1**. HOW displays the Class Object Properties dialog box. In the dialog box, change Class1 to **Authors**. Similarly, change the Class2 class object's name to **Books**. The AuthorTrak domain now looks as shown in Figure 26.6.

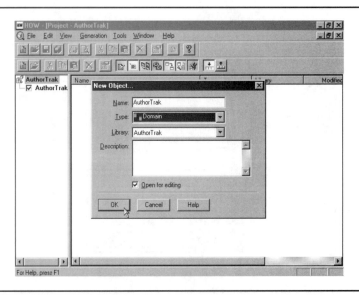

Figure 26.3   Creating a business domain.

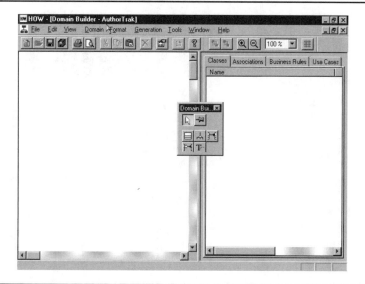

Figure 26.4   The Domain Builder.

In this step, you created a domain and added a couple of class objects to the domain. In the next step, you add attributes for the class objects.

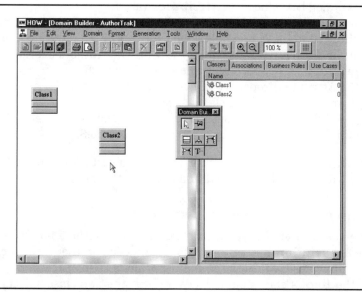

Figure 26.5   Adding class objects to the domain.

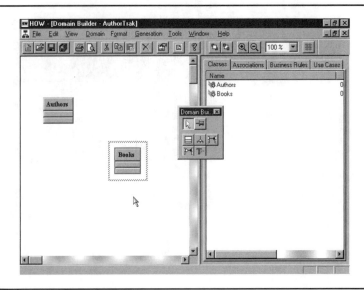

Figure 26.6   The AuthorTrak domain.

Create Attributes for the Class Objects

To add attributes for the class object Authors, use the following steps:

1. Double-click **Authors** within the Domain Builder. HOW displays the Class Object Properties dialog box. Click the **Attributes** tab.
2. To add a new attribute, click **New**. HOW displays the Attribute Properties dialog box.
3. Type **Author_Id** in the Name field. Choose **Integer** from the Type drop-down list-box. Since the Author_ID is a primary key for the Authors class object, check the **Part of primary key** checkbox as shown in Figure 26.7.
4. To close the Attribute Properties dialog box, click OK. Similarly, add the attribute **Author_Name** to the Authors class object.
5. Similarly, add the attributes (Book_Id and Book_Name) for the Books class object. The Domain Builder now looks as shown in Figure 26.8.

In this step, you added attributes for the class objects Authors and Books. In the next step, you will establish an association between the class objects.

Establish an Association between the Class Objects

To establish an association between the class objects, use the following steps:
1. Click the **Association** icon in the toolbar, and click on the Authors class object.
2. Click once anywhere within the Domain Builder's open space.
3. Click on the **Books** class object. HOW relates the two class objects Authors and Books.

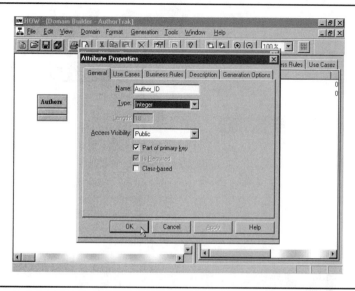

Figure 26.7   **Adding the Author_Id attribute.**

4. To change the assocation's name, double-click on the Association. HOW, in turn, displays the Class Association Properties dialog box. Change the text **relates to** to **has** and close the dialog box by clicking OK. The Domain Builder now looks as shown in Figure 26.9.

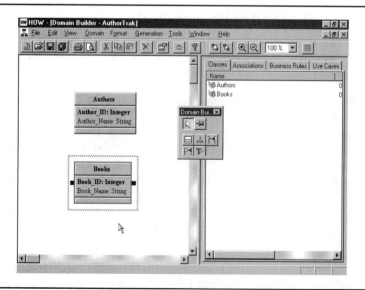

Figure 26.8   **The class objects Authors and Books within the Domain Builder.**

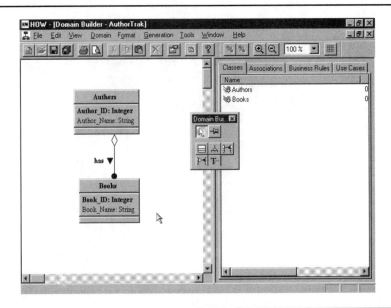

Figure 26.9   Changing the association's name.

In this step, you established an association between the class objects Authors and Books. In the next step, you create a data model based on the AuthorTrak domain.

Generate a Data Model Based on the Domain

Before generating the data model, you must specify the data modeling tool you would like to use. This example uses ERwin 2.6. To specify the data modeling tool, use the following steps:

1. Select **Data Model Maps** from the **Generation** menu. HOW displays the Data Model Maps dialog.
2. Click **AuthorTrak** in the list the dialog box displays and then click OK. HOW, in turn, displays the Data Model Map Properties–AuthorTrak dialog box.
3. Choose **ERwin 2.6** from the Associated Tool drop-down listbox.
4. Use the **Browse** button to specify the path for the AuTrak.erx file as shown in Figure 26.10.
5. To close the Data Model Map Properties–AuthorTrak dialog box, click OK.
6. To close the Data Model Map dialog box, click OK.

To generate the logical data model based on the domain, use the following steps:

1. Select **Synchronize Data Models** from the **Generation** menu. HOW displays the Synchronizing ERwin Objects dialog box as shown in Figure 26.11.

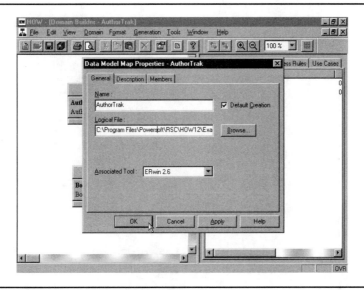

Figure 26.10   **Generating the ERwin 2.6 data model.**

2. To synchronize the data model, click **Sync**. HOW synchronizes the data model, creates a logical data model file, and displays the log, as shown in Figure 26.12.

3. To close the log dialog, click OK.

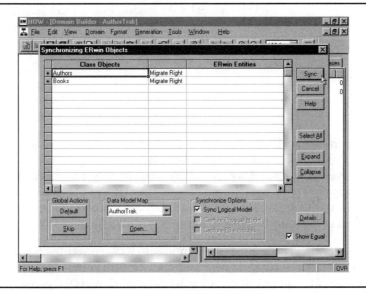

Figure 26.11   **The Synchronizing ERwin Objects dialog box.**

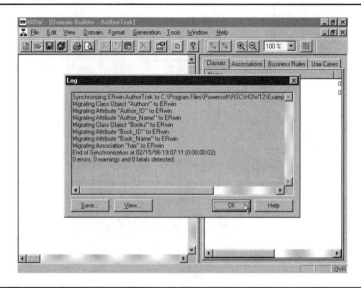

Figure 26.12 HOW displays a log file after synchronizing the data model.

To view the ERwin data model, use the following steps:

1. Select **Edit Data Model** from the **Generation** menu. HOW launches ERwin.
2. Import the .ERX file into ERwin.

In this step, you generated the logical data model. In the next steps, you will generate the physical data model and bring the physical data model information into HOW.

Synchronize the Data Model and Bring the Physical Data Model Information into HOW

To generate and bring the physical data model information into HOW, use the following steps:

1. Select **Synchronize Data Models** from the **Generation** menu. HOW displays the Synchronizing ERwin Objects dialog box.
2. Make sure you check the **Capture Physical Model** checkbox. By doing so, you bring the physical data model information into HOW.
3. To synchronize the data model, click **Sync**. HOW synchronizes the data model, creates a physical data model file, and displays a log. To close the log, click OK.

To view the physical data model information HOW generates for the class objects, double-click on any of the class objects and click the **Physical Data Model Info** tab. Figure 26.13 shows the physical data model information HOW generated for the Authors class object.

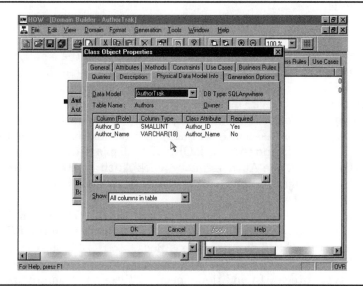

Figure 26.13   The Physical Data Model information for the Authors class object.

In this step, you synchronized the data model and brought the physical data model information into HOW. In the next step, you create the windows, controls, and queries.

Create the Windows and Controls

To create the windows and controls, use the following steps:

1. Select **New Object** from the **File** menu. HOW, in turn, displays the New Object dialog box.
2. Choose **Window** from the Type drop-down listbox and type the window's name, **Authors,** in the Name field. In addition, you can add a description for the window in the Description field. Click OK.
3. HOW displays the Windows Properties dialog box. Click the **Controls** tab. To add a data control, click **Add**. HOW displays the Add Control dialog box.
4. Type the data control's name, **Authors**, in the Name field. You can also add a description for the data control within the Description field. To close the dialog box, click OK. To close the Window Properties dialog box, click OK. HOW adds the window and data control to its object repository.
5. Similarly, you can create another window, **Books,** and add a data control to the window.

In this step, you created the windows and controls for the application. In the next step, you create the queries.

Create the Queries

To create the queries, use the following steps:

1. Select **New Object** from the **File** menu. HOW displays the New Object dialog box.
2. Choose **Query** from the Type drop-down listbox and type the query's name, **Authors,** in the Name field. In addition, you can add a description for the query within the Description field. Click OK.
3. HOW displays the Select Domain dialog box. Before you can specify the attributes for the query, you must associate the query with a domain. Click **Authors** in the Select Domain dialog box and then click OK. HOW displays the Query Builder window.
4. To add attributes for the Authors query, click **Author_ID** and **Author_Name** in the Authors class object in the Domain space. HOW adds the two attributes within the Attributes window.
5. To save the query, select **Save** from the **File** menu. HOW, in turn, adds the query to its object repository. To close the query, select **Close** from the **File** menu.
6. Similarly, create and add another query, Books, to HOW's object repository. When creating the Books query, use the **Arguments** tab to specify the argument a_author_ID of type integer. In addition, specify a filter condition by using the **Filter By** tab. Select **Add Attribute** from the **Query** menu. HOW displays the Add Attribute tab. Click the **Via Association** tab. Choose **Books** from the Class Object drop-down listbox. Choose **has(Authors to Books)** from the Association dropdown listbox. Choose **Author_ID** from the Foreign Keys listbox and click OK. To add the operand, double-click in the Operand textbox and add the argument a_author_ID by using the Expression Builder.

In this step, you created the queries for the application. In the next step, you specify the navigations between the windows to establish the program's flow.

Create the Tasks that Use the Windows, Controls, Queries, and the Given Navigations between the Windows

Creating a task includes the following steps:

1. Create and define the tasks.
2. Add the windows to the tasks.
3. Associate the queries with the window's data controls.
4. Add entry and exit points to the tasks.

To create a task, use the following steps:

1. Select **New Object** from the **File** menu. HOW, in turn, displays the New Object dialog box.
2. Choose **Task** from the Type drop-down listbox and type the task's name, **Display Books for Authors,** in the Name field. In addition, you can add a description for the task in the Description field. Click OK.
3. HOW displays the Task Builder. By using the Task Builder, you can add components like windows and queries to the task.

To add windows to the task, drag the windows **Authors** and **Books** in the Task Builder window's empty space.

To associate queries with the data controls within the windows, click the **Queries** tab. Drag the **Authors** query from the **Queries** tab onto the data control in the **Authors** class object. HOW adds the query, as shown in Figure 26.14.

Similarly, you can add the other query, **Books,** onto the data control in the **Books** class object.

To add the entry and exit points, use the following steps:

1. Click on the **Entry Point** icon within the Task Builder toolbar, and then click anywhere in the Task Builder window's open space.
2. Click on the **Exit Point** icon within the Task Builder toolbar, and then click anywhere in the Task Builder window's open space. HOW adds the **Entry** and **Exit Point** icons as shown in Figure 26.15.

You have created the tasks for the application.

Specify the Navigation between the Windows to Establish the Program's Flow

To establish the program flow, use the following steps:

1. Click the **Navigation** icon in the Task Builder's toolbar.
2. Click on the **Entry** icon, and then click on the Authors window. HOW adds the navigation from the **Entry** icon to the Authors window.

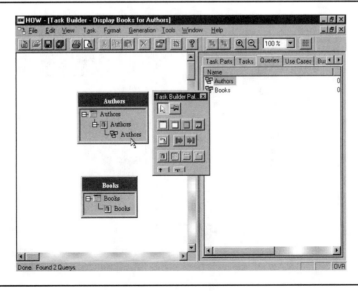

Figure 26.14   Adding the Authors query to the Authors data control.

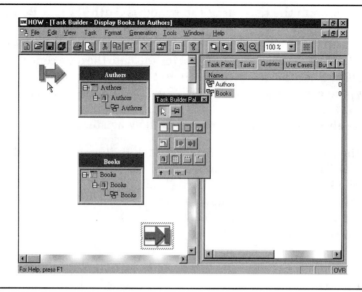

Figure 26.15 Adding the Entry and Exit Point icons.

3. Click on the Authors window, and then the Books window. HOW adds the navigation from the Authors window to the Books window.

4. Click on the Books window, and then the **Exit** icon. HOW, in turn, adds the navigation from the Books window to the **Exit** icon as shown in Figure 26.16.

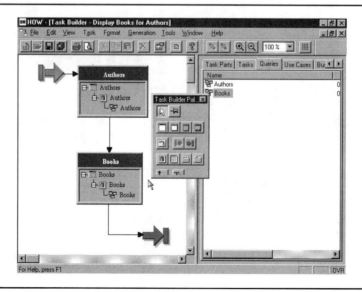

Figure 26.16 Establishing the program's flow.

In this step, you established the navigation between the application's windows. In the next step, you specify values for the parameters and add links.

Add Parameters and Links

To add a parameter to the Books window, use the following steps:

1. Double-click on the Books window object. In the Window Properties dialog box, click the **Parameters** tab.
2. To add a new parameter, click **New**. Within the Parameters Properties dialog box, type the parameter's name **p_Author_ID** within the Name field. Choose **Integer** from the Type drop-down listbox. You can also add a description for the parameter in the Description field. To close the Parameter Properties dialog box, click OK. To close the Window Properties dialog, click OK.

To assign a value to the above parameter, use the following steps:

1. Double-click on the navigation link between the Authors and Books window objects. Click the **Input Value Assignment Map** tab. Click on **Books.p_Author_ID**, then click **Open**. HOW displays the Expression Builder.
2. Assign an expression to Books.p_Author_ID by double-clicking **Authors.Author_ID** in the list of available values. To verify the expression, click **Verify**. To close the dialog, click OK. To close the Navigation Properties dialog, click OK.

To define a link from the Books window object to the Books data control, use the following steps:

1. Double-click on the **Books** window object. Click the **Links** tab, then click **New**.
2. Click on the **Books** data control in the Destination list. HOW displays the parameter **a_author_ID** for the data control within the Value Assignment Maps. Click on this parameter, then click OK. HOW adds the link as shown in Figure 26.17.

In this step, you added a parameter to the Books window object, established a value for this parameter, and defined a link between the Books window object and the Books data control.

Generate the PowerBuilder Application

To generate the PowerBuilder application from the HOW objects you built, use the following steps:

1. Select **Generate PowerBuilder Objects** from the **Generation** menu. HOW displays the Generate PowerBuilder Code dialog box with all the objects highlighted as shown in Figure 26.18.
2. To direct HOW to generate the PowerBuilder objects, click **Generate**.
3. HOW generates all the PowerBuilder objects and displays a log. To close the log, click OK.

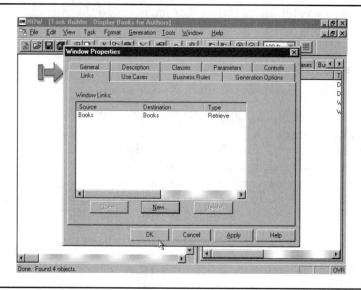

Figure 26.17 Adding a link.

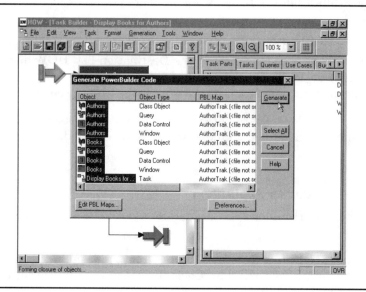

Figure 26.18 Generating the PowerBuilder objects.

You are now ready to run the application.

Run the Application

To run the PowerBuilder application, use the following steps:

1. Within HOW, select **Edit PowerBuilder Object** from the **Generation** menu. HOW runs PowerBuilder.
2. To run the application, click the **Run** icon.

You can now examine the objects that HOW generated when building the Power-Builder application.

Examine the Objects that HOW Generates

HOW generates a partitioned, *n*-tier application that takes advantage of the PFC services. The presentation logic is different from the data access and business logic. Figure 26.19 shows the library of PowerBuilder objects HOW generates for the AuthorTrak application.

The following is an example of the code HOW generates for the w_authors window's **open** event. Note the w_authors window is inherited from w_sheet, a PFC window:

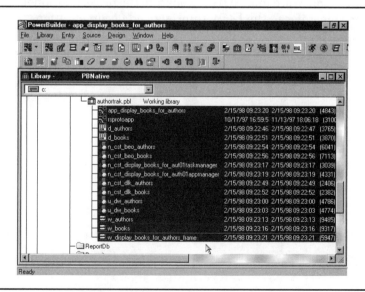

Figure 26.19   The PowerBuilder objects for AuthorTrak.

```
//@(data)(recreate=yes)<Parameters>
//@(data)-

//@(data)(recreate=yes)<Links>
SetLinkage(TRUE)
//@(data)-

//@(data)(recreate=yes)<GenerationOptions>
of_SetResize(TRUE)
SetTransactionManagement(TRUE)
inv_txsrv.SetLoadUpdateList(TRUE)
//@(data)-

//@(text)(recreate=yes)<resizevalues>
inv_resize.of_SetMinSize(1300, 400)
inv_resize.of_Register (dw_authors, 'ScaleToRight')
//@(text)-

//@(text)(recreate=yes)<RetrieveNoArgs>
inv_linkage.Retrieve(dw_authors )
//@(text)-
```

Generate Documentation for the Project by Using HOW

You can use Microsoft Word and HOW to generate the project documentation. For more information on this, refer to the HOW tutorials and documentation.

What's on the CD-ROM?

The CD-ROM accompanying this book includes:

- Source code from the book
- English Wizard from Linguistic Technology Corporation
- Demo Utilities Toolkit from SoftTree Technologies
- PB Developer Tools & Services from Digital Process
- Introduction to Interspace from PlanetWorks
- PowerDoc from Catapult Systems

SOURCE CODE FROM THE BOOK

The CD-ROM includes selected code and examples from the book. To review the code, you must install PowerBuilder 6 on your machine. All the source code exists in the bookcode directory within the respective chapter sub-directories on the CD-ROM.

ENGLISH WIZARD

English Wizard is a remarkable software component, from Linguistic Technology Corporation, that lets users access relational databases by using plain English. Users express their database requests by using ordinary English, and the English Wizard handles all the messy details of translating English to the language required to access the database (SQL) and returns the answer. Imagine asking "Which of my customers bought high margin products but not extended services?"—in exactly those words, and getting the answer, instantly, irrespective of whether the database is located on the desktop, the network, or even the Internet. English Wizard accepts either typed or voiced input supported by its integration with most popular voice recognition software products.

To install the corresponding product demo, run any of the following programs from the EngWiz directory on the CD-ROM:

Client32.exe English Wizard Client for 32-bit Windows 95 and NT

Client16.exe English Wizard Client for 16-bit Windows 3.x

WebServer.exe English Wizard Web/Server

Exposé.exe Exposé

TIP These demo programs run only on Windows NT or Windows 95 platform.

The CD-ROM also includes the following white papers in the EngWiz directory:

EngWiz.rtf Tell Me More about English Wizard

DataWare.rtf Proliferating the Data Warehouse beyond the Power User

Internet.rtf Effective Use of Relational Databases on the Internet

DEMO UTILITIES TOOLKIT

PowerDrops

The demo program from SoftTree Technologies presents examples of how you can include custom drop-down windows, substituting the PowerBuilder DropDownDataWindows, to use calendars, graph selections, custom windows, and more. Include a single line of code for each DataWindow where you want to include the custom drop-down windows.

PowerGraph

This demo program presents some examples of graphs built by using PowerGraph. Since the program makes no external function calls, the code is portable across all the platforms that support PowerBuilder. You can use PowerGraph to design your own graph styles that are not regularly available in PowerBuilder.

PowerUndo

This demo program presents an example of implementing word-processor style undo/redo features for the PowerBuilder DataWindows.

You will find all the demo programs on the CD-ROM in the SoftTree directory. Run the following programs for the corresponding product demo:

D:\Softtree\PwrGraph\demo.exe PowerGraphs Toolkit

D:\Softtree\PwrDrop\Dddwdemo.exe PowerDrops Toolkit

D:\Softtree\PwrDrop\undodem.exe PowerUndo Toolkit

TIP The above path assumes the D drive is mapped to your CD-ROM. These demo programs run only on Windows NT or Windows 95 platform. Also, to run these demo programs, you must install the PowerBuilder 6 32-bit deployment kit.

PB DEVELOPER TOOLS & SERVICES

PB Developer Tools & Services, from Digital Process, provides a couple of useful Developer demo applications and a PFC shell application:

Dp_xref.exe   An application that creates a table of all the object cross references in a PB application.

Dp_exec.exe   An application that helps compile all the stored procedures and triggers within a batch mode that may be located in multiple text (.sql) files in multiple directories.

Dp_demop.exe   This is a shell application demonstrating how quickly you can create a new PFC based MDI application by simply making a copy of DP's GEN application object found in dp_pfc.pbl. You will find most of the application-specific setup in a single convenient place—the application's OPEN event.

All of the files for the demo are located in the CD-ROM's DigiProc directory. For instructions on installing the demo, use the readme.txt as the starting point.

INTERSPACE

Interspace, from PlanetWorks, provides an application architecture and development framework that simplifies building new, net-enabled applications by using Power-Builder. The CD-ROM includes a story board that explains the value of using Planet-Works' Interspace product with the best of breed enterprise middleware.

To learn more about Interspace, load the intro.htm in your browser from your CD-ROM's planetwk directory.

POWERDOC

The CD-ROM also includes an evaluation copy of PowerDoc from Catapult Systems. PowerDoc automatically extracts objects, controls, attributes, pictures, events, Power-Scripts, SQL, functions, variables, structures, comments, and produces comprehensive technical documentation in Microsoft Word. The evaluation copy, however, only documents one object of each type per PBL.

Read the readme.txt file located in your CD-ROM's PowerDoc directory. To install PowerDoc's evaluation copy, run setup.exe.

TIP Before installing PowerDoc, you must install Microsoft Word for Windows.

Index

A

accelerator keys, 248
AcceptText( ), 62, 67, 69
Activate event, 193, 194
AddData( ), 327
Addseries( ), 327
AncestorReturn Value, 684
Any datatype, 267–271
API. *See also* MAPI; ORCA
  email APIs, 446
  ODBC API, 518–521
  Source Code Control API, 647
  Windows API, 454–461
APOL library, 32, 780
AppendMenu( ), 228, 232
application architectures, 7–32
  class libraries, 28–32
  COM, 25–26
  CORBA, 27
  DCOM, 26–27
  object generation
    infrastructure, 27
  object orientation, 17–25
  services architecture, 12–17
  tiered architecture, 8–12
application design and
    performance, 665–674
  bind PBLs into executable,
    668–670
  DataWindows, 672–673

DropDownListBoxes, 673
inheritance and
  performance, 673–674
number of EXEs, 668
partitioning, 666
and PBLs, 668–670
PowerBuilder controls,
  671–672
PowerScript functions vs.
  external functions, 668
preloading objects, 671
static vs. dynamic interfaces,
  673
storing application
  components, 670–671
and validation, 667–668
when to perform validation,
  667
when to use database
  triggers, 666
when to use stored
  procedures, 666–667
application development,
  675–684. *See also*
  applications
coding tips, 676–683
managing PowerBuilder
  libraries, 675–676
new features in
  PowerBuilder 6, 683–684

scope of variables/functions,
  675
application layer (OSI), 500
application lead, 646
application module directory
  tree, 647
application NVO, 294–297
applications. *See also*
  distributed application
  development
  architectures, 7–32
  design and performance,
    665–674
  development, 675–684
  test stages, 616–617
application server, 646
appProfile( ), 588–589
Arabic language support, 5
ARCH (Archiver), 545
architectures. *See also*
  application
  architectures
  creating DataWindow
  architecture, 168–170
ArrangeSheets( ), 234
asynchronous operation
  SQL Anywhere, 540–541
  SQL Server, 570
asynchronous processing,
  737–749

AutoCommit, 567–573
Avg( ), 327

B
backup/recovery, 536–538
base classes, 18
binding, 24–25, 266–267
bitmaps within DataWindows,
    152–160
    Bitmap( ), 157–158
    Display As Picture,
        153–157
    display using computed
        field, 157–158
    indicate current row,
        158–160
    PrintBitmap, 353, 364
    stop light reports, 168
black box testing, 618
buffers, 96–98, 143–144
    DataWindow as data buffer,
        143–144
    sharing data, 138
built-in functions, 253
business objects NVO, 299
button object, 89–90

C
C++ classes, defining with
    User Objects, 320
C_mkdir( ), 380
CA_Librarian, 656
CA-PAN/LCM, 656
CA-PANVALET, 656
calling events/functions,
    196–197
CASE, 447–449. *See also*
    ORCA
    tools, 448
case statement, 85
category, 322–323
CategoryCount( ), 330
CategoryName( ), 330
changemenu( ), 249
Check( ), 235
checkbox code tables, 146
CheckBox window control, 201
child DataWindows, 91–96
    exclusive DDDWs, 94–96
child window, 190

standards, 595, 596
CKPT (Checkpoint), 545
class libraries, 28–32. *See also*
    PFC
    web.pb class library, 802
ClassName( ), 268, 271, 309
Clicked, 193, 218
client
    application, 161
    configuration and
        performance, 662–663
client/server open
    development environment
    (CODE), 448–449
clock, 184–186
CloseChannel( ), 463, 790
Close event, 193
CloseQuery event, 193, 194
CloseUserObject( ), 309
CloseUserObjectWithParm( ),
    309
CloseWithReturn( ), 190
CODE (client/server open
    development
    environment), 448–449
code
    coding tips, 676–683
    maintenance, 20
    modularization, 588–590
    reliability, 19
    reusability, 18
    sharing, 18–19
code tables, 146–152
    checkbox edit style, 146
    DDDW edit style, 146–147,
        152
    DDLB edit style, 147
    dynamically changing,
        151–152
    edit style code tables,
        147–149
    radiobutton edit styles, 151
    spin controls, 149–150
    and validation, 71
CodeView, 420
columns
    computed columns/fields,
        79–85
    Data Pipeline column
        definition, 690–691

finding required columns,
    71–72
and key modification, 88–89
OLE columns, 160–167
protecting columns, 70
sliding columns, 61
specify key columns, 89
specify updatable columns,
    89
status, 105–106
and update flags, 106
Where clause, 86–88
COM (Component Object
    Model), 25–26
CommandButton window
    control, 201
CommandParm( ), 383
comments, 590–591
Common Object Request
    Broker Architecture. *See*
    CORBA
component generators,
    613–614
Component Object Model
    (COM), 25–26
composite reports, 41–45, 345
    number of nested reports
        supported, 45
computed columns and fields,
    79–85
    displaying bitmaps, 157
    stop light reports, 168
computer-aided software
    engineering. *See* CASE
Configuration Builder, 656
ConnectDBs( ), 695
connection object, 707
Control menu, 228–229
Constructor window event,
    218
contents file, 424
context-sensitive help,
    424–426
controls. *See also*
    DataWindow controls;
    window controls
    naming conventions,
        593–594
CORBA (Common Object
    Request Broker

Architecture), 27, 508–509
CornerStone library, 32, 780
Count( ), 324
Count(*), 137, 142
Create( ), 112
CrosstabAvg( ), 342
CrosstabCount( ), 342
CrosstabMax( ), 342
CrosstabMin( ), 342
Crosstab presentation style, 45, 47–48, 340–342
CrosstabSum( ), 342
cumulative sum, 85
cursors, 136–137
  scrolling, 521, 541, 570, 579
customizable Web jumps, 789
custom user events, 195

D
Daemon processes, 576
data access, 16–17
database. *See also* Oracle; SQL Anywhere; SQL Server
  connectivity considerations, 679–680
  design and performance, 665
  error handling, 598–599
  functions and secure mode, 790
  gateways, 509–510
  Informix, 574–581
  ObjectCycle database, 650
  support, 715
  when to use triggers, 666
database objects
  naming conventions, 594
Database Profile Painter, 526–529
DataCount( ), 330
datalink layer, 501
data manipulation language (DML), 128
Data Pipeline, 685–701
  attributes, 700
  column definition, 690–691
  Commit, 689
  creating a Data Pipeline, 685–691

events, 700
executing a Data Pipeline, 691–700
extended attributes, 690
functions, 700
key, 690
max errors, 690
objects, 700–701
options, 689
table, 689
within an application, 692–700
within development environment, 691–692
data source options, 36–41
  external data sources, 39–41
  query, 39
  Quick Select, 36–39
  SQL Select, 39
  stored procedures, 41
DataStores, 144–145
  sharing data, 140
datatypes
  naming conventions, 592–593
  window datatypes, 199–200
data validation. *See* validation
DataWindow. *See also* DataWindow controls
  as a data buffer, 143–144
  code tables, 146–152
  create dynamically, 111–112
  creating an architecture, 168–170
  DataStore objects, 143–145
  design considerations, 36, 127
  direct data access, 128
  enhancements, 4
  error handling, 108–110
  and graphs, 326–327
  large result sets, 135–138
  modify dynamically, 112–121
  OLE columns, 160–167
  and performance, 672–674
  print multiple DataWindows, 358–363
  print single DataWindow, 354–358

Retrieve As Needed, 140–143, 681–682
  sharing result sets, 138–140
  stop light reports, 168
  synchronization, 749–760
  using DDDWs, 152
  when to use, 127
DataWindow controls, 35–36, 96–127
  associating transaction objects, 103–104
  buffers, 96–98
  Drag-and-drop, 98–100
  dynamic DataWindows, 111–121
  Equality Required, 125–126
  Override Edit, 125
  Prompt for Criteria, 121, 124–126
  Query mode, 121–124, 125–126
  save data to other file formats, 126–127
  transaction processing, 100–111
DataWindow objects, 35, 36–96
  button object, 89–90
  child DataWindow, 91–96
  computed columns/fields, 79–85
  data sources, 36–41
  data validation, 61–72
  display formats, 73–79
  edit masks, 73–79
  filters, 58–60
  group box object, 90
  groups, 57–58
  new object in DataWindow, 89–91
  presentation styles, 41–57
  sliding columns, 61
  sorting, 60
  update properties, 85–89
DataWindow plug-in, 781–783
  and secure mode, 792
DataWindow window control, 201
dbCancel( ), 141
DBErrorCode( ), 109

DBError event, 109–110
DBErrorMessage( ), 109
DBWR (Database Writer), 545
DCE (Distributed Computing Environment), 508
DCOM (Distributed Component Object Model), 25, 26–27
DDDW (DropDownDataWindow), 91–96
  code tables, 146–147, 152
  exclusive, 94–96
  vs. DDLB, 152
DDE (Dynamic Data Exchange), 432–435, 462–467
  client/server, 467
  Microsoft Excel, 462–464
  Microsoft Word, 462–467
  PowerBuilder functions, 462, 463
  and secure mode, 790
DDL statements and static SQL, 135
DDLB (DropDownListBox), 201, 202
  code tables, 147
  editable DDLB, 203
  noneditable DDLB, 202–203
  and performance, 673
  vs. DDDW, 152
Deactivate event, 193
deadlocks, 599
debugging, 393–420
  CodeView, 420
  custom debug methods, 415–418
  DebugBreak( ), 404
  HeapWalker, 418
  Just In Time Debugging, 402–403
  messageboxes, 417
  runtime debug, 404–407
  Spy, 418
  third-party debug tools, 418–420
  Trace debug, 407–415, 683
  utilities, 418–419
  Windows Profiler, 420, 683

  write variables to a file, 415–417
Debug painter, 393–402
  Breakpoints, 394–396
  Call Stack, 394, 402
  Objects In Memory, 394, 402
  Source, 394, 399–400
  Source Browser, 394, 401
  Source History, 394, 402
  Variables, 394, 396–399
  Watch, 394, 396
Delete! buffer, 96–98, 138
Delete( ), 139
DeleteRow( ), 96
Describe( ), 112–114, 677
Destructor window event, 218
developer, 646
direct data access, 128
directory I/O, 380–385
directory structure, 644–645
DirList( ), 274, 283, 790
Disable( ), 249
Display As Picture, 153–157
display formats, 73–78
  changing, 76–78
distributed application development, 717. *See also* DPB
asynchronous processing, 737–749
creating shared objects, 718–727
DataWindow synchronization, 749–760
development methodology, 718
improved support, 4
server push, 728–737
Distributed Component Object Model (DCOM), 25, 26–27
Distributed Computing Environment (DCE), 508
Distributed PowerBuilder. *See* DPB
Distributed Relational Database Architecture (DRDA), 509

DLL (Dynamic Link Library), 489–498, 607–608, 643
  and applications, 490–491
  directory I/O, 380
  error handling, 603
  module definition file, 492–493
  and performance, 668–670
  source file, 493–497
  writing your own, 490, 491–498
DLLEntryPoint( ), 491
DLLMain( ), 491, 495
DML (data manipulation language), 128
Doc-To-Help, 428
documentation test, 621–622
DOS/File I/O, 17
DoubleClicked event, 193
double list paradigm, 223
DPB (Distributed PowerBuilder), 705–713
  class and concepts, 706–711
  client application, 711
  connection object, 707, 708
  Jaguar CTS, 714
  MTS, 714–715
  networking with, 504
  overview, 705–706
  platforms and drivers, 712
  proxy object, 710
  remote user object, 709–710
  server application, 711
  technology support, 715–716
  transaction servers, 714–715
  transport object, 707, 709
  uses of DPB, 712
Drag( ), 99, 309
drag-and-drop, 17, 98–100
  events, 98
  functions, 99
DragAuto, 98
DragDrop, 98, 193, 218
DragEnter, 98, 193, 218
DraggedObject( ), 99, 309
DragIcon, 98
DragLeave, 98, 193, 218
DragWithin, 98, 193, 218

DRDA (Distributed Relational Database Architecture), 509
drill-down graphs, 331–333
DropDownDataWindow. *See* DDDW
DropDownListBox. *See* DDLB
DropDownPictureListBox window control, 201, 206–208
drop-down toolbars, 241–242
dual, 556
dynamic binding, 25, 266–267
Dynamic Data Exchange. *See* DDE
dynamic DataWindows, 111–121
Dynamic Link Library. *See* DLL

E
EasyHelp/Web, 428
EDI (electronic data interchange) functionality, 17
EditMask window control, 201
edit masks, 73–76
    code tables, 149–150
    spin controls, 78–79, 149–150
edit style code tables, 147–149
email, 13–16, 431–446
    APIs, 446
    MAPI, 431–432
    messaging standards, 431–432
    PowerBuilder Library for Lotus Notes, 443–446
    PowerBuilder's DDE interface, 432–435
    PowerBuilder's MAPI interface, 435–443
    VIM, 431–432
    X.400, 432
embedded SQL, 107–108, 127
    dynamic SQL, 130–135
    static SQL, 128–130, 135
    when to use, 127
Enable( ), 249

encapsulation, 21–22
    custom encapsulation, 320
    inherent encapsulation, 317–320
    in PowerBuilder, 22
    programming standards, 590
    and User Objects, 317–320
environment adapter NVO, 298
ENVY/Developer, 656
Equality Required, 125, 126
errors/error handling, 597–605
    database error handling, 598–599
    and Data Pipeline, 690
    data validation, 69
    DataWindows, 108–110
    embedded SQL, 107–108
    error actions, 605
    Error event, 599–600
    ExternalException event, 599–601
    ImportFile, 604
    ItemError event, 69
    location of error logs, 605
    nested error handling, 603–604
    ORCA errors, 452, 453
    security/error test, 619–620
    standards, 597–605
    and synchronizer, 794–795
    system error handling, 601–603
    when calling DLLs, 603
events, 26
    calling, 196–197
    control events, 217
    Data Pipeline events, 700
    drag-and-drop, 98
    menu events, 234–235
    window events, 192–195
ExecRemote( ), 463
executable file, 606–610. *See also* Project painter
    library search path, 608
    machine code vs. p–code, 607

optimizing .PBLs, 610
    .PBDs or .DLLs, 607–608
    resource files, 608–609
    and Windows 95, 612–613
Execute Immediate command, 131
execution speed and inheritance, 20
ExtDeviceMode( ), 351–352
extension class, 31
external data sources, 39–41
external functions, 254–257
    declaring, 255–257
    parameter passing, 262–263
    vs. PowerScript functions, 271
external interfaces, 454–498
    cross-platform issues, 498
    DDE, 462–467
    OCXs, 484–489
    OLE, 467–484
    testing, 619
    Windows API, 454–461
    Windows DLLs, 489–498

F
FAR PASCAL_export( ), 492
fields, computed, 79–85
    displaying bitmaps, 157–158
file and I/O, 350, 373–392
    directory I/O, 380–385
    environment variables, 378–380
    functions, 373–374
    ImportFile( ), 376–377
    initialization files, 385–392
    reading large files, 374–375
    registry functions, 392
    simulating ImportFile function, 377–378
    Windows SDK functions, 391–392
    writing a file copy function, 375–376
FileClose( ), 374
FileDelete( ), 374, 381
FileExists( ), 374
file handle, 373

FileLength( ), 374, 375
FileOpen( ), 374
FileRead( ), 374
FileSeek( ), 374
file types, 642–644
FileWrite( ), 374
Filter( ), 60
  and sharing data, 139
Filter! buffer, 96–98, 138
FilteredCount( ), 60
filters, 58–60
Find( ), 145
FindCategory( ), 330
FindRequired( ), 71–72
FindSeries( ), 330
ForeHelp, 428
form modcl, 222–223
foundation class, 30–31
  description, 8
frame, 173–174
  creating a clock, 184–186
freeform presentation style,
  48–49
FreePower, 419
functions, 253
  Any datatype, 267–271
  built-in functions, 253
  calling, 196–197, 266–267
  Data Pipeline functions,
  700–701
  declaring external
  functions, 255–257
  drag-and-drop, 99
  dynamic vs. static binding,
  266–267
  external functions, 254–257,
  262–263, 668
  external vs. PowerScript, 271
  global functions, 253
  global vs. object functions,
  263–264
  graph functions, 326–327
  and inheritance, 264–265
  menu functions, 234,
  236–237
  object-level functions,
  253–254
  and object-oriented
  programming, 263–271

and overloading, 196,
  265–266
passing parameters,
  257–263
posting functions, 195–196
PowerScript functions,
  257–262, 271, 668
private function, 254
protected function, 254
public function, 254
scope of, 675
and secure mode, 790–791
types of functions, 253
user-defined functions,
  195–196, 253
visibility, 591

G

GarbageCollect( ), 683
garbage collection, 683
GarbageCollectSetTimeLimit( ),
  683
gateways, 509–510
GetActiveSheet( ), 178, 187
GetCommandDDE( ), 463
GetCommandDDEOrigin( ),
  463
GetCurrDrive( ), 382–383
GetData( ), 330
GetDataDDE( ), 463, 790
GetDataDDEOrigin( ), 463,
  790
GetDataPieExplode( ), 334
GetDataStyle( ), 330, 334
GetDynamicDate( ), 133
GetDynamicDateTime( ), 133
GetDynamicNumber( ), 133
GetDynamicString( ), 133
GetDynamicTime( ), 133
GetFileOpenName( ), 374, 790
GetFileSaveName( ), 374
GetFirstSheet( ), 175–176,
  187
getfocus event and MicroHelp,
  186
GetFocus, 218
GetFormat( ), 76
GetFreeGDI( ), 302
GetFreeMem( ), 302

GetFreeSpace( ), 621
GetFreeSystemResources( ),
  301, 621
GetFreeUser( ), 302
GetItemStatus( ), 106
GetNextSheet( ), 175–176, 187
GetPrivateProfileInt, 391
GetPrivateProfileString, 391
GetProfileInt, 391
GetRemote( ), 463, 790
GetSeriesStyle( ), 330, 334
GetSystemDirectory( ), 380
GetSystemMenu( ), 228
GetValidate( ), 66
GetWindowsDirectory( ), 380
global functions, 253
  vs. object functions,
  263–264
global structures, 252
graph( ), 327
graphical user interface. See
  GUI
graph presentation style, 49
graphs, 321–339
  category, 322–323
  change visual attributes,
  329–330
  data attributes, 330–331
  in the DataWindow,
  326–327
  display attributes list, 329
  drill-down graphs, 331–333
  in help files, 424
  manipulating graphs,
  328–331
  overlays, 324–325
  parts of a graph, 321–322
  printing, 364
  series, 324
  3-D graphs, 333–339
  value, 323–324
  in the window, 327–328
Graph window control, 201
grClipboard( ), 364
grid presentation style, 49–50
group box object, 90
GroupBox window control,
  201
GroupCalc( ), 58

group presentation style, 50
groups, 57–58
GUI (graphical user interface)
  standards, 596–597
  tab–folder interface, 224–225
  and three-tiered
    architecture, 10
  and two-tiered architecture,
    9–10

H

Handle( ), 254, 255, 460
hard-coded references,
  586–588
hasChanged( ), 21
HeapWalker, 418
Hebrew language support, 5
HelpBreeze, 428
help files, 421–428
  application help, 424–427
  contents file, 424
  context-sensitive help,
    424–427
  graphics, 424
  keyword help, 424–425
  Microsoft Windows 95 help,
    422–424
  project file, 424
  third-party products,
    427–428
  topic file, 422–426
Hide( ), 240, 249
Hide event, 193
hierarchy, 18. *See also*
  inheritance
  User Objects, 315–317
HotLinkAlarm event, 193
HOW, 803–822
  add parameters/links, 819
  building PowerBuilder
    applications, 805–806
  create attributes, 810
  create domain, 808–809
  create project/library,
    806–808
  create queries, 816
  create tasks, 816–817
  create windows and
    controls, 815

editions, 804
establish association
  between class objects,
  810–812
establish program flow,
  817–819
examine the objects, 821
generate the application,
  819
generate data model,
  812–813
generate documentation, 822
installing, 804
run the application, 821
synchronize data model,
  814–815
Hscrollbar window control,
  201
HTML table generation,
  797–798

I

IDT (Internet Developer
  Toolkit), 781
ImportClipboard( ), 139
ImportFile( ), 376–377
  display error messages, 604
  simulating, 377–378
ImportString( ), 139
Informix, 574–581
  connecting to from
    PowerBuilder, 578–579
  database architecture,
    575–576
  datatypes, 580–581
  PowerBuilder system
    tables, 579–580
  SPL, 577
  SQL optimization, 577
  stored procedures, 577
  triggers, 577
inheritance, 18–21
  advantages, 18–20
  design considerations, 20–21
  disadvantages, 20
  and functions, 264–265
  and menus, 229–234
  and performance, 673–674
  in PowerBuilder, 20

and User Objects, 313–314,
  315–317
INI files
  format, 385–386
  initialization, 386–389
  and menus, 242, 244–247
  ODBC connectivity,
    522–523
  standard initialization files,
    385
  types of, 386
  updating, 389–391
inparmtype, 132
Insert( ), 139
InsertMenu( ), 228, 232
InsertRow( ), 91, 94
  the primary buffer, 96
integration test, 618–619
IntelliMouse support, 684
interfaces
  consistency, 19
  static vs. dynamic, 673
Internet Developer Toolkit
  (IDT), 781
Internet tools, 4, 781
  customizable Web jumps,
    789
  DataWindow plug-in,
    781–783, 792
  HTML table generation,
    797–799
  secure mode, 789–792
  synchronizer, 792–797
  web.pb, 799–802
  Window ActiveX control,
    786–788, 791
  Window plug-in, 783–786,
    791
IntHigh( ), 254–255, 460
IntLow( ), 254–255, 460
IsRowModified( ), 106
IsRowNew( ), 106
ItemError event, 69
Itemfocuschanged( ), 278

J

Jaguar CTS, 714
  three-tiered architecture,
    11–12

Java ActiveX objects, 26
Java applets, 26
Java Virtual Machine (JVM), 613
Just In Time Debugging, 402–403
JVM (Java Virtual Machine), 613

K
Kerberos Authentication Security Service, 16–17
Key event, 193

L
label presentation style, 50
large result sets, controlling, 135–138
    Count(*), 137
    cursors, 136–137
    Retrieve As Needed, 136, 140–143, 681–682
    RetrieveRow event, 137–138
    Retrieve To Disk, 136
LastFile( ), 182
LastSheet( ), 181–182
LCKn (Locks), 545
LGWR (Log Writer), 545
LibEntry, 491
LibMain( ), 491
    and source file, 493
LibraryExport( ), 112
libraries
    functions and secure mode, 790
    managing, 675–676
    ObjectCycle client library, 650
    PFC libraries, 762
    and Project painter, 612
    third-party class libraries, 780
library management, ORCA, 450
library search path, 608
Line window control, 201
linkage service, 768–769
ListBox window control, 201

list model, 221–222
ListView window control, 201, 212–215
load-balancing of database servers, 599
locking options, 541, 570
logical unit of work (LUW), 111
Long( ), 254
LookupDisplay( ), 322, 327
loop control statements, 676
LoseFocus, 218
Lotus Notes, 442–446
LowerBound( ), 677
LUW (logical unit of work), 111

M
mailAddress( ), 436, 790
mailAddress(mailmessage), 436
mailDeleteMessage( ), 436, 790
mailDeleteMessage(messageid), 436
mailFileDescription, 435
mailFileType, 439
mailGetMessages( ), 436, 437, 790
mailGetMessages(return-unreadonly), 437
mailHandle( ), 437, 790
mailLogoff( ), 437, 790
mailLogon(userid, password, logonoption), 437
mailLogonOption, 439
mailMessage, 436
mailReadMessage( ), 438, 439, 790
mailReadMessage(messageid, mailmessage, mailreadoption, mark), 437–438
mailReadOption, 439
mailRecipient, 436
mailRecipientDetails(mail recipient, allowupdates), 438
mailRecipientType, 439

mailResolveRecipient(recipient name, allowupdates), 438
mailReturnCode, 439–440
mailSend(mailmessage), 438–439
main window, 187–188
    standards, 595, 596
MakeDir( ), 380
management, 646–647
MAPI (Messaging API), 431–432
    PowerBuilder's interface, 435–443
mark, 438
master/detail model, 221
MDI (multiple document interface) applications, 171–187
    components, 173–176
    creating/manipulating, 176–178
    displaying time, 184–186
    frame, 173–174, 191
    menus, 178–183, 237–239
    MicroHelp, 186–187
    multiple task application, 172–173
    sheets, 174–184
    single task application, 172
    standards, 596
    toolbars, 178, 184
    types of applications, 172
MDI frame, 173–174, 191
memory conservation, 197–199
menu bar, 227–228
menus, 227–250
    accelerator keys, 248
    and child windows, 190, 228
    design considerations, 250
    drop-down toolbars, 241–242
    inheritance, 229–234
    integrating with an .INI file, 242, 244–247
    and MDI application, 178–183
    menu bar, 227–228
    menu events, 234–235

menu functions, 234, 236–237
MenuItem properties, 248–250
popup menus, 228–229
shortcut keys, 248
toolbars, 239–242
types of, 227–229
within MDI applications, 237–239
messagebox-like window, 19
messageboxes, 417
Messaging API. *See* MAPI
methods, 26
private, 27
protected, 27
public, 27
MicroHelp, 186–187
Microsoft Excel, 462–465
maximizing, 464
Microsoft's Messaging API. *See* MAPI
Microsoft Transaction Server (MTS), 714–715
Microsoft Word, 462–467
maximizing, 464
passing data from PowerBuilder, 465–467
middleware, 504–512
database gateways, 509–510
DCE and CORBA, 508–509
DRDA, 509
RPCs and message-passing, 505–508
TP monitors, 510–512
migration. *See* software migration
modeling tool, 4
MLE (MultiLineEdit), 201, 204
tab stops, 204–205
modem communication functionality, 17
Modify( ), 48, 86
add object to a DataWindow, 115
Any datatype, 268
and child DataWindow, 93

and compound commands, 677
modify attributes of DataWindow, 115
modify DataWindow, 112–113, 115–120
printing DataWindows, 360
and Prompt for Criteria, 124
remove an object from a DataWindow, 115
Month( ), 341
Move( ), 309
mouse, 186–187, 193
MouseDown event, 193
MouseMove event, 193
MouseUp event, 193
MTS (Microsoft Transaction Server), 714–715
MultiLineEdit. *See* MLE
multimedia, 17
multimedia NVO, 299
multiple document interface. *See* MDI
multiple platforms support, 715
multiple protocol support, 501–502
multiple task, 172

N

Named Pipes, 504
naming conventions, 591–594
controls, 593–594
database objects, 594
datatypes, 592–593
objects, 591–592
variables, 592
native data, 161
nested reports, 41. *See also* composite reports
network layer (OSI), 501
network operating system. *See* NOS
networks, 499–512
architecture and performance, 663–664
database gateways, 509–510

DCE and CORBA, 508–509
and distributed applications, 504
DRDA, 509
interfacing with NOS, 503–504
middleware, 504–512
and multiple protocols, 501–502
network packet size, 664
OSI model, 499–501
RPCs and message-passing, 505–508
TP monitors, 510–512
NextDay( ), 489
nonvisual objects. *See* NVOs
NOS (network operating system), 503–504
NOS adapter NVO, 300
n-tier architecture, 717
number of peak users, 663–664
numinputs, 132
numoutputs, 133
N-Up presentation style, 51
NVOs (nonvisual objects), 292–302
application NVO, 294–297
building an NVO, 292
business objects, 299
create/destroy, 293–294
description, 292
email adapter NVO, 300
environment adapter NVO, 298
multimedia objects, 299
NOS adapter NVO, 300
Print adapter NVO, 300
SystemResource NVO, 300–302
vs. functions, 292
vs. visual User Objects, 292

O

ObjectAtPointer( ), 331
object/component library, 8
ObjectCycle, 647, 648–654
client library, 650
database, 650

ObjectCycle (*cont.*)
default login parameters, 651
manager, 650
SDK, 650
server, 650
source control management, 716
to unregister application, 652
using, 650–654
object framework, 8
object generation infrastructure, 27
object hierarchy. *See* inheritance
object-level functions, 253–254
object-level structures, 253
object library, 8
object link, 161
object linking and embedding. *See* OLE
object manager, 646
object orientation concepts, 17–25
binding, 24–25
encapsulation, 21–22
inheritance, 18–21
object generation infrastructure, 27
polymorphism, 23–24
objects
connection object, 707
creating shared objects, 718–727
Data Pipeline objects, 700
naming conventions, 591–592
PFC object hierarchy, 778
PFC objects, 773–777
preloading, 671
printing PowerBuilder objects, 363–364
proxy object, 710
remote user object, 709–710
sharing PowerBuilder objects, 32
transaction objects, 102–104
transport object, 707, 709

OCX (OLE custom controls), 484–489
ODBC (open database connectivity), 515
advantages, 516
conformance levels, 518–522
connecting from PowerBuilder, 525–529
disadvantages, 516
.INI file settings, 522–523
PowerBuilder's support, 522
registry settings, 523–524
setting up on the client, 530–531
SQL processing, 517–518
OLE (object linking and embedding), 467–468
common terms, 161
linking vs. embedding, 166–167
Microsoft OLE 2 features, 468–469
OLE client library, 161
OLE columns, 160–167
OLE functions and secure mode, 790
OLE server library, 161
OLE 2 presentation style, 51–56
OLE 2 window control, 201, 208
PowerBuilder OLE 2 container application support, 471–475
PowerBuilder OLE 2 control properties, 469, 470
PowerBuilder OLE 2 functions, 469, 471
PowerBuilder OLE 2 sample code, 475–484
and secure mode, 790
OLEActivate( ), 167
OLE custom controls (OCX), 484–489
OLEDraw( ), 167
OpenChannel( ), 463
Open Client, 504

open database connectivity. *See* ODBC
Open event, 192–194
open repository CASE API. *See* ORCA
OpenSheetWithParm( ), 176–177
Open Systems Interconnect (OSI) model, 499–501
OpenUserObject( ), 309
OpenUserObjectWithParm( ), 309
OpenWithParm( ), 337
Oracle, 544–562
connecting to from PowerBuilder, 557–561
database architecture, 544–546
datatypes, 562
lock selected rows, 557
PL/SQL, 546
PowerBuilder supported, 544
PowerBuilder system tables, 561–562
sequences, 556
SQL optimization, 546
stored procedures, 547–556
triggers, 546–547
ORCA (open repository CASE API), 447, 449–453
architecture, 449
errors, 452, 453
features, 449–451
functions, 451–452
PowerBuilder ORCA header file, 452–453
to download documentation, 453
Original! buffer, 96–98
OSI (Open Systems Interconnect) model, 499–501
Other event, 193, 218
outparmtype, 133
Oval window control, 201
overlays, 324–325
overloading, 23, 24, 196, 265–266

Override Edit, 125–126
overriding, 24
owner link, 161

P

packet size, 664
parameter passing, 257
  external functions, 262–263
  PowerScript functions,
    257–262
Parent reference, 586, 587
ParentWindow reference, 586,
  588
partitioning application
  components, 666
Paste command, 166
Paste Link command, 166
PBDs, 607–608, 643
  and performance, 668–670
PBLs, 643
  optimizing, 610
  and performance, 668–670
PBSync (PowerBuilder
  synchronization tool), 614
perceived performance, 661.
  See also performance
  and Retrieve As Needed, 143
performance, 661
  application performance,
    661
  changing validation rules, 67
  client configuration,
    662–663
  database design, 665
  network architecture,
    663–664
  new features in
    PowerBuilder 6, 683–684
  and ODBC, 516
  perceived performance, 143,
    661
  performance test, 620–621,
    625, 627–630
  PowerBuilder application
    design issues, 665–674
  PowerBuilder application
    development, 675–684
  and Retrieve As Needed,
    142–143

and RetrieveRow event,
  137–138
and sharing data, 139
PFC (PowerBuilder
  Foundation Classes), 30,
  761
  application services,
    763–768
  DataWindow service,
    768–769
  extension class, 31–32
  foundation class, 30–31
  new services, 4
  PFC extension layers,
    762–763
  PFC libraries, 762
  PFC object hierarchy, 778
  PFC objects, 773–777
  PFC process flows, 779–780
  PFC services architecture,
    761–762
  third-party class libraries,
    32, 780
  third-party PFC-based
    products, 780
  where to find PFC PBLs, 31
  window service, 769–773
physical layer, 501
PictureButton window
  control, 201
PictureListBox window
  control, 201, 206–208
Picture window control, 201
pipelines. *See* Data Pipeline
PLAN (PowerBuilder Library
  Application for Lotus
  Notes) toolkit, 443–446
platforms and drivers, 712
Platinum CCC/Life Cycle
  Manager, 656
PL/SQL (procedural Language
  extension to SQL), 546
plug-in
  DataWindow, 781–783, 792
  Window, 783–786, 791
PMON (Process Monitor),
  545
PointCast Network, 728
PointerX, 309

PointerY, 309
polymorphism, 23–24,
  265–266
  in PowerBuilder, 24
  and User Objects, 314–315
PopMenu( ), 229
PopulateError( ), 418
popup menus, 228–229
popup window, 188–190
  standards, 595, 596
Post( ), 460
PostEvent( ), 194
posting functions, 195–196
PostMessage( ), 462
PowerBuilder
  browser, 684
  class libraries, 28–32
  connecting to ODBC,
    525–529
  Library for Lotus Notes,
    443–446
  DDE interface, 432–435
  MAPI interface, 435–443
  object generation
    infrastructure, 27
  object-oriented system
    concepts, 17–25
  ORCA header file, 452
  set catalog tables' owner,
    542
PowerBuilder Foundation
  Classes. *See* PFC
PowerBuilder 6
  support for ODBC, 522
  synchronization tool, 614
  what's new, 4–5, 683–684
PowerBuilder Virtual
  Machine (PVM), 613
PowerClass library, 32, 780
PowerScript functions,
  257–262
  vs. external functions, 271
PowerTOOL library, 32
preloading
  data, 682
  objects, 671
presentation format, 161
presentation layer (GUI), 9
presentation layer (OSI), 500

presentation styles, 41–57
  composite, 41–45
  Crosstab, 45, 47–48
  freeform, 48–49
  graph, 49
  grid, 49–50
  group, 50
  label, 50
  N-Up, 51
  OLE 2, 51–56
  RichText, 57
  Tabular, 57
Primary! buffer, 96–98, 138
Print( ), 348, 353, 354
print adapter NVO, 300
PrintBitmap( ), 353, 364
PrintCancel, 353
PrintClose, 353
PrintDataWindow( ), 353, 354, 364
PrintDefineFont, 353
PrintEnd Event, 353
printing, 350–373
  changing print settings, 364–365
  description, 351–352
  dialog boxes, 365–373
  functions, 352, 353–354
  graphs, 364
  multiple DataWindows, 358–363
  page area, 352
  PowerBuilder objects, 363–364
  Print All, 364
  print options dialog box, 365–368
  print preview/zoom dialog box, 368–372
  reports, 345–348
  single DataWindows, 354–358
printing a DataWindow
  DataWindow as a buffer, 143–144
  to print all rows, 142
  and Retrieve As Needed, 142
PrintLine, 353

PrintOpen( ), 347, 348
PrintOpen, 353
PrintOval, 353
PrintPage, 354
PrintPage Event, 353
PrintRect, 353
PrintRoundRect, 354
PrintScreen( ), 348, 364
PrintSend, 353
PrintSetSpacing, 353
PrintSetup, 353
PrintStart Event, 353
PrintText, 353
PrintX, 353, 354
PrintWidth, 353
PrintY, 353, 354
private function, 254
private method, 27
ProfileInt( ), 242, 390
ProfileString( ), 242, 244, 390, 588–589
profiling, 407–408, 683
  Windows Profiler, 420
program complexity and inheritance, 20
programming standards, 585–591
  code modularization, 588–590
  comments, 590–591
  encapsulation, 590
  function visibility, 591
  hard-coded references, 586–588
program size and inheritance, 20
project file, 424
Project painter, 610–612
  building the executable, 611
  choosing libraries, 612
  filenames, 611
  options, 611–612
Prompt for Criteria, 121, 124–125
  and Query Mode, 125
properties, 26
protected function, 254
protected method, 27
protocols, multiple, 501–502

proxy object, 710
public function, 254
public method, 27
push technology, 728
PVCS, 647, 656, 657–658
PVM (PowerBuilder Virtual Machine), 613

Q
QBE (Query By Example), 121
query
  and Count(*), 137
  ODBC SQL processing, 517–518
  ORCA object query, 451
  Prompt for Criteria, 125
  query mode, 121–124
  query objects as data source, 39
  query optimizer, 534–535
  query selection dialog box, 220–221
Query By Example (QBE), 121
Quick Select, 36–39

R
radiobuttons, 201, 203
  code tables, 151
RbuttonDown event, 193, 218
RDBMSs
  fine-tune performance, 665
  and gateways, 510
  and ODBC, 515–516
  stored procedures, 41
  three-tiered architecture, 10
  two-tiered architecture, 9–10
RECO (Recoverer), 545
Rectangle window control, 201
registration database, 161
RegistryDelete, 392, 790
registry functions, 392
  and secure mode, 790
RegistryGet, 392, 790
RegistryKeys, 392, 790
RegistrySet, 392
registry settings, 523–524

RegistryValues, 392, 790
regression test, 622–623
RemoteExec event, 193
RemoteHotlinkStart event, 193
RemoteHotlinkStop event, 193
RemoteRequest event, 193
RemoteSend event, 193
remote user object, 709–710
RemoveFile( ), 381–382
Repair( ), 700, 701
reports, 339–349
  composite reports, 41–45, 345
  crosstab style report, 340–342
  InfoMaker, 339–340
  printing, 345–348
  Report painter, 339–340
  Rich Text Format, 342–345
  saving reports, 348–349
  stop light reports, 168
ReselectRow( ), 110
Reset( ), 139, 327
ResetUpdate( ), 106
Resize event, 193
resource files, 608–609
RespondRemote( ), 463
response window, 190–191
  standards, 595, 596
result sets
  controlling large sets, 135–138
  to disable data sharing, 139
  sharing sets, 138–140
Retrieve( ), 79–80, 91, 93–94, 104–105
  and error handling, 108–109
  to execute new SQL statement, 124
  the primary buffer, 96
  and Retrieve As Needed, 141
  and sharing data, 139
  to trap SQL statements, 110
Retrieve As Needed, 136, 140–143, 681–682

RetrieveRow event, 137–138
Retrieve To Disk, 136
RichTextEdit (RTE), 201, 205
RichText Format (RTF), 342–345
RichText presentation style, 57
RoboHelp, 427–428
RoundRectangle window control, 201
Rowcount( ), 141–142, 327
RowFocusChanging event, 70–71
RowsCopy( ), 97, 140, 144
RowsDiscard( ), 98
RowsMove( ), 98, 144
RPCs, 505–508
RTE (RichTextEdit), 201, 205
RTF (Rich Text Format), 342–345
Run( ), 464

S
SAG (SQL Access Group)
  dynamic SQL, 130–135
  embedded SQL, 127–135
  and ODBC, 518
  static SQL, 128–130, 135
sample( ), 495
SaveAs, 126–127
scrolling, 201, 521, 541, 570, 579
SDI (single document interface), 187, 594
SDLC (systems development life cycle), 615–616
secure mode, 789–792
security
  security/error test, 619–620
  SQL Anywhere (database), 539–540
Security( ), 236, 240
selection dialog box, 220–221
  query, 220–221
  standard, 220
Send( ), 460, 790
SendMessage( ), 462
sequences, 556
series, 324

SeriesCount( ), 330
SeriesName( ), 330
server application, 161
server databases. *See* Informix; Oracle; SQL Anywhere; SQL Server
server push, 728–737
services architecture, 12–17
  data access, 16–17
  DOS/file I/O, 17
  drag-and-drop, 17
  EDI, 17
  email, 13–16
  fax, 17
  modem, 17
  multimedia, 17
session handle, 449–450
session layer (OSI), 500
SetActionCode( ), 278
SetColumn( ), 67
SetDataDDE( ), 463, 790
SetDataPieExplode( ), 334
SetDataStyle( ), 334
SetDynamicParm( ), 133
SetFilter( ), 60
  and sharing data, 139
SetFormat( ), 76
SetItem( ), 62
SetItemStatus( ), 106
SetMicroHelp( ), 186, 235
SetPosition( ), 309
SetProfileString( ), 242, 390
SetRedraw( ), 360, 677
SetRemote( ), 463, 467
SetRow( ), 67
SetRowFocusIndicator( ), 158–160
SetSeriesStyle( ), 334
SetSort( ), 60
  and sharing data, 139
SetTrans( ), 103–104, 108, 679, 790
  and LUW, 111
SetTransObject( ), 103–104, 679–680, 790
  and LUW, 111
SetValidate( ), 66
SGA (system global area), 544–546

ShareData( ), 138
ShareDataOff( ), 139
sharing
  between DataStores, 140
  code, 18–19
  creating shared objects,
    718–727
  disable data sharing, 139
  PowerBuilder objects, 32
  result sets, 138–140
sheets, 174–178
  finding active sheets, 178
  managing sheets, 175–176
  and menus, 179–183
  minimize sheets, 177
  OpenSheetWithParm( ),
    176–177
  to prevent maximizing, 178
shortcut keys, 248
Show( ), 182, 193, 249
  and Open event, 194
  and the toolbar, 240
Show event, 193
ShowHelp( ), 425
single document interface
    (SDI), 187, 594
SingleLineEdit (SLE), 201,
    204
single task, 172
SLE (SingleLineEdit), 201,
    204
sliding columns, 61
  Left, 61
  Up-All Above, 61
  Up-Directly Above, 61
SMON (System Monitor), 545
software migration, 640–660
  application lead, 646
  application module
    directory tree, 647
  application server, 646
  developer, 646
  directory structure, 644–645
  external version control,
    655–656
  file types and locations,
    642–644
  migration forms, 658–660

ObjectCycle, 647, 648–654
object manager, 646
PVCS procedures, 657
software development life
    cycle, 640–642
software migration life
    cycle, 641
source code locations,
    646–647
temporary holding area, 647
version control, 646,
    647–656
version control manager,
    646
version control repository,
    646
sort, 60
  and groups, 58
  sort criteria and query
    mode, 122–123
Sort( ), 58
  and sharing data, 139
Source Code Control API, 647
space( ), 380
spin controls, 78–79
  code tables, 149–150
SPL, 577
Spy, 418
SQL. *See also* embedded SQL
  ODBC SQL processing,
    517–518
  optimization, 546, 564, 577
  PL/SQL, 546
  SPL, 577
  static SQL, 128–130, 135
  TRANSACT-SQL, 564
  to trap statements, 110
  and Update Properties,
    85–89
SQL Access Group. *See* SAG
SQL Anywhere, 532–544
  administrator, 535
  asynchronous operation,
    540–541
  backup/recovery, 536–538
  binary datatypes, 544
  character datatypes, 543
  connecting to, 540

cursor scrolling, 541
database architecture,
    533–534
datatypes supported,
    543–544
date/time datatypes, 543
identifier delimiters, 541
locking options, 541
numeric datatypes, 543
optimizer, 534–535
PowerBuilder catalog
    owner, 542
PowerBuilder system
    tables, 542
security, 539–540
SQL Central, 535
stored procedures, 538
tables displayed, 541
triggers, 538–539
user-defined datatypes, 544
SQLAllocConnect( ), 518
SQLAllocEnv( ), 518
SQLAllocStmt( ), 518
SQLBindCol( ), 518
SQLBrowseConnect( ), 520
SQLCancel( ), 518
SQL Central, 535–538
SQLCode, 107–108, 109
SQLColAttributes( ), 518
SQLColumnPrivileges( ), 520
SQLColumns( ), 519
SQLConfigDataSource( ), 531
SQLConnect( ), 518
SQLDataSources( ), 520
SQLDBCode, 107–108, 109
SQLDescribeCol( ), 519
SQLDescribeParam( ), 520
SQLDisconnect( ), 519
SQLDriverConnect( ), 519
SQLError( ), 519
SQLErrText, 107–108, 109
SQLExecDirect( ), 519
SQLExecute( ), 519
SQLExtendedFetch( ), 520
SQLFetch( ), 519
SQLForeignKeys( ), 520
SQLFreeConnect( ), 519
SQLFreeEnv( ), 519

SQLFreeStmt( ), 519
SQLGetAvailableDrivers( ), 531
SQLGetConnectOption( ), 519
SQLGetCursorName( ), 519
SQLGetData( ), 519
SQLGetFunction( ), 520
SQLGetInfo( ), 520
SQLGetInstalledDrivers( ), 531
SQLGetStmtOption( ), 520
SQLGetTypeInfo( ), 520
SQLInstallDriver( ), 531
SQLInstallDriverManager( ), 531
SQLMoreResults( ), 521
SQLNativeSql( ), 521
SQLNumParams( ), 521
SQLNumResultCols( ), 519
SQLParamData( ), 520
SQLParamOptions( ), 521
SQLPrepare( ), 519
SQLPreview DataWindow event, 110
SQLPrimaryKeys( ), 521
SQLProcedureColumns( ), 521
SQLProcedures( ), 521
SQLPutData( ), 520
SQLRemoveDefaultData-Source( ), 531
SQLRemoveDSNFromIni( ), 531
SQLRowCount( ), 519
SQL Select data source, 39
SQL Server (Microsoft and Sysbase), 562–574
    connecting to from PowerBuilder, 565–573
    database architecture, 563–564
    datatypes, 573–574
    extension to SQL, 564
    handling deadlocks, 599
    PowerBuilder system tables, 573
    SQL optimization, 564
    stored procedures, 564–565
    triggers, 564–565
SQLSetConnectOption( ), 520

SQLSetCursorName( ), 519
SQLSetParam( ), 519
SQLSetPos( ), 521
SQLSetScrollOptions( ), 521
SQLSetStmtOption( ), 520
SQLSpecialColumns( ), 520
SQLStatistics( ), 520
SQLTablePrivileges( ), 521
SQLTables( ), 520
SQLTransact( ), 519
SQLWriteDsnToIni( ), 531
standards
    error-handling, 597–605
    GUI standards, 596–597
    naming conventions, 591–594
    programming standards, 585–591
    Window type standards, 594–596
Start( ), 700
StartHotLink( ), 463, 790
StartServerDDE( ), 463, 790
static binding, 25, 266–267
StaticText window control, 201
StopHotLink( ), 463
stop light reports, 168
StopServerDDE( ), 463, 790
stored procedures, 41, 130
    Informix, 577
    Oracle, 547–556
    SQL Anywhere, 538
    SQL Server, 564–565
    when to use, 666–667
structures, 251–253
    creating/declaring, 251–252
    global structures, 252
    object-level structures, 253
    types of, 252–253
Sum( ), 324, 327
superclasses, 18
synchronization tool, 614
synchronizer, 792–797
    logging errors, 794–795
    as stand-alone application, 796
Sync ActiveX control, 796

SyntaxFromSQL( ), 111–112
system architecture, 7
system error handling, 601–603
system global area (SGA), 544–546
SystemKey event, 193
SystemResource NVO, 300–302
systems development life cycle (SDLC), 615–616
system test, 620, 623

T
tab-folder interface, 224–226
Tab window control, 201, 205–206
tables. *See also* code tables
    displayed within Database painter, 541
tabular presentation style, 57
TeamWare, 656
technology support, 715–716
testing PowerBuilder applications, 614
    application test stages, 616–617
    black box testing, 618
    documentation test, 621–622
    external interface test, 619
    integration test, 618–619
    performance test, 620–621
    regression test, 622–623
    relative to SDLC, 615–616
    sample stress/performance test, 625–639
    security/error test, 619–620
    system test, 620, 623
    testing tools, 623–625
    unit test, 617–618, 623
    user acceptance test, 622
    white box testing, 618
This reference, 586–587
3-D graphs, 333–339
tiered architecture, 8–9
    three tiers, 10–12, 717
    two tiers, 9–10

time, displaying, 164–186
Timer event, 193
ToolbarAlignment attribute, 239
ToolbarFrameTitle attribute, 239
ToolbarHeight attribute, 239
ToolbarItemDown attribute, 239
ToolbarItemDownName attribute, 239
ToolbarItemName attribute, 239
ToolbarItemOrder attribute, 239
ToolbarItemSpace attribute, 239
ToolbarItemText attribute, 239
ToolbarItemVisible attribute, 239
ToolbarMoved event, 193
toolbars, 239–241
  attribute list, 239
  drop-down toolbars, 241–242
  and MDI application, 178, 184
ToolbarSheetTitle attribute, 239
topic files, 422–423
  and graphics, 424
TP (transaction processing) monitors, 510–512
Trace debugger, 407–415, 683
TRANSACT-SQL, 564
transaction processing, 100–111
  attributes, 102
  error handling, 107–110
  LUW, 111
  Retrieve( ), 104–105
  TP monitors, 510–512
  transaction objects, 102–104
  Update( ), 104–107
  update flags, 106–107
transaction servers, 713–715
transport layer (OSI), 500
transport object, 707, 709

TreeView window control, 201, 208–212
triggers
  Informix, 577
  Oracle, 546–547
  SQL Anywhere, 538–539
  SQL Server, 564–565
  when to use, 666
TypeOf( ), 99, 309

U
UNICODE support, 4, 715
unit test, 617–618, 623
UNIX
  and multiple protocols, 501
  platform support, 715
  and TP monitors, 512
  Winsock, 504
Update( ), 104–106, 790
  and AcceptText( ), 67, 107
  and DataWindow buffers, 96–97
  and error handling, 108–109
  and sharing data, 139
  to trap SQL statements, 110
  update flags, 106
  and Update Properties, 85–89
update flags, 106–107
Update Properties, 85–89
  key columns, 89
  key modification, 88–89
  table to update, 86
  updatable columns, 89
  Where clause, 86–88
UpperBound( ), 677
user acceptance test, 622
user-defined functions, 253
User Objects, 271–320
  add to Window painter toolbar, 307
  class:custom, 292–302
  class:standard, 302–304
  class User Object, 271, 292–304
  defining C++ classes, 320
  dynamic User Objects, 307–313

and encapsulation, 317–320
  executing functions, 307
  and inheritance, 313–314, 315–317
  NVOs (nonvisual objects), 292–302
  and object-oriented programming, 313–320
  and polymorphism, 314
  types of User Objects, 271
  visual User Object, 271–292
  visual:custom, 280–290
  visual:external, 290–292
  visual:standard, 271–280
  windows and User Objects, 304–307
UserObject window control, 201
users, number of, 663–664

V
validation, 61–73
  change rules dynamically, 66–67
  code tables, 71
  datatype validation, 64
  error handling, 69
  finding columns, 71–72
  ItemChanged event, 67
  ItemError event, 69
  process flow, 67–68
  protecting columns, 70
  RowFocusChanging event, 70–71
  rules, 64–67
  to trigger, 62
  when to perform, 667–668
value, 323–324
variables
  naming conventions, 592
  PowerBuilder variables, 197–199
  scope of, 675
vendor-independent messaging (VIM), 431–432
version control, 646, 647–656
  default version control, 648
  ObjectCycle, 647, 648–654

repository, 646
Source Code Control API,
    647
vendor's version control,
    655–656
version control manager,
    646
within PowerBuilder, 647
VIM (vendor-independent
    messaging), 431–432
virtual class, 18
Visual Help, 428
Vscrollbar window control,
    201

W
Web( ), 491
    and source file, 493
web.pb, 799–802
    web.pb class library, 802
    web.pb wizard, 800
Web jumps, 789
Where clause, 86–88
    key columns option, 86
    key/modified columns
        option, 86
    Key/updatable columns
        option, 86
    Original! buffer, 96
    Prompt for criteria, 121,
        124–125
    Query Mode, 121–124, 125
white box testing, 618
Window ActiveX control,
    786–788
    and secure mode, 791
window controls, 200–217
    control array, 215
    control events, 217, 218
    DropDownListBox, 202–203

DropDownPictureListBox,
    206–208
list of, 201
ListView, 212–215
MultiLineEdit, 204–205
OLE 2, 208
PictureListBox, 206–208
Radiobuttons, 203
RichTextEdit, 205
SingleLineEdit, 204
tab, 205–206
TreeView, 208–212
window events, 192–195
    Activate event, 194
    CloseQuery event, 194
    custom user events, 195
    list of, 193
    Open event, 192, 194
window paradigms, 219–226
    double list, 223
    form, 222–223
    list, 221–222
    master/detail, 221
    selection dialog box,
        220–221
    tab-folder, 224–226
Window plug-in, 783–786
    and secure mode, 791
windows, 187. *See also*
        window controls; window
        events; window
        paradigms
    calling events/functions,
        196–197
    child window, 190
    and graphs, 327–328
    main window, 187–188
    MDI frame, 191
    popup window, 188–190
    posting functions, 195–196

PowerBuilder functions,
    195–196
PowerBuilder variables,
    197–199
response window, 190–191
selecting a window type,
    187
types of windows, 187
type standards, 594–596
and User Objects, 304–305
window attributes, 217–219
window controls, 200–217
window datatypes, 199–200
window events, 192–195
window paradigms,
    219–226
Windows API, 454–461
    mapping PowerBuilder
        messages, 456
    messages, 455
    message structure, 460–461
    trapping a message,
        457–459
    user-defined messages, 460
Windows 95, 612–613
    help file, 422–424
Windows Profiler, 420, 683
Windows SDK
    functions, 391–392
    PowerBuilder and C SDK
        datatype mapping, 497
    and SystemResource NVO,
        300–302
Winsock, 504
WritePrivateProfileString, 391
WriteProfileString, 391

X
X.400, 432